FOURTH EDITION

THRIVING IN
College and Beyond

Research-Based Strategies for Academic Success and Personal Development

Joseph B. Cuseo • **Aaron Thompson** • **Michele Campagna** • **Viki Sox Fecas**

Emeritus,
Marymount College

Eastern Kentucky University

Montclair State University

University of South Carolina—
Columbia

Kendall Hunt
publishing company

Book Team

Chairman and Chief Executive Officer   Mark C. Falb
President and Chief Operating Officer   Chad M. Chandlee
Vice President, Higher Education   David L. Tart
Director of Publishing Partnerships   Paul B. Carty
Developmental/Product Supervisor   Lynnette M. Rogers
Vice President, Operations   Timothy J. Beitzel
Senior Production Editor   Stefani DeMoss
Permissions Coordinator   Caroline Kieler
Cover Designer   Heather Richman

Kendall Hunt
publishing company

www.kendallhunt.com
Send all inquiries to:
4050 Westmark Drive
Dubuque, IA 52004-1840

Copyright ©2007, 2010, 2013, 2016 by Kendall Hunt Publishing Company

ISBN: 978-1-4652-9093-9

Printed in the United States of America

Brief Contents

Contents

Preface

WELCOME TO OUR BOOK

Plan and Purpose of This Book

This book is designed to help you make a smooth transition to college as well as equip you with strategies for success that you can use throughout college and beyond. Its aim is to promote the academic excellence and personal development of all students—whether you're a student who is (a) transitioning to college directly from high school or from a full-time or part-time job, (b) living on or off campus, or (c) attending college on a full-time or part-time basis. Whatever your previous educational record may have been, college is a new ball game played on a different field with different rules and expectations. If you haven't been a particularly successful student in the past, this book will help you become a successful student in the future. If you have been a successful student in high school, this book will make you an even stronger student in college.

One of the book's major goals is to help you put into practice a powerful principle of human learning and personal success: *mindfulness*. When you're mindful, you're aware of *what* you're doing and *if* you're doing it in the most effective way. Mindfulness or self-awareness is the critical first step toward self-improvement and success in any aspect of your life. If you develop the habit of remaining aware of whether you're "doing college" strategically (e.g., by using the key strategies identified in this book), you will have taken a huge step toward college success.

Rather than trying to figure out how to do college on your own through random trial-and-error, this book gives you a game plan for getting it right from the start and an inside track for getting off to a fast start. Its plan is built on a solid foundation of research that equips you with a comprehensive set of well-documented strategies for doing college successfully.

Specific action strategies make up the heart of this book. You will find that these practical strategies aren't presented simply as a laundry list of what-to-do tips dispensed by authority figures who think they know what's best for you. Instead, the recommendations are accompanied by evidence-based reasons for *why* they're effective and they're organized into broader *principles* that tie the strategies together into a meaningful plan. It's not only important for you to know *what* to do, but also *why* to do it. If you understand the reason behind a suggested strategy, you're more likely to take that strategy seriously and implement it effectively.

When specific strategies are organized into general principles, they become more powerful because you're able to see how the same principle may be generalized and applied across different subjects and situations. Understanding the key principles that underlie effective strategies also empower you to create additional strategies of your own that follow or flow from the same general principle. This promotes deeper, more powerful learning than simply collecting a bunch of tips about what you should or shouldn't do in college. We believe that you're ready and able to meet the challenge of deeper learning.

Since the strategies cited in this book are research-based, you'll find references cited regularly throughout all the chapters and a sizable reference section at the end of each chapter. Your professors will expect you to think critically and support your

> "More than 30 years of research has shown that mindfulness is figuratively and literally enlivening. It's the way you feel when you're feeling passionate."
>
> —Dr. Ellen Langer, Harvard University, mindfulness researcher and author of The Power of Mindful Learning

> "Important achievements require a clear focus, all-out-effort, and a bottomless trunk full of strategies."
>
> —Carol Dweck, Stanford professor, and author of Mindset: The New Psychology of Success

> "The man who also knows why will be his own boss. As to methods there may be a million and then some, but principles are few. The man who grasps principles can successfully select his own methods. The man who tries methods, ignoring principles, is sure to have trouble."
>
> —Ralph Waldo Emerson, 19th-century author, poet, and philosopher

ideas with evidence. As authors, we should do the same and model that behavior for you.

You will find that the references cited represent a balanced blend of older, "classic" studies and more recent "cutting edge" research from a variety of fields. The time span of references cited serves to highlight the long-standing relevance of the ideas presented and their power to withstand the test of time. It also underscores the fact that the subject of success in college and beyond, like any other academic subject in the college curriculum, rests on a solid body of research and scholarship that spans multiple decades.

Introduction

Welcome to College

In the introduction to this book, you'll learn why college has the potential to be the most enriching experience of your life and one that will benefit you throughout life. The first year of college is a particularly critical stage of your educational development. It's a transitional stage during which students encounter the greatest challenges, the most stress, the most academic difficulties, and the highest risk of dropping out. However, it's also the year when students experience the greatest amount of learning and personal growth. These findings highlight the power of the first-year experience, the value of first-year courses designed to promote college success, and the importance of books like this.

In the introduction, you'll find convincing evidence that new students who participate in first-year experience courses (college-success courses) are more likely to stick with college, complete their degree, and get the most out of their college experience.

> "I could really relate to everything we talked about. It is a great class because you can use it in your other classes."
>
> "Everything we learned we will apply in our lives."
>
> "This is the only course I've ever taken that was about me."
>
> —Comments made by students when evaluating their first-year experience course

Preview of Content

Chapter 1

Touching All the Bases
Using Powerful Principles of Student Success and Key Campus Resources

This chapter focuses on the "big picture"—the most powerful principles you can implement to promote your own success and the key campus resources to use to help you succeed. It describes *what* these key principles and resources are, *why* they're effective, and *how* to capitalize on them.

Chapter 2

Liberal Arts and General Education
What it Means to be a Well-Educated Person in the 21st Century

The liberal arts represent the core of your college experience; they provide foundational, versatile skills that spell success in all college majors, careers, and life roles. In this chapter, you will gain a deeper understanding and appreciation of the liberal arts and acquire strategies for making the most of general education. You will learn about what it means to have a global perspective, how to develop yourself as a whole person, and how to enhance the overall quality (and marketability) of your college education.

Chapter 3
Goal Setting and Motivation
Moving from Intention to Action

The path to personal success begins with goals and finding the means (succession of steps) to reach those goals. People who set specific goals are more likely to succeed than people who simply tell themselves they're going to try hard and do their best. This chapter lays out the key steps involved in the process of setting effective goals, identifies key self-motivational strategies for staying on track and sustaining progress toward our goals, and describes how personal qualities such as self-efficacy, grit, and growth mindset are essential for achieving goals.

Chapter 4
Time Management
Prioritizing Tasks, Preventing Procrastination, and Promoting Productivity

Time is a valuable personal resource—if you gain greater control of it, you gain greater control of your life. Time managed well not only enables you to get work done in a timely manner, it also enables you to set and attain personal priorities and maintain balance in your life. This chapter offers a comprehensive set of strategies for managing time, combating procrastination, and ensuring that you spend time in a way that aligns with your educational goals and priorities.

> In high school, a lot of the work was done while in school, but in college all of your work is done on your time. You really have to organize yourself in order to get everything done."
>
> —First-year student's response to a question about what was most surprising about college life

Chapter 5
Deep Learning
Strategic Note-Taking, Reading, and Studying

This chapter helps you apply research on human learning and the human brain to become a more effective and efficient learner. It takes you through three key stages of the learning process—from the first stage of acquiring information through lectures and readings, through the second stage of studying and retaining the information you've acquired, to the final stage of retrieving (recalling) the information you studied. The ultimate goal of this chapter is to supply you with a set of powerful strategies that makes your learning *deep* (not surface-level memorization), *durable* (long-lasting), and *retrievable* (accessible to you when you need it).

Chapter 6
Test-Taking Skills and Strategies
What to do Before, During, and After Exams

This chapter supplies you with a systematic set of strategies for improving your performance on different types of tests, including multiple-choice and essay exams. It identifies strategies that can be used before, during, and after exams, as well as practical tips for becoming more "test wise" and less "test anxious."

Chapter 7
Three Key Academic Success and Lifelong Learning Skills
Information Literacy, Writing, and Speaking

Research, writing, and speaking effectively are flexible, transferable skills that can be applied to improve performance across all majors, all careers, and throughout life. In this chapter, you will acquire strategies to research and evaluate information, write papers and reports, and use writing as a learning and thinking tool. You will also learn how to make effective oral presentations, overcome speech anxiety, and gain self-confidence about speaking in public.

Chapter 8
Higher-Level Thinking
Moving Beyond Basic Knowledge to Critical and Creative Thinking

National surveys consistently show that the primary goal of college faculty is teaching students how to think critically. This chapter will help you understand what critical thinking is and empower you to think critically and creatively. You will acquire thinking strategies that move you beyond memorization to higher levels of thought and learn ways to demonstrate higher-level thinking on college exams and assignments.

Chapter 9
Social and Emotional Intelligence
Relating to Others and Regulating Emotions

This chapter identifies effective strategies for communicating with and relating to others, as well as strategies for understanding and managing our emotions—such as stress, anxiety, anger, and depression. Implementing the strategies discussed in this chapter will enhance the quality of your college experience and your overall quality of life.

Chapter 10
Diversity
Learning about and from Human Differences

This chapter clarifies what "diversity" really means and demonstrates how experiencing diversity can deepen learning, promote critical and creative thinking, and contribute to your personal and professional development. Strategies are provided for overcoming cultural barriers and biases that block our development of rewarding relationships with diverse people and learning from others whose cultural backgrounds differ from our own. Simply stated, we learn more from people who are different from us than we do from people similar to us. There's more diversity among college students today than at any other time in history. This chapter will help you capitalize on this learning opportunity.

Chapter 11
Educational Planning and Academic Decision-Making
Making Wise Choices about College Courses and a College Major

Making strategic choices about your courses and your major is essential to reaching your educational goals. You want to be sure your choice of a major is compatible with your personal interests, talents, and values. You should also have a strategic plan in mind (and in hand) that will enable you to strike a healthy balance between exploring your major options and making a final commitment. This chapter will help you strike this balance and make educational decisions that put you in the best position to reach your long-term goals.

 **Reflection P.1**

What percentage of first-year college students do you think have already decided on a major?

What percentage of these "decided" students do you think will eventually change their mind and end up with a different major by the time they graduate?

(See Chapter 11, p. 270 for answers to these questions.)

Chapter 12
Career Exploration, Preparation, and Development
Finding a Path to Your Future Profession

It may seem unusual to find a chapter on career success in a book for beginning college students. Even though career entry may be years away, career exploration and preparation should begin in the first term of college. Career planning gives you a practical, long-range goal to strive for and gets you thinking about how the skills you're using and developing in college align with the skills that promote your professional success beyond college. Career planning is really a form of *life* planning; the sooner you begin this process, the sooner you start gaining control of your future and start steering it in the direction you want it to go.

> It is hard to know how any student could truly understand whom [he or she] wants to be without thinking carefully about what career to pursue."
> —Derek Bok, president emeritus, Harvard University

Chapter 13
Financial Literacy
Managing Money and Minimizing Debt

Research shows that accumulating high levels of debt in college is associated with higher stress, lower academic performance, and greater risk of withdrawing from college. The good news is that research also shows that students who learn to use effective money management strategies are able to minimize unnecessary spending, reduce accumulation of debt and stress, and improve the quality of their academic performance. This chapter identifies effective strategies for tracking income and expenses, minimizing and avoiding debt, balancing time spent on schoolwork and employment, and making wise financial choices in college.

Chapter 14
Health and Wellness
Body, Mind, and Spirit

Humans cannot reach their full potential without attending to their physical well-being. Sustaining health and attaining peak levels of performance depend on how well we treat our *body*—what we put into it (healthy food), what we keep out of it (unhealthy substances), what we do with it (exercise), and how well we rejuvenate it (sleep). This chapter examines strategies for maximizing wellness by maintaining a balanced diet, attaining quality sleep, promoting total fitness, and avoiding risky behaviors that jeopardize our health and impair our performance.

 **Reflection P.2**

What does being "well-rounded" and living a "well-balanced" life mean to you?

Sequence of Chapter Topics

The chapters in this book are arranged in an order that allows you to ask and answer the following sequence of questions:

1. Why am I here?
2. Where do I want to go?
3. What must I do to get there?
4. How do I know when I've arrived?

The early chapters help you get oriented to the college environment, excite you about the college experience, and help you decide where college will take you. These chapters provide a mental map of your trip through college, help you set educational goals, and increase your awareness of key campus resources to get you there. Once you get a clear sense of why college is worth doing and where it will take you, you should become more enthused about taking action on the strategies suggested throughout the remainder of the book.

The middle chapters are devoted to helping you handle the practical, daily responsibilities you encounter in college and getting these day-to-day tasks done. The body of the book equips you with strategies for note-taking, reading, writing, learning, thinking, and test-taking.

The book's concluding chapters move you beyond specific day-to-day academic responsibilities and move you toward future planning and promoting your social, emotional, and physical well-being.

Process and Style of Presentation

As important as *what* information is contained in a book is *how* that information is presented. When writing this text, we made an intentional attempt to present information in a way that would: (a) stimulate your motivation to learn, (b) deepen your understanding of what you're learning, and (c) strengthen your retention (memory) for what you've learned.

We attempted to do this by incorporating the following principles of motivation, learning, and memory throughout the text.

- Each chapter begins with a **Preview** of the chapter's key goals and content, followed by an **Ignite Your Thinking** question designed to stimulate your thoughts and feelings about the upcoming material. This pre-reading exercise is designed to "warm up" or "tune up" your brain, preparing it to connect the ideas you're about to encounter in the chapter with the ideas you already have in your head. It's an instructional strategy that implements one of the most powerful principles of learning: we learn most effectively by relating what we're going to learn to what we've already learned and stored in our brain.

- Within each chapter, we periodically interrupt your reading with opportunities for **Reflection** that prompt you to pause and think about the material you've just read. These timely pauses for thought should keep you alert and mentally active throughout the reading process. They serve to intercept "attention drift" that normally takes place when the brain continually receives and processes information for an extended period, such as it does when reading (Willis, 2007). These reflections also deepen your understanding of the material because they ask you to *write* in response to your reading. Writing stimulates deeper learning and higher levels of thinking than simply underlining or highlighting sentences. We recommend keeping a record of your written responses to the textbook's reflection questions in a *learning journal*.

- **Exercises** at the *end* of each chapter ask you to reflect further on the knowledge you've acquired and transform that knowledge into informed action. We achieve *wisdom* when we move beyond simply acquiring knowledge to *applying* the knowledge—putting it into practice to help us become more wise, effective, and successful human beings (Staudinger, 2008).

  The strategic positioning of the *Ignite Your Thinking* questions at the beginning of each chapter, the *Reflections* interspersed throughout the chapter, and the application *Exercises* at the end of the chapter will keep you actively involved at three key stages of the reading process: the beginning, middle, and end.

- **Online self-assessment activities** are included in each chapter that relate to the topic being discussed. These self-assessment activities will provide you with a deeper understanding about how the chapter topics relate directly to your learning experiences. Upon completing these activities, personalized strategies for increasing your effectiveness will be recommended to you.

- Information is presented through **multiple modes of input**, which include: diagrams, pictures, cartoons, words of wisdom from famous and successful people, advice from current and former college students, and personal stories drawn from the authors' experiences. When you receive information through different formats, you process that information through multiple sensory modalities (input channels). This deepens learning by enabling your brain to lay down multiple memory tracks (traces) of the information it's taking in (Willis, 2007).

What follows is a list of the book's seven key instructional features. As you read these features, make a quick note in the side margin about how effective you think this feature will be in terms of motivating you to read and learn from the book.

1. Research and Scholarly Support

The book's ideas and recommendations are grounded in research and scholarship drawn from a variety of academic fields. You will find references cited regularly throughout the chapters and a sizable reference section at the end of the chapter. The sheer quantity of references cited serves as testimony to the fact that the subject matter of this book is built on a solid body of research and scholarship, just like any other academic subject studied in the college curriculum. You'll also find that the references include a balanced blend of older, "classic" scholarship and more recent "cutting edge" research.

2. Boxed Summaries

At different points in the text, you will find boxes containing summaries of top tips for success. These summaries pull together key strategies relating to the same concept and organize them in the same place physically, which will help you organize and retain them mentally.

3. Quotes

Throughout the book, quotes from successful and influential people appear in the side margins that relate to and reinforce ideas covered at that point of the chapter.

You'll find quotes from famous individuals who have lived in different historical periods and who have specialized in a variety of fields, including politics, philosophy, religion, science, business, music, art, and athletics. The wide-ranging time frames, cultures, and fields of study represented by the people quoted demonstrate that their words of wisdom are timeless and universal. It's our hope that the words of these highly successful and respected individuals will inspire you to put their words in practice.

You can also learn a lot from the first-hand experiences of current and former students. Throughout the book, you'll find comments and advice from students at different stages of the college experience, including college graduates (alumni). Studies show that students can learn a great deal from their peers—especially from more experienced peers who've "been there, done that." By hearing about their success stories and stumbling blocks, you can benefit from their college experiences to improve your college experience.

4. Authors' Experiences

In each chapter, you will find at least one author's experience related to the chapter topic. We share our own experiences as college students, our professional experiences working with students as instructors and advisors, and our personal experiences in other areas of our lives. Studies show that when people hear stories shared by others, their understanding and memory for key ideas contained in the stories is deepened and strengthened (McDrury & Alterio, 2002). We share our stories for the purpose of personalizing the book and with the hope that you'll learn from our experiences—including learning from our mistakes!

 Reflection P.3

Have you received any tips or advice from friends or family about what to do, or what not to do, in college?

If you have, what kind of advice did you receive and who gave it to you?

If you haven't, why do you think none of your friends or family members have offered you any advice?

5. Concept Maps (Graphic Organizers): Verbal-Visual Aids

Throughout the book, you will find ideas visually organized into diagrams, charts, and figures. When important concepts are represented in a visual-spatial format, we're more likely to retain them because two different memory traces are recorded in our brain: verbal (words) and visual (images).

6. Cartoons: Emotional-Visual Aids

You will find cartoons sprinkled throughout the text to lighten up the reading and provide you with a little entertainment. More importantly, the cartoons relate to an important concept and are also intended to strengthen your retention of that concept by reinforcing it with a visual image (drawing) and an emotional experience (humor). If the cartoon triggers at least a snicker, your body will release adrenaline—a hormone that facilitates memory formation. If it generates actual laughter, it will also stimulate your brain to release endorphins—natural, morphine-like chemicals that lower stress and elevate mood.

7. Learning More through the World Wide Web

At the end of each chapter are web-based resources containing additional information relating to the chapter's major ideas. One of the major goals of a college education is to prepare students to become independent, self-directed learners. We hope that the information presented in each chapter's topic will stimulate your interest and motivation to learn more about the topic. If it does, you can use the online resources cited at the end of the chapter to access additional information.

 Reflection P.4

Look back at the seven features of this book that have just been described. Which of these features do you think will be most effective for stimulating your interest in reading and learning from the book?

> I've gained more insight into who I am as a person."
>
> I've gotten a better sense of how to manage my life."
>
> —Comments made by first-year students in a course that used this book

We firmly believe that the content of this book, and the manner in which the content is delivered, will empower you not only to survive college, but to *thrive* in college and beyond. The skills and strategies found on the following pages promote success throughout life. Self-awareness, effective planning and decision making, learning deeply and remembering longer, thinking critically and creatively, speaking and writing persuasively, managing time and money effectively, communicating and relating effectively with others, and maintaining health and wellness are more than college success skills—they are *life* success skills.

> Learning doesn't stop after college; it's a lifelong process. If you strive to apply the ideas in this book, you'll develop habits that will enable you to thrive in college and beyond.

AUTHOR'S EXPERIENCE

I've learned a lot from teaching the first-year seminar (college success course) and from writing this book. Before I taught this course, I didn't have a clear idea about the meaning, purpose, and value of a college education, or why general education was so important for achieving personal and professional success. By preparing for this course, I also learned new strategies for improving my memory and my writing, as well as for managing my time, money, and health. I continue to use these strategies in my personal and professional life. My only regret is that I didn't take a course like this when I was a college freshman. If I had, I would have been able to apply these life-success skills earlier in my life.

—*Joe Cuseo*

References

McDrury, J., and Alterio, M. G. (2002). *Learning through storytelling: Using reflection and experience in higher education contexts.* Palmerston North, New Zealand: Dunmore Press.

Staudinger, U. M. (2008). A psychology of wisdom: History and recent developments. *Research in Human Development, 5,* 107–120.

Willis, J. (2007). *Brain-friendly strategies for the inclusion classroom.* Alexandria, VA: Association for Supervision and Curriculum Development.

Acknowledgments

I'd like to take this opportunity to thank several people who have played an important role in my life and whose positive influence made this book possible. My parents, Mildred (nee, Carmela) and Blase (nee, Biaggio) Cuseo, for the many sacrifices they made to support my education. My wife, Mary, for her patience, love, and meticulous editorial feedback. My uncle, Jim Vigilis, for being a second father and life coach to me during my formative years. Jim Cooper, my best friend, for being a mentor to me in graduate school. My students, who taught me a lot and contributed their insightful perspectives, poignant poems, and illustrations to this book. Finally, thanks to all the author-centered professionals at Kendall Hunt who gave me the freedom to write a book I believe in and reflect who I am.

—Joe Cuseo

I would like to thank my wife Holly and my children Sonya, Sara, Michael, Maya, Isaiah, and Olivia for being my continual inspiration and source of unconditional love. I would also like to thank my father and mother (Big "A" and Margaret) for instilling in me that education is the key to most all that is valuable in our society. In addition, I would like to acknowledge the support that Eastern Kentucky University gave me. They provided me with a great undergraduate education and wonderful employment. Thanks Rhonda for your always continued friendship and support. In addition, I want to thank Bob King at the Kentucky Council on Postsecondary Education who is a good friend and good boss and believes deeply that high-quality education of all is the ultimate path to a truly civilized nation. I would also like to thank my coauthors and Kendall Hunt for the opportunity to be part of a great team. Lastly, I would like to thank my mentors and students who gave me encouragement and motivation.

—Aaron Thompson

My thanks go out to my family, Dominic, Nicolas, and Brianna, for their continuous support. Special thanks go out to my parents, Sal and Yolanda, who despite only their elementary school education drilled in me that I needed to have both *educación y ganas* (education and desire/drive) if I were going to achieve my dreams. That has always stayed with me. Over the years that lesson has shaped the work that I do and has inspired my contributions to this book. I thank the colleagues and students who have motivated and supported my efforts. I am especially grateful to my coauthors, Aaron and Joe, and to Paul at Kendall Hunt for their sharing and collaboration.

—Michele Campagna

If not for the love and support of my parents, Wyman and Fae Sox, and son, Matt Fecas, my involvement in this project would never have happened. Thanks also to Kendall Hunt's Paul Carty's wisdom in assembling the writing team and assigning a crackerjack editorial team. I also tremendously value my colleagues for their encouragement and feedback through the writing and review process.

—Viki Sox Fecas

About the Authors

Joe Cuseo holds a doctoral degree in Educational Psychology and Assessment from the University of Iowa and is Professor Emeritus of Psychology. For more than 25 years, he directed the first-year seminar—a core college success course required of all new students.

He's a 14-time recipient of the "faculty member of the year award" on his home campus—a student-driven award based on effective teaching and academic advising; a recipient of the "Outstanding First-Year Student Advocate Award" from the National Resource Center for The First-Year Experience and Students in Transition; and a recipient of the "Diamond Honoree Award" from the American College Personnel Association (ACPA) for contributions made to student development and the Student Affairs profession.

Currently, Joe serves as an educational advisor and consultant for AVID—a nonprofit organization whose mission is to promote the college access and college success of underserved student populations. He has delivered hundreds of campus workshops and conference presentations across North America, as well as Europe, Asia, Australia, and the Middle East.

Aaron Thompson, Ph.D., is executive vice president and chief academic officer at the Kentucky Council on Postsecondary Education and a professor of sociology in the Department of Educational Leadership and Policy Studies at Eastern Kentucky University. Thompson has a Ph.D. in sociology in the areas of organizational behavior and race and gender relations. Thompson has researched, taught, and/or consulted in the areas of assessment, diversity, leadership, ethics, research methodology and social statistics, multicultural families, race and ethnic relations, student success, first-year students, retention, and organizational design. He is nationally recognized in the areas of educational attainment, academic success, and cultural competence.

Dr. Thompson has worked in a variety of capacities within two-year and four-year institutions. He got his start in college teaching at a community college. His latest coauthored books are *The Sociological Outlook*; *Infusing Diversity and Cultural Competence Into Teacher Education*; *Diversity and the College Experience*; *Thriving in the Community College and Beyond: Research-Based Strategies for Academic Success and Personal Development*; *Humanity, Diversity, & the Liberal Arts: The Foundation of a College Education*; *Focus on Success*; and *Black Men and Divorce*. He has more than 30 publications and numerous research and peer-reviewed presentations. Thompson has traveled throughout the United States and internationally, giving more than 800 workshops, seminars, and invited lectures in the areas of race and gender diversity, living an unbiased life, overcoming obstacles to gain success, creating a school environment for academic success, cultural competence, workplace interaction, organizational goal setting, building relationships, the first-year seminar, and a variety of other topics. He has been or is a consultant to educational institutions, corporations, nonprofit organizations, police departments, and other governmental agencies.

Michele Campagna, Ed.D., is the executive director of the Center for Advising and Student Transitions at Montclair State University in New Jersey. Dr. Campagna provides leadership for a comprehensive and holistic program designed to retain and engage first-year, freshman, sophomore, and transfer students. Dr. Campagna has over 20 years of experience teaching various types of first-year seminar courses and directing services for students in transition at both two-year and four-year institutions.

Dr. Campagna holds an Ed.D. in higher education and is a recipient of the "Outstanding First-Year Student Advocate Award" from the National Resource Center for the First-Year Experience and Students in Transition. She is the author of "New Student Experience: A Holistic and Collaborative Approach to First-Year Retention" in *Exploring the Evidence: Campus-Wide Initiatives in the First College Year*, published by the National Resource Center for the First-Year Experience and Students in Transition. Dr. Campagna has presented at many statewide and national conferences on designing and implementing student engagement and retention initiatives, strategic planning, assessment, and diversity.

Viki Sox Fecas has a Ph.D. in educational administration from the University of South Carolina (USC). In her role as program manager for freshman and pre-freshman programs, she coordinated the career component for all 150+ sections of the number one-ranked University 101 program in the country. She served as a career resource for international scholars visiting the National Resource Center (NRC).

Viki has served as an adjunct professor in the Higher Education and Student Affairs graduate program at USC. She was recognized as the *Outstanding Freshman Advocate* in 1996. She took University 101 as a freshman at USC, and has been teaching for over 20 years, including sections dedicated to transfer students. Her research interests center around the transition of college students, with a special interest in transfer students. She has written career chapters for the U101 *Transitions* book and *Your College Experience*. She has been a regular presenter at both the National First-Year Experience and Students in Transition Conferences sponsored by the NRC.

Introduction

Ready for takeoff,
On my adventure today,
As I take a seat in my chair
And clear the way.

Eager people around,
With destinations to go,
As a woman at the front says,
"Please find a seat in any row."

Some people are anxious,
Waiting to take flight,
To soar above the rest,
With aspirations in sight

Our first day of college,
A chance to start anew,
To find out who we are,
And learn what is true.

—Waiting to Take Flight, *a poem by Kimberly Castaneda, first-year student*

Congratulations! We applaud your decision to continue your education. Your previous enrollment in school was required, but your decision to continue your education in college is entirely *your choice*. By choosing to enter *higher education*, you've chosen to learn and think at a higher level than you did in high school. You're about to begin an exciting and challenging journey that has the potential to be the most enriching experience of your life.

 Reflection I.1

Why have you decided to attend college?

What are you most *looking forward to* about college?

After college, it's probably safe to say that you will never again be a member of an organization or community with as many resources and services available to you that have been intentionally designed to promote your learning, development, and success. If you capitalize on the resources available to you, and if you utilize effective college-going strategies—such as those suggested in this book—you can create a life-changing experience for yourself that will enhance your quality of life for the remainder of your life. See **Box I.1** for a snapshot summary of the multiple, lifelong benefits of a college education and college degree. (Supporting references are cited at the bottom of the box.)

Box I.1

The Power of College: Economic and Personal Benefits of a College Education

Approximately 31% of Americans hold a four-year college degree (Lumina Foundation, 2015). When they are compared with people from similar social and economic backgrounds who did not continue their education beyond high school, research reveals that a college education is well worth it—both in terms of both personal development and career advancement.

Summarized below are positive outcomes associated with a college education and a college degree. Their wide-ranging impact on the whole person and society at large serve as testimony to the power of the college experience.

"It's an irrefutable fact that college gives you a significant and persistent advantage decade after decade."

—*Mary C. Daly, Vice President of the Federal Reserve Bank of San Francisco (quoted in the* Los Angeles Times, *April 15, 2015)*

1. Economic and Career Benefits
   - Job security and stability—college graduates have lower rates of unemployment and lower risk of being laid off work
   - Higher income—the gap between the earnings of high school and college graduates is large and *growing*. Individuals holding a bachelor's degree earn an average salary that's $17,500 higher than high school graduates. When these differences are

Box I.1 *(continued)*

calculated over a lifetime, the income of families headed by people with a bachelor's degree earn an income that's over a million dollars more than families headed by people with a high school diploma. (See **Figure I.1**.)

- Better retirement and pension benefits
- Career versatility and mobility—greater ability to move out of one position into another (a college graduate has more job options)
- Career advancement—greater opportunity to move up to higher-level professional positions (in other words a college graduate has more opportunities for job promotions)

- Career satisfaction—college graduates are more likely to be in careers that interest them and in positions they find stimulating, challenging, and personally fulfilling
- Career autonomy—college graduates have more opportunities to work independently (without supervision) and make their own on-the-job decisions
- Career prestige—college graduates are more likely to hold higher-status positions, (i.e., jobs considered to be desirable and highly regarded by society)

FIGURE I.1

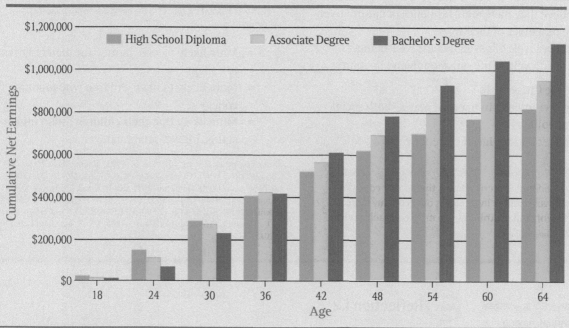

©Kendall Hunt Publishing Company

2. **Advanced Intellectual Skills**
   College graduates possess:
   - Greater knowledge
   - More effective problem-solving skills—better ability to deal with complex and ambiguous (uncertain) problems
   - Greater openness to new ideas

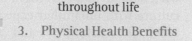

> "Without exception, the observed changes [during college] involve greater breadth, expansion, and appreciation for the new and different . . . and the evidence for their presence is compelling."
>
> —*Ernest Pascarella and Pat Terenzini,* How College Affects Students

- More advanced levels of moral reasoning
- More effective consumer choices and decisions
- Wiser long-term investments
- Clearer sense of self-identity—greater awareness and knowledge of personal talents, interests, values, and needs
- Greater likelihood of learning continually throughout life

3. **Physical Health Benefits**
   - Better health insurance—college graduates are more likely to have insurance coverage and have more comprehensive coverage
   - Better dietary habits

(continued)

Box I.1 *(continued)*

- Exercise more regularly
- Have lower rates of obesity
- Live longer and healthier lives

4. Social Benefits
   - Greater social self-confidence
   - Better ability to understand and communicate effectively with others
   - Greater popularity
   - More effective leadership skills
   - Higher levels of marital satisfaction

5. Emotional Benefits
   - Lower levels of anxiety
   - Higher levels of self-esteem
   - Greater sense of self-efficacy—college graduates believe they have more influence or control over the outcomes of their lives
   - Higher levels of psychological well-being
   - Higher levels of life satisfaction and happiness

6. Effective Citizenship
   - Greater interest in national issues—both social and political
   - Greater knowledge of current events

The evidence is overwhelming that higher education improves people's lives, makes our economy more efficient, and contributes to a more equitable society."
—The College Board

- Higher voting participation rates
- Higher rates of participation in civic affairs and community service

7. Higher Quality of Life for Their Children
   - Less likely to smoke during pregnancy
   - Provide better health care for their children
   - Spend more time with their children
   - More likely to involve their children in stimulating educational activities that advance their cognitive (mental) development

My three-month-old boy is very important to me, and it is important I graduate from college so my son, as well as I, live a better life."
—First-year student's response to the question: "What is most important to you?"

- More likely to save money for their children to go to college
- More likely to have children who graduate from college
- More likely that their children attain higher-status, higher-salary careers

Sources: Andres & Wyn (2010); Astin (1993); Baum, Ma, & Payea (2013); Bowen (1977, 1997) ; Carnevale, Strohl, & Melton (2011); Dee (2004); Feldman & Newcomb (1994); Hamilton (2011, 2014); Knox, Lindsay, & Kolb (1993); Lumina Foundation (2013, 2015); Pascarella & Terenzini (2005); Pew Research Center (2014); Seifert, et al. (2008); SHEEO (2012); The College Board (2013); The Hamilton Project (2014); Tomsho (2009); U.S. Bureau of Labor Statistics (2015).

For the individual, having access to and successfully graduating from an institution of higher education has proved to be the path to a better job, to better health and to a better life."
—The College Board

 Reflection I.2

Glance back at the seven major benefits or positive outcomes of a college education listed in **Box I.1**. If you were to rank them in terms of their importance to you, which three would rank at the top your list? Why?

The Importance of the First Year of College

Your transition into higher education represents an important life transition. Somewhat similar to an immigrant moving to a new country, you're moving into a new culture with unfamiliar expectations, regulations, customs, and language (Chaskes, 1996). (For definitions and "translations" of the new language you'll encounter in college, see the Glossary and Dictionary of College Vocabulary, pp. 385–392.)

The *first* year of college is undoubtedly the most important year of the college experience because it's a *transitional* stage. Students report the most change, the most learning, and the most development during their first year of college (Flowers, et al., 2001; HERI, 2014; Light, 2001). Other research suggests that the academic habits students develop in their first year are likely to persist throughout their remaining years of college (Schilling, 2001). When graduating seniors look back at their college experience, many of them say that their first year was the time of greatest change and the time when they made the most significant improvements in their approach to learning. Here's how one senior put it during a personal interview:

Interviewer: What have you learned about your approach to learning [in college]?

Student: I had to learn how to study. I went through high school with a 4.0 average. I didn't have to study. It was a breeze. I got to the university and there was no structure. No one took attendance to make sure I was in class. No one checked my homework. No one told me I had to do something. There were no quizzes on the readings. I did not work well with this lack of structure. It took my first year and a half to learn to deal with it. But I had to teach myself to manage my time. I had to teach myself how to study. I had to teach myself how to learn in a different environment (Chickering & Schlossberg, 1998, p. 47).

In some ways, the first-year experience in college is similar to ocean surfing or downhill skiing: It can be filled with the most exciting thrills—greatest learning and development, but also the most dangerous spills—it's the year when students experience the most stress, the most academic difficulties, and the highest college withdrawal rates (American College Testing, 2015; Morrow & Ackerman, 2012). The ultimate goal of downhill skiing and surfing is to experience the thrills, avoid the spills, and finish the run on your feet and feeling exhilarated. The same can be said for the first year of college; studies show that if students complete their first-year experience in good standing, their chances for successfully completing college increase dramatically (American College Testing, 2009).

You'll find that the research cited and the advice provided in this book point to one major conclusion: Success in college depends on you—you make it happen by what you do and how well you capitalize on the resources available to you. Don't let college happen *to* you; make it happen *for* you—take charge of your college experience and take advantage of the college resources that are at your command.

After reviewing 40 years of research on how college affects students, two distinguished researchers reached the following conclusion:

The impact of college is largely determined by individual effort and involvement in the academic, interpersonal, and extracurricular [co-curricular] offerings on a campus. Students are not passive recipients of institutional efforts to "educate" or "change" them, but rather bear major responsibility for any gains they derive from their postsecondary [college] experience (Pascarella & Terenzini, 2005, p. 602).

Compared to your previous experiences in school, college will provide you with a broader range of courses to choose from, more resources to capitalize on, and more decision-making opportunities. Your particular college experience will end up being different than any other college student because you have the freedom to actively shape and create it in a way that's uniquely your own.

Reflection I.3

Why have you decided to attend the particular college or university you're enrolled in now?

Are you happy to be here?

> **"** One of the major transitions from high school to college involves the unlearning of past attitudes, values, and behaviors and the learning of new ones. This represents a major social and psychological transition and a time when students may be more ready to change than at any other point in their college career."
>
> —*Ernest Pascarella & Patrick Terenzini,* How College Affects Students

> **"** What students do during college counts more than who they are or where they go to college."
>
> —*George Kuh, author,* Student Success in College

Importance of a First-Year Experience Course (also known as a First-Year Seminar)

If you're reading this book, you are already beginning to take charge of your college experience because you're likely to be enrolled in a course that's designed to promote your college success. Research strongly indicates that new students who participate in first-year experience courses are more likely to continue in college until they complete their degree and perform at a higher level. These positive effects have been found for:

- All types of students (under-prepared and well-prepared, minority and majority, residential and commuter, male and female),
- Students at all types of colleges (two-year and four-year, public and private),
- Students attending colleges of all sizes (small, mid-sized, and large), and
- Students attending colleges in all locations (urban, suburban, and rural).

(Sources: Barefoot, et al., 1998; Boudreau & Kromrey, 1994; Cuseo, 2011; Cuseo & Barefoot, 1996; Fidler & Godwin, 1994; Glass & Garrett, 1995; Grunder & Hellmich, 1996; Hunter & Linder, 2005; Keup & Barefoot, 2005; Padgett, Keup, & Pascarella, 2013; Porter & Swing, 2006; Shanley & Witten, 1990; Sidle & McReynolds, 1999; Starke, Harth, & Sirianni, 2001; Thomson, 1998; Tobolowsky, 2005).

There has been more research on the first-year experience course and more evidence supporting its positive impact on student success than any other course in the college curriculum. Give this course your best effort and take full advantage of what it has to offer. If you do, you'll take an important first step toward excelling in college and in life beyond college.

Enjoy the trip!

> "Being in this class has helped me a lot. What I learned I will apply to all my other classes."
>
> "I am now one of the peer counselors on campus, and without this class my first semester, I don't think I could have done as well, and by participating in this class again (as a teaching assistant), it reinforced this belief."
>
> —*Comments made by students when evaluating their first-year experience course*

References

American College Testing. (2015). *College student retention and graduation rates from 2000 through 2015*. Retrieved from http://www.act.org/research/policymakers/pdf/retain_2015.pdf.

Andres, L., & Wyn, J. (2010). *The making of a generation: The children of the 1970s in adulthood*. Buffalo, NY: University of Toronto Press.

Astin, A. W. (1993). *What matters in college?* San Francisco: Jossey-Bass.

Barefoot, B. O., Warnock, C. L., Dickinson, M. P., Richardson, S. E., & Roberts, M. R. (Eds.). (1998). *Exploring the evidence: Vol. 2. Reporting outcomes of first-year seminars* (Monograph No. 29). Columbia: National Resource Center for the First-Year Experience and Students in Transition, University of South Carolina.

Baum, S., Ma, J., & Payea, K. (2013). *Education pays 2013: The benefits of higher education for individuals and society*. Washington, DC: The College Board. Retrieved from http://trends.collegeboard.org/sites/default/files/education-pays-2013-full-report-022714.pdf.

Boudreau, C., & Kromrey, J. (1994). A longitudinal study of the retention and academic performance of participants in a freshman orientation course. *Journal of College Student Development, 35*, 444–449.

Bowen, H. R. (1977). *Investment in learning: The individual and social value of American higher education*. San Francisco: Jossey-Bass.

Bowen, H. R. (1997). *Investment in learning: The individual and social value of American higher education* (2nd ed.). Baltimore: Johns Hopkins Press.

Carnevale, A. P., Strohl, J., & Melton, M. (2011). *What's it worth? The economic value of college majors*. Washington, DC: Center on Education and the Workforce, Georgetown University. Retrieved from https://cew.georgetown.edu/wp-content/uploads/2014/11/whatsitworth-complete.pdf.

Chaskes, J. (1996). The first-year student as immigrant. *Journal of The Freshman Year Experience & Students in Transition, 8*(1), 79–91.

Chickering, A. W., & Schlossberg, N. K. (1998). Moving on: Seniors as people in transition. In J. N. Gardner, G. Van der Veer, et al. (Eds.), *The senior year experience* (pp. 37–50). San Francisco: Jossey-Bass.

Cuseo, J. B., & Barefoot, B. O. (1996). A natural marriage: The extended orientation seminar and the community college. In J. Henkin (Ed.), *The community college: Opportunity and access for America's first-year students* (pp. 59–68). Columbia: National Resource Center for the First-Year Experience and Students in Transition, University of South Carolina.

Dee, T. (2004). Are there civic returns to education? *Journal of Public Economics, 88,* 1697–1720.

Feldman, K. A., & Newcomb, T. M. (1994). *The impact of college on students.* New Brunswick: Transaction Publishers.

Fidler, P., & Godwin, M. (1994). Retaining African-American students through the freshman seminar. *Journal of Developmental Education, 17,* 34–41.

Flowers, L., Osterlind, S., Pascarella, E., & Pierson, C. (2001). How much do students learn in college? Cross-sectional estimates using the College Basic Academic Subjects Examination. *Journal of Higher Education, 72,* 565–583.

Glass, J., & Garrett, M. (1995). Student participation in a college orientation course: Retention, and grade point average. *Community College Journal of Research and Practice, 19,* 117–132.

Grunder, P., & Hellmich, D. (1996). Academic persistence and achievement of remedial students in a community college's success program. *Community College Review, 24,* 21–33.

Hamilton, W. (2011, December 29). "College still worth it, study says." *Los Angeles Times,* p. B2.

Hamilton, W. (2014, June 25). "College still good bet, study says." *Los Angeles Times,* p. B4.

HERI (Higher Education Research Institute). (2014). *Your first college year survey 2014.* Los Angeles, CA: Cooperative Institutional Research Program, University of California-Los Angeles.

Hunter, M. A., & Linder, C. W. (2005). First-year seminars. In M. L. Upcraft, J. N. Gardner, B. O. Barefoot, et al. (Eds.), *Challenging and supporting the first-year student: A handbook for improving the first year of college* (pp. 275–291). San Francisco: Jossey-Bass.

Keup, J. R., & Barefoot, B. O. (2005). Learning how to be a successful student: Exploring the impact of first-year seminars on student outcomes. *Journal of the First-Year Experience, 17*(1), 11–47.

Knox, W. E., Lindsay, P., & Kolb, M. N. (1993). *Does college make a difference? Long-term changes in activities and attitudes.* Westport, CT: Greenwood.

Light, R. J. (2001). *Making the most of college: Students speak their minds.* Cambridge, MA: Harvard University Press.

Lumina Foundation. (2013). *A stronger nation through higher education.* Indianapolis IN: Author. Retrieved from http://www.pesc.org/library/docs/about_us/whitepapers/a-stronger-nation-2013lumina.pdf.

Lumina Foundation. (2015). *A stronger nation through higher education.* Indianapolis IN: Author. Retrieved from http://www.luminafoundation.org/files/publications/A_stronger_nation_through_higher_education-2015.pdf.

Morrow, J., & Ackermann, M. E. (2012). Intention to persist and retention of first-year students: The importance of motivation and sense of belonging. *College Student Journal, 46*(3), 483–491.

Padgett, R. D., Keup, J. R., & Pascarella, E. T. (2013). The impact of first-year seminars on college students' life-long learning orientations. *Journal of Student Affairs Research and Practice, 50*(2), 133–151.

Pascarella, E., & Terenzini, P. (2005). *How college affects students: A third decade of research* (Vol. 2). San Francisco: Jossey-Bass.

Pew Research Center. (2014, February). *The rising cost of not going to college.* Retrieved from http://www.pewsocialtrends.org/2014/02/11/the-rising-cost-of-not-going-to-college/.

Porter, S. R., & Swing, R. L. (2006). Understanding how first-year seminars affect persistence. *Research in Higher Education, 47*(1), 89–109.

Schilling, K. (2001, August). *Plenary address.* Presented at The Summer Institute on First-Year Assessment, Asheville, North Carolina.

Seifert, T. A., Goodman, K. M., Lindsay, N., Jorgensen, J. D., Wolniak, G. C., Pascarella, E. T., & Blaich, C. (2008). The effects of liberal arts experiences on liberal arts outcomes. *Research in Higher Education, 49,* 107–125.

Shanley, M., & Witten, C. (1990). University 101 freshman seminar course: A longitudinal study of persistence, retention, and graduation rates. *NASPA Journal, 27,* 344–352.

SHEEO (State Higher Education Executive Officers). (2012). *State higher education finance, FY 2011.* Retrieved from http://www.sheeo.org/sites/default/files/publications/SHEF_FY11.pdf.

Sidle, M., & McReynolds, J. (1999). The freshman year experience: Student retention and student success. *NASPA Journal, 36,* 288–300.

Starke, M. C., Harth, M., & Sirianni, F. (2001). Retention, bonding, and academic achievement: Success of a first-year seminar. *Journal of the First-Year Experience and Students in Transition, 13*(2), 7–35.

The College Board. (2013). *Education pays: The benefits of higher education for individuals and society.* Retrieved from https://trends.collegeboard.org/sites/default/files/education-pays-2013-full-report.pdf.

The Hamilton Project. (2014). *Major decisions: What graduates earn over their lifetimes.* Washington, DC: Brookings Institution. Retrieved from http://www.hamiltonproject.org/papers/major_decisions_what_graduates_earn_over_their_lifetimes/.

Thomson, R. (1998). University of Vermont. In B. O. Barefoot, C. L. Warnock, M. P. Dickinson, S. E. Richardson, & M. R. Roberts (Eds.), *Exploring the evidence: Vol. 2. Reporting outcomes of first-year seminars* (Monograph No. 29, pp. 77–78). Columbia: National Resource Center for the First-Year Experience and Students in Transition, University of South Carolina.

Tobolowsky, B. F. (2005). *The 2003 national survey on first-year seminars: Continuing innovations in the college curriculum* (Monograph No. 41). Columbia: National Resource Center for the First-Year Experience and Students in Transition, University of South Carolina.

Tomsho, R. (2009, April 22). Study tallies education's gap on GDP. *Wall Street Journal.* Retrieved from http://www.wsj.com/articles/SB124040633530943487.

U.S. Bureau of Labor Statistics. (2015). *Employment projections.* United States of Department of Labor. Retrieved from http://www.bls.gov/emp/ep_chart_001.htm.

Touching All the Bases

USING POWERFUL PRINCIPLES OF STUDENT SUCCESS AND KEY CAMPUS RESOURCES

This chapter focuses on the "big picture"—the most powerful principles you can implement to promote your own success and the key campus resources you can use to help you succeed. It describes *what* these key principles and resources are, *why* they're effective, and *how* to capitalize on them.

Alert you to the most powerful strategies and resources that you can use immediately to get off to a fast start in college and use continually to achieve excellence throughout your college experience.

 Reflection 1.1

1. In what three major ways do you think college will differ from high school?

2. What three personal characteristics, qualities, or strategies do you think will be most important for college success?

Powerful Principles of College Success

Research points to four powerful principles of college success:

1. Active Involvement (Engagement)
2. Capitalizing on Campus Resources (Resourcefulness)
3. Interpersonal Interaction and Collaboration (Social Integration)
4. Reflection and Self-Awareness (Mindfulness)

(Sources: Astin, 1993; Barber, et al., 2013; Kuh, et al., 2005; Light, 2001; Pascarella & Terenzini, 1991, 2005; Tinto, 1993.)

FIGURE 1.1: The Diamond of College Success

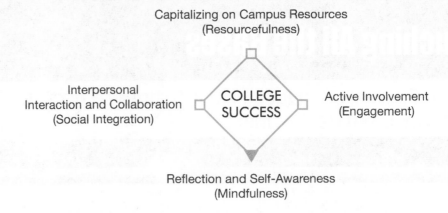

©Kendall Hunt Publishing Company

These four principles are presented in the opening chapter of this book because they represent the foundational basis for all success strategies discussed throughout the book.

Touching the First Base of College Success: Active Involvement (Engagement)

Research indicates that active involvement may be the most powerful principle of human learning and college success (Astin, 1993; Kuh, et al., 2005). To succeed in college, you can't be a passive spectator; you need to be an active player.

Active involvement includes the following key components:

- The amount of *time* you devote to the college experience—inside and outside the classroom
- The degree of *effort or energy* (mental and physical) you invest in the learning process.

Think of something you do with intensity, passion, and commitment. If you were to approach college in the same way, you would be faithfully implementing the principle of active involvement. Here's how you can apply both key components of active involvement—time and energy—to the major learning challenges you'll face in college.

Time in Class

Not surprisingly, the total amount of time you spend on learning is associated with how much you learn and how deeply you learn. This association leads to a straight-forward recommendation: Attend all your classes in all your courses. It may be tempting to skip or cut classes because college professors are less likely to monitor your attendance or take roll than high school teachers. However, don't let this new freedom fool you into thinking that missing classes will not affect your course grades. Over the past 75 years, numerous studies have shown a direct relationship between class attendance and course grades—as one goes up or down, so does the other (Credé, Roch, & Kieszczynka, 2010; Launius, 1997; Shimoff & Catania, 2001; Tagliacollo, Volpato, & Pereira, 2010). **Figure 1.2** depicts the results of a study conducted at the City Colleges of Chicago, which shows the relationship be-

Tell me and I'll listen. Show me and I'll understand. Involve me and I'll learn.

—*Teton Lakota Indian saying*

My biggest recommendation: GO TO CLASS. I learned this the hard way my first semester. You'll be surprised what you pick up just by being there. I wish someone would have informed me of this before I started school."

—*Advice to new students from a college sophomore*

FIGURE 1.2: **Relationship between Class Attendance Rate and Course Final Grades**

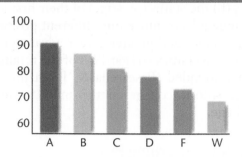

tween students' class attendance during the first five weeks of the term and their final course grades.

Look at going to class like going to work. If you miss work days, it lowers your pay; if you miss classes, it lowers your grades.

Eighty percent of success is showing up."

—Woody Allen, Oscar & Golden Globe winning film director, writer, and author

Reflection 1.2

During your senior year in high school, about how many hours per week did you spend on schoolwork outside of class?

Time Spent on Coursework Outside of Class

In college, you will spend much less time sitting in class than you did in high school; however, you will be expected to spend much more time working on your courses outside of class. Less than 40% of beginning college students report having studied six or more hours per week during their final year in high school (Pryor, et al., 2012) and only one-third expect to spend more than 20 hours per week preparing for class in college (National Survey of Student Engagement, 2009).

Unfortunately, less than 10% of beginning college students say they will study at least two hours out of class for every hour spent in class—which is what most college faculty believe is necessary to do well in college (Kuh, 2005). This has to change if college students are to earn good grades. Just as successful athletes need to put in time and effort to improve their physical performance, successful students need to do the same to improve their academic performance. Studies repeatedly show that the more time college students spend on academic work outside of class, the higher grades they earn in their college courses (National Survey of Student Engagement, 2009). In one study of more than 25,000 college students it was found that the percentage of students receiving "A" grades was almost three times higher for students who spent 40 or more hours per week on academic work than it was for students who spent between 20 and 40 hours. For students who spent 20 or fewer hours per week on academic work, the percentage of them receiving a grade of "C" or below was almost twice as high as it was for students who spent 40 or more hours on academic work (Pace, 1990, 1995).

If you need further motivation to achieve good grades, keep in mind that higher grades earned in college translates into career success after college. Research on college graduates indicates that the higher their grades were in college, the higher: (a) their starting salary, (b) the status (prestige) of their first job, and (c) their career mobility (ability to change jobs or move into different positions). This relationship between higher college grades and greater career advantages exists for students at all types of colleges and universities—regardless of the reputation or prestige of the institution the students attended (Pascarella & Terenzini, 1991, 2005). In other words, how well students do in college matters more to their career success than where they went to college.

Active Involvement in the Learning Process

College success will require that you work harder (put in more time than high school) and smarter (learn more strategically and effectively). Probably the most powerful principle of effective learning is active involvement (engagement); there's simply no such thing as "passive learning." You can ensure you're actively involved in the learning process by engaging in some form of *action* on what you're learning, such as the actions listed below.

- *Writing.* For example, when reading, take notes on what you're reading rather than passively highlighting sentences.
- *Speaking.* For example, rather than studying silently, explain what you're learning to a study-group partner.
- *Organizing.* For example, create an outline, diagram, or concept map that pulls together the ideas you're learning.

Active Listening and Note-Taking in Class

You will find that many college professors rely heavily on the lecture method—they profess their knowledge by speaking for long stretches of time and expect students to listen and take notes on the knowledge they dispense. This method of instruction places great demands on your ability to listen actively and take notes that are both accurate and complete. Research consistently shows that most test questions on college exams come from professors' lectures and students who take better class notes get better grades (Brown, 1988; Cuseo, et al., 2013; Kiewra, 2000).

The best way to apply the principle of active involvement during a class lecture is to engage in the physical action of writing notes. Writing down what your instructor is saying in class "forces" you to pay closer attention to what is being said and reinforces your retention of what was said. By taking notes, you not only hear the information (auditory memory), you also see it on paper (visual memory) and feel it in the muscles of your hand as you write it (motor memory).

Note

Your role in the college classroom is not that of a passive spectator or an absorbent sponge who sits back and soaks up information through osmosis. Instead, it's like being an aggressive detective or investigative reporter on a search-and-record mission. Your job is to actively search for information by picking your instructor's brain, picking out the instructor's key points, and recording your "pickings" in your notebook.

Box 1.1 contains a summary of top strategies for classroom listening and note-taking that you can put into action right now.

" I never had a class before where the teacher just stands up and talks to you. He says something and you're writing it down, but then he says something else."

—*First-year college student (Erickson, Peters, & Strommer, 2006)*

" All genuine learning is active, not passive. It is a process in which the student is the main agent, not the teacher."

—*Mortimer Adler, American professor of philosophy and educational theorist*

" I thought I would get a better education if the school had a really good reputation. Now, I think one's education depends on how much effort you put into it."

—*First-year college student*

Box 1.1

Top Tips for Active Listening and Note-Taking in the College Classroom

One task that you'll be expected to perform during the very first week of college is taking notes in class. Studies show that professors' lecture notes are the number one source of test questions (and test answers) on college exams. You can improve the quality of your note-taking and your course grades by using the following strategies.

1. Get to every class. Whether or not your instructors take roll, you're responsible for all material covered in class. Remember that a full load of college courses (15 units) only requires that you be in class about 13 hours per week. If you consider your class work to be a full-time job, any job that requires you to show up for only 13 hours a week is a pretty sweet deal; it's a deal that supplies you with much more educational freedom than you had in high school. To miss classes in college when you're required to spend so little time in class per week is an abuse of this educational freedom. It's also an abuse of the money that you, your family, and taxpaying American citizens are paying to support your college education.

2. Get to every class on time. During the first few minutes of a class session, instructors often share valuable information—such as important reminders, reviews, and previews.

3. Get organized. Bring the right equipment to class. Get a separate notebook for each class, write your name on it, date each class session, and store all class handouts in it.

4. Get in the right position.
   - The ideal place to sit in class is at the front and center of the room—where you're in the best position to hear and see what's going on.
   - The ideal posture to adopt is sitting upright and leaning forward—because your body influences your mind; if your body is in an alert and ready position, your mind is likely to follow.
   - The ideal social position to occupy in class is near motivated classmates who will not distract you, but motivate you to listen actively and take notes aggressively.

   Note: These attention-focusing strategies are particularly important in large classes where you're likely to feel more anonymous, less accountable, and less engaged.

5. Get in the right frame of mind. Come to class with the attitude that you're there to pick your instructor's brain, pick up answers to test questions, and pick up points to elevate your course grade.

6. Get it down (in writing). Actively look, listen, and record important points at all times in class. Pay special attention to whatever information instructors put in writing, whether it appears on the board, on a slide, or in a handout.

7. Don't let go of your pen (or keyboard). When in doubt, write it out (or type it out); it's better to have it and not need it than to need it and not have it.

   Note: Most college professors don't write all important information on the board for you; instead, they expect you to listen carefully and write it down yourself.

8. Finish strong. During the last few minutes of class, instructors often share valuable information, such as timely reminders, reviews, and previews.

9. Stick around. When class ends, don't bolt out of the room; instead, hang out for a few moments and quickly review your notes (by yourself or with a classmate). This quick end-of-class review will help your brain retain the information it just received. If you detect any gaps or confusing points in your notes, try to consult with your instructor immediately after class.

For more detailed ideas and strategies on listening and note taking, see Chapter 5, pp. 100–106.

 Reflection 1.3

Do you feel prepared to do the type of note-taking required in college classes? What adjustments or changes will you need to make in your previous classroom learning habits to meet the challenge?

Finish class with a rush of attention, not a rush out the door!

Active Class Participation

You can implement the principle of active involvement in the college classroom by not only taking notes in class, but also by being an engaged participant who comes to class well prepared (e.g., having done the assigned reading), asks relevant questions, and contributes thoughtful comments during class discussions. Class participation increases your ability to stay alert and attentive in class, and it sends a clear message to your instructors that you are a motivated student who wants to learn. Class participation is also likely to account for a portion of your grade in many courses, so your attentiveness and involvement in class can have a direct, positive effect on your college grades.

Active Reading

Note-taking not only promotes active listening in class, it also promotes active reading out of class. Taking notes on what you're reading (or on information you've highlighted while reading) keeps you actively involved in the reading process because it requires more mental and physical energy than merely reading the material or passively highlighting sentences.

College professors also expect you to relate or connect what they talk about in class to the reading they've assigned. Thus, it's important to start developing good reading habits now. You can do so by using the top tips suggested in **Box 1.2**.

Box 1.2

Top Tips for Strengthening Textbook Reading Comprehension and Retention

1. Get the textbooks required for your courses as soon as possible and get your reading assignments done on time. Information from reading assignments ranks right behind lecture notes as a source of test questions on college exams. Many professors deliver their lectures with the expectation that you've done the assigned reading and assume you can build on that knowledge to understand their lectures. If you haven't done the reading, you'll have more difficulty following what your instructor is saying in class.

Thus, by not doing the assigned reading you pay a double penalty: you miss information found in the reading that's not covered in class which will likely appear on exams, and you miss understanding ideas presented in class that build on the reading.

> I recommend that you read the first chapters right away because college professors get started promptly with assigning certain readings. Classes in college move very fast because, unlike high school, you do not attend class five times a week but two or three times a week."
> —Advice to new college students from a first-year student

Box 1.2 *(continued)*

2. Read with the right equipment.
   - Bring a writing tool (pen, pencil, or keyboard) to record important information and a storage space (notebook or computer) in which you can save and later retrieve information acquired from your reading for later use on tests and assignments.
   - Have a dictionary nearby to quickly find the meaning of unfamiliar words that may interfere with your ability to comprehend what you're reading. Looking up definitions of unfamiliar words helps you understand what you're reading and also builds your vocabulary. A strong vocabulary will improve your reading comprehension in all college courses, as well as your performance on standardized tests, such as those required for admission to graduate and professional schools.
   - Check the back of your textbook for a glossary (list) of key terms included in the book. Each college subject and academic discipline has its own special language, and decoding it is often the key to understanding the concepts covered in the course. The glossary that appears at the end of your textbook is more than an ancillary add-on; it's a valuable tool that you can use to improve your comprehension of course concepts. Consider making a photocopy of the glossary at the back of your textbook so you can access it easily while you're reading—without having to repeatedly stop, hold your place, and go to the back of the text to find it.

3. Get in the right position. Sit upright and have light coming from behind you, over the side of your body opposite your writing hand. This will reduce the distracting and fatiguing effects of glare and shadows.

4. Get a sneak preview. Approach the chapter by first reading its boldface headings and any chapter outline, summary, or end-of-chapter questions that may be provided. This will supply you with a mental map of the chapter's important ideas before you start your trip through it. Getting an overview of the chapter will help you keep track of its major ideas (the "big picture") and reduce your risk of getting lost in all the smaller details you encounter along the way.

5. Finish each of your reading sessions with a short review. Rather than using the last few minutes of a reading session to cover a few more pages, end it with a review of what you've highlighted or noted as important information. Since most forgetting takes place immediately after you stop processing (taking in) information and start doing something else, it's best to use your last minutes of reading time to "lock in" the most important information you've just read.

Note *When reading, your goal should be to discover or uncover the most important ideas, so the final step in the reading process should be to review (and lock in) the most important ideas you've discovered.*

Note: For a more detailed discussion of reading comprehension and retention, see Chapter 5 (pp. 106–112).

Touching the Second Base of College Success: Capitalizing on Campus Resources (Resourcefulness)

Successful people are *resourceful*; they seek out and take advantage of resources to help them reach their goals. Your campus is chock full of resources that have been intentionally designed to support your quest for educational and personal success. Studies show that students who utilize campus resources report higher levels of satisfaction with college and get more out of the college experience (Pascarella & Terenzini, 1991, 2005).

Note

Capitalizing on campus services is not only valuable, it's also "free"; the cost of these services has already been covered by your college tuition. By investing time and energy in campus resources, you maximize the return on your financial investment in college—you get a bigger bang for your buck.

"Do not be a PCP (Parking Lot → Classroom → Parking Lot) student. The time you spend on campus will be a sound investment in your academic and professional success."

—Drew Appleby, professor of psychology

Utilizing campus resources is a natural extension of the principle of active involvement. Successful students are *involved* students, both inside and outside the classroom. Out-of-class involvement includes involvement with campus resources. The first step toward making effective use of campus resources is becoming aware of the full range of resources available to you and what they can do for you. Listed below are key campus services that are likely to be available to you and what they can do for you.

Learning Center (a.k.a. Academic Success Center)

This campus is designed to strengthen your academic performance. The individual and group tutoring provided here will help you master difficult course concepts and assignments, and the people working here are professionally trained to help you learn *how to learn*. Just as professors are experts in the subjects they teach: learning resource professionals are experts in the process of learning. They are professionals who can equip you with effective learning strategies that can be used in all courses, as well as specific strategies for dealing with the demands of certain courses and teaching styles. You're also likely to find trained peer tutors in this center who can often help you understand concepts better than more experienced professionals because they're closer to you in age and experience.

Studies show that college students who capitalize on academic support services outside the classroom achieve higher grades and are more likely to complete their college degree, particularly if they begin their involvement with these support services during their first year of college (Bailey, 2009; Cuseo, 2003). Students who seek and receive assistance from the Learning Center also show significant improvement in academic self-efficacy—that is, they develop a stronger sense of personal control over their academic performance and higher expectations for academic success (Smith, Walter, & Hoey, 1992).

Despite the powerful advantages associated with student use of academic support services, these services are typically underused by college students—especially by students who need them the most (Cuseo, 2003; Walter & Smith, 1990). Unfortunately, some college students believe that seeking academic help is admitting they're not smart, self-sufficient, or able to succeed on their own. Don't buy into this myth. In high school, students may only go to an office on campus if they're required to (e.g., if they forgot to do something or did something wrong). In college, students go to campus offices to enhance their success by taking advantage of the services and support they provide.

Note

Using academic support services doesn't mean you're helpless, need remedial repair work, or require academic life support because you're on the verge of flunking out. Instead, it's a sign that you're a motivated and resourceful student who is striving for academic excellence.

Writing Center

Many college campuses offer specialized support for students seeking to improve their writing skills. Typically referred to as the Writing Center, this is the place on campus where you can receive assistance at any stage of the writing process, whether it be collecting and organizing your ideas, composing your first draft, or proofreading your final draft. Since writing is an academic skill that you'll use throughout your college experience, if you improve your writing skills, you're likely to improve your overall academic performance. Thus, the Writing Center can be one of your most valuable campus resources.

> "Where I learn the material best is tutoring because they go over it and if you have questions, you can ask. They have time for you or will make time for you."
>
> —First-year college student

> "At colleges where I've taught, we found that the grade point average of students who used the Learning Center was higher than the college average, and honors students were more likely to use the center than other students."
>
> —Joe Cuseo, professor of psychology and lead author of this text

 Reflection 1.4

How much writing did you typically do in your high school courses?

How much confidence do you have in your writing skills right now?

Disability Services (a.k.a. Disability Resource Center)

If you have a physical or learning disability that's interfering with your performance in college, or you think you may have such a disability, Disability Services is the campus resource to consult for assistance and support. Programs and services typically provided by this office include:

- Assessment for learning disabilities;
- Verification of eligibility for disability support services;
- Authorization of academic accommodations for students with disabilities; and
- Specialized counseling, advising, and tutoring.

College Library

This is your campus resource for finding information and completing research assignments (e.g., term papers and group projects). Librarians are professional educators who provide instruction outside the classroom; you can learn from them just as you can learn from faculty inside the classroom. They can help you develop research skills for accessing, retrieving, and evaluating information. These are lifelong learning skills that promote your educational success at all stages of the college experience as well as your professional and personal success beyond college.

> The next best thing to knowing something is knowing where to find it."
>
> *—Dr. Samuel Johnson, English literary figure and original author of the Dictionary of the English Language (1747)*

Academic Advisement

Whether or not you have an assigned academic advisor, the Academic Advisement Center is your campus resource for help with course selection, educational planning, and choosing or changing a major. Studies show that students who develop clear educational and career goals are more likely to persist in college and complete their college degree (Braxton, Hirschy, & McClendon, 2011; Kuh, et al., 2011; Lotkowski, Robbins, & Noeth, 2004). Research also indicates that most beginning college students need help clarifying their educational goals, deciding on a major, and identifying career options (Cuseo, 2005; Tinto, 2012). As a first-year college student, being undecided or uncertain about your educational and career goals is nothing to be embarrassed about. However, you should start thinking about your future now. Connect early and often with an academic advisor to help you clarify your educational goals and choose a field of study that best complements your interests, talents, and values.

Office of Student Life or Student Development

This is your campus resource for involvement in student life outside the classroom, including student clubs and organizations, recreational programs, leadership activities, and volunteer experiences. Research consistently shows that experiential learning outside the classroom contributes as much to your personal development and career success as class work (Kuh, 1995; Kuh, et al., 1994; Pascarella & Terenzini, 2005). This is one reason why most campuses no longer refer to out-of-class experiences as "*extra*curricular" activities; instead they are referred to as "*co*-curricular" experiences—which conveys the message they're equally important as classroom-based learning. Studies show that students who become actively involved in campus life are more likely to:

- Enjoy their college experience;
- Graduate from college; and
- Develop leadership skills that enhance career performance beyond college (Astin, 1993).

Note

Co-curricular experiences are also resume-building experiences, and campus professionals with whom you interact regularly while participating in co-curricular activities (e.g., director of student activities or dean of students) can be valuable resources for personal references and letters of recommendation.

Devoting some out-of-class time to co-curricular experiences should not interfere with your academic performance. Keep in mind that in college you'll be spending much less time in the classroom than you did in high school. As mentioned previously, a full load of college courses (15 units) requires that you be in class for about 13 hours per week. This can leave you with sufficient time to become involved in learning experiences on or off campus. Research indicates that students' academic performance and progress to degree completion aren't impaired if they spend 20 or fewer hours on co-curricular and part-time work experiences (Advisory Committee on Student Financial Assistance, 2008). In fact, they earn higher grades than students who don't get involved in any out-of-class activities (Pascarella, 2001; Pascarella & Terenzini, 2005).

Although co-curricular involvement is valuable, limit your involvement to no more than two or three major campus organizations at a time. Restricting the number of your out-of-class activities will not only enable you to keep up with your studies, it will be more impressive to future schools or employers because a long list of involvement in numerous activities may send the message that you're padding your resume with activities you participated in superficially (or never participated in at all).

> "
> Just a [long] list of club memberships is meaningless; it's a fake front. Remember that quality, not quantity, is what counts."
>
> *—Lauren Pope, former director of the National Bureau for College Placement*

Reflection 1.5

If you were to join one campus club or student organization, what would it be?
How would participating in this club or organization contribute to your educational development?

Financial Aid Office

If you have questions concerning how to obtain assistance in paying for college, the staff in this office can guide you through the application process. The paperwork needed to apply for and secure financial aid can sometimes be confusing or overwhelming. Don't let the process of applying for financial aid intimidate you or prevent you from seeking financial aid because professional financial aid counselors can walk you through the process. They can also help you find:

- Part-time employment on campus through a work–study program;
- Low-interest student loans; and
- Grants and scholarships.

If you have any doubt about whether you're using the most effective plan for financing your college education, make an appointment to see a professional in your Financial Aid Office right now.

Health Center

The transition from high school to college often involves adjustments and decisions that affect students' health and well-being. Students who develop good health habits are better able to cope with stress and reach peak levels of performance. The Health Center is your campus resource for establishing productive habits to maintain physical health and attain optimal wellness. It's also the place to go for help with illnesses, sexually transmitted infections or diseases, and eating or nutritional disorders.

Career Development Center (a.k.a. Career Center)

Research indicates that students are more likely to stay in college and graduate when they have some sense of how their present academic experience relates to their future career goals (Braxton, et al., 2011; Kuh, et al., 2011; Tinto, 1993). Studies also show that most new students are uncertain about what career they will pursue (Gordon & Steele, 2003). So, if you're uncertain about your future career, welcome to a club to which many other first-year students belong.

The Career Development Center is the place to go for help in finding a meaningful connection between your current college experience and your future career goals. Here's where you'll find such services as personal career counseling, workshops on career exploration and development, and career fairs where you'll be able to meet professionals working in different fields. Although it may seem like your career is light years away, the process of exploring, planning, and preparing for career success should begin now—in your first year of college.

Counseling Center

Here's where you can get ideas and strategies for managing college stress, gaining greater self-awareness, and reaching your full potential. Personal counselors are professionals who do more than just help students maintain mental health; they also develop students' emotional intelligence, interpersonal skills, and personal growth.

Note

Personal counseling is not just for students experiencing emotional problems. It's for all students who want to enrich the quality of their life.

Touching the Third Base of College Success: Interpersonal Interaction and Collaboration (Social Integration)

Students who become socially integrated or connected with other members of the college community are more likely to complete their first year of college and go on to complete their college degree (Pascarella & Terenzini, 2005; Tinto, 1993). (For effective ways to make interpersonal connections with key members of your college community, see **Box 1.3**.)

Box 1.3

Social Integration: Making Connections with Members of Your College Community

Listed below are top tips for making key social connections in college. Start developing these relationships right now so you can build a base of social support to help you succeed during the critical first year of college.

- Connect with a student development professional you may have met during orientation.
- Join a college club, student organization, campus committee, intramural team, or volunteer service group whose members share the same personal or career interests as you. If you can't find a club or organization you were hoping to join, consider starting it on your own. For example, if you're an English major, consider starting a Writing Club or a Book Club.
- Connect with a peer leader who has been trained to assist new students (e.g., orientation week leader, peer tutor, or peer mentor).
- Connect with classmates and team up with them to take notes, complete reading assignments, study for exams, or take classes together. Look especially to team up with a peer who may be in more than one class with you. (For more detailed information on forming collaborative learning teams, see Chapter 5, pp. 121–123.)
- Connect with peers who live near you or who commute to school from the same community in which you live. If your schedules are similar, consider carpooling together.
- Connect with faculty members—particularly in a field that you're considering as a major. Visit them during office hours, converse briefly with them after class, or communicate with them via e-mail.
- Connect with an academic advisor to discuss and develop your educational plans.
- Connect with academic support professionals in your college's Learning Center for personalized academic assistance or tutoring related to any course in which you'd like to improve your performance or achieve academic excellence.
- Connect with a college librarian to get early assistance or a head start on any research project that you've been assigned.
- Connect with a personal counselor or campus minister to discuss college adjustment or personal challenges you may be experiencing.

 Reflection 1.6

If you were to join a student club or campus organization right now, what would it be? Why?

How likely is it that you will join this club or organization?

Four particular forms of interpersonal interaction have been found to promote student learning and motivation in college:

1. Student–faculty interaction,
2. Student–advisor interaction,
3. Student–mentor interaction, and
4. Student–student (peer) interaction.

Strategies for capitalizing on each of these key forms of interaction are provided below.

Interacting with Faculty Members

College success is strongly influenced by the frequency and quality of student–faculty interaction *outside the classroom*. Out-of-class contact with faculty is associated with the following positive outcomes for college students:

* Improved academic performance;
* Increased critical thinking skills;
* Greater satisfaction with the college experience;
* Increased likelihood of completing a college degree; and
* Stronger desire to pursue education beyond a four-year degree (Astin, 1993; Pascarella & Terenzini, 1991, 2005).

These positive outcomes are so powerful and widespread that we encourage you to immediately begin making connections with your professors outside of class time. Here are some of the easiest ways to do so.

1. **Seek contact with your instructors right after class.** If something covered in class captures your interest, approach your instructor to discuss it further. You could ask a quick question about something you weren't sure you understood, or have a short conversation about how the material covered in class really hit home for you or connected with something you learned in another course. Interacting briefly with instructors after class can help them get to know you as an individual and help you gain the confidence to approach them during office hours.

2. **Connect with course instructors during their office hours.** One of the most important pieces of information you'll find on a course syllabus is your instructor's office hours. College professors specifically reserve times in their weekly schedule to be available to students in their office. (Make note of them and make an earnest attempt to capitalize on them.) Try to visit the office of each of your instructors at least once, preferably early in the term, when quality time is easier to find. Don't wait until later in the term when major exams and assignments start piling up. Even if your early contact with instructors is only for a few minutes, it can be a valuable icebreaker that helps them get to know you as a person and helps you feel more comfortable interacting with them in the future.

   Making office visits *with other classmates* is an effective way to get additional assistance in preparing for exams and completing assignments—for the following reasons:

   * You're more likely to feel comfortable about venturing onto your instructor's "turf" in the company of peers than entering this unfamiliar territory on your own. As the old expression goes, "There's safety in numbers."
   * When you make an office visit as a team, the information shared by the instructor is heard by more than one person; your teammates may pick up some useful information that you may have missed, misinterpreted, or forgotten to write down (and vice versa).
   * You save time for your instructors by allowing them to help more than one student at a time. This means they won't have to engage in as many "repeat performances" for individual students seeking help at separate times.
   * You send a message to the instructor that you're a motivated student who's serious about the course, because you've taken the time—ahead of time—to connect with your peers and prepare for the office visit.

> "[In high school] the teacher knows your name. But in college they don't know your name; they might see your face, but it means nothing to them unless you make yourself known."
> —*First-year college student*

> "I wish that I would have taken advantage of professors' open-door policies when I had questions, because actually understanding what I was doing, instead of guessing, would have saved me a lot of stress and re-doing what I did wrong the first time."
> —*College sophomore*

> "Two heads are better than one, not because either is infallible, but because they are unlikely to go wrong in the same direction."
> —*C.S. Lewis, English novelist and essayist*

3. **Connect with your instructors through e-mail.** Electronic communication is another effective tool for experiencing the benefits of student–faculty interaction outside the classroom, particularly if your professor's office hours conflict with your class schedule, work responsibilities, or family commitments. If you're a commuter student who doesn't live on campus, or if you're an adult student juggling family and work commitments along with your academic schedule, e-mail communication may be an especially effective and efficient way to interact with faculty. E-mail may also be a good way to initially communicate with instructors and build self-confidence to eventually seek out face-to-face interaction with them. In one national survey, almost half of college students reported that e-mail enabled them to communicate their ideas with professors on subjects they would not have discussed in person (Pew Internet & American Life Project, 2002). However, if you miss class, don't use e-mail to ask such questions as:

©Kendall Hunt Publishing Company

Did I miss anything important in class today?

- Did I miss anything important in class today?
- Could you send me your PowerPoint slides from the class I missed?

Also, when using e-mail to communicate with your instructors, be sure to:

- Include your full name in the message.
- Mention the class or course in which you're enrolled.
- Use complete sentences, correct grammar, and avoid informal "hip" expressions (e.g., "yo," "whatup").
- Spell check and proofread your message before sending it.
- Include your full contact information. (If you're communicating via Facebook, watch your screen name; for example, names like "Sexsea" or "Studly" wouldn't be appropriate.)
- Give your instructor time to reply. (Don't expect an immediate response, particularly if you send your message in the evening or on a weekend.)

Lastly, when you're *in class*, use personal technology responsibly and sensitively by adhering to the guidelines provided in **Box 1.4**.

Box 1.4

Guidelines for Civil and Responsible Use of Personal Technology in the College Classroom

Behavior that interferes with the right of others to learn or teach in the classroom is referred to as *classroom incivility*. Listed below are forms of classroom incivility that involve student use of personal technology. Be sure to avoid them.

Using Cell Phones

Keeping a cell phone on in class is a clear form of classroom incivility because it can interfere with the right of others to learn. In a study of college students who heard a cell phone ringing during class and were later tested on

information presented in class, they scored approximately 25% lower for information that was presented at the time the cell phone rang. This drop in performance was found even if the material was covered by the professor just prior to the cell phone ringing and if it was projected on a slide while the phone rang. The study also showed that students' attention to information presented in class is significantly reduced when classmates frantically search through handbags or pockets to find and silence a ringing (or vibrating) phone (Shelton, et al., 2009). These findings clearly suggest that cell phone use in class disrupts the learning process and the civil thing to do is:

- Turn your cell phone off before entering class, or keep it out of the classroom altogether. (You can use *studiousapp.com* to automatically silence your phone

Box 1.4 *(continued)*

at times of the day when you're in class.) In rare cases where you may need to leave class to respond to an emergency, ask your instructor for permission in advance.

- Don't check your cell phone during the class period by turning it off and on.
- Don't look at your cell phone at any time during an exam because your instructor may suspect that you're looking up answers to test questions.

> The right to do something does not mean that doing it is right."
>
> —*William Safire, American author, journalist, and presidential speech writer*

Text Messaging

Although this form of electronic communication is silent, it still can distract or disturb your classmates. It's also discourteous or disrespectful to instructors when you put your head down and turn your attention away from them while they're speaking in class. The bottom line: Be sensitive to your classmates and your instructor—don't text in class!

Surfing the Web

Although this can be done without creating distracting sounds, it still can create visual distractions. Unless you're taking class notes on it, keep your laptop closed to avoid distracting your classmates and raising your instructors' suspicion that you're a disinterested or disrespectful student.

Final Note: In addition to technological incivilities, other discourteous classroom behaviors include personal grooming, holding side conversations, and doing homework for other classes. Even if your attendance is perfect, "little things" you do in class that reflect inattention or disinterest can send a strong message to your instructors that you're an unmotivated or discourteous student.

 Reflection 1.7

Have you observed any recent examples of classroom incivility that you thought were particularly distracting or discourteous? What was the uncivil behavior and what consequences did it have on others?

Interacting with Academic Advisors

If you need some help understanding college policies and procedures, or navigating the bureaucratic maze of course options and course requirements, an academic advisor is the person to see. Advisors also serve as key referral agents who can direct you to, and connect you with, key campus support services that best meet your educational needs and career goals.

Your academic advisor should be someone whom you feel comfortable speaking with, someone who knows your name, and someone who's familiar with your personal interests and abilities. Give advisors the opportunity to get to know you personally, and seek their input on courses, majors, and any academic difficulties you may be experiencing.

If you've been assigned a specific advisor and cannot develop a good relationship with this person, ask the director of advising or academic dean if you could make a change. Consider asking your peers or peer leaders for their recommendations.

If your college does not assign you a personal advisor, but offers advising services in an Advising Center on a drop-by or drop-in basis, you may see a different advisor each time you visit the center. If you're not comfortable working with different advisors from one visit to the next, find one you like and make that person your advisor by scheduling appointments in advance. This will enable you to consistently connect with the same advisor and develop a close, ongoing relationship with that person.

Note

Advisors can be much more than course schedulers; they can be mentors. Unlike your course instructors—who may change from term to term—your academic advisor may be the one professional on campus with whom you have regular contact and a continuous relationship throughout your college experience.

 **Reflection 1.8**

Do you have a personally assigned advisor?

If yes, do you know who this person is and where he or she can be found?

If you don't have a personally assigned advisor, where will you go if you have questions about your class schedule or educational plans?

Interacting with a Mentor

A mentor may be described as an experienced guide who takes a personal interest in you and helps you progress toward your goals. For example, in the movie *Star Wars*, Yoda served as a mentor for Luke Skywalker. Research demonstrates that when first-year college students have a mentor, they feel more valued and are better able to stay on track until they complete their degree (Campbell & Campbell, 1997; Crisp & Cruz, 2009; Komarraju, Musulkin, & Bhattacharya, 2010). A mentor can help you anticipate issues, resolve problems, and be someone with whom you can share your struggles as well as your success stories and personal accomplishments. Keep an eye out for a person on campus with whom you can develop this type of relationship. A variety of people have the potential to be a mentor for you, including:

- Your instructor in a first-year seminar or experience course
- Your academic advisor
- Faculty member in your major field of interest
- Peer mentor or peer leader
- Academic support professional (e.g., professional working in the Learning Center)
- Career counselor
- Personal counselor
- Student development professional (e.g., the director of student life or residential life)
- Campus minister or chaplain
- Financial aid counselor
- Professionals working in a career you're interested in pursuing

 **Reflection 1.9**

Think about your first interactions with faculty, staff, and administrators on campus. Did you meet anyone who took interest in you and who might be a potential mentor for you?

Interaction with Peers (Student–Student Interaction)

Your peers can be more than competitors or a source of negative peer pressure; they can also be collaborators, a source of positive social influence, and a resource for college success. Peer support is important at any stage of the college experience, but it's especially valuable during the first term of college. It's at this stage when new students have a strong need for belongingness and social acceptance because they're in the midst of a major life transition. As a new student, it may be useful to view your first-year experience through the lens of psychologist Abraham Maslow's hierarchy of human needs (see **Figure 1.3**). According to Maslow, humans only reach their full potential and achieve peak performance after their more basic emotional and social needs have been met (e.g., needs for personal safety, social acceptance, and self-esteem). Making early connections with your peers helps you meet these basic human needs, provides you with a base of social support that eases your integration into the college community, and prepares you to move up to higher levels of the need hierarchy (e.g., achieving academic excellence and reaching your educational goals).

Getting involved with campus organizations or activities is one way to connect with other students. Also, try to interact with experienced students who have spent more time at college than you. Sophomores, juniors, and seniors can be valuable social resources for a new student. In particular, seek out contact with students who have been selected and trained as peer mentors or peer leaders.

FIGURE 1.3: **Abraham Maslow's Hierarchy of Needs**

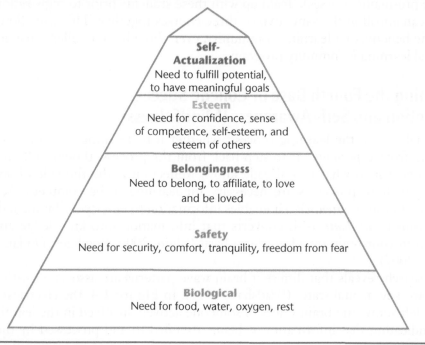

Research clearly demonstrates that college students learn as much from peers as they do from instructors and textbooks (Astin, 1993; Pascarella, 2006). One study of more than 25,000 college students revealed that when peers interact with one another while learning, they achieve higher levels of academic performance and are more likely to persist to degree completion (Astin, 1993).

Be observant—keep an eye out for peers who are successful. Start building your social support network by surrounding yourself with success-seeking and success-achieving students. Learn from them, emulate their productive habits and strategies, and use them as a social resource to promote your own success.

> "Surround yourself with only people who are going to lift you higher."
>
> —Oprah Winfrey, actress and talk-show host

 Reflection 1.10

Think about classmates in courses you're taking this term. Would you be willing to ask any of them if they'd like to form a learning team? Why?

Your campus may offer you the opportunity to participate in a *learning community* program, in which the same group of students takes the same block of courses together during the same term. If this opportunity is available to you, take advantage of it because research suggests that students who participate in learning community programs are more likely to:

- Become actively involved in classroom learning,
- Form their own learning groups outside of class,
- Experience greater intellectual growth, and
- Continue their college education (Tinto, 1997, 2000).

If learning community programs are not offered on your campus, consider creating informal learning communities on your own by finding other students who are likely to be enrolling in the same courses as you (e.g., the same general education or pre-major courses). Team up with these students prior to registration to see if you can enroll in the same two or three courses together. This will allow you to reap the benefits of a learning community, even though your college may not offer a formal learning community program.

Touching the Fourth Base of College Success: Reflection and Self-Awareness (Mindfulness)

The final step in the learning process, whether it be learning in the classroom or learning from experience, is to step back from the process, thoughtfully review it, and connect it to what you already know. Reflection is the flip side of active involvement; both processes are necessary for learning to be complete. Active involvement ensures *attention*—it enables information to enter your brain, and reflection ensures *consolidation*—it converts that information into knowledge and helps retain it in your brain on a long-term basis (Bligh, 2000; Roediger, Dudai, & Fitzpatrick, 2007).

Research reveals that different brain wave patterns are associated with each of these two key mental states (Bradshaw, 1995). In **Figure 1.4**, the electrical pattern on the left shows the brain waves of someone actively involved in the learning process, indicating that information is being attended to and processed by the brain. The electrical pattern on the right shows the brain waves of a person reflecting on information after it's been actively processed and moving that information into long-term memory. The brain wave patterns in these two different stages of the learning process indicate that deep, long-lasting learning takes place through a combination of (a) active involvement—characterized by high-amplitude "beta" brain waves—and (b) thoughtful reflection—characterized by high-frequency "alpha" brain waves (similar to someone in a meditative state).

FIGURE 1.4

Beta Waves: High-Amplitude Brain Waves Associated with a Mental State of *Active Involvement.*

Alpha Waves: High-Frequency Brain Waves Associated with a Mental State of *Reflective Thinking.*

©Kendall Hunt Publishing Company

Self-Awareness

In addition to reflecting on what you're learning, it's also important to reflect on yourself. This process is known as *introspection*—it involves turning inward to gain deeper self-awareness and understanding of who you are, what you're doing, and where you're going. Two forms of self-awareness are particularly important for success in college: (a) self-monitoring and (b) self-assessment.

Self-Monitoring

One characteristic of successful learners is that they self-monitor (check themselves) while learning to remain aware of:

* Whether they're using effective learning strategies (e.g., if they're giving their undivided attention to what they're learning)
* Whether they're truly comprehending what they are learning (e.g., if they're understanding it at a deep level or memorizing it at a surface level)
* How they're regulating or adjusting their learning strategies to meet the demands of different academic tasks and subjects (e.g., if they're reading technical material in a science textbook, they read at a slower rate and check their understanding more frequently than when reading a novel) (Weinstein, Acee, & Jung, 2011).

You can begin to establish good self-monitoring habits by getting in the routine of periodically pausing to reflect on the strategies you're using to learn and how you "do" college. For instance, you can ask yourself the following questions:

* Am I listening attentively to what my instructor is saying in class?
* Am I comprehending what I'm reading outside of class?
* Am I effectively using campus resources designed to support my success?
* Am I interacting with campus professionals who can contribute to my current success and future development?
* Am I interacting and collaborating with peers who can support (not sabotage) my learning and development?
* Am I effectively implementing college success strategies (such as those identified in this book)?

> "
> We learn neither by thinking nor by doing; we learn by thinking about what we are doing."
>
> *—George Stoddard, Professor Emeritus, University of Iowa*

<u>Note</u>

Successful students and successful people are mindful—*they watch what they're doing and remain aware of whether they're doing it effectively and to the best of their ability.*

Self-Assessment

Simply defined, self-assessment is the process of reflecting on and evaluating your personal characteristics. The following are key target areas for self-assessment because they enable you to accurately identify and achieve your educational and personal goals:

> "Successful students know a lot about themselves."
>
> —*Claire Weinstein and Debra Meyer, professors of educational psychology at the University of Texas*

- **Personal interests.** What you like to do or enjoy doing.
- **Personal values.** What's important to you and what you care about doing.
- **Personal abilities or aptitudes.** What you do well or have the potential to do well.
- **Learning habits.** What approaches, methods, or techniques you use to learn.
- **Learning styles.** How you like or prefer to learn.
- **Personality traits.** Your temperament, emotional characteristics, and social tendencies (e.g., whether you lean toward being outgoing or reserved).

(To help you get a better understanding of your personality type and how it connects to your learning style and personal interests, log into *Human eSources* and complete the "Do What You Are" self-assessment tool.)

 Reflection 1.11

How would you rate your academic self-confidence at this point in your college experience? (Circle one.)

very confident   somewhat confident   somewhat unconfident   very unconfident

Why?

Chapter Summary and Highlights

The key ideas contained in this chapter are summarized in the following self-assessment checklist of success-promoting principles and practices.

A Checklist of Success-Promoting Principles and Practices

1. **Active Involvement (Engagement)**
   Inside the classroom, I will:

   - ☐ *Get to class.* I'll treat it like a job and be there on all days I'm expected to.
   - ☐ *Get involved in class.* I'll come prepared, listen actively, take notes, and participate.

   Outside the classroom, I will:

   - ☐ *Read actively.* I'll take notes while I read to increase attention and retention.
   - ☐ *Double up.* I'll spend twice as much time on academic work outside of class as I spend in class. If I'm a full-time student, I'll make it a full-time job and put in a 40-hour workweek (with occasional "overtime" as need).

2. **Capitalizing on Campus Resources (Resourcefulness)**
   I will capitalize on academic and student support services available to me, such as the:
   - ☐ Learning Center
   - ☐ Writing Center
   - ☐ College Library
   - ☐ Academic Advisement Center
   - ☐ Office of Student Life
   - ☐ Financial Aid Office
   - ☐ Counseling Center
   - ☐ Health Center
   - ☐ Career Development Center

3. **Interpersonal Interaction and Collaboration (Social Integration)**
   I will interact and collaborate with the following members of my college community:
   - ☐ **Peers.** I'll join student clubs and participate in campus organizations.
   - ☐ **Faculty members.** I'll connect with my course instructors and other faculty members after class, in their offices, or via e-mail.
   - ☐ **Academic advisors.** I'll see an advisor for more than course registration, and I'll find an advisor whom I can relate to and develop an ongoing relationship.
   - ☐ **Mentors.** I'll try to find someone on campus who can serve as an experienced guide and role model for me.

4. **Reflection and Self-Awareness (Mindfulness)**
   I will engage in:
   - ☐ **Reflection.** I'll step back from what I'm learning, review it, and connect it to what I already know.
   - ☐ **Self-Monitoring.** I'll maintain self-awareness of how I'm learning in college and if I'm using effective strategies.
   - ☐ **Self-Assessment.** I'll reflect on and evaluate my personal interests, talents, learning styles, and learning habits.

In short, successful students are:

- **Involved.** They *get into* it by investing time and effort in the college experience;
- **Interactive.** They *team up* for it by interacting and collaborating with others;
- **Resourceful.** They *get help* with it by capitalizing on their surrounding resources; and
- **Reflective.** They *step back* from it to think about their performance and themselves.

Reflection 1.12

Identify one way in which you will put each of the following four principles of college success into practice during the next few weeks?

1. Active Involvement (Engagement)

2. Capitalizing on Campus Resources (Resourcefulness)

3. Interpersonal Interaction and Collaboration (Social Integration)

4. Reflection and Self-Awareness (Mindfulness)

Learning More through the World Wide Web: Internet-Based Resources

For additional information on strategies for college success, see the following websites:

http://www.cgcc.edu/success

http://www.dartmouth.edu/~acskills/success/

www.studygs.net

References

Advisory Committee on Student Financial Assistance. (2008, September). *Apply to succeed: Ensuring community college students benefit from need-based financial aid.* Washington, DC: Author. Retrieved from https://www2.ed.gov/about/bdscomm/list/acsfa/applytosucceed.pdf.

Astin, A. W. (1993). *What matters in college?* San Francisco: Jossey-Bass.

Bailey, G. (2009). *University of North Carolina, Greensboro application for NADE certification, tutoring program.* NADE Certification Council Archives. Searcy, AR: Harding University.

Barber, J. P., King, P. M., & Baxter Magolda, M. B. (2013). Long strides on the journey toward self-authorship: Substantial developmental shifts in college students' meaning making. *The Journal of Higher Education, 84*(6), 866–999.

Bligh, D. A. (2000). *What's the use of lectures?* San Francisco: Jossey Bass.

Bradshaw, D. (1995). Learning theory: Harnessing the strength of a neglected resource. In D. C. A. Bradshaw (Ed.), *Bringing learning to life: The learning revolution, the economy and the individual* (pp. 79–92). London: Falmer Press.

Braxton, J. M., Hirschy, A. S., & McClendon, S. A. (2011). *Understanding and reducing college student departure.* ASHE-ERIC Higher Education Report, Volume 30, Number 3.

Brown, R. D. (1988). Self-quiz on testing and grading issues. *Teaching at UNL (University of Nebraska–Lincoln), 10*(2), 1–3.

Campbell, T. A., & Campbell, D. E. (1997, December). Faculty/student mentor program: Effects on academic performance and retention. *Research in Higher Education, 38*, 727–742.

Credé, M., Roch, S. G., & Kieszczynka, U. M. (2010). Class attendance in college: A meta-analytic review of the relationship of class attendance with grades and student characteristics. *Review of Educational Research, 80*(2), 272–295.

Crisp, G., & Cruz, I. (2009). Mentoring college students: A critical review of the literature between 1990 and 2007. *Research in Higher Education, 50*, 525–545.

Cuseo, J. B. (2003). Comprehensive academic support for students during the first year of college. In G. L. Kramer, et al. (Eds.), *Student academic services: An integrated approach* (pp. 271–310). San Francisco: Jossey-Bass.

Cuseo, J. B. (2005). "Decided," "undecided," and "in transition": Implications for academic advisement, career counseling, and student retention. In R. S. Feldman (Ed.), *Improving the first year of college: Research and practice* (pp. 27–50). Mahwah, NJ: Lawrence Erlbaum.

Cuseo, J. B., Thompson, A., Campagna, M., & Fecas, V. S. (2013). *Thriving in college & beyond: Research-based strategies for academic success and personal development* (3rd ed.). Dubuque, IA: Kendall Hunt.

Erickson, B. L., Peters, C. B., & Strommer, D. W. (2006). *Teaching first-year college students.* San Francisco: Jossey-Bass.

Gordon, V. N., & Steele, G. E. (2003). Undecided first-year students: A 25-year longitudinal study. *Journal of the First-Year Experience and Students in Transition, 15*(1), 19–38.

Kiewra, K. A. (2000). Fish giver or fishing teacher? The lure of strategy instruction. *Teaching at UNL (University of Nebraska–Lincoln), 22*(3), 1–3.

Komarraju, M., Musulkin, S., & Bhattacharya, G. (2010). Role of student–faculty interactions in developing college students' academic self-concept, motivation, and achievement. *Journal of College Student Development, 51*(3), 332–342.

Kuh, G. D. (1995). The other curriculum: Out-of-class experiences associated with student learning and personal development. *Journal of Higher Education, 66*(2), 123–153.

Kuh, G. D. (2005). Student engagement in the first year of college. In M. L. Upcraft, J. N. Gardner, B. O. Barefoot & Associates (Eds.), *Challenging and supporting the first-year student: A handbook for improving the first year of college* (pp. 86–107). San Francisco: Jossey-Bass.

Kuh, G. D., Douglas, K. B., Lund, J. P., & Ramin-Gyurnek, J. (1994). *Student learning outside the classroom: Transcending artificial boundaries.* ASHE-ERIC Higher Education Report No. 8. Washington, DC: George Washington University, School of Education and Human Development.

Kuh, et al. (2005). *What matters to student success: A review of the literature.* National Postsecondary Education Cooperative.

Kuh, G. D., Kinzie, J., Buckley, J. A., Bridges, B. K., & Hayek, J. C. (2011). *Piecing together the student success puzzle: Research, propositions, and recommendations.* ASHE Higher Education Report (Vol. 116). John Wiley & Sons.

Launius, M. H. (1997). College student attendance: Attitudes and academic performance. *College Student Journal, 31*(1), 86–93.

Light, R. J. (2001). *Making the most of college: Students speak their minds.* Cambridge, MA: Harvard University Press.

Lotkowski, V. A., Robbins, S. B., & Noeth, R. J. (2004). *The role of academic and non-academic factors in improving student retention.* ACT Policy Report. Retrieved from https://www.act.org/research/policymakers/pdf/college_retention.pdf.

National Survey of Student Engagement. (2009). *NSSE Annual Results 2009. Assessment for improvement: Tracking student engagement over time.* Bloomington, IN: Author.

Pace, C. (1990). *The undergraduates: A report of their activities.* Los Angeles: University of California, Center for the Study of Evaluation.

Pace, C. (1995, May). *From good processes to good products: Relating good practices in undergraduate education to student achievement.* Paper presented at the meeting of the Association for Institutional Research, Boston.

Pascarella, E. T. (2001, November/December). Cognitive growth in college: Surprising and reassuring findings from the National Study of Student Learning. *Change,* 21–27.

Pascarella, E. T. (2006). How college affects students: Ten directions for future research. *Journal of College Student Development, 57*(5), 508–520.

Pascarella, E., & Terenzini, P. (1991). *How college affects students: Findings and insights from twenty years of research.* San Francisco: Jossey-Bass.

Pascarella, E., & Terenzini, P. (2005). *How college affects students: A third decade of research* (Vol. 2). San Francisco: Jossey-Bass.

Pew Internet & American Life Project. (2002). *The Internet goes to college: How students are living in the future with today's technology.* Retrieved from http://www.pewinternet.org/files/old-media/Files/Reports/2002/PIP_College_Report.pdf.

Pryor, J. H., De Angelo, L., Palucki-Blake, B., Hurtado, S., & Tran, S. (2012) *The American freshman: National norms fall 2011.* Los Angeles: Higher Education Research Institute, UCLA.

Roediger, H. L., Dudai, Y., & Fitzpatrick, S. M. (2007). *Science of memory: concepts.* New York: Oxford University Press.

Shelton, J. T., Elliot, E. M., Eaves, S. D., & Exner, A. L. (2009). The distracting effects of a ringing cell phone: An investigation of the laboratory and the classroom setting. *Journal of Environmental Psychology,* (March). Retrieved from http://news-info.wustl.edu/news/page/normal/14225.html.

Shimoff, E., & Catania, C. A. (2001). Effects of recording attendance on grades in Introductory Psychology. *Teaching of Psychology, 23*(3), 192–195.

Smith, J. B., Walter, T. L., & Hoey, G. (1992). Support programs and student self-efficacy: Do first-year students know when they need help? *Journal of the Freshman Year Experience, 4*(2), 41–67.

Tagliacollo, V. A., Volpato, G. L., & Pereira, A., Jr. (2010). Association of student position in classroom and school performance. *Educational Research, 1*(6), 198–201.

Tinto, V. (1993). *Leaving college: Rethinking the causes and cures of student attrition* (2nd ed.). Chicago: University of Chicago Press.

Tinto, V. (1997). Classrooms as communities: Exploring the educational character of student persistence. *The Journal of Higher Education, 68,* 599–623.

Tinto, V. (2000). Linking learning and leaving: Exploring the role of the college classroom in student departure. In J. M. Braxton (Ed.), *Reworking the student departure puzzle* (pp. 81–94). Nashville: Vanderbilt University Press.

Tinto, V. (2012). *Completing college: Rethinking institutional action.* Chicago: The University of Chicago Press.

Walter, T. L., & Smith, J. (1990, April). *Self-assessment and academic support: Do students know they need help?* Paper presented at the annual Freshman Year Experience Conference, Austin, Texas.

Weinstein, C. E., Acee, T. W., & Jung, J. (2011). Self-regulation and learning strategies. New *Directions for Teaching and Learning, 126,* 45–53.

Chapter 1 Exercises

1.1 Quote Reflections

Review the sidebar quotes contained in this chapter and select two that were especially meaningful or inspirational to you.

For each quote, provide a three- to five-sentence explanation of why you chose it.

1.2 Reality Bite

Alone and Disconnected: Feeling like Calling It Quits

Josephine is a first-year student in her second week of college. She doesn't feel like she's fitting in with other students on her campus. She also feels a little guilty about the time she's taking time away from family and friends back home, and she fears that her ties with them will be weakened or broken if she continues spending so much time at school and on schoolwork. Josephine is feeling so torn between college, her family, and her old friends that she's beginning to have second thoughts about returning to college next term.

Reflection and Discussion Questions

1. What would you say to Josephine that might persuade or motivate her to stay in college?

2. What could Josephine do to get more connected with her college community and feel less disconnected from her family and hometown friends?

3. What could Josephine do for herself right now to minimize the conflict she's experiencing between her commitment to college and her commitment to family and high school friends?

4. Can you relate to Josephine's situation? If yes, in what way? If no, why not?

1.3 Birds of a Different Feather: High School vs. College

The following list identifies 12 key differences between high school and college. Rate each difference on a scale from 1 to 4 in terms of how aware you were of this difference when you began college:

> 1 = totally unaware
>
> 2 = not fully aware
>
> 3 = somewhat aware
>
> 4 = totally aware.

a)   In high school, class schedules are typically made for students.

b)   In college, students make their own class schedules—either on their own or in consultation with an academic advisor.

Awareness Rating _____

a)   In high school, classes are scheduled back-to-back at the same time every day with short breaks in between.

b)   In college, courses are scheduled at various times throughout the day (and night) and larger time gaps can exist between successive classes in a student's schedule.

Awareness Rating _____

a)   In high school, class attendance is mandatory and checked regularly.

b)   In college, class attendance is not always mandatory; in many classes, attendance isn't taken at all.

Awareness Rating _____

> "In college, if you don't go to class, that's up to you. Your professor doesn't care really if you pass or fail."
>
> —First-year student

a) In high school, teachers often write all important information they cover in class on the board.

b) In college, professors frequently expect students to write down important information contained in their lectures without explicitly writing it on the board or including it on PowerPoint slides.

Awareness Rating _____

a) In high school, teachers often re-teach material in class that students were assigned to read.

b) In college, professors often don't cover the same material in class that appears in assigned reading, yet information from the assigned reading still appears on exams.

Awareness Rating _____

a) In high school, teachers often take class time to remind students of assignments and their due dates.

b) In college, professors list their assignments and due dates on the course syllabus and expect students to keep track of them on their own.

Awareness Rating _____

> College teachers don't tell you what you're supposed to do. They just expect you to do it. High school teachers tell you about five times what you're supposed to do."
> —College sophomore

a) In high school, homework assignments (e.g., math problems) are typically turned into the teacher who checks and grades the student's work.

b) In college, assigned work is often not turned in to be checked or graded; students are expected to have the self-discipline to do the work on their own.

Awareness Rating _____

a) In high school, students spend most of their learning time in class; they spend much less time studying outside of class than they spend learning in class.

b) In college, students typically spend no more than 15 hours per week in class and are expected to spend at least twice as much time studying out of class for every hour they spend in class.

Awareness Rating _____

a) In high school, tests are given frequently and cover limited amounts of material.

b) In college, exams are given less frequently (e.g., midterm and final) and tend to cover large amounts of material.

Awareness Rating _____

> In high school, they're like, 'Okay, well, I'll give you another day to do it.' In college, you have to do it that day ... teachers are like, 'If you don't do it, that's your problem."
> —First-year student

a) In high school, make-up tests and extra credit opportunities are often available to students.

b) In college, if an exam or assignment is missed, rarely do students have a chance to make it up or recapture lost points through extra credit work.

Awareness Rating _____

a) A grade of "D" in high school is still passing.

b) In college, a grade-point average below "C" puts a student on academic probation, and if it doesn't improve to C or higher, the student may be academically dismissed.

Awareness Rating _____

a) In high school, students go to offices on campus only if they have to, or if they're required to (e.g., if they forgot to do something or did something wrong).

b) In college, students go to campus offices to enhance their success by taking advantage of the support services provided in these offices.

Awareness Rating _____

1.4 Syllabus Review

Review the syllabus (course outline) for all classes you're enrolled in this term, and answer the following questions.

Self-Assessment Questions

1. Is the overall workload what you expected? Are you surprised by the amount of work required in any particular course(s)?

2. At this point in the term, what do you see as your most challenging or demanding course or courses? Why?

3. Do you think you can handle the total workload required by the full set of courses you're enrolled in this term?

4. What adjustments or changes do you think you'll make to your previous learning and study habits to accommodate your academic workload this term?

1.5 Creating a Master List of Resources on Your Campus

1. Construct a master list of all support services that are available to you on your campus by consulting the following sources:
   - Information published in your college catalog and student handbook
   - Information posted on your college's website
   - Information obtained by visiting with a professional in different offices or centers on your campus

2. Your final product will be a list that includes the following:

Campus Support Service	Type of Support Provided	Contact Person	Campus Location
_____	_____	_____	_____
_____	_____	_____	_____
_____	_____	_____	_____
_____	_____	_____	_____

etc.

Note:
- You can team up with other classmates to work collaboratively on this assignment. Members of your team could identify different campus resources to research and then share their findings with teammates.
- After completing this assignment, save your master list of support services for future use.

1.6 Utilizing Campus Resources in Your First Term

Look back at the campus resources you identified in the previous exercise, or those described on pp. 8–11 of this chapter. Which of these resources do you plan to use this term?

Why did you identify these resources as your top priorities right now?

Ask your course instructor for recommendations about what campus resources you should consult during your first term on campus. Compare their recommendations with your selections.

Liberal Arts and General Education

WHAT IT MEANS TO BE A WELL-EDUCATED PERSON IN THE 21ST CENTURY

The liberal arts represent the core of your college experience; they provide foundational, versatile skills that spell success in all college majors, careers, and life roles. In this chapter, you will gain a deeper understanding and appreciation of the liberal arts and acquire strategies for making the most of general education. You will learn about what it means to have a global perspective, how to develop yourself as a whole person, and how to enhance the overall quality (and marketability) of your college education.

Chapter Preview

Appreciate the meaning, purpose, and value of general education.

Learning Goal

Ignite Your Thinking

 Reflection 2.1

Before starting to read this chapter, answer the following question:

Which one of the following statements best captures the meaning and purpose of the term *liberal arts*?

1. Learning to be more artistic

2. Learning about things that are theoretical rather than practical

3. Learning to be less politically conservative

4. Learning to be a liberal spender

5. Learning skills for freedom

(The answer to this question appears later in the chapter.)

The *Meaning* and *Purpose* of the Liberal Arts

If you're uncertain about what "liberal arts" means, you're not alone. National surveys show that the vast majority of college students don't have a clear idea about what the liberal arts stand for and why they're valuable (Hersh, 1997). Many students think it's "learning for its own sake" (Humphreys, 2006), or that is has something to do with liberal politics—as illustrated by the following true story.

I was once advising a student (Laura)—a business major. While helping her develop a plan for graduation, I informed her she needed to take a course in philosophy. After I made this point, here's how our conversation went.

Laura (in a somewhat irritated tone): I'm a business major. Why do I have to take philosophy?

Dr. Cuseo: Because philosophy is an important part of a liberal arts education.

Laura (in a very agitated tone): I'm not liberal and I don't want to be liberal! I'm conservative and so are my parents; we all voted Republican in the last election.

—*Joe Cuseo*

Laura probably would have picked option (1) as her answer to the multiple-choice question posed at the start of this chapter; she would have been wrong because the correct choice is option (5). Literally translated, the term "liberal arts" derives from two Latin roots: *liberalis*—meaning to "liberate" or "free," and *artes*—meaning "skills" (Kimball, 1986). Thus, the liberal arts are "skills for freedom."

The roots of the liberal arts date back to the origin of modern civilization—to the ancient Greek and Roman democracies—where citizens were given the freedom to elect their own leaders, thus "liberating" them from uncritical dependence on autocrats or dictators (Bishop, 1986). Citizens of a democracy need to be skilled in the arts of critical thinking and communication to make wise choices about whom they elect as leaders and lawmakers and to participate effectively in the democratic process (Humphreys, 2006).

The political ideals of the ancient Greeks and Romans were shared by the founding fathers of the United States who believed that an educated citizenry was essential for sustaining America's new democracy. Thomas Jefferson, principal author of the U.S. Declaration of Independence, stated: "If a nation expects to be ignorant and free, it expects what never was and never will be."

Thus, the liberal arts are rooted in the belief that education and freedom are inescapably intertwined (Truman, 1948). Citizens educated in the liberal arts acquire the breadth of knowledge and depth of thinking to vote wisely and the communication skills to argue persuasively. To this day, the liberal arts continue to be a hallmark of the American college and university system that distinguishes it from systems in other countries around the world (Conley, 2005).

Note

The original purpose of college education in America was not just career preparation; it was preparation for citizenship and leadership in a democratic nation.

Over time, the concept of the liberal arts expanded to take on a broader meaning of liberating people to become self-directed thinkers—capable of making personal decisions based on well-reasoned ideas and values (Gamson, 1984; Katz, 2008)—rather than by blind obedience to authority or social conformity. In addition to resisting manipulation by dictatorial politicians, self-directed critical thinkers are also able to resist manipulation by other societal forces, including:

- Authority figures—resisting excessive use or abuse of authority by parents, teachers, or law enforcers;
- Peers—resisting negative forms of social conformity and peer pressure; and
- Media—detecting and rejecting manipulative advertisements and misleading persuasive messages.

"Advertisers rely on a half-educated public . . . because such people are easy to deceive with an effective set of logical and psychological tricks."

—*Robert Harris*, On the Purposes of a Liberal Arts Education

"I want knowledge so I don't get taken advantage of in life."

—*First-year college student*

In short, the liberal arts empower you to become a well-informed citizen and critical thinker who is armed and ready to ask the question: "Why?" It's the component of your college education that equips you with an inquiring mind and the mental tools to think independently.

The Liberal Arts Curriculum

Based on the educational philosophy of the ancient Greeks and Romans, the first liberal arts curriculum (collection of courses) originated during the Middle Ages and consisted of the following subjects: Logic, Language, Rhetoric—the art of argumentation and persuasion, Music, Mathematics, and Astronomy (Association of American Colleges & Universities, 2002, 2007; Ratcliff, 1997). It was a curriculum designed to: (a) supply students with a broad base of knowledge so they would be well informed in a variety of subjects and (b) equip them with a flexible set of thinking skills for thinking deeply and critically about any subject.

The range of courses offered by today's colleges and universities is much broader than the original seven subjects that comprised the medieval curriculum. However, the original goal of the liberal arts curriculum has withstood the test of time. It continues to provide students a broad base of knowledge spanning multiple subject areas, plus transferable thinking and communication skills that can be applied across different topics and situations (Humphreys, 2006).

Today, the liberal arts curriculum is sometimes referred to as *general education* to capture the fact that it supplies students with general knowledge and skills rather than narrow, specialized knowledge associated with a specific major or career. General education is what all college students experience, no matter what their particular major or specialized field of study happens to be (Association of American Colleges & Universities, 2002).

The liberal arts are also referred to on some campuses as: (a) the *core curriculum* —what's central or essential for all students to learn, or (b) *breadth requirements*— the broad range of subject areas and skill sets that every college graduate should possess.

 Reflection 2.2

On your campus, what term is used to refer to the fields of study that all students must take in order to graduate?

Whatever term is used to describe the liberal arts on your campus, the bottom line is that they provide the foundation of a college education on which all academic specializations (majors) are built. The liberal arts signify what all college graduates should know and be able to do in order to succeed in any occupational path they choose to pursue.

Note

The liberal arts are what distinguish a college education from vocational training; they define what it means to be a well-educated person.

Major Bodies of Knowledge in the Liberal Arts Curriculum

The divisions of knowledge comprising today's liberal arts curriculum have expanded well beyond the seven subjects found in the original curriculum of medieval universities. The liberal arts divisions may vary somewhat from campus to campus; variation across campuses also exists in terms of the specific courses students are required to take within each of these divisions of knowledge. Despite campus-to-campus variation in the exact number and nature of courses required for general education, the liberal arts curriculum on every college and university continue to represent what the campus believes are the foundational fields of knowledge and the transferable skills that all of its graduates should possess.

The breadth of knowledge you acquire through the liberal arts allows you to stand on the shoulders of intellectual giants from a wide range of fields and capitalize on their collective wisdom. What follows is a description of the general divisions of knowledge that comprise the liberal arts curriculum on most campuses today. As you read through the specific fields of study within each of these divisions of knowledge, make note of those subjects in which you've never had a course.

> "Challenging the meaning of life is the truest expression of the state of being human."
>
> *—Viktor Frankl, Austrian neurologist, psychiatrist, and Holocaust survivor*

Humanities

Courses in this division of the liberal arts focus on the human experience and the "big questions" that humans have always tried to answer, such as: "Why are we here?" "What is the purpose of our existence?" "What does it mean to be human?" "What constitutes living a 'good life'?" and "Is there life after death?" Listed below are the primary subjects in the Humanities, followed by the type of skills these subjects are designed to develop.

> "It was books that taught me that the things that tormented me the most were the very things that connected me with all the people who were alive, and who have ever been alive."
>
> *—James Baldwin, African-American novelist, essayist, playwright, and poet*

- *Literature.* Reading critically and appreciating the artistic merit of different literary genres—e.g., novels, short stories, poems, plays, and essays.
- *Philosophy.* Thinking rationally, acquiring wisdom (the ability to use knowledge prudently), and living an ethical life.
- *Theology.* Appreciating the ways in which humans believe and express their faith in a transcendent (supreme) being.
- *English Composition.* Writing clearly, thoughtfully, and convincingly.
- *Speech.* Speaking informatively, eloquently, and persuasively.
- *Languages.* Communicating in languages other than one's native tongue.

©Ekaterina Pokrovskays/Shutterstock.com

Fine Arts

Courses in this division of the liberal arts focus largely on the art of human expression, asking such questions as: "How do humans create, and appreciate what is beautiful?" "How do humans express themselves aesthetically (through the senses), imaginatively, and stylistically?" Listed below are the primary subdivisions of the Fine Arts, followed by the type of skills these subjects are designed to develop.

- *Visual Arts.* Expression and appreciation of creativity through visual representation (drawing, painting, sculpture, photography, and graphic design).
- *Musical Arts.* Expression and appreciation of creativity through rhythmical arrangement of sounds.

- *Performing Arts.* Appreciation and expression of creativity through drama and dance.

Mathematics

Courses in this division of the liberal arts develop skills relating to numerical calculations, quantitative reasoning, and data analysis. Listed below are subjects that typically comprise the general education in mathematics, followed by the type of skills these subjects are designed to develop.

- *Algebra.* Mathematical reasoning and logical thinking expressed through symbolic representation of numbers in the language of letters.
- *Statistics.* Mastering methods for summarizing quantitative data; estimating probabilities; representing and understanding numerical information depicted in graphs, charts, and tables; and drawing accurate inferences from statistical data.
- *Calculus.* Advanced mathematical skills for calculating areas enclosed by curves and rates at which the quantity of one entity changes in relation to another.

Natural Sciences

Courses in this division of the liberal arts curriculum focus on systematic observation of the physical world and underlying explanations of natural phenomena, asking such questions as: "What causes the physical events that take place in the natural world?" "How can we predict and control natural events?" "How do we promote harmonious interaction between humans and the natural environment in ways that support their mutual survival and well-being?" Listed below are the primary subject areas in the Natural Sciences and the type of skills these subjects are designed to develop.

- *Biology.* Understanding the structures and processes of all forms of life.
- *Chemistry.* Understanding the composition of natural and synthetic substances, how these substances can be altered, and how new substances may be synthesized.
- *Physics.* Understanding the properties of physical matter, their principles of energy and motion, and how they are affected by electrical and magnetic forces.
- *Geology.* Examining the composition of the earth and the natural processes that shaped its development.
- *Astronomy.* Exploring the makeup and motion of celestial bodies that comprise the cosmos.

Social and Behavioral Sciences

Courses in this division of the liberal arts focus on the systematic observation of human behavior, both individually and in groups, asking such questions as: "What causes people to behave the way they do?" "How can we predict, control, and improve human behavior and social interaction?" Listed below are subjects that typically comprise the Social and Behavioral Sciences and the type of skills these subjects are designed to develop.

> Dancing is silent poetry."
> —Simonides, ancient Greek poet

> The universe is a grand book which cannot be read until one learns to comprehend the language of which it is composed. It is written in the language of mathematics."
> —Galileo Galilei, 17th-century Italian physicist, mathematician, astronomer, and philosopher

> The media through which we get our information about the world are full of charts, graphs, and statistical information. Important decisions you will make about such matters as a medical treatment, home buying or voting will depend on your math skills."
> —Robert Shoenberg, Senior Fellow, Association of American Colleges and Universities

> There are in fact two things, science and opinion; the former begets knowledge, the latter ignorance."
> —Hippocrates, ancient Greek philosopher, physician, and the "father of western medicine"

©Yuri Arcurs/Shutterstock.com

The natural sciences division of the liberal arts curriculum focuses on the observation of the physical world and the explanation of natural phenomena.

- *History.* Understanding past events, their causes, and their influence on current events.
- *Political Science.* Understanding how societal authority is organized and used to govern people, make collective decisions, and maintain social order.
- *Psychology.* Understanding the human mind, its conscious and subconscious processes, and the underlying causes of human behavior.
- *Sociology.* Understanding how people behave in groups, and the organizations and institutions that comprise society (e.g., families, schools, hospitals, and corporations).
- *Anthropology.* Understanding the cultural origins, physical origins, and development of the human species
- *Geography.* Understanding how the place (physical location) where humans live shapes, and is shaped by, their culture.
- *Economics.* Examining how society's material needs are met through allocation of its limited resources and how monetary wealth generated by its production of goods and services are distributed, priced, and consumed.

"Man, the molecule of society, is the subject of social science."

—Henry Charles Carey, 19th-century American economist

Physical Health and Wellness

Courses in this division of the liberal arts focus on maintaining optimal health and attaining peak levels of human performance, asking such questions as: "How does the body function most effectively?" "What can humans do to minimize illness, maximize wellness, and improve the overall quality of their lives?" Listed below are the primary subject areas in this division of the curriculum and the type of skills they're designed to develop.

- *Physical Education.* Understanding how exercise enhances health and the quality of human performance.
- *Nutrition.* Understanding how the body uses food as nourishment for maintaining health and as fuel for generating energy.
- *Sexuality.* Understanding the biology and psychology of sexual relationships.
- *Drug Education.* Understanding how chemical substances alter the body and mind, and affect physical health, mental health, and human behavior.

"To eat is a necessity, but to eat intelligently is an art."

—La Rochefoucauld, 17th-century French author

Reflection 2.3

Look back at the subject areas of the liberal arts. For those subjects in which you've never had a course, identify a field of study that strikes you as particularly interesting or potentially useful, and provide a brief explanation why.

Most of the courses you will take to fulfill general education requirements will be taken during your first two years of college. Don't be dismayed if some of these requirements look similar to courses you had in high school. College courses are not videotape replays of high school courses; you will learn these subjects in greater depth and with higher levels of critical thinking than you did previously (Conley, 2005). Research reveals that the greatest gains in learning and thinking students make in college take place during their first two years in college (Pascarella & Terenzini, 2005)—the years when most liberal arts courses are taken.

In addition to acquiring this broad base of knowledge, the liberal arts also discipline your mind to *think* in a variety of ways. This is why different academic divisions in college are often referred to as *disciplines*—by studying them, you begin to develop the "mental discipline" that faculty in these fields have spent years of their lives developing. For instance, when you study history, algebra, biology, and art, you discipline your mind to think chronologically (history), symbolically (algebra), scientifically (biology), and aesthetically (art).

The Liberal Arts Liberate You from Narrowness and Broaden Your Perspectives

In addition to developing your ability to think critically, the liberal arts ensure that you think comprehensively. The wide range of subjects you encounter in the general education curriculum equip you with a wide-angle lens to view the world from a panoramic perspective (Braskamp, 2008). The key components of this broader perspective are organized and illustrated in **Figure 2.1**. The center circle in the figure represents the self. Fanning out to the right of the self are increasingly wider arches that represent the broadening elements of a *social–spatial perspective*. This perspective takes you from micro to macro, expanding your view to progressively larger social groups and more distant places, ranging from the narrowest perspective (the individual) to the broadest perspective (the universe). This expanded social–spatial perspective provides you with a world view, enabling you to step outside yourself and see yourself in relation to other people and other places.

FIGURE 2.1: **Broadening Perspectives Developed by the Liberal Arts**

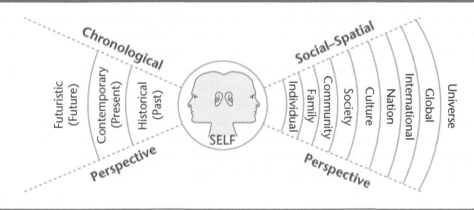

©Kendall Hunt Publishing Company

In Figure 2.1, to the left of the self are three arches that comprise the *chronological perspective* and embrace three key dimensions of time: *past* (historical), *present* (contemporary), and *future* (futuristic). A chronological perspective gives you hindsight—seeing where the world has been, insight—seeing the world's current condition, and foresight—seeing where the world is going. It stretches your perspective beyond the here and now, enabling you to view the world from the perspective of humans who have lived before you and will live after you.

In a nutshell, the social–spatial perspective widens your frame of reference and the chronological perspective lengthens it. Together, these two broadening perspectives developed by the liberal arts allow you to appreciate the human experience of people living long ago and far away.

The Social–Spatial Perspective: Moving Beyond the Self to the Wider World

The Perspective of *Family*

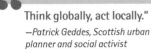

"I noticed before when I wasn't going to college, they [my family] didn't look at me as highly as a person. But now since I have started college, everybody is lifting me up and saying how proud they [are] of me."

—First-year student

One of the ways in which a liberal arts education broadens your perspective is by deepening your understanding of how the family influences development of the individual. The people who raised you and with whom you were raised have shaped the person you are today. Moreover, your family members not only influence you, you influence them. For example, your decision to go to college is likely to influence your parents' view of you and may influence whether other members of your immediate or extended family attend college. If you have children, your college knowledge will likely impact their development because research shows that children of college graduates experience improved intellectual development, better physical health, and greater economic security (Bowen, 1977, 1997; Pascarella & Terenzini, 1991, 2005).

The Perspective of *Community*

"Think globally, act locally."

—Patrick Geddes, Scottish urban planner and social activist

In addition to being nested in a family, you're also nested in a larger social unit—your community. A community may be defined as a group of people that share the same environment, interests, beliefs, and values (Canuto & Yaeger, 2000). This circle of community members includes your friends as well as people in the communities where you live, work, and go to school. If you want to make the world a better place, the place to start is by engaging in service and leadership in your local communities. As William Cronon (1998) notes: "In the act of making us free, it [liberal arts education] also binds to the communities that gave us our freedom in the first place; it makes us responsible to those communities. It is about exercising our freedom in such a way as to make a difference in the world and make a difference for more than just ourselves." Studies show that compared to other citizens, college graduates have higher rates of participation in civic affairs and community service (Bowen, 1977, 1997; Pascarella & Terenzini, 2005).

One way in which we can demonstrate civic engagement is by stepping beyond our narrow self-interests and volunteering to help other members of our community, particularly those in need. Engaged citizens are *humane*—they have genuine compassion for others less fortunate than themselves—and *humanitarian*—they devote time and effort to promote the welfare of other human beings.

Note

A college education is not only about learning how to earn a better living; it's also about learning how to be a better human being.

The Perspective of *Society*

Moving beyond our local communities, we're also members of a larger *society*—a group of people organized under the same social system. Society is comprised of groups of people stratified (divided) into different social classes with unequal amounts of economic resources and social privileges (Feagin & Feagin, 2012). Members of society have different levels of socioeconomic status (SES) depending on their level of education, personal income, and occupational prestige—all three of which tend to be interrelated. For instance, young adults from high-income families are more than seven times more likely to have earned a college degree and hold a prestigious job than those from low-income families (Olson, 2007). These differences may be explained, at least in part, by the fact that young adults from families with higher income levels and SES are privileged with two major forms of capital, each of which contributes to their higher rates of college attendance and college completion: (a) economic capital—the *material* resources they possess—such as, homes, health benefits, discretionary income for travel, technology, tutors, and other enriching educational experiences; and (b) social capital—*who* they know (Bourdieu, 1986)—such as, contacts with employers, college counselors, college admissions officials, and "power players" in the legal and political system.

The societal perspective developed by the liberal arts helps us understand how such stratification has advantaged or disadvantaged us as individuals and increases our empathy for less privileged members of society.

The *National* Perspective

In addition to being members of a society, we're also citizens of a *nation*. Citizens in a democratic nation are expected to be informed and engaged participants in its system of governance—as voters—and in its judicial system—as jurors. When voter turnouts are low, citizens with more moderate political views tend to be the ones who don't turn out to vote, resulting in people with more extreme views getting a larger percentage of the vote. Thus, low turnouts can result in a more polarized political system that's less conducive to balanced, bipartisan representation and negotiation. Also, when voter turnouts are low, political candidates are more likely to use extreme media tactics—such as attack ads and smear campaigns—to instill public fear of opposing candidates (Bolles, 1998).

It's noteworthy that American citizens between the ages of 18 and 24 have the lowest voter turnout rate of any age group that's eligible to vote (Cummings & Wise, 2006). If you're in this age group, don't contribute to this disturbing statistic. Remember that the right to vote is the hallmark of a democratic nation. Having the privilege of citizenship in a free nation brings with it the responsibility of learning about and participating in the country's governance through the voting process. "Civic responsibility must be learned, for it is neither natural nor effortless. It takes work to inform oneself sufficiently to cast an intelligent vote" (Bok, 2006). Recent surveys reveal that employers of college graduates feel the same way: 83% of them agree that college students should take classes that build civic knowledge and judgment (Hart Research Associates, 2013).

Remember that a foundational purpose of the liberal arts is to educate citizens broadly and deeply so they can vote wisely and ensure the quality of a democracy. The signers of the Declaration of Independence believed that the pursuit of personal happiness was not possible without pursuit of the national good; the well-being of the individual and the well-being of the whole (nation) were inescapably interrelated (Kluger, 2013).

> "It [a liberal arts education] shows you how to accommodate yourself to others, how to throw yourself into their state of mind, how to come to an understanding of them. You are at home in any society; you have common ground with every class."
>
> —*John Henry Newman*, The Idea of a University

> "Get involved. Don't gripe about things unless you are making an effort to change them. You can make a difference if you dare."
>
> —*Richard C. Holbrooke, former director of the Peace Corps and American ambassador to the United Nations*

Note

Investing in a college education isn't only an investment in yourself, it's also an investment in your country.

 **Reflection 2.4**

Did you vote in the last presidential election? If yes, why? If no, why not?

The *International* Perspective

Moving beyond our particular country of citizenship, we're also members of an international world that includes close to 200 nations (Rosenberg, 2014). Citizens in every nation today are affected by events that cross national borders. Boundaries between nations are melting away as a result of increased international travel, increased international trading, and the growth of multinational corporations (Friedman, 2005). In addition, rapid advances in electronic technology have created more opportunities for citizens of different nations to communicate than at any other time in world history (Dyrden & Vos, 1999; Smith, 1997). The worldwide web (www) has made today's world "a small world after all" and success in it requires an international perspective. The liberal arts curriculum helps you develop this perspective by supplying you with cross-cultural knowledge that takes you beyond the boundaries of your own nation.

The *Global* Perspective

Even broader than the international perspective is the global perspective. It transcends nations to embrace all forms of human and nonhuman life that inhabit planet earth, and examines how these diverse life forms interface with its natural resources (minerals, air, and water). Humans share the earth with approximately 10 million animal species and more than 300,000 forms of vegetative life (Myers, 1997), all of which have needs that must be met and balanced in order to ensure the health and sustainability of our planet (Knoll, 2003). Just as we need to avoid egocentrism—thinking that the self is the center of the universe—we also need to avoid *anthropocentrism*—believing that humans are the only significant life form on the planet while ignoring (or abusing) other elements of the natural world (Grey, 1993).

A global perspective includes consideration of the industrial and economic pursuits that impact the earth's sustainability. As "global citizens" of the same planet, we have an environmental responsibility to address issues that threaten Mother Earth's natural resources and life forms that depend on its resources for survival. Global research indicates that the earth's atmosphere is gradually thickening and trapping more heat as a result of buildup in gases created by our burning fossil fuels for industrial purposes (Intergovernmental Council on Climate Change, 2013; IPCC, 2014). The consensus among today's scientists is that this buildup of human-made pollution is responsible for temperatures rising (and sometimes falling) around the world, resulting in more extreme weather conditions and more frequent natural disasters—such as droughts, wildfires, hurricanes, and dust storms (Joint Science Academies Statement, 2005; National Resources Defense Council, 2005, 2012). Solving the problem of climate change requires a global perspective and worldwide appreciation of how waste admissions generated on earth need to be held to an environmentally sustainable level (Daly, 1999; Goodland, 2002). Such a planetwide perspective is promoted by the liberal arts.

The Perspective of the *Universe (Cosmos)*

Beyond the global perspective is the broadest of all perspectives—the perspective of the universe. This cosmic perspective positions us to view earth as a single planet sharing a solar system with multiple planets and our planet as one celestial body sharing a galaxy with millions of other celestial bodies, which includes stars, moons, meteorites, and asteroids (Encrenaz, et al., 2004).

It's noteworthy that astronomy was one of the seven essential subjects included in the original liberal arts curriculum developed during the Middle Ages. The timeless intrigue of the cosmos is supported by the ongoing work of modern-day cos-

"A liberal [arts] education frees a person from the prison-house of class, race, time, place, background, family, and nation."

—Robert Hutchins, former dean of Yale Law School and president of the University of Chicago

"[College] graduates need to develop a sense of global citizenship . . . to care about people in distant places, to understand the nature of global economic integration, to appreciate the interconnectedness and interdependence of people, and to protect planet Earth."

—Yong Zhao, noted Chinese painter, calligrapher, and poet

"Treat the Earth well. It was not given to you by your parents. It was loaned to you by your children."

—Kenyan proverb

"In astronomy, you must get used to viewing the earth as just one planet in the larger context of the universe."

—Physics professor

mologists. Reflecting on the massive, mysterious nature of the universe, how it began, where it may be going, and whether it will ever end, are considered by many to be spiritual questions (Zohar & Marshall, 2000). Similarly, astronauts who have traveled beyond the earth's force of gravity to view the universe from a cosmic perspective have described it as a "spiritual" experience.

Whether you view the universe through the physical telescope of astronomy or the spiritual scope of reflective contemplation, it qualifies as the broadest of all social–spatial perspectives developed by the liberal arts.

The Chronological Perspective: Embracing the Past, Present, and Future

In addition to broadening your perspective of the world—equipping you with knowledge about other people and places, the liberal arts also stretches your perspective of time—enabling you to learn about the past and its relationship to the present and future. Described below are the three key dimensions of a chronological perspective: historical, contemporary, and futuristic.

Historical Perspective

Humans are products of both their social and natural history. A historical perspective gives you insight into the root causes of the current human condition and world situation. We need to remember that the earth is estimated to be more than 4.5 billion years old and our human ancestors date back more than 250,000 years (Knoll, 2003). Viewed from this historical perspective, the lifespan of humans living today represents just a very small frame of time in a very long chronological reel. Every modern convenience we now enjoy reflects the collective knowledge and cumulative efforts of humans that have taken place over thousands of years of history. By studying the past, we build on our ancestors' successes and avoid repeating their mistakes. For instance we have built on the architectural experiences of ancient Egyptian pyramid makers to construct more advanced buildings today, and by understanding the causes and consequences of the Holocaust, we reduce the risk that an atrocity of such size and scope will ever happen again. The liberal arts curriculum lengthens your chronological perspective and deepens your understanding of the historical roots of today's world.

Reflection 2.5

What historical event or development in your lifetime do you think is having the most impact on today's world and will continue to impact the world of the future?

Contemporary Perspective

Today's news is tomorrow's history. A contemporary perspective gives us insight into current issues and events. Taking a critical perspective on current events is particularly important because news reporting in today's media has become more politically biased. Current political campaigns also use more manipulative media advertisements, relying on short sound bites, one-sided arguments, and powerful visual images designed to appeal to emotions and discourage deep thinking (Boren, 2008; Goleman, 1992). Thus, the original goal of the liberal arts to develop a well-informed, critical-thinking citizenry may be more essential today than at any time

> "Man must rise above the Earth—to the top of the atmosphere and beyond—for only thus will he fully understand the world in which he lives."
> —Socrates, classic Greek (Athenian) philosopher and founding father of Western philosophy

> "We all inherit the past. We all confront the challenges of the present. We all participate in the making of the future."
> —Ernest Boyer & Martin Kaplan, Educating for Survival

> "Those who cannot remember the past are damned to repeat it."
> —George Santayana, Spanish-born American philosopher

> "Yesterday is gone. Tomorrow has not yet come. We have only today. Let us begin."
> —Mother Teresa of Calcutta, Albanian, Catholic nun and winner of the Nobel Peace Prize

in American history. The liberal arts will strengthen your contemporary perspective and supply you with the skills and wisdom to make a difference in today's world (Harris, 2001; Miller, 1988).

 Reflection 2.6

Do you keep up with current events? What news source(s) do you rely on?

Futuristic Perspective

A futuristic perspective frees us from the here and now, allowing us to envision what our world may be like in the years ahead. This perspective allows us to confront the future challenges facing humankind, asking such questions as: "Will we leave the world a better place for future generations, including our children and grandchildren?" "How can we avoid short-term, shortsighted thinking and take a long-range perspective that enables us to anticipate the consequences of our current actions on future generations?"

The liberal arts help us remain mindful that our human lifespan is incredibly short when compared to the lifespan of humanity. Viewing humanity from this extended perspective underscores our moral responsibility to use the limited time we have on earth to promote the quality and sustainability of life for future generations of humans.

To sum up, the chronological perspective brings our view of the past, present, and future into focus on a single screen. It enables us to see how the current world is a short snippet in a much longer temporal sequence that's been shaped by past events and will shape future events. When you combine the past-present-future dimensions of a chronological perspective with the broad-based dimensions of a social–spatial perspective, you're positioned to see the multiple layers of context within which specific issues in today's world are embedded. (These layers of context are illustrated in **Figures 2.2** and **2.3**.)

> "Education is our passport to the future, for tomorrow belongs to the people who prepare for it today."
>
> *—Malcolm X, African American Muslim minister, public speaker, and human rights activist*

FIGURE 2.2: Nested Social–Spatial Perspectives: Interconnected People and Places

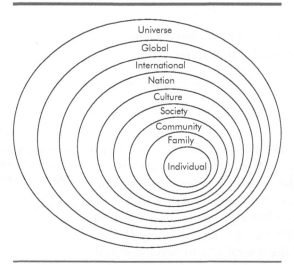

©Kendall Hunt Publishing Company

FIGURE 2.3: Nested Chronological Perspectives: Interconnected Times

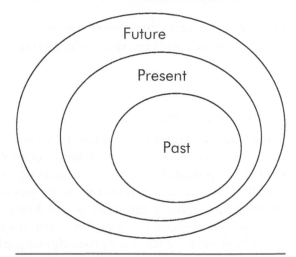

©Kendall Hunt Publishing Company

The Synoptic Perspective: Integrating Multiple Perspectives into a Coherent Whole

A liberal arts education not only involves taking multiple perspectives, but also integrating those perspectives into a meaningful whole (King, et al., 2007; Nussbaum, 1997). Understanding how the perspectives of time, place, and person connect to create a unified whole is referred to as a *synoptic* perspective (Cronon, 1998; Heath, 1977). The word derives from a combination of two roots: *syn*—meaning "together" (as in the word "synthesize")—and *optic*—meaning "to see." Thus, a "synoptic" perspective literally means to "see things together" or "see the whole." Said in another way, it's a big picture perspective that allows you to "connect the dots" and see how the trees form the forest.

A synoptic perspective enables us to see how we, as individuals, fit into the larger scheme of things (Daly, 1992; Heath, 1976). When we view ourselves as nested within an interconnected web of other people, places, and times, we become aware of our common humanity (Bronfenbrenner, 2005). This increased sense of connection with humankind reduces our sense of isolation and alienation (Bellah, et al., 1985); it also increases our ability to empathize and identify with people whose life experiences differ radically from our own. In his book, *The Perfect Education*, Kenneth Eble eloquently describes this benefit of a liberal arts education:

> *"It can provide that overarching life of a people, a community, a world that was going on before the individual came onto the scene and that will continue on after [s]he departs. By such means we come to see the world not alone. Our joys are more intense for being shared. Our sorrows are less destructive for our knowing universal sorrow. Our fears of death fade before the commonness of the occurrence"* (Eble, 1966, pp. 214–215).

The Liberal Arts Develop the *Whole Person*

In addition to expanding your knowledge of the world around you, the liberal arts expand your knowledge of the world within you. Well-educated people not only look outward to learn about the world around them, they also look inward to learn about themselves. Scholars consider introspection (the ability to inspect and understand yourself) to be a major form of human intelligence, referring to it as "intrapersonal intelligence" (Gardner, 1999, 2006).

"Know thyself"—the famous exhortation of Socrates (ancient and influential Greek philosopher)—is one of the primary goals of the liberal arts (Cross, 1982; Tubbs, 2011). To know thyself—to be fully self-aware—requires knowledge of the *whole* self. The liberal arts liberate us from a narrow or single-dimensional view of ourselves, enabling us to become aware of the multiple components that comprise the "self."

As illustrated in **Figure 2.4**, the self is a multidimensional entity comprised of multiple identities, all of which are interrelated and interdependent. We are not just thinking (intellectual) beings or working (vocational) beings; we're also social, emotional, physical, ethical, and spiritual beings.

> "A truly great intellect is one which takes a connected view of old and new, past and present, far and near, and which has an insight into the influence of all these on one another, without which there is no whole, and no center."
> —*John Henry Newman*, The Idea of a University

> "Integration of learning is the ability to connect information from disparate contexts and perspectives—for example, to connect one field of study with another, the past with the present, one part with the whole—and vice versa."
> —*Wabash National Study of Liberal Arts Education*

> "A liberal arts education can help us develop a more comprehensive understanding of the universe and ourselves."
> —*Spencer Mc Williams*, Liberal Arts Education: What Does it Mean? What is it Worth?

> "I want to see how all the pieces of me come together to make me, physically and mentally."
> —*College sophomore*

©Kendall Hunt Publishing Company

Know Thyself

Self-awareness is one of the most important outcomes of the liberal arts and general education.

FIGURE 2.4: **Key Elements of Holistic (Whole-Person) Development**

©Kendall Hunt Publishing Company

Comprehensive self-awareness and self-development includes the following dimensions of self.

1. **Intellectual:** acquiring broad-based knowledge, learning how to learn, and learning how to think critically.
2. **Emotional:** understanding, managing, and expressing emotions.
3. **Social:** improving the quality and depth of interpersonal relationships.
4. **Ethical:** building moral character—making sound ethical judgments, developing a clear value system for guiding personal decisions, and demonstrating consistency between your convictions (beliefs) and your commitments (actions).
5. **Physical:** acquiring knowledge about the human body and applying that knowledge to prevent disease, promote wellness, and achieve peak performance.
6. **Spiritual:** devoting attention to the "big questions," such as the meaning or purpose of life, the inevitability of death, and the origins of human life and the natural world.
7. **Vocational:** exploring career options and pursuing a career path that capitalizes on your talents, interests, and values.
8. **Personal:** developing a strong sense of personal identity, a coherent self-concept, and the capacity to manage personal affairs and resources.

(For a more detailed description of these eight elements of self-development, see **Exercise 2.4**, pp. 51–54.)

> "Everyone is a house with four rooms: a physical, a mental, an emotional, and a spiritual. Most of us tend to live in one room most of the time but unless we go into every room every day, even if only to keep it aired, we are not complete."
>
> —*Native American proverb*

 Reflection 2.7

Which one of the eight dimensions of self listed above are you most interested in developing or improving while you're in college? Why?

(Complete Exercise 2.3 at the end of this chapter to identify areas of the liberal arts that can bolster your strengths and uncover your blind spots.)

As can be seen in Figure 2.4, the different dimensions of self are interrelated. They do not operate independently but interdependently; they intersect with each other to influence an individual's development and overall well-being (Kegan, 1994; Love & Love, 1995). Our intellectual performance is influenced by our emotional state (e.g., whether we're enthusiastic or anxious); our emotional state is influenced by our social relationships (e.g., whether we are supported or ostracized); and our social relationships are influenced by our physical self-concept (e.g., whether we have a positive or negative body image). If one link in the chain is strengthened or weakened, other dimensions of the self are likely to be simultaneously strengthened or weakened. This ripple effect is supported by research on college students, which indicates that when they develop intellectually, they also develop higher levels of self-esteem and social self-confidence (Pascarella & Terenzini, 1991, 2005).

National surveys show that the number-one reason why students go to college is to get a good job (Pryor, et al., 2012). While finding a job and earning a decent living are certainly important, occupational or career development represents just one element of self-development. It also represents just one of many roles or responsibilities that humans are required to perform in life. A college education will not just enrich you economically; it will enrich you personally, enabling you to become a fuller, more complete human being.

The Co-Curriculum: Using the *Whole Campus* to Develop the *Whole Person*

The power of the liberal arts is magnified when you take advantage of the total campus environment (Shoenberg, 2005). A college education involves more than just taking courses and piling up credits; it also involves taking advantage of the learning opportunities available to you outside the classroom—known as the *co-curriculum*. Co-curricular experiences include educational discussions you have with your peers and professors outside of class, as well as your participation in campus events, programs, and organizations sponsored by the Office of Student Life or Student Development.

Learning from courses (the curriculum) is primarily vicarious—that is, you learn from or through somebody else—by listening to professors in class and by reading outside of class. This *academic* learning is certainly valuable, but it needs to be complemented by *experiential* learning—that is, learning that takes place directly from first-hand experiences. For example, leadership is not learned solely by listening to lectures and reading books about leadership. To fully develop your leadership skills, you need to have actual leadership experiences, such as "leading a [discussion] group in class, holding office in student government or by being captain of a sports team" (Association of American Colleges & Universities, 2002).

> "
> The comprehensiveness of general education does not relate simply to knowledge, but to the entire environment in which learning takes place. From the beginning, general education curricula [the liberal arts] have been concerned with the student's total learning environment; the entire community is considered as a resource for general education."
>
> —*George Miller,* The Meaning of General Education

Note

General education includes both the curriculum and the co-curriculum; they work together to produce college graduates who are both well-rounded and globally minded.

Listed in **Box 2.1** are some of the major co-curricular programs and services offered on most colleges and university campuses; they are organized according to the primary dimension of the self they're designed to develop.

BOX 2.1

Dimensions of Holistic (Whole-Person) Development Promoted by Co-Curricular Programs and Student Development Services

Intellectual Development
- Learning center
- College library
- Academic advising
- Tutoring services
- Information technology services
- Campus speakers
- Academic skills-development workshops
- Concerts, theater productions, and art shows

Ethical Development
- Judicial review board
- Student government
- Integrity committees and task forces

Physical Development
- Student health services
- Wellness programs
- Campus athletic activities and intramural sports

Spiritual Development
- Campus ministry
- Peer ministry
- Religious services

> "To educate liberally, learning experiences must be offered which facilitate maturity of the whole person. These are goals of student development and clearly they are consistent with the mission and goals of liberal education."
> —*Theodore Berg*, Student Development and Liberal Education

Vocational Development
- Career development services
- Internships program
- Service learning experiences
- Work-study programs
- Major and career fairs

Personal Development
- Financial aid services and workshops
- Self-management workshops (e.g., managing time and money)
- Student development workshops and retreats

 Reflection 2.8

What student club or organization on your campus do you think would contribute most to your self-development?

The list in Box 2.1 represents just a sample of the total number of out-of-class programs and services that may be available on your campus. As you can see from the list's length, colleges and universities have been intentionally designed to promote student development in multiple ways.

Note

The power of general education is magnified when you learn from both the breadth of courses in the liberal arts curriculum and the diversity of experiences available through the co-curriculum. By combining the two, you use the whole college to develop yourself as a whole person.

The Liberal Arts Develop Transferable Skills that Can be Applied in Multiple Contexts

In addition to providing you with a broad base of knowledge and multiple perspectives for viewing yourself and the world around you, the liberal arts also equips you with a set of skills that can be adapted for use in a wide variety of settings. This is another way in which the liberal arts are liberating—they supply you with a set of versatile skills that aren't tied to any particular subject area or career field—skills that can be transferred freely and used to enhance your performance in different situations. These key transferable skills are listed in **Box 2.2**.

BOX 2.2

Transferable Skills Developed by the Liberal Arts

As you read the skills below, rate yourself on each of them, using the following scale:

4 = very strong, 3 = strong, 2 = needs some improvement, 1 = needs much improvement

1. Critical and Creative Thinking. Ability to evaluate the validity of ideas and arguments and the capacity to think innovatively.
2. Communication. Ability to express and comprehend ideas through various media, including:
   - *Written* Communication. Writing in a clear, creative, and persuasive manner
   - *Oral* Communication. Speaking concisely, confidently, and eloquently
   - *Reading*. Comprehending, interpreting, and evaluating the literal and figurative meaning of language written in various styles and subjects
   - *Listening*. Comprehending spoken language actively, accurately, and empathically

"

Effectively managing personal affairs, from shopping for household products to electing health care providers to making financial decisions, often requires people to acquire new knowledge from a variety of media, use different types of technologies and process complex information."

—The Partnership for 21st Century Skills

   - *Technology*. Using electronic media to effectively deliver and process ideas
3. Quantitative Skills. Ability to calculate, analyze, summarize, interpret, and evaluate quantitative information or statistical data.
4. Information Literacy Skills. Ability to access, retrieve, and evaluate information from various sources, including in print and online (technology-based) systems.

"

Ability to recognize when information is needed and the ability to locate, evaluate, and use it effectively."

—Definition of "information literacy," American Library Association Presidential Committee on Information Literacy

 Reflection 2.9

Reflect on the four skill areas developed by a liberal arts education (communication, information literacy, computation, and higher-level thinking). In which areas do you think you need the most improvement? How will you improve them?

The skills listed in Box 2.2 have two powerful qualities:

1. Flexibility: they are *portable* skills that "travel well"—you can carry them with you and apply them across a wide range of subject areas, work situations, and life roles.
2. Durability: they are *sustainable* skills—they have long-lasting value and can be used continually throughout life.

Using an athletic analogy, what the liberal arts do for the mind is similar to what cross-training does for the body. Cross-training engages the body in a wide range of exercises that promotes total physical fitness and develops a broad set of physical skills—strength, endurance, flexibility, and agility—which can be applied to improve performance in any sport or athletic endeavor. Similarly, the liberal arts engage the mind in a wide range of mental skills that can be used to improve performance in any major or career. As one scholar put it:

> *"Good learning habits can be transferred from one subject to another. When a basketball player lifts weights or plays handball in preparation for basketball, no one asks, "What good is weightlifting or handball for a basketball player?" because it is clear that these exercises build muscles, reflexes, and coordination that can be transferred to basketball—building them perhaps better than endless hours of basketball practice would. The same is true of the mind. Exercise in various areas builds brainpower for whatever endeavor you plan to pursue"* (Harris, 2001).

> "You know you've got to exercise your brain just like your muscles."
>
> —*Will Rogers, Native American humorist and actor*

AUTHOR'S EXPERIENCE

I must confess that I graduated from college without ever truly understanding the true meaning and purpose of the liberal arts. When I became a college professor, two of my colleagues from the Office of Student Affairs asked me to help them create a first-year experience (college success) course. I agreed and volunteered to teach the course, which included a unit on the Meaning and Value of a Liberal Arts Education. When I researched the topic to prepare for class, I began to realize what the liberal arts were all about and what they did for me. It became clear that the lasting power of my college education didn't lie in all the factual information I'd studied (and forgotten), but in the transferable skills and "habits of mind" I took with me as a college graduate and have continued to use throughout my professional and personal life.

— *Joe Cuseo*

Note

You're likely to forget much of the specialized, factual information learned in college. However, you will retain the ways of thinking, habits of mind, and communication skills developed by the liberal arts, and you will continue to use them in multiple life roles throughout life.

The Liberal Arts Develop Skills for Success in Your College Major

Studies show that students often view general education as something to "get out of the way" or "get behind them" before they can get into their major and career (Association of American Colleges & Universities, 2007). Don't buy into the belief that liberal arts courses represent a series of hoops and hurdles that must be surmounted or circumnavigated before you get to do what really matters. Don't just get these courses "out of the way," get "into them" and take away from them the skills that will enable you to succeed in your major.

Recall our story at the very start of this chapter about Laura, the student with a business major who questioned why she had to take a course in philosophy. Laura's philosophy course not only fulfilled a general education requirement, it also developed critical thinking and ethical reasoning skills that she could apply to understand business issues more deeply and respond to them more humanely. It also enabled her to gain understanding of important philosophical issues embedded in business practice, such as: (a) underlying assumptions and values of capitalism relative to other economic systems, (b) business ethics—such as, fair hiring and advertising practices, and (c) business justice—such as, equitable distribution of profits among workers, executives, and shareholders.

Similarly, other subjects in the liberal arts curriculum provide business majors (and the many non-business majors who end up working in business organizations) with essential knowledge and deep thinking skills needed to succeed in the corporate world, such as:

- **History and Political Science:** understanding governmental policies that impact business operations and regulations.
- **Psychology and Sociology:** understanding how different sources of individual and group motivation affect worker productivity and consumer purchasing habits.
- **Speech, English Composition, and Literature:** speaking confidently and persuasively at meetings; writing clear and concise memos; reading and interpreting business reports accurately and critically.
- **Mathematics:** analyzing and interpreting statistical data from marketing surveys.
- **Natural Science:** determining effective and efficient ways for companies to conserve energy and sustain natural resources.
- **Fine Arts:** designing visually engaging advertisements and marketing strategies.

The liberal arts are also relevant to successful performance in fields other than business. For example, a historical perspective and ethical perspective are important in all majors and professions because every one of them has a history and none of them are value-free.

The Liberal Arts Enhance Career Preparation and Career Success

The world has changed dramatically in the 21st century and the world of work has changed with it. What are today's employers looking for in the people they hire? They are seeking workers who can problem-solve and manage projects; they want employees with effective interpersonal skills who can work well with groups; they also want their new hires to be skilled communicators who are able to adapt to a variety of environments.

In particular, employers report that the following skills and perspectives are necessary to ensure that college graduates are well prepared for work in the 21st century (Association of American Colleges & Universities, 2007; Colby, et al., 2011).

- Integrative learning: ability to apply knowledge and skills to real-world settings
- Knowledge of human cultures, the physical world, and the natural world, which includes understanding of:
  - Concepts and new developments in science and technology
  - Global issues and developments and their implications for the future
  - The role of the United States in the world
  - Cultural values and traditions in America and other countries
- Intellectual and practical skills, such as the ability to:
  - Communicate orally and in writing
  - Think critically and analytically
  - Locate, organize, and evaluate information from multiple sources
  - Innovate and think creatively
  - Solve complex problems
  - Work with numbers and statistics
- Personal and social responsibility:
  - Teamwork skills and the ability to collaborate with others in diverse group settings
  - A sense of integrity and ethics

> "
> A general education supplies a context for all knowledge and especially for one's chosen area. Every field gives only a partial view of knowledge and an exclusive or overemphasis on one field of study distorts the understanding of reality."
>
> —*Robert Harris*, On the Purpose of a Liberal Arts Education

> "
> Virtually all occupational endeavors require a working appreciation of the historical, cultural, ethical, and global environments that surround the application of skilled work."
>
> —*Robert Jones, author*, Liberal Education for the Twenty-first Century: Business Expectations

> "
> From Utah to the Ukraine and from Milwaukee to Manila, industry is demanding that our graduates have better teamwork skills, communication abilities, and an understanding of the socioeconomic context in which engineering is practiced."
>
> —*Ernest Smerdon, president of the American Society for Engineering Education*

The foregoing skills and qualities are best developed by a well-rounded education that combines general education through the liberal arts and specialized education in a specific major. Interviews with hundreds of recent college graduates and employers indicate that both groups believe the best preparation for career entry is an education that provides career-specific preparation *plus* broad-based knowledge and flexible skills (Hart Research Asscociates, 2006, 2013). In fact, 93% of employers agree that a candidate's capacity to think critically, communicate clearly, and solve complex problems is *more* important than his or her undergraduate major (Hart Research Associates, 2013).

 Reflection 2.10

Among the above four bulleted areas of knowledge and skills emphasized by today's employers, which one were you most surprised to see? Why?

The Liberal Arts Prepare You for Lifelong Learning

The current global economy has progressed from being agrarian (farm-based) to industrial (machine-based) to technological (information-based). The technological revolution is generating information and new knowledge at a faster rate than at any other time in human history (Dupuy & Vance, 1995). When knowledge is produced and communicated at such rapid rates, existing knowledge quickly becomes obsolete (Naisbitt, 1982). Studies show that today's workers change jobs 12 times in the two decades following college and the job-changing rate is highest for younger workers (AAC&U, 2007; U.S Bureau of Labor Statistics, 2015). These findings point to the need for college graduates to have transferable skills and a broad knowledge base to adapt to the demands of new positions they're likely to take on during the course of their career.

In order to perform their jobs and advance in their careers, workers in today's complex, fast-changing world must continually update their skills and learn new skills (Niles & Harris-Bowlsbey, 2012; Almeida, Behrman, & Robalino, 2012). This need for lifelong learning creates demand for workers who have *learned how to learn* and how to continue learning throughout life. This is a signature feature of the liberal arts and a key attribute of successful college graduates. (It's also the reason why college graduation is referred to as *commencement*—a beginning, not an end.)

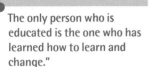

"The only person who is educated is the one who has learned how to learn and change."

—Carl Rogers, influential humanistic psychologist and Nobel Peace Prize nominee

AUTHOR'S EXPERIENCE

One life role that the liberal arts helped prepare me for was that of a parent. Courses I took in psychology and sociology proved to be useful in helping me understand my son's development and how I could best support him at different stages of his life. Surprisingly, however, there was one course I took that I never expected would help me as a parent, but it turned out to be critical. That course was statistics, which I took merely to fulfill a general education requirement in mathematics. It was not a particularly enjoyable course; in fact, some of my classmates sarcastically referred to it as "sadistics." What I learned in that statistics course became very valuable to me many years later when my 14-year-old son (Tony) developed leukemia—a cancer that attacks blood cells. Tony had a particularly perilous form of leukemia—one that 65% died from within seven years. This statistic was based on patients receiving the traditional treatment of chemotherapy, which was the type of treatment that my son's doctors began using when his cancer was first detected.

Another set of doctors strongly recommended that Tony's cancer be treated with a bone marrow transplant, which involved using radiation to destroy and replace all of his own bone marrow with bone marrow from a matched donor. My wife and I got opinions from doctors at two major cancer centers—one from a center that specialized in chemotherapy, and one from a center that specialized in bone marrow transplants. The chemotherapy doctors felt strongly that drug treatment would be the better way to treat and cure my son; however, the bone marrow transplant doctors felt just as strongly that his chances of survival would be much better if he had a transplant. Thus, my wife and I had to decide between two opposing recommendations, each made by a respected group of doctors.

To help us reach a decision, I sought out research studies on the effectiveness of chemotherapy and bone marrow transplants for treating my son's particular type of cancer and carefully reviewed all their statistical findings. I remembered from my statistics course that when an average is calculated for a group of people (e.g., average cure rate for people with leukemia) it tends to lump together individuals from different subgroups (e.g., males and females; children, teenagers and adults). Sometimes, an average statistic calculated for a whole group tends to mask or camouflage differences among the subgroups that comprise the whole group. With this in mind, I dug deeper to find any subgroup statistics that were embedded in the reports. I found two subgroups of patients with my son's form of cancer that had a higher rate of cure with chemotherapy than the general (whole-group) average of 35%. One subgroup included patients with a low number of abnormal cells at the time their cancer was first diagnosed, and the other subgroup consisted of patients whose cancer cells dropped rapidly after their first week of chemotherapy. My son belonged to both of these subgroups, which meant that his chance for cure with chemotherapy was higher than the overall 35% average. Furthermore, I found that the statistics for successful bone marrow transplants were based only on patients whose body accepted the donor's bone marrow. Since the statistics didn't include patients who died from the transplant, rather than from the cancer itself, the success rate for bone marrow patients wasn't as high as it appeared to be at first glance. Based on my interpretation of these statistics, my wife and I decided to have my son treated with chemotherapy instead of a bone marrow transplant.

My son has now been cancer free for almost 10 years; it looks like we made the right decision. I never imagined, however, that a statistics course, which I took many years ago to fulfill a general education requirement, would help me fulfill my role as a parent and help me make a life-or-death decision about my only son.

—*Joe Cuseo*

Note

General education is not just "learning for its own sake." The skills developed by the liberal arts are also practical skills that can be transferred and applied to different life roles throughout life. They provide a mental gift that keeps on giving.

Chapter Summary and Highlights

The liberal arts broaden your worldview by expanding (a) your social–spatial perspective to include increasingly larger social groups and more distant places—ranging from micro (the individual) to macro (the universe)—and (b) your chronological perspective—ranging from the past to the present to the future. The liberal arts also promote your development as a whole person—intellectually, socially, emotionally, physically, and spiritually.

The power of the liberal arts is magnified when you take advantage of the total campus environment, including learning opportunities outside the classroom—known as the *co-curriculum*. Co-curricular experiences include out-of-class discussions with peers and professors, as well as participation in campus events, programs, and organizations sponsored by the Office of Student Life or Student Development. Capitalizing on experiential learning opportunities outside the classroom enables you to use the whole campus to develop yourself as a whole person.

The liberal arts represent the foundation of a college education upon which all academic majors are built. They promote success in any major and career by supplying you with a set of versatile, lifelong learning skills that can be applied in multiple settings.

Despite popular beliefs to the contrary, the liberal arts have many practical benefits, including promoting career mobility and career advancement. Most importantly, the liberal arts prepare you for life roles other than an occupation, including roles such as family member, community member, and citizen. In short, the liberal arts prepare you for life.

Learning More through the World Wide Web: Internet-Based Resources

For additional information on liberal arts and general education, see the following websites.

"What is a liberal arts education?"
http://www.iseek.org/education/liberalarts.html

Understanding Liberal Education:
https://www.aacu.org/leap/what-is-a-liberal-education

Skills for Success in the 21st Century:
http://edglossary.org/21st-century-skills/

The Value of the Liberal Arts in the Global Economy:
http://www.huffingtonpost.com/edward-j-ray/the-value-of-a-liberal-arts-education_b_3647765.html

References

Almeida, R., Behrman, J., & Robalino, D. (Eds.). (2012). *The right skills for the job?: Rethinking training policies for workers.* Washington, DC: World Bank Publications.

Association of American Colleges & Universities. (2002). *Greater expectations: The commitment to quality as a nation goes to college.* Washington, DC: Author. Retrieved from http://www.greaterexpectaions.org/.

Association of American Colleges and Universities (AAC&U). (2007). *College learning for the new global century.* A report from the National Leadership Council for Liberal Education & America's Promise. Washington, DC: Association of American Colleges and Universities.

Bellah, R. N., Madsen, R., Sullivan, W. M., Swidler, A., & Tipton, S. M. (1985). *Habits of the heart: Individualism and commitment in American life.* Berkeley: University of California Press.

Bishop, S. (1986). Education for political freedom. *Liberal Education, 72*(4), 322–325.

Bok, D. (2006). *Our underachieving colleges.* Princeton, NJ: Princeton University Press.

Bolles, R. N. (1998). *The new quick job-hunting map.* Toronto, Ontario, Canada: Ten Speed Press.

Boren, D. (2008). *A letter to America.* Norman, OK: University of Oklahoma Press.

Bourdieu, P. (1986). The forms of capital. In J. Richardson (Ed.), *Handbook of theory and research for the social psychology of education* (pp. 241–258). Westport, CT: Greenwood Press.

Bowen, H. R. (1977). *Investment in learning: The individual and social value of American higher education.* San Francisco: Jossey-Bass.

Bowen, H. R. (1997). *Investment in learning: The individual and social value of American higher education* (2nd ed.). Baltimore: The Johns Hopkins Press.

Braskamp, L. A. (2008). Developing global citizens. *Journal of College and Character, 10*(1), 1–5.

Bronfenbrenner, U. (Ed.). (2005). *Making human beings human: Bioecological perspectives on human development.* Thousand Oaks, CA: Sage.

Canuto, M. A., & Yaeger, J. (Eds.). (2000). *The archaeology of communities.* New York: Routledge.

Colby, A., Ehrlich, T., Sullivan, W. M., & Dolle, J. R. (2011). *Rethinking undergraduate business education: Liberal learning for the profession.* The Carnegie Foundation for the Advancement of Teaching. San Francisco: Jossey-Bass.

Cronon, W. (1998). "Only connect": The goals of a liberal education. *The American Scholar, 67*(4), 73–80.

Cross, K. P. (1982). Thirty years passed: Trends in general education. In B. L. Johnson (Ed.), *General education in two-year colleges* (pp. 11–20). San Francisco: Jossey-Bass.

Cummings, M. C., & Wise, D. (2006). *Democracy under pressure* (10th ed.). Belmont, CA: Wadsworth.

Daly, W. T. (1992, July/August). The academy, the economy, and the liberal arts. *Academe,* 10–12.

Daly, H. E. (1999). *Ecological economics and the ecology of economics.* Cheltenham, UK: Edward Elgar Publishing.

Dryden, G., & Vos, J. (1999). *The learning revolution: To change the way the world learns.* Torrance, CA and Auckland, New Zealand: The Learning Web.

Dupuy, G. M., & Vance, R. M. (1995, October). *Launching your career: A transition module for seniors.* Paper presented at the Second National Conference on Students in Transition, San Antonio, Texas.

Eble, K. E. (1966). *A perfect education.* New York: Macmillan.

Encrenaz, T., Bibring, J. P., Blanc M., Barucci, M. A., Roques, F., & Zarka, P. (2004). *The solar system.* Berlin, Germany: Springer.

Feagin, J. R., & Feagin, C. B. (2012). *Racial and ethnic relations* (9th ed.). Saddle River, NJ: Prentice Hall.

Friedman, T. L. (2005). *The world is flat: A brief history of the twenty-first century.* New York: Farrar, Straus & Giroux.

Gamson, Z. F. (1984). *Liberating education.* San Francisco: Jossey-Bass.

Gardner, H. (1999). *Intelligence reframed: Multiple intelligences for the twenty-first century.* New York: Basic Books.

Gardner, H. (2006). *Five minds for the future.* Cambridge, MA: Harvard Business School Press.

Goodland, R. (2002). Sustainability: Human, social, economic, and environmental. In T. Munn (Ed.), *Encyclopedia of global environmental change* (pp. 488–489). Hoboken, NJ: Wiley.

Grey, W. (1993). Anthropocentrism and deep ecology. *Australasian Journal of Philosophy, 71,* 463–475.

Harris, R. (2001). *On the purpose of a liberal arts education.* Retrieved from http://www.virtualsalt.com/libarted.htm.

Hart Research Associates. (2006). *How should college prepare students to succeed in today's global economy?* Washington, DC: American Association of Colleges & Universities. Retrieved from http://www.aacu.org/leap/documents/2009_EmployerSurvey.pdf.

Hart Research Associates. (2013). *It takes more than a major: Employer priorities for college learning and student success.* Washington, DC: Author.

Heath, H. (1977). *Maturity and competence: A transcultural view.* New York: Halsted Press.

Hersh, R. (1997). Intentions and perceptions: A national survey of public attitudes toward liberal arts education. *Change, 29*(2), 16–23.

Humphreys, D. (2006). *Making the case for liberal education: Responding to challenges.* Washington DC: AAC&U. Retrieved from http://www.aacu.org/leap/documents/LEAP_MakingtheCase_Final.pdf.

Intergovernmental Council on Climate Change. (2013). *Climate change 2013: The physical science basis.* Working Group I Contribution to the Fifth Assessment Report of the Intergovernmental Council on Climate Change. Switzerland: Intergovernmental Panel on Climate Change. Retrieved from http://www.ipcc.ch/report/ar5/wg1/.

IPCC. (2014). *Climate change 2014: Synthesis report.* Contribution of Working Groups I, II and III to the Fifth Assessment Report of the Intergovernmental Panel on Climate Change [Core Writing Team, R. K. Pachauri and L. A. Meyer (Eds.)]. IPCC, Geneva, Switzerland. Retrieved from http://www.ipcc.ch/pdf/assessment-report/ar5/syr/AR5_SYR_FINAL_Front_matters.pdf.

Joint Science Academies Statement. (2005). *Global response to climate change.* Retrieved from http://nationalacademies.org/onpi/06072005.pdf.

Katz, S. N. (2008, May 23). Taking the true measure of liberal education. *Chronicle of Higher Education, 32.*

Kegan, R. (1994). *In over our heads: The mental demands of modern life.* Cambridge, MA: Harvard University Press.

Kimball, B. (1986). *Orators and philosophers: A history of the idea of liberal arts.* New York: Teachers College Press.

King, P. N., Brown, M. K., Lindsay, N. K., & Vanhencke, J. R. (2007). Liberal arts student learning outcomes: An integrated approach. *About Campus,* September/October, 2–9.

Kluger, J. (2013). The pursuit of happiness. *Time, 21*(3), 24–40.

Knoll, A. H. (2003). *Life on a young planet: The first three billion years of evolution on earth.* Princeton, NJ: Princeton University Press.

Love, P., & Love, A. G. (1995). *Enhancing student learning: Intellectual, social, and emotional integration.* ASHE-ERIC Higher Education Report No. 4. Washington, DC: The George Washington University. Graduate School of Education and Human Development.

Miller, G. (1988). *The meaning of general education.* New York: Teachers College Press.

Myers, N. (1997). The rich diversity of biodiversity issues. In M. L. Reaka-Kudla, D. E. Wilson, & E. O. Wilson (Eds.), *Biological diversity II: Understanding and protecting our biological resources* (pp. 125–134). National Academic of Sciences, Washington, DC: Joseph Henry Press.

Naisbitt, J. (1982). *Megatrends: Ten new directions transforming our lives.* New York: Warner Books.

National Resources Defense Council. (2005). *Global warming: A summary of recent findings on the changing global climate.* Retrieved from http://www.nrdc.org/globalwarming/science/2005.asp.

National Resources Defense Council. (2012). *Global warming: An introduction to climate change.* Retrieved from http://www.nrdc.org/globalwarming/.

Niles, S. G., & Harris-Bowlsbey, J. (2012). *Career development interventions in the twenty-first century.* Upper Saddle River, NJ: Pearson Education.

Nussbaum, M. C. (1997). *Cultivating humanity: A classical defense of reform in liberal education.* Cambridge, MA: Harvard University Press.

Olson, L. (2007). What does "ready" mean? *Education Week, 40,* 7–12.

Pascarella, E., & Terenzini, P. (1991). *How college affects students: Findings and insights from twenty years of research.* San Francisco: Jossey-Bass.

Pascarella, E. T., & Terenzini, P. T. (2005). *How college affects students: A third decade of research* (volume 2). San Francisco: Jossey-Bass.

Pryor, J. H., De Angelo, L., Palucki-Blake, B., Hurtado, S., & Tran, S. (2012). *The American freshman: National norms fall 2011.* Los Angeles: Higher Education Research Institute, UCLA.

Ratcliff, J. L. (1997). What is a curriculum and what should it be? In J. G. Gaff, J. L. Ratcliff, and Associates (Eds.), *Handbook of the undergraduate curriculum: A comprehensive guide to purposes, structures, practices, and change* (pp. 5–29). San Francisco: Jossey-Bass.

Rosenberg, M. (2014). *The number of countries in the world.* Retrieved from http://geography.about.com/cs/countries/a/numbercountries.htm.

Shoenberg, R. (2005). *Why do I have to take this course? A student guide to making smart educational choices.* Washington, DC: American Association of Colleges & Universities.

Smith, D. (1997). How diversity influences learning. *Liberal Education, 83*(2), 42–48.

Truman, H. S. (1948). *Higher education for democracy.* New York: Harper & Brothers.

Tubbs, N. (2011). Know thyself: Macrocosm and microcosm. *Studies in Philosophy and Education, 30*(1), 53–66.

U.S. Bureau of Labor Statistics. (2015). *Job openings and labor turnover survey.* Washington DC: Bureau of Labor Statistics. Retrieved from http://www.bls.gov/jlt/.

Zohar, D., & Marshall, I. (2000). *SQ: Connecting with your spiritual intelligence.* New York: Bloomsbury.

Chapter 2 Exercises

2.1 Quote Reflections

Review the sidebar quotes contained in this chapter and select two that were especially meaningful or inspirational to you.

For each quote, provide a three- to five-sentence explanation why you chose it.

2.2 Reality Bite

Dazed and Confused: General Education "versus" Career Specialization

Joe Tech was really looking forward to college because he thought he would have freedom to select the courses he wanted and the opportunity to get into the major of his choice (computer science). However, he's shocked and disappointed with his first-term schedule of classes because it consists mostly of required general education courses that seem totally unrelated to his major. He's also frustrated because some of these courses are about subjects he already took in high school (English, History, and Biology). He's beginning to think he would be better off quitting college and going to a technical school for a year or two so he can get right into computer science and immediately begin acquiring the skills he'll need to work in the computer industry.

Reflection and Discussion Questions

1. If Joe decides to get a technical certificate and not pursue a college degree, how do you see it affecting his future:
   a) in the short run, and
   b) in the long run?

2. Do you see any way Joe might strike a balance between pursuing his career interest and obtaining his college degree so that he could work toward achieving both goals at the same time?

3. Can you relate to Joe's story in any way, or do you know anyone else who is having a similar experience?

2.3 Do What You Are Self-Assessment

Complete the "Do What You Are" self-assessment which produced a report exclusively for you.

What do those results tell you about yourself?

Which areas of the liberal arts can bolster your strengths and which can help you uncover your blind spots?

2.4 Holistic Development Needs and Priorities: A Self-Assessment

Development of the whole self is an essential goal of the liberal arts and general education. As you read through the specific skills and qualities associated with the following dimensions of holistic ("whole person") development, rate each one in terms of its *importance to you* on a scale of 1 to 5, with 5 being highest and 1 lowest.

Skills and Qualities Associated with the Dimensions of Holistic (Whole-Person) Development

1. *Intellectual* Development: Acquiring a broad base of knowledge, learning how to learn deeply and think critically.

   Specific Objectives and Attributes:

   ___ Becoming aware of your intellectual abilities, interests, and learning styles

   ___ Improving your focus of attention and concentration

   ___ Moving beyond memorization to learning at a deeper level

   ___ Improving your ability to retain knowledge on a long-term basis

   ___ Acquiring effective research skills for finding information from a variety of sources and systems

> Intellectual growth should commence at birth and cease only at death."
>
> —Albert Einstein, Nobel Prize-winning physicist

___ Learning how to view issues from multiple angles or perspectives (psychological, social, political, economic, etc.)

___ Responding constructively to differing viewpoints or opposing arguments

___ Critically evaluating ideas in terms of their truth and value

___ Detecting and rejecting persuasion tactics that appeal to emotion rather than reason

___ Thinking creatively and innovatively

2. *Emotional* Development: Understanding, managing, and expressing emotions.

Specific Objectives and Attributes:

___ Dealing with personal emotions in an honest, nondefensive manner

___ Maintaining a healthy balance between emotional control and emotional expression

___ Responding with empathy and sensitivity to emotions experienced by others

___ Using effective stress-management strategies to control anxiety and reduce tension

___ Dealing effectively with depression

___ Dealing effectively with anger

___ Responding constructively to frustrations and setbacks

___ Dealing effectively with fear of failure and lack of self-confidence

___ Maintaining optimism and enthusiasm

___ Accepting feedback from others in a constructive, nondefensive manner

> It's not stress that kills us, it is our reaction to it."
>
> —Hans Selye, Canadian endocrinologist and author of Stress Without Distress

3. *Social* Development: Improving the quality and depth of interpersonal relationships.

Specific Objectives and Attributes:

___ Increasing social self-confidence

___ Improving listening and conversational skills

___ Overcoming shyness

___ Relating to others in an open, nondefensive and nonjudgmental manner

___ Forming meaningful friendships

___ Learning how to resolve interpersonal conflicts effectively

___ Developing greater empathy for others

___ Relating effectively to others from different cultural backgrounds and lifestyles

___ Collaborating effectively with others when working in groups or teams

___ Strengthening leadership skills

> Chi rispetta sara rippetato."
> ("Respect others and you will be respected.")
>
> —Italian proverb

4. *Ethical* (Character) Development: Developing a clear value system for guiding personal decisions, making sound ethical judgments, and demonstrating consistency between convictions (beliefs) and commitments (actions).

Specific Objectives and Attributes:

___ Gaining deeper awareness of your personal values and ethical priorities

___ Making personal choices and life decisions based on a meaningful value system

___ Developing the capacity to think and act with personal integrity and authenticity

___ Resisting social pressure to act in ways that are inconsistent with your values

___ Treating others in a fair and just manner

___ Exercising personal freedom responsibly without infringing on the rights of others

___ Increasing awareness of and commitment to human rights and social justice

___ Developing the courage to challenge or confront others who violate human rights and social justice

___ Using electronic technology in a civil and ethical manner

___ Becoming a more engaged and responsible citizen

> If you don't stand for something you will fall for anything."
>
> —Malcolm X, African American Muslim minister, public speaker, and human rights activist

5. *Physical* Development: Acquiring knowledge about the human body and how to apply that knowledge to prevent disease, preserve wellness, and promote peak performance.

    Specific Objectives and Attributes:

    ___ Becoming more aware of your physical condition and state of health
    ___ Applying knowledge about exercise and fitness to improve your physical and mental health
    ___ Developing sleep habits that maximize physical and mental well-being
    ___ Maintaining a healthy balance between work, recreation, and relaxation
    ___ Applying knowledge about nutrition to reduce risk of illness and promote peak performance levels
    ___ Becoming knowledgeable about nutritional imbalances and eating disorders
    ___ Developing a positive physical self-image
    ___ Increasing knowledge about the effects of drugs and how they affect the body and mind
    ___ Becoming more knowledgeable about human sexuality and sexual diversity
    ___ Understanding how biological differences between the sexes affect how males and females communicate and relate to each other

> "A man too busy to take care of his health is like a mechanic too busy to take care of his tools."
>
> *—Spanish proverb*

6. *Spiritual* Development: Devoting attention to the "big questions" about the meaning or purpose of life, the inevitability of death, and the origins of human life and the natural world.

    Specific Objectives and Attributes:

    ___ Developing or refining your philosophy of life
    ___ Exploring the unknown or what cannot be completely understood scientifically
    ___ Appreciating the mysteries associated with the origin of the universe
    ___ Searching for the connection between the self and the larger world or cosmos
    ___ Searching for the mystical or supernatural—that which transcends the boundaries of the natural world
    ___ Examining questions relating to death and life after death
    ___ Exploring questions about the possible existence of a supreme being or higher power
    ___ Gaining knowledge about different approaches to spirituality and their underlying beliefs or assumptions
    ___ Understanding the difference and relationship between faith and reason
    ___ Becoming more aware and accepting of diverse religious beliefs and practices

> "We are not human beings having a spiritual experience. We are spiritual beings having a human experience."
>
> *—Pierre Teilhard de Chardin, French philosopher, geologist, paleontologist, and Jesuit priest*

7. *Vocational* Development: Exploring career options and pursuing a career path that is compatible with your interests, talents, and values.

    Specific Objectives and Attributes:

    ___ Understanding the relationship between majors and careers
    ___ Using effective strategies for exploring and identifying potential careers
    ___ Identifying career options that capitalize on your personal interests, talents, needs, and values
    ___ Acquiring work experience related to your vocational interests
    ___ Creating an effective resume or portfolio
    ___ Developing effective strategies for selecting personal references and acquiring letters of recommendation
    ___ Implementing effective job search strategies
    ___ Learning how to write persuasive letters of inquiry and letters of application for employment positions
    ___ Acquiring networking skills for connecting with potential employers
    ___ Developing strategies for performing successfully in job interviews

> "Your work is to discover your work and then with all your heart to give yourself to it."
>
> *—Hindu Siddhartha Prince Gautama Siddharta, a.k.a. Buddha, founder of the philosophy and religion of Buddhism*

8. *Personal* Development: Developing a strong sense of personal identity, a coherent self-concept, and the ability to manage personal affairs and resources.

    Specific Objectives and Attributes:

    ___ Discovering your identity and clarifying your self-concept (answering the question: Who am I?)
    ___ Finding a sense of purpose and direction in life (answering the question: Who will I become?)

____ Developing greater self-respect and self-esteem

____ Increasing self-confidence

____ Developing self-efficacy—belief that the outcomes of your life are within your control and can be influenced by personal initiative and effort

____ Strengthening skills for managing personal resources (e.g., time and money)

____ Becoming more independent, self-directed, and self-reliant

____ Setting realistic goals and priorities

____ Developing the self-motivation and self-discipline needed to reach long-term goals

____ Developing the resiliency to overcome obstacles and convert setbacks into comebacks

- Based on your total score in each area, what aspect(s) of self-development appear to be most and least important to you? How would you explain (or what do you think accounts for) this discrepancy?
- Add up your total score for each of the eight (8) areas of holistic development.
  a) Do your totals in each of the eight areas suggest that all aspects of self-development are about equally important to you and that you're striving to become a well-rounded person?
  b) If yes, why? If no, why not?

2.5 Identify Courses that Broaden Your Perspectives

Using your *College Catalog* or *University Bulletin*, identify one course that you could take that develops each of the key broadening perspectives associated with the liberal arts listed in the box below.

Broadening Social–Spatial Perspectives	Course Developing this Perspective
(See pages 34–37 for specific descriptions of these perspectives.)	*(Read the course descriptions in your Catalog or Bulletin to identify a general education requirement that develops this perspective.)*
Self	
Family	
Community	
Society	
Nation	
International	
Global	
Universe	
Broadening Chronological Perspectives	Course Developing this Perspective
(See pages 37–38 for detailed description of these perspectives.)	*(Read the course descriptions in your Catalog or Bulletin to identify a general education requirement that develops this perspective.)*
Historical	
Contemporary	
Futuristic	

2.6 Identifying Co-Curricular Experiences that Develop the Whole Self

Using your *Student Handbook*, identify a co-curricular program or experience you could engage in that would contribute to each of the key dimensions of holistic (whole person) development listed in the box below.

Dimensions of Self	Co-curricular Experience Developing this Dimension of Self
(See page 40 for a description of these dimensions of self-development.)	*(Consult your Student Handbook to identify a co-curricular experience that contributes to this dimension of self-development.)*
Intellectual (Cognitive)	
Emotional	
Social	
Ethical	
Physical	
Spiritual	
Vocational	
Personal	

2.7 Identifying Personally Enriching Curricular and Co-Curricular Opportunities

Your College Satisfiers section of your "Do What You Are" report identified experiences that you would find enriching based on your self-assessment results. What curricular and co-curricular opportunities exist on your campus that match these descriptors?

How can connecting with these opportunities assist you in reaching your personal goals?

Goal Setting and Motivation

MOVING FROM INTENTION TO ACTION

The path to personal success begins with goals and finding the means (succession of steps) to reach those goals. People who set specific goals are more likely to succeed than people who simply tell themselves they're going to try hard and do their best. This chapter lays out the key steps involved in the process of setting effective goals, identifies key self-motivational strategies for staying on track and sustaining progress toward our goals, and describes how personal qualities such as self-efficacy, grit, and growth mindset are essential for achieving goals.

Help you set meaningful goals and maintain motivation to achieve your goals.

 Reflection 3.1

Complete the following sentence:

For me, success is . . .

Chapter Preview

> "
> What keeps me going is goals."
>
> —Muhammad Ali, philanthropist, social activist, and Hall of Fame boxer crowned "Sportsman of the 20th Century" by Sports Illustrated

Learning Goal

Ignite Your Thinking

> "
> Stopping a long pattern of bad decision-making and setting positive, productive priorities and goals."
>
> —College sophomore's answer to the question: "What does being successful mean to you?"

The Relationship between Goal Setting and Success

Achieving success begins with setting goals. Research shows that people who set goals and develop plans to reach them are more likely to reach them (Halvorson, 2010), and successful people set goals on a regular basis (Locke & Latham, 1990). In fact, the word "success" derives from the Latin root "successus"—meaning "to follow or come after"—as in the word "successive." Thus, by definition, success involves a sequence of actions that leads to a desired outcome; the process starts with identifying an end (goal) and then finding a means (sequence of steps) to reach that goal.

> "
> The tragedy of life doesn't lie in not reaching your goal. The tragedy of life lies in having no goal to reach."
>
> —Benjamin Mays, minister, scholar, activist, president of Morehouse College

Motivation begins with dreams and great intentions that get turned into realistic goals. Depending on the length of time it takes to reach them and the order in which they are to be achieved, goals may be classified into three general categories: long-range, mid-range, and short-range. Short-range goals need to be completed before a mid-range goal can be reached, and mid-range goals must be reached before a long-range goal can be achieved. For example, if your long-range goal is a successful career that requires a college degree, your mid-range goal is completing all the coursework required for a degree that will allow you entry into that career. To reach your mid-range goal of a college degree, you need to start by successfully completing the courses you're taking this term (your short-range goal).

This goal-setting process is called *means-end analysis*; it involves working backward from your long-range goal (the end) and identifying what mid-range and short-range subgoals (the means) must be reached in order to achieve your long-range goal (Brooks, 2009; Newell & Simon, 1959). Engaging in this means-end analysis doesn't mean you're locking yourself into a premature plan that will restrict your flexibility or options. It's just a process that gets you to: (a) think about where you want to go, (b) provides some sense of direction about how to get there, and (c) starts moving you in the right direction.

> " You've got to be careful if you don't know where you're going because you might not get there."
> —Yogi Berra, Hall of Fame baseball player

Characteristics of a Well-Designed Goal

Studies show that people who set specific, well-designed goals are more likely to succeed than are people who simply tell themselves they're going to try hard and do their very best (Halvorson, 2010; Latham & Locke, 2007). The acronym SMART is a well-known mnemonic device (memory strategy) for recalling all the key components of a well-designed goal (Doran, 1981; Meyer, 2003). **Box 3.1** describes the different components of a SMART goal.

Box 3.1

The *SMART* Method of Goal Setting

A *SMART* goal is one that's:

Specific—it states precisely what the goal is, targets exactly what needs to be done to achieve it, and provides a clear picture of what successfully reaching the goal looks like.

Example: By spending 25 hours per week on my coursework outside of class and by using the effective learning strategies (such as those recommended in this book), I'll achieve at least a 3.0 grade point average this term. (Note that this is a much more specific goal than saying, "I'm really going to work hard this term.")

> " Dreams can be fulfilled only when they've been *defined*."
> —Ernest Boyer, former United States Commissioner of Education

Meaningful (and Measurable)—the goal really matters to you (not someone else) and the progress you're making toward the goal can be clearly measured (tracked).

Example: Achieving at least a 3.0 grade point average this term is important to me because it will enable me to get into the field I'd like to major in. I'll measure my progress toward this goal by calculating the grade I'm earning in each of my courses this semester at regular intervals throughout the term.

Note: At *www.futureme.org* you can set up a program to send future emails to yourself that remind you to check and reflect on whether you're making steady progress toward the goals you set.

Actionable (i.e., Action-Oriented)—the actions or behaviors that will be taken to reach your goal are clearly specified.

Example: I will achieve at least a 3.0 grade point average this term by (a) attending all classes, (b) taking detailed notes in all my classes, (c) completing all reading assignments before their due dates, and (d) avoiding cramming by studying in advance for all my major exams.

Box 3.1 *(continued)*

*R*ealistic—there is a good chance of reaching the goal, given the time, effort, and skills needed to get there.

Example: Achieving a 3.0 grade point average this term is a realistic goal because my course load is manageable, I will be working no more than 15 hours per week at my part-time job, and I'll be able to get help from campus support services for any academic skills or strategies I need to strengthen.

*T*ime-framed—the goal has a deadline plus a timeline or timetable that includes short-range (daily), mid-range (weekly), and long-range (monthly) steps.

Example: To achieve at least a 3.0 grade point average this term, first I'll acquire all the information I need to learn by taking complete notes in my classes and complete all reading assignments (short-range step). Second, I'll learn the information I've acquired from my notes and readings, break it into parts, and study the parts in separate sessions in advance of major exams (mid-range step). Third, on the day before

exams, I'll review all the information I previously studied in parts so I avoid cramming and get a good night's sleep (long-range step).

Note: The SMART process can be used to set goals in any area of your life or dimension of personal development, such as:

- self-management (e.g., time-management and money-management goals),
- physical development (e.g., health and fitness goals),
- social development (e.g., relationship goals),
- emotional development (e.g., stress-management or anger-management goals),
- intellectual development (e.g., learning and critical thinking goals),
- career development (e.g., career exploration and preparation goals), or
- any other element of holistic (whole-person) development discussed in Chapter 2 (see p. 40).

 Reflection 3.2

If you were to set a SMART goal for some aspect of your life right now, what would it be and why would you set it?

In addition to the effective goal-setting properties associated with the SMART method, research reveals that the following goal-setting features characterize people who set and reach important goals.

1. Effective goal-setters set *improvement (get-better) goals* that emphasize progress and growth, rather than *perfection (be-good) goals*. Studies show that when people pursue get-better goals, they pursue them with greater interest and intensity, and they are more likely to enjoy the process (Halvorson, 2010). This is likely because get-better goals give us a sense of accomplishment about how far we've come—even when we still have a long way to go.

2. Effective goal-setters focus on outcomes they have *influence or control over*, not on outcomes that are beyond their control. For example, a controllable goal for an aspiring actress would be to improve her acting skills and opportunities, rather than to become a famous movie star—which will depend on factors that are beyond her control.

3. Effective goal-setters set goals that are *challenging and effortful*. Goals worth achieving require that we stretch ourselves and break a sweat; they require endurance, persistence, and resiliency. Studies of successful people in all occupations indicate that when they set goals that are attainable but also *challenging*, they pursue those goals more strategically, with more intensity, and with greater commitment (Locke & Latham, 2002; Latham & Locke, 2007). There's an-

> Nothing ever comes that is worth having, except as a result of hard work."
>
> *—Booker T. Washington, born-in-slavery Black educator, author, and advisor to Republican presidents*

> Accomplishing something hard to do. Not something that has just been handed to me."
>
> *—First-year student's response to the question: "What does being successful mean to you?"*

other advantage of setting challenging goals: Achieving them supplies us with a stronger sense of accomplishment, satisfaction, and self-esteem.

4. Effective goal-setters anticipate *obstacles* they may encounter along the path to their goal and have a plan in place for dealing with them. Successful people often imagine what things will be like if they don't reach their goals, which drives them to anticipate problems and setbacks before they arise (Gilbert, 2006; Harris, Griffin, & Murray, 2008). They're optimistic about succeeding, but they're not blind optimists; they realize the road will be tough and they have a realistic plan in place for dealing with the rough spots (Oettingen, 2000; Oettingen & Stephens, 2009). Thus, a well-designed goal should not only include specific information about how the goal will be achieved, but also specific plans to handle anticipated impediments along the way—for example, identifying what resources and social support networks may be used to keep you on track and moving forward.

Capitalize on resources that can help you stay on track and moving toward your goal. Research indicates that success in college involves a combination of what students do for themselves (personal responsibility) and how they capitalize on resources available to them (Pascarella & Terenzini, 1991, 2005). Successful people are *resourceful*; they seek out and take advantage of resources to help them reach their goals. Use your campus (and community) resources to help you achieve your long-range goals (e.g., academic advising and career counseling).

Don't forget that your peers can serve as a resource to help you reach your goals. Much has been said about the dangers of "peer pressure," but much less attention has been paid to the benefits of "peer power." The power of social support groups for helping people achieve personal goals is well documented by research in different fields (Brissette, Cohen, & Seeman, 2000; Ewell, 1997). There's also a long historical trail of research pointing to the power of peers for promoting the development and success of college students (Astin, 1993; Feldman & Newcomb, 1994; Pascarella & Terenzini, 2005). Be sure to ask yourself: Who can help me stick to my plan and complete the steps needed to reach my goal? You can harness the power of social support by surrounding yourself with peers who are committed to successfully achieve their educational goals and by avoiding "toxic" people who are likely to poison your plans or dampen your dreams.

Find motivated peers with whom you can make mutually supportive "pacts" to help one another reach your respective goals. These mutual support pacts may be viewed as "social contracts" signed by "co-witnesses" who help them stay on track and moving toward their long-range goals. Studies show that making a commitment to a goal in the presence of others increases our commitment to that goal because our successful pursuit of it is viewed not only through our own eyes, but through the eyes of others as well (Hollenbeck, Williams, & Klein, 1989; Locke, 2000).

> "Develop an inner circle of close associations in which the mutual attraction is not sharing problems or needs. The mutual attraction should be values and goals."
>
> —*Denis Waitley, former mental trainer for U.S. Olympic athletes and author of* Seeds of Greatness

Reflection 3.3

What *obstacles* or *impediments* do you anticipate may interfere with your goal of succeeding in college and completing your college degree?

What *campus resources* do you think would be most helpful for dealing with your anticipated obstacles?

What *social support networks* (family members, friends, or mentors) do you think could help you overcome your anticipated obstacles?

Strategies for Maintaining Motivation and Progress toward Your Goals

The word "motivation" derives from the Latin *movere*, meaning "to move." Success comes to those who overcome inertia—they start moving toward their goal—then they maintain momentum until their goal is reached. Goal-setting only creates the potential for success; it takes motivation to turn this potential into reality by converting intention into action. We can have the best-designed goals and know the way to succeed, but if we don't have the *will* to succeed, there's no way we will succeed. Studies show that goal-setting is just the first step in the process; it must be accompanied by a strong commitment to achieve the goal that has been set (Locke, 2000; Locke & Latham, 1990).

> You can lead a horse to water, but you can't make him drink."
> —*Author unknown*

Reaching challenging goals requires that you maintain motivation and sustain effort over an extended period of time. Listed below are strategies for doing so.

Put your goals in writing and make them visible. Written goals can serve almost like a written contract that holds you accountable for following through on your commitments. By placing written goals where you can't help but see them on a daily basis (e.g., your laptop, refrigerator, and bathroom mirror), you're less likely to "lose sight" of them and more likely to continue pursuing them. What's kept in sight is kept in mind.

Note

The next best thing to doing something you intend to do is to write down your intention to do it.

Keep your eye on the prize. Visualize reaching your long-range goals; picture it by creating vivid mental images of your future success. For example, if your goal is to achieve a college degree, visualize a crowd of cheering family, friends, and faculty at your graduation. (You could even add musical accompaniment to your visualization by playing a motivational song in your head—e.g., "We are the Champions" by Queen). Imagine cherishing this proud memory for the rest of your life and being in a career your college degree enabled you to enter. Picture a typical workday going something like this: You wake up on a Monday morning and are excited about the upcoming workweek. When you're at work, time seems to fly by; before you know it, the day is over. When you go home after work and reflect on your day, you feel great about what you did and how well you did it.

Visualize completing the steps leading to your goal. For visualization to be really effective, you need to visualize not just the success itself (the end goal), but also the steps you'll take along the way. "Just picturing yourself crossing the finish line doesn't actually help you get there—but visualizing how you run the race (the strategies you will use, the choices you will make, the obstacles you will face) not only will give you greater confidence, but also leave you better prepared for the task ahead" (Halvorson, 2010, p. 208).

Thus, reaching a long-term goal requires focusing on the prize—your dream and *why* it's important to you; this "big picture" view provides the inspiration. At the same time, however, you have to focus on the little things—*what* it will take to get there—the nitty-gritty of due dates, to-do lists, and day-to-day tasks. This is the

You've got to think about 'big things' while you're doing small things, so that all the small things go in the right direction."

—Alvin Toffler, American futurologist and author who predicted the future effects of technology on our society

perspiration that transforms inspiration into action, enabling you to plug away and stay on track until your goal is achieved.

It could be said that successfully achieving a long-term goal requires two lenses, each of which provides you with a different focus point: (a) a wide-angle lens that gives you a big-picture view of a future that's far ahead of you (your ultimate goal), and (b) a narrow-angle lens that allows you to focus intently on the here and now—on the steps that lie immediately ahead of you. Alternating between these two perspectives allows you to view your small, short-term chores and challenges (e.g., completing an assignment that's due next week) in light of the larger, long-range picture (e.g., college graduation and a successful future).

AUTHOR'S EXPERIENCE

I once helped coach a youth soccer team (five to six year olds) and noticed that many of the less successful players tended to make one of either two mistakes when they tried to advance the ball toward the goal. Some spent too much time looking down, focusing on the ball at their feet, trying to be sure that they didn't lose control of it. By not occasionally lifting their head and looking ahead, they often missed open territory, open teammates, or an open goal. Other unsuccessful players made the opposite mistake: They spent too much time with their heads up, trying to see where they were headed. By not periodically glancing down at the ball in front of them, they often lost control of it, moved ahead without it, or sometimes stumbled over it and fell flat on their face. In contrast, the more successful players had developed the habit of shifting their focus between looking down to maintain control of the ball immediately in front of them and lifting their eyes to see where they were headed.

The more I thought about how these successful soccer players alternated their perspective between looking at the ball right in front of them and looking at the goal farther ahead, it struck me that this was a metaphor for success in life. Successful people alternate between long-range and short-range perspectives; they don't lose sight of how executing the tasks immediately in front of them connect with the ultimate goal further ahead of them.

—Joe Cuseo

Note

Keep pursuit of your future dreams and completion of your current tasks in dual focus. Integrating these two perspectives provides you with the inspiration to set goals and the determination to reach them.

Writing my resume was a real ego booster—I've actually done stuff!"

—College student (quoted in Brooks, 2009)

Keep a record of your progress. Research indicates that the mere act of monitoring and recording progress toward your goals increases your motivation to continue pursuing them (Locke & Latham, 2005; Matsui, Okada, & Inoshita, 1983). Keeping a regular record of your personal progress increases motivation by providing you with frequent *feedback* about whether you're on track and positive *reinforcement* for staying on track (Bandura & Cervone, 1983; Schunk, 1995).

Mark down your accomplishments in red on a calendar, or keep a journal of the short- and mid-range goals you've reached. These markings serve as benchmarks, supplying you with concrete evidence and a visible reminder of your progress. You can also mark your progress on a chart or graph, or list your achievements in a resume or portfolio. Place these displays of progress where you can see them on a daily basis and use them as a source of motivation to keep striving toward your ultimate goal (Halvorson, 2010).

This practice of ongoing (daily) assessment of our personal progress toward goal completion is a simple, yet powerful form of self-reflection that's associated with success. Research on successful people reveals that they reflect regularly on their daily progress to ensure they're on track and progressing steadily toward their goals (Covey, 1990).

Reward yourself for reaching milestones on the path toward your goal. Reaching a long-range goal is clearly rewarding because it marks the end of the trip and arrival at your desired destination. However, reaching short- and mid-range goals are not as self-rewarding because they're merely the means to the end. Thus, you need to make intentional attempts to reward yourself for climbing these smaller, yet essential stepping stones on the path to the mountain peak.

Engaging in the behaviors needed to persist and persevere through all the intermediate steps needed to reach a long-range goal is more likely to take place if these behaviors are followed by reward (positive reinforcement). The process of setting small goals, moving steadily toward them, and rewarding yourself for reaching them is a simple, yet powerful self-motivational strategy. It helps you maintain momentum over an extended period of time, which is exactly what's required to reach a long-range goal. When you achieve short- and mid-range goals, check them off as milestones and reward yourself for reaching them (e.g., celebrate successful completion of midterms or finals by treating yourself to something you really enjoy).

> "Whoever wants to reach a distant goal must take many small steps."
> —*Helmut Schmidt, former chancellor of West Germany*

 ## Reflection 3.4

For you, what would be effective rewards for making progress toward your goals and serve as motivators to keep you going?

(Take a look at the results of your "Do What You Are" report. What does it say about your character traits with respect to goal setting, as well as your motivational strengths and blind spots?)

Characteristics of Successful People

Achieving success involves effective use of goal-setting and motivational strategies, but it takes something more. Ultimately, success emerges from the inside out; it flows from personal qualities and attributes found within a person. Studies of successful people who achieve their goals reveal they possess the following personal characteristics. Keep these characteristics in mind as you set and pursue your goals.

Internal Locus of Control

Successful people have what psychologists call an "internal locus of control"; they believe that the locus (location or source) of control for events in their life is *internal*—"inside" them and within their control—rather than *external*—outside them and beyond their control. They believe that success is influenced more by attitude, effort, commitment, and preparation than by inherited ability, inborn intelligence, luck, chance, or fate (Rotter, 1966; Carlson, et al., 2009; Jernigan, 2004).

> "If you do not find it within yourself, where will you go to get it?"
> —*Zen saying (Zen is a branch of Buddhism that emphasizes seeing deeply into the nature of things and ongoing self-awareness)*

Research shows that individuals with a strong internal locus of control display the following positive qualities:

1. Greater independence and self-direction (Van Overwalle, Mervielde, & De Schuyer, 1995),
2. More accurate self-assessment of strengths and weaknesses (Hashaw, Hammond, & Rogers, 1990), and
3. Higher levels of learning and achievement (Wilhite, 1990).

Self-Efficacy

An internal locus of control contributes to the development of another positive trait that psychologists refer to as *self-efficacy*—the belief that you have power to produce a positive effect on the *outcomes* of your life (Bandura, 1994). People with low self-efficacy tend to feel helpless, powerless, and passive; they think (and allow) things to happen to them rather than taking charge and making things happen for them. College students with a strong sense of self-efficacy believe they're in control of their educational success and can shape their future, regardless of their past experience or current circumstances.

People with a strong sense of self-efficacy initiate action and exert effort. They believe success is something that's earned and the harder they work at it, the more likely they'll get it. If they encounter setbacks or bad breaks along the way, they don't give up or give in; they persevere and push on (Bandura, 1986, 1997).

Students with a strong sense of *academic self-efficacy* have been found to:

1. Put considerable effort into their studies;
2. Use active-learning strategies;
3. Capitalize on campus resources; and
4. Persist in the face of obstacles (Multon, Brown, & Lent, 1991; Zimmeman, 1995, 2000).

Students with a strong sense of self-efficacy also possess a strong sense of personal responsibility. As the breakdown of the word "responsible" implies, they are "response" "able"—they believe they're able to respond to personal challenges, including academic challenges.

 ## Reflection 3.5

In what area or areas of your life do you feel that you've been able to exert the most control and achieve the most positive results?

In what area(s) do you wish you had more control and were achieving better results?

What strategies have you used in the area of your life where you've been able to exert the most personal control and achieve the most positive outcomes?

Could you apply any of these same strategies to those areas in which you need to gain more control?

Grit

When you expend significant effort, energy, and sacrifice over a sustained period of time to achieve a goal, you're demonstrating grit (Stoltz, 2014). People with grit have been found to possess the following qualities (Duckworth, et al., 2007).

Persistence. They hang in there and persevere until they reach their goals. When the going gets tough, they don't give up; they step it up. They have the fortitude to persist in the face of frustration and adversity.

> "I'm a great believer in luck, and I find the harder I work the more I have of it."
>
> —*Thomas Jefferson, third president of the United States*

> "Grit is perseverance and passion for long-term goals. Sticking with your future day in, day out, not just for the week, not just for the month, but for years and working really hard to make that future a reality."
>
> —*Angela Duckworth, psychologist, University of Pennsylvania*

Tenacity. They pursue their goals with relentless determination. If they encounter something along the way that's hard to do, they work harder to do it.

Resilience. They bounce back from setbacks and keep striving to reach their goals. They adopt the mindset that they'll bounce back from setbacks and turn them into comebacks. How you react mentally and emotionally to a setback affects what action you take in response to it. For instance, you can react to a poor test grade by knocking yourself down with self-putdowns ("I'm a loser") or by building yourself back up with positive self-talk ("I'm going to learn from my mistakes on this test and rebound with a stronger performance on the next one").

As you can see in **Figure 3.1**, information passes through the emotional center of the human brain (lower, shaded area) before reaching the center responsible for rational thinking and future planning (upper area). As a result, when we encounter setbacks, our initial (and subconscious) tendency is to react emotionally and defensively. To counteract this tendency, we need to slow down, calm down, and make a conscious attempt to respond rationally to setbacks—thinking about how we can overcome them, learn from them, and make use of them to continue progressing toward our goal.

FIGURE 3.1: **The Brain's Emotional Filter**

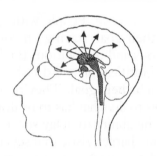

Information entering the human brain is first processed emotionally (lower shaded area) before reaching higher areas of rational thinking and future planning.

©Kendall Hunt Publishing Company

It's noteworthy that the word "problem" derives from the Greek root *proballein*, meaning "to throw forward." This suggests that a problem is an opportunity to move ahead. You can take this approach to problems by rewording or rephrasing the problem you're experiencing in terms of a positive goal statement. (For example, "I'm flunking math" can be reframed as: "My goal is to get a grade of C or better on the next exam to pull my overall course grade into passing territory.")

Similarly, the root of the word "failure" is *fallere*—meaning to trip or fall. Thus, failing at something doesn't mean we've been defeated; it just means we've stumbled and taken a temporary spill. Success can still be achieved after a fall if we don't give up, but get up and get back to taking the next step needed to reach our goal. By viewing poor academic performances and other setbacks (particularly those occurring early in your college experience) not as failures but as learning opportunities, you put yourself in a position to bounce back and transform your setbacks into comebacks. Here are some notable people who did so:

- Louis Pasteur, famous bacteriologist, failed his admission test to the University of Paris;
- Albert Einstein, Nobel Prize–winning physicist, failed math in elementary school;

> "How smart you are will influence the extent to which you experience something as difficult (for example, how hard a math problem is), but it says nothing about how you will deal with difficulty when it happens. It says nothing about whether you will be persistent and determined or feel overwhelmed and helpless."
>
> —*Heidi Grant Halvorson, social psychologist, and author of* Succeed: How We Can Reach Your Goals

> "The harder you fall, the higher you bounce."
>
> —*Chinese proverb*

> "What happens is not as important as how you react to what happens."
>
> —*Thaddeus Golas,* Lazy Man's Guide to Enlightenment

> "When written in Chinese, the word 'crisis' is composed of two characters. One represents danger, and the other represents opportunity."
>
> —*John F. Kennedy, 35th president of the United States*

- Thomas Edison, prolific inventor, once expelled from school as "uneducable";
- Johnny Unitas, Hall of Fame football player, cut twice from professional football teams early in his career; and
- Michael Jordan, Hall of Fame basketball player, cut from his high school team as a sophomore.

Note

Don't let early setbacks bring you down emotionally or motivationally. Reflect on them, learn from them, and make sure they don't happen again.

 Reflection 3.6

What would you say is the biggest setback or obstacle you've overcome in your life thus far?

How did you overcome it? (What enabled you to get past it, or what did you do to prevent it from stopping you?)

> "Self-discipline is the ability to make yourself do the thing you have to do, when it ought be done, whether you like it or not."
>
> —Thomas Henry Huxley, 19th-century English biologist

Self-Discipline. People with grit have *self-control*—they keep their actions aligned with their goal, staying on course and moving in the right direction—despite distractions and temptations (Halvorson, 2010). They resist the impulse to pursue instant gratification and do what they feel like doing instead of what needs to be done to reach their goal. They're able to sacrifice immediate, short-sighted needs and desires to do what has to be done to get where they want to be in the long run.

The ability to delay short-term (and short-sighted) gratification is a distinctive human characteristic that sets us apart from other animals. As can be seen in **Figure 3.2**, the upper front part of the human brain, which is responsible for long-range planning and impulse control, is much larger in humans than chimpanzees—one of the most intelligent of all nonhuman animals.

FIGURE 3.2: Where Thoughts, Emotions, and Drives are Experienced in the Brain

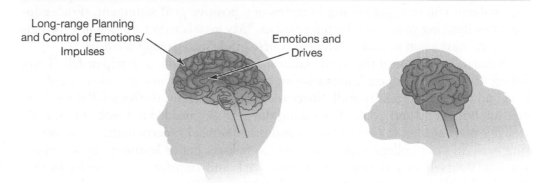

The part of the brain responsible for long-range planning and controlling emotions and impulses is much larger in humans than in other animals, including the highly intelligent chimpanzee.

Setting long-range goals is important but having the self-discipline to reach them is another matter. Each day, whether we're aware of it or not, we're tempted to make choices and decisions that interfere with our ability to reach our goals. We need to remain mindful about whether these choices are moving us in the direction of our goals or taking us off course.

AUTHOR'S EXPERIENCE

When I entered college in the mid-1970s, I was a first-generation student from an extremely impoverished background. Not only did I have to work to support my education, I also needed to assist my family financially. I stocked grocery store shelves at night during the week and waited tables at a local country club on the weekends. Managing my time, school, work, and life required a lot of self-discipline. However, I always understood that my goal was to graduate from college and all of my other commitments supported that goal. One of my greatest achievements in life was to keep my mind and body focused on the ultimate prize of getting a college education. That achievement has paid off for me many times over the course of my life.

—*Aaron Thompson*

Note

Doing what you have *to do now allows you to do what you* want *to do later. Sacrifices made for a short time can bring benefits that last a lifetime.*

 ## Reflection 3.7

Think about something in your life that you sacrificed for and persisted at for the longest period of time before getting there. Do you see ways in which you could apply the same approach to achieving your goals in college?

Growth Mindset

A *mindset* is a powerful belief. People with a *growth mindset* believe that intelligence and other positive qualities can be grown or developed. People with a *fixed mindset* believe just the opposite: they think that intelligence and personal characteristics are deep-seated traits that are set and unlikely to change (Dweck, 2006).

Listed below are opposing pairs of traits—one representing a fixed mindset (FM) and the other representing a growth mindset (GM). As you read through them, honestly assess whether you lean more toward a fixed or growth mindset by circling either FM or GM for each pair of traits.

I try to get better at what I do. (GM)
I try to show others (including myself) how good I am. (FM)

I try to validate myself by proving how smart or talented I am. (FM)
I validate myself by stretching myself to become smarter and more talented. (GM)

I believe that if I cannot learn to do something easily, I'm not smart. (FM)
I believe that I can learn to do something well even if it doesn't come easily at first. (GM)

I evaluate my performance by comparing it to the performance of others. (FM)
I evaluate my performance by comparing it to my past performances. (GM)

I believe I have a certain amount of intelligence and not much can be done to change it. (FM)

I believe that the amount of intelligence I start with isn't the amount I'll end up with. (GM)

I think that intelligence and personal qualities are inherited and hard to change. (FM)

I think that intelligence and personal qualities are learned and changeable. (GM)

I think success is a matter of having ability. (FM)
I think success is a matter of getting ability. (GM)

I focus on demonstrating my skills to others. (FM)
I focus on developing my skills. (GM)

I focus on proving myself (as being good or smart). (FM)
I focus on improving myself (by getting better). (GM)

I feel smart when I complete tasks quickly and without mistakes. (FM)
I feel smart when I work on something for awhile before figuring it out. (GM)

I avoid seeking constructive criticism from others because it will expose my weaknesses. (FM)

I seek out constructive criticism from others to improve myself. (GM)

I feel threatened by the success of others. (FM)
I feel I can be inspired by and learn from the success of others. (GM)

I tend to peak early and don't continually progress to higher levels of achievement. (FM)

I tend to keep progressing toward increasingly higher levels of achievement. (GM)

I think success should be effortless. (FM)
I think success should be effortful. (GM)

I view challenges as threatening because they may prove I'm not smart. (FM)
I view challenges as opportunities to develop new skills. (GM)

I believe effort creates talent. (GM)
I believe effort is for those who can't make it on talent. (FM)

I focus on self-improvement—about becoming the best I can be. (GM)
I focus on self-validation—about proving I'm already good. (FM)

I look at grades as labels that judge or measure my intelligence. (FM)
I look at grades as a source of feedback for improving my performance. (GM)

> "If you believe you can develop yourself, then you're open to accurate information about your current abilities, even if it's unflattering."
>
> —*Carol Dweck*, Growth Mindset: The New Psychology of Success

> "No matter what your ability is, effort is what ignites that ability and turns it into accomplishment."
>
> —*Carol Dweck, Stanford psychologist*

> "SUCCESS is peace of mind which is a direct result of self-satisfaction in knowing you made the effort to become the best that you are capable of becoming."
>
> —*John Wooden, college basketball coach and author of the* Pyramid of Success

 Reflection 3.8

Look back at the above pairs of statements and compare the total number of fixed mindset (FM) and growth mindset (GM) statements you circled.

Do your totals suggest that, in general, you lean more toward a growth or fixed mindset?

Do you see any patterns in your responses that suggest you're more likely to hold a growth mindset for certain characteristics or situations and a fixed mindset for others?

Numerous studies show that a growth mindset is strongly associated with goal achievement and personal success (Dweck, 2006). In one study, the mindset of pre-med students taking a difficult chemistry course was measured at the start of the semester and their performance was tracked throughout the term. Students with a growth mindset consistently earned higher grades in the course. Even when students with a growth mindset did poorly on a particular test, they improved on the next one. In contrast, the performance of students with a fixed mindset showed no pattern of improvement from one exam to the next (Dweck, 2006).

In another study, students with a growth mindset (who believed their goal in college courses was to improve their grade as the course progressed) were compared to students with a fixed mindset (who believed their goal was to prove how smart they were). Students with a growth mindset achieved higher overall course grades and did so because they improved with each exam. They didn't have higher grades on the first exam, but began earning higher grades on later exams. The opposite pattern was true for fixed mindset students—their performance actually remained the same or declined over time—particularly if their first exam score was low (Halvorson, 2010).

It's been found that students can have different mindsets for different subjects and situations. Some students may have a fixed mindset for learning math, but a growth mindset for learning other subjects. However, the most important thing to remember about mindsets is: although they're powerful, they're just beliefs held in our mind. Thus, mindsets can be changed from fixed to growth for any subject or situation. By so doing, we increase the likelihood of achieving our goals and reaching our full potential (Dweck, 2006).

Studies of highly successful people—whether they be scientists, musicians, writers, chess masters, or basketball stars—consistently show that achieving performance excellence success requires ongoing effort and dedicated practice (Charness & Schultetus, 1999; Levitin, 2006). This is even true of extremely successful people who may appear to be naturally gifted or talented. For example, before they burst into musical stardom, the Beatles performed live an estimated 1,200 times over a four-year period; many of these performances lasted five hours or more per night. They performed (practiced) for more hours during those first four years than most bands perform during their entire career. Similarly, before Bill Gates became a computer software giant and creator of Microsoft, he logged almost 1,600 hours of computer time during one seven-month period alone, averaging eight hours a day, seven days a week (Gladwell, 2008). These extraordinary success stories remind us that reaching our goals and achieving excellence takes dedication, determination, and perseverance.

> "
> When we change the way we look at things, the things we look at change."
> —*Max Planck, Nobel Prize-winning physicist*

Chapter Summary and Highlights

A key to success is challenging ourselves to set ambitious, yet realistic goals. Studies consistently show that goal-setting is a more effective self-motivational strategy than simply telling ourselves to "try hard" or "do our best." Achieving success begins with setting goals and successful people set goals on a regular basis.

The acronym "SMART" is a popular mnemonic device (memory strategy) for recalling all the key components of a well-designed goal. A **SMART** goal is one that is:

Specific—it states precisely what the goal is and what you will do to achieve it.
Meaningful (and Measurable)—it's a goal that really matters to you and your progress toward reaching it can be steadily measured or tracked.

*A*ctionable (or *A*ction-Oriented)—it identifies concrete actions and specific behaviors you'll engage in to reach the goal.

*R*ealistic—the goal is attainable and you're aware of the amount of time, effort, and skill it will take to attain it, as well as obstacles you'll need to overcome along the way.

*T*ime-framed—the goal has a deadline and a timeline that includes a sequence of short-range, mid-range, and long-range steps.

In addition to the effective goal-setting properties associated with the SMART method, research reveals that the following goal-setting features characterize people who set and reach important goals.

1. Effective goal-setters set *improvement (get-better) goals* that emphasize progress and growth, rather than *perfection (be-good) goals*.
2. Effective goal-setters focus on what outcomes they can *influence* or *control*, not on outcomes that are beyond their control.
3. Effective goal-setters set goals that are *challenging and effortful*.
4. Effective goal-setters anticipate *obstacles* they may encounter along the path to their goal and have a plan in place for dealing with them.

Setting goals ignites motivation, but maintaining motivation after it's been ignited requires use of effective self-motivational strategies. You can maintain your motivation by using such strategies as:

- Visualizing reaching your long-range goals;
- Putting your goals in writing;
- Creating a visual map of your goals;
- Keeping a record of your progress toward your goals;
- Rewarding yourself for milestones you reach along the path to your goals;
- Converting setbacks into comebacks by learning from mistakes and maintaining positive expectations.

Studies of successful people who achieve their goals reveal they possess the following personal characteristics.

Internal Locus of Control. They believe that the locus (location or source) of control for events in their life is *internal*—"inside" them and within their control—rather than *external*—outside them and beyond their control.

Self-Efficacy. They believe they have power to produce a positive effect on the *outcomes* of their lives. They believe success is something that's earned and the harder they work at it, the more likely they'll get it.

Grit. They expend significant effort, energy, and sacrifice over an extended period of time to achieve their goals. People with grit have been found to possess the following qualities:

- *Persistence*—when the going gets tough, they don't give up, they step it up; they have the fortitude to persist in the face of frustration and adversity.
- *Tenacity*—they pursue their goals with relentless determination; if they encounter something along the way that's hard to do, they work harder to do it.
- *Resilience*—they bounce back from setbacks and turn them into comebacks.

- *Self-Discipline*—they have *self-control*—they resist the impulse to pursue instant gratification and do what they feel like doing instead of what should be done to reach their goal; they're able to sacrifice immediate, short-sighted needs and desires to do what has to be done to get where they want to be in the long run.

Growth Mindset. They believe that intelligence and other positive qualities can be grown or developed. In contrast, people with a "fixed mindset" believe that intelligence and personal characteristics are deep-seated traits that are set and unlikely to change.

Note

Achieving success isn't a short sprint; it's a long-distance run that takes patience and perseverance. Goal-setting is the key that gets us off the starting blocks and motivation is the fuel that keeps us going until we cross the finish line.

Learning More through the World Wide Web: Internet-Based Resources

For additional information on goal-setting and motivation, see the following websites.

Goal Setting:
https://www.mindtools.com/page6.html

Self-Motivational Strategies:
www.selfmotivationstrategies.com

Self-Efficacy:
www.psychologytoday.com/blog/flourish/201002/if-you-think-you-can-t-think-again-the-sway-self-efficacy

Grit and Resilience:
https://undergrad.stanford.edu/resilience

Growth Mindset:
www.ted.com/talks/carol_dweck_the_power_of_believing_that_you_can_improve?language=en

References

Astin, A. W. (1993). *What matters in college?* San Francisco: Jossey-Bass.

Bandura, A. (1986). *Social foundations of thought and action: A social cognitive theory.* Englewood Cliffs, NJ: Prentice Hall.

Bandura, A. (1994). Self-efficacy. In V. S. Ramachaudran (Ed.), *Encyclopedia of human behavior* (Vol. 4, pp. 71–81). New York: Academic Press.

Bandura, A. (1997). *Self-efficacy: The exercise of control.* New York: Freeman.

Bandura, A., & Cervone, D. (1983). Self-evaluative and self-efficacy mechanisms governing the motivational effects of goal systems. *Journal of Personality and Social Psychology, 45*(5), 1017–1028.

Brissette, I., Cohen, S., & Seeman, T. E. (2000). Measuring social integration and social networks. In S. Cohen, L. G. Underwood, & B. H. Gottlieb (Eds.), *Social support measurement and intervention* (pp. 53–85). New York: Oxford University Press.

Brooks, K. (2009). *You majored in what? Mapping your path from chaos to career.* New York: Penguin.

Carlson, N. R., Miller, H., Heth, C. D., Donahoe, J. W., & Martin, G. N. (2009). *Psychology: The science of behaviour* (7th ed.). Toronto, ON: Pearson Education Canada.

Charness, N., & Schultetus, R. S. (1999). Knowledge and expertise. In F. T. Durso, R. S, Nickerson, R. W. Schvaneveldt, S. T. Dumais, D. S. Lindsay, & M. T. H. Chi (Eds.), *Handbook of applied cognition* (pp. 57–81). Chichester, United Kingdom: John Wiley & Sons.

Covey, S. R. (1990). *Seven habits of highly effective people* (2nd ed.). New York: Fireside.

Duckworth, A.L., Peterson, C., Matthews, M.D., & Kelly, D.R. (2007). Grit: Perseverance and passion for long-term goals. *Journal of Personality and Social Psychology, 92*(6), 1087–1101.

Dweck, C. S. (2006). *Mindset: The new psychology of success.* New York: Random House.

Ewell, P. T. (1997). Organizing for learning. *AAHE Bulletin, 50*(4), 3–6.

Feldman, K. A., & Newcomb, T. M. (1994). *The impact of college on students.* New Brunswick, NJ: Transaction Publishers. (Original work published 1969).

Gilbert, P. T. (2006). *Stumbling on happiness.* New York: Alfred A. Knopf.

Gladwell, M. (2008). *Outliers: The story of success.* New York: Little, Brown.

Halvorson, H. G. (2010). *Succeed: How we can reach our goals.* New York: Plume.

Harris, P., Griffin, D., & Murray, S. (2008). Testing the limits of optimistic bias: Event and person moderators in a multilevel framework. *Journal of Personality and Social Psychology, 95,* 1225–1237.

Hashaw, R. M., Hammond, C. J., & Rogers, P. H. (1990). Academic locus of control and the collegiate experience. *Research & Teaching in Developmental Education, 7*(1), 45–54.

Hollenbeck, J. R., Williams, C. R., & Klein, H. J. (1989). An empirical examination of the antecedents of commitment to difficult goals. *Journal of Applied Psychology, 74*(1), 18–23.

Jernigan, C. G. (2004). What do students expect to learn? The role of learner expectancies, beliefs, and attributions for success and failure in student motivation. *Current Issues in Education* [On-line], 7(4). Retrieved from cie.asu.edu/ojs/index.php/cieatasu/article/download/824/250.

Latham, G., & Locke, E. (2007). New developments in and directions for goal-setting research. *European Psychologists, 12,* 290–300.

Levitin, D. J. (2006). *This is your brain on music: The science of a human obsession.* New York: Dutton.

Locke, E. A. (2000). Motivation, cognition, and action: An analysis of studies of task goals and knowledge. *Applied Psychology: An International Review, 49,* 408–429.

Locke, E. A., & Latham, G. P. (1990). *A theory of goal setting and task performance.* Englewood Cliffs, NJ: Prentice Hall.

Locke, E. A., & Latham, G. P. (2002). Building a practically useful theory of goal setting and task motivation. *American Psychologist, 57,* 705–717.

Locke, E. A., & Latham, G. P. (2005). Goal setting theory: Theory building by induction. In K. G. Smith & M. A. Mitt (Eds.), *Great minds in management: The process of theory development.* New York: Oxford.

Matsui, T., Okada, A., & Inoshita, O. (1983). Mechanism of feedback affecting task performance. *Organizational Behavior and Human Performance, 31,* 114–122.

Meyer, P. J. (2003). "What would you do if you knew you couldn't fail? Creating S.M.A.R.T. Goals." In *Attitude is everything: If you want to succeed above and beyond.* Meyer Resource Group, Incorporated.

Multon, K. D., Brown, S. D., & Lent, R. W. (1991). Relation of self-efficacy beliefs to academic outcomes: A meta-analytic investigation. *Journal of Counseling Psychology, 38*(1), 30–38.

Newell, A., & Simon, H. A. (1959). *The simulation of human thought.* Santa Monica, CA: Rand Corporation.

Oettingen, G. (2000). Expectancy effects on behavior depend on self-regulatory thought. *Social Cognition, 14,* 101–129.

Oettingen, G., & Stephens, E. (2009). Mental contrasting future and reality: A motivationally intelligent self-regulatory strategy. In G. Moskowitz & H. Grant (Eds.), *The psychology of goals.* New York: Guilford.

Pascarella, E., & Terenzini, P. (1991). *How college affects students: Findings and insights from twenty years of research.* San Francisco: Jossey-Bass.

Pascarella, E., & Terenzini, P. (2005). *How college affects students: A third decade of research* (Vol. 2). San Francisco: Jossey-Bass.

Rotter, J. (1966). Generalized expectancies for internal versus external controls of reinforcement. *Psychological Monographs: General and Applied, 80*(609), 1–28.

Schunk, D. H. (1995). Self-efficacy and education and instruction. In J. E. Maddux (Ed.), *Self-efficacy, adaptation, and adjustment: Theory, research, and application* (pp. 281–303). New York: Plenum Press.

Snyder, C. R. (1995). Conceptualizing, measuring, and nurturing hope. *Journal of Counseling and Development, 73* (January/February), 355–360.

Stoltz, P. G. (2014). *Grit: The new science of what it takes to persevere, flourish, succeed.* San Luis Obispo: Climb Strong Press.

Van Overwalle, F. I., Mervielde, I., & De Schuyer, J. (1995). Structural modeling of the relationships between attributional dimensions, emotions, and performance of college freshmen. *Cognition and Emotion, 9*(1), 59–85.

Wilhite, S. (1990). Self-efficacy, locus of control, self-assessment of memory ability, and student activities as predictors of college course achievement. *Journal of Educational Psychology, 82*(4), 696–700.

Zimmerman, B. J. (1995). Self-efficacy and educational development. In A. Bandura (Ed.), *Self-efficacy in changing societies.* New York: Cambridge University Press.

Zimmerman, B. J. (2000). Self-efficacy: An essential motive to learn. *Contemporary Educational Psychology, 25,* 82–91.

Chapter 3 Exercises

3.1 Quote Reflections

Review the sidebar quotes contained in this chapter and select two that were especially meaningful or inspirational to you.

For each quote, write a three- to five-word sentence explaining why you chose it.

3.2 Reality Bite

No Goals, No Direction

Amy Aimless decided to go to college because it seemed like that's what she was expected to do. All of her closest friends were going and her parents have talked to her about going to college for as long as she can remember.

Now that she's in her first term, Amy isn't sure she made the right decision. She has no educational or career goals, nor does she have any idea about what her major might be. None of the subjects she took in high school and none of the courses she's taking during her first term in college have really sparked her interest. Since she has no goals or sense of purpose, she's beginning to think that being in college is a waste of her time and her parents' money, so she's considering withdrawing at the end of the term.

Reflection and Discussion Questions

1. Would you agree that Amy shouldn't have begun college in the first place? Why?

2. What suggestions do you have for Amy that might help her find some sense of educational purpose or direction?

3. Would you agree that Amy is currently wasting her time and her parents' money? Why?

4. Can you relate to Amy's story, or do you know other students who are in a similar predicament? (Briefly describe why or how.)

3.3 Clarifying Your Goals

Take a moment to answer the following questions as honestly as possible:

- What are my highest priorities?
- What competing needs and priorities do I need to keep in check?
- How will I maintain balance across different aspects of my life?
- What am I willing and able to give up in order to achieve my educational and personal goals?
- How can I maintain motivation on a day-to-day basis?
- Who can I collaborate with to reach my goals and what will that collaboration involve?

3.4 Reducing the Gap between Your Ideal Future and Your Current Reality

Think of an aspect of your life where there's a significant gap between what you'd like it to be (the ideal) and where you are (the reality).

Use the following form to identify a goal you could pursue to reduce this gap.

Goal: _____

What specific *actions* will be taken?

When will these actions be taken?

What *obstacles or roadblocks* do you anticipate?

What *resources* could you use to overcome your anticipated obstacles or roadblocks?

How will you *measure your progress*?

How will you know when you *reached or achieved* your goal?

3.5 Converting Setbacks into Comebacks: Transforming Pessimism into Optimism through Positive Self-Talk

In *Hamlet,* Shakespeare wrote: "There is nothing good or bad, but thinking makes it so." His point was that experiences have the potential to be positive or negative, depending on how people interpret them and react to them.

Listed below is a series of statements representing negative, motivation-destroying interpretations and reactions to a situation or experience:

a) "I'm just not good at this."

b) "There's nothing I can do about it."

c) "Nothing is going to change."

d) "This always happens to me."

e) "Everybody is going to think I'm a loser."

For each of the preceding statements, replace the negative statement with a statement that represents a more positive, self-motivating interpretation or reaction.

3.6 Self-Assessment of Hope

Studies of people who have changed their lives in productive ways indicate they exhibit "high hope" by engaging in certain behaviors that enable them to find the will and the way to reach their personal goals (Snyder, 1995). A sample of hopeful behaviors is listed below. Assess yourself on these behaviors, using the following scale:

1 = Never
2 = Rarely
3 = Frequently
4 = Almost Always

Behavior Exhibited by People Possessing High Levels of Hope

____ When I think of goals, I think of challenges, rather than setbacks and failures.

____ I seek out stories about how other people have succeeded to inspire me and give me new ideas on how to be successful.

____ I find role models I can emulate and who can advise, guide, or mentor me.

____ I tell my friends about my goals and seek their support to help me reach my goals.

____ I use positive self-talk to help me succeed.

____ I think that mistakes I make along the way to my goals are usually the result of using a wrong strategy or making a poor decision, rather than lack of talent or ability on my part.

____ When I struggle, I remember past successes and things I did that worked.

____ I reward myself when reaching smaller, short-term goals I accomplish along the way to larger, long-term goals.

Adapted from: Snyder, C. R. (1995). Conceptualizing, measuring, and nurturing hope. *Journal of Counseling and Development, 73*(January/February), 355–360.

For any item you rated "1" or "2," explain:

a) *Why* you "rarely" or "never" engage in the practice;

b) *If* you intend to engage in the practice more frequently in the future;

c) *How likely* is it that you'll engage in the practice more frequently in the future;

d) *When* do you plan to begin engaging in the practice.

CHAPTER 4

Time Management

PRIORITIZING TASKS, PREVENTING PROCRASTINATION,
AND PROMOTING PRODUCTIVITY

Chapter Preview

Time is a valuable personal resource—if you gain greater control of it, you gain greater control of your life. Time managed well not only enables you to get work done in a timely manner; it also enables you to set and attain personal priorities and maintain balance in your life. This chapter offers a comprehensive set of strategies for managing time, combating procrastination, and ensuring that you spend time in a way that aligns with your educational goals and priorities.

Learning Goal

Equip you with a powerful set of strategies for setting priorities, planning time, and completing tasks in a timely and productive manner.

Ignite Your Thinking

 Reflection 4.1

Complete the following sentence with the first thought that comes to your mind:

For me, time is . . .

The Importance of Time Management

To have any realistic chance of attaining our goals, we need an intentional and strategic plan for spending our time in a way that aligns with our goals and enables us to make steady progress toward them. Thus, setting goals, reaching goals, and managing time are interrelated skills.

Most college students struggle to at least some extent with time management, particularly first-year students who are transitioning from the lockstep schedules of high school to the more unstructured time associated with college course schedules. National surveys indicate that almost 50% of first-year college students report difficulty managing their time effectively (HERI, 2014). In college, time-management skills grow in importance because students' time is less structured or controlled by school authorities or family members and more responsibility is placed on students to make their own decisions about how their time will be spent. Furthermore, the academic calendar and class scheduling patterns in college differ radically from high school. There's less "seat time" in class each week and college students are expected to do much more academic work on their courses outside of class time, which leaves them with a lot more "free time" to manage.

> The major difference [between high school and college] is time. You have so much free time on your hands that you don't know what to do for most of the time."
>
> —*First-year college student (Erickson & Strommer, Teaching College Freshmen)*

77

Simply stated, college students who have difficulty managing their time have difficulty managing college. One study compared college sophomores who had an outstanding first year (both academically and personally) with sophomores who struggled in their first year. Interviews with both groups revealed there was one key difference between them: sophomores who experienced a successful first year repeatedly brought up the topic of time during the interviews. The successful students said they had to think carefully about how they spent their time and that they needed to budget their time. In contrast, sophomores who experienced difficulty in their first year of college hardly talked about the topic of time during their interviews, even when they were specifically asked about it (Light, 2001).

Studies also indicate that people of all ages report time management to be a critical element of their life. Working adults report that setting priorities and balancing multiple responsibilities (e.g., work and family) can be a stressful juggling act (Harriott & Ferrari, 1996). For them, time management and stress management are interrelated. These findings suggest that time management is more than just a college success skill; it's also a life management and life success skill that benefits both our family life and work life (Gupta, Hershey, & Gaur, 2012). When we gain greater control of our time, we gain greater control and a greater sense of satisfaction with all areas of our life. In fact, studies show that people who manage their time well report feeling happier (Myers, 1993, 2000).

AUTHOR'S EXPERIENCE

I started the process of earning my doctorate a little later in life than other students. I was a married father with a pre-school daughter (Sara). Since my wife left for work early in the morning, it was always my duty to get up and get Sara's day going in the right direction. In addition, I had to do the same for myself. Three days of my week were spent on campus in class or in the library. (We didn't have quick access to research on home computers then as you do now.) The other two days of the workweek and the weekend were spent on household chores, family time, and studying.

I knew that if I was to have any chance of finishing my Ph.D. in a reasonable amount of time, I had to adopt an effective schedule for managing my time. Each day of the week, I held to a strict routine. I got up in the morning, ate breakfast while reading the paper, got Sara ready for school, and got her to school. Once I returned home, I put a load of laundry in the washer, studied, wrote, and spent time concentrating on what I needed to do to be successful from 8:30 a.m. to 12:00 p.m. every day. At lunch, I had a pastrami and cheese sandwich and a soft drink while rewarding myself by watching *Perry Mason* reruns until 1:00 p.m. I then continued to study until it was time to pick up Sara from school. Each night I spent time with my wife and daughter and then prepared for the next day. I lived a life that had a preset schedule. By following that schedule, I was able to successfully complete my doctorate in a reasonable amount of time while giving my family the time they needed. (By the way, I still watch *Perry Mason* reruns.)

—Aaron Thompson

Strategies for Managing Time and Tasks

Effectively managing our time and our tasks involves three key processes:

1. **Analysis**—breaking down time to see how much of it we have and what we're spending it on;
2. **Itemizing**—identifying and listing the tasks that we need to complete and when we need to complete them; and
3. **Prioritizing**—ranking our tasks in terms of their importance and attacking them in order of their importance.

The following strategies can be used to implement these three processes and should help you open up more time in your schedule, enabling you to discover new ways to use your time more productively.

Become more aware of how your time is spent by breaking it into smaller units. How often have you heard someone say, "Where did all the time go?" or "I just can't seem to find the time!" One way to find out where all our time goes and find more time to get things done is by doing a *time analysis*—a detailed examination of how much total time we have and where we're spending it—including patches of wasted time when we get little done and nothing accomplished. This time analysis only has to be done for a week or two to give us a pretty good idea of where our time is going and to find better ways to use our time productively.

(Complete the online Exercise 4.5 at the end of this chapter to gain insights into how you organize your time and the approach you take to completing tasks.)

Identify *what* specific tasks you need to accomplish and *when* you need to accomplish them. When we want to remember items we need to buy at the grocery store or people we want to invite to a party, we make a list. This same list-making strategy can be used for tasks we need to complete so we don't forget about them, or forget to do them on time. One characteristic of successful people is that they are list makers; they make lists for things they want to accomplish each day (Covey, 2004).

Note

When we write out things we need to do, we're less likely to block them out and forget to do them.

 Reflection 4.2

Do you make a to-do list of things you need to get done each day? (Circle one.)

never   seldom   often   almost   always

If you circled "never" or "seldom," why don't you?

Take advantage of time-planning and task-management tools, such as the following:

- *Small, portable planner.* You can use this device to list all your major assignments and exams for the term, along with their due dates. By pulling together all work tasks required in each of your courses and getting them in one place, it will be much easier to keep track of what you have to do and when you have to do it throughout the entire term. It will also sync with the same calendar programs available on your desktop or laptop.

- *Large, stable calendar.* In the calendar's date boxes, record your major assignments for the term. The calendar should be posted in a place you can see it every day (e.g., bedroom or refrigerator). If you repeatedly see the things you have to do, you're less likely to overlook them, forget about them, or subconsciously push them out of your mind because you'd really prefer not to do them.

- *Smartphone.* This device can be used for more than checking social networking sites and sending or receiving text messages. It can be used as a calendar tool to record due dates and set up alert functions to remind you of deadlines. Many smartphones also allow you to set up task or "to-do" lists and set priorities for each item entered. A variety of apps are now available for planning tasks and

©artzenter/Shutterstock.com

Using a calendar is an effective way to itemize your academic commitments.

tracking time spent on tasks (for example, see: http://www.rememberthemilk. com). Take advantage of these cutting-edge tools, but at the same time, keep in mind that planners don't plan time, people do. Effectively planning time and tasks flows from a clear vision of your goals and priorities.

AUTHOR'S EXPERIENCE

My mom ensured I got up for school on time. Once I got to school the bell would ring to let me know to move on to the next class. When I returned home, I had to do my homework and chores. My daily and weekly schedules were dictated by someone else.

When I entered college, I quickly realized that I needed to develop my own system for being organized, focused, and productive without the assistance of my mother or school authorities. Since I came from a modest background, I had to work my way through college. Juggling schedules became an art and science for me. I knew the things that I could not miss, such as work and school, and the things I could miss—TV and girls. (OK, TV, but not girls.)

After college, I spent 10 years in business—a world where I was measured by being on time and delivering a productive "bottom line." It was during this time that I discovered a scheduling book. When I became a professor, I had other mechanisms to make sure I did what I needed to do when I needed to do it. This was largely based on when my classes were offered. Other time was dedicated to working out and spending time with my family. Now, as an administrator, I have an assistant who keeps my schedule for me. She tells me where I am going, how long I should be there, and what I need to accomplish while I am there. Unless you take your parents with you or have the luxury of a personal assistant, it's important to schedule your time. Use a planner!

—*Aaron Thompson*

 Reflection 4.3

Do you have a calendar that you carry with you or use the calendar tool on your phone? If yes, why? If no, why not?

Prioritize: rank tasks in order of their importance. After you itemize your work tasks by identifying and listing them, the next step is to *prioritize* them—determine the order or sequence in which they get done. Prioritizing basically involves ranking tasks in terms of their importance, with the highest-priority tasks placed at the top of the list to ensure they're tackled first.

How do you decide on what tasks are to be ranked highest and tackled first? Here are two key criteria (standards of judgment) for determining your highest-priority tasks:

> Things that matter most must never be at the mercy of things that matter least."
>
> –*Johann Wolfgang von Goethe, German poet, dramatist, and author of the epic* Faust

- **Urgency.** Tasks that are closest to their deadline or due date should receive highest priority. Finishing an assignment that's due tomorrow should receive higher priority than starting an assignment that's due next month.
- **Gravity.** Tasks that carry the greatest weight (count the most) should receive highest priority. If an assignment worth 100 points and an assignment worth 10 points are due at the same time, the 100-point task should receive higher priority. We want to be sure to invest our work time on tasks that matter most. Similar to investing money, we should invest our time on tasks that yield the greatest pay-off.

Note

Put first things first: Plan your work by identifying your most important and most urgent tasks, and work your plan by attacking these tasks first.

An effective strategy for prioritizing tasks is to divide them into "A," "B," and "C" lists (Lakein, 1973; Morgenstern, 2004). The "A" list is reserved for *essential* (nonnegotiable) tasks—those that that *must* be done now. The "B" list is for *important* tasks—those that *should* be done soon. The "C" list is for *optional* tasks—those that *could* or *might* be done if there's time remaining after the more important tasks on lists A and B have been completed. Organizing tasks and time in this fashion helps you decide how to divide your labor in a way that ensures you "put first things first." You shouldn't waste time doing unimportant things to deceive yourself into thinking that you're "getting stuff done"—when, in reality, all you're doing is "keeping busy" and distracting yourself (and subtracting time) from doing the things that should be done.

Note

Developing awareness of how our time is spent is more than a brainless, clerical activity. When it's done well, it becomes an exercise in self-awareness and values clarification—how we spend our time is a true test of who we are and what we really value.

Create a Time-Management Plan

You may have heard of the old proverb, "A stitch in time saves nine." Planning your time represents the "stitch" (unit of time) that saves you nine additional stitches (units of time). Similar to successful chess players, successful time managers plan ahead and anticipate their next moves.

Don't buy into the myth that taking time to plan takes time away from getting started and getting things done. Time-management experts estimate that the amount of time planning your total work actually reduces your total work time by a factor of three: for every one unit of time you spend planning, you save three units of time working (Goldsmith, 2010; Lakein, 1973). For example, 5 minutes of planning time will typically save you 15 minutes of total work time, and 10 minutes of planning time will save you 30 minutes of work time.

Planning your time saves you time because it ensures you start off in the right direction. If you have a plan of attack, you're less vulnerable to "false starts"—starting your work and then discovering you're not on the right track or not doing things in the right sequence, which forces you to retreat and start all over again.

Once you have accepted the idea that taking time to plan your time will save you time in the long run, you're ready to create a plan for effectively managing time. Listed below are specific strategies for doing so.

Be mindful of time by wearing a watch or carrying a phone that can accurately and instantly tell you the date and time. This may seem like an obvious "no-brainer," but time can't be managed if we don't know what time it is, and we can't plan a schedule if we don't know what day it is. Consider setting the time on your watch or phone slightly ahead of the actual time to help ensure that you arrive to class, work, or meetings on time. You can also equip your phone with apps to remind you of times when tasks are to be completed (e.g., remindme.com or studious app.com).

Carry a *small calendar, planner, appointment book* or *cell phone* at all times, and develop a daily routine of using the calendar or task list functions on your cell phone. This will allow you to record appointments that you may make on the run during the day as well as enable you to jot down creative ideas or memories of things you need to do—which can sometimes pop into your mind at the most unexpected times.

> "
> When I have lots of homework to do, I suddenly go through this urge to clean up and organize the house. I'm thinking, 'I'm not wasting my time. I'm cleaning up the house and that's something I have to do.' But all I'm really doing is avoiding school work."
> —*College sophomore*

> "
> If you fail to plan, you are planning to fail."
> —*Benjamin Franklin, renowned author, inventor, civic activist, and a founding father of the United States*

Take *portable work* with you during the day that you can work at any place at any time. This will enable you to take advantage of "dead time" such as time spent sitting and waiting for appointments or transportation. Portable work allows you to resurrect dead time and transform it into productive work time. Not only is this a good time-management strategy, it's a good stress-management strategy because you replace the frustration and boredom associated with having no control over "wait time" with a sense of accomplishment.

Make good use of your *free time between classes* by working on assignments and studying in advance for upcoming exams. See **Box 4.1** for a summary of how you can use your out-of-class time to improve your academic performance and course grades.

Box 4.1

Making Productive Use of "Free Time" Outside the Classroom

Students' class schedules in college differ radically from high school. College students are often pleasantly surprised by how much "free time" they have because they're spending much less time in class. However, students are expected to spend two or more hours outside of class for every hour they spend in class. Thus, using out-of-class time strategically and productively is critical to ensuring college success.

Compared to high school, "homework" in college typically doesn't involve turning in assignments on a daily or weekly basis. Academic work done outside the college classroom may not even be collected and graded. Instead, it's often assigned for your own benefit to help you prepare for upcoming exams and complete written reports (e.g., assigned reading and assigned problems in math and science). Rather than formally assigning and collecting this work as homework, your professors expect that you will do this work on your own and without supervision.

In high school we were given a homework assignment every day. Now we have a large task assigned to be done at a certain time. No one tells [us] when to start or what to do each day."

—*First-year college student*

Listed in this box are strategies for working independently and in advance of college exams and assignments. By building time for each of these activities into your regular schedule, you'll make more productive use of out-of-class time, decrease your level of stress, and strengthen your academic performance.

Doing Out-of-Class Work in Advance of Exams

- **Complete reading assignments** relating to lecture topics *before* the topic is discussed in class. This will make lectures easier to understand and enable you to participate intelligently in class (e.g., by asking meaningful questions and making informed comments during class discussions).
- **Review class notes** from your last class before the next class to build a mental bridge from one class to the next. Many students don't look at their class notes until they study them right before an exam. Don't be one of those students; instead, review your notes before the next class. Rewrite any class notes that may have been sloppily written the first time. If you find notes related to the same point all over the place, reorganize them into the same section. Lastly, if you find any information gaps or confusing points in your notes, seek out the course instructor or a trusted classmate to clear them up before the next class takes place.

  By reviewing your class notes on a regular basis, you will improve your ability to understand each upcoming lecture and reduce the total time you'll need to spend studying your notes the night before an exam.

- **Review your reading notes and highlights** to improve retention of important material. If you find certain points in your reading to be confusing, discuss them with your course instructor during office hours or with a fellow classmate outside of class.
- **Integrate class material with reading material.** Connect related information from your lecture notes and reading notes and get them in the same place (e.g., on the same index card).
- Use a "part-to-whole" study method whereby you study material from your class notes and assigned

Box 4.1 *(continued)*

reading in small pieces (parts) during short, separate study sessions in advance of the exam; then make your last study session before the exam a longer review session during which you restudy all the small parts (the whole) at the same time. Don't buy into the myth that studying in advance is a waste of time because you'll forget everything you studied by test time. As will be fully explained in Chapter 5, material studied in advance of an exam remains in your brain and is still there when you later review it. Even if it doesn't immediately come back to mind when you first start reviewing it, you'll relearn it much faster than you did the first time.

Doing Out-of-Class Work in Advance of Term Papers and Research Reports

Work on large, long-range assignments due at the end of the term by breaking them into smaller, short-term tasks completed at separate times during the term. For instance, a large term paper may be broken up into the following smaller tasks and completed in separate installments.

1. Search for and decide on a topic.
2. Locate sources of information on the topic.
3. Organize information obtained from your sources into categories.
4. Develop an outline of your paper's major points and the order or sequence in which you plan to present them.
5. Construct a first draft of your paper (and, if necessary, a second or third draft).
6. Write a final draft of your paper.
7. Proofread your final draft for spelling and grammatical errors before turning it in.

(For a detailed discussion of strategies for writing papers and reports, see Chapter 7, pp. 163–169.)

 Reflection 4.4

Do you have time gaps between your classes this term? If you do, what have you been doing during these "free" periods between classes?

What would you say is your greatest between-class time waster?

Do you see a need to stop or eliminate it?

If yes, what could you do to convert your wasted time into productive time?

A good time-management plan transforms intention into action. Once you've planned the work, the next step is to work the plan. A time-management plan turns into an action plan when you: (a) preview what you intend to do, (b) review whether you actually did what you intended to do, and (c) close the gap between your intentions and actions. The action plan begins with your *daily to-do list*, bringing that list with you as the day begins, and checking off items on the list as they're completed during the day. At the end of the day, the list is reviewed to determine what got done and what still needs to be done. The uncompleted tasks then become high priorities on the following day's to-do list.

If, at the end of each day, you find many unchecked items still remaining on your daily to-do list, this probably means you're spreading yourself too thin by trying to do too many things in a single day. You may need to be more realistic about how much you can accomplish per day by shortening your daily to-do lists. Not being able to complete many of your intended daily tasks may also mean that you need to modify your time-management plan by adding more work time or subtracting some nonwork activities that are drawing time and attention away from your work (e.g., responding to phone calls and text messages during your planned work times). If you're consistently falling short of achieving your daily goals, honestly ask yourself if you're spending too much time on less important things (e.g., TV, video games, Facebook).

 Reflection 4.5

At the end of a typical day, how often do you find that you accomplished most of the tasks you intended to accomplish? (Circle one.)

                    never   seldom   often   almost   always

If you circled "never" or "seldom," what strategies could you use to move the bar toward "often" or "almost always"?

 Murphy's Laws:

1. Nothing is as simple as it looks.
2. Everything takes longer than it should.
3. If anything can go wrong, it will.

—Author unknown (Murphy's Laws were named after Captain Edward Murphy, a naval engineer)

 It is important to allow time for things you enjoy doing because this is what will keep you stable."

—Advice to new college students from a first-year student

A good time-management plan includes reserving time for the unexpected. Always hope for the best, but prepare for the worst. Your plan should include a buffer zone or safety net that contains extra time in case you encounter unforeseen developments or unexpected emergencies. Just as you should plan to have extra funds in your account to pay for unexpected expenses (e.g., auto repair), you should plan to have extra time in your schedule for unexpected events (e.g., personal illness or family emergency).

A good time-management plan should also contain time for work and play. Your plan shouldn't consist solely of a daunting list of work tasks you have to do; it should also include fun things you like to do. Plan time to relax, refuel, and recharge. Your overall time-management plan shouldn't turn you into an obsessive-compulsive workaholic. Instead, it should represent a balanced blend of work and play, including activities that promote your mental and physical wellness—such as recreation and reflection. Consider following the daily "8-8-8 rule"—eight hours for sleep, eight hours for school, and eight hours for other activities.

If you schedule things you like to do, you're more likely do to the things you have to do. You're much more likely to faithfully execute your plan if play time is scheduled along with work time and if you use play as a reward for completing your work.

Note

An effective time management plan helps you stress less, learn more, and earn higher grades while reserving time for other things that are important to you; it enables you to attain and maintain balance in your life.

 Reflection 4.6

What activities do you engage in for fun or recreation?

What do you do to relax or relieve stress?

Do you build these activities into your daily or weekly schedule?

A good time-management plan has some flexibility. A time-management plan shouldn't enslave you to a rigid work schedule. The plan should be flexible enough to allow you to occasionally bend it without breaking it. Just as work commitments and family responsibilities can crop up unexpectedly, so, too, can opportunities for fun and enjoyable activities. Your plan should allow you the freedom to modify your schedule to take advantage of these enjoyable opportunities and experiences. However, you should plan to make up the work time you lost. In other words, you can borrow or trade work time for play time, but don't "steal" it; plan to pay back the work time you borrowed by substituting it for play time that was planned for another time. If you decide not to do work you planned, the next best thing to do is re-plan when you'll do it.

Note

When you create a personal time-management plan, remember it's your *plan—you own it and you run it. It shouldn't run you.*

Dealing with Procrastination

A major enemy of effective time management is procrastination. Procrastinators don't abide by the proverb: "Why put off till tomorrow what can be done today?" Instead, their philosophy is just the opposite: "Why do today what can be put off till tomorrow?" Adopting this philosophy promotes a perpetual pattern of postponing what needs to be done until the last possible moment, forcing the procrastinator to rush frantically to finish work on time and turn in work that's inferior or incomplete (or not turn in anything at all).

> "Many people take no care of their money 'til they come nearly to the end of it, and others do just the same with their time."
>
> —*Johann Wolfgang von Goethe, German poet, dramatist, and author of the epic* Faust

©Kendall Hunt Publishing Company

Next time I'll start sooner!

A procrastinator's idea of planning ahead and working in advance often boils down to this scenario.

> "I believe the most important aspect of college life is time management. DO NOT procrastinate because, although this is the easy thing to do at first, it will catch up with you and make your life miserable."
>
> —*Advice to new college students from a student completing his first year*

    Research shows that 80% to 95% of college students procrastinate (Steel, 2007) and almost 50% report that they procrastinate consistently (Onwuegbuzie, 2000). Procrastination is such a serious issue for college students that some campuses have opened "procrastination centers" to help them (Burka & Yuen, 2008).

Myths That Promote Procrastination

To have any hope of putting a stop to procrastination, procrastinators need to let go of two popular myths or misconceptions about time and performance.

Myth 1. "I work better under pressure" (e.g., on the day or night before something is due). Procrastinators often confuse desperation with motivation. Their belief that they work better under pressure is usually a rationalization to justify the fact that they *only* work under pressure—when they have to work because they've run out of time and are under the gun of a looming deadline.

It's true that when people are under pressure, they will start working and work with frantic energy, but that doesn't mean they're working more *effectively* and producing work of better *quality*. Because procrastinators are playing "beat the clock," they focus less on doing the job well and more on beating the buzzer. This typically results in a work product that's incomplete or inferior to what could have been produced if they had begun the work process sooner.

Myth 2. "Studying in advance is a waste of time because you will forget it all by test time." This myth is used by procrastinators to justify putting off all studying until the night before an exam. As will be discussed in Chapter 5, studying that's distributed (spread out) over time is more effective than massed (crammed) studying all at one time. Furthermore, last minute studying before exams often involves pulling "late-nighters" or "all-nighters" that result in sleep loss. This fly-by-night strategy deprives the brain of dream sleep (a.k.a. REM sleep), which it needs to retain information and manage stress (Hobson, 1988; Voelker, 2004). Research indicates that procrastinators suffer from higher rates of stress-related physical disorders, such as insomnia, stomach problems, colds, and flu (McCance & Pychyl, 2003). Working under time pressure also increases performance pressure by leaving the procrastinators with (a) no margin of error to correct mistakes, (b) no time to seek help on their work, and (c) no chance to handle random catastrophes or setbacks that may arise at the last minute.

Psychological Causes of Procrastination

Sometimes, procrastination has deeper psychological roots. People may procrastinate for reasons that relate more to emotional issues than poor time-management habits. Studies show that some people procrastinate as a psychological strategy to protect their self-esteem. Referred to as *self-handicapping* (Rhodewalt & Vohs, 2005), this strategy is used by some procrastinators, often unconsciously, to give themselves a "handicap" or disadvantage. By starting their work at the last possible moment, if their performance turns out to be less than spectacular, they can always conclude (rationalize) that it was because they were performing under a handicap—lack of time rather than lack of ability (Chu & Cho, 2005).

For example, if they receive a low grade on a test or paper, they can "save face" (self-esteem) by concluding that it was because they waited until the last minute and didn't put much time or effort into it. In other words, they had enough ability or intelligence to earn a high grade; they just didn't put in enough time. Better yet, if they happen to get a good grade—despite their last-minute, last-ditch effort—it proves just how smart they are. It shows they were able to earn a high grade, even without putting in much time at all. Thus, self-handicapping creates a fail-safe or win-win scenario that always protects the procrastinators' self-image.

> "Haste makes waste."
> —Benjamin Franklin

> "Procrastinators would rather be seen as lacking in effort than lacking in ability."
> —Joseph Ferrari, professor of psychology and procrastination researcher

Reflection 4.7

Do you tend to put off work for so long that getting it done turns into an emergency or panic situation?

If your answer is yes, why do you think you put yourself in this position?

If your answer is no, what motivates or enables you to avoid this scenario?

In addition to self-handicapping, other psychological factors have been found to contribute to procrastination, including the following:

- **Fear of failure.** The procrastinator feels better about not turning in work than turning it in and getting negative feedback (Burka & Yuen, 2008; Solomon & Rothblum, 1984);
- **Perfectionism.** The procrastinator has unrealistically high personal standards or expectations, which leads to the belief that it's better to postpone work or not do it than to risk doing it less than perfectly (Kachgal, Hansel, & Nuter, 2001);
- **Fear of success.** The procrastinator fears that doing well will show others that he has the ability to achieve success, leading others to expect him to maintain those high standards in the future (Beck, Koons, & Milgram, 2000; Ellis & Knaus, 2002);
- **Indecisiveness.** The procrastinator has difficulty making decisions, including decisions about what to do first, when to do it, or whether to do it (Anderson, 2003; Steel, 2007), so they delay doing it or don't do it at all; and
- **Thrill seeking.** The procrastinator is hooked on the adrenaline rush triggered by rushing around to get things done just before a deadline (Szalavitz, 2003).

> Striving for excellence motivates you; striving for perfection is demoralizing."
> —*Harriet Braiker, psychologist and best-selling author*

If these psychological issues are at the root of procrastination, they must be uprooted and dealt with before the problem can be solved. This may take some time and assistance from a counseling psychologist (either on or off campus) who is professionally trained to deal with emotional issues, including those that underlie procrastination.

Reflection 4.8

How often do you procrastinate? (Circle one.)

    rarely   occasionally   frequently   consistently

When you do procrastinate, what's the usual cause?

Strategies for Preventing and Overcoming Procrastination

Consistently use effective time-management strategies. When effective time-management practices (such as those cited in this chapter) are implemented consistently, they turn into regular habits. Research indicates that procrastinators are less likely to procrastinate when they convert their intentions or vows ("I swear I'm

"We are what we repeatedly do. Excellence, then, is not an act, but a habit."

—Aristotle, influential Ancient Greek philosopher

"The secret to getting ahead is getting started."

—Mark Twain (Samuel Clemens), American humorist and author of the Adventures of Huckleberry Finn (1885), a.k.a. "the Great American Novel"

"Did you ever dread doing something, then it turned out to take only about 20 minutes to do?"

—Conversation between two college students overheard in a coffee shop

going to start tomorrow") into concrete action plans (Gollwitzer, 1999; Gollwitzer & Sheeran, 2006). When they repeatedly practice effective time-management strategies with respect to tasks they tend to procrastinate on, their bad procrastination habits gradually fade and are replaced by good time-management habits (Ainslie, 1992; Baumeister, Heatherton, & Tice, 1994).

Make the start of work as inviting or appealing as possible. Starting work—getting off the starting blocks—is often the major stumbling block for procrastinators. It's common for procrastinators to experience what's known as "start-up stress"—when they're about to start a task, they start having negative feelings about it—expecting it to be difficult, stressful, or boring (Burka & Yuen, 2008).

If you have trouble starting your work, sequence your work tasks in a way that allows you to start on tasks you find more interesting or are more likely to do well. Beginning with these tasks can give you a "jump start," enabling you to overcome inertia and create momentum. You can ride this initial momentum to motivate you to attack less appealing or more daunting work tasks that come later in your work sequence, which often turn out not to be as unpleasant or time-consuming as you thought they would be. Like many events in life, anticipation of the event turns out to be worse than the event itself. In one study of college students who didn't start a project until just before its due date, it was found that that they experienced anxiety and guilt while they were procrastinating, but once they began working, these negative emotions subsided and were replaced by more positive feelings of progress and accomplishment (McCance & Pychyl, 2003).

You can also reduce start-up stress by beginning your work in an environment you find pleasant and relaxing (e.g., working in your favorite coffee shop while sipping your favorite beverage). In other words, if you have trouble starting work, start it in a place you enjoy while doing something you enjoy.

Organization matters. Research indicates that disorganization is a factor that contributes to procrastination (Steel, 2007). How well you organize your workplace and manage your work materials can reduce your tendency to procrastinate. Having the right materials in the right place at the right time can make it easier to get started. Once you decide to start working, you don't want to delay acting on that decision by looking for the tools you need to work with. If you're a procrastinator, this slight delay may provide the time (and excuse) to change your mind and not start working.

Note

The less time and effort it takes to start working, the more likely the work will be started.

One simple, yet effective way to organize academic materials is to develop your own file system. Start by filing (storing) materials from different courses in different colored folders or notebooks. This not only enables you to keep all materials related to the same course in the same place, it also gives you immediate access to them when you need them. A file system helps get you organized, gets rid of the stress associated with having things all over the place, and reduces your risk of procrastinating by reducing the time and effort it takes to get started.

Location matters. *Where* you choose to work can influence *whether* your work gets done. Research indicates that distractions promote procrastination (Steel, 2007). Thus, working in an environment that minimizes distraction and maximizes concentration will reduce the risk of procrastination.

Arrange your work environment in a way that minimizes social distractions (e.g., people nearby who are not working), and media distractions (e.g., cell phones, e-mails, text messages, music, and TV). Remove everything from your work site that's not relevant or directly related to the work you're doing.

Your concentration will also improve if you work in an environment that allows you easy access to (a) work-support materials (e.g., class notes, textbooks, and a dictionary), and (b) social-support networks (e.g., working with a group of motivated students who help you stay focused, on task, and on track toward completing your work).

 Reflection 4.9

List your two most common sources of distraction while working. Next to each distraction, identify a strategy you might use to reduce or eliminate it.

Source of Distraction   *Strategy for Reducing this Distraction*

1.

2.

If you have difficulty maintaining or sustaining commitment to your work until it's finished, schedule easier and more interesting work tasks *in the middle or toward the end* **of your planned work time.** Some procrastinators have difficulty starting work, others have trouble continuing and completing the work they've started (Pierro, et al., 2011). As previously mentioned, if you have trouble starting work, it might be best for you to start with tasks you find most interesting or easiest. In contrast, if you tend to experience procrastination by not completing your work once you've started, it might be better to schedule tasks of greater interest and ease at later points during your work session. Doing so can restore or revive your interest and energy. Tackling enjoyable and easier tasks last can also provide you with an incentive or reward for completing your less enjoyable and more difficult tasks first. (Take a look at the Persistence Preference results of your My PEPS Learning Style Inventory. What do the results say about your inclination to finish tasks and activities?)

If you're close to completing a task, "go for the kill"—finish it then and there —rather than stopping and completing it later. Completing a task that's almost done allows you to build on the momentum you've already generated. In contrast, postponing work on a task that's near completion means that you have to overcome inertia and regenerate momentum all over again. As the old saying goes, "There's no time like the present."

Furthermore, finishing a task gives you a sense of *closure*—the feeling of personal accomplishment and self-satisfaction that comes from knowing you've "closed the deal." Checking off a completed task can motivate you to keep going and complete the unfinished tasks ahead of you.

Divide large work tasks into smaller, bite-sized pieces. Work becomes less overwhelming and stressful when it's handled in small chunks or segments. You can conquer procrastination for large tasks by using a "divide and conquer" strategy: divide the large task into smaller, more manageable subtasks; then tackle and complete these subtasks one at a time.

Don't underestimate the power of short work sessions. They're often more effective than longer sessions because it's easier to maintain concentration and mo-

> "To reduce distractions, work at a computer on campus rather than using one in your room or home."
>
> —*Advice to new college students from a student finishing her first year in college*

> "I'm very good at starting things but often have trouble keeping a sustained effort."
>
> —*First-year college student*

> "Just do it."
>
> —*Commercial slogan of Nike, athletic equipment company named after the Greek goddess of victory*

> "To eat an elephant, first cut it into small pieces."
> —*Author unknown*

mentum for shorter periods of time. By dividing work into short sessions, you can take quick jabs at a tall task, poke holes in it, and shrink its overall size with each successive jab. This reduces the pressure of having to deliver one, big knockout punch right before the final bell (deadline date).

AUTHOR'S EXPERIENCE

The two biggest projects I've had to complete in my life were writing my doctoral thesis and writing this book. The strategy that enabled me to complete both of these large tasks was to set short-term deadlines for myself (e.g., complete five to ten pages each week). I psyched myself into thinking that these little, self-imposed due dates were really drop-dead deadlines that I had to meet. This strategy allowed me to divide one monstrous chore into a series of smaller, more manageable mini-tasks. It was like taking a huge, indigestible meal and breaking it into small, bite-sized pieces that could be easily ingested and gradually digested over time.

—*Joe Cuseo*

> I long to accomplish some great and noble task, but it is my chief duty to accomplish small tasks as if they were great and noble."
> —*Helen Keller, seeing- and hearing-impaired author and activist for the rights of women and the handicapped*

Chapter Summary and Highlights

Effective goal-setting gets you going, but effective time management gets things done. To manage time effectively, we need to

- *Analyze* it. Break down time and become aware of how we spend it;
- *Itemize* it. Identify the tasks we need to accomplish and their due dates; and
- *Prioritize* it. Tackle our tasks in order of their importance.

Developing a comprehensive time-management plan for academic work involves long-, mid-, and short-range steps that involve:

- Planning the total term (long-range steps);
- Planning your week (mid-range steps); and
- Planning your day (short-range steps).

A good time-management plan includes the following features:

- It transforms intention to action.
- It includes time to take care of unexpected developments.
- It contains time for work and play.
- It gives you the flexibility to accommodate unforeseen opportunities.

The enemy of effective time management is procrastination. Overcoming it involves letting go of two major myths:

- Better work is produced "under pressure"—on the day or night before it's due.
- Studying in advance is a waste of time—because you'll forget it all by test time.

Effective strategies for beating the procrastination habit include the following:

- Organize your work materials to make it easy and convenient for you to start working.
- Organize your work place or space so that you work in a location that minimizes distractions and temptations not to work.

- Intentionally arrange your work schedule so that you are working on more enjoyable or stimulating tasks at times when you're less vulnerable to procrastination.
- If you're close to finishing a task, finish it, because it's often harder to restart a task than to complete one that's already been started.
- Divide large tasks into smaller, more manageable units and tackle them in separate work sessions.

Mastering the skill of managing time is critical for success in college and beyond. Time is one of our most powerful personal resources; the better we manage it, the more likely we are to achieve our goals and gain control of our life.

> Doesn't thou love life? Then do not squander time, for that is the stuff life is made of."
>
> *—Benjamin Franklin, 18th-century inventor, newspaper writer, and cosigner of the Declaration of Independence*

Learning More through the World Wide Web: Internet-Based Resources

For additional information on managing time, and preventing procrastination, see the following websites:

Time-Management Strategies for All Students:
www.studygs.net/timman.htm

www.pennstatelearning.psu.edu/resources/study-tips/time-mgt

Time-Management Strategies for Adult Students:
www.essortment.com/lifestyle/timemanagement_sjmu.htm

Beating Procrastination:
www.mindtools.com/pages/article/newHTE_96.htm

http://success.oregonstate.edu/learning-corner/time-management/managing-procrastination

References

Ainslie, G. (1992). Specious reward: A behavioral theory of impulsiveness and impulse control. *Psychological Bulletin, 82*, 463–496.

Anderson, C. J. (2003). The psychology of doing nothing: Forms of decision avoidance result from reason and emotion. *Psychological Bulletin, 129*, 139–167.

Baumeister, R. F., Heatherton, T. F., & Tice, D. M. (1994). *Losing control: How and why people fail at self-regulation*. San Diego, CA: Academic Press.

Beck, B. L., Koons, S. R., & Milgram, D. L. (2000). Correlates and consequences of behavioural procrastination: The effects of academic procrastination, self-consciousness, self-esteem and self-handicapping. [Special issue], *Journal of Social Behaviour & Personality, 15*(5), 3–13.

Burka, J. B., & Yuen, L. M. (2008). *Procrastination: Why you do it, what to do about it now*. Cambridge, MA: De Capo Press.

Chu, A. H. C., & Cho, J. N. (2005). Rethinking procrastination: Positive effects of "active" procrastination behavior on attitudes and performance. *The Journal of Social Psychology, 145*(3), 245–264.

Covey, S. R. (2004). *Seven habits of highly effective people* (3rd ed.). New York: Fireside.

Ellis, A., & Knaus, W. J. (2002). *Overcoming procrastination* (Rev. ed.). New York: New American Library.

Goldsmith, E. B. (2010). *Resource management for individuals and families* (4th ed.). Upper Saddle River, NJ: Prentice Hall.

Gollwitzer, P. M. (1999). Implementation intentions: Strong effects of simple plans. *American Psychologist, 54*(7), 493–503.

Gollwitzer, P. M., & Sheeran, P. (2006). Implementation intentions and goal achievement: A meta-analysis of effects and processes. *Advances in Experimental Social Psychology, 38*, 69–119.

Gupta, R., Hershey, D. A., & Gaur, J. (2012). Time perspective and procrastination in the workplace: An empirical investigation. *Current Psychology, 31*(2), 195–211.

Harriot, J., & Ferrari, J. R. (1996). Prevalence of procrastination among samples of adults. *Psychological Reports, 78*, 611–616.

HERI (Higher Education Research Institute). (2014). *Your first college year survey 2014*. Los Angeles, CA: Cooperative Institutional Research Program, University of California–Los Angeles.

Hobson, J. A. (1988). *The dreaming brain*. New York: Basic Books.

Kachgal, M. M., Hansen, L. S., & Nutter, K. T. (2001). Academic procrastination prevention/intervention: Strategies and recommendations. *Journal of Developmental Education, 25*(1), 2–12.

Lakein, A. (1973). *How to get control of your time and your life*. New York: New American Library.

Light, R. J. (2001). *Making the most of college: Students speak their minds*. Cambridge, MA: Harvard University Press.

McCance, N., & Pychyl, T. A. (2003, August). *From task avoidance to action: An experience sampling study of undergraduate students' thoughts, feelings and coping strategies in relation to academic procrastination*. Paper presented at the Third Annual Conference for Counseling Procrastinators in the Academic Context, University of Ohio, Columbus.

Morgenstern, J. (2004). *Time management from the inside out: The foolproof system for taking control of your schedule—and your life* (2nd ed.). New York: Henry Holt & Co.

Myers, D. G. (1993). *The pursuit of happiness: Who is happy—and why?* New York: Morrow.

Myers, D. G. (2000). *The American paradox: Spiritual hunger in an age of plenty*. New Haven, CT: Yale University Press.

Onwuegbuzie, A. J. (2000). Academic procrastinators and perfectionistic tendencies among graduate students. *Journal of Social Behavior and Personality, 15*, 103–109.

Pierro, A., Giacomantonio, M., Pica, G., Kruglanski, A. W., & Higgins, E. T. (2011). On the psychology of time in action: regulatory mode orientations and procrastination. *Journal of Personality and Social Psychology, 101*(6), 1317–1331.

Rhodewalt, F., & Vohs, K. D. (2005). Defensive strategies, motivation, and the self. In A. Elliot & C. Dweck (Eds.). *Handbook of competence and motivation* (pp. 548–565). New York: Guilford Press.

Solomon, L. J., & Rothblum, E. D. (1984). Academic procrastination: Frequency and cognitive-behavioral correlates. *Journal of Counseling Psychology, 31*(4), 503–509.

Steel, P. (2007). The nature of procrastination: A meta-analytic and theoretical review of quintessential self-regulatory failure. *Psychological Bulletin, 133*(1), 65–94.

Szalavitz, M. (2003, July/August). Tapping potential: Stand and deliver. *Psychology Today*, 50–54.

Voelker, R. (2004). Stress, sleep loss, and substance abuse create potent recipe for college depression. *Journal of the American Medical Association, 291*, 2177–2179.

Chapter 4 Exercises

4.1 Quote Reflections

Review the sidebar quotes contained in this chapter and select two that were especially meaningful or inspirational to you.

For each quote, provide a three- to five-sentence explanation why you chose it.

4.2 Reality Bite

Procrastination: The Vicious Cycle

Delayla has a major paper due at the end of the term. It's now past midterm and she still hasn't started to work on it. She keeps telling herself, "I should have started sooner," but she continues to postpone her work and is becoming increasingly anxious and guilty. To relieve her growing anxiety and guilt, Delayla starts doing other tasks instead, such as cleaning her room and returning e-mails. This makes her feel a little better because these tasks keep her busy, take her mind off the term paper, and give her the feeling that at least she's getting something accomplished. Time continues to pass; the deadline for the paper grows dangerously close. Delayla now finds herself in the position of having lots of work to do and little time in which to do it.

Adapted from *Procrastination: Why You Do It, and What to do about It* (Burka & Yuen, 2008).

Reflection and Discussion Questions

1. What do you expect Delayla will do at this point? Why?

2. What grade do you think she'll end up receiving on her paper?

3. Other than simply starting sooner, what else could Delayla (and other procrastinators like her) do to break the cycle of procrastination?

4. Can you relate to this student's predicament, or do you know other students who often find themselves in this predicament?

4.3 Procrastination Self-Assessment

Look at the results of your My PEPS Learning Style Inventory, under the section of Persistence Preference.

What did you learn about your inclination to finish tasks and activities?

How likely are you to procrastinate?

How could you incorporate some of the suggestions offered to you increase your persistence?

4.4 Developing a Task-Management Plan for Your First Term in College

1. Review the *course syllabus (course outline)* for each class you are enrolled in this term and highlight all major exams, tests, quizzes, assignments, and papers and the dates on which they are due.

2. Obtain a *large calendar* for the academic term (available at your campus bookstore or learning center) and record all the highlighted information for your exams and assignments for all your courses in the calendar boxes that represent their due dates. To fit this information within the calendar boxes, use creative abbreviations to represent different tasks, such as RA for reading assignment, E for exam, and TP for term paper. When you're done, you'll have a detailed chart or map of deadline dates and a master schedule for the entire term.

3. Activate the calendar and task lists functions on your smartphone. Enter your schedule, important dates, deadlines, and set alert reminders. By carrying your phone with you regularly, you will always have this information at your fingertips.

1. Is your overall workload what you expected? Are your surprised by the amount of work time you will need to devote to your courses?

2. At this point in the term, what course is demanding the greatest amount of out-of-class work time? Have you been able to put in this time?

3. What adjustments or changes (if any) could you make to your personal schedule this term to create more time to handle your academic workload?

4.5 Time Management Self–Awareness

Take the online *My PEPS Learning Style Inventory* tool that accompanies this text.

Did the results provide you with helpful insights on how you organize your time and the approach you take to completing tasks? If yes, why? If no, why not?

4.6 Time Analysis Inventory

1. Go to the following website: http://tutorials.istudy.psu.edu/timemanagement/TimeEstimator.html

2. Complete the time management exercise at this site. The exercise asks you to estimate the hours per day or week that you engage in various activities (e.g., sleeping, employment, and commuting). When you enter the amount of time devoted to each activity, this website will automatically compute the total number of remaining hours you have available in the week for academic work.

3. After completing your entries, answer the following questions (or provide your best estimate).
   a) How many hours per week do you have available for academic work?
   b) Do you have two hours available for academic work outside of class for each hour you spend in class? If you don't, what activities could be eliminated or reduced to create more time for academic work outside of class?

4.7 Developing a Time–Management Plan for Your First Term in College

Keep in mind the task-management plan you developed in Exercise 4.4, use the following *Week-at-a-Glance Grid* to map out your typical or average week for this term. Start by recording what you usually do on these days, including the times you're in class, when you work, and when you relax or recreate. You can use abbreviations (e.g., CT for class time, HW for homework, J for job, and R&R for rest and relaxation). List the abbreviations you created at the bottom of the page so that your instructor can follow them.

> The amount of free time you have in college is much more than in high school. Always have a weekly study schedule to go by. Otherwise, time slips away and you will not be able to account for it."
>
> —*Advice to new college students from a first-year student (Rhoads, 2005)*

If you're a *full-time* student, plan for 25 *hours* in your week for homework (HW). (If you're a *part-time* student, find 2 *hours* you could devote to homework *for every hour* you're in class—for example, if you're in class 9 hours per week, find 18 hours of homework time).

These homework hours could take place at any time during the week, including weekends. If you combine 25 hours per week of out-of-class school work with the amount of time you spend in class each week, you'll end up with a 40-hour academic workweek—comparable to a full-time job—which is how college should be viewed.

Week-at-a-Glance Grid

	Sunday	Monday	Tuesday	Wednesday	Thursday	Friday	Saturday
7:00 a.m.							
8:00 a.m.							
9:00 a.m.							
10:00 a.m.							
11:00 a.m.							
12:00 p.m.							
1:00 p.m.							
2:00 p.m.							
3:00 p.m.							
4:00 p.m.							
5:00 p.m.							
6:00 p.m.							
7:00 p.m.							
8:00 p.m.							
9:00 p.m.							
10:00 p.m.							
11:00 p.m.							

Reflections

1. How likely are you to put this time-management plan into practice?
   Circle one: Definitely   Probably   Unlikely

2. What would *promote or encourage* you to put this plan into practice?

3. What would *prevent or discourage* you from putting this plan into practice?

4. How do you think other students would answer the above-three questions?

Deep Learning

STRATEGIC NOTE-TAKING, READING, AND STUDYING

This chapter helps you apply research on human learning and the human brain to become a more effective and efficient learner. It takes you through three key stages of the learning process—from the first stage of acquiring information through lectures and readings, to the second stage of studying and retaining the information you've acquired, through the final stage of retrieving (recalling) the information you studied. The ultimate goal of this chapter is to supply you with a set of powerful strategies that makes your learning *deep* (not surface-level memorization), *durable* (long-lasting), and *retrievable* (accessible to you when you need it).

Chapter Preview

Develop a repertoire of effective strategies for studying smarter, learning deeply, and retaining longer what you have learned.

Learning Goal

 Reflection 5.1

Ignite Your Thinking

What would you say is the key difference between learning and memorizing?

Learning is the fundamental mission of all colleges and universities. One of the major goals of a college education is to help students become independent, self-directed learners. Learning doesn't stop after college graduation; it's a lifelong process that is essential for success in the 21st century. The ongoing information technology revolution, coupled with global interdependence, is creating a greater need for effective learning skills that can be used throughout life in different and cultural and occupational contexts. Today's employers value job applicants who have "learned how to learn" and will continue to be "lifelong learners" (SECFHE, 2006).

What Is Deep Learning?

When students learn deeply, they dive below the surface of shallow memorization; they go further by building mental bridges between what they're trying to learn and what they already know (Piaget, 1978; Vygotsky, 1978). Knowledge isn't acquired by simply pouring information into the brain as if it were an empty jar. It's a matter of attaching or connecting new ideas to ideas that are already stored in the brain. When this happens, facts are transformed into *concepts*—networks of connected or interrelated ideas. In fact, when something is learned deeply, the human brain actually makes a physical (neurological) connection between separate nerve cells (LeDoux, 2002). (See **Figure 5.1**.)

FIGURE 5.1: Network of Brain Cells

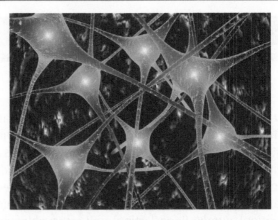

Deep learning involves making connections between what you're trying to learn and what you already know. When you learn something deeply, it's stored in the brain as a link in an interconnected network of brain cells.

©Jurgen Ziewe/Shutterstock.com

Studies suggest that most college students don't engage in deep learning (Arum & Roksa, 2011; Kuh, 2005; Nathan, 2005). They may show up for class most of the time, cram for their exams, and get their assignments done right before they're due. These learning strategies may enable students to survive college, but not thrive in college and achieve academic excellence.

Stages in the Learning and Memory Process

Learning deeply and retaining what you've learned is a process that involves three key stages:

1. **Sensory input (perception).** Taking information into the brain;
2. **Memory formation (storage).** Transforming that information into knowledge and storing it in the brain; and
3. **Memory recall (retrieval).** Bringing that knowledge back to mind when you need it.

These three stages are summarized visually in **Figure 5.2**. These stages of the learning and memory process are similar to the way information is processed by a computer: (1) information is entered onto the screen (input), (2) that information is saved in a memory file (storage), and (3) the saved information is recalled and used when it's needed (retrieval). This three-stage process can serve as a framework for using the two major routes through which knowledge is acquired in college: from lectures and readings.

FIGURE 5.2: **Key Stages in the Learning and Memory Process**

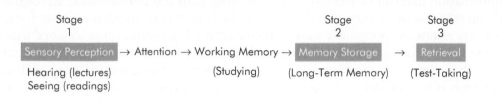

©Kendall Hunt Publishing Company

Effective Lecture-Listening and Note-Taking Strategies

The importance of developing effective listening skills in the college classroom was highlighted in a classic study of more than 400 students who were given a listening test at the start of their college experience. At the end of their first year in college, 49% of those students who scored low on the listening test were on academic probation—compared to only 4.4% of students who scored high on the listening test. On the other hand, 68.5% of students who scored high on the listening test were eligible for the honors program at the end of their first year—compared to only 4.17% of those students who had low listening test scores (Conaway, 1982).

 Reflection 5.2

Do you think writing notes in class helps or hinders your ability to pay attention to and learn from your instructors' lectures?

Why?

Studies show that information delivered during lectures is the number one source of test questions (and answers) on college exams (Brown, 1988; Kuhn, 1988). When lecture information isn't recorded in students' notes and appears on a test, it has only a 5% chance of being recalled (Kiewra, et al., 2000). Students who write notes during lectures achieve higher course grades than students who just listen to lectures (Kiewra, 1985, 2005), and students with a more complete set of lecture notes are more likely to demonstrate higher levels of overall academic achievement (Johnstone & Su, 1994; Kiewra & DuBois, 1998).

Contrary to a popular belief that writing while listening interferes with the ability to listen, students report that taking notes actually increases their attention and concentration in class (Hartley, 1998; Hartley & Marshall, 1974). Studies also show that when students write down information that's presented to them, they're more likely to remember the most important aspects of that information when tested later (Bligh, 2000). One study discovered that students with grade point averages (GPAs) of 2.53 or higher record more information in their notes and retain a larger percentage of the most important information than do students with GPAs of less than 2.53 (Einstein, Morris, & Smith, 1985). These findings aren't surprising when you consider that *hearing* information, *writing* it, and then *seeing* it after it's been written produces three different memory traces (tracks) in the brain, thus tripling your chances of remembering it.

Furthermore, when notes are taken, you're left with a written record of lecture information that can be studied later to improve your test performance. In contrast, if you take few or no notes, you're left with little or no information to study for upcoming exams. As previously noted, the majority of questions on professors' exams come from information contained in their lectures. So, come to class with the attitude that your instructors are dispensing answers to test questions as they speak and your job is to pick out and record these answers so you can pick up points on the next exam.

Note

Points your professors make in class that make it into your notes turn into points earned on your exams (and higher grades in your courses).

You can get the most out of lectures by employing effective strategies at three key times: *before*, *during*, and *after* class.

Pre-Lecture Strategies: What to Do *Before* Class

1. **Check your syllabus to see where you are in the course and determine how the upcoming class fits into the total course picture.** By checking the course syllabus before individual class sessions you'll see how each part (class) relates to the whole (course). This strategy capitalizes on the brain's natural tendency to seek larger patterns and see the "big picture." The human brain is naturally inclined to connect parts into a meaningful whole (Caine & Caine, 2011). It looks for patterns and connections rather than isolated bits and pieces of information (Jensen, 2008). In **Figure 5.3**, notice how your brain naturally ties together and fills in the missing information to perceive a whole pattern that is meaningful.

FIGURE 5.3: **Triangle Illusion**

You perceive a white triangle in the middle of this figure. However, if you use three fingers to cover up the three corners of the white triangle that fall outside the other (background) triangle, the white triangle suddenly disappears. What your brain does is take these corners as starting points and fills in the rest of the information on its own to create a complete or whole pattern that has meaning to you. (Also, notice how you perceive the background triangle as a complete triangle, even though parts of its three sides are missing.)

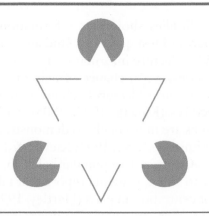

2. **Get to class early so that you can review your notes from the previous class session and from any reading assignments relating to the day's lecture topic.** Research indicates that when students review information related to an upcoming lecture topic, they take more accurate and complete lecture notes (Jairam & Kiewra, 2009; Kiewra, 2005). Thus, a good way to improve your ability to learn from lectures is to review your notes from the previous class session and read textbook information related to the lecture topic—*before* hearing the lecture. Reviewing previously learned information activates your prior

knowledge, enabling you to connect lecture material to what you already know—a powerful way to promote deep learning (Bruner, 1990; Piaget, 1978; Vygotky, 1978).

3. **Adopt a seating location that maximizes attention and minimizes distraction.** Many years of research show that students who sit in the front and center of class tend to earn higher exam scores and course grades (Tagliacollo, Volpato, & Pereira, 2010; Benedict & Hoag, 2004; Rennels & Chaudhair, 1988). These results have been found even when students are assigned seats by their instructor, so it's not just a matter of more motivated and studious students sitting in the front of the room. Instead, the better academic performance achieved by students sitting front and center stems from learning advantages associated with this seating location.

    Front-and-center seating benefits your academic performance by improving your vision of material written on the board or screen and your ability to hear the instructor's lectures. In addition, sitting in the front means you don't have to peer over or around the heads of other students. This results in more direct eye contact with the instructor, which increases your focus of attention, reduces your sense of anonymity, and increases your level of involvement in class.

    Lastly, sitting in the front of class can also reduce your level of anxiety about speaking in class because you will not have numerous classmates sitting in front of you turning around to look at you when you speak.

    The *bottom line*: When you enter a classroom, get in the habit of heading for a seat in the front and center of class. In large classes, it's even more important to get "up close and personal" with your instructors—not only to improve your attention, note-taking, and class participation—but also to improve your instructors' ability to remember who you are and how well you performed in class. This will work to your advantage when you ask your instructors for letters of recommendation.

4. **Sit by people who will enable (not disable) your ability to listen and learn.** Intentionally sit near classmates who will not distract you or interfere with the quality of your note-taking. The human attention span has a limited capacity; we can give all or part of our attention to whatever task we're performing. Actively listening to and taking notes on lecture information is a demanding task that demands undivided attention.

> "
> I like to sit up front so I am not distracted by others and I don't have to look around people's heads to see the chalkboard."
> —*First-year college student*

> "
> I tend to sit at the very front of my classrooms. It helps me focus and take notes better. It also eliminates distractions."
> —*First-year college student*

Note

When you enter class, you have a choice about where you're going to sit. Choose wisely by selecting a location that will maximize your attentiveness to the instructor and your effectiveness as a note-taker.

The evolution of student attention from the back to the front of class.

 Reflection 5.3

When you enter a classroom, where do you usually sit?

Why do you sit there? Is it a conscious choice or more like an automatic habit?

Do you think that the seat you usually choose places you in the best possible position for listening and learning in the classroom?

5. **Adopt a seating posture that screams attention.** Sitting upright and leaning forward increases attention because these signs of physical alertness reach the brain and stimulate mental alertness. If your body is in an alert and ready position, your mind picks up these physical cues and follows your body's lead. Baseball players get into a ready position before a pitch is delivered to ready themselves to catch batted balls; similarly, learners who assume a ready position in the classroom put themselves in a better position to catch ideas batted around in class. Studies show that when humans are mentally alert and ready to learn, a greater amount of C-kinase (a brain chemical) is released at the connection point between brain cells, which increases the likelihood that neurological (learning) connections are formed between them (Howard, 2014).

    Another advantage to being attentive in class is that it sends a clear message to your instructor that you're a courteous and conscientious student. This can influence your instructor's perception and evaluation of your academic performance; if at the end of the course you're on the border between a higher and lower grade, you're more likely to get the benefit of the doubt.

Listening and Note-Taking Strategies: What to Do *During* Class

1. **Give lectures your undivided attention.** As previously noted, research shows that in all subject areas, the majority of test questions appearing on college exams come from the professor's lectures and students who take better class notes get better course grades (Brown, 1988; Cuseo, et al., 2013; Kiewra, 2000). Studies also show that the more time students spend surfing the web or using Facebook during lectures, the lower their test scores. These results hold true for all students, regardless of how they scored on college admissions tests (Ravizza, Hambrick, & Fenn, 2014).

    Remember that like all humans, not all professors are created equal. You'll have some that are more dynamic and easier to pay attention to than others. It's the less dynamic ones that will tempt you to lose attention and stop taking notes. Don't let the less engaging or less entertaining professors lower your course grades. Instead, view them as a challenge; step up your focus of attention, continue taking notes to keep yourself engaged, and leave the course with the satisfaction of earning a good grade.

2. **Take your own notes in class.** Don't rely on someone else to take notes for you. Taking notes in your own words focuses your attention and ensures the notes you take make sense to you. Research indicates that students who record and review their own notes on information presented to them earn higher scores on memory tests for that information than do students who review notes taken by others (Jairam & Kiewra, 2009; Kiewra, 2005). Taking your own notes in your own words makes them *meaningful to you*. While it's a good idea to col-

laborate with classmates to compare notes for completeness and accuracy, or to pick up points you may have missed, you shouldn't rely on someone else to do your note-taking for you.

3. **Take notes in longhand rather than typing them on a laptop.** Studies show that when students use a keyboard to type notes, they're more likely to mindlessly punch in the exact words used by the instructor, rather than transforming the instructor's words into words that are meaningful to them. When tested on understanding and memory for key concepts presented in class, students who took notes in longhand outperformed those who typed notes on a keyboard (Mueller & Oppenheimer, 2014). This may be due to the fact that the movements made during handwriting leave a motor (muscle) memory trace in the brain, which deepens learning and strengthens memory (Herbert, 2014).

4. **Be alert to cues for the most important information contained in lectures.** Since the human attention span is limited, it's impossible to attend to and make note of everything. Thus, we need to use our attention *selectively* to detect and select information that matters most. Here are some strategies for identifying and recording the most important information delivered by professors during lectures:

- Pay particular attention to information your instructors put *in print*—on the board, on a slide, or in a handout. If your instructor has taken the time and energy to write it out or type it out, this is usually a good clue that the information is important and you'll likely see it again—on an exam.

- Pay special attention to information presented during the *first and last few minutes of class*. Instructors are most likely to provide valuable reminders, reviews, and previews at the start and end of a class session.

- Look for *verbal and nonverbal cues* that signal the instructor is delivering important information. Don't just tune in when your professors are writing something down and tune out at other times. It's been found that students record almost 90% of material written on the board, but less than 50% of important ideas that professors state but don't write on the board (Johnstone & Su, 1994; Locke, 1977; Titsworth & Kiewra, 2004). So, don't fall into the reflex-like routine of just taking notes when you see your instructor writing notes. Instead, listen actively to ideas you *hear* your instructor saying and take notes on these ideas as well. **Box 5.1** contains strategies for detecting clues to important information that professors are delivering orally in class.

Box 5.1

Detecting When Instructors Are Delivering Important Information during Lectures

Look for *verbal* cues, such as:

- Phrases signaling important information (e.g., "The point here is . . ." or "What's most significant about this is . . .").
- Information that's repeated or rephrased in a different way (e.g., "In other words, . . .", or "To put it another way . . .").
- Stated information that's followed by a question to check understanding (e.g., "Is that clear?" "Do you follow that?" "Does that make sense?" or "Are you with me?").

Watch for *vocal (tone of voice)* cues, such as:

- Information delivered in a louder tone or at a higher pitch than usual—which may indicate excitement or emphasis.
- Information delivered at a slower rate or with more pauses than usual—which may be your instructor's way of giving you more time to write down these important ideas.

(continued)

Box 5.1 *(continued)*

Keep an eye out for *nonverbal* cues, such as:

- Information delivered by your instructor with more than the usual:
  a) Facial expressiveness (e.g., raised or furrowed eyebrows);
  b) Body movement (e.g., gesticulation and animation);
  c) Eye contact (e.g., looking directly and intently at the faces of students to see if they're following or understanding what's being said).

- Your instructor moving closer to the students (e.g., moving away from the podium or blackboard).
- Your instructor orienting his or her body directly toward the class (i.e., both shoulders directly or squarely facing the class).

5. **Keep taking notes even if you don't immediately understand what your instructor is saying.** If you are uncertain or confused about the material being presented, don't stop taking notes. Having notes on that material will at least leave you with a record to review later—when you have more time to think about it and make sense of it. If you still don't understand it after taking time to review it, seek clarification from your instructor, a classmate, or your textbook.

6. **Take organized notes.** If your instructor continues to make points relating to the same idea, take notes on that idea within the same paragraph. When the instructor shifts to a new idea, skip a few lines and shift to a new paragraph. Be alert to phrases that your instructor may use to signal a shift to a new or different idea (e.g., "Let's turn to . . ." or "In addition to . . ."). Use these phrases as cues for taking notes in paragraph form.

   By recording different ideas in different paragraphs, the organizational quality of your notes improves as will your comprehension and retention of them. Be sure to leave extra space between paragraphs (ideas) to give yourself room to add information that you may have initially missed, or to later translate the professor's words into your own words.

Another popular strategy for taking organized notes is the *Cornell Note-Taking System*. This system is summarized in **Box 5.2** (p. 105).

Post-Lecture Strategies: What to Do *After* Class

1. **As soon as class ends, quickly check your notes for missing information or incomplete thoughts.** Information delivered during a lecture is likely to be fresh in your mind immediately after class. A quick check of your notes at this time will allow you to take advantage of your short-term memory. By reviewing and reflecting on your notes, you can help move that information into long-term memory before forgetting takes place. This quick review can be done alone or, better yet, with a motivated classmate. If you both have gaps in your notes, check them out with your instructor before he or she leaves the classroom. Even though it may be weeks before you'll be tested on the material, the quicker you pick up missed points and clear up sources of confusion, the better; it will help you understand upcoming material—especially upcoming material that builds on previously covered material. Catching confusion early in the game also enables you to avoid the mad last-minute rush of students seeking help from the instructor just before test time. You want to reserve the critical time just before exams to study notes you know are complete and accurate,

Box 5.2

The Cornell Note-Taking System

1. On the page on which you're taking notes, draw a horizontal line about 2 inches from the bottom edge of the paper.
2. If there's no vertical line on the left side of the page, draw one line about 2½ inches from the left edge of the paper (as shown in the scaled-down illustration here).
3. When your instructor is lecturing, use the large space to the right of the vertical line (area A) to record your notes.
4. After a lecture, use the space at the bottom of the page (area B) to summarize the main points you recorded on that page.
5. Use the column of space on the left side of the page (area C) to write questions that are answered in the notes on the right.
6. Quiz yourself by looking at the questions listed in the left margin while covering the answers to them that are found in your class notes on the right.

Note: You can use this note-taking and note-review method on your own, or you could team up with two or more students and do it collaboratively.

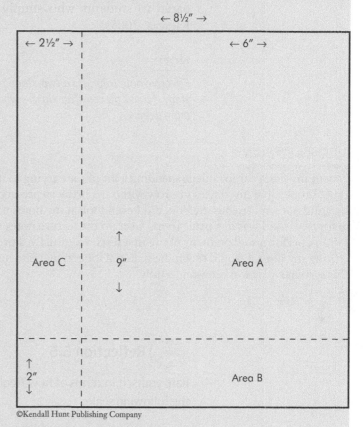

©Kendall Hunt Publishing Company

rather than rushing around trying to find missing information and seeking last-minute help on concepts presented weeks earlier.

 Reflection 5.4

Do you tend to stick around a few minutes after class sessions end to review your notes and clear up missing information or confusing points?

If you don't, why not?

2. **Before the next class session meets, reflect on and review your notes to make sense of them.** Your professors will often lecture on information that you may have little prior knowledge about, so it's unrealistic to expect that you will understand everything that's being said the first time you hear it. Instead, set aside time to reflect on and review your notes as soon as possible after class has ended. During this review process, take notes on your notes by:

   • Translating technical information into your own words to make it more meaningful to you; and
   • Reorganizing your notes to get ideas related to the same point in the same place.

Studies show that students who organize their lecture notes into meaningful categories demonstrate superior recall of that information on memory tests—compared to students who simply review the notes they took in class (Howe, 1970; Kiewra, 2005).

Note

Effective note taking is a two-stage process: Stage 1 involves actively taking notes in class and stage 2 takes places after class—when you take time to reflect on your notes and process them more deeply.

AUTHOR'S EXPERIENCE

I spent my first year in college spending a lot of time trying to manipulate my schedule to create large blocks of free time. I took all of my classes in a row without a break to preserve some time at the end of the day for relaxation and hanging out with friends. Seldom did I even look at my notes until it was time to be tested on them. Thus, on the day before the test I was in a panic trying to cram the lecture notes into my head for the upcoming exam. Needless to say, I didn't perform well on many of my first tests. Eventually, a professor told me that if I spent some time each day re-writing my notes I would retain the material longer, increase my grades, and decrease my stress at test time. I employed this system and it worked wonderfully.

—Aaron Thompson

 Reflection 5.5

Rate yourself in terms of how frequently you use these note-taking strategies according to the following scale:

4 = always, 3 = sometimes, 2 = rarely, 1 = never

1. I take notes aggressively in class.	4	3	2	1
2. I sit near the front of class.	4	3	2	1
3. I sit upright and lean forward while in class.	4	3	2	1
4. I take notes on what my instructors say, not just what they write on the board.	4	3	2	1
5. I pay special attention to information presented at the start and end of class.	4	3	2	1
6. I take notes in paragraph form.	4	3	2	1
7. I review my notes immediately after class to check that they are complete and accurate.	4	3	2	1

Strategic Reading

Expect to do more reading in college than you did in high school and be ready to be held accountable for the reading you're assigned. Information from assigned readings ranks right behind information from lectures as a source of test questions on college exams (Brown, 1988; Cuseo, et al., 2013). There is strong evidence that completing and comprehending assigned readings is associated with higher course grades (Sappington, Kinsey, & Munsayac, 2002). You're likely to find exam questions relating to reading assignments that your professors didn't talk much about in class (or even mention in class). College professors often expect you to relate or connect their lectures with material they've assigned you to read. Furthermore, professors often deliver class lectures with the assumption that students have done the assigned reading, so if you haven't done it, you're more likely to have difficulty following what your instructor is saying in class. Thus, you should not only do the assigned reading but also do it according to the schedule the instructor has established. By completing assigned reading in a timely manner, you will (a) be better positioned to understand class lectures, (b) acquire information that's likely to appear on exams but not covered in class, and (c) improve the quality of your participation in class.

The following research-based strategies can be used to improve your reading comprehension and retention.

> Employ your time in improving yourself by other men's writing so that you shall come easily by what others have labored for."
>
> —*Socrates, classic Greek (Athenian) philosopher and founding father of Western philosophy*

Pre-Reading Strategies: What to Do *Before* Reading

1. **Before jumping into your assigned reading, first see how it fits into the overall organizational structure of the book and course.** You can do this efficiently by taking a quick look at the book's table of contents to see where the chapter you're about to read is placed in the overall sequence of chapters. Look especially at its relationship to the chapters that immediately precede and follow it. This strategy will give you a sense of how the particular part you're focusing on connects with the bigger picture. Research shows that if students have advanced knowledge about how material they're about to learn is organized—if they see how its parts relate to the whole *before* they start learning the specific parts—they're better able to comprehend and retain the material (Ausubel, Novak, & Hanesian 1978; Chen & Hirumi, 2009). Thus, the first step toward improving reading comprehension and retention of a book chapter is to see how it relates to the book as a whole.

 **Reflection 5.6**

When you open a textbook to read a chapter, how do you start the reading process? What's the first thing you do?

2. **Preview the chapter by first reading its boldface headings and any chapter outline, objectives, summary, or end-of-chapter questions that may be included.** Before tackling the chapter's specific content, get in the habit of previewing what's in the chapter to get a general sense of its overall organization. If you dive into the specific details first, you may lose sight of how the smaller details relate to the larger picture. Since the brain's natural tendency is to perceive and comprehend whole patterns rather than isolated bits of information, start by seeing how the parts of the chapter relate to the whole. Just as looking at the whole picture of a completed jigsaw puzzle beforehand helps you connect its parts, so too does getting a picture of the whole chapter before reading its parts.

3. **Take a moment to think about what you may already know that relates to the main topic of the chapter.** This strategy will activate the areas of your brain where your prior knowledge about that topic is stored, thereby preparing it to make meaningful connections with the material you're about to read.

Strategies to Do *During* the Reading Process

1. **Read selectively to locate the most important information.** Effective reading begins with a plan for identifying what should be noted and remembered. Here are three key strategies you can use while reading to help you determine what information you should focus on and retain.

   - **Use boldface or dark-print headings and subheadings as cues for identifying important information.** These headings organize the chapter's major points; you can use them as "traffic" signs to direct you to the most important information in the chapter. Better yet, turn the headings into questions and read to find answers to them. This question-and-answer routine ensures that you read actively and with a purpose. (You can set up this strategy while previewing the chapter by placing a question mark after each heading contained in the chapter.) Creating and answering questions while reading also keeps you motivated because the questions stimulate curiosity and a desire to find answers to them (Walter, Knudsvig, & Smith, 2003). Another advantage of posing and answering questions about what you're reading is that it's an effective way to prepare for exams—you're practicing exactly what you'll be expected to do on exams—answering questions.

   - **Pay close attention to information that's *italicized*, <u>underlined</u>, CAPITALIZED, or bulleted.** These features call attention to key terms that must be understood and built on before you can proceed to understand higher-level concepts covered later in the reading. Don't simply highlight these words because their special appearance suggests they're important. Read these terms carefully and be sure you understand them before you continue reading.

   - **Pay special attention to the first and last sentences in each paragraph.** These sentences provide an important introduction and conclusion to the key point contained in the paragraph. It's a good idea to reread the first and last sentences of each paragraph before you move on to the next paragraph, particularly when reading material that's cumulative (builds on previously covered material), such as science and math.

Note

Your goal when reading is not just to cover the assigned pages, but to uncover the most important ideas contained on those pages.

2. **Take written notes on important information you find in your reading.** A good way to stop and think deeply about key ideas in your reading is to take notes on those ideas in your own words. Research shows that the common student practice of just highlighting the text (the author's words) is not a particularly effective strategy (Dunlosky, et al., 2013). Highlighting is a passive learning process, whereas note-taking actively engages you in the reading process and enables you to transform the text into your own words. Don't slip into the habit of using your textbook simply as a coloring book in which the artistic process of highlighting information in spectacular, kaleidoscopic colors distracts you from the more important process of learning actively and thinking deeply about what you're reading. Highlighting is okay as long it's not the only thing you do while reading; take time to make notes on the material you've highlighted—in your own words—to ensure that you reflect on it and make it personally meaningful. Taking notes on information delivered during lectures will improve your performance on exams; taking notes on your reading assignments will do the same.

"I would advise you to read with a pen in your hand, and enter in a little book of short hints of what you find that is curious, or that might be useful; for this will be the best method of imprinting such particulars in your memory, where they will be ready."

—Benjamin Franklin, 18th-century inventor, newspaper writer, and cosigner of the Declaration of Independence

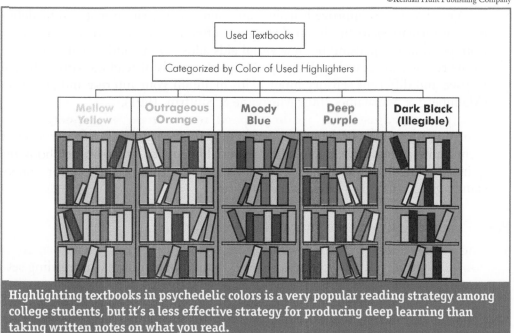

Highlighting textbooks in psychedelic colors is a very popular reading strategy among college students, but it's a less effective strategy for producing deep learning than taking written notes on what you read.

> I had the worst study habits and the lowest grades. Then I found out what I was doing wrong. I had been highlighting with a black magic marker."
>
> —*Jeff Altman, American comedian*

When you transform what someone else has written into your own words, you're implementing a powerful principle of deep learning: relating what you're trying to learn to what you already know (Demmert & Towner, 2003). A good time for pausing and writing a brief summary of what you've read in your own words is when you encounter a boldface heading because it indicates you're about to encounter a new topic; this is the ideal time to deepen your knowledge of what you just finished reading and use that knowledge to help you understand what's coming next.

 Reflection 5.7

When reading a textbook, do you usually have the following tools on hand?

Highlighter:	yes	no
Pen or pencil:	yes	no
Notebook:	yes	no
Class notes:	yes	no
Dictionary:	yes	no
Glossary:	yes	no

If you don't usually have one or more of the above tools on hand while reading, which one(s) do you plan to have on hand in the future?

3. **Make use of visual aids that accompany the written text.** Don't fall into the trap of thinking that visual aids can or should be skipped because they're merely supplemental or ornamental. Visual aids, such as charts, graphs, diagrams, and concept maps, are powerful learning and memory tools for a couple of reasons: (a) they enable you to "see" the information in addition to reading (hearing) it, and (b) they pull together separate ideas into a unified snapshot.

Visual aids also improve learning and memory of written material by delivering information to the brain through a different sensory modality. In addition, periodically pausing to view visual aids adds variety and a change of pace to the reading process. Breaking up sustained periods of reading with a change of pace and different sensory input helps maintain your interest and attention (Malmberg & Murname, 2002; Murname & Shiffrin, 1991).

4. **Regulate or adjust your reading speed to the type of subject matter you're reading.** As you know, academic subjects vary in terms of their level of technicality and complexity. Reading material in a math or science textbook requires reading at a slower rate with more frequent pauses to check for understanding than reading a novel or a short story.

Post-Reading Strategies: What to Do *After* Reading

1. **End your reading sessions with a short review of the key information you've highlighted and taken notes on.** Rather than ending your reading session by trying to cover a few more pages, reserve the last five minutes to review the key ideas you already covered. Most forgetting of information takes place immediately after we stop focusing on the information and turn our attention to another task (Averell & Heathcote, 2011; Baddeley, 1999). By taking a few minutes at the end of a reading session to review the most important information you've just read, you help your brain "lock" that information into long-term memory before getting involved with another task.

The graph in **Figure 5.4** represents the results of a classic experiment that tested how well information is recalled at various times after it was originally learned. As you can see on the far left of the graph, most forgetting occurs soon after information has been taken in (e.g., after 20 minutes, more than 60% of it was

FIGURE 5.4: **The Forgetting Curve**

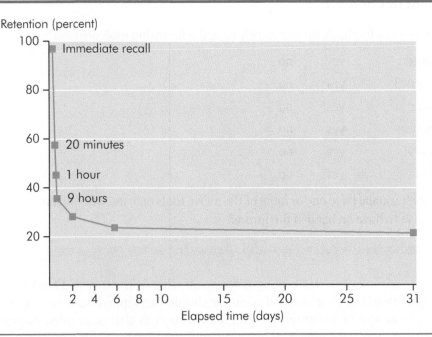

Source: Hermann Ebbinghaus, *Memory: A Contribution to Experimental Psychology*, 1885–1913.

forgotten). The results of this classic study have been confirmed multiple times (Schacter, 2001) and they underscore the importance of reviewing key information acquired through reading *immediately* after you've read it. By doing so, your memory for that information improves dramatically because you're intercepting the human "forgetting curve" at its steepest point of memory loss—just after information has been taken in.

2. After completing a reading assignment, if you're still confused about an important idea or concept contained in the reading, go to another source. The problem may not be you—it may be the way the author has presented or explained it. You may be able to clear up your confusion by simply consulting another source or resource, such as those listed below.

   • **Look at how another book explains it.** Not all textbooks are created equal; some do a better job of explaining certain concepts than others. Check to see whether your library or campus bookstore has other texts dealing with the same subject as your course. A different book may be able to explain a hard-to-understand concept much better than your assigned textbook.

   • **Seek help from your instructor.** If you completed the reading assignment and made every effort to understand a particular concept but still can't grasp it, most instructors should be willing to assist you.

   • **Seek help from learning assistance professionals or peer tutors in your Learning Center (Academic Support Center).** This is your key campus resource for help with reading assignments, particularly if your instructor is unavailable or unwilling to provide assistance.

Box 5.3

SQ3R: A Method for Improving Reading Comprehension and Retention

A popular system for organizing and remembering key reading strategies, such as those discussed in this chapter, is the *SQ3R* system. SQ3R is an acronym for five steps that can be taken to increase textbook reading comprehension and retention, particularly when reading highly technical or complex material. The following sequences of steps comprise this method:

1. Survey
2. Question
3. Read
4. Recite
5. Review

S = Survey: Get a preview and overview of what you're about to read.

1. Use the chapter's title to activate your thoughts about the subject and get your mind ready to receive information related to it.

2. Read the introduction, chapter objectives, and chapter summary to become familiar with the author's purpose, goals, and key points.

3. Note the boldface headings and subheadings to get a sense of the chapter's organization before you begin reading. This supplies you with a mental structure or framework for making sense of the information you're about to read.

4. Take note of any graphics—such as charts, maps, and diagrams; they provide valuable visual support and reinforcement for the material you're reading.

5. Pay special attention to reading aids (e.g., italics and boldface font); use them to identify, understand, and remember key concepts.

Q = Question: Stay active and curious.

As you read, use boldface headings to formulate questions and read to find answers to those questions. When your mind is actively searching for answers, it becomes more engaged in the learning process. As you read, add any questions of your own that come to mind.

(continued)

Box 5.3 *(continued)*

*R = R*ead: Find answers to questions you've created.

Read one section at a time—with your questions in mind—and search for answers to these questions.

*R = R*ecite: Rehearse your answers.

After you complete reading each section, recall the questions you asked and see if you can answer them from memory. If not, look at the questions again and practice your answers until you can recall them without looking.

Don't move onto the next section until you're able to answer all questions in the section you've just completed.

*R = R*eview: Look back and get a second view of the whole picture.

Once you've finished the chapter, review all the questions you've created for different parts or sections. See whether you can still answer them without looking. If not, go back and refresh your memory.

 Reflection 5.8

Rate yourself in terms of how frequently you use the following reading strategies, using the following scale:

4 = always, 3 = sometimes, 2 = rarely, 1 = never

1. I read chapter outlines and summaries before I start reading the chapter content.	4	3	2	1
2. I preview a chapter's boldface headings and subheadings before I begin to read the chapter.	4	3	2	1
3. I adjust my reading speed to the type of subject I am reading.	4	3	2	1
4. I look up the meaning of unfamiliar words and unknown terms that I come across before I continue reading.	4	3	2	1
5. I take written notes on information I read.	4	3	2	1
6. I use the visual aids included in my textbooks.	4	3	2	1
7. I finish my reading sessions with a review of important information that I noted or highlighted.	4	3	2	1

Strategic Studying: Learning More Deeply and Remembering Longer

Studying isn't a short sprint that takes place just before test time. Instead, it's more like a long-distance run that takes place over time. Studying the night before an exam should be the last step in a sequence of test-preparation steps that take place well before test time, which include: (a) taking accurate and complete notes in class, (b) doing the assigned reading, and (c) seeking help from professors or peers along the way for any concepts that are unclear or confusing. After these steps have been taken, you are then well-positioned to study the material you've acquired and learn it deeply.

Described below is a series of study strategies you can use to promote deep and durable (long-lasting) learning.

Give Studying Your Undivided Attention

The human attention span has limited capacity—we have only so much of it available to us at any point in time and we can give all or part of it to whatever task(s) we're working on. As the phrase "paying attention" suggests, it's like paying money; we only have so much of it to spend. Thus, if attention while studying is spent on other activities at the same time (e.g., watching TV or messaging friends), there's a deduction in the amount of attention paid to studying. In other words, studying doesn't receive our undivided attention.

Multitasking while studying interferes with learning by dividing up attention and driving down comprehension and retention.

Studies show that when people multitask they don't pay equal attention to all tasks at the same time; instead, they divide their attention by shifting it back and forth between tasks (Howard, 2014). Their performance on the task that demands the most concentration or deepest thinking is the one that suffers the most (Crawford & Strapp, 1994). When performing complex mental tasks that cannot be done automatically or mindlessly, the brain needs quiet, internal reflection time for permanent connections to form between brain cells—which is what must happen if deep, long-lasting learning is to take place (Jensen, 2008). If the brain must simultaneously engage in other tasks or process other sources of external stimulation, this connection-making process is interfered with and learning is impaired.

So, give study time your undivided attention by unplugging all your electronic accessories. You can even use apps to help you do so (e.g., to silence your phone). Another strategy would be to set aside a short time block of time to check electronic messages after you've completed a longer block of study time (e.g., as a study break); this allows you to use social media as a reward *after* putting in a stretch of focused study time. Just don't do both at the *same* time.

> You can do several things at once, but only if they are easy and undemanding. You are probably safe carrying on a conversation with a passenger while driving on an empty highway [but] you could not compute the product of 17 x 24 while making a left turn into dense traffic, and you certainly should not try."
>
> —*Daniel Kahneman, professor emeritus of Psychology, and author of* Thinking Fast and Slow

Make Meaningful Associations

Deep learning doesn't take place by simply absorbing information like a sponge—in exactly the same, prepackaged form as you received it from a textbook or lecture.

> "When you have to do work, and you're getting it. It's linking what I already know to what I didn't know."
>
> —*Student's description of a "good class"*

Instead, deep learning involves actively translating the information you receive into a form that makes sense to you (Biggs & Tang, 2007; Mayer, 2002).

Note

Deep learning is not about teachers transmitting information to students; it's about students transforming *that information into* knowledge *that's meaningful to them.*

The brain's natural learning tendency is to translate unfamiliar information into a familiar form that makes sense and has personal meaning. This is illustrated in the experience.

AUTHOR'S EXPERIENCE

When my son was about three years old, we were riding in the car together and listening to a song by the Beatles titled, *Sergeant Pepper's Lonely Hearts Club Band*. You may be familiar with this tune, but in case you're not, there's a part in it where the following lyrics are sung repeatedly: "Sergeant Pepper's Lonely, Sergeant Pepper's Lonely, Sergeant Pepper's Lonely . . ."

When this part of the song was being played, I noticed that my three-year-old son was singing along. I thought it was pretty amazing for a boy his age to be able to understand and repeat those lyrics. However, when that part of the song came on again, I listened to him more closely and noticed he wasn't singing "Sergeant Pepper's Lonely, Sergeant Pepper's Lonely . . ." Instead, he was singing: "Sausage Pepperoni, Sausage Pepperoni . . ." (which were his two favorite pizza toppings).

My son's brain was doing what all human brains tend to naturally do. It took unfamiliar information—song lyrics that didn't make any sense to him—and transformed it into a form that was meaningful to him.

—*Joe Cuseo*

You can experience the brain's natural inclination for meaning-making by reading the following passage, which once appeared anonymously online.

> *Aoccdrnig to rscheearch at Cmabridge Uinverstisy, it deos't mattaer in what order the ltteers in a word are, the only iprmoetnt thing is that the frist and lsat ltteer be at the rghit pclae. The rset can be a total mses and you can still raed it wouthit a porbelm. This is bcusae the human mind deos not raed ervey lteter by istlef, but the word as a wlohe. Amzanig huh?*

Notice how easily you made meaning out of unfamiliar, misspelled words by naturally transforming them into familiar, meaningful words—which were already stored in your brain. Whenever you're learning something new, capitalize on the brain's natural tendency to find meaning by trying to connect what you're trying to understand to what you already know.

Learning the specialized terminology associated with different academic disciplines may seem like learning a foreign language for a student with little or no experience with these terms. However, before you start brutally beating these terms into your brain through sheer repetition, try to find meaning in them. One way to do so is by looking up the term's word root in the dictionary or by identifying its prefix or suffix, which may give away the term's meaning. For instance, suppose you're taking a biology course and studying the autonomic nervous system—the part of the nervous system that operates without conscious awareness or voluntary control (e.g., your heart and lungs). The meaning of this biological term is found in its prefix "auto," meaning self-controlling or "automatic" (e.g., automatic transmission). Once you find meaning in a term, you can learn it faster and retain it longer than by memorizing it through sheer repetition.

If looking up an academic term's root, prefix, or suffix doesn't reveal its meaning, see if you can make it meaningful to you in some other way. Suppose you looked up the root of the term "artery" and nothing about the origins of this term helped you understand its meaning or purpose. You could create your own meaning for this term by taking its first letter (a), and have it stand for "*a*way"—to help you remember that arteries carry blood away from the heart. By so doing, you take a meaningless term and make it personally meaningful and memorable.

⊜ Reflection 5.9

Think of a technical academic term or concept you're learning in a course this term, and create a meaningful association you could use to remember it.

Another way you can make learning meaningful is by *comparing and contrasting* what you're learning with what you already know. When you're studying, get in the habit of asking yourself the following questions:

a) How is this idea similar or comparable to something that I've already learned? (Compare)
b) How is this idea different from what I've already learned? (Contrast)

Research indicates that this simple strategy is one of the most powerful ways to promote learning of academic information (Marzano, Pickering, & Pollock, 2001). When you ask yourself the question, "How is this similar to and different from concepts I already know?" you make the learning process more meaningful and relevant because you're relating what you're trying to learn to what you already know or have already experienced.

Note

When learning, go for meaning first, memorization last. If you can connect what you're trying to learn to what you already know, the deeper you'll learn it and the longer you'll remember it.

Integrate Information from Lectures and Readings

Connect ideas from your lecture notes and reading assignments that relate to the same concept. Get them in the same place by recording them on the same index card under the same category heading. Index cards can be used like a portable file cabinet, whereby each card functions like the hub of a wheel, around which individual pieces of related information can be attached like spokes. In contrast, when ideas pertaining to the same point or concept are spread all over the place, they're more likely to take that form in your mind—leaving them mentally disconnected and leaving you more confused or overwhelmed (and stressed out).

Note

Deep learners ask questions like: How can this specific piece of information be categorized or classified into a larger concept? How does this particular idea relate to or "fit into" something bigger?

> "The extent to which we remember a new experience has more to do with how it relates to existing memories than with how many times or how recently we have experienced it."
>
> —*Morton Hunt,* The Universe Within: A New Science Explores the Human Mind

Distribute Study Time across Separate Study Sessions

Learning deeply depends not only on *how* you learn (your method), but *when* you learn (your timing). Equally important as how much time you spend studying is how you distribute or spread out your study time. Research consistently shows that for students of all abilities and ages, distributing study time across several shorter sessions results in deeper learning and longer retention than channeling all study time into one long session (Brown, Roediger, & McDaniel, 2014; Carey, 2014; Dunlosky, et al., 2013). Distributed practice improves your learning and memory in two major ways:

- It minimizes loss of attention due to fatigue or boredom.
- It reduces mental interference by giving the brain some downtime to cool down and lock in information it has received before being interrupted by the need to deal with additional information (Malmberg & Murnane, 2002; Murname & Shiffrin, 1991). Memory works like a muscle: after it's been exercised, if given some "cool down" time before it's exerted again, it builds greater strength—that is, stronger memory for what it previously learned (Carey, 2014). On the other hand, if the brain's downtime is interfered with by the arrival of additional information, it gets overloaded and its capacity for handling information becomes impaired. That's what cramming does—it overloads the brain with lots of information in a limited period of time. In contrast, distributed study does just the opposite—it uses shorter sessions with downtime between sessions—giving the brain time to slow down and retain the information it's previously processed (studied) and more time to move that information from short-term to long-term memory (Willis, 2006).

>
> Hurriedly jam-packing a brain is akin to speed-packing a cheap suitcase—it holds its new load for a while, then most everything falls out."
>
> —*Benedict Carey, author,* How We Learn: Throw Out the Rule Book and Unlock Your Brain's Potential

Distributed study is also less stressful and more motivating than cramming. You're more likely to start studying when you know you won't be doing it for a long stretch of time (or lose any sleep doing it). It's also easier to sustain attention for tasks that are done for a shorter period of time.

Although cramming just before exams is better than not studying at all, it's far less effective than studying that's spread out across time. Instead of frantically cramming total study time into one long session ("massed practice"), use *distributed practice*—"distribute" or space out your study time over several shorter sessions.

Reflection 5.10

Are you more likely to study in advance of exams or cram just before exams?

How do you think most students would answer this question?

Use the "Part-to-Whole" Study Method

A natural extension of distributed practice is the part-to-whole method. This method involves breaking up the material you need to learn into smaller parts and studying those parts in separate sessions in advance of the exam; then you use your last study session just before the exam to review (restudy) the parts you previously studied in separate sessions. Thus, your last session isn't a cram session or even a study session; it's a review session.

Research shows that students of all ability levels learn material in college courses more effectively when it's studied in small units and when progression to the next unit takes place only after the previous unit has been mastered or understood (Pascarella & Terenzini, 1991, 2005).

Don't buy into the myth that studying in advance is a waste of time because you'll forget it all by test time. (Procrastinators often use this argument to rationalize their habit of putting off studying until the very last moment, which forces them to cram frantically the night before exams.) Even if you aren't able to recall what you previously studied when you look at it again closer to test time, research shows that once you start reviewing it, you can relearn it in a fraction of the time it took the first time. Since it takes much less time to relearn the material because the brain still has a memory trace for information studied in the earlier sessions (Kintsch, 1994), it proves you didn't completely forget it and that studying it in advance wasn't a waste of time. Another key advantage of breaking material you're learning into smaller parts and studying those parts in advance of major exams is that it allows you to check your understanding of the part you studied before moving on to learning the next part. This is a particularly important advantage in courses where learning the next unit of material builds on your understanding the previous unit (e.g., math and science).

Capitalize on the Power of Visual Learning

The human brain consists of two hemispheres (half spheres)—left and right (see **Figure 5.5**). Each of these hemispheres specializes in a different type of learning. The left hemisphere specializes in verbal learning; it deals primarily with words. In contrast, the right hemisphere specializes in visual–spatial learning; it deals primarily with perceiving images, patterns, and objects that occupy physical place or space. If you involve both hemispheres of the brain while studying, two different memory traces are recorded—one in each major hemisphere (half) of the brain. This process of laying down dual memory traces (verbal and visual) is referred to as *dual coding* (Paivio, 1990). Since two memory traces are better than one, dual coding results in deeper learning and longer retention.

FIGURE 5.5

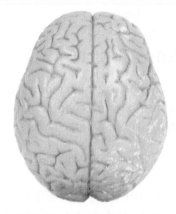

The human brain is comprised of two half spheres (hemispheres): the left hemisphere specializes in verbal learning, and the right hemisphere specializes in visual learning.

©JupiterImages Corporation.

To capitalize on the advantage of dual coding, be sure to use all the visual aids available to you, including those found in your textbook and those provided by your instructor in class. You can also create your own visual aids by representing what you're learning in the form of pictures, symbols, or concept maps—such as flow-charts, timelines, spider webs, wheels with hubs and spokes, or branching tree diagrams. (See **Figure 5.6** for an example of a concept map.) When you transform material you're learning into a visual pattern, you're putting it into a form that's compatible with the brain's tendency to store information in neurological networks (Willis, 2006). Drawing also keeps you actively engaged in the process of learning, and by representing verbal information in visual form, you double the number of memory traces recorded in your brain. As the old saying goes, "A picture is worth a thousand words."

Note

Don't forget that drawings and visual illustrations can be more than just forms of artistic expression; they can also be powerful learning tools—you can draw to learn!

FIGURE 5.6: **Concept Map for the Human Nervous System**

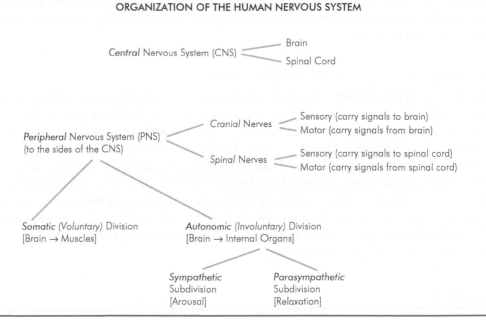

©Kendall Hunt Publishing Company

 **Reflection 5.11**

Think of a course you're taking this term in which related pieces of information could be joined together to form a concept map. Make a rough sketch of this map that includes the information you need to remember.

Build Variety into the Study Process

Infusing variety and change of pace into your study routine can increase your motivation to study and your concentration while studying. Here are some practical strategies for doing so.

Mix it up: periodically shift the type of academic tasks you perform during a study session. Changing the nature of the academic work you do while studying increases your alertness and concentration by reducing *habituation*—attention loss that occurs after repeatedly engaging in the same type of mental task (Thompson, 2009). You can combat attention loss due to habituation by varying the type of tasks you perform during a study session. For instance, you can shift periodically among tasks that involve reading, writing by hand, typing on a keyboard, reviewing, reciting, and solving problems. Similar to how athletes benefit from mixing different types of drills into their workouts (e.g., separate drills for building strength, speed, and endurance), studies of human learning show that "interleaving" (mixing) different academic subjects or academic skills while studying results in deeper learning and stronger memory (Brown, Roediger, & McDaniel, 2014; Carey, 2014).

Study in different places. In addition to spreading out your studying at different times, it's also a good idea to spread it out in different places. Studying in different locations provides different environmental contexts for learning; this reduces the amount of mental interference that normally builds up when all information is studied in the same place (Rankin, et al., 2009). The great public speakers in ancient Greece and Rome used this method of changing places to remember long speeches by walking through different rooms while rehearsing their speech, learning each major part of their speech in a different room (Higbee, 2001).

Although it's useful to have set times for studying so that you get into a regular work routine, this doesn't mean you learn best by always studying in the same place. Periodically changing the academic tasks you perform while studying, as well as the environment in which you perform them, has been found to improve attention to (and retention of) what you're studying (Carey, 2014; Druckman & Bjork, 1994).

Break up long study sessions with short study breaks that involve physical activity (e.g., a short jog or brisk walk). Study breaks that include physical activity refresh the mind by giving it a rest from studying. Physical activity also stimulates the mind by increasing blood flow to your brain—helping you retain what you've studied and regain concentration for what you'll study next.

Learn with and through a variety of senses. When memory is formed in the brain, different sensory aspects of it are stored in different areas. For example, if your brain receives auditory input (e.g., hearing your own words or the words of others), visual input (viewing images, maps, or charts), and motor input (movement made when writing, drawing, or manipulating), that inputted information reaches your brain through multiple sensory modalities and is better retained because it: (a) creates more interconnections in areas of the brain where that information is stored, and (b) provides multiple cues for retrieving (recalling) the information (Willis, 2006; Shams & Seitz, 2011; Zull, 2002). Different forms of sensory input are stored as multiple neurological tracks in different parts of the brain, which deepens learning and strengthens memory.

> I have to *hear* it, *see* it, *write* it, and *talk* about it."
>
> —First-year college student responding to the question: "How do you learn best?"

Don't forget that movement is also a sensory channel. When you move, your brain receives kinesthetic stimulation—the sensations generated by your muscles. Memory traces for movement are commonly stored in an area of your brain (the cerebellum) that plays a major role for all types of learning (Middleton & Strick, 1994; Jensen, 2005). Thus, incorporating movement into the process of learning improves your ability to retain what you're studying by adding a motor (muscle) memory trace of it to your brain. You can use movement to help you learn and retain academic information by using your body to act out what you're studying or symbolize it with your hands (Kagan & Kagan, 1998). Suppose you're trying to remember five points about something (e.g., five consequences of the Civil War). When you're studying these points, count them on your fingers as you try to recall each of them.

> When I have to remember something, it's better for me to do something with my hands so I could physically see it happening."
>
> —First-year college student

(Complete Exercise 5.5 at the end of this chapter. If your results on the "My PEPs Learning Style Inventory" indicate that you have kinesthetic and tactile preferences, such learning-through-movement activities may be particularly effective ways to strengthen your learning.)

I was talking about memory in class one day and mentioned that when I can't recall how to spell a word, its correct spelling comes back to me after I start writing it. One of my students raised her hand and said the same thing happens to her when she forgets a phone number—it comes back to her when she starts punching it in. Both of these experiences point to the power of movement for promoting learning and memory.

—*Joe Cuseo*

Also, remember that talking involves muscle movement of your lips and tongue. Thus, speaking aloud when you're studying, either to a friend or to yourself, can improve memory by supplying kinesthetic stimulation to your brain (in addition to the auditory stimulation your brain receives from hearing what you're saying).

Figure 5.7 shows a map of the outer surface of the human brain; you can see how different parts of the brain are specialized to receive input from different sensory modalities. When multiple sensory modalities are used while learning, multiple memory traces of what you're studying are recorded in separate areas of the brain, resulting in deeper learning and stronger memory for what's been studied.

FIGURE 5.7: A Map of the Functions Performed by the Outer Surface of the Human Brain

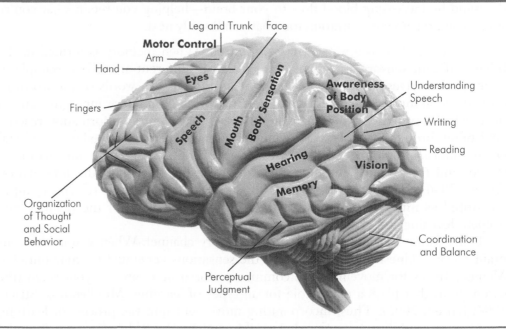

Brain image modified from ©David Huntley/Shutterstock.com

Learn with Emotion

Neural connections run between the emotional and memory centers of the brain (Zull, 1998). Thus, the emotions we're experiencing while learning can affect how deeply we learn. Research indicates that emotional intensity, excitement, and enthusiasm strengthen memory of academic information just as they do for memory of life events and personal experiences. When we're emotionally excited about what we're learning, adrenaline is released and is carried through the bloodstream to the brain. Once adrenaline reaches the brain, it increases blood flow and glucose production, which stimulates learning and strengthens memory (LeDoux, 1998; Rosenfield, 1988). Thus, if you become passionate and enthused about what you're learning, you're more likely to learn it deeply and remember it longer (Howard, 2014; Minninger, 1984).

One way to do this is by keeping in mind the importance or significance of what you're learning. For instance, if you're learning about photosynthesis, remind yourself that you're not just learning a chemical reaction, you're learning about the driving force that underlies all plant life on the planet. If you don't know why the concept you're studying is significant, find out—do a computer search, talk it over with your instructor, or ask an advanced student majoring in the field.

Note

Make learning a "total body experience." Put your whole self into it—your mind, your body, and your heart.

Learn Collaboratively

Simply defined, collaborative learning is the process of two or more people working *interdependently* to advance each other's success—as opposed to working independently or competitively. Learning is strengthened when it takes place in a social context that involves interpersonal interaction. As scholars put it, human knowledge is "socially constructed" or built up through dialogue and an exchange of ideas; conversations with others become internalized as ideas in your mind and influence your way of thinking (Bruffee, 1993). Thus, by having frequent, intelligent conversations with others, you broaden your knowledge base, deepen your learning, and elevate the quality of your thinking.

> **"**
> If you want to go quickly, go by yourself—if you want to go farther, go in a group."
> —*African proverb*

Research from kindergarten through college shows that students who learn collaboratively in teams experience significant gains in both academic performance and interpersonal skills (Cross, Barkley, & Major, 2005; Gilles & Adrian, 2003; Johnson, Johnson, & Smith, 1998). In one national study that involved in-depth interviews with more than 1,600 college students, it was discovered that almost all students who struggled academically had one particular study habit in common: they always studied alone (Light, 2001).

> **"**
> TEAM = <u>T</u>ogether <u>E</u>veryone <u>A</u>chieves <u>M</u>ore"
> —*Author unknown*

To maximize the power of collaboration, use the following pair of guidelines to choose teammates who will enhance the quality and productivity of your learning team:

1. Observe your classmates with an eye toward identifying potentially good teammates. Look for motivated students who will actively contribute to your team's success (rather than those whom you suspect may just be hitchhikers looking for a free ride).

2. Don't team up exclusively with peers who are familiar with or similar to you in terms of their personal characteristics, backgrounds, and experiences. This familiarity can actually interfere with your team's performance by turning your learning team into a social group or gabfest that gets off track and onto topics that have nothing to do with studying (e.g., what you did last weekend or what you're planning to do next weekend). Instead, include teammates who differ from you with respect to such characteristics as: age, gender, race or ethnicity, and cultural or geographical background. Such variety brings different life ex-

periences, styles of thinking strategies and learning styles to your team, which enriches your team's diversity and learning capacity.

Note

Capitalize on the advantages of collaborating with peers of varied backgrounds and lifestyles. Studies show that we learn more from people who are different from us than from people similar to us (Pascarella, 2001; Thompson & Cuseo, 2014).

Keep in mind that collaborative learning can be much more than just forming study groups the night before an exam. You can team up with classmates more regularly to work on a variety of academic tasks, such as those listed below.

Note-Taking Teams. Immediately after class sessions end, take a couple of minutes to team up with other students to compare and share notes. Since listening and note-taking are demanding tasks, it's likely that a classmate will pick up an important point you missed and vice versa. By teaming up *immediately after class*, if you and your teammates find missing or confusing information, quickly consult with the instructor before leaving the room.

AUTHOR'S EXPERIENCE

During my first term in college, I was having difficulty taking complete notes in my biology course because the instructor spoke rapidly and with an unfamiliar accent. I noticed another student (Alex) sitting in the front row who was trying to take notes as best he could; however, he was experiencing the same difficulty as me. Following one particularly fast and complex lecture, we looked at each other and noticed we were both shaking our heads in frustration. We started talking about how frustrated we were and decided to join forces after every class to compare notes and identify points we missed or found confusing. First, we helped each other by comparing and sharing our notes in case one of us got something the other missed. If there were points we both missed or couldn't figure out, we went to the front of class together to consult with the instructor before he left the room. At the end of the course, Alex and I finished with the highest grades in the course.

—*Joe Cuseo*

Reading Teams. After completing reading assignments, team up with classmates to compare your highlighting and margin notes. See what you both identified as the most important material to be studied for upcoming exams.

Writing Teams. Students can provide each other with feedback to revise and improve their own writing. Studies show that when peers assess each other's writing, the quality of their individual writing gets better and they develop a more positive attitude about the writing process (Topping, 1998). You can form peer-writing teams to help at any or all of the following stages in the writing process:

1. Topic selection and refinement: to help one another come up with a list of possible topics and subtopics to write about;
2. Pre-writing: to clarify your writing purpose and audience;
3. First draft: to improve your general writing style and tone; and
4. Final draft: to proofread, detect, and correct clerical errors before submitting your written work.

Library Research Teams. Many first-year students are unfamiliar with the process of using a college or university library to conduct academic research. Some experience "library anxiety" and avoid even stepping foot into the library, particularly if it's a large and intimidating place (Malvasi, Rudowsky, & Valencia, 2009). Forming library research teams is an effective way to develop a social support group that can make library research less intimidating by converting it from a solitary experience done alone to a collaborative venture done as a team. Working together with peers on any research task can reduce anxiety, create collective energy, and result in a final product that's superior to what could have been produced by a single person working independently.

Note

It's perfectly acceptable and ethical to team up with others to search for information and share resources. This isn't cheating or plagiarizing—as long as your final product is completed individually and what you turn into the instructor represents your own work.

Study Teams. When seniors at Harvard University were interviewed, nearly every one of them who had participated in study groups considered the experience to be crucial to their academic progress and success (Light, 1990, 1992, 2001).

Additional research on study groups indicates that they are effective only if each member has done the required course work in advance of team meetings—for example, if all teammates attended class consistently and completed required readings (Light, 2001). To fully capitalize and maximize the power of study teams, each team member should study individually *before* studying with the group and come to the group prepared with answers and ideas to share with teammates, as well as specific questions or points of confusion about which they hope to receive help from other members of the team. This ensures that all team members are individually accountable for their own learning and equally responsible for contributing to their teammates' learning.

> I would suggest students get to know [each] other and get together in groups to study or at least review class material. I find it is easier to ask your classmates with whom you are comfortable 'dumb' questions."
>
> —*Advice to first-year students from a college sophomore (Walsh, 2005)*

Note

Don't forget that team learning goes beyond late-night study groups. Students could and should form learning teams in advance of exams to help each other with other academic tasks—such as note-taking, reading, writing, and library research.

Test-Review Teams. After receiving your results on course examinations (and assignments) you can collaborate with peers to review your performance as a team. When you compare your answers to the answers of other students, you're better able to identify what you did well and where you lost points. By seeing the answers of teammates who received maximum credit on certain questions, you get a clearer picture of what went wrong and what you can do to get it right next time.

Reflection 5.12

Think about the students in your classes this term. Are there classmates who would be good candidates to connect with and form learning teams?

Self-Monitor: Reflect on What You're Learning and Assess Whether You're Learning It Deeply

Deep learners are *reflective* learners—they are self-aware and mindful of how well they're learning what they're studying. They reflect, check, and self-assess whether they're really getting it. They monitor their comprehension by asking questions such as: "Am I actually understanding this?" and "Do I really know it?"

> When you know a thing, to recognize that you know it; and when you do not, to know that you do not know; that is knowledge."
>
> —*Confucius, influential Chinese thinker and educator*

How do you know if you really know it? Probably the best answer to this question is: "I find *meaning* in it—I can relate to it personally or put it in terms that make sense to me" (Ramsden, 2003). Listed below are some strategies for checking whether you're truly (deeply) understanding what you're learning. These strategies can be used as indicators or checkpoints for determining whether you're just memorizing or learning at a deep level. They will help you answer the question: "How do I know if I really know it?"

- **Can you think of an *analogy* between the concept you're learning and something you already know or understand?** (e.g., This concept is like ____ or is similar to ____.)
- **Can you paraphrase (restate or translate) what you're learning in your own words?** If you can take what you're learning and complete the following sentence: "In other words, . . .", it's very likely you've moved beyond surface memorization (and mental regurgitation) to a deeper level of comprehension, because you've transformed what you're learning into a form that makes sense to you. You know you know it if you're not stating it the same way your instructor or textbook stated it, but restating it in words that are your own.
- **Can you explain what you're learning to someone who is unfamiliar with it?** One of the best ways to gain awareness of how well we know or don't know something is to explain it to someone who's never heard it before (just ask any teacher). Studies show that students gain a deeper level of understanding for what they're learning when they're asked to explain it to someone else (Chi, et al., 1994). If you can explain it to someone who's unfamiliar with it, that's a good sign you've moved to deeper comprehension because you're able to translate it into language that's understandable to anyone.
- **Can you think of an *example* of what you've learned?** If you can come up with an instance or illustration of what you're learning—that's your own—not one given by your instructor or textbook, this is a good sign that you truly understand it. It shows you've taken an abstract academic concept and connected it to a concrete experience (Bligh, 2000).
- **Can you apply what you're learning to solve a new problem that you haven't seen before?** The ability to apply what you've learned in a different situation is a good indicator of deep learning (Erickson & Strommer, 2005). Learning specialists refer to this mental process as *decontextualization*—taking what you learned in one context (situation) and transferring it to another context (Bransford, Brown, & Cocking, 2000). For instance, you know you've learned a mathematical concept deeply when you can use that concept to solve math problems different from those solved by your instructor or textbook. This is why math instructors rarely include on exams the exact problems they solved in class or were solved in your textbook. They're not trying to "trick" you at test time; they're trying to see whether you've learned the concept deeply.

"You do not really understand something unless you can explain it to your grandmother."

—Albert Einstein, considered the Father of Modern Physics

"I learn best through teaching. When I learn something and teach it to someone else, I find that it really sticks with me a lot better."

—College sophomore

"Most things used to be external to me—out of a lecture or textbook. It makes learning a lot more interesting and memorable when you can bring your experiences into it. It makes you want to learn."

—Returning adult student

Reflection 5.13

Rate yourself in terms of how frequently you use the following learning strategies:

4 = always, 3 = sometimes, 2 = rarely, 1 = never

1. I block out all distracting sources of outside
    stimulation when I study.   4   3   2   1

2. I try to find meaning in technical terms by looking at their prefix or suffix, or by looking up their etymology (word origin).   4   3   2   1

3. I compare and contrast what I'm currently studying with what I've already learned.   4   3   2   1

4. I organize the information I'm studying into categories or classes.   4   3   2   1

5. I pull together information from my class notes and readings that relate to the same concept or general category.   4   3   2   1

6. I distribute (spread out) my study time over several short sessions in advance of exams and use my last study session before the test to review the information I previously studied.   4   3   2   1

7. I participate in study groups with my classmates.   4   3   2   1

Chapter Summary and Highlights

This chapter identified key principles of human learning and supplied specific strategies for learning effectively in college and throughout life. Deep learning goes beyond surface-level memorization. It's connecting new ideas to ideas that have already been learned. Deep learners build mental bridges between what they're trying to learn and what they already know.

Information delivered during lectures is the information that's most likely to appear as items on college exams. Students who don't take good lecture notes have a slim chance of recalling the information at test time. Thus, effective note taking is critical to successful academic performance in college.

Information from reading assignments is the second most common source of test questions on college exams. Professors often don't discuss information in class that's contained in assigned reading. Thus, doing the assigned reading, and doing it in a way that maximizes comprehension and retention, is essential for academic success in college.

Learning from lectures requires active involvement (e.g., actively taking notes while listening to lectures) as does learning from reading (e.g., actively taking notes while reading). Active involvement during the learning process engages your attention and enables information to enter the brain. Reflection on what you have learned keeps it in the brain by locking it into memory. Self-awareness also promotes deep learning. By reflecting on whether you truly understand what you're studying, you become a more self-aware learner and a more successful student.

Cramming total study time into one long session ("massed practice") immediately before exams doesn't promote deep learning or long-term retention. Research consistently shows that *distributed practice*, whereby study time is "distributed" or spread out over several shorter sessions, is more effective—particularly if the last study session just before an exam is used to review (restudy) the parts that were previously studied in separate sessions. Learning is also deepened by engaging as many senses as possible during the learning process.

Lastly, deep learning is enhanced when done *collaboratively*. Research from kindergarten through college shows that students who learn in teams experience significant gains in both academic performance and interpersonal skills.

Learning More through the World Wide Web: Internet-Based Resources

For additional information on learning deeply and strategically, see the following websites:

Strategic Learning & Study Strategies:
http://www.dartmouth.edu/~acskills/success/

http://www.isu.edu/success/strategies/handouts.shtml

Brain-Based Learning:
http://www.brainrules.net/the-rules

Learning Math and Overcoming Math Anxiety:
www.mathacademy.com/pr/minitext/anxiety

www.onlinemathlearning.com/math-mnemonics.html

References

Arum, R., & Roska, J. (2011). *Academically adrift: Limited learning on college campuses.* Chicago: The University of Chicago Press.

Ausubel, D., Novak, J., & Hanesian, H. (1978). *Educational psychology: A cognitive view* (2nd ed.). New York: Holt, Rinehart & Winston.

Averell, L., & Heathcote, A. (2011). The form of the forgetting curve and the fate of memories. *Journal of Mathematical Psychology, 55*(1): 25–35.

Baddeley, A. D. (1999). *Essentials of human memory.* Hove: Psychology.

Benedict, M. E., & Hoag, J. (2004). Seating location in large lectures: Are seating preferences or location related to course performance? *Journal of Economics Education, 35,* 215–231.

Biggs, J., & Tang, C. (2007). *Teaching for quality learning at university* (3rd ed.) Buckingham: SRHE and Open University Press.

Bligh, D. A. (2000). *What's the use of lectures?* San Francisco: Jossey Bass.

Bransford, J. D., Brown, A. L., & Cocking, R. R. (2000). *How people learn: Brain, mind, experience and school.* Washington, DC: National Academies Press.

Brown, R. D. (1988). Self-quiz on testing and grading issues. *Teaching at UNL (University of Nebraska–Lincoln), 10*(2), 1–3.

Brown, P. C., Roediger III, H. L., & McDaniel, M. A. (2014). *Make it stick: The science of successful learning.* Cambridge, MA: The Belknap Press of Harvard University Press.

Bruffee, K. A. (1993). *Collaborative learning: Higher education, interdependence, and the authority of knowledge.* Baltimore: Johns Hopkins University Press.

Bruner, J. (1990). *Acts of meaning.* Cambridge, MA: Harvard University Press.

Caine, R., & Caine, G. (2011). *Natural learning for a connected world: Education, technology and the human brain.* New York: Teachers College Press.

Carey, B. (2014). *How we learn.* London: Random House.

Chen, B., & Hirumi, A. (2009). Effects of advance organizers on learning for differentiated learners in a fully web-based course. *International Journal of Instructional Technology & Distance Learning.* Retrieved from http://itdl.org/Journal/Jun_09/article01.htm.

Chi, M., de Leeuw, N., Chiu, M. H., & LaVancher, C. (1994). Eliciting self-explanations improves understanding. *Cognitive Science, 18,* 439–477.

Conaway, M. S. (1982). Listening: Learning tool and retention agent. In A. S. Algier & K. W. Algier (Eds.), *Improving reading and study skills* (pp. 51–63). San Francisco: Jossey-Bass.

Crawford, H. J., & Strapp, C. M. (1994). Effects of vocal and instrumental music on visuospatial and verbal performance as moderated by studying preference and personality. *Personality and Individual Differences, 16*(2), 237–245.

Cross, K. P., Barkley, E. F., & Major, C. H. (2005). *Collaborative learning techniques: A handbook for college faculty.* San Francisco: Jossey-Bass.

Cuseo, J. B., Thompson, A., Campagna, M., & Fecas, V. S. (2013). *Thriving in college & beyond: Research-based strategies for academic success and personal development* (3rd ed.). Dubuque, IA: Kendall Hunt.

Demmert, W. G., Jr., & Towner, J. C. (2003). *A review of the research literature on the influences of culturally based education on the academic performance of Native American students.* Retrieved from the Northwest Regional Educational Laboratory, Portland, Oregon, website http://www.nrel.org/indianaed/cbe.pdf.

Druckman, D., & Bjork, R. A. (Eds.). (1994). *Learning, remembering, believing: Enhancing human performance.* Washington, DC: National Academies Press.

Dunlosky, J., Rawson, K. A., Marsh, E. J., Nathan, M. J., & Willingham, D. T. (2013). Improving students' learning with effective learning techniques: Promising directions from cognitive and educational psychology. *Psychological Science in the Public Interest, 14*(1), 4–58.

Einstein, G. O., Morris, J., & Smith, S. (1985). Note-taking, individual differences, and memory for lecture information. *Journal of Educational Psychology, 77*(5), 522–532.

Erickson, B. L., & Strommer, D. W. (2005). Inside the first-year classroom: Challenges and constraints. In M. L. Upcraft, J. N. Gardner, & B. O. Barefoot & Associates (Eds.), *Challenging and supporting the first-year student: A handbook for improving the first year of college* (pp. 241–256). San Francisco: Jossey-Bass.

Gilles, R. M., & Adrian, F. (2003). *Cooperative learning: The social and intellectual outcomes of learning in groups.* London: Farmer Press.

Hartley, J. (1998). *Learning and studying: a research perspective.* London: Routledge.

Hartley, J., & Marshall, S. (1974). On notes and note taking. *Universities Quarterly, 28,* 225–235.

Herbert, W. (2014). *Ink on paper: Some notes on note taking.* Association for Psychological Science (APS). Retrieved from http://www.psychologicalscience.org/index.php/news/were-only-human/ink-on-paper-some-notes-on-note-taking.html.

Higbee, K. L. (2001). *Your memory: How it works and how to improve it.* New York: Marlowe.

Howard, P. J. (2014). *The owner's manual for the brain: Everyday applications of mind-brain research* (4th ed.). New York: HarperCollins.

Howe, M. J. (1970). Note-taking strategy, review, and long-term retention of verbal information. *Journal of Educational Psychology, 63,* 285.

Jairam, D., & Kiewra, K. A. (2009). An investigation of the SOAR study method. *Journal of Advanced Academics* (August), 602–629.

Jensen, E. (2005). *Teaching with the brain in mind* (2nd ed.). Alexandria, VA: ASCD.

Jensen, E. (2008). *Brain-based learning.* Thousand Oaks, CA: Corwin Press.

Johnson, D., Johnson, R., & Smith, K. (1998). Cooperative learning returns to college: What evidence is there that it works? *Change, 30,* 26–35.

Johnstone, A. H., & Su, W. Y. (1994). Lectures: a learning experience? *Education in Chemistry, 31*(1), 65–76, 79.

Kagan, S., & Kagan, M. (1998). *Multiple intelligences: The complete MI book.* San Clemente, CA: Kagan Cooperative Learning.

Kiewra, K. A. (1985). Students' note-taking behaviors and the efficacy of providing the instructor's notes for review. *Contemporary Educational Psychology, 10,* 378–386.

Kiewra, K. A. (2000). Fish giver or fishing teacher? The lure of strategy instruction. *Teaching at UNL (University of Nebraska–Lincoln), 22*(3), 1–3.

Kiewra, K. A. (2005). *Learn how to study and SOAR to success.* Upper Saddle River, NJ: Pearson Prentice Hall.

Kiewra, K. A., & DuBois, N. F. (1998). *Learning to learn: Making the transition from student to lifelong learner.* Needham Heights, MA: Allyn and Bacon.

Kiewra, K. A., Hart, K., Scoular, J., Stephen, M., Sterup, G., & Tyler, B. (2000). Fish giver or fishing teacher? The lure of strategy instruction. *Teaching at UNL (University of Nebraska–Lincoln), 22*(3).

Kintsch, W. (1994). Text comprehension, memory, and learning. *American Psychologist, 49,* 294–303.

Kuh, G. D. (2005). Student engagement in the first year of college. In M. L. Upcraft, J. N. Gardner, B. O. Barefoot & Associates (Eds.), *Challenging and supporting the first-year student: A handbook for improving the first year of college* (pp. 86–107). San Francisco: Jossey-Bass.

Kuhn, L. (1988). What should we tell students about answer changing? *Research Serving Teaching, 1*(8).

LeDoux, J. (1998). *The emotional brain: The mysterious underpinnings of emotional life.* New York: Simon & Schuster.

LeDoux, J. (2002). *Synaptic self: How our brains become who we are.* New York: Penguin Books.

Light, R. L. (1990). *The Harvard assessment seminars.* Cambridge, MA: Harvard University Press.

Light, R. L. (1992). *The Harvard assessment seminars, second report.* Cambridge, MA: Harvard University Press.

Light, R. J. (2001). *Making the most of college: Students speak their minds.* Cambridge, MA: Harvard University Press.

Locke, E. (1977). An empirical study of lecture note-taking among college students. *Journal of Educational Research, 77,* 93–99.

Malmberg, K. J., & Murnane, K. (2002). List composition and the word-frequency effect for recognition memory. *Journal of Experimental Psychology: Learning, Memory, and Cognition, 28,* 616–630.

Malvasi, M., Rudowsky, C., & Valencia, J. M. (2009). *Library Rx: Measuring and treating library anxiety, a research study.* Chicago: Association of College and Research Libraries.

Marzano, R. J., Pickering, D. J., & Pollock, J. (2001). *Classroom instruction that works: Research-based strategies for increasing student achievement.* Alexandria, VA: Association for Supervision and Curriculum Development.

Mayer, R. E. (2002). Rote versus meaningful learning. *Theory into Practice, 41*(4), 226–232.

Middleton, F., & Strick, P. (1994). Anatomical evidence for cerebellar and basal ganglia involvement in higher brain function. *Science, 226*(5184), 458–461.

Minninger, J. (1984). *Total recall: How to boost your memory power.* Emmaus, PA: Rodale.

Mueller, P. A., & Oppenheimer, D. M. (2014). The pen is mightier than the keyboard: Advantages of longhand over laptop note taking. *Psychological Science, 25*(6), 1159–1168.

Murname, K., & Shiffrin, R. M. (1991). Interference and the representation of events in memory. *Journal of Experimental Psychology: Learning, Memory, & Cognition, 17,* 855–874.

Nathan, R. (2005). *My freshman year: What a professor learned by becoming a student.* Ithaca, New York: Cornell University Press.

Paivio, A. (1990). *Mental representations: A dual coding approach.* New York: Oxford University Press.

Pascarella, E. T. (2001, November/December). Cognitive growth in college: Surprising and reassuring findings from the National Study of Student Learning. *Change*, 21–27.

Pascarella, E., & Terenzini, P. (1991). *How college affects students: Findings and insights from twenty years of research*. San Francisco: Jossey-Bass.

Pascarella, E., & Terenzini, P. (2005). *How college affects students: A third decade of research* (Vol. 2). San Francisco: Jossey-Bass.

Piaget, J. (1978). *Success and understanding*. Cambridge, MA: Harvard University Press.

Ramsden, P. (2003). *Learning to teach in higher education* (2nd ed.). London: RoutledgeFalmer.

Ravizza, S. M., Hambrick, D. Z.. & Fenn, K. M. (2014). Non-academic internet use in the classroom is negatively related to classroom learning regardless of intellectual ability. *Computers & Education*, 78, 109–114.

Rennels, M. R., & Chaudhair, R. B. (1988). Eye-contact and grade distribution. *Perceptual and Motor Skills, 67* (October), 627–632.

Rosenfield, I. (1988). *The invention of memory: A new view of the brain*. New York: Basic Books.

Sappington, J., Kinsey, K., & Munsayac, K. (2002). Two studies of reading compliance among college students. *Teaching of Psychology, 29*(4), 272–274.

Schacter, D. L. (2001). *The seven sins of memory: how the mind forgets and remembers*. Boston: Houghton Mifflin.

SECFHE. (2006). *A national dialogue: The Secretary of Education's Commission on the future of higher education*. (U.S. Department of Education Boards and Commissions: A Draft Panel Report). Retrieved from http://www.ed.gov/about/bdscomm/list/hiedfuture/reports/0809-draft.pdf.

Shams, W., & Seitz, K. (2011). Influences of multisensory experience on subsequent unisensory processing. *Frontiers in Perception Science, 2*(264), 1–9.

Tagliacollo, V. A., Volpato, G. L., & Pereira, A., Jr. (2010). Association of student position in classroom and school performance. *Educational Research, 1*(6), 198–201.

Thompson, A., & Cuseo, J. (2014). *Diversity and the college experience*. Dubuque, IA: Kendall Hunt.

Thompson, R. F. (2009). Habituation: A history. *Neurobiology of Learning and Memory, 92*(2), 127–134.

Titsworth, S., & Kiewra, K. A. (2004). Organizational lecture cues and student notetaking. *Contemporary Educational Psychology, 29*, 447–461.

Topping, K. (1998). Peer assessment between students in colleges and universities. *Review of Educational Research, 68*(3), 249–276.

Vygotsky, L. S. (1978). Internalization of higher cognitive functions. In M. Cole, V. John-Steiner, S. Scribner, & E. Souberman (Eds. & Trans.), *Mind in society: The development of higher psychological processes* (pp. 52–57). Cambridge, MA: Harvard University Press.

Walsh, K. (2005). *Suggestions from more experienced classmates*. Retrieved from http://www.uni.edu/walsh/introtips.html.

Walter, T. W., Knudsvig, G. M., & Smith, D. E. P. (2003). *Critical thinking: Building the basics* (2nd ed.). Belmont, CA: Wadsworth.

Willis, J. (2006). *Research-based strategies to ignite student learning: Insights from a neurologist and classroom teacher*. Alexandria, VA: ASCD.

Zull, J. E. (1998). The brain, the body, learning, and teaching. *The National Teaching & Learning Forum, 7*(3), 1–5.

Zull, J. E. (2002). *The art of changing the brain: Enriching the practice of teaching by exploring the biology of learning*. Sterling, VA: Stylus.

Chapter 5 Exercises

5.1 Quote Reflections

Review the sidebar quotes contained in this chapter and select two that were especially meaningful or inspirational to you. For each quote, provide a three- to five-sentence explanation why you chose it.

5.2 Reality Bite

Too Fast, Too Frustrating: A Note-Taking Nightmare

Susan Scribe is a first-year student majoring in journalism. She's currently enrolled in an introductory course that is required for her major (Introduction to Mass Media). The instructor in this course lectures at a rapid rate and uses vocabulary that goes right over her head. Since she cannot get all her instructor's words down on paper and cannot understand half the words she does manage to write down, she becomes frustrated and stops taking notes. She wants to do well in this course because it's the first course in her major, but she's afraid she'll fail it because her class notes are so pitiful.

Reflection and Discussion Questions

1. Can you relate to this case personally, or do know any students who are in the same boat as Susan?
2. What would you recommend that Susan do at this point? Why?

5.3 Self-Assessment of Learning Habits

Look back at the ratings you gave yourself for effective note-taking (Reflection 5.5, p. 106), reading (Reflection 5.8, p. 112), and studying (Reflection 5.13, pp. 124–125). Add up your total score for these three sets of learning strategies (the maximum score for each set is 28):

Note Taking = _____

Reading = _____

Studying = _____

Total Learning Strategy Score = _____

Self-Assessment Questions

1. In which learning strategy area did you score lowest?
2. Do you think the area in which you scored lowest has anything to do with your lowest course grade at this point in the term?
3. Of the seven strategies listed under the area you scored lowest, which could you immediately put into practice to improve your performance in the course you're having most difficulty with this term?
4. What's the likelihood that you will put the preceding strategies into practice this term?

5.4 Consulting with a Learning Specialist

Make an appointment to visit your Learning Center or Academic Support Center on campus to discuss the results of your note-taking, reading, and studying self-assessment in Exercise 5.3 (or any other learning self-assessment you may have taken). Ask for recommendations about how you can improve your learning habits in your lowest score area. Following your visit, answer the following questions.

1. Who did you meet with in the Learning Center?

2. What steps were recommended to you for improving your academic performance?

3. How likely is it that you will take the steps mentioned in the previous question?
   a) definitely
   b) probably
   c) possibly
   d) unlikely

   Why?

4. Do you plan to see a learning specialist again? (If yes, why? If no, why not?)

5.5 Learning Style Assessment

Take the *My PEPs Learning Style Inventory* that accompanies this textbook.

What do the results suggest are your strongest learning styles?

For which classes would the suggestions offered be most helpful to you this semester?

Test-Taking Skills and Strategies

WHAT TO DO BEFORE, DURING, AND AFTER EXAMS

This chapter supplies you with a systematic set of strategies for improving your performance on different types of tests, including multiple-choice and essay exams. It identifies strategies that can be used before, during, and after exams, as well as practical tips for becoming more "test wise" and less "test anxious."

Chapter Preview

Acquire effective strategies to improve your performance on multiple-choice, true–false, and essay tests.

Learning Goal

 Reflection 6.1

Ignite Your Thinking

On which of the following types of tests do you tend to perform better?

a)   Multiple-choice tests

b)   Essay tests

Why?

Learning in college courses typically takes place in a three-stage process: (1) acquiring information from lectures and readings; (2) studying that information and storing it in your brain as knowledge; and (3) demonstrating that knowledge on exams. The following sections of this chapter contain strategies relating primarily to the third stage of this learning process and they are divided into three categories:

*   Strategies to use *in advance* of a test,
*   Strategies to use *during* a test, and
*   Strategies to use *after* test results are returned.

Pre-Test Strategies: What to Do *in Advance* of Exams

Your ability to remember material on an exam that you studied prior to the exam depends not only on how long and how well you studied, but also on the type of exam questions used to test your memory (Roediger, 2008). You may be able to remember what you've studied if you're tested in one format (e.g., multiple-choice) but not if tested in a different format (e.g., essay). Thus, the type of questions that will appear on an upcoming exam should influence the type of study strategies you use to prepare for the exam. Test questions can be classified into the following two major categories, depending on the type of memory required to answer them.

1. *Recognition* test questions ask you to select or choose the correct answer from choices that are provided for you. Falling into this category are multiple-choice, true–false, and matching questions. These test questions don't require you to supply or produce the correct answer on your own; instead, you're asked to recognize or pick out the correct answer—similar to picking out the "correct" criminal from a lineup of potential suspects.

2. *Recall* test questions require you to retrieve information you've studied and reproduce it on your own. As the word "recall" implies, you have to re-call ("call back") information and supply it yourself—as opposed to picking it out from information supplied for you. Recall test questions include essay and short-answer questions that require you to provide your own answer—in writing.

Since recognition test questions (e.g., multiple-choice or true–false) ask you to recognize or pick out the correct answer from answers provided for you, reading your class notes and textbook highlights and identifying key information may be an effective study strategy—because it matches the type of mental activity you'll be performing on the exam—reading test questions and identifying correct answers provided to you.

On the other hand, recall test questions, such as essay questions, require you to retrieve information and generate your own answers. They don't involve answer recognition; they require answer *production*—you produce the answer in writing. If you study for essay tests by just looking over your class notes and reviewing your reading highlights, you're using a study strategy that doesn't align with or match what you'll be expected to do on the test itself, which is to supply the correct information yourself. To prepare for essay-test questions, you need to practice *retrieval* —recalling the information on your own—without looking at it.

Two essay-test preparation strategies that ensure you engage in memory retrieval are: (1) recitation and (2) creation of retrieval cues. Each of these strategies is described below.

Recitation

Stating aloud the information we want to remember—without looking at that information—is a memory-improvement strategy known as *recitation*. Memory is strengthened substantially when we reproduce on our own what we're trying to remember, instead of simply looking it over or rereading it (Roediger & Karpicke, 2006). Research consistently indicates that this type of self-testing may be the most powerful of all test-preparation strategies (Carey, 2014). Recitation strengthens memory and better prepares you for essay tests because it:

- Requires *more mental effort* to dig out (retrieve) the answer on its own, which strengthens memory for the answer and allows the brain to practice exactly what it's expected to do on essay tests.
- Gives you clear *feedback* about whether or not you know the material. If you can't retrieve and recite it without looking at it, you know for sure that you won't be able to recall it at test time and need to study it further. You can pro-

vide yourself with this feedback by putting the question on one side of an index card and the answer on the flip side. If you find yourself flipping over the index card to look at the answer in order to remember it, this shows you can't retrieve the information on your own and you need to study it further. (To create electronic flash cards, see: www.studystack.com or studyblue.com)

- Encourages you to *use your own words*. If you can paraphrase it—rephrase what you're studying in your own words—it's a good indication you really understand it; and if you really understand it, you're more likely to recall it at test time.

Recitation can be done silently, by speaking aloud, or by writing out what you're trying to recall. Speaking aloud or writing out what you're reciting are particularly effective essay-test preparation strategies because they involve physical activity, which ensures that you're actively involved and engaged in the learning process.

(Check the results of your "My PEPs Learning Style Inventory." How does the recitation technique match up with your auditory preference? What recommendations would work best for you?)

Creating Retrieval Cues

Suppose you're trying to remember the name of a person you know; you know you know it, but just can't recall it. If a friend gives you a clue (e.g., the first letter of the person's name or a name that rhymes with it), it's likely to suddenly trigger your memory of that person's name. What your friend did was provide a retrieval cue. A *retrieval cue* is a type of memory reminder (like a string tied around your finger) that brings back to mind what you've temporarily forgotten.

Research shows that students who can't remember previously studied information are better able to recall that information if they're given a retrieval cue. In a classic study, students studied a long list of items, some of which were animals (e.g., giraffe, coyote, and turkey). After they finished studying, students were given a blank sheet of paper and asked to write down the names of those animals. None of the students were able to recall all of the animals that appeared on the list they previously studied. However, when the word "animals" was written on top of the answer sheet to provide students with a retrieval cue, they were able to recall many of the animals they had forgotten (Tulving, 1983). Research findings such as these suggest that category names can serve as powerful retrieval cues. By taking pieces of information you need to recall on an essay-test and organizing it into categories, you can then use the category names as retrieval cues at test time. Retrieval cues work because memories are stored in the brain as part of an interconnected network. So, if you're able to recall one piece or segment of the network (the retrieval cue), it can trigger recall of other pieces of information linked to it in the same network (Willingham, 2009).

 Reflection 6.2

Think about items of information you need to remember in a course you're taking this term. Group these items into a category that can be used as a retrieval cue to help you remember them.

1. What's the course?

2.   What's the category you've created as a retrieval cue?

3.   What items of information would this retrieval cue help you recall?

Another strategy for creating retrieval cues is to come up with your own catchword or catchphrase to "catch" or batch together all related ideas you're trying to remember. Acronyms can serve as catchwords, with each letter acting as a retrieval cue for a batch of related ideas. For instance, suppose you're studying for an essaytest in abnormal psychology that will include questions testing your knowledge of different forms of mental illness. You could create the acronym SCOT as a retrieval cue to help you remember to include the following key elements of mental illness in your essay answers: Symptoms (S), Causes (C), Outcomes (O), and Therapies (T).

Strategies to Use *Immediately Before* a Test

1.   **Before the exam, take a brisk walk or light jog.** Physical activity increases mental alertness by increasing oxygen flow to the brain; it also decreases tension by increasing the brain's production of emotionally "mellowing" brain chemicals (e.g., serotonin and endorphins).

2.   **Come fully armed with all the test-taking tools you need.** In addition to the basic supplies (e.g., no. 2 pencil, pen, blue book, Scantron, calculator, etc.), bring backup equipment in case you experience equipment failure (e.g., an extra pen in case your first one runs out of ink or extra pencils in case your original one breaks).

3.   **Get to the classroom as early as possible.** Arriving early allows you to take a few minutes to get into a relaxed pretest state of mind by thinking positive thoughts, taking slow, deep breaths, and stretching your muscles.

(Take a look at the "structure preference" results from your "My PEPs Learning Style Inventory." What do they suggest you do when starting an exam?)

4.   **Sit in the same seat you normally occupy in class.** Research indicates that memory is improved when information is recalled in the same place where it was originally received or reviewed (Sprenger, 1999). Thus, taking a test in the same place where you heard the information delivered will likely improve your test performance.

Studies also show that when students take a test on material in the same environment where they studied the material, they tend to remember more of it at test time than do students who study the material in one place and take a test on that material in a different place (Smith & Vela, 2001). While it's unlikely you will be able to do all your studying in the same room where your test will be taken, it may be possible to do a short, final review session in your classroom or in an empty classroom with similar features. This should strengthen your memory because the physical features of the room become associated with the material you're trying to remember. Seeing these features again at test time can help trigger your memory of that material.

A classic, fascinating study supporting this recommendation was once conducted on a group of deep sea divers. Some divers learned a list of words on a beach, while the others learned the list underwater. They were later tested for their memory of the words. Half the divers who learned the words on the beach remained there to take the test; the other half were tested underwater. Half the

> "Avoid flipping through notes (cramming) immediately before a test. Instead, do some breathing exercises and think about something other than the test."
>
> —*Advice to first-year students from a college sophomore*

divers who studied the words underwater took the test in the same place; the other half took the test on the beach. The results showed that the divers who took the test in the same place where they learned the list recalled 40% more of the items than the divers who did their learning and testing in different places (Godden & Baddeley, 1975). This study provides strong evidence that memory is strengthened when studying and testing takes place in the same location.

Other intriguing studies have shown that if students are exposed to a certain aroma while they're studying (e.g., the smell of chocolate) and are later exposed to that same smell during a memory test for what they studied, they display better memory for the information they studied (Schab & Crowder, 2014). One possible, practical application of this finding to improve your memory during a test is to put on a particular cologne or perfume while studying, and put in on again on the day of the test. This may improve your memory for the information you studied by matching the scent of your study environment with the scent of your test environment. Although this strategy may seem silly, keep in mind that the area of the human brain where humans perceive smell has connections with the brain's memory centers (Jensen, 2005). These neurological connections probably explain why people often report that certain smells can trigger long-ago memories (e.g., the smell of a summer breeze triggering memories of summer games played during childhood).

Since smell is related to memory, you may be able to use smell as a retrieval cue to stimulate recall for information you've studied. In so doing, you may improve your performance on essay tests.

Box 6.1

Nutritional Strategies for Strengthening Academic Performance

Is there a "brain food" that can enhance our test performance? Can we "eat to learn" or "eat to remember"? Some animal studies suggest that memory can be improved by consumption of foods containing lecithin—a substance that helps the brain produce acetylcholine—a chemical that plays an important role in the formation of memories (Ueda, et al., 2011; Ulus & Wurtman, 1977). Fish contains high amounts of lecithin, which may explain why fish is sometimes referred to as "brain food."

Despite the results of some animal studies, not enough human research evidence is available to conclude that consuming certain foods will dramatically increase our ability to retain information or knowledge. However, the following nutritional strategies can improve mental performance on days when our knowledge is tested.

1. Eat breakfast on the day of the exam. Studies show that when students eat a nutritious breakfast on the day they are tested, they achieve higher test scores (Phillips, 2005; Schroll, 2006). Breakfast on the day of an exam should include grains, such as whole wheat toast, whole grain cereal, oatmeal, or bran, because those foods contain complex carbohydrates that deliver a steady stream of energy to the body throughout the day. These complex carbohydrates also help your brain produce a steady stream of serotonin—a brain chemical that reduces tension and anxiety.

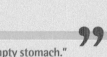

No man can be wise on an empty stomach."
—George Eliot, 19th-century English novelist

2. Make the meal you eat before an exam a light meal. The meal you consume nearest test time should not be a large one because it will elevate your blood sugar to a high level, causing large amounts of insulin must be released into the bloodstream to reduce the blood sugar level. This draws blood sugar away from the brain, causing mental fatigue.

(continued)

Box 6.1 *(continued)*

3. If you need an energy boost prior to an exam, eat a piece of fruit rather than a candy bar. Candy bars are processed sweets that infuse synthetic sugar into the bloodstream, which provides a short and sudden burst of energy. That's the good news; the bad news is that this short-term rush of blood sugar and sudden jolt of energy can also increase bodily tension followed by a sharp drop in energy and feelings of sluggishness (Haas, 1994; Thayer, 1997). The key is to find a food that elevates energy without elevating tension and sustains this energy level over an extended period of time. The best nutritional option for producing such a steady, sustained state of higher energy is *natural* sugar contained organically in a piece of fruit, not processed sugar artificially slipped into a candy bar.

4. Avoid consuming caffeine before an exam. Although caffeine increases alertness, it's a stimulant that elevates bodily tension and nervousness. These are feelings you don't want to experience during a test, particularly if you're prone to test anxiety. Also, caffeine is a diuretic, which means it will increase your urge to urinate. You certainly want to avoid this urge during an exam—when you're confined to a classroom and can't afford to take time to tend to urological needs (or be distracted by them).

©Kendall Hunt Publishing Company

Consuming large doses of caffeine or other stimulants before exams is likely to increase your alertness, but it's also likely to increase your level of stress and test anxiety.

Strategies to Use *During* Exams

1. **As soon as you receive a copy of the test, write down any hard-to-remember terms, formulas, and equations and any memory-retrieval cues you may have created before you start the exam.** This will help ensure you don't forget this important information when you start focusing your attention on the test itself.

2. **First answer questions you know well and carry the most points.** Before automatically attacking the first question that appears on test, take a moment to check out the overall layout of the test and note the questions that are worth the most points and the questions you're best prepared to answer. Tackle these questions first. Put a checkmark next to questions whose answers you're unsure of and come back to them later—after you've answered the questions you're sure of—to ensure you get these points added to your total test score before you run out of test time.

3. If you experience "memory block" for information you know, use the following strategies to unlock it.

   * Mentally put yourself back in the environment in which you studied. Recreate the situation by mentally picturing the place where you first heard or saw the information and where you studied it—including sights, sounds, smells, and time of day. This memory-improvement strategy is referred to as *guided retrieval*, and research supports its effectiveness for recalling information of any kind, including information recalled by eyewitnesses to a crime (Glenberg, 1997; Glenberg-Robertson, 1998).

   * Think of any idea or piece of information that relates to the information you can't remember. Studies show that when students forget information they studied, they're more likely to suddenly remember that information if they first recall a piece related to it in some way (Reed, 2013). This strategy works because related pieces of information are typically stored in the same area of the brain—as part of an interconnected neural network.

   * Take your mind off the question by turning to another question. This frees your subconscious to focus on the forgotten information, which can suddenly trigger your conscious memory of it. Moving on to other test questions also allows you to find information included in later test questions that may enable you to recall information related to the earlier question that you previously forgot.

   * Before turning in your test, carefully review and double-check your answers. This is the critical last step in the test-taking process. Sometimes the performance pressure and anxiety associated with test taking can cause students to overlook details, misread instructions, unintentionally skip questions, or make absentminded mistakes. So take time to look over your answers and check for any mindless mistakes you may have made. Avoid the temptation to immediately cut out of class after answering the last test question because you're pooped out or stressed out. When you think about the amount of time and effort you put into preparing for the exam, it's foolish not to take a little more time to detect and correct any silly mistakes you may make that could cost you points and lower your test score.

Reflection 6.3

I'm most likely to experience memory block during exams in the following subjects:

During tests, when I experience memory block, I usually . . .

Strategies for Answering Multiple-Choice Test Questions

You're likely to encounter multiple-choice questions on college tests (particularly in large classes), on certification or licensing exams for particular professions (e.g., nursing and teaching), as well as on admissions tests for graduate school (e.g., master's and doctoral degree programs) and professional school (e.g., law school and medical school). Since you're likely to take multiple-choice tests frequently in college and beyond, this section of the text is devoted to a detailed discussion of strategies for taking such tests. These strategies are also applicable to *true–false* questions, which are really essentially multiple-choice questions with two choices: true or false.

1. **Read all choices listed and use a *process-of-elimination* approach.** Search for the correct answer by first eliminating choices that are clearly wrong; continue to do so until you're left with one choice that represents the best option. Keep in mind that the correct answer is often the one that has the highest probability or likelihood of being true; it doesn't have to be absolutely true—just truer than all the other choices listed.

A *process-of-elimination* approach is an effective test-taking strategy to use when answering difficult multiple-choice questions.

2. **For a choice to be correct, the *entire statement* must be true.** If any part of the statement is inaccurate or false, eliminate it because it's an incorrect answer.

3. **Use *test-wise* strategies when you cannot narrow down your choice to one answer.** Your first strategy on any multiple-choice question should be to choose an answer based on your knowledge of the material, not by guessing the correct answer based on how the question is worded. However, if you've relied on your knowledge, used the process-of-elimination strategy to eliminate clearly wrong choices, and you're still left with two or more answers that appear to be correct, then you should turn to being *test wise*—use the wording or placement of the test question itself to increase your chances of selecting the correct answer (Flippo & Caverly, 2009). Here are three test-wise strategies you can use for multiple-choice questions when more than one choice appears to be correct:

    *   **Pick the answer that contains qualifying words.** Correct answers are more likely to contain modifying words such as "usually," "probably," "often," "likely," "sometimes," "perhaps," or "may." Knowledge often doesn't come neatly packaged as absolute or unqualified truths, so choices are more likely to be false if they make broad generalizations or contain words such as "always," "every," "never," "only," "must," and "completely."
    *   **Pick the longest answer.** True statements often require more words to make them true.
    *   **Pick a middle answer rather than the first or last answer.** If you've narrowed down the correct answer to either "a" or "c," your best bet may be to go with "c." Similarly, if you've narrowed your choices to "b" or "d," go with "b." Studies show that instructors have a tendency to place the correct answer in the middle, rather than as the first or last choice (Miller, Linn, & Gronlund, 2012)—perhaps because they think the correct answer will be too obvious or stand out if it's placed at the top or bottom of the list.

4. **Check to be sure that your answers are aligned with the right questions.** When looking over your test before turning it in, search carefully for questions you may have skipped and intended to go back to later. Sometimes you may skip a test question on a multiple-choice test and forget to skip the number of that question on the answer form. This will throw off all your other answers by one space or line and result in a disastrous "domino effect" of wrong answers that can do major damage to your total test score. To prevent this from happening, check the alignment of all your answers to be sure there are no blank spaces on your column of answers and that your order of answers line up with the order or test questions.

5. **Don't feel that you must remain locked into your first answer.** When reviewing your answers on multiple-choice and true–false tests, don't be afraid to change an answer after you've given it more thought. Don't buy into the common belief that your first answer is always your best answer. There have been numerous studies on the topic of changing answers on multiple-choice and true–false tests, dating all the way back to 1928 (Higham & Gerrard, 2005). These studies consistently show that most changed test answers go from being incorrect to correct, resulting in improved test scores (Bauer, Kopp, & Fischer, 2007; Prinsell, Ramsey, & Ramsey, 1994). In one study of more than 1,500 students' midterm exams in an introductory psychology course, it was discovered that when students changed answers, 75% of the time they changed from an incorrect to correct answer (Kruger, Wirtz, & Miller, 2005). These results probably reflect the fact that students often catch mistakes when reading the question again or when they find some information later in the test that causes them to reconsider (and correct) their first answer to an earlier test question.

If you have good reason to think an answer change should be made, don't be afraid to make it. The only exception to this general rule is when you find yourself changing many of your original answers; this may indicate that you were not well prepared for the exam and are just doing a lot of guessing and second-guessing.

 ## Reflection 6.4

On multiple-choice exams, do you ever change your original choice?

If you do make changes, what's your usual reason for doing so?

Strategies for Answering Essay Questions

Along with multiple-choice questions, essay questions are among the most common types of test questions on college exams. The following strategies are recommended for strengthening your performance on essay questions.

1. **Look for "mental action" verbs in the question that point to the type of thinking your instructor expects you to demonstrate in your answer. Box 6.2** contains a list of thinking verbs you're likely to see in essay questions and the type of mental action typically called for by each of these verbs. As you read this list, place a check mark next to the verbs that represent a type of thinking you've rarely or never been asked to do in the past.

Box 6.2

Mental Action Verbs Commonly Found in Essay-Test Questions

Analyze. Break the topic down into its key parts and evaluate the parts in terms of their accuracy, strengths, and weaknesses.

Compare. Identify the similarities and differences between major concepts.

Contrast. Identify the differences between ideas, particularly sharp differences and clashing viewpoints.

Describe. Provide details (e.g., who, what, where, and when).

Discuss. Analyze (break apart) and evaluate the parts (e.g., strengths and weaknesses).

Document. Support your judgment and conclusions with scholarly references or research evidence.

Explain. Provide reasons that answer the questions "why?" and "how?"

> I keep six honest serving men. They taught me all I knew. Their names are what and why and how and when and where and who."
> —*Rudyard Kipling, "The Elephant's Child,"* The Just-So Stories

Illustrate. Supply concrete examples or specific instances.

Interpret. Draw your own conclusion and explain why you came to that conclusion.

Support. Back up your ideas with logical reasoning, persuasive arguments, or statistical evidence.

Reflection 6.5

Which of the mental actions listed in **Box 6.2** was most often required on your high school writing assignments?

Which was least often (or never) required?

2. **Make an outline of your key ideas before you start writing sentences.** First, do a quick "information dump" by jotting down the main points you plan to make in your essay answer in outline form. Outlines are effective for several reasons:

   - **An outline ensures you don't forget to include your most powerful points.** The points listed in your outline serve as memory-retrieval cues that help you remember the "big picture" before getting lost in all the details.
   - **An outline earns you points by improving your answer's organizational quality.** In addition to reminding you of the points you need to make, an outline gives you a plan for ordering your ideas in a sequence that flows smoothly from beginning to middle to end. One factor instructors consider when awarding points for an essay answer is how well that answer is organized. An outline will make your answer's organization clearer and more coherent to the reader, which will increase the amount of points you're awarded.
   - **An outline helps reduce test anxiety.** By organizing your points ahead of time, you can focus on expressing (writing) those points without the added stress of figuring out what you're going to say at the same time you're trying to figure out *how* to say it.

- **An outline can add points to answers you don't have time to complete.** If you run out of test time before writing out your full answer to an essay question, an outline shows your instructor what you planned to include in your written answer. The outline itself is likely to earn you some points because it demonstrates your knowledge of the major points called for by the question.

Exhibit 1

Identical twins
Adoption
Parents/family tree

6/6

1. *There are several different studies that scientists conduct, but one study that they conduct is to find out how genetics can influence human behavior in <u>identical twins</u>. Since they are identical, they will most likely end up very similar in behavior because of their identical genetic makeup. Although environment has some impact, genetics are still a huge factor and they will, more likely than not, behave similarly. Another type of study is with <u>parents and their family trees</u>. Looking at a subject's family tree will explain why a certain person is bipolar or depressed. It is most likely caused by a gene in the family tree, even if it was last seen decades ago. Lastly, another study is with adopted children. If an <u>adopted child</u> acts a certain way that is unique to that child, and researchers find the parents' family tree, they will most likely see similar behavior in the parents and siblings as well.*

2. *The monistic view of the mind-brain relationship is so strongly opposed and criticized because there is a belief or assumption that <u>free will</u> is taken away from people. For example, if a person commits a horrendous crime, it can be argued "monistically" that the chemicals in the brain were the reason, and that a person cannot think for themselves to act otherwise. This view limits responsibility.*

No freewill
No afterlife

   Another reason that this view is opposed is because it has been said that <u>there is no afterlife</u>. If the mind and brain are one and the same, and there is <u>NO</u> difference, then once the brain is dead and is no longer functioning, so is the mind. Thus, it cannot continue to live beyond what we know today as life. <u>And</u> this goes against many religions, which is why this reason, in particular, is heavily opposed.

6/6

A college sophomore's answers to short essay questions that demonstrate effective use of bulleted lists or short outlines (in the side margin) to ensure recall of key points.

---

3. **Get directly to the point on each question.** Avoid elaborate introductions that take up your test time (and your instructor's grading time) but don't earn you any points. An answer that begins with the statement "This is an interesting question that we had a great discussion on in class . . ." is pointless because it doesn't add points to your test score. Timed essay tests often leave you pressed for time; don't waste that time on flowery introductions that contribute nothing to your test grade.

   One effective way to get directly to the point on essay questions is to include part of the question in the first sentence of your answer. For example, suppose the test question asks you to, "Argue for or against capital punishment by explaining how it will or will not reduce the nation's homicide rate." Your first sentence could be, "Capital punishment will not reduce the homicide rate for the following reasons . . ." Thus, your first sentence becomes your thesis statement—it points you directly to the major points you're going to make in your answer and earns immediate points for your answer.

4. **Answer essay questions with as much detail as possible.** Don't assume that your instructor already knows what you're talking about or will be bored by details. Instead, take the approach that you're writing to someone who knows little or nothing about the subject—as if you're an expert teacher who is explaining it from scratch.

Note

As a general rule, it's better to over-explain than under-explain your answers to essay questions.

5. **Support your points with evidence—facts, statistics, quotes, or examples.** When you're answering essay questions, take on the mindset of a lawyer: make your case by presenting concrete evidence (exhibit A, exhibit B, etc.).
6. **Leave space between your answers to each essay question.** This strategy will enable you to easily add information to your original answer if you recall something later in the test that you would like to include.
7. **Proofread your answers for spelling and grammar.** Before turning in your test, proofread what you've written and correct any spelling or grammatical errors you find. Catching and correcting clerical errors will improve your test score. Even if your instructor doesn't explicitly state that grammar and spelling count toward your grade, these mechanical mistakes are still likely to influence your professor's overall evaluation of your written work.
8. **Neatness counts.** Many years of research indicate that neatly written essays are scored higher than sloppy ones, even if the answers are essentially the same (Huck & Bounds, 1972; Hughes, et al., 1983; Pai, et al., 2010). These findings aren't surprising when you consider that grading essay answers is a time-consuming, labor-intensive task that requires your instructor to plod through multiple answers written by students with multiple styles of handwriting—ranging from crystal clear to quasi-cryptic. If you make your instructor's job a little easier by writing as clearly as possible and cleaning up any sloppy markings before turning in your test, you're likely to earn more points for your answers.

 Reflection 6.6

What do you usually do with tests and assignments after they're returned to you? Why?

> "When you make a mistake, there are only three things you should do about it: admit it; learn from it; and don't repeat it."
>
> *—Paul "Bear" Bryant, legendary college football coach*

Post-Test Strategies: What to Do *After* Receiving Your Test Results

Successful test performance involves both forethought (preparation before the test) and afterthought (reflection after the test). Often, when students get a test back, they check to see what grade they got, then stuff it in a binder or toss it into the nearest wastebasket. Don't fall prey to this unproductive habit; instead, use your test results as feedback to improve your future performance. Reflect on your results and ask yourself: How can I learn from this? How can I put it to use to correct my mistakes and repeat my successes? Remember: A test score isn't an end result; it may tell you where you are now, but it doesn't tell you where you'll end up. Use your results as a means to another end—a higher score on the next test.

Note

If you do poorly on an exam, don't get bitter—get better. View your mistakes in terms of what they can do for *you, not* to *you. A poor test performance can be turned into a productive learning experience, particularly if it occurs early in the course when you're still learning the rules of the game. You can use your test results as a valuable source of feedback for improving your future performance and final course grade.*

In the movie and record industry, if the first cut isn't successful, additional "takes" ("take two," "take three," etc.) are made until it's done right. Successful students do the same thing: If they make a mistake on "take one," they stick with it and continue working to improve their performance on the next take.

©Lightspring/Shutterstock.com

In the movies, a clipboard is used to signal the next take (shooting) if the previous take was unsuccessful. Take the same approach to your test performances. If you make a mistake, consider it "take one," learn from it, and approach the next take with the mindset that you're going to improve your previous performance.

> A man who has committed a mistake and doesn't correct it is committing another mistake."
>
> —Confucius, ancient Chinese philosopher and educator

Listed below are strategies you can use to transform your test results into performance-enhancing feedback.

1. **When you get a test back, determine where you gained points and lost points.** Pinpoint what went right so you do it again, and troubleshoot what went wrong so you don't make the same mistake again. On test questions where you lost points, use the strategies summarized in **Box 6.3** to pinpoint the source of the problem.

Box 6.3

Strategies for Pinpointing the Source of Lost Points on Exams

On test questions where you lost points, identify the stage in the learning process where the breakdown occurred by asking yourself the following questions.

- Did I have the information I needed to answer the question correctly? If you didn't have the information needed to answer the question, where should you have acquired it in the first place? Was it information presented in class that didn't get into your notes? If yes, consider adopting strategies for improving your classroom listening and note-taking (such as those found on pp. 100–106). If the missing information was contained in your assigned reading, check whether you're using effective reading strategies (such as those listed on pp. 106–112).
- Did I have the information but didn't study it because I didn't think it was important? If you didn't expect the information to appear on the test, review the strategies for detecting the most important information delivered during class lectures and in reading assignments. (See strategies on pp. 103–104 and p. 108.)
- Did I study it, but didn't retain it? Not remembering information you studied may mean one of three things:
  a) You didn't learn it deeply and didn't lay down a strong enough memory trace in your brain for you to recall it at test time. This suggests you need to put in more study time or use a different study strategy to learn it more deeply. (See pp. 113–115 for specific strategies.)
  b) You may have tried to cram in too much study time just before the exam and may have not given your brain time enough to "digest" (consolidate) the information and store it in long-term memory. The solution may be to distribute your study time more evenly in advance of the next exam and take advantage of the "part-to-whole" study method. (See pp. 116–117.)

(continued)

Box 6.3 *(continued)*

c)   You studied hard and didn't cram, but you may need to study smarter or more strategically. (See strategies on pp. 116–123.)

- Did I study the material but didn't really understand it or learn it deeply? This suggests you may need to self-monitor your comprehension more carefully while studying to track whether you're truly understanding the material and moving beyond "shallow" or "surface" learning. (See pp. 123–124.)

- Did I know the material but lost points due to careless test-taking mistakes? If this happened, the solution may simply be to take more time to review your test after completing it and check for absent-minded errors before turning it in. Or, your careless errors may have resulted from test anxiety that interfered with your concentration and memory. If you think this was the factor, consider using strategies for reducing test anxiety. (See pp. 145–147.)

2. **Get feedback from your instructor.** Start by noting any written comments your instructor made on your exam; keep these comments in mind when you prepare for the next exam. You can seek additional feedback by making an appointment to speak with your instructor during office hours. Come to the appointment with a positive mindset about improving your next test performance, not complaining about your last test grade.

3. **Seek feedback from professionals in your Learning Center or Academic Support Center.** Tutors and other learning support professionals can also be excellent sources of feedback about adjustments you can make in your test-preparation and test-taking strategies. Ask these professionals to take a look at your tests and seek their advice about how to improve your test performance.

4. **Seek feedback from your classmates.** Your peers can also be a valuable source of information on how to improve your performance. You can review your test with other students in class, particularly with students who did well. Their test answers can provide you with models of what type of work your instructor expects on exams. You might also consider asking successful students what they did to be successful, such as how they prepared for the test and what they did during the test.

   Teaming up after tests and assignments *early in the term* is especially effective because it enables you to get a better idea of what the instructor will expect from students throughout the remainder of the course. You can use this information as early feedback to diagnose your initial mistakes, improve your next performance, and raise your overall course grade—while there's still plenty of time in the term to do so. (See **Box 6.4** for a summary of the type of feedback you should seek from others to best strengthen your academic performance.)

 Reflection 6.7

How would you rate your general level of test anxiety during exams? (Circle one.)

high   moderate   low

What types of tests or subjects tend to produce the most test stress or anxiety for you?

Why?

Box 6.4

Key Features of Performance-Enhancing Feedback

When asking for feedback from others on your academic performance, seek feedback that has the following performance-improvement features:

- Effective feedback is *specific.* Seek feedback that identifies precisely what you should do to improve your performance and how you should go about doing it. After a test, seek feedback that provides you with more than information about what your grade is, or why you lost points. Seek specific information about what particular adjustments you can make to improve your next performance.

- Effective feedback is *prompt.* After receiving your grade on a test or assignment, *immediately* review your performance and seek feedback as soon as possible. This is the time when you're likely most motivated to find out what you got right and wrong, and it's also the time when you're most likely to retain the feedback you receive.

- Performance-enhancing feedback is *proactive.* Seek feedback *early* in the learning process. Be sure to ask for feedback at the start of the term. This will leave you with plenty of time and opportunity to use the feedback throughout the term to accumulate points and earn a higher final grade.

Strategies for Reducing Test Anxiety

High levels of anxiety can interfere with the ability to recall information that's been studied and increases the risk of making careless concentration-related errors on exams—such as, overlooking key words in test questions (Fernández-Castillo & Caurcel, 2014; Tobias, 1993). Studies also show that students who experience high levels of test anxiety are more likely to use ineffective "surface"-level study practices that rely on memorization, rather than more effective "deep-learning" strategies that involve seeking meaning and understanding (Biggs & Tang, 2007; Ramsden, 2003). The strategies listed below can help you recognize and minimize test anxiety.

1. **Understand what test anxiety is and what it's not.** Don't confuse anxiety with stress. Stress is a physical reaction that prepares your body for action by arousing and energizing it; this heightened level of arousal and energy can actually strengthen your performance. In fact, to be totally stress-free during an exam may mean that you're too laid back and could care less about how well you're doing. Peak levels of performance—whether academic or athletic—are not achieved by completely eliminating stress. Research shows that experiencing a *moderate* level of stress (neither too high nor too low) during exams and other performance-testing situations serves to maximize alertness, concentration, and memory (Sapolsky, 2004). The key is to keep stress at a manageable level so you can capitalize on its capacity to get you pumped up or psyched up, but prevent it from reaching a level where you become stressed out or psyched out.

   If you often experience the following physical and psychological symptoms during tests, it probably means your stress level is too high and may be accurately called *test anxiety*.

   - You feel bodily symptoms of tension during the test, such as pounding heartbeat, rapid pulse, muscle tension, sweating, or a queasy stomach.
   - You have difficulty concentrating or maintaining your focus of attention while answering test questions.
   - Negative thoughts and feelings rush through your head, such as fear of failure or self-putdowns (e.g., "I always mess up on exams.")

- You rush through the test just to get it over with and get rid of the uncomfortable feelings you're experiencing.
- Even though you studied and know the material, you go blank during the exam and forget much of what you studied. However, after turning in the exam and leaving the test situation, you're often able to remember the information you were unable to recall during the exam.

2. **Use effective test-preparation strategies prior to the exam.** Test anxiety research indicates that college students who prepare well for exams and use effective study strategies prior to exams—such as those discussed in Chapter 5—experience less test anxiety during exams (Cassady & Johnson, 2002). Studies also show that there is a strong relationship between test anxiety and procrastination—that is, students who put off studying to the very last minute are more likely to report higher levels of test anxiety (Carden, Bryant, & Moss, 2004). The high level of pretest tension caused by last minute rushing to prepare for an exam often carries over to the test itself, resulting in higher levels of tension during the exam. Furthermore, late night cramming deprives the brain of stress-relieving dream (REM) sleep (Voelker, 2004), causing the sleep-deprived student to experience higher levels of anxiety the following day—the day of the test.

3. **Stay focused on the test in front of you, not the students around you.** Don't spend valuable test time looking at what others are doing and wondering whether they're doing better than you are. If you came to the test well prepared and still find the test difficult, it's very likely that other students are finding it difficult too. If you happen to notice that other students are finishing before you do, don't assume they breezed through the test or that they're smarter than you. Their faster finish may simply reflect the fact that they didn't know many of the answers and decided to give up and get out, rather than prolong the agony.

4. **During the exam, concentrate on the here and now.** Devote your attention fully to answering the test question that you're currently working on; don't spend time thinking (and worrying) about the test's outcome or what your grade will be.

5. **Focus on the answers you're getting right and the points you're earning, rather than worrying about what you're getting wrong and how many points you're losing.** Our thoughts can influence our emotions (Ellis, 2004), and positive emotions—such as those associated with optimism and a sense of accomplishment—can improve mental performance by enhancing the brain's ability to process, store, and retrieve information (Fredrickson & Branigan, 2005). One way to maintain a positive mindset is to keep in mind that college exams are often designed to be more difficult than high school tests, so it's less likely that students will get 90% to 100% of the total points. You can still achieve a good grade on a college exam without having to achieve a near-perfect test score.

6. **Don't forget that it's just a test, not a measure of your intelligence, academic ability, or self-worth.** No single exam can measure your true intellectual capacity or academic talent. In fact, the test grade you receive may not be a true indicator of how much you've actually learned. A low test grade also doesn't mean you're not capable of doing better work or destined to end up with a poor grade in the course—particularly if you adopt a "growth mindset" that views mistakes as learning opportunities (see pp. 67–69) and uses test results as feedback for improving future performance (see pp. 142–145).

"

If you focus on growth . . . on making progress instead of proving yourself, you are less likely to get depressed because you won't see setbacks and failures as reflecting your own self worth." And you are less likely to stay depressed, because feeling bad makes you want to work harder and keep striving."

—Heidi Grant Halvorson, psychologist and author of Succeed: How We Can Reach Our Goals

7. **If you continue to experience test anxiety after trying to overcome it on your own, seek assistance from a professional in your Learning (Academic Support) Center or the Counseling Center.** You can try to overcome test anxiety (or any other personal issue) through the use of self-help strategies. However, if the problem persists after you've done your best to overcome it, there's no need to keep struggling on your own; instead, it's probably time to seek help from others. This doesn't mean you're weak or incompetent; it means you have the emotional intelligence and resourcefulness to realize your limitations and capitalize on the support networks available to you.

Chapter Summary and Highlights

Effective performance on college exams involves strategies used in advance of the test, during the test, and after test results are returned. Good test performance starts with good test-preparation and awareness of the type of test questions you will be expected to answer (e.g., multiple-choice or essay). Test questions can be classified into two major categories, depending on the type of memory required to answer them: (1) *recognition* questions and (2) *recall* questions. Each of these types of questions tests your knowledge and memory in a different way.

Recognition test questions ask you to select or choose the correct answer from choices provided for you. Falling into this category are multiple-choice, true–false, and matching questions. These test questions don't require you to supply or produce the correct answer on your own; instead, you recognize or pick out the correct answer. Since recognition test questions ask you to recognize or select the correct answer from among answers provided for you, reviewing your class notes and textbook highlights may be an effective study strategy for multiple-choice and true–false test questions because it matches the type of mental activity you'll be asked to perform on the exam—which is to read test questions and look for the correct answer.

Recall test questions, on the other hand, require you to retrieve information you've studied and reproduce it on your own. This means you have to recall (re-call or "call back") the information you studied and supply it yourself. Recall test questions include essay and short answer questions; these questions don't involve answer recognition, but answer *production*—you produce the answer in writing. Studying for these types of test questions require *retrieval*—such as reciting the information without looking at it.

Effective test performance not only involves effective test-preparation strategies, but also effective test-taking strategies. For multiple-choice tests, effective test-taking strategies include using a *process-of-elimination* approach to weed out incorrect answers before identifying the best option, and *test-wise* strategies that use the wording of test questions to increase the likelihood of choosing the correct answer (e.g., choosing the longest answer and eliminating answers that contain absolute truths or broad generalizations).

Lastly, effective test performance involves carefully reviewing test results and using them as feedback to improve your future performance and final course grade. When test results are returned, determine where you earned and lost points. Pinpoint what went right so you continue doing it, and troubleshoot what went wrong so you prevent it from happening again.

Learning More through the World Wide Web: Internet-Based Resources

For additional information on strategic test-taking and managing test anxiety, see the following websites:

Test-Taking Strategies:
https://miamioh.edu/student-life/rinella-learning-center/academic-counseling/self-help/test-taking/index.html

https://www.stmarys-ca.edu/academics/academic-resources-support/student-academic-support-services/tutorial-academic-skills-8

Overcoming Test Anxiety:
http://www.studygs.net/tstprp8.htm

http://www.sic.edu/files/uploads/group/34/PDF/TestAnxiety.pdf

References

Bauer, D., Kopp, V., & Fischer, M. R. (2007). Answer changing in multiple choice assessment: change that answer when in doubt—and spread the word! *BMC Medical Education, 7*, 28–32.

Biggs, J., & Tang, C. (2007). *Teaching for quality learning at university* (3rd ed.) Buckingham: SRHE and Open University Press.

Carden, R., Bryant, C., & Moss, R. (2004). Locus of control, test anxiety, academic procrastination, and achievement among college students. *Psychological Reports, 95*(2), 581–582.

Carey, B. (2014). *How we learn.* London: Random House.

Cassady, J. C., & Johnson, R. E. (2002). Cognitive test anxiety and academic performance. *Contemporary Educational Psychology, 27*(2), 270–295.

Ellis, A. (2004). *Rational emotive behavior therapy: It works for me—It can work for you.* Amherst, NY: Prometheus Books.

Fernández-Castillo, A., & Caurcel, M. J. (2014). State test-anxiety, selective attention and concentration in university students. *International Journal of Psychology, 50*(4), 265–271.

Flippo, R. F., & Caverly, D. C. (2009). *Handbook of college reading and study strategy research* (2nd ed.). New York: Lawrence Erlbaum Associates.

Fredrickson, B. L., & Branigan, C. (2005). Positive emotions broaden the scope of attention and thought-action repertoires. *Cognition & Emotion, 19*, 313–332.

Glenberg, A. M. (1997). What memory is for. *Behavioral and Brain Sciences, 20*, 1–55.

Glenberg, A. M., Schroeder, J. L., & Robertson, D. A. (1998). Averting the gaze disengages the environment and facilitates remembering. *Memory & Cognition, 26*(4), 651–658.

Godden, D., & Baddeley, A. (1975). Context dependent memory in two natural environments. *British Journal of Psychology, 66*(3), 325–331.

Haas, R. (1994*). Eat smart, think smart.* New York: HarperCollins.

Higham, P. A., & Gerrard, C. (2005). Not all errors are created equal: Metacognition and changing answers on multiple-choice tests. *Canadian Journal of Experimental Psychology/Revue canadienne de psychologie expérimentale, 59*(1), 28.

Huck, S., & Bounds, W. (1972). Essay grades: An interaction between graders' handwriting clarity and the neatness of examination papers. *American Educational Research Journal, 9*(2), 279–283.

Hughes, D. C., Keeling, B., & Tuck, B. F. (1983). Effects of achievement expectations and handwriting quality on scoring essays. *Journal of Educational Measurement, 20*(1), 65–70.

Jensen, E. (2005). *Teaching with the brain in mind* (2nd ed.). Alexandria, VA: Association for Supervision and Curriculum Development.

Kruger, J., Wirtz, D., & Miller, D. (2005). Counterfactual thinking and the first instinct fallacy. *Journal of Personality and Social Psychology, 88*, 725–735.

Miller, M. D., Linn, R. L., & Gronlund, N. E. (2012). *Measurement and assessment in teaching* (7th ed.). Englewood Cliffs, NJ: Pearson.

National Resource Center for the First-Year Experience and Students in Transition. (2004). *The 2003 Your First College Year (YFCY) Survey.* Columbia, SC: Author.

Pai, M. R., Sanji, N., Pai, P. G. & Kotian, S. (2010). Comparative assessment in pharmacology multiple choice questions versus essay with focus on gender differences. *Journal of Clinical and Diagnostic Research* [serial online], *4*(3), 2515–2520.

Phillips, G. W. (2005). Does eating breakfast affect the performance of college students on biology exams? *Bioscene, 30*(4), 15–19.

Prinsell, C. P., Ramsey, P. H., & Ramsey, P. P. (1994). Score gains, attitudes, and behaviour changes due to answer-changing instruction. *Journal of Educational Measurement, 31*, 327–337.

Ramsden, P. (2003). *Learning to teach in higher education* (2nd ed.). London: RoutledgeFalmer.

Reed, S. K. (2013). *Cognition: Theory and applications* (3rd ed.). Belmont, CA: Wadsworth/Cengage.

Roediger, III, H. L. (2008). Relativity of remembering: Why the laws of memory vanished. *Annual Review of Psychology, 59*, 225–254.

Roediger, III, H. L., & Karpicke, J. (2006). The power of testing memory: Basic research and implications for educational practice. *Perspectives on Psychological Science, 1*(3), 181–210.

Sapolsky, R. (2004). *Why zebras don't get ulcers*. New York: W. H. Freeman.

Schab, F. R., & Crowder, R. G. (2014). *Memory for odors*. New York: Psychology Press.

Schroll, R. M. (2006). Effects of breakfast on memory retention of students at the college level. *Saint Martin's University Biology Journal, 1*, 35–50.

Smith, S., & Vela, E. (2001). Environmental context-dependent memory: A review and meta-analysis. *Psychonomic Bulletin & Review, 8*(2), 203–220.

Sprenger, M. (1999). *Learning and memory: The brain in action*. Alexandria, VA: Association for Supervision and Curriculum Development.

Thayer, R. E. (1997). *The origin of everyday moods: Managing energy, tension, and stress*. New York: Oxford University Press.

Tobias, S. (1993). *Overcoming math anxiety*. New York: W.W. Norton.

Tulving, E. (1983). *Elements of episodic memory*. Oxford: Clarendon Press/Oxford University Press.

Ueda, Y., Wang, M. F., Irei, A. V., Sarukura, N., Sakai, T., & Hsu, T. F. (2011). Effect of dietary lipids on longevity and memory in SAMP8 mice. *Journal of Nutritional Science Vitaminol, 57*(1), 36–41.

Ulus, I. H., Scally, M. C., & Wurtman, R. C. (1977). Choline potentiates the dinduction of adrenal tyrosine hydroxylase by reserpine, probably by enhancing the release of acetylcholine. *Life Sci, 21*, 145–148.

Voelker, R. (2004). Stress, sleep loss, and substance abuse create potent recipe for college depression. *Journal of the American Medical Association, 291*, 2177–2179.

Willingham, D. B. (2009). *Cognition: The thinking animal*. Upper Saddle River, NJ: Pearson.

Chapter 6 Exercises

6.1 Quote Reflections

Review the sidebar quotes contained in this chapter and select two that were especially meaningful or inspirational to you.

For each quote, provide a three- to five-sentence explanation why you chose it.

6.2 Reality Bite

Bad Feedback: Shocking Midterm Grades

Fred has enjoyed his first weeks on campus. He has met lots of people and really likes being in college. He's also very pleased to discover that, unlike high school, his college schedule doesn't require him to be in class for five to six hours per day. That's the good news. The bad news is that unlike high school, where his grades were all As and Bs, Fred's first midterm grades in college are three Cs, one D, and one F. He's stunned and a bit depressed by his midterm grades because he thought he was doing well. Since he never received grades this low in high school, he's beginning to think that he's not college material and may flunk out.

Reflection Questions

1. What factors may have caused or contributed to Fred's bad start?

2. What are Fred's options at this point?

3. What do you recommend Fred do right now to get his grades up and avoid being placed on academic probation?

4. What might Fred do in the future to prevent this midterm setback from happening again?

6.3 Self–Assessment of Test-Taking Habits and Strategies

Rate yourself in terms of how frequently you use these test-taking strategies according to the following scale:

4 = always, 3 = sometimes, 2 = rarely, 1 = never

1.	I take tests in the same seat I usually sit in to take class notes.	4	3	2	1
2.	I answer easier test questions first.	4	3	2	1
3.	I use a process-of-elimination approach on multiple-choice questions to eliminate choices until I find one that is correct or appears to be the most accurate option.	4	3	2	1
4.	Before answering essay questions, I look for key action words indicating what type of thinking I should display in my answer (e.g., "analyze," "compare").	4	3	2	1
5.	On essay questions, I outline or map out the major ideas I'll include in my answer before I start writing sentences.	4	3	2	1
6.	I look for information included on the test that may help me answer difficult questions or that may help me remember information I've forgotten.	4	3	2	1
7.	I leave extra space between my answers to essay questions in case I want to come back and add more information later.	4	3	2	1
8.	I carefully review my work, double-checking for errors and skipped questions before turning in my tests.	4	3	2	1

Self-Assessment Reflections

Which of the above strategies do you already use?

Of the ones you don't use, which one are you *most* likely to implement and *least* likely to implement? Why?

6.4 Midterm Self-Evaluation

At this point in the term, you may be experiencing the "midterm crunch"—a wave of midterm exams and due dates for assignments. This is a good time to step back and assess your academic progress.

Using the form below, list the courses you're taking this term and the grades you are currently receiving in each of these courses. If you don't know what your grade is, take a few minutes to check your syllabus for your instructor's grading policy and add up your scores on completed tests and assignments; this should give you at least a rough idea of where you stand in your courses. If you're having difficulty determining your grade in a course, even after checking your course syllabus and returned tests or assignments, ask your instructor how you could estimate your current grade.

	Course No.	Course Title	Grade
1.			
2.			
3.			
4.			
5.			

Reflection Questions

1. Were these the grades you *expected*? If not, were they better or worse than you anticipated?
2. Were these the grades you were *hoping* for? Are you pleased or disappointed?
3. Do you see any patterns in your performance that suggest what you're doing well and what you need to improve?
4. If you had to pinpoint one action you could immediately take to improve your lowest course grades, what would it be?

6.5 Calculating Your Midterm Grade Point Average

Use the information below to calculate what your grade point average (GPA) would be if your current course grades turn out to be your final grades for the term.

How to Compute Your Grade Point Average (GPA)

Most colleges and universities use a grading scale ranging from 0 to 4 to calculate a student's grade point average (GPA) or QPA (quality point average). Some schools use a grading system that involves only letters (A, B, etc.), while other institutions use letters as well as pluses and minuses (A-, B+, etc.). Check you college catalog or student handbook to determine what grading system is used at your campus.

The typical point value (points earned) by different letter grades are listed below.

Grade = Point Value

A = 4.0
A– = 3.7
B+ = 3.3
B = 3.0
B– = 2.7
C+ = 2.3
C = 2.0
C– = 1.7
D+ = 1.3
D = 1.0
D– = .7
F = 0

1. Calculate the grade points you're earning in each of your courses this term by multiplying the course's number of units (credits) by the point value of the grade you're now earning in the course. For instance, if you have a grade of B in a three-unit course, that course is earning you 9 grade points; if you have a grade of A in a two-unit course, that course is earning you 8 grade points.

2. Calculate your grade point average by using the following formula:

$$\text{GRADE POINT AVERAGE (GPA)} = \frac{\text{Total Number of Grade Points for all Courses}}{\text{Divided by Total Number of Course Units}}$$

For instance, see the fictitious example below:

Course	Units	×	Grade	=	Grade Points
Roots of Rock 'n' Roll	3	×	C (2)	=	6
Daydreaming Analysis	3	×	A (4)	=	12
Surfing Strategies	1	×	A (4)	=	4
Wilderness Survival	4	×	B (3)	=	12
Sitcom Analysis	2	×	D (1)	=	2
Love and Romance	3	×	A (4)	=	12
	16				48

$$\text{GPA} = \frac{48}{16} = 3.0$$

Reflection Questions

1. What is your GPA at this point in the term?

2. At the start of this term, was this the GPA you expected to attain? If there is a gap between the GPA you expected to achieve and the GPA you now have, what do you think accounts for this discrepancy?

3. Do you think your actual GPA at the end of the term will be higher or lower than it is now? Why?

Note: It's very typical for GPAs to be lower in college than they were in high school, particularly during the first year of college. Here are the results of one study that compared students' high school GPAs with their GPAs after their first year of college:

*   A total of 29% of beginning college students had GPAs of 3.75 or higher in high school, but only 17% had GPAs that high at the end of their first year of college.

*   A total of 46% had high school GPAs between 3.25 and 3.74, but only 32% had GPAs that high after the first year of college (National Resource Center for the First-Year Experience and Students in Transition, 2004).

Three Key Academic Success and Lifelong Learning Skills

INFORMATION LITERACY, WRITING, AND SPEAKING

Chapter Preview

Research, writing, and speaking effectively are flexible, transferable skills that can be applied to improve performance across all majors, all careers, and throughout life. In this chapter, you will acquire strategies to research and evaluate information, write papers and reports, and use writing as a learning and thinking tool. You will also learn how to make effective oral presentations, overcome speech anxiety, and gain self-confidence about speaking in public.

Learning Goal

Acquire skills for accessing and referencing ideas obtained through scholarly research, as well as strategies for effectively communicating your own ideas through writing and speaking.

 Reflection 7.1

Ignite Your Thinking

What would you say is the difference between acquiring factual knowledge and learning a transferable skill?

The Importance of Research and Communication Skills

We're now living in the "information" and "communication" age; more information is being produced, reproduced, and communicated in today's world than at any other time in human history (Cairncross, 2001; Friedman, 2005). Because information is being generated and disseminated at such a rapid rate, "information literacy"—the ability to search for, locate, and evaluate information for relevance and accuracy—has become an essential 21st-century skill for managing and making sense of the overload of information currently available to us. Oral and written communication skills have also become increasingly important for career success in today's work world. College graduates with well-developed communication skills have a clear advantage in today's job market (AAC&U, 2013; National Association of Colleges & Employers, 2014). If you dedicate yourself to improving your information literacy, writing, and speaking skills, you'll improve both your academic performance in college and your career performance beyond college.

> Employers are far more interested in the prospect's ability to think and to think clearly, to write and speak well, and how (s)he works with others than in his major or the name of the school (s)he went to. Several college investigating teams found that these were the qualities on which all kinds of employers, government and private, base their decisions."
>
> —*Lauren Pope, author,* Looking Beyond the Ivy League

Information Literacy: Research Strategies for Locating and Evaluating Information

In addition to writing assignments relating to course readings and class lectures, you're likely to be assigned research reports that require you to locate and evaluate information on your own. As noted in Chapter 2, one of the major goals of a college education is to empower students to become self-reliant, lifelong learners. One key characteristic of a self-reliant, lifelong learner is *information literacy*—the ability to locate, evaluate, and use information (National Forum on Information Literacy, 2015). When you become information literate, you become a critical consumer of information who knows where and how to find credible information whenever you need it.

Described below is a six-step process for locating, evaluating, and using information to write research papers and reports in college (and beyond). This process can also be used to research information for oral presentations and group projects.

1. Define Your Research Topic or Question

The first step in the information search process is to be sure you've selected a research topic that's acceptable to your instructor, and a topic that's neither: (a) too *narrow*, leaving you with an insufficient amount of information to write about; or (b) too *broad*, leaving you with too much information to cover. If you have any doubts about your topic's acceptability or scope, before going any further, seek feedback from your instructor or from a professional in your college library.

Note

Librarians are information literacy experts and educators. Be sure to capitalize on the one-on-one instructional support they can provide for you outside the classroom.

2. Identify Resources for Locating Information

Two major resources are available to you for locating information:

- Print resources—such as, card catalogs, published indexes, and guidebooks; and
- Online resources—such as, online card catalogs, Internet search engines, and electronic databases.

Before beginning the information search process, be sure you know what sources your instructor requires or prefers.

Different information search tools are likely to generate different types of information; therefore, it's best to rely on more than one search tool. See **Box 7.1** for a summary of key information search tools and terms.

Box 7.1

Key Information Search Tools and Terms

As you read the following list of terms, place a check mark next to each term you're familiar with, and a plus sign next to those you've use before.

Abstract: a concise summary of the source's content, usually appearing at the beginning of an article; this information can help you decide quickly whether the source is relevant to your research topic.

Catalog: a library database containing information about what information sources the library owns and where they're located. Most catalogs are now in electronic form and can be searched by typing in a topic heading, author, or keyword.

Box 7.1 *(continued)*

Citation: a reference to an information source (e.g., book, article, or web page) that provides enough information to allow the reader to retrieve the source. Citations used in a college research paper must be presented in a standard format, such as APA or MLA format. (For further details, see p. 159.)

Database: a collection of data (information) that's been organized to make it easily accessible and retrievable. A database may include:

a) *reference citations*—such as, author, date, and publication source,

b) *abstracts*—summary of the contents of a scholarly article,

c) *full-length documents*, or

d) a combination of (a), (b), and (c).

Descriptor (a.k.a. Subject Heading): a key word or phrase in the index of a database (card or catalog) describing the subjects or content areas found within it, enabling you to quickly locate sources relevant to your research topic. For example, "emotional disorders" may be a descriptor for a psychology database that enables you to find information related to anxiety and depression. (Some descriptors or subject headings are accompanied by suggestions for using different search words to explore the topic you're investigating.)

Index: an alphabetical listing of topics contained in a database.

Keyword: a word used to search multiple databases that matches the search word to information found in different databases. A keyword is very specific; information relating to your topic that doesn't exactly match the key word isn't likely to be retrieved. For example, if the key word is "college," it may not supply you with potentially useful sources that have "university" instead of "college" in their titles.

Search Engine: a computer-run program that allows you to search for information across the entire Internet or at a particular website. For regularly updated summaries of different electronic search engines, how they work, and the type of information they generate, check: "search enginewatch.com/reports" and "researchbuzz.com."

Search Thesaurus: a list of words or phrases with similar meaning, allowing you to identify which of these words or phrases to use as key words, descriptors, or subject headings in the database. This feature enables you to choose the best search terms before beginning the search process.

Subscription Database: a database that can only be accessed with a paid subscription. You may be able to access many of these databases at no personal cost because your college or university library has subscribed to them.

URL (Uniform Resource Locator): an Internet address consisting of a series of letters and/or numbers that pinpoints the exact location of an information resource (e.g., http://www. thrivingincollege.com).

Wildcard: a symbol, such as an asterisk (*), question mark (?), or exclamation point (!), that can be used to substitute different letters into a search word or phrase, allowing an electronic search to be performed on all variations of the word represented by the symbol. For example, an asterisk at the end of the key word, *econom*, may be used to search all information sources containing the words "economy," "economical," or "economist."

Source: Hacker & Fister (2014)

For a more extensive glossary of Internet terms, see: Matisse's Glossary of Internet Terms at http://www. matisse.net/files/glossary.html.

 Reflection 7.2

Look back at the terms listed in **Box 7.1**. What terms were already familiar to you? Which of these tools have you used before?

When you locate a source, your first step is to evaluate its relevance to your paper's topic. One strategy for efficiently determining the relevance of a source is to ask if it will help you answer at least one or more of the following questions about your topic: Who? What? When? Where? Why? How?

3. Evaluate the Credibility and Quality of Your Sources

The primary purpose of searching for sources is to seek *documentation*—references you will use to support or confirm your conclusions. Since sources of information can vary widely in terms of their accuracy and quality, you need to think critically and make sound judgments to determine which of them are valid and reputable. The Internet has made this judgment process more challenging because most of its posted information is "self-published" and not subjected to the same quality control measures as information published in professional journals and books—which go public only after they're reviewed by a neutral panel of experts and carefully edited by professional editors. Listed below are criteria you can use to critically evaluate the sources you locate.

Credibility: Is the source written by an authority or expert in the field (e.g., someone with an advanced educational degree or professional experience relating to the topic)? For example, if your topic relates to an international issue, a highly credible source would be an author who has an advanced degree in international relations, or extensive professional experience in international affairs.

Scholarly: Does the information appear in a scholarly publication that's been reviewed by a panel or board of impartial experts in the field? Scholarly publications are written in a formal style that include references to other published sources, and they're "peer reviewed" or "peer refereed," meaning that they've been evaluated and approved for publication by other experts in the field. Professional journals are peer reviewed (e.g., *New England Journal of Medicine*) but not popular magazines (e.g., *Newsweek*) or popular websites (e.g., Wikipedia.org). Subscription databases accessible through your college or university library are more likely to contain peer-reviewed sources than free databases available to you on the world wide web. You may, however, use websites like "Google Scholar" (scholar.google.com) to find some scholarly sources that can be accessed for free.

Note

Wikipedia isn't considered to be a scholarly source, but you can track down scholarly references mentioned at this site, read them, and cite them in your report.

Currency: Has the source been published or posted recently? In certain fields of study, such as science and technology, recent references may be strongly preferred because new data is generated rapidly in these fields and information can become quickly outdated. In other fields, such as history and philosophy, older references may be viewed as classics, and citing them is perfectly acceptable. If you're not sure if current references are strongly preferred, check with your instructor before you begin the search process.

Objectivity: Is the author likely to be impartial or unbiased toward the subject? Consider how the professional position or personal background of authors may influence their ideas or their interpretation of evidence. Scholars should be impartial and objective in their pursuit of truth; they should not be in a position to gain fiscally, personally, or politically by drawing a certain conclusion about their topic of investigation. You should always be skeptical about the objectivity of web-based information sources whose address ends with ".com" because these are "com"mercial sites whose primary purpose is to sell products and make money, not to educate the public and engage in the objective pursuit of truth. To assess the objectivity of websites, always ask yourself why the site was created, what its objective or purpose is, and who sponsors it.

Even scientific research may lack objectivity. For instance, if you find an article on climate change written by scientists who work for or with an industry that risks incurring costs or losing revenue by switching to a more ecologically efficient source of energy, it would be reasonable to suspect that these researchers have a conflict of interest and may be biased toward reaching a conclusion that will benefit their employer (and themselves). When evaluating an article, ask yourself the following questions to check for bias: (a) Is the author a member of a special interest group or organization that could affect the article's objectivity? (b) Does the author consider alternative or opposing viewpoints, and deal with those viewpoints fairly? (c) Does the author use words that convey rationality and objectivity, or are they characterized by emotionality and an inflammatory tone?

If you think an article may lack complete objectivity, but still find that it's well written and contains good information or arguments, you can cite it in your paper. However, be sure you demonstrate critical thinking by noting that its conclusions may have been biased by the author's background or position.

4. Include a Sufficient Quantity and Variety of Sources

The quality of your research will be judged on the credibility of your sources as well as their number and variety.

Have you cited a sufficient number of references? As a general rule, it's better to include a larger than smaller set of references because it provides your paper with a broader base of support and a wider range of perspectives. In addition, using multiple sources allows you to demonstrate the higher-level thinking skill of synthesis—the ability to integrate information from numerous sources.

Have you used different *types* of sources? For some research reports, the variety of references cited may be as important as their sheer quantity. You can intentionally vary your sources by drawing on different types of references, such as:

- Books
- Scholarly journals—written by professionals and research scholars in the field
- News magazine and newspaper articles—written by journalists
- Course readings and class notes
- Personal interviews and personal experiences.

You can also vary your references by using both (a) *primary* sources—firsthand information or original documents (e.g., research experiments or novels), and (b) *secondary* sources—publications that build on or respond to primary sources (e.g., textbook or newspaper articles that critically review a novel or movie).

Lastly, you can vary your references by blending older, classic sources with newer, cutting-edge references. This combination will enable you to demonstrate how certain ideas have changed or evolved over time.

5. Use Your Sources as Stepping Stones to Your Own Ideas and Conclusions

It's your name that appears on the front cover of your research report, so it should be something more than an accumulation or amalgamation of other peoples' ideas. Simply collecting and compiling the ideas of others will result in a final product that reads more like a high school book report than a college research paper. Look at your sources as raw material you shape into a finished product that has your stamp on it. Don't just report or describe information drawn from other sources; instead, react to the information you cite, interpret it, and use it as evidence to support your own interpretations and conclusions.

6. Cite Your Sources with Integrity

College students with integrity don't cheat on exams and then rationalize that their cheating is acceptable because "others are doing it," nor do they plagiarize the work of others and pawn it off as their own. By accurately citing and referencing your sources, you demonstrate intellectual honesty by giving credit where credit is due. You credit others whose ideas you've borrowed and you credit yourself for the careful research you've done.

When should sources be cited? Simply put: You must cite anything included in your paper that was obtained from a source other than yourself. This includes other people's words, ideas, statistics, research findings, and visual work (e.g., diagrams, pictures, or drawings). There's only one exception to this rule: Information that's *common knowledge*—that is, information most people already know does not have to be cited. Common knowledge includes things like well-known facts (e.g., the earth is the third planet from the sun) and familiar dates (e.g., the Declaration of Independence was signed in 1776).

The Internet has given us easy access to an extraordinary amount of information and has made research much easier—that's the good news. The bad news is that it has also made proper citation more challenging. Determining the true "owner" or original author of posted information isn't as clear cut as it is for published books and articles. If you can't find the name of an author, at least cite the website, the date of the posted information (if available), and the date you accessed or downloaded it. If you have any doubt about an online source, print it out and check it out with your instructor or a professional librarian.

Note

*As a general rule, if you're unsure about whether a source should be cited, it's better to cite it and risk being corrected for over-citing than it is to run the risk of being accused of plagiarism— a serious violation of academic integrity that can have grave consequences. (See **Box 7.2** on p. 159 for specific details about what constitutes or defines plagiarism and specific ways to avoid it.)*

Where and how should sources be cited? Your sources should be cited in two places: (a) the *body* of your paper, and (b) the *reference section* at the end of your paper (also known as a "bibliography" or "works cited" section). How your sources should be cited depends on the referencing style of the particular academic field or discipline in which you are writing your paper, so be sure you know the citation style your instructor prefers. It's likely you will be expected to use either (or both) of two referencing styles in college:

> "When a student violates an academic integrity policy, no one wins, even if the person gets away with it. It isn't right to cheat and it is an insult to everyone who put the effort in and did the work. I learned my lesson and have no intention of ever cheating again."
>
> —First-year college student's reflection on an academic integrity violation

- *MLA* style—the style adopted by the Modern Language Association—which is commonly used in the Humanities and Fine Arts (e.g., English and Music); or
- *APA* style—the style adopted by the American Psychological Association—which is most commonly used in the Social and Natural Sciences (e.g., Sociology and Anthropology), and is the style used in this book.

You may be asked to use other styles in advanced courses in specialized fields, such as *The Chicago Manual of Style* for papers in history, or the Council of Biology Editors (CBE) style for papers in the biological sciences. Software programs are now available that automatically format references according to a particular citation style, such as CiteFast (www.citefast.com) and EasyBib (www.easybib.com). If you use these programs, be sure to proofread the results because they can sometimes generate inaccurate or incomplete citations (Hacker & Fister, 2014).

> Although it may seem like a pain to write a works cited page, it is something that is necessary when writing a research paper. You must acknowledge every single author of whose information you used. The authors spent much time and energy writing their book or article [so] you must give them the credit that they deserve."
>
> —*First-year student's reflection on a plagiarism violation*

Reflection 7.3

Prior to college, did you write papers that required citation of references? If yes, do you know what referencing style you used?

Box 7.2

Plagiarism: A Violation of Academic Integrity

What Exactly Is Plagiarism?

Plagiarism is a violation of academic integrity that involves intentional or unintentional use of someone else's work without acknowledging it, which gives the reader the impression that it's your own work.

Common Forms of Plagiarism

1. Paying someone, or paying a service, for a paper and turning it in as your own work.
2. Submitting an entire paper, or portion thereof, that was written by someone else.
3. Copying sections of someone else's work and inserting it into your own work.
4. Cutting paragraphs from separate sources and pasting them into the body of your own paper.
5. Paraphrasing or rewording someone else's words or ideas without citing that person as a source. (Good strategies for paraphrasing without plagiarizing may be found at: http://www.upenn.edu/academic integrity/ai_paraphrasing.html.)
6. Placing someone else's exact words in the body of your paper and not placing quotation marks around them.

7. Failing to cite the source of factual information in your paper that's not common knowledge.

Good examples of different forms of plagiarism may be found at: http://www.princeton.edu/pr/pub/integrity/pages/plagiarism/

Final Notes:
- If you include information in your paper and just list its source in your reference (works cited) section—without citing the source in the *body* of your paper—this still qualifies as plagiarism.
- Be sure only to include sources in your reference section that you actually used and cited in the body of your paper. Although including sources in your reference section that aren't cited in your paper isn't technically a form of plagiarism, it may be viewed as being deceitful because you're "padding" your reference section, giving the reader the impression that you incorporated more sources into your paper than you actually did.

Sources: Academic Integrity at Princeton (2011); Purdue University Online Writing Lab (2015)

 **Reflection 7.4**

Reflect back at the different forms of plagiarism described in **Box 7.2**. Were there any you were surprised to see, or didn't realize was a form of plagiarism?

Writing Skills and Strategies

The Power of Writing

Writing is a versatile academic skill that can be used to strengthen your performance across the curriculum, including general education courses and courses in your major. It's the primary route through which you will communicate your knowledge and the quality of your thinking. No matter how many great ideas you have in your head, if you can't get those ideas out of your head and onto paper, you'll never receive full credit for them in college courses that will require you to write. Improving your writing will not only improve your written communication skills, it will enable you to better demonstrate your knowledge and elevate your course grades.

In addition to strengthening your academic performance in college, your ability to write clearly, concisely, and persuasively will promote your professional success beyond college. When college alumni were asked about what professional skills they were using in the workplace, more than 90% of them ranked "need to write effectively" as a skill that was of "great importance" to their current work (Worth, cited in Light, 2001). In fact, the letter of application (cover letter) you write to apply for employment positions after college graduation is likely to be the first impression you'll make on a potential employer. Thus, a well-written letter of application may be your first step toward converting your college degree into your first career position.

> "Want one more reason for developing strong writing skills? *Money.* Good writing skills are consistently one of the most sought-after skills by employers."
>
> *—Karen Brooks, career development specialist and author,* You Majored in What? Mapping Your Path From Chaos to Career

Note

Strengthening your writing skills will strengthen your academic performance throughout college and your professional performance throughout all stages of your career.

Writing to Learn

As mentioned in Chapter 1, humans learn most effectively when they're actively involved in the learning experience and when they reflect on that experience after it has taken place. Writing is a powerful tool for helping you reflect on and learn from any experience, inside or outside the classroom. Research shows that writing is positively related to deep learning and personal development (National Survey of Student Engagement, 2008).

Scholars have coined the term "writing to learn" to capture the idea that writing is not just a communication skill learned in English composition classes, but also a learning strategy that can deepen understanding of any academic subject or life experience (Ackerman, 1993; Applebee, 1984; Elbow, 1973; Zinnser, 1993). Just as you can learn to be a better writer, you can write to be a better learner.

Writing-to-learn strategies differ from traditional writing assignments, such as essays or term papers, in two key ways:

1. They're shorter—requiring less amount of time to complete.
2. They're written primarily for the benefit of the writer—to stimulate thinking and learning (Tchudi, 1986; Tynjälä, Mason, & Lonka, 2012).

Writing-to-learn strategies can be used for a wide range of learning tasks and purposes, such as those listed below. As you read the following list, place a check mark next to any strategy you rarely or never use.

1. Writing to Listen

Writing can improve your attention and listening skills during classroom lectures, study group sessions, or office visits with your instructors. Writing requires physical action, essentially forcing you to focus attention on your own thoughts and activate your thinking. For instance, immediately after each class session, you could write a "one-minute paper" (that only takes a minute or less to complete) to assess whether you've actively listened to and grasped the most important message delivered in class that day (e.g., "What was the most significant concept I learned in class today?" or, "What was the most confusing thing discussed in today's class that I should ask my instructor to clarify?").

2. Writing to Read

Just as writing can promote active listening in class, it can also promote active reading outside of class. Taking notes on *what* you're reading while you're reading implements the effective learning principle of active involvement because it requires more mental and physical energy than merely reading and highlighting sentences.

3. Writing to Remember

Afraid you'll forget a great idea or to do something that's really important? As you already know, the best way to prevent this from happening is to write it down! Writing lists or memos to yourself is an old-fashion but sure-fire way not to forget things you want to remember. When you've recorded an idea in print, you've created a permanent record of it that will enable you to access it and review it at any time. Furthermore, the act of writing itself creates motor (muscle) memory for the information you're writing, which enables you to better retain and retrieve the information you've written. Writing also improves memory by allowing you to *see* the information you're trying to remember, which registers it in your brain as a visual memory trace.

> "
> I would advise you to read with a pen in your hand, and enter in a little book of short hints of what you find that is curious, or that might be useful; for this will be the best method of imprinting such particulars in your memory, where they will be ready."
>
> *—Benjamin Franklin, 18th-century inventor, politician, and co-signer of the Declaration of Independence*

AUTHOR'S EXPERIENCE

Whenever I have trouble remembering the spelling of a word, I take a pen or pencil and start to write the word out. I'm surprised by how many times the correct spelling comes back to my mind once I begin writing the word. The more I think about it, this memory "flashback" probably happens because when I start using the muscles in my hand to write the word, it activates "muscle memories" in my brain from previous times when I wrote the word with its correct spelling.

—Joe Cuseo

4. Writing to Organize

Writing summaries and outlines, or writing ideas on index cards that relate to the same concept, are effective ways of organizing information you're trying to learn. These forms of writing also require synthesis, which is a higher-level thinking skill.

5. Writing to Study

Writing study guides or practice answers to potential test questions is an effective learning strategy that can be used while studying alone or preparing to study in groups. It's a particularly effective way to prepare for essay tests because it enables you to study in a way that closely matches what you'll be expected to do on the test, which is to write out answers to test questions.

6. Writing to Understand

Paraphrasing or restating what you're learning by writing it in your own words is an effective way to provide yourself with feedback about whether you're truly understanding it (not just memorizing it)—because you're transforming what you are learning into words that are meaningful to you. In addition, writing slows down the thinking process, making it more deliberate, systematic, and attentive to specific details. Lastly, writing leaves you with a tangible product of your thinking that can be viewed, reviewed, and used as feedback to further improve the quality of your thoughts (Applebee, 1984; Langer & Applebee, 2007). In other words, writing allows you to "think out loud on paper" (Bean, 2003, p. 102).

7. Writing to Create

Writing can also trigger discovery of new ideas that come to mind *during* the act of writing itself. Writing isn't just the end result or final product of thinking; it's also a means or process of stimulating thinking.

Creative ideas can be generated through *freewriting*—a process whereby you quickly jot down free-flowing thoughts on paper, without worrying about spelling and grammar. Freewriting can be used as a warm-up exercise to help you generate ideas for a research topic, to keep track of original ideas that emerge during group brainstorming, or to record creative ideas that suddenly pop into mind at unexpected times.

8. Writing to Discuss

Prior to participating in class discussions or small group work, you can gather your thoughts in writing before expressing them orally. This will ensure that you've carefully reflected on your ideas, which, in turn, should improve the quality of ideas you contribute. Gathering your thoughts in writing before speaking will also make you a less anxious, more confident speaker because you have a good idea about what you're going to say before you start saying it. Furthermore, your written notes can give you a script to build on, or fall back on, in case you experience speech anxiety (or memory loss) while expressing your ideas.

9. Writing for Problem Solving

Writing can be used to capture your thought process while solving problems in math and science. By writing down the thoughts going through your head at each major step in the problem-solving process, you become more self-aware of how your thinking progresses. Plus, you're left with a written record of your train of thought, which can be reviewed later to help you remember the path of thought that you took to solve the problem successfully. You can use this knowledge to repeat the same thought process to solve similar problems in the future.

Try to get into the habit of periodically stepping back to reflect on your thinking process. Reflect on what type of thinking you're using (e.g., analysis, synthesis, or evaluation) and record your reflections in writing. You could even keep a "thinking log" or "thinking journal" to increase self-awareness of the thinking skills and strategies you're developing. (These thinking skills can also be listed on your resume and mentioned in job interviews.)

"I write to understand as much as to be understood."

—*Elie Wiesel, world-famous American novelist, Nobel Prize winner, and Holocaust survivor*

"There is in writing the constant joy of sudden discovery, of happy accident."

—*H. L. Mencken, 20th-century American journalist and social critic*

"There are some kinds of writing that you have to do very fast, like riding a bicycle on a tightrope."

—*William Faulkner, Nobel Prize-winning author*

Reflection 7.5

Which of the above-listed writing activities have you done? For those you haven't tried, which one would be the most beneficial for you to start doing now? Why?

Writing Papers and Reports

Studies show that only a small percentage of high school students engage in writing assignments that are as lengthy and challenging as those required in college. Most high school writing assignments involve summaries or descriptive reports, whereas in college, students are expected to engage in expository (persuasive) writing that requires them to express ideas and prove a point by supporting it with compelling evidence (The University of Texas at El Paso, 2008).

Reflection 7.6

Reflect back on your writing assignments in high school experience.

a) What was the longest paper you wrote?

b) What types of thinking were you usually asked to demonstrate in your writing assignments (e.g., summarize, analyze, or criticize)?

Writing lengthy papers almost always take more time than you think it will; it's a multistage process that cannot be completed in one night. Breaking down the writing task into separate stages and completing these stages in advance of the paper's due date is an effective way to strengthen the quality of your final product (Boice, 1994). These stages include:

- Knowing your writing goal or purpose
- Generating ideas to write about
- Organizing your ideas into major categories

©Kendall Hunt Publishing Company

Dividing large writing assignments into smaller, manageable steps can reduce late-night frustration and the risk of permanent computer damage.

- Ordering your categories of ideas into a logical sequence
- Expressing your ideas in the form of well-written sentences and paragraphs
- Revising your writing after editing and proofreading

What follows is a systematic, 10-step process for completing these stages. Following this stepwise process should make your writing of papers and reports more manageable, less stressful, and more successful.

1. **Know the purpose of the writing assignment.** The critical first step in the process of writing an effective paper is having a clear understanding of its purpose or goal. This will help you stay on track and moving in the right direction. It also helps you get going in the first place, because one of the major causes of writer's block and writer procrastination is uncertainty about the goal or purpose of the writing task (Knaus, 2010).

   Before you start writing anything, be sure you have a clear understanding of your instructor's expectations. You can do this by asking yourself these three questions about the writing assignment:

   - What is the major objective or intended outcome of this assignment?
   - What type of thinking am I being asked to demonstrate?
   - What criteria (standards) will my instructor use to evaluate and grade my performance?

2. **Focus first on generating ideas.** In the initial stages of the writing process, the only thing you should be concerned about is getting ideas you have in your head out of your head and on to paper. Don't worry about how well the ideas are written. Writing scholars refer to this process as *focused freewriting*—you write freely for a certain period just to come up with ideas—not to write complete, eloquent, and grammatically correct sentences (Bean, 2011). Beginning first by just generating ideas can jump-start the writing process and enable you to overcome writer's block (Zinsser, 1993). The simple act of writing down your thoughts can, in itself, stimulate additional thoughts. If you're not sure what ideas you have, start writing because it will activate ideas, which, in turn, will lead to new ideas. (Sometimes, changing your writing environment or format can also stimulate production of new ideas, such as shifting to a new location or shifting from writing ideas in pen or pencil to typing them on your computer.)

3. **Categorize your ideas.** After you've completed generating ideas, the next step is to sort them out and figure out how they can be pieced together. This organizational process involves two key sub-steps.

   - Group together ideas relating to the same point or concept. For instance, if your topic is terrorism and you find three ideas on your list referring to what motivates terrorists, group those ideas together under the category of "motivational causes." Similarly, if you find ideas on your list that relate to preventing or deterring terrorism, group those ideas under the category of "potential solutions." Consider recording separate ideas on sticky notes and placing sticky notes containing specific ideas relating to the same general category on separate index cards. You can then arrange and rearrange the cards until you find an order that works best—which will lead you to the step below.
   - Arrange your categories of ideas in an order that flows smoothly and logically from start to finish. Try to come up with a sequence that has a meaningful beginning, middle, and end. Index cards come in handy when trying to find the best progression of your major ideas because the cards can be ar-

> "Begin with the end in mind."
> —*Stephen Covey*, The Seven Habits of Highly Effective People

> "A writer is not so much someone who has something to say as he is someone who has found a process that will bring about new things he would not have thought of if he had not started to say [write] them."
> —*William Stafford, American author and recipient of the National Book Award for Poetry*

ranged and rearranged easily until you discover an order that produces the smoothest, most logical sequence. Your sequence of index cards can also be used to create an outline for your paper that contains all its major categories of ideas and the order in which they'll appear in your paper.

AUTHOR'S EXPERIENCE

When I wrote this chapter, I began by writing down ideas on separate pieces of paper. Second, I took pieces of paper relating to the same general category (e.g., information literacy or writing), and put them into separate piles. Third, I took the piles of general categories and broke them into smaller piles of sub-categories (e.g., piles relating to different stages of the writing process). Fourth, I arranged the piles in an order or sequence that seemed to flow logically from start to finish.

Some of this sorting and ordering was done while I was sitting at a table in a Chicago airport. A gentleman at a nearby table caught my eye and said: "I see you're organizing all your receipts." I responded: "Actually, I'm organizing all my ideas."

—Joe Cuseo

Another effective way to organize and sequence ideas is by arranging them in a drawing or diagram. When ideas are laid out in such a visual-spatial format, the product is referred to as a "concept map" or "graphic organizer." **Figure 7.1** illustrates a concept map that organizes the main ideas related to higher-level thinking—a topic covered in Chapter 8. This type of concept map is known as a "clock map" because its main ideas are organized like the numbers of a clock that begins at the top and moves sequentially in a clockwise direction. Concept maps can be created in any pattern that works well for the material you're trying to organize and sequence. (To see a variety of concept-mapping formats and apps, go to: *www.graphic.org/concept.html*)

FIGURE 7.1: Concept Map Used to Organize and Sequence Major Ideas Relating to Higher-Level Thinking

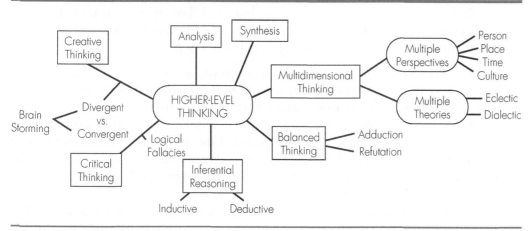

©Kendall Hunt Publishing Company

4. **Write a first draft of your paper that focuses on expressing your main ideas in a logical sequence of paragraphs.** The previous steps in the writing process are often referred to as *prewriting* because they focus on generating and organizing ideas before they're put into complete sentences (Murray, 2004). In your *first draft*, you begin the actual writing process by converting your major ideas into sentences. The purpose of this first draft is to simply "talk through"

your key ideas on paper. In later drafts, you will convert this informal writing into more formal and polished prose.

Your first draft should transform your major ideas into paragraphs that are arranged in a smooth and logical sequence. Here are some strategies for doing so.

- Use the first section of the paper to provide a meaningful introduction, overview, or preview of the major points you'll make in the remainder (body) of the paper. Your opening paragraph is critical because it shapes the reader's first impression and sets the stage for what will follow. Your opening paragraph should include a *thesis statement*—a short summary (one to three sentences) of the key point you intend to make or the central question you will answer in the body of your paper. In short, a thesis statement answers the following question about your paper: "What's your point?" It's the compass that guides your thinking and guides the reader's thinking throughout the paper, keeping you both on the same page and moving in the right direction toward the same destination (your conclusion).
- Keep ideas relating to different points in different paragraphs. A paragraph should represent a chain of sentences that are linked to the same thought or idea. If you shift to a new idea, shift to a new paragraph.
- Whenever possible, start new paragraphs with a *topic sentence* that introduces the new idea you're about to make and connects it to the major point being made in your paper—your thesis statement. Topic sentences help bring coherence to your paper by showing the reader how separate paragraphs relate to your central idea (your thesis).
- Use the final paragraph (or two) of your paper to "tie it altogether" and finish strong; drive home your key point with the major evidence you've gathered to support it.

After all your paragraphs have been written, your paper should have three identifiable parts:

a) *Introduction*—an opening section that includes your thesis statement.
b) *Body*—a series of paragraphs that follows and flows from your introduction.
c) *Conclusion*—a final section that summarizes your major points and relates them to the thesis statement in your introduction.

5. **Write more than one draft.** Don't expect to write a perfect draft of your paper on the first try. Even professional writers report that it takes them more than one draft (often three or four) before they produce their final draft. Although the final product of award-winning writers may seem impeccably written, what preceded it was a messy process that included lots of revisions between the first try and the final product (Bean, 2011). Just as actors and actresses need multiple takes (take 2, take 3, etc.) to get their spoken lines right, so do writers need multiple takes (drafts) to get their written lines right.

After you've completed your first draft, step away from it for a while. Return to it later with a fresh mind and new eyes that look to improve your product in the next draft. In particular, review your thesis statement to be sure that it still serves as an accurate compass for the direction your paper has taken. It's okay to go back and tweak your original thesis statement to more closely match the conclusion in your final draft (Bean, 2011). However, if you find yourself radically changing your thesis statement, this suggests you strayed too far from it and may need to replace it with one that aligns more directly with the body of your paper, or make changes in the body of the paper so it aligns more closely with your original thesis statement.

> "You don't write because you want to say something, you write because you have something to say."
>
> —F. Scott Fitzgerald, renowned novelist and author of The Great Gatsby

> "I'm not a writer; I'm a rewriter."
>
> —James Thurber, award-winning American journalist and author

6. **Critically review your own writing.** After you have completed at least two drafts of your paper and created what looks like a final product, take a look at it from a different perspective—as reader and editor, rather than writer. It's noteworthy that the term "revision" literally means to re-vision (view again). At this stage in the process, you're re-viewing your writing as if the words were written by someone else and your role now is to be a critic. If you find words and sentences that aren't clearly capturing or reflecting what you intended to say, this is the stage in the writing process to make major revisions. (Make sure your paper is double-spaced so that you have enough room for making changes and additions.)

When critiquing and editing your paper, use the same criteria (judgment standards) your instructor is likely to use. If your instructor has shared these criteria with the class, use them to critique and improve your paper. Your paper will probably be evaluated with respect to the following features, so keep them in mind when critiquing your work.

- **Documentation.** Are all of your paper's major points and final conclusions supported by evidence—such as:
  a) direct quotes from authoritative sources,
  b) specific examples,
  c) statistical data,
  d) scientific research findings, or
  e) firsthand experiences?

- **Overall Organization.** Take a panoramic or aerial view of your paper to see if you can clearly identify its three major parts: the beginning (introduction), the middle (body), and the end (conclusion). Do these three parts unite to form a connected whole? Also, check to be sure there's *continuity* from one paragraph to the next throughout your paper: Does your train of thought stay on track from start to finish? If you find yourself getting off track at certain points in your paper, eliminate that information or rewrite it in a way that re-routes your thoughts back onto its main track (your thesis statement).

- **Sentence Structure.** Refine and fine tune your sentences. Keep an eye out for *sentence fragments*—"sentences" missing either a noun or a verb—and *run-on sentences*—two sentences that are not separated by a period or conjunction (e.g., "and" or "but").

  Check for sentences that are too long—rambling sentences that go on and on without any punctuation, leaving readers without time to pause and catch their breath. If you find long-winded sentences, (a) punctuate them with a comma to give the reader a short pause, (b) punctuate them with a semicolon (;) to provide a longer pause than a comma (but not as long as a period), or (c) divide them into two shorter sentences (separated by a period).

  Also, check for *choppy sentences* that "chop up" what you've written into such short segments that it disrupts the natural rhythm of reading, forcing the reader to stop and restart. If you find choppy sentences in your writing, combine them to form larger sentence, and, if necessary, punctuate them with a comma or semicolon—instead of a period.

  A good strategy for helping you determine if your sentences flow smoothly is to read them aloud. Note the places where you naturally tend to pause and where you tend to keep going. Your natural pauses may serve as cues for places where your sentences need punctuation, and your natural runs may indicate sentences that are flowing smoothly and should be left alone.

- **Word Selection.** Are certain words or terms showing up so frequently in your paper that they sound repetitious? If you find any, replace the redundancy with variety by substituting words that have the same or similar meaning. This substitution process can be made easier by using a thesaurus, which may be conveniently available on your computer's word processing program.

7. **Seek feedback on your writing from a trusted peer or writing professional.** You should be the first reader of your paper, but you don't have to be the only reader before it's formally submitted and graded. No matter how honest or objective we try to be about our own writing, we may still be blind to its weaknesses. We all have a tendency to see what we hope or want to see in our work, especially after we've put a great deal of time, effort, and energy into the process of creating it. Consider getting a second opinion on your paper by seeking feedback from a trusted friend or a tutor in the Writing or Learning Center. This isn't cheating or plagiarism—as long as it's you who makes the changes and does the re-writing in response to the feedback you've received.

   You can seek feedback at any stage of the writing process—whether it be for help with understanding the assignment, brainstorming ideas, writing a first draft, or reviewing your final draft. Seeking help from the Writing or Learning Center is not just for students experiencing writing problems or writer's block. If you're already a good writer, the quality of your written work can get even better by seeking and receiving feedback from others. Even professional writers share their drafts with other writers to obtain feedback at different stages in the writing process (Leahy, 1990).

   Consider pairing up with a writing partner to exchange and assess each other's papers by using the same criteria your instructor will use to evaluate and grade your work. Studies show that when students at all levels of writing ability receive feedback from others prior to submitting a paper, the quality of their writing improves, as does their grade on the writing assignment (Patchan, Charney, & Schunn, 2009; Thompson, 1981).

8. **In your final draft, be sure that your conclusion and introduction are connected or aligned.** The most important component of your conclusion involves revisiting or restating your initial thesis and answering the question you originally posed in your introduction. Connecting your thesis statement and concluding statement provides a pair of meaningful bookends to your paper, anchoring it at its two most pivotal points: beginning and end. Making this connection ensures you've ended up at the destination you planned to reach when you started out. It also enables you to maximize the power of the two most important impressions your paper can make on the reader: the *first* impression and the *last* impression.

9. **Carefully proofread your paper for clerical and technical mistakes before submitting it.** Proofreading is the critical last step in the editorial process. It's a step that's essential for catching small, technical errors that were likely overlooked during earlier stages of the writing process—when your attention was focused on the paper's content and organization. Proofreading may be viewed as a micro form of editing, during which you shift the focus of your editorial attention to minute mechanics related to referencing, grammar, punctuation, and spelling.

   Don't forget that your computer's spell-checker may not catch words that are actually incorrectly spelled in the context you're using them. For instance, a spell-checker wouldn't detect the fact that there are five "correctly" spelled words that are actually misspellings in the context of the following sentence: "*Where you're* high-*heal* shoes when we *meat* for the executive *bored* meeting."

> "
> End with the beginning in mind."
>
> —*Joe Cuseo, non-award-winning author of the book you're now reading*

(A career counselor once reported that a student forgot to proofread her job application before submitting it; her roommate read it and laughingly noticed that she mistakenly applied for a job in "pubic service" instead of public service [Brooks, 2009].)

Note

Careful proofreading represents the last important step in the process of writing a high-quality paper. To skip this simple, final step and lose points on something you spent so much time creating would be a crying shame.

10. **After your paper is graded and returned to you, carefully review your instructor's written comments.** Some things you can only learn *after* receiving feedback about your performance. Use your instructor's comments as constructive feedback to improve your performance on future assignments. If the instructor didn't provide sufficient feedback and you're still unclear about what to do to improve your work, make an appointment for an office visit. If your instructor is willing to meet with you during office hours and review your paper with you, take full advantage of this opportunity. Besides receiving personalized feedback that can improve your future writing, your office visit sends a clear message to the instructor that you're a student who is serious about learning and achieving academic excellence.

> Spell checkers aren't always reliable, so ask someone for suggestions or read papers out loud to yourself."
>
> —*Advice to first-year students from a college sophomore*

Public Speaking: Making Oral Presentations and Delivering Speeches

The Importance of Oral Communication

In addition to writing, the second major channel you'll use in college to communicate your ideas and knowledge is speaking—whether it be raising your hand and speaking up in class, participating in small group discussions, or making formal presentations individually or as part of a group presentation. When graduating seniors at Harvard University were asked about what specific strategies they would recommend to first-year students for overcoming shyness and developing social self-confidence, their most frequent recommendation was to take classes in which you are expected to speak up (Light, 1992).

Developing your ability to speak in a clear, concise, and confident manner will strengthen your academic performance in college and your career performance after college. The oral communication skills you display during job interviews will likely play a pivotal role in determining whether you're initially hired. Speaking skills will also increase your prospects for career advancement by strengthening your professional presentations and performance at meetings. Research repeatedly shows that employers place a high value on oral communication skills and rank them among the top characteristics they seek in prospective employees (AAC&U, 2013; National Association of Colleges & Employers, 2014).

> As you move up through your career path, you're judged on your ability to articulate a point of view."
>
> —*Donald Keogh, former president of the Coca-Cola Company*

Reflection 7.7

How many times have you made an oral presentation or delivered a speech?

Does your college require a course in speech or public speaking? If yes, when do you plan to take it? If no, would you consider taking an elective course in public speaking? (Why?)

(To assess your verbal skills, complete Exercise 7.5 at the end of this chapter.)

Strategies for Making Effective Oral Presentations

Listed below are strategies for delivering oral presentations and speeches. Since speaking and writing both involve communicating thoughts verbally, you'll find that many of the strategies suggested here for improving oral reports are similar to those for improving written reports. Thus, you'll be able to "double dip" by using the following oral presentation strategies to strengthen your written presentations and vice versa.

1. **Know the purpose of your presentation.** Oral presentations usually fall into one of the following two categories, depending on their purpose or objective:

    a) *informative* presentations—intended to provide the audience with accurate information to increase their knowledge or supply them with practical information they can use, or

    b) *persuasive* (expository) presentations—intended to persuade (convince) the audience to agree with a particular position or buy into a certain viewpoint.

    Be sure you're clear about what you're expected to accomplish and keep that objective in mind as you develop your presentation. When deciding on what specific information to include, always ask yourself: Is this information relevant to the intended purpose of my presentation?

    In college, most of your oral presentations will likely fall into the persuasive category, which means that you will search for information, draw conclusions about your research, and document your conclusions with evidence. Similar to writing research papers, persuasive presentations usually require you to think at a higher level, cite sources, and demonstrate academic integrity.

2. **Select a topic that matters to you and you're passionate about.** If you're given a choice about the topic of your presentation, seize this opportunity to pursue a subject that captures your interest and enthusiasm. By doing so, your interest and enthusiasm will show through in your delivery, which will increase your audience's attention, your self-confidence, and the overall quality of your presentation.

3. **Create an outline of your major ideas.** Get your major points down on index cards or PowerPoint slides and arrange them in an order that provides the best sequence or flow of your ideas from start to finish. Use the major points you've recorded on separate index cards or slides as memory "cue cards" to trigger your recall of specific details relating to each of your major points.

4. **Rehearse and revise.** Just as you should write several drafts of a paper before turning it in, an oral presentation should be rehearsed and revised before delivering it. Rehearsal will help ensure that your presentation isn't interrupted by long pauses, stops and starts, and distracting "fillers" (e.g., "uh," "umm," "like," "you know," "whatever"). Rehearsal will also help reduce your level of speech anxiety. Studies show that fear of public speaking is often really a fear of failure—fear of being negatively evaluated by the audience (Finn, Sawyer, & Behnke, 2009). If your oral presentation is well prepared and well rehearsed, your fear of receiving a negative evaluation should decrease, along with your level of speech anxiety.

    When rehearsing your presentation, pay special attention to the following parts:

    - The *introduction*. This part of your speech should be particularly well-rehearsed because it provides the audience with a sense of direction and positive anticipation for what's to come. Like a well-designed written report,

> "Enthusiasm is everything."
>
> —*Pelé, Brazilian soccer player (arguably the most famous player in the sport's history)*

> "The only time I get nervous is when I am not very familiar with my topic or if I'm winging my assignment and I'm not prepared."
>
> —*First-year student commenting on her previous oral presentations*

> "One important key to success is self-confidence. An important key to self-confidence is preparation."
>
> —*Arthur Ashe, former world number 1 professional tennis player and first black player ever selected to the United States Davis Cup team*

the introduction to your oral report should include a thesis statement—a statement about *why* you're speaking about this topic and what you intend to accomplish by the end of your presentation. It should also "hook" the audience and stimulate their interest in what you're about to say.

- *Transition statements* that signal you're moving from one major idea to another. These statements serve to highlight the key components of your presentation and show how its separate parts are connected.

- The *conclusion*. This is your chance to finish strong and create a powerful last impression that drives home your presentation's most important points. Your conclusion should include a statement that refers back to, and reinforces, your original thesis statement, thereby connecting your ending with your beginning.

> "First, I tell 'em what I'm gonna tell 'em; then I tell 'em; then I tell 'em what I told 'em."
> —*Anonymous country preacher's formula for successful sermons*

Lastly, when you rehearse your presentation, be aware of the total time it takes to complete it. Be sure it falls within the time range set by your instructor and that it's neither too short nor too long.

5. **Get feedback on your presentation before officially delivering it.** Ask a friend or group of friends to listen to your presentation and request their input. Not only can peers provide valuable feedback, they can provide you with a "live audience" for your rehearsal. This makes your rehearsal more realistic and effective because your practice environment closely matches your performance environment.

Another way to obtain feedback prior to your presentation is to have a friend make a video recording of your rehearsed presentation. This will enable you to step outside of yourself and observe your presentation as the audience would. This "out-of-body experience" can dramatically increase awareness of your nonverbal communication (body language) habits.

When you first see how you look and hear how you sound on videotape, you may be quite surprised (or shocked), but that's a normal reaction. After a while, the initial shock will fade and you'll feel more comfortable viewing, reviewing, and improving your presentation.

 Reflection 7.8

Have you ever received feedback on the quality of your speaking skills from a teacher, a peer, or by observing yourself on video?

If you have, what did you learn about your speaking habits and how to improve them?

If you haven't, would you be willing to seek feedback from others on your oral presentation skills?

6. **Observe presentations made by other students and learn from them.** Note the things that effective speakers seem to do when delivering their speeches and use them as clues to improve the quality of your own presentations.

7. **During delivery of your speech, maximize eye contact with your audience.** You can occasionally look at your notes and slides during your presentation and use them as cue cards to help you recall the key points you intend to make; however, they shouldn't be used as a script that you read verbatim.

PowerPoint presentations have the potential to become deadly boring when the speaker's "presentation" involves looking at and reading slides off a screen, rather than looking at and speaking to the audience. (See **Box 7.3** for tips on using, not abusing, PowerPoint.)

Effective oral presentations should not be written out entirely in advance and read (or memorized) word for word (Luotto, Stoll, & Hoglund-Ketttmann, 2001), nor should they be impromptu presentations delivered off the top of the speaker's head. Instead, they should be *extemporaneous* presentations, which fall between "winging it" and reading or memorizing it word-by-word. Extemporaneous speaking includes advanced preparation and the use of notes or slides as memory retrieval cues, but allows you some freedom to ad lib or improvise. If you happen to forget the exact words you planned to use, you can freely substitute different words to make the same point—without stumbling or stressing out—and without your audience even noticing you made any substitutions. The key to extemporaneous speaking is to rehearse and remember your major points, not the exact words you will use to express each and every point. This will ensure your presentation comes across as natural and authentic, rather than mechanical or robotic.

Box 7.3

Tips for Using (Not Abusing) PowerPoint

- List information on your slides as bulleted points, not complete sentences. The more words included on your slides, the more time your audience will spend reading the slides rather than listening to you. You can help keep the focus on *you* (not your slides) by showing only one point on your slide at a time. This will keep the audience members focused on the point you're discussing and prevent them from reading ahead.

Note *Your PowerPoint slides are not your presentation; they're merely cue cards that trigger the ideas you will discuss in relation to the slides.*

❝A presentation is about explaining things to people that go above and beyond what they get in the slides. If it weren't, they might just as well get your slides and read them in the comfort of their own office, home, boat, or bathroom."

—*Jesper Johansson, senior security strategist for Microsoft and author of* Death by PowerPoint *(personal blog) (2005)*

- List only three to five points on each slide. Research indicates that humans can retain only about four points or bits of information in their short-term memory (Cowan, 2001).
- Use the titles of slides as general headings or categories for your major ideas.

- Use a font size of at least 18 points to ensure that people in the back of the room can read what's printed on each slide.
- Don't use color just for decoration (which can be a source of distraction), but as a visual aid to highlight how points are organized on a slide. For example, a dark or bold blue heading could be used to highlight the title of the slide—to represent a major point, and sub-points could be listed as bullets in a lighter shade of blue.
- Incorporate visual images into your presentation. Don't hesitate to use pictures, graphs, cartoons, and objects or artifacts that relate to and reinforce your major points.

Note *The true power of PowerPoint may be that it allows you to illustrate visually what you're discussing verbally. Take advantage of this PowerPoint feature to display images and pictures that relate to your spoken words.*

- If you include words or images on a slide that are not your own work, demonstrate academic integrity by noting its source at the bottom of the slide.
- Before going public with your slides, proofread them with the same care as you would a written paper.

Sources: Hedges (2014); Johansson (2005); *Ten Commandments of PowerPoint Presentations* (2015)

Managing Speech Anxiety

If you're uncomfortable about public speaking, you're certainly not alone. It's such a common feeling, it should be considered "normal." National surveys show that fear of public speaking affects people of all ages, including adolescents and young adults (Brewer, 2001; Croston, 2012). A significant number of college students also experience *classroom communication apprehension*—anxiety about speaking in classroom settings (Wrench, McCroskey, & Richmond, 2008).

Keep in mind that it's natural to experience at least some anxiety in any performance situation. This isn't necessarily a bad thing, because if your stress is kept at a moderate level, it can actually increase your energy, concentration, and memory (Rosenfield, 1988; Sapolsky, 2004). However, if it reaches the level of fear, leaving you unwilling or unable to stand up in front of a group to make an oral presentation, you may be experiencing speech anxiety or "stage fright." Listed below are strategies for controlling speech anxiety and keeping it at a moderate and productive level.

1. **In the minutes just prior to your speech, focus on relaxation.** Take deep breaths, or use any stress management strategy that works well for you. (See Chapter 9, pp. 220–223, for an assortment of effective stress management methods.)
2. **Avoid consuming caffeine or other "energy drinks" prior to speaking.** These substances will elevate your level of physiological arousal during your speech, which, in turn, can elevate your level of psychological arousal (anxiety).
3. **Come to your speech with a positive mindset.** Simply stated, positive thoughts trigger positive emotions (Ellis, 2000). Here are some strategies for putting yourself in a positive frame of mind:
    *   Adopt the mindset that your speech is nothing more than a formal conversation with a group of friends. To help get you into this conversational mindset, make eye contact with small sections of the audience while delivering your speech. When you shift to a new idea or part of your speech, shift your focus of attention to a different section of the audience. This strategy will help relax you by making the audience seem smaller, and it will ensure that you make periodic eye contact with different sections of the audience.
    *   Expect to give a good speech, but not a perfect speech. Don't think you're going to deliver a presentation like a TV reporter who is smoothly delivering (actually reading) the nightly news. A few verbal mistakes or lapses of memory are common during speeches, just as they are during normal conversations. You can still receive an excellent grade on an oral presentation without delivering a flawless performance.
    *   Keep in mind that the audience to whom you are speaking is not made up of expert speakers. Most of them have no more public speaking experience than you do, nor are they experienced critics. These are your peers and they know that standing up in front of class and delivering a formal speech isn't an easy thing to do. They're likely to be very accepting of any mistakes you make, as they hope you'll do for them when it's their turn to stand and deliver.
4. **During delivery of your speech, focus on the *message* (your ideas), not the *messenger* (yourself).** By keeping your attention on the ideas you're communicating, you'll be less self-conscious and anxious about the impression you're making on the audience or the audience's impression (evaluation) of you.

Like any fear, fear of public speaking tends to subside after getting your "feet wet" and doing it for the first time. The anticipation of the experience is often worse than the experience itself. Anxious feelings experienced before and during a speech are often replaced by feelings of accomplishment, pride, and self-confidence after the speech is completed.

AUTHOR'S EXPERIENCE

I was required to take a course in public speaking by the end of my sophomore year. I was extremely nervous about standing up and delivering a speech in front of a large group, so I avoided taking the course as long as I possibly could. Finally, as a second semester sophomore, I delivered my first oral presentation. When it was done, I felt like I just got a huge gorilla off my back.

After giving that first speech, I noticed I was more confident about asking questions in my classes, speaking up during group discussions, and expressing myself in situations where a large number of people were present. Eventually, I became a college professor whose lifelong career has involved speaking in front of people. I now make presentations on college campuses across the United States and other countries.

Every now and then I think about that first speech I delivered as a college sophomore and realize that it may have been a turning point in my life. It gave me the opportunity to overcome my speech anxiety and gave me the self-confidence to succeed in my eventual career. It also gave me the confidence and courage to deliver a meaningful and moving eulogy at my father's funeral.

—Joe Cuseo

Chapter Summary and Highlights

This chapter began with a question about what you thought was the difference between acquiring factual knowledge and learning a transferable skill. You may have known the difference before reading this chapter, or discovered it while reading the chapter. Either way, you know now that a transferable skill has more flexibility and versatility than factual knowledge because it can be transferred and applied to a wide variety of situations throughout life. The transferable skills discussed in this chapter—research (information literacy), writing, and speaking—are powerful, durable skills that can be applied across different academic subjects you encounter in college and different career positions you hold after college.

Research, writing, and speaking are also complementary skills that can be used together to achieve educational and professional success. Research skills enable you to acquire high-quality information generated by others. Writing and speaking skills actively engage you with the ideas you acquire through research, and enable you to effectively communicate your interpretation of those ideas as well as your own ideas. Said in another way, *research* skills enable you to locate, evaluate, and integrate information, while *writing* and *speaking* skills enable you to comprehend, communicate, and demonstrate your mastery of that information to others. These three skills have always been important for achieving educational and professional success, but they've become even more important in the current information and communication age, and are more highly valued by today's employers than perhaps at any other time in history.

Work hard at developing the transferable skills discussed in this chapter and take full advantage of the campus resources designed to help you develop these skills. The time and energy you invest in developing your research, writing, and speaking skills will supply you with lifelong benefits.

Learning More through the World Wide Web: Internet-Based Resources

For additional information on research, writing, and oral communication skills, see the following websites:

Information Literacy (Information Search) Strategies:
https://liblearn.osu.edu/tutor/rightstuff.html

Writing Strategies:
www.enhancemywriting.com

http://writingcenter.fas.harvard.edu/pages/strategies-essay-writing

Academic Integrity and Character:
http://www.academicintegrity.org/icai/integrity-1.php

http://www.calea.org/calea-update-magazine/issue-100/who-s-watching-character-and-integrity-21st-century

Public Speaking Skills:
www.public-speaking.org/public-speaking-articles.htm

https://www.hamilton.edu/oralcommunication/tips-for-effective-delivery

References

Academic Integrity at Princeton. (2011). *Examples of plagiarism*. Retrieved from www.princeton.edu/pr/pub/integrity/.

Ackerman, J. M. (1993). The promise of writing to learn. *Written Communication, 10*(3) 334–370.

Applebee, A. N. (1984). Writing and reasoning. *Review of Educational Research, 54*(4), 577–596.

AAC&U (Association of American Colleges and Universities). (2013*). It takes more than a major: Employer priorities for college learning and success*. Washington, DC: Author.

Bean, J. C. (2003). *Engaging ideas: The professor's guide to integrating writing, critical thinking and active learning in the classroom*. San Francisco: Jossey-Bass.

Bean, J. C. (2011). *Engaging ideas: The professor's guide to integrating writing, critical thinking and active learning in the classroom* (2nd ed.). San Francisco: Jossey-Bass.

Boice, R. (1994). *How writers journey to comfort and fluency: A psychological adventure*. Westport, CT: Greenwood.

Brewer, G. (2001, March 19). "Snakes top list of Americans' fears: Public speaking, heights and being closed in small spaces also create fear in many Americans." *Gallup News Service*. Retrieved from www.gallup.com/poll/1891/snakes-top-list-americans-fears.aspx.

Brooks, K. (2009). *You majored in what? Mapping your path from chaos to career*. New York: Penguin.

Cairncross, F. C. (2001). *The death of distance: How the communication revolution is changing our lives*. Cambridge, MA: Harvard Business School Press.

Cowan, N. (2001). The magical number 4 in short-term memory: A reconsideration of mental storage capacity. *Behavioral and Brain Sciences, 24*, 87–114.

Croston, G. (2012). The thing we fear more than death. *Psychology Today*. Retrieved from https://www.psychology today.com/blog/the-real-story-risk/201211/the-thing-we-fear-more-death.

Elbow, P. (1973). *Writing without teachers*. New York: Oxford University Press.

Ellis, A. (2000). *How to control your anxiety before it controls you*. New York: Citadel Press/Kensington Publishing.

Finn, A. N., Sawyer, C. R., & Behnke, R. R. (2009). A model of anxious arousal for public speaking. *Communication Education, 58*, 417–432.

Friedman, T. L. (2005). *The world is flat: A brief history of the twenty-first century*. New York: Farrar, Straus & Giroux.

Hacker, D., & Fister, B. (2014). *Research and documentation in the electronic age* (6th ed.). Boston: Bedford/St. Martin's.

Hedges, K. (2014). *Six ways to avoid death by PowerPoint*. Retrieved from http://www.forbes.com/sites/work-in-progress/2014/11/14/six-ways-to-avoid-death-by-powerpoint/.

Johansson, J. (2005). *Death by PowerPoint*. Retrieved from http://articles.tech.republic.com5100-22_11-5875608.html.

Knaus, B. (2010). Ten top tips to end writer's procrastination. *Psychology Today* (June 18). Retrieved from https://www.psychologytoday.com/blog/science-and-sensibility/201006/ten-top-tips-end-writer-s-block-procrastination.

Langer, J. A., & Applebee, A. N. (2007). *How writing shapes thinking: A study of teaching and learning*. WAC Clearinghouse Landmark Publications in Writing Studies. Retrieved from http://wac.colostate.edu/books/langer_applebee/.

Leahy, R. (1990). What the college writing center is—and isn't. *College Teaching, 38*(2), 43–48.

Light, R. L. (1992). *The Harvard assessment seminars, second report*. Cambridge, MA: Harvard University Press.

Light, R. L. (2001). *Making the most of college: Students speak their minds*. Cambridge, MA: Harvard University Press.

Luotto, J. A., Stoll, E. L., & Hoglund-Ketttmann, N. (2001). *Communication skills for collaborative learning* (2nd ed.). Dubuque, IA: Kendall/Hunt.

Murray, D. M. (2004). *Write to learn* (8th ed.). Fort Worth: Harcourt Brace.

National Association of Colleges & Employers. (2014). *Job outlook 2014 survey*. Bethlehem, PA: Author.

National Forum on Information Literacy. (2015). *Information literacy skills*. Retrieved from http://infolit.org/information-literacy-projects-and-programs.

National Survey of Student Engagement. (2008). *NSSE Annual Results 2008. Promoting engagement for all students: The imperative to look within*. Bloomington, IN: Author.

Patchan, M. M., Charney, D., & Schunn, C. D. (2009). A validation study of students' end comments: Comparing comments by students, a writing instructor, and a content instructor. *Journal of Writing Research*, *1*(2) 124–152.

Purdue University Online Writing Lab. (2015). *Avoiding plagiarism*. Retrieved from https://owl.english.purdue.edu/owl/resource/589/01/.

Rosenfield, I. (1988). *The invention of memory: A new view of the brain*. New York: Basic Books.

Sapolsky, R. (2004). *Why zebras don't get ulcers*. New York: W. H. Freeman.

Tchudi, S. N. (1986). *Teaching writing in the content areas: College level*. New York: National Educational Association.

The Ten Commandments of PowerPoint Presentations. (2015). Retrieved from http://avalaunchmedia.com/blog/using-power-point-for-presentations.

The University of Texas at El Paso. (2008). *High school writing v. college writing*. Retrieved from http://utminers.utep.edu/omwilliamson/univ1301/high_school_writing_vs.htm.

Thompson, R. F. (1981). Peer grading: Some promising advantages for composition research and the classroom. *Research in the Teaching of English*, *15*(2), 172–174.

Tynjälä, P., Mason L., & Lonka, K. (Eds.). (2012). *Writing as a learning tool: Theory and practice*. Dordrecht, The Netherlands: Kluwer Academic Publishers.

Wrench, J. S., McCroskey, J. C., & Richmond, V. P. (2008). *Human communication in everyday life: Explanations and applications*. Boston, MA: Allyn & Bacon.

Zinsser, W. (1993). *Writing to learn*. New York: HarperCollins.

Chapter 7 Exercises

7.1 Quote Reflections

Review the sidebar quotes contained in this chapter and select two that were especially meaningful or inspirational to you.

For each quote, provide a three- to five-sentence explanation of why you chose it.

7.2 Reality Bite

Crime and Punishment: Plagiarism and Its Consequences

In an article that appeared in an Ohio newspaper, titled "Plagiarism persists in classrooms," an English professor is quoted as saying: "Technology has made it easier to plagiarize because students can download papers and exchange information and papers through their computers. But technology has also made it easier to catch students who plagiarize." This professor works at a college that subscribes to a website that matches the content of students' papers with content from books and online sources. Many professors now require students to submit their papers through this website. If students are caught plagiarizing, for a first offense, they typically receive an F for the assignment or the course. A second offense can result in dismissal or expulsion from college, which has already happened to a few students.

Reflection and Discussion Questions

1. What do you suspect are the primary motives or reasons why students plagiarize from the web?

2. What would you say is a fair or just penalty for those found guilty of a first plagiarism violation? What do you think would be fair penalty for a second violation?

3. How might web-based plagiarism be minimized or prevented from happening in the first place?

7.3 Internet Research

Go to *www.itools.com/search*. This website allows you to conveniently access multiple search engines, web directories, and newsgroups. Type in the name of a subject or topic you'd like to research and select three of the multiple search engines listed at this site.

1. What differences did you find in the type of information generated by the three search engines?

2. Did any of these search engines locate better or more comprehensive information than the others?

3. Would you return to this website again to help you with future research?

7.4 Is It or Is It Not Plagiarism?

The following four incidents were brought to a judicial review board to determine if plagiarism had occurred and, if so, what the penalty should be. After reading each case, answer the questions listed below it.

CASE 1. A student turned in an essay that included substantial material copied from a published source. The student admitted that he didn't cite the sources properly, but argued that it was because he misunderstood the directions, not because he was attempting to steal someone else's ideas.

Is this plagiarism?

How severe is it? (Rate it on a scale from 1 = low to 5 = high)

What should the consequence or penalty be?

How could the accusation of plagiarism been avoided?

CASE 2. A student turned in a paper that was identical to a paper submitted by another student for a different course.

Is this plagiarism?

How severe is it? (Rate it on a scale from 1 = low to 5 = high)

What should the consequence or penalty be?

How could the accusation of plagiarism been avoided?

CASE 3. A student submitted a paper he wrote in a previous course as an extra credit paper for a course.

Is this plagiarism?

How severe is it? (Rate it on a scale from 1 = low to 5 = high)

What should the consequence or penalty be?

How could the accusation of plagiarism been avoided?

CASE 4. A student submitted a paper in an art history class that contained some ideas from art critics she read about and whose ideas she agreed with. The student didn't cite the critics as sources, but claimed it wasn't plagiarism because their ideas were merely their own subjective judgments or opinions, not facts or findings; furthermore, they were opinions she agreed with.

Is this plagiarism?

How severe is it? (Rate it on a scale from 1 = low to 5 = high)

What should the consequence or penalty be?

How could the accusation of plagiarism been avoided?

Look back at these four cases. Which of them do you think represents the most severe and least severe violation of academic integrity? Why?

7.5 Assessing Your Linguistic Intelligence

1. Complete the MI (Multiple Intelligence) Advantage self-assessment and review your results.

2. What does your report say about your linguistic intelligence?

3. What strengths does the report point out? What areas of development does it suggest?

7.6 Preparing an Oral Presentation on Student Success

1. Scan this textbook and identify a chapter topic or chapter section that you find interesting or important.

2. Create an *introduction* for an oral presentation on this topic that:
   a) Provides an overview or sneak preview of what you will cover in your presentation;
   b) Creates a favorable first impression that grabs the attention of your audience (your classmates); and
   c) Demonstrates the topic's relevance or importance for your audience.

3. Create a *conclusion* to your presentation that:
   a) Relates back to your introduction;
   b) Highlights your most important point or points; and
   c) Leaves a memorable last impression.

Higher-Level Thinking

MOVING BEYOND BASIC KNOWLEDGE TO CRITICAL AND CREATIVE THINKING

National surveys consistently show that the primary goal of college faculty is teaching students how to think critically. This chapter will help you understand what critical thinking is and empower you to think critically and creatively. You will acquire thinking strategies that move you beyond memorization to higher levels of thought and learn ways to demonstrate higher-level thinking on college exams and assignments.

Equip you with higher-level thinking skills for achieving excellence in college and beyond.

 Reflection 8.1

To me, critical thinking is . . .

(At a later point in this chapter, we'll ask you to flashback to the response you made here.)

What Is Higher-Level Thinking?

Contestants on TV quiz shows like *Jeopardy* are asked questions that call for knowledge of facts: Who? What? When? or Where? If game show contestants were asked higher-level thinking questions, they'd be responding to questions such as: "Why?" "How?" "What if?" Higher-level thinking (a.k.a. higher-order thinking) refers to a more advanced level of thought than that used to acquire factual knowledge. It involves reflecting on knowledge and taking it to a higher level—evaluating its validity, integrating it with something else you've learned, or creating new ideas. As its name implies, higher-level thinking involves raising the bar and jacking up your thinking to a level that goes beyond merely remembering, reproducing, or regurgitating factual information.

The number one educational goal of college professors is to help students think at a higher or more advanced level. In national surveys of college professors teaching freshman-level through senior-level courses in various academic fields, more than 95% of faculty report that the most important goal of a college education is to develop students' ability to think critically (Gardiner, 2005; Milton, 1982). Similarly, college professors teaching introductory courses for freshmen and sophomores report that the primary educational purpose of their courses is to develop

> "To me, thinking at a higher level means to think and analyze something beyond the obvious and find the deeper meaning."
>
> *—First-year college student*

students' critical thinking skills (Higher Education Research Institute, 2009; Stark, et al., 1990). Simply stated, professors are more concerned with teaching you *how* to think than teaching you *what* to think (i.e., what facts to remember).

Compared to high school, college courses focus less on memorizing information and more on thinking about issues, concepts, and principles (Conley, 2005). Remembering information in college may get you a grade of "C," demonstrating comprehension of that information may get you a "B," and going beyond comprehension to demonstrate higher-level thinking will earn you an "A." This is not to say that acquiring knowledge and basic comprehension are unimportant; they provide the stepping stones needed to climb to higher levels of thinking—as illustrated in **Figure 8.1**.

> "What is the hardest task in the world? To think."
>
> —*Ralph Waldo Emerson, celebrated 19th-century American essayist and lecturer*

FIGURE 8.1: **The Relationship between Knowledge, Comprehension, and Higher-Level Thinking**

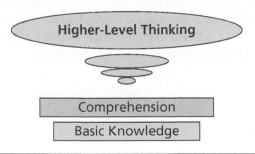

©Kendall Hunt Publishing Company

Note

College professors expect students to do more than just retain or reproduce information; they want you to demonstrate higher levels of thinking with respect to what you learned (e.g., analyze it, evaluate it, apply it, or integrate it with other concepts you've learned).

Studies show that memory for factual information acquired in college fades quickly with the passage of time. However, higher-level thinking is a *skill* (like learning to ride a bike) that's retained on a long-term basis and used for an entire lifetime (Pascarella & Terenzini, 1991, 2005).

Defining and Describing the Major Forms of Higher-Level Thinking

When your college professors ask you to "think critically," they're usually asking you to use one or more of the seven forms of thinking listed in **Box 8.1**. As you read the descriptions of each form of thinking, note whether you've heard of it before.

Box 8.1

Seven Major Forms of Higher-Level Thinking

1. Analysis (Analytical Thinking). Breaking down information to identify its essential parts and underlying elements.
2. Synthesis (Integrative Thinking). Building up ideas by connecting them to form a larger whole or more comprehensive system.
3. Application (Applied Thinking). Putting thinking into practice to solve problems and resolve issues.
4. Multidimensional Thinking. Viewing issues from a variety of vantage points to gain a more complete or comprehensive perspective.

> "In college . . . you will be expected to get inside what you are learning to apply it, make comparisons and connections, draw implications, and use ideas."
> —*Robert Shoenberg, author,* Why Do I Have to Take This Course?

5. Balanced Thinking. Carefully considering arguments for and against a particular position or viewpoint.
6. Critical Thinking (Evaluation). Judging the quality of arguments, conclusions, and thought processes—including all forms of thinking on this list.
7. Creative Thinking. Generating ideas that are unique, original, or distinctively different.

 Reflection 8.2

Look back at the seven forms of thinking described in **Box 8.1**. Which of these forms of thinking have you used on high school exams or assignments?

Analysis (Analytical Thinking)

The mental process of analysis is similar to the physical process of peeling an onion. When you analyze something, you take it apart and pick out its key parts, main points, or underlying elements. For example, if you were to analyze a chapter in this book, you would do more than cover its content; you would try to uncover or discover its main ideas by detecting its essential points and distinguishing them from background information or incidental details.

> "In physics, you have to be analytical and break it [the problem] down into its parts."
> —*Physics student (quoted in Donald, 2002)*

In an art course, you would use analytical thinking to identify the underlying elements or separate components of a painting or sculpture (e.g., its structure, texture, tone, and form). In the natural and social sciences, you would use analysis to identify underlying reasons or causes for natural (physical) phenomena and social events—known as "causal analysis." For instance, a causal analysis of the September 11, 2001, attack on the United States would involve identifying the key factors that led to the attack or the underlying reasons why the attack took place.

 Reflection 8.3

A TV commercial for a particular brand of liquor (which shall remain nameless) once showed a young man getting out of his car in front of a house where a party is going on. The driver gets out of his car, takes out a knife, slashes his tires, and goes inside to join the party. Using the higher-level thinking skill of analysis, what would you say are the underlying or embedded messages in this commercial?

Synthesis (Integrative Thinking)

When you engage in *synthesis*, you're using a thought process that's basically the opposite of analysis. Instead of breaking down or taking apart ideas, you piece them together to form an integrated whole—like piecing together parts of a puzzle. Connecting ideas learned in different courses is a form of synthesis, such as integrating ethical concepts learned in a philosophy course with marketing concepts learned in a business course to develop a comprehensive set of ethical guidelines for marketing and advertising products.

Although synthesis and analysis are seemingly opposite thought processes, they complement one another. Analysis enables you to disassemble information into its key parts; synthesis allows you to reassemble those parts into a new whole. For instance, when writing this book, we analyzed published material in many fields (e.g., psychology, history, philosophy, and biology) to detect pieces of information in these different fields that were most relevant to promoting the success of college students. We then synthesized or reassembled these parts to create a new whole—the textbook you're now reading.

Note

Synthesis is not just a summary of ideas produced by someone else; it's a thought process that integrates isolated pieces of information to generate a comprehensive product of your own.

Application (Applied Thinking)

When you learn something deeply, you transform information into knowledge; when you translate knowledge into practice, you engage in a higher-level thinking process known as *application*. It's a powerful form of higher-level thinking that allows you to transfer your knowledge to real-life situations and put it to use for practical purposes. For instance, you're engaging in application if you use the knowledge you've acquired about human relations in Chapter 9 to become more assertive, or when you take knowledge acquired in an accounting course to help manage your personal finances.

Always be on the lookout for ways to take action on the knowledge you've acquired by applying it to your personal life experiences and current events or issues. When you use your knowledge for the practical purpose of doing something good, such as bettering yourself or others, you not only demonstrate application; you also demonstrate *wisdom* (Staudinger, 2008).

"As gold which he cannot spend will make no man rich, so knowledge which he cannot apply will make no man wise."

—Dr. Samuel Johnson, famous English literary figure and original author of the Dictionary of the English Language (1747)

"To me, thinking at a higher level is when you approach a question or topic thoughtfully, when you fully explore every aspect of that topic from all angles."

—First-year college student

Multidimensional Thinking

When you view yourself and the world around you from different perspectives or vantage points to gain a comprehensive perspective, you're engaging in *multidimensional thinking*. For instance, multidimensional thinkers are able to think from the following four key perspectives and see how each of them influences, and is influenced by, the issue they're examining.

1. Perspective of **Person (Self)**: How does this issue affect individuals on a personal basis?
2. Perspective of **Place**: What impact does this issue have on people living in different areas of the country or different parts of the world?
3. Perspective of **Time**: How will future generations of people be affected by this issue?

4. Perspective of **Culture**: How is this issue likely to be interpreted or experienced by groups of people who share different social customs and traditions? (the perspective of culture)

Important issues don't exist in isolation but as parts of a complex, interconnected system that involves interplay of multiple factors and perspectives. For example, global warming (climate change) is an issue that involves the gradual thickening and trapping of more heat in the earth's atmosphere as a result of a buildup in gases generated by the burning of fossil fuels for industrial purposes (Intergovernmental Council on Climate Change, 2013). The consensus among today's scientists is that this buildup of human-made pollution is causing temperatures to rise (and sometimes fall) around the world, resulting in more extreme weather conditions and more frequent natural disasters—such as droughts, wildfires, hurricanes, and dust storms (Joint Science Academies' Statement, 2005; National Resource Defense Council, 2005, 2012). As depicted in **Box 8.2**, understanding and addressing this issue requires understanding interrelationships among the multiple perspectives of person, place, time, and culture.

Box 8.2

Understanding Climate Change from Four Key Perspectives

Person

Climate change involves humans at a personal level because individual efforts to conserve energy in our homes and our willingness to purchase energy-efficient products can play a major role in resolving this issue.

Place

Climate change is an international phenomenon that extends beyond the boundaries of any one country; it affects all countries in the world and its solution requires the joint effort of different nations around the world to reduce their level of carbon emissions.

Time

If the current trend toward higher global warming isn't addressed soon, it could seriously threaten the lives of future generations inhabiting the planet.

Culture

Industries in technologically and industrially advanced cultures are primarily responsible for contributing to the problem of climate change, yet its potentially adverse effects will be greater for less technologically advanced cultures because they lack the resources to respond to it (Joint Science Academies' Statement, 2005). Industrially advanced cultures will need to use their advanced resources and technology to devise alternative methods for generating energy in ways that reduce the risk of global warming for all cultures.

 Reflection 8.4

Think of a current national or international problem (other than climate change) whose solution requires multiple perspective-taking or systems thinking.

Balanced Thinking

When we seek out and carefully consider arguments *for* and *against* a particular position, we're engaging in balanced thinking. The process of finding supporting evidence or reasons for a position is referred to as *adduction*—when you adduce, you identify reasons *for* a position; the process of finding evidence or reasons that contradicts a position is called *refutation*—when you refute, you provide a rebuttal *against* a particular position.

Balanced thinking involves both adduction and refutation. Each position's stronger arguments are acknowledged, and its weaker ones are refuted (Fairbairn & Winch, 1996). The goal of a balanced thinker is not to stack up evidence for one position or the other but to be an impartial judge looking at supporting and opposing evidence for both sides of an issue, and striving to draw a conclusion that's neither biased nor one-sided. When you consider the strengths and weaknesses of opposing arguments at the same time, it reduces the likelihood that you'll fall prey to an overly simplistic form of thinking typical of many first-year students—known as *dualistic* thinking—seeking the "truth" in the form of clear-cut, black-or-white answers or solutions to complex issues—where one position or theory is "right" and the others "wrong" (Perry, 1970, 1999).

Don't be surprised and frustrated if you find scholars disagreeing about what particular positions or theories are more accurate or account for most of the "truth" in their field. This is a healthy thought process known as *dialectic* or *dialogic* thinking (deriving from the root "dialogue" or "conversation"). It's a productive form of intellectual dialogue (Paul & Elder, 2014) that acknowledges different sides of a complex issue and results in a more balanced, integrated understanding of it. In a study of leaders who excel in the field of business, it was discovered that one of their distinguishing qualities was their capacity for "integrative thinking"—the ability to hold opposing or conflicting ideas in their head and use that tension to create a new and superior idea—much like how humans use their opposable thumbs to excel at manual tasks (Martin, 2007).

Keep in mind that your first step in the process of solving problems and seeking truth shouldn't be to immediately jump in and take an either-or (for-or-against) position. Instead, take a balanced thinking approach by looking at arguments for and against each position, acknowledge the strengths and weaknesses of both sides of the argument, and seek to integrate the best points of both arguments.

Lastly, balanced thinking involves more than just totaling the number of arguments for and against a position; it also involves *weighing* the strength of each argument. Arguments can vary in terms of their degree of importance or level of support. When weighing arguments, ask yourself, "What is the quality and quantity of evidence supporting it?" Consider whether the evidence is:

1. **Definitive**—so strong or compelling that a definite conclusion should be reached;
2. **Suggestive**—strong enough to suggest that a tentative or possible conclusion may be reached; or
3. **Inconclusive**—too weak to reach any conclusion.

When making class presentations and writing papers or reports, be mindful of how much weight should be assigned to different arguments and explain how their weight has been factored into your conclusion.

In some cases, after reviewing both supporting and contradictory evidence for opposing positions, balanced thinking may lead you to suspend judgment and withhold drawing a conclusion that favors one position over another. A balanced thinker may occasionally reach the following conclusion: "The evidence doesn't strongly favor one position over the other" or "More information is needed before I can make a final judgment or reach a firm conclusion." These aren't wishy-washy answers; they're legitimate conclusions to reach after all the evidence has been carefully considered. In fact, it's better to hold an undecided but informed viewpoint

"The test of a first-rate intelligence is the ability to hold two opposed ideas in mind at the same time and still retain the ability to function."

—*F. Scott Fitzgerald, regarded as one of the greatest American writers of the 20th century*

"[Successful] business leaders have the capacity to hold two diametrically opposing ideas in their heads. And then, without panicking or settling for one alternative or the other, they're able to produce a synthesis that is superior to either opposing idea."

—*Roger Martin, Dean of the Rotman School of Management, University of Toronto*

"For years I really didn't know what I believed. I always seemed to stand in the no man's land between opposing arguments, yearning to be won over by one side or the other but finding instead degrees of merit in both. But in time I came to accept, even embrace, what I called "my confusion" and to recognize it as a friend and ally, with no apologies needed."

—*"In Praise of the 'Wobblies'" by Ted Gup, journalist, who has written for Time Magazine, National Geographic, and The New York Times*

based on balanced thinking than to hold definite opinions that are uninformed, biased, or based on emotion—such as those often expressed by people on radio talk shows.

If you find that the more you learn, the more complicated things seem to become, this is good news. It means you're moving from simplistic to complex thinking that's more multidimensional and balanced.

> The more you know, the less sure you are."
> —*Voltaire, French historian, philosopher, and advocate for civil liberty*

 Reflection 8.5

Consider the following positions:

1. Course requirements should be eliminated; college students should be allowed to choose the classes they want to take for their degree.

2. Course grades should be eliminated; college students should take classes on a pass–fail basis.

Using balanced thinking, identify one or more arguments *for* and *against* each of these positions?

Note

Balanced thinking enables you to become a more complex and comprehensive thinker capable of viewing issues from opposing sides and multiple perspectives.

Critical Thinking (Evaluation)

When we *evaluate* or *judge* the quality of an argument or work product, we're engaging in a form of higher-level thinking known as *critical thinking*. It's a skill highly valued by professors teaching students at all stages in the college experience and all subjects in the college curriculum (Higher Education Research Institute, 2009; Stark, et al., 1990). By working on developing your critical thinking skills as a first-year student, you will significantly improve your academic performance throughout your college experience.

> Critical thinking is an evaluative thought process that requires deep thinking."
> —*First-year college student*

Many students misinterpret critical thinking to mean "being critical"—criticizing something or somebody. Although critical thinking does involving making an evaluation or judgment, the evaluation can be either positive or negative. For instance, a movie critic can give a good (thumbs up) or bad (thumbs down) review of a film.

Critical thinking is used for many purposes beyond critiquing films, art, or music. It's a skill that enables you to "read between the lines" and cut through the fog or smog of ideas and arguments—including your own. Whether the evaluation is positive or negative (or some combination thereof), critical thinking involves backing up your evaluation with specific, well-informed reasons or evidence that support the critique. Failure to do so makes the criticism unfounded—that is, lacking any foundation or basis of support.

You can start developing the mental habit of critical thinking by using the following criteria as standards for evaluating ideas or arguments:

1. **Validity (Truthfulness).** Is it true or accurate?
2. **Morality (Ethics).** Is it fair or just?
3. **Beauty (Aesthetics).** Does it have artistic merit or value?

4. **Practicality (Usefulness).** Can it be put to use for practical or beneficial purposes?

5. **Priority (Order of Importance or Effectiveness).** Is it better than other ideas and alternative courses of action?

 **Reflection 8.6**

Flash back to **Reflection 8.1** on p. 179. How does your response compare with the definition of critical thinking just provided?

How are they similar?

How do they differ?

Critical Thinking and Inferential Reasoning

When we make arguments or arrive at conclusions, we use a mental process called *inferential reasoning*. We start with a premise (a statement or observation) and use it to infer (step to) a conclusion. Two major ways in which we use inferential reasoning to make arguments and reach conclusions are: (a) through logical reasoning, and/or (b) citing empirical (observable) evidence.

1. *Logical Reasoning.* Reaching a conclusion by showing that it logically follows from or is logically consistent with an established premise. In other words, if statement "A" is true, it can be concluded that statement "B" is also true.

    For example:
    Statement A. The constitution guarantees all U.S. citizens the right to vote. (Premise)
    Statement B. Women and people of color are citizens of the U.S.; therefore, they should have the right to vote. (Conclusion)

2. *Empirical (observable) evidence.* Reaching a conclusion by showing that it is supported with statistical data or scientific research findings. In other words, based on evidence "A," it can be concluded that "B" is true.

    For example:
    Statement A. There is statistical evidence that a much higher percentage of people who smoke experience cancer and heart disease. (Premise)
    Statement B. Based on this statistical evidence, smoking is a major health risk. (Conclusion)

Although using logic and empirical evidence are different routes to conclusions, they can be combined to support the same conclusion. For instance, in this book, we use both logical arguments and empirical evidence (research and statistics) to support our conclusions and recommendations. Similarly, advocates for lowering the legal drinking age to 18 have used the following forms of logical reasoning and empirical evidence to support their position:

a) Logical reasoning: 18-year-olds in the United States are considered to be legal adults with respect to such rights and responsibilities as voting, serving on juries, joining the military, and being held responsible for committing crimes; therefore, 18-year-olds should have the right to drink.

b) Empirical evidence: In other countries where drinking is allowed at age 18, statistics show that they have fewer binge-drinking and drunk-driving problems than the United States.

Reflection 8.7

Can you think of arguments *against* lowering the drinking age to 18 that are based on logical reasoning and empirical evidence?

Drawing inferences based on logic and empirical evidence are the primary thought processes that humans use to reach conclusions about themselves and the world around them. Inferential reasoning is also the form of thinking you will use to make arguments and reach conclusions in your college courses. You'll often be required to take positions and support your conclusions with sound reasoning and solid evidence. Adopt the mindset that you're a courtroom lawyer and be ready to prove your case with logical arguments and empirical evidence (exhibit A, exhibit B, etc.).

Logical Fallacies: Inferential Reasoning Errors

Unfortunately, errors can be made in the inferential reasoning processes, which are commonly referred to as *logical fallacies*. Listed below is a summary of the major types of logical fallacies. Be mindful of them in your thinking and when evaluating the thinking of others. As you read the following reasoning errors, briefly note in the margin whether you've ever witnessed it or committed it.

- **Non sequitur.** Drawing a conclusion that doesn't follow from or connect with the premise—the initial statement or observation. ("Non sequitur" derives from Latin, which literally means, "it does not follow.") Example: There was a bloody glove found at the murder scene and it doesn't fit the defendant, therefore the defendant must be innocent.
- **Selective Perception.** Seeing only examples and instances that support one's position while overlooking or ignoring those that contradict it. Example: Believers of astrology who only notice and point out people whose personalities happen to fit their astrological sign, but overlook those who don't.
- **Dogmatism.** Stubbornly clinging to a personal point of view unsupported by evidence while remaining closed-minded (nonreceptive) to other viewpoints better supported by evidence. Example: Arguing that adopting a national health system is a form of socialism that cannot work in a capitalistic economy, while ignoring the fact that there are other nations in the world that have both a national health care system and a capitalistic economy.
- **Double Standard.** Having two sets of judgment standards—a higher standard for judging others and a lower standard for judging oneself. Example: Critically evaluating and challenging the opinions of others, but not our own.
- **Wishful Thinking.** Thinking something is true not because of logic or evidence, but because the person *wants* it to be true. Example: A teenage girl who believes she will not become pregnant, even though she and her boyfriend are having sex without any form of contraception.

> A very bad (and all too common) way to misread a newspaper: To see whatever supports your point of view as fact, and anything that contradicts your point of view as bias."
>
> *—Daniel Okrent, first public editor of The New York Times*

> Facts do not cease to exist because they are ignored."
>
> *—Aldous Huxley, English writer and author of Brave New World*

> Belief can be produced in practically unlimited quantity and intensity, without observation or reasoning, and even in defiance of both by the simple desire to believe."
>
> *—George Bernard Shaw, Irish playwright and Nobel Prize winner for literature*

- **Hasty Generalization.** Reaching a conclusion prematurely on the basis of a limited number of instances or experiences. Example: Concluding that people belonging to a racial or ethnic group are all "that way" on the basis of personal experiences with only one or two individuals.
- **Jumping to a Conclusion.** Making a leap of logic to a conclusion that's based on a single reason or factor while ignoring other possible reasons or contributing factors. Example: A shy person immediately concludes that a person who doesn't make eye contact with her doesn't like her, without considering the possibility that the lack of eye contact may be due to the fact that the other person was distracted or shy himself.
- **False Cause and Effect (a.k.a. Correlational Error).** Concluding that if two things co-occur at about the same time or in close sequence, one must *cause* the other. Example: The old belief that sexual activity causes acne because when children become teenagers, they are more sexually active and also are more likely to develop acne.
- **False Analogy.** Concluding that because two things are alike in one respect, they must be alike in another respect. This is the classic error of "comparing apples and oranges"—they're both alike in that they are fruits but they're not alike in other ways. Example: People who argue that government is a form of business, therefore it should be run like a business or run by a businessman. While it's true that government and business are societal institutions that have some similarities (e.g., budgets and payrolls), government is not a profit-making enterprise and has purposes that aren't fiscal in nature.
- **Glittering Generality.** Making a positive, general statement that isn't supported by specific details or evidence. Example: A letter of recommendation that describes the recommended person as a "wonderful person" with a "great personality," but provides little or no evidence to back up the claim.
- **Straw Man Argument.** Distorting an opponent's argument or position and then attacking it. Example: Attacking an opposing political candidate for restricting civil liberties when, in fact, the opponent only supported a ban on concealed weapons.
- **Ad Hominem Argument.** Attacking the person, not the person's argument. (Literally translated, ad hominem means "to the man.") Example: Discounting a young person's argument by saying: "you're too young and inexperienced to know what you're talking about," or discounting an older person's argument by stating: "you're too old-school to understand this issue."
- **Red Herring.** Bringing up an irrelevant issue that disguises or distracts attention from the real issue being discussed or debated. (The term "red herring" derives from an old practice of dragging a herring—a strong-smelling fish—across a trail to distract the scent of pursuing dogs.) Example: People who responded to criticism of former President Richard Nixon's involvement in the Watergate scandal by arguing, "He was a good president who accomplished many great things while he was in office." (Nixon's effectiveness as a president is an irrelevant issue or a red herring; the real issue being discussed is Nixon's behavior in the Watergate scandal.)
- **Smoke Screen.** Intentionally disguising or camouflaging the truth by providing confusing or misleading explanations. Example: A politician who opposes gun control legislation by arguing that it's a violation of the constitutional right to bear arms, when in reality, the reason for his position is that he's receiving financial support from gun manufacturing companies.

- **Slippery Slope.** Using fear tactics to argue that not accepting a position will result in a "domino effect"—bad things will happen one after another—like a series of falling dominoes. Example: Arguing that "if America allows communism to happen anywhere, it will eventually happen everywhere."

- **Rhetorical Deception.** Using deceptive language to conclude that something is true without actually providing reasons or evidence. Example: Using glib words such as: "*Clearly* this is . . ." "It's *obvious* that . . ." or "Any *reasonable* peson can see . . .," without explaining why it's so "clear," "obvious," or "reasonable."

- **Circular Reasoning (a.k.a. "Begging the Question").** Drawing a conclusion by merely rewording or restating one's position without providing any supporting reasons or evidence, thus leaving the original question unanswered. This logical fallacy basically offers a conclusion that's simply a circular restatement of the premise—it's true because it's true. Example: Concluding that "stem cell research isn't ethical because it's morally wrong."

- **Appealing to Authority or Prestige.** Believing that if an authority figure or celebrity says it's true, it must be true. Example: Buying product X simply because a famous actor or athlete endorses it. Or, concluding that a course of action should be taken simply because the president says so.

- **Appealing to Tradition or Familiarity.** Concluding that if something has been considered to be true for a long time, or has always been done in a certain way, it must true or must be the best way to do it. Example: "Throughout history, marriage has been a relationship between a man and a woman; therefore, gay marriage should be illegal."

- **Appealing to Popularity or the Majority (a.k.a. Jumping on the Bandwagon).** Believing that if an idea is popular or held by the majority of people, it must be true. Example: "So many people believe in psychics, it must be true; they can't all be wrong."

- **Appealing to Emotion.** Believing in something based on the emotional intensity of our reaction to an argument, rather than the quality of reasoning or evidence used to support the argument. Example: "If I feel strongly about something, it must be true" or believing that I should "always trust my feelings" and "just follow my heart."

 **Reflection 8.8**

Glance back at the reasoning errors just discussed. Identify the two most common errors you've witnessed or experienced?

What were the situations in which these errors took place? Why do you think they took place?

(Check the results of your My PEPs Learning Style Inventory and My MI Advantage for the personalized strategies suggested to you to become a more successful learner. Have you tried these strategies or plan to try them? If not, analyze your reasons. Can you identify any logical fallacies in your reasoning?)

> "Political talk shows have become shouting matches designed to push emotional hot buttons and drive us further apart. We desperately need to exchange ideas with one another rationally and courteously."
>
> —David Boren, President, University of Oklahoma, and longest-serving chairman of the U.S. Senate Intelligence Committee

AUTHOR'S EXPERIENCE

When I teach classes or give workshops, I often challenge students or participants to debate me on either politics or religion. I ask them to choose a political party affiliation, a religion, or a branch of religion for their debate topic, or their stance on a social issue for which there are political or religious viewpoints. The ground rules are as follows: They choose the topic for debate; they can only use facts to support their argument, rebuttal, or both, and they must respond in a rational manner—without letting emotions drive their answers.

When I conduct this exercise, I usually discover that the topics people feel most strongly about are often those they haven't critically evaluated. For instance, people say they are Democrat, Republican, independent, and so on, and argue from this position; however, few of them have taken the time to critically examine whether their stated affiliation is actually consistent with their personal viewpoints. They almost always answer "no" to the following questions: "Have you read the core document (e.g., party platform) that outlines the party stance?" and "Have you engaged in self-examination of your party affiliation through reasoned discussions with others who say they have the same or a different political affiliation?"

> "Too often we enjoy the comfort of opinion without the discomfort of thought."
>
> —*John F. Kennedy, 35th U.S. president*

—*Aaron Thompson*

Creative Thinking

> "The principle mark of genius is not perfection but originality, the opening of new frontiers."
>
> —*Arthur Koestler, Hungarian novelist and philosopher*

> "The blues are the roots. Everything else are the fruits."
>
> —*Willie Dixon, blues songwriter; commenting on how all forms of contemporary American music contain elements of blues music, which originated among African American slaves*

> "Imagination should give wings to our thoughts, but imagination must be checked and documented by the factual results of the experiment."
>
> —*Louis Pasteur, French microbiologist, chemist, and founder of pasteurization (a method for preventing milk and wine from going sour)*

> "Creativity isn't 'crazytivity'."
>
> —*Edward De Bono, internationally known authority on creative thinking*

Creative thinking leads you to ask the question: "Why not?" (e.g., "Why not do it a different way?"). When you generate something new or different—an original idea, strategy, or work product—you're thinking creatively.

The process of creative thinking may be viewed as an extension or higher form of synthesis. Like synthesis, separate ideas are integrated, but they're combined in a way that results in something distinctively different (Anderson & Krathwohl, 2001). For instance, the musical genre of hard rock was created by combining elements of blues and rock and roll, and folk rock was born when Bob Dylan combined musical elements of acoustic blues and amplified rock (Shelton, et al., 2003). Robert Kearns (subject of the film, "Flash of Genius") combined preexisting mechanical parts to create the intermittent windshield wiper (Seabrook, 2008).

Keep in mind that creative thinking is not restricted to the arts; it can occur in all subject areas—even in fields that seek precision and definite answers. In math, creative thinking involves using new approaches or strategies for arriving at a correct solution to a problem. In science, creativity takes place when a scientist first uses imaginative thinking to create a hypothesis or logical hunch ("What might happen if . . . ?") and then conducts an experiment to test out whether the hypothesis turns out to be true.

It could be said that thinking critically involves looking "inside the box" to evaluate the quality of its content. Thinking creatively involves looking "outside the box" to imagine other packages containing different content. Creative and critical thinking are two of the most important forms of higher-level thinking and they can work together in a cyclical and complementary fashion. Creative thinking is used to ask new questions and generate new ideas; critical thinking is used to evaluate or critique the ideas we generate (Paul & Elder, 2004). For an idea to be truly creative, it must not just be different or unusual, it must also be effective or significant (Sternberg, 2001; Runco, 2004). If our critique of what we've created reveals that it lacks quality or is ineffective, we shift back to creative thinking to generate something new and improved.

Or, the starting point for the cyclical process of creative and critical thinking may be reversed, whereby we begin by using critical thinking to evaluate an old idea or approach. If our evaluation indicates that it's not very good, we turn on the creative thinking process to come up with a new idea or different approach; then we turn back to critical thinking to evaluate the quality of the new idea we created.

Brainstorming is a problem-solving process that illustrates how creative and critical thinking work hand-in-hand. The steps or stages involved in the process of brainstorming are summarized in **Box 8.3**.

Box 8.3

The Process of Brainstorming

1. Generate as many ideas as you can, jotting them down rapidly without stopping to evaluate their validity or practicality. Studies show that worrying about whether an idea is correct often blocks creativity (Basadur, Runco, & Vega, 2000). So, at this stage of the process, just let your imagination run wild; don't be concerned about whether the idea you generate is impractical, unrealistic, or outrageous.
2. Review the ideas you generated and use them as a springboard to trigger additional ideas, or combine them into larger ideas.
3. After you run out of ideas, critically evaluate the list of ideas you've generated and eliminate those that you think are least effective.
4. From the remaining list of ideas, choose the best idea or best combination of ideas.

Note that the first two steps in the brainstorming process involve *divergent thinking*—a form of creative thinking that allows you to go off in different directions and generate diverse ideas. In contrast, the last two steps in the process involve *convergent thinking*—a form of critical thinking in which you converge (focus in) and narrow down the ideas, evaluating each of them for their effectiveness.

As this multistage process suggests, creativity doesn't just happen suddenly or effortlessly (the so-called "stroke of genius"); instead, it takes sustained mental effort (Paul & Elder, 2004; De Bono, 2007). Although creative thinking may occasionally involve spontaneous or intuitive leaps, it typically involves careful reflection and evaluation of whether any of those leaps actually land you on a good idea.

AUTHOR'S EXPERIENCE

I was once working with a friend to come up with ideas for a grant proposal. We started out by sitting at his kitchen table, exchanging ideas while sipping coffee; then we both got up and began to pace back and forth, walking all around the room while bouncing different ideas off each other. Whenever a new idea was thrown out, one of us would jot it down (whoever was pacing closer to the kitchen table at the moment).

After we ran out of ideas, we shifted gears, slowed down, and sat down at the table together to critique the ideas we generated during our "binge-thinking" episode. After some debate, we finally settled on an idea that we judged to be the best of all the ideas we produced, and we used this idea for the grant proposal—which, ultimately, was awarded to us.

Although I wasn't fully aware of it at the time, the stimulating thought process my friend and I were engaging in was called brainstorming: first we engaged in creative thinking—our fast-paced, idea-production stage followed by critical thinking—our slower-paced, idea-evaluation stage.

—*Joe Cuseo*

> "Creativity is allowing oneself to make mistakes; art is knowing which ones to keep."
>
> *—Scott Adams, creator of the Dilbert comic strip and author of The Dilbert Principle*

Note

Creative thinking is about generating new answers and solutions. Critical thinking is about evaluating the quality of answers and solutions we generate.

 **Reflection 8.9**

Do you consider yourself to be a creative thinker? Why?

What could you do to improve your ability to think creatively?

Using Higher-Level Thinking Skills to Improve Academic Performance

Thus far, this chapter has focused primarily on helping you get a clear idea of what higher-level thinking is and what its major forms are. The remainder of the chapter focuses on helping you develop habits of higher-level thinking that can be applied to improve your performance in college and beyond.

Connect ideas you acquire in class with related ideas found in your assigned reading. When you discover information in your reading that relates to something you've learned about in class (or vice versa), make a note of it in the margin of your textbook or your class notebook. By integrating knowledge you've obtained from these two major sources, you're engaging in the higher-level thinking skill of synthesis, which you can then demonstrate on exams and assignments to improve your course grades.

When listening to lectures and completing reading assignments, pay attention not only to the content being covered but also the thought process used to cover the content. Periodically ask yourself what form of higher-level thinking your instructors are using during class presentations and authors are using when you're reading their writing. The more conscious you are of the type of higher-level thinking skills you're being exposed to, the more likely you are to develop those thinking skills yourself and demonstrate them on exams and assignments.

Periodically pause to reflect on your own thinking process. When working on different academic tasks, ask yourself what type of thinking you're doing (e.g., analysis, synthesis, or evaluation). Thinking about and becoming aware of how you're thinking while you're thinking is a mental process called *metacognition* (Flavell, 1979; Hartman, 2001). It's a mental habit that's associated with higher-level thinking and improved problem-solving skills (Halpern, 2013; Resnick, 1986).

One simple yet powerful way to help you reflect on your thinking is through self-questioning. Since thinking often involves talking to ourselves silently (or aloud), if you ask yourself high-quality, thought-provoking questions, you can train your mind to think at a higher level. A good question can launch you on a quest or voyage to answer it by using higher-level thinking skills. Getting in the habit of asking yourself higher-level thinking questions while learning will increase the likelihood you'll display higher levels of thinking during class discussions, as well as on course exams and assignments.

Box 8.4 contains key questions you can use to trigger different forms of higher-level thinking. The questions are constructed as incomplete sentences so you can fill in the blank with any topic or concept you're studying in any course you may be taking. Research indicates that when students get in the habit of using question stems such as these, they develop and demonstrate higher levels of thinking in college courses (King, 1990, 1995, 2002). As you read the questions under each of the

> If you do not ask the right questions, you do not get the right answers."
>
> —*Edward Hodnett, British poet*

seven forms of higher-level thinking in the following box, think about how they may be applied to material you're learning in courses this term.

Box 8.4

Self-Questioning Strategies to Trigger Different Forms of Higher-Level Thinking

1. ANALYSIS (ANALYTICAL THINKING)—breaking down information into its essential elements or parts.

   Trigger Questions:
   - What are the main ideas contained in _____?
   - What are the important aspects of _____?
   - What are the key issues raised by _____?
   - What are the major purposes of _____?
   - What hidden assumptions are embedded in _____?
   - What are the reasons behind _____?

2. SYNTHESIS (INTEGRATIVE THINKING)—integrating separate pieces of information to form a more complete and coherent product or pattern.

   Trigger Questions:
   - How can this idea be joined or connected with _____ to create a more complete or comprehensive answer?
   - How could these different _____ be grouped together into a more general class or category?
   - How could these separate _____ be reorganized or rearranged to produce a comprehensive understanding of the big picture?

3. APPLICATION (APPLIED THINKING)—using knowledge for practical purposes to solve problems and resolve issues.

   Trigger Questions:
   - How can this idea be used to _____?
   - How can this theory be put into practice to _____?
   - What could be done to improve or strengthen _____?
   - What could be done to prevent or reduce _____?

4. MULTIDIMENSIONAL THINKING—thinking that involves viewing yourself and the world around you from different angles or vantage points.

   Trigger Questions:
   - Have I taken into consideration all factors that could influence _____ or be influenced by _____?
   - How would _____ affect different dimensions of myself (emotional, physical, etc.)?
   - What broader impact would _____ have on the social and physical world around me?
   - How might people living in different times (e.g., past and future) experience _____?
   - How would people from different cultural backgrounds interpret or react to _____?

5. BALANCED THINKING—carefully considering reasons for and against a particular position or viewpoint.

   Trigger Questions:
   - Have I considered both sides of _____?
   - What are the strengths (advantages) and weaknesses (disadvantages) of _____?
   - What evidence supports and contradicts _____?
   - What are arguments for and counterarguments against _____?

6. CRITICAL THINKING (EVALUATION)—making critical judgments or assessments.

   Trigger Questions for Evaluating *Empirical Evidence*:
   - What examples support the argument that _____?
   - What research evidence is there for _____?
   - What statistical data document or back up this _____?

   Trigger Questions for Evaluating *Logical Consistency*:
   - If ____ is true, does it follow that _____ is also true?
   - If I believe in _____, should I practice _____?
   - To draw this conclusion means I'm assuming that _____?

   Trigger Questions for Evaluating *Morality (Ethics)*:
   - Is _____ fair?
   - Is _____ just?
   - Is this action consistent with the professed or stated values of _____?

   Trigger Questions for Evaluating *Beauty (Aesthetics)*:
   - Does _____ meet established criteria for judging artistic beauty?
   - What is the aesthetic merit or value of _____?
   - Does _____ contribute to or detract from the beauty of the environment?

(continued)

Box 8.4 *(continued)*

Trigger Questions for Evaluating *Practicality (Usefulness)*:

- Will _____ work?
- What practical value does this _____ have?
- What potential benefits and drawbacks would result if this _____ were put into practice?

Trigger Questions for Evaluating *Priority (Order of Importance or Effectiveness)*:

- Which one of these _____ is the most important?
- Is this _____ the best option or choice available?
- How do these _____ rank from first to last (best to worst) in terms of their effectiveness?

7. CREATIVE THINKING—generating ideas that are unique, original, or distinctively different.

Trigger Questions:

- What could be invented to _____?
- Imagine what would happen if _____?
- What might be a different way to _____?

- How would this change if _____?
- What would be an innovative approach to _____?

Note: Save these higher-level thinking questions and use them when completing different academic tasks required in your courses (e.g., preparing for exams, writing papers or reports, and participating in class discussions or study group sessions). Get in the habit of periodically stepping back to reflect on your thinking and ask yourself what form of thinking you're engaging in (analysis, synthesis, application, etc.). You could even keep a "thinking log" or "thinking journal" to increase self-awareness of the thinking strategies you're using and developing. This strategy will not only help you acquire higher-level thinking skills, it will also help you communicate these skills in job interviews and letters of application for career positions.

Reflection 8.10

Review the higher-level thinking skills listed in questions in **Box 8.4** above. Identify one trigger question listed under each of the seven forms of thinking and fill in the blank with an idea or issue being covered in a course you're taking this term.

Strategies for Increasing Creativity

In addition to self-questioning strategies, the following attitudes and practices can be used to stimulate creative thinking.

"All thinking begins with wonder."

—Socrates, classic Greek (Athenian) philosopher and founding father of Western philosophy

- **Be flexible.** Think about ideas and objects in alternative and unconventional ways. The power of flexible and unconventional thinking was well illustrated in the movie *Apollo 13*, based on the true story of an astronaut who saved his life by creatively using duct tape as an air filter. The inventor of the printing press (Johannes Gutenberg) made his groundbreaking discovery while watching a machine being used to crush grapes at a wine harvest. He thought that the same type of machine could be used for a different purpose—to press letters onto paper (Dorfman, Shames, & Kihlstrom, 1996).

- **Be experimental.** Play with ideas; try them out to see whether they'll work or work better than the status quo. Studies show that creative people tend to be mental risk-takers who are willing to experiment with different ideas and techniques (Sternberg, 2001). Consciously resist the temptation to settle for the security of familiarity. When people cling rigidly to what's conventional or traditional, they're clinging to the comfort or security of what's most familiar and predictable; this often blocks originality, ingenuity, and openness to change.

Tom Kelley, cofounder of the famous IDEO design firm in Palo Alto, California, has found that innovative thinking emerges from an exploratory mindset that's "open to new insights every day" (Kelley & Littman, 2005).

- **Get mobile.** Stand up and move around while you're thinking. Research shows that taking a walk—either inside or outside—stimulates the production of creative ideas (Oppezzo & Schwartz, 2014). Even by standing up, our brain gets approximately 10% more oxygen than it does when sitting down (Sousa, 2011). Since oxygen provides fuel for the brain, our ability to think creatively is energized when we're up on our feet and moving around.

- **Get it down.** Creative ideas can often pop into our mind at the most unexpected times. Scholars refer to the sudden birth of creative ideas as *incubation*—just like incubated eggs can hatch at any time, so too can original ideas suddenly hatch and pop into our consciousness. However, just as great ideas can suddenly come to mind, they can also slip out of mind as soon as we start thinking about something else. You can prevent this slippage from happening by having the right equipment on hand to record your creative ideas before they slip away. Carry a pen and a small notepad, a packet of sticky notes, or a portable electronic recording device at all times to immediately record original ideas the instant you have them.

- **Get diverse.** Seek ideas from diverse social and informational sources. Bouncing your ideas off of different people and getting their feedback about your ideas is a good way to generate mental energy, synergy (multiplication of ideas), and serendipity (accidental discoveries). Studies show that creative people venture well beyond the boundaries of their particular area of training or specialization (Baer, 1993; Kaufman & Baer, 2002). They have wide-ranging interests and knowledge, which they draw upon and combine to generate new ideas (Riquelme, 2002). So, be on the lookout to combine the knowledge and skills you acquire from different subjects and different people, and use them to create bridges to new ideas.

> "I make progress by having people around who are smarter than I am—and listening to them. And I assume that everyone is smarter about something than I am."
> —Henry Kaiser, successful industrialist, known as the father of American shipbuilding

- **Take breaks.** If you're having trouble discovering a solution to a problem, stop working on it for a while and come back to it later. Creative solutions often come to mind after you stop thinking about the problem you're trying to solve. What often happens when you work intensely on a problem or challenging task for a sustained period of time, your attention can get rigidly riveted on just one approach to its solution (German & Barrett, 2005; Maier, 1970). By taking your mind off of it and returning to it later, your focus of attention is likely to shift to a different feature or aspect of the problem. This new focus may enable you to view the problem from a different angle or vantage point, which can lead to a breakthrough idea that was blocked by your previous perspective (Anderson, 2010). Furthermore, taking a break allows the problem to incubate in your mind at a lower level of consciousness and stress, which can sometimes give birth to a sudden solution.

> "Eureka! (literally translated: "I have found it!")
> —Attributed to Archimedes, ancient Greek mathematician and inventor when he suddenly discovered (while sitting in a bathtub) how to measure the purity of gold

- **Reorganize the problem.** When you're stuck on a problem, try rearranging its parts or pieces. Reorganization can transform the problem into a different pattern that may enable you to suddenly see a solution you previously overlooked—similar to how changing the order of letters in a word jumble can help you find the hidden word. You can use the same strategy to change the wording of any problem you're working on, or by recording ideas on index cards (or sticky notes) and laying them out in different sequences and patterns.

> "Creativity consists largely of re-arranging what we know in order to find out what we do not know."
> —George Keller, prolific American architect and originator of the Union Station design for elevated train stations

If you're having trouble solving a problem that involves a sequence of steps (e.g., a math problem), try reversing the sequence and start by working from the end or middle. The new sequence makes you to take a different approach to the problem; this forces you to come at it from a different direction, which can lead you to an alternative path to its solution.

 Reflection 8.11

The popularity of sticky notes is no doubt due to their versatility—you can post them on almost anything, remove them from where they were stuck (without a mess), and re-stick them somewhere else.

Think creatively for a minute. In what ways might you use sticky notes in a course or to handle a challenge?

> "Genius is 1% inspiration and 99% perspiration."
>
> —*Thomas Edison, scientist and creator of more than 1,000 inventions, including the light bulb, phonograph, and motion picture camera*

- **Be persistent.** Studies show that creativity takes time, dedication, and hard work (Ericsson, 2006; Ericsson & Charness, 1994). Creative insights typically don't occur effortlessly, but emerge after repeated reflection and sustained commitment.

Chapter Summary and Highlights

"Higher-level thinking" (also known as "higher-order thinking") refers to a more advanced level of thought than that used to acquire factual knowledge. It involves reflecting on knowledge acquired and taking it to a higher level—by performing additional mental action on it—such as evaluating its validity, integrating it with other ideas, or applying it to solve problems.

In this chapter, seven major forms of higher-level thinking skills were identified along with strategies for developing each of them:

1. *Analysis (Analytical Thinking)*—breaking down information to identify its key parts and underlying elements;
2. *Synthesis (Integrative Thinking)*—building up ideas by connecting them to form a larger whole or more comprehensive system;
3. *Application (Applied Thinking)*—putting knowledge into practice to solve problems and resolve issues;
4. *Multidimensional Thinking*—taking multiple perspectives (i.e., viewing issues from different vantage points);
5. *Balanced Thinking*—carefully considering arguments for and against a particular argument or position;
6. *Critical Thinking*—evaluating (judging the quality of) arguments, conclusions, and ideas; and
7. *Creative Thinking*—generating ideas that are unique, original, or distinctively different.

Besides achieving academic excellence in college, there are other key benefits of developing higher-level thinking skills.

1. **Higher-level thinking is essential for success in today's "information age" —a time when new information is being generated at faster rates than at any other time in human history. The majority of new workers in the information age no longer work with their hands; they will work with their heads**

(Miller, 2003). Employers now value college graduates who have inquiring minds and possess higher-level thinking skills (AAC&U, 2013; Peter D. Hart Research Associates, 2006).

2. **Higher-level thinking skills are vital for citizens in a democratic nation.** Authoritarian political systems, such as dictatorships and fascist regimes, suppress critical thought and demand submissive obedience to authority. In contrast, citizens of a democracy are able to control their political destiny by making wise choices about the political leaders they elect. Thus, effective use of higher-level thinking skills, such as critical thinking, is an essential civic responsibility for people living in a democratic nation.

3. **Higher-level thinking is an important safeguard against prejudice, discrimination, and hostility.** Racial, ethnic, and national prejudices are often rooted in narrow, self-centered, or group-centered thinking (Paul & Elder, 2014). Oversimplified, dualistic thinking can lead individuals to categorizing others into either "in" groups (us) or "out" groups (them). Such dualistic thinking can lead, in turn, to ethnocentrism—the tendency to view one's own racial or ethnic group as the superior "in" group and see other groups as inferior "out" groups. Development of higher-level thinking skills, such as taking multiple perspectives and using balanced thinking, counteracts the type of dualistic, ethnocentric thinking that leads to prejudice, discrimination, and hate crimes.

4. **Higher-level thinking helps preserve mental and physical health.** Simply put: Those who use their mind don't lose their mind. As they age, mentally active people are less likely to suffer memory loss or experience dementia (Wilson, et al., 2002). Thinking is not only a mental activity; it's also a physical activity that exercises the brain, much like physical activity exercises muscles in other parts of the body. Thinking requires higher levels of energy, which stimulates biological activity among brain cells, invigorates them, and reduces the likelihood they will deteriorate with age.

Contrary to common belief, problem solving and other forms of higher-level thinking will not "fry" your brain but will stimulate and exercise it, reducing the likelihood that you'll experience Alzheimer's disease and other causes of memory loss in later life.

Learning More through the World Wide Web: Internet-Based Resources

For additional information on thinking skills, see the following websites:

Higher-Level Thinking Skills:
http://edorigami.wikispaces.com/Bloom%27s+Digital+Taxonomy

Critical Thinking:
www.criticalthinking.org

Creative Thinking:
www.amcreativityassoc.org

Thinking Errors:
www.psychologytoday.com/blog/what-mentally-strong-people-dont-do/201501/10-thinking-errors-will-crush-your-mental-strength

www.factcheck.org (site for evaluating the factual accuracy of statements made by politicians in TV ads, debates, speeches, interviews, and news releases)

References

Anderson, J. R. (2010). *Cognitive psychology and its implications.* New York: Worth Publishers.

Anderson, L. W., & Krathwohl, D. R. (Eds.). (2001). *A taxonomy for learning, teaching, and assessing: A revision of Bloom's taxonomy of educational objectives.* New York: Addison Wesley Longman.

Association of American Colleges and Universities (AAC&U). (2013). *It takes more than a major: Employer priorities for college learning and success.* Washington, DC: Author.

Baer, J. M. (1993). *Creativity and divergent thinking.* Hillsdale, NJ: Erlbaum.

Basadur, M., Runco, M. A., & Vega, L. A. (2000). Understanding how creative thinking skills, attitudes and behaviors work together: A causal process model. *Journal of Creative Behavior, 34*(2), 77–100.

Conley, D. T. (2005). *College knowledge: What it really takes for students to succeed and what we can do to get them ready.* San Francisco: Jossey-Bass.

De Bono, E. (2007). *How to have creative ideas.* London, UK: Vermillion.

Donald, J. G. (2002). *Learning to think: Disciplinary perspectives.* San Francisco: Jossey-Bass.

Dorfman, J., Shames, J., & Kihlstrom, J. F. (1996). Intuition, incubation, and insight. In G. Underwood (Ed.), *Implicit cognition* (pp. 257–296). New York: Oxford University Press.

Ericsson, K. A. (2006). The influence of experience and deliberate practice on the development of superior expert performance. In K. A. Ericsson, N. Charness, P. Feltovich, and R. R. Hoffman (Eds.). *Cambridge handbook of expertise and expert performance* (pp. 685–706). Cambridge, UK: Cambridge University Press.

Ericsson, K. A., & Charness, N. (1994). Expert performance: Its structure and acquisition. *American Psychologist, 49*(8), 725–747.

Fairbairn, G. J., & Winch, C. (1996). *Reading, writing and reasoning: A guide for students* (2nd ed.). Buckingham: OU Press.

Flavell, J. H. (1979). Metacognition and cognitive monitoring: A new area of cognitive-developmental inquiry. *American Psychologist, 34*(10), 906–911.

Gardiner, L. F. (2005). Transforming the environment for learning: A crisis of quality. *To Improve the Academy, 23,* 3–23.

German, T. P., & Barrett, H. C. (2005). Functional fixedness in a technologically sparse culture. *Psychological Science, 16,* 1–5.

Halpern, D. F. (2013). *Thought & knowledge: An introduction to critical thinking* (5th ed.). New York: Psychology Press.

Hartman, H. J. (Ed.). (2001). *Metacognition in learning and instruction: Theory, research and practice.* Dordrecht: Kluwer Academic Publishers.

Higher Education Research Institute (HERI). (2009). *The American college teacher: National norms for 2007–2008.* Los Angeles: HERI, University of California, Los Angeles.

Intergovernmental Council on Climate Change. (2013). *Climate change 2013: The physical science basis.* Working Group I Contribution to the Fifth Assessment Report of the Intergovernmental Council on Climate Change. Switzerland: Intergovernmental Panel on Climate Change. Retrieved from http://www.ipcc.ch/report/ar5/wg1/.

Joint Science Academies' Statement. (2005). *Global response to climate change.* Retrieved from http://nationalacademies.org/onpi/06072005.pdf.

Kaufman, J. C., & Baer, J. (2002). Could Steven Spielberg manage the Yankees? Creative thinking in different domains. *Korean Journal of Thinking & Problem Solving, 12*(2), 5–14.

Kelley, T., & Littman, J. (2005). *The ten faces of innovation: IDEO's strategies for beating the devil's advocate & driving creativity throughout your organization*. New York: Currency/Doubleday.

King, A. (1990). Enhancing peer interaction and learning in the classroom through reciprocal questioning. *American Educational Research Journal, 27*(4), 664–687.

King, A. (1995). Guided peer questioning: A cooperative learning approach to critical thinking. *Cooperative Learning and College Teaching, 5*(2), 15–19.

King, A. (2002). Structuring peer interaction to promote high-level cognitive processing. *Theory into Practice, 41*(1), 33–39.

Maier, N. R. F. (1970). *Problem solving and creativity in individuals and groups*. Belmont, CA: Brooks/Cole.

Martin, R. L. (2007). *The opposable mind: How successful leaders win through integrative thinking*. Boston: Harvard Business School Press.

Miller, M. A. (2003, September/October). The meaning of the baccalaureate. *About Campus*, 2–8.

Milton, O. (1982). *Will that be on the final?* Springfield, IL: Charles C. Thomas.

National Resources Defense Council. (2005). *Global warming: A summary of recent findings on the changing global climate*. Retrieved from http://www.nrdc.org/globalwarming/science/2005.asp.

National Resources Defense Council. (2012). *Global warming: An introduction to climate change*. Retrieved from www.nrdc.org/globalwarming.

Oppezzo, M., & Schwartz, D. L. (2014). Give your ideas some legs: The positive effect of walking on creative thinking. *Journal of Experimental Psychology: Learning, Memory, and Cognition, 40*(4), 1142–1152.

Pascarella, E., & Terenzini, P. (1991). *How college affects students: Findings and insights from twenty years of research*. San Francisco: Jossey-Bass.

Pascarella, E., & Terenzini, P. (2005). *How college affects students: A third decade of research* (Vol. 2). San Francisco: Jossey-Bass.

Paul, R., & Elder, L. (2004). *The nature and functions of critical and creative thinking*. Dillon Beach, CA: Foundation for Critical Thinking.

Paul, R., & Elder, L. (2014). *Critical thinking: Tools for taking charge of your professional and personal life*. Upper Saddle River, NJ: Pearson Education.

Perry, W. G. (1970, 1999). *Forms of intellectual and ethical development during the college years: A scheme*. New York: Holt, Rinehart & Winston.

Peter D. Hart Research Associates. (2006). *How should colleges prepare students to succeed in today's global economy?* The Association of American Colleges and Universities by Peter D. Hart Research Associates, Inc.

Resnick, L. B. (1986). *Education and learning to think*. Washington, DC: National Academy Press.

Riquelme, H. (2002). Can people creative in imagery interpret ambiguous figures faster than people less creative in imagery? *Journal of Creative Behavior, 36*(2), 105–116.

Runco, M. A. (2004). Creativity. *Annual Review of Psychology, 55*, 657–687.

Seabrook, J. (2008). *Flash of genius and other true stories of invention*. New York: St. Martin's Press.

Shelton, et al. (2003). Evaluation of parameters affecting quantitative detection of Escherichia coli O157 in enriched water samples using immunomagnetic electrochemiluminescence. *J. Microbiology Methods*, (Dec.), *55*(3), 717–725.

Sousa, D. A. (2011). *How the brain learns*. Thousand Oaks, CA: Sage.

Stark, J. S., Lowther, R. J., Bentley, M. P., Ryan, G. G., Martens, M. L., Genthon, P. A., et al. (1990). *Planning introductory college courses: Influences on faculty*. Ann Arbor: National Center for Research to Improve Postsecondary Teaching and Learning, University of Michigan. (ERIC Document Reproduction Services No. 330 277 370.)

Staudinger, U. M. (2008). A psychology of wisdom: History and recent developments. *Research in Human Development, 5*, 107–120.

Sternberg, R. J. (2001). What is the common thread of creativity? *American Psychologist, 56*(4), 360–362.

Wilson, R., Mendes, C., Barnes, L., et al. (2002). Participation in cognitively stimulating activities and risk of incident Alzheimer's disease. *Journal of the American Medical Association, 287*(6), 742–748.

Chapter 8 Exercises

8.1 Quote Reflections

Review the sidebar quotes contained in this chapter and select two that were especially meaningful or inspirational to you.

For each quote, provide a three- to five-sentence explanation why you chose it.

8.2 Reality Bite

Trick or Treat: Confusing Test or Challenging Test?

Students in Professor Plato's philosophy course just got their first exam back and they're going over the test together in class. Some students are angry because they feel the professor deliberately included "trick questions" to confuse them. Professor Plato responds by saying that his test questions were not designed to trick the class but to "challenge them to think."

Reflection and Discussion Questions

1. What do you think may have led some students to conclude that the professor was trying to trick or confuse them?
2. What type of test questions do you suspect the professor created to "challenge students to think"?
3. On future tests, what might the students do to reduce the likelihood that they'll feel tricked again?
4. On future tests, what might Professor Plato do to reduce the likelihood that students will complain about being asked "trick questions"?

8.3 Faculty Interview

Make an appointment to visit a faculty member on campus, either in a course you're taking this term, or in a field of study you're likely to pursue as your major. During your visit, ask the following questions:

1. In your field of study, what key questions do scholars ask?
2. How are answers to these questions investigated and discovered?
3. How do scholars in your field demonstrate critical and creative thinking?
4. What types of thinking skills does it take for students to succeed or excel in your field?

8.4 Self-Assessment of Higher-Level Thinking Characteristics

Thinking at a higher level is not just an intellectual process, it's also a personal attribute. Listed below are attributes of higher-level thinkers, accompanied by specific behaviors associated with each attribute. As you read the behaviors under each of the general attributes, place a checkmark (✓) next to any behavior that's true of you now and an asterisk (*) next to any behavior you think you need to work on.

1. *Tolerant and Accepting*
   ___ Don't tune out ideas that conflict with your own
   ___ Keep your emotions under control when someone criticizes your personal viewpoint
   ___ Feel comfortable discussing controversial issues
   ___ Try to find common ground with others holding opposing viewpoints

2. *Inquisitive and Open Minded*

___ Eager to continue learning new things from different people and different experiences

___ Willing to seek out others who hold viewpoints different than your own

___ Find differences of opinion and opposing viewpoints to be interesting and stimulating

___ Attempt to understand why people have opposing viewpoints

3. *Reflective and Tentative*

___ Take time to consider all perspectives or sides of an issue before drawing conclusions, making choices, or reaching decisions

___ Give fair consideration to ideas that others may instantly disapprove of or find distasteful

___ Acknowledge the complexity, ambiguity, and uncertainty of certain issues, and am willing to say: "I need to give this more thought" or "I need more evidence before I can draw a conclusion."

___ Periodically reexamine your own viewpoints to determine whether they should be maintained or changed

4. *Honest and Courageous*

___ Willing to examine your views to see if they're biased or prejudiced

___ Willing to challenge others' ideas that are based on personal bias or prejudice

___ Willing to express viewpoints that may not conform to those of the majority

___ Willing to change previously held opinions and personal beliefs when they're contradicted by sound arguments or new evidence

Look back at the list and count the number of checkmarks and asterisks you placed in each of the four general areas:

	Checkmarks	Asterisks
Tolerant and Accepting:	_____	_____
Inquisitive and Open Minded:	_____	_____
Reflective and Tentative:	_____	_____
Honest and Courageous:	_____	_____

Reflection Questions

- Under which of the four attributes did you place (a) the most *checkmarks*, (b) the most *asterisks*? What do you think accounts for the difference?

- What could you do in college to strengthen your weakest area (the attribute below which you had the most asterisks)?

8.5 Demonstrating Higher-Level Thinking in Your Courses

Look at the syllabus for three courses you're enrolled in this term and find an assignment or exam that counts the most toward your final course grade. (If you're taking fewer than three courses, you can choose more than one assignment or exam from the same course.)

Course	Major Assignment or Test
1. _____	_____
2. _____	_____
3. _____	_____

Using the grid that follows, place a checkmark in each box that represents the form of higher-level thinking you think you can demonstrate on each of these major assignments or tests. (For a quick review of the major forms of higher-level thinking, see the higher-level thinking definitions on p. 181.)

	Course 1	Course 2	Course 3
Analysis Thinking			
Synthesis Thinking			
Application Thinking			
Multidimensional Thinking			
Balanced Thinking			
Critical Thinking			
Creative Thinking			

For each course, select one box you checked and describe how you would demonstrate this form of higher-level thinking on the particular assignment or test you chose. For instance, if you checked a box indicating that you will use multidimensional thinking, describe what perspectives or factors you will take into consideration.

Course 1 exam or assignment: _____

Form of higher-level thinking to be demonstrated:

How I plan to demonstrate this form of thinking:

Course 2 exam or assignment: _____

Form of higher-level thinking to be demonstrated:

How I plan to demonstrate this form of thinking:

Course 3 exam or assignment: _____

Form of higher-level thinking to be demonstrated:

How I plan to demonstrate this form of thinking:

Social and Emotional Intelligence

RELATING TO OTHERS AND REGULATING EMOTIONS

This chapter identifies effective strategies for communicating with and relating to others, as well as strategies for understanding and managing our emotions—such as stress, anxiety, anger, and depression. Implementing the strategies discussed in this chapter will enhance the quality of your college experience and your overall quality of life.

Strengthen social intelligence through use of effective interpersonal communication and human relations skills, and enhance emotional intelligence by effectively recognizing one's own emotions and the emotions of others.

 Reflection 9.1

When you think about someone being "intelligent," what personal characteristics come to mind?

If your answer to the preceding question focused on "intellectual" characteristics, your response reflected the traditional definition of intelligence. Human intelligence was once considered to be a general intellectual trait that could be measured by a single intelligence test score. Scholars have since discovered that the singular word "intelligence" needs to be replaced with the plural "intelligences" to reflect the fact that humans can and do display intelligence in many forms other than that measured by an IQ test. One of these other forms of human intelligence is referred to as *social intelligence* (a.k.a. "interpersonal intelligence"); it refers to the ability to communicate and relate effectively to others (Gardner, 1993, 1999; Goleman, 2006). It's been long known than interpersonal skills are essential for effective leadership (Avolio, Walumbwa, & Weber, 2009), and more recent research indicates that social intelligence is a better predictor of personal and professional success than intellectual ability (Carneiro, Crawford, & Goodman, 2006; Goleman, 2006).

Another newly identified form of human intelligence is *emotional intelligence*—the ability to recognize our own emotions and the emotions of others, and behave in ways that have a positive impact on how others feel (Matthews, Zeidner, & Rob-

> "The most important single ingredient in the formula of success is knowing how to get along with people."
>
> —Theodore (Teddy) Roosevelt, 26th president of the United States and winner of the Nobel Peace Prize

"The Internet supposedly increases communication and brings humanity closer together. Instead, in my generation, I'm noticing quite the opposite. There seems to be less face-to-face communication. Everyone is hooked on social networking websites. We cowardly avoid interaction where there are no facial expressions or tones."

—*First-year college student*

"We have been given two ears and but a single mouth in order that we may hear more and talk less."

—*Zeno of Citium, Ancient Greek philosopher and founder of Stoic philosophy*

erts, 2007; Salovey & Mayer, 1990). Research on emotional intelligence also reveals that it's a better predictor of personal and occupational success than performance on intellectual tests (Goleman, 1995, 2000). Research also shows that emotional self-awareness—a key element of emotional intelligence—is a characteristic of effective leaders (Avolio & Luthans, 2006; Goleman, Boyatzis, & McKee, 2013).

The Importance of Social Relationships and Social Intelligence

Studies show that people with stronger social support networks are happier (Myers, 1993, 2000) and live a longer life (Giles, et al., 2005). The need to develop strong social support networks is particularly important in today's high-tech world of virtual reality and online (vs. in-person) communication, both of which make it easier to avoid face-to-face interaction with other people and increase the risk of social isolation and loneliness (Putman, 2000).

 Reflection 9.2

Who are the people in your life that you tend to turn to for social support when you're experiencing stress or need personal encouragement?

The quality of our social relationships rests heavily on two key skills:

1. *interpersonal communication* skills—how well we communicate (verbally and non-verbally) when interacting with others, and
2. *human relations* skills—how well we relate to and treat others (i.e., people skills).

Interpersonal Communication Skills

Listed below are strategies for strengthening interpersonal communication skills. Some of these strategies may seem very simple or obvious, but they are powerful. Perhaps it's because they're so simple that people simply overlook look them and forget to use them consistently. Don't be fooled by the seeming simplicity of the following suggestions and don't underestimate the positive impact they have on the quality of your interpersonal interactions and relationships.

1. Take *listening* seriously. When people hear the term "communication skills," the skills of speaking and writing usually come to mind. However, the root of the word "communicate" is *communicare*, meaning "to share or divide out," which suggests that communication is a two-way process that involves skills not only for delivering information, but receiving it as well. In fact, studies show that listening is the most frequently used communication skill; we spend more time listening than speaking, reading, and writing (Purdy & Borisoff, 1996). One study found that college students spend an average of 52.5% of each day listening (Barker & Watson, 2000). When people are asked to identify what they like most about their best friend, "a good listener" ranks among the top characteristics cited (Berndt, 1992). Effective listening skills is also a top-ranking characteristic of effective leaders (Johnson & Bechler, 1998), and it ranks among the top skills employers look for when hiring and promoting employees (Gabric & McFadden, 2001; Wolvin, 2010).

2. **Use *active* listening strategies.** We can listen to and understand spoken words at a rate four or more times faster than the average rate at which people speak (Barker & Watson, 2000). This leaves plenty of time for our attention to drift and fall into the trap of *passive listening*—hearing the words with our ears, but not thinking about those words with our mind because our mind is somewhere else. To combat this tendency, we need to engage in *active listening*, which involves: (a) making an effortful attempt to focus full attention on the speaker's message (as opposed to just waiting for our turn to talk or thinking about what we're going to say next); (b) being an empathic listener who attends to the speaker's feelings and nonverbal messages; and (c) being an engaged listener who checks for understanding, expresses interest, and encourages elaboration.

Note

When you listen actively and closely to others, it sends them the message that you respect them and their thoughts and feelings are worthy of receiving your undivided attention.

Active listening doesn't happen naturally; it's a skill developed through effort and practice that eventually becomes a regular habit. To develop the habit of active listening, engage in the following practices:

*   While listening, monitor your understanding of what's being said. Good listeners take personal responsibility for following the speaker's message; in contrast, poor listeners put all the responsibility on the speaker to make the message clear and interesting. One way to check if you've followed the message is to occasionally summarize or paraphrase what you heard the speaker saying in your own words (e.g., "What I hear you saying is . . ."). This not only ensures you understand the message, it also sends the speaker the message that you're really listening to what's being said and taking it seriously.
*   Check to be sure you're understanding what the person is *feeling* in addition to what the person is saying (e.g., "I'm sensing that you're feeling . . ."). Be sensitive to nonverbal messages, such as tone of voice and body language; they can often provide clues to the feelings behind the speaker's words. (For instance, speaking at a high rate and with high volume may indicate frustration or anger and speaking at a low rate and with low volume may indicate dejection or depression.)
*   When you ask questions, allow the speaker time to formulate a thoughtful response. Be patient with some period of silence. If the silence continues, rephrase the question in a different way.
*   Avoid the urge to interrupt the speaker when you think you have something important to say. Wait until the speaker has paused or completed her train of thought.
*   If the speaker pauses and you start to say something at the same time the speaker begins to speak again, don't overpower him by speaking louder; let him continue before you express your ideas.
*   Be sure your nonverbal messages send the speaker the message that you're interested and nonjudgmental. (For positive, nonverbal communication signals to send while listening, see **Box 9.1**.)

Box 9.1

Nonverbal Behaviors Associated with Active Listening

It's estimated that more than two-thirds of all human communication is nonverbal, and it's been found that nonverbal messages communicate stronger and truer messages than spoken language (Driver, 2010; Navarro, 2008). When there's inconsistency between an individual's verbal and nonverbal message (e.g., one shows interest, the other disinterest), we're more likely to perceive the nonverbal message as the true message (Ekman, 2009). Thus, "body language" may be the most powerful way a listener can communicate genuine interest in the speaker's message, as well as interest in and respect for the speaker. (Similarly, when we're speaking, awareness of our listeners' body language can provide us with important clues about whether we're holding or losing their interest.)

The most important thing in communication is to hear what isn't being said."

—Peter F. Drucker, Austrian author and founder of the study of "management"

Good listeners listen with their whole body and they use body language to signal their attention and interest. The different body language signals we should send while listening may be summarized in the acronym SOFTEN:

S = Smile. Smiling sends signals of acceptance and interest. However, smiling should be periodic, not continuous. (A sustained smile can come across as an insincere or artificial pose.)

Sit Still. Fidgeting or squirming sends the message that you're bored or growing inpatient (and can't wait to move onto something else).

O = Open Posture. Avoid closed-posture positions, such as crossing your arms or folding your hands; they can send the message that you're not open to what the speaker is saying or passing judgment on what's being said.

F = Forward Lean. Leaning *forward* sends the message that you're looking forward to what the speaker is going to say next. In contrast, leaning back can send a signal that you're backing off from (losing interest in) what's being said, or that you're evaluating (psychoanalyzing).

Face the Speaker Directly. Line up your shoulders with the speaker's shoulders rather than turning one shoulder away—which sends the message that you want to get away or are giving the speaker the "cold shoulder."

T = Touch. An occasional light touch on the arm or hand can be a good way to communicate warmth—but not repeated touching, stroking, or rubbing—which could be interpreted as inappropriate intimacy (or sexual harassment).

E = Eye Contact. Lack of eye contact sends the message that you're looking around for something more interesting or stimulating than the speaker. However, eye contact shouldn't be continuous because that borders on staring or glaring. Instead, strike a happy medium by making *periodic* eye contact.

N = Nod Your Head. Nodding slowly and periodically while listening sends the signal that you're following what's being said and affirming the person saying it. However, avoid rapid and repeated head nodding; this sends the message that you want the speaker to hurry up and finish up so you can start talking!

Sources: Barker & Watson (2000); Nichols (2009); Purdy & Borisoff (1996)

 Reflection 9.3

Are there any effective nonverbal listening messages cited in **Box 9.1** that you weren't already aware of, or that you need to work on?

An interesting exercise you can use to gain greater awareness of your nonverbal communication habits is to choose a couple of people whom you trust, and who know you well, and ask them to imitate your body language. This exercise can frequently be revealing (and sometimes very entertaining).

3. **Be open to listening to different conversational topics and viewpoints.** Don't be a close-minded or selective listener who listens to others like you're listening to a radio—selecting or tuning into only those stations that immediately capture your own interests or reinforce your opinions—while tuning out or turning off everything else. This is an issue of social etiquette and social ethics. It's also a learning issue because we learn the most from others whose interests and viewpoints don't duplicate our own. Thus, ignoring or blocking out information and ideas about topics that don't immediately interest you or support your particular perspective is not only a poor social skill; it's also a poor learning strategy.

When others express ideas you don't agree with, you still owe them the courtesy of listening to what they have to say (and not immediately shaking your head, frowning, or interrupting them). After others finish expressing their point of view, you should then feel free to express your own. You certainly have the right to express your viewpoints, as long as you don't express them in such an opinionated way that it makes others feel their views weren't heard or welcomed.

 Reflection 9.4

On what topics do you hold strong opinions?

When you express these opinions, how do others usually react to you?

4. **Communicate your ideas precisely and concisely.** When we speak, our goal should be to get to our point, make it, get "off stage," and give someone else a chance to talk. Nobody appreciates "stage hogs" who dominate the conversation and gobble up more than their fair share of conversation time.

You can make your spoken messages less time-consuming and more to the point by avoiding tangents, unnecessary details, and empty fillers (e.g., "like," "kinda like," "I mean," "I'm all," and "you know"). Fillers such as these just "fill up" time and waste conversation time while adding nothing substantial or meaningful to the conversation. Excessive use of fillers can also result in listeners losing patience, interest, and respect for the speaker (Daniels & Horowitz, 1997).

5. **Take time to gather your thoughts before expressing them.** It's better to think silently *before* speaking aloud than to think aloud *while* talking. Giving forethought to what you're going to say will enable you to speak economically and open up more time for others to speak.

6. **Be comfortable with silent spells that may take place during conversations.** Silence can sometimes make us feel uncomfortable (like being in an elevator with a stranger). To relieve the discomfort of silence, it's tempting to rush in and say anything to get the conversation going again. Although this may be well intended, it can result in speaking before (and without) thinking. Probably more often than not, it's better to hold back our words and think them through before blurting them out.

Silent spots in a conversation shouldn't always be viewed as a "communication breakdown." Instead, they may indicate that the people involved in the conversation are pausing to think deeply about what each other is saying and are comfortable enough with each other to allow these reflective pauses to take place.

> Be sincere; be brief; be seated."
> —*Franklin D. Roosevelt, 32nd president of the United States*

> It does not require many words to speak the truth."
> —*Chief Joseph, leader of the Nez Percé, Native American Indian tribe*

> To talk without thinking is to shoot without aiming."
> —*An English proverb*

> I have never been hurt by anything I didn't say."
> —*Calvin Coolidge, 30th U.S. president*

Reflection 9.5

Would you say that you're a good conversationalist?

If yes, what makes you so?

If no, what prevents you from being one?

> "We should be aware of the magic contained in a name. The name sets that individual apart; it makes him or her unique among all others. Remember that a person's name is to that person the sweetest and most important sound in any language."
>
> —*Dale Carnegie, author of the best-selling book,* How to Win Friends and Influence People, *and founder of* The Dale Carnegie Course—*a worldwide leadership training program for business professionals*

Human Relations Skills (a.k.a. "People Skills")

In addition to communicating well with others, another key component of social intelligence is *human relations* skills—how well we relate to and treat others. Listed below are specific strategies for strengthening human relations skills.

Learn and remember the *names* of people you meet. When you refer to a person by name, you affirm that person's individuality and unique identity. You've likely heard people say they just don't have a good memory for names, which implies that they will never be good at remembering names. However, the truth is that the ability to remember names is not some kind of natural talent or inherited ability that you either have or don't have. Instead, it's an acquired skill that's developed through intentional effort and effective use of memory improvement strategies, such as those described below.

- Pay close attention to the names of people you meet when you first meet them. The key first step to remembering someone's name is to actually hear it and get it into our brain in the first place. As obvious as this may seem, when we first meet someone, instead of listening actively and carefully for their name, we're often more focused on the first impression we're making on the person, or what we're going to say next. Consequently, when we *forget* someone's name, what really happened is that we didn't *get* the name (into our brain) in the first place because we were distracted by other thoughts.

- Strengthen your memory for the person's name by saying it soon after you first hear it. For instance, if your friend Gertrude has just introduced you to Geraldine, you might say: "Geraldine, how long have you known Gertrude?" When you recall a person's name shortly after you've heard it, you prevent memory loss at the time when it's most likely to occur—during the first minutes after information is taken into the brain. Using the person's name soon after you've heard it also serves to make that person feel welcomed and validated.

- Associate the person's name with other information you've learned or know about the person. For instance, you can associate the person's name with (a) your first topic of conversation, (b) some physical characteristic of the person, or (c) the place where you met. By making a mental connection between the person's name and another piece of information, you capitalize on the brain's natural tendency to store (retain) information as part of an interconnected network, rather than as isolated bits of information.

- Keep a name journal that includes the names of new people you meet, along with information about them (e.g., what they do and what their interests are). We write down things we don't want to forget to do, so why not do the same for the names of people we want to remember? Whenever you meet someone new,

> "When I joined the bank, I started keeping a record of the people I met and put them on little cards, and I would indicate on the cards when I met them, and under what circumstances, and sometimes [make] a little notation which would help me remember a conversation."
>
> —*David Rockefeller, prominent American banker, philanthropist, and former CEO of the Chase Manhattan Bank*

make note of that person's name by recording it in a name journal and accompany it with a short note of where you met and what you talked about.

Note

Remembering names is not only a social skill that can bring you friends and improve your social life, it's also a powerful professional tool that can promote your career success in whatever field you choose to pursue.

Refer to people by name when you greet and interact with them. Once you've learned a person's name, use it when you interact with the person. Saying, "Hi, Waldo" will mean a lot more to Waldo than simply saying "Hi" or the impersonal "Hi, there"—which sounds like you've just seen an unidentifiable entity "out there" in public space—similar to addressing a letter "to whom it may concern." By continuing to use people's names after you've learned them, you send the message you haven't forgotten who they are, and at the same time, you strengthen your memory of their names.

Remember information others share with you and refer to it when you interact with them. Ask people questions about their personal interests, plans, and experiences. Listen closely to their answers, especially to what seems most important to them, what they care about, or what interests them, and use this information in your future conversations with them. For one person that topic may be politics, for another it may be sports, for another it may be relationships.

When you see the person again, bring up something that was discussed in your last conversation. Get beyond the stock, generic questions that people routinely ask after they say "Hello" (e.g., "What's up? What's going on?"). Instead, ask about something specific you discussed with them last time you spoke (e.g., "How did you make out on that math test last week?"). Our memories often reflect our priorities—we remember what's important to us. When you remember what others share with you, it shows them they're important to you.

Furthermore, when you show interest in others, you'll find that others start showing more interest in you. You're also likely to hear others say that you're a good listener and a great conversationalist.

(Complete Exercise 9.3 at the end of this chapter to assess your strengths and blind spots when it comes to forming and maintaining interpersonal relationships.)

> "You can make more friends in 2 months by becoming interested in other people than you can in 2 years by trying to get other people interested in you."
>
> —*Dale Carnegie,* How to Win Friends and Influence People

Strategies for Meeting People and Forming Friendships

An important aspect of the college experience is meeting new people, learning from them, and forming lifelong friendships. Listed below are practical strategies for increasing the number and variety of people you meet and the quality of friendships you form.

1. **Place yourself in situations and locations where you will come in regular contact with others.** Social psychologists have found that physical propinquity is the first step in the process of forming friendships—that is, people are more likely to become friends if they continue to find themselves in the same place at the same time (Latané, et al., 1995; Oloritun, et al., 2013). You can apply this principle by spending as much time on campus as possible and spending time in places where others are likely to be present (e.g., by eating your meals in the student cafeteria and studying in the college library). If you have the opportunity to live on campus, do so, because studies show that it helps students make

social connections and increases their satisfaction with the college experience (Pascarella & Terenzini, 2005; Tinto, 2012). If you're a commuter student, make your college experience as similar as possible to that of a residential student. When your schedule permits, spend time on campus doing things other than attending class (e.g., study in the library and participate in campus events).

 Reflection 9.6

Have you attended any college parties on or off campus?

If yes, what were they like?

If no, why haven't you?

2. **Put yourself in social situations where you're likely to meet people who share your interests, goals, and values.** Research supports the proverb: "Birds of a feather flock together." People tend to form friendships with others who share similar interests, values, or goals (AhYun, 2002). Friendships are more likely to form among people who have interests and values in common because they're more likely to spend time together doing things relating to their shared interests, and because they're more likely to validate each other's shared values (Festinger, 1954; Suls, Martin, & Wheeler, 2002).

   One straightforward way to find others with whom you have something in common is by participating in campus clubs and organizations that reflect your interests and values. (If you can't find one, start one of your own.) Also, keep track of social events that are likely to attract others who share your interests, values, or goals by regularly checking your college newspaper, posted flyers on campus, and the Student Information Desk in your Student Activities Center. However as you know, meeting new people and "fitting in" doesn't mean blind conformity, caving into peer pressure, or doing things that conflict with your values and compromise your integrity.

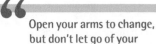
"Open your arms to change, but don't let go of your values."

—*Dalai Lama, the current Dalai Lama, Tibetan Buddhist guru*

"I'm genuine. I don't change depending on who I'm around."

—*College sophomore*

 Reflection 9.7

Since you've begun college, have you experienced any "peer pressure" (good or bad)?

What was the situation?

How did you respond?

3. **Meeting others through social websites.** Facebook and other social websites represent an additional way to meet new people, join groups on campus, and check for announcements of parties or other social events. However, be careful about the people you respond to, and the screen name you use, and the messages you post on your page or "wall." Don't forget that cyberspace is public space and it can be accessed by people beyond your social circle. For instance,

©pixinity/Shutterstock.com

An important aspect of the college experience is meeting new people and forming lasting friendships.

some schools and employers review social networking sites (e.g., Facebook and Twitter) to check entries; they use the information they find to help them screen prospects and accept or reject applicants (Grasz, 2014).

Dating and Romantic Relationships

Traditionally, romantic relationships begin through the process of dating. College students take different approaches to dating, ranging from not dating at all to dating with the intent of exploring or cementing long-term relationships. These different dating approaches are summarized in **Box 9.2**.

Box 9.2

Different Approaches to Dating among College Students

Postponing Dating. Students taking this approach feel that the demands of college work and college life are too time-consuming to take on the additional social and emotional burden of dating while in college.

It's hard enough to have fun here with all the work you have to do. There's no reason to have the extra drama [of dating] in your life."

—College sophomore

Hooking Up. Students who prefer this approach believe that formal dating is unnecessary; they feel that their social and sexual needs are better met more causally by associating with friends and acquaintances. Instead of going out on a one-on-one date, they prefer to first meet

and connect with romantic partners in larger group settings, such as college parties.

Now all a guy has to do to hookup on a Saturday night is to sit on the couch long enough at a party. Eventually a girl will plop herself down beside him . . . he'll make a joke, she'll laugh, their eyes will meet, sparks will fly, and the mission is accomplished. And you want me to tell this guy to call a girl, spend $100 on dinner and hope for a goodnight kiss?"

—College student

Casual Dating. Students using this approach like to date primarily for the purpose of enjoying themselves, rather than getting "tied down" to any particular person. These are "casual daters" who prefer to go out on a short series of dates with one person, then stop and shift to someone else; or, they may date different individuals at the same time. Their primary goal is to meet new people and

(continued)

Box 9.2 *(continued)*

discover what characteristics they find attractive in others.

Exclusive Dating. Students adopting this approach prefer to date one person for an extended period of time. Although marriage is not the goal, an exclusive dater takes casual dating one step further: they date for the purpose of getting a better idea about what characteristics they're seeking in a long-term mate or spouse.

Courtship. Students involved in this form of dating intend to continue the relationship until it culminates in marriage or a formal, long-term commitment.

Source: Adapted from research reviewed by Seirup (2004).

 Reflection 9.8

How would you define *love*? Would you say it's a feeling? An action? Both?

What do you think are the best signs that two people are "in love"?

What would you say are the most common reasons why people "fall out of love"?

Romantic Relationships

Dating relationships may eventually evolve into romantic relationships. Research on romantic relationships reveals they typically progress through the following stages (Bassham, et al., 2013; Ruggiero, 2011).

Stage 1. Passionate Love (Infatuation)

This is the very first stage of a romantic relationship, and it's characterized by the following features.

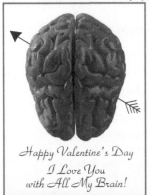

©MarkusManson/Shutterstock.com, compilation ©Kendall Hunt Publishing Company

Happy Valentine's Day I Love You with All My Brain!

Despite expressions like "I love you with all my heart," romantic love takes place in the brain and is accompanied by major changes in the production of brain chemicals.

- *Erotic* love: relationship involves intense physical arousal and passion; attention is focused primarily on the partner's physical appearance and physical attraction between the partners is at a peak.
- *Impulsivity*: partners can quickly "fall into" love or be suddenly "swept off their feet" (e.g., "love at first sight").
- *Obsession*: partners can't stop thinking about each other (they're "madly in love").
- *Intense emotions*: a surge of chemicals are released in the body and brain (similar to a drug-induced state), namely:
  1) a rush of adrenalin—a bodily hormone that triggers faster heart rate and breathing; and
  2) increased production of dopamine—a brain chemical that triggers feelings of excitement, euphoria, joy, and general well being (Bartels & Zeki, 2000).
- *Idealism*: The partners perceive each other and the relationship as being "perfect." They may say things like: "We're made for each other." "Nobody else has a relationship like ours." "We'll be together forever." Such idealistic thinking can make love "blind"—the partner's flaws and weaknesses are not seen (although they may be obvious to those outside of the relationship). One or both of the partners may be in relationship *denial*, whereby problems that threaten

the security of the relationship are simply denied (pushed out of conscious awareness).

- *Attachment and Dependency*: The lovers feel insecure without each other and can't bear being separated (e.g., "I can't live without him"). As a result of such attachment and dependency, love at this stage follows the principle: "I love you because I am loved" and "I love you because I need you." It's hard to determine if the person is in love with the other person or is in love with the idea or feeling of being in love (Fromm, 1970).

- *Possessiveness and Jealousy*: Each lover feels that he or she has exclusive rights to the partner and may quickly become suspicious about the partner's fidelity, as well as jealous of anyone else who interacts with the partner in a friendly or affectionate manner. This possessiveness can be unjustified and irrational ("insane jealousy"), whereby the lover suspects the partner is "cheating" when there's no real evidence that any cheating is taking place.

- *Love Sickness*: If the relationship breaks up, intense depression or "love withdrawal" tends to follow the breakup, similar to withdrawal from a pleasure-producing drug. Studies show that the most common cause of despair or depression among college students is a romantic breakup (Foreman, 2009).

Stage 2. Mature Love

The partners gradually "fall out" of first-stage (puppy) love and progress or "fall into" a more mature (advanced) stage of love that has the following characteristics.

- The partners become less selfish and self-centered and more selfless and other-centered. Love is no longer just a noun—an emotion or feeling within the person (e.g., "I'm in love"), but also an action verb—a way in which the partners act toward each other and treat one another (e.g., "we love each other"). More emphasis is placed on caring for the partner, rather than being cared for. This more mature stage of love follows two principles:

  1) "I am loved because I love"—not, "I'm in love because I am loved" and
  2) "I need you because I love you"—not, "I love you because I need you" (Fromme, 1980).

- There's less of an emotional high experienced at this stage than early stages of the relationship. After the passage of time and experience with the partner, the original "mad rush" of hormones and euphoria-producing brain chemicals gradually levels off—similar to how the effects of a drug level off after it's been taken for an extended period of time (Fisher, 2004; Peele & Brodsky, 1991). The intense emotional "ups and downs" of early stage love are now replaced by feelings of emotional serenity (mellowness) and evenness—a less extreme, but more consistently pleasant emotional state characterized by slightly elevated levels of different brain chemicals (endorphins, rather than dopamine). Unlike infatuation or early-stage love, this pleasant emotional state does not decline with time; in fact, it may actually grow stronger as the relationship continues and matures (Bartels & Zeki, 2000).

- Physical passion decreases. The "flames of the flesh" don't burn as intensely as in first-stage love, but a romantic afterglow continues. This afterglow is characterized by more emotional intimacy or psychological closeness between the partners and greater self-disclosure, mutual trust, and interpersonal honesty—all of which enhance both the physical and psychological quality of the relationship (Viorst, 1998).

> "I learned love and I learned you. I learned that, in order to love someone, you must be blind to the physical and the past. You must see their emotional and mental strengths and weaknesses, passions and dislikes, hobbies and pastimes."
>
> —*Letter written by first-year student*

> "Two become one, yet remain one."
>
> —*Erich Fromm, in the book,* The Art of Loving

- Interest is now focused on the partner as a whole person, not just on the partner's physical qualities. The partners have a less idealistic, more realistic view of one another in which they recognize and accept each other's strengths and weaknesses. The partners genuinely like one another as persons (not just as lovers) and consider the other to be their "best" or "closest" friend.
- The partners have mutual trust and confidence in each other's commitment; they aren't plagued by feelings of suspicion, distrust, or petty jealousy. Each partner may have interests and close friends outside the relationship without the other becoming jealous (Hatfield & Rapson, 1993, 2000).
- The partners have mutual concern for each other's growth and fulfillment. Rather than being envious or competitive, they take joy in each other's personal successes and accomplishments.
- The relationship contains a balanced blend of independence and interdependence—referred to as the "paradox (contradiction) of love"—because both partners maintain their independence and individuality yet feel more complete and fulfilled when they're together. The partners maintain their sense of personal identity and self-worth, but when they're together, their respective identities become more complete.

 Reflection 9.9

Rate your degree of agreement or disagreement with the following statements:

1. "All you need is love."

   Strongly agree   Agree   Not sure   Disagree   Strongly disagree

   Reason for rating:

2. "Love is just a four-letter word."

   Strongly agree   Agree   Not sure   Disagree   Strongly disagree

   Reason for rating:

3. "Love stinks."

   Strongly agree   Agree   Not sure   Disagree   Strongly disagree

   Reason for rating:

Managing Interpersonal Conflict

Disagreement and conflict among people are inevitable aspects of social life. Research shows that even the most happily married couples don't experience perpetual marital bliss; they have occasional disagreements and discord (Gottman, 1994, 1999).

Interpersonal conflict is something we can't expect to escape or eliminate; the best we can do is defuse it, contain it, and prevent it from reaching unmanageable levels. The interpersonal communication and human relations skills already discussed in this chapter can help minimize conflicts. In addition to these general social skills, the following set of specific strategies may be used to handle interpersonal conflicts constructively and compassionately.

1. **Make your point** *assertively*—not passively, aggressively, or passive–aggressively. When you're *passive*, you don't stand up for your personal rights; you allow others to take advantage of you by letting them push you around. You say nothing when you should say something. You say "yes" when you want to say "no." When you handle conflict passively, you tend to become angry, bitter, or resentful because you keep it all inside (Alberti & Emmons, 2008).

   In contrast, when you're *aggressive*, you stand up for your rights, but at the same time you violate the rights of the person with whom you have a conflict by threatening, dominating, humiliating, or bullying. You use intense, emotionally loaded words to attack the person (e.g., "You spoiled brat" or "You're a self-centered sociopath"). You may manage to get what you want but at the other person's expense and at the risk of losing a friend. Later, you tend to feel guilty about overreacting or coming on too strong (e.g., "I knew I shouldn't have said that").

Note

When dealing with interpersonal conflict, the goal should be reconciliation not retaliation.

When you're *passive–aggressive*, you get back at or get even with the other person by: (a) withholding or taking away something (e.g., not speaking to the other person or withdrawing attention and affection), or (b) indirectly hinting that you're angry (e.g., making cynical comments or using sarcastic humor).

When you're *assertive*, you're not aggressive, passive, or passive–aggressive. You handle conflict in a way that protects or restores your rights without taking away or stepping on the rights of others. You handle conflict in a direct, even-tempered manner, not in an angry or agitated fashion. Rather than yelling or screaming, you speak in a normal volume and you communicate at a normal distance—you don't get into the face of the other person.

Listed below are specific strategies you can use to resolve conflicts *assertively*.

- **Focus on the *behavior* causing the conflict, not the person.** Avoid labeling the person as "selfish," "mean," or "inconsiderate." If you're upset because your roommate doesn't do his share of cleaning, stay away from aggressive labels such as "slob" or "slacker." Attacking with such negative labels makes the person feel like a verbal punching bag. It puts the person on the defensive and is likely to launch a retaliatory assault on your personal flaws. Before you know it, you're likely to find yourself in a full-out war of words and mutual character assassinations that escalate well beyond a small-scale skirmish about the specific conflict in question.

  Rather than focusing on the person's general character, focus on the specific action or behavior that's causing the problem (e.g., failing to do the dishes or leaving dirty laundry around the room). This lets the other person know exactly what behavior needs to be changed to resolve the conflict. It's much easier to change a specific behavior than it is to change a person's entire character or personality.

- **Use "I" messages that focus on how the other person's behavior affects you.** Rather than targeting the other person, "I" messages focus on *you*—what you are perceiving and feeling. This sends a message that's less accusatory and threatening to the other person. For example, suppose you receive a course grade that's lower than what you actually earned. You think a mistake was made, so you decide to ask your instructor about it. The conversation should not begin by saying to the instructor: "You made a mis-

"Don't find fault. Find a remedy."

—*Henry Ford, founder of Ford Motor Company and one of the most widely admired people of the 20th century*

take" or "You gave me the wrong grade." These messages are likely to put your professor immediately on the defensive and ready to defend the grade you received. Your professor will be less threatened and more likely to listen to and consider your complaint if you initiate the conversation with an "I" statement, such as: "I think an error may have been made in my final grade."

"I" messages are less aggressive because you're targeting the issue and how it's affecting you, not the other person (McKay, Davis, & Fanning, 2009). By saying: "I feel angry when . . ." rather than "You make me angry when . . . ," you send the message that you're taking responsibility for the way you feel rather than guilt-tripping the person for making you feel that way. In contrast, "you" messages are more likely to launch the person on a counter-offensive in an attempt to retaliate rather than cooperate (Bippus & Young, 2005).

Here are some specific tips for getting maximum mileage out of "I" messages.

a) Be *specific* about what *emotion* you're experiencing. Saying, "I feel neglected when you don't write or call" identifies what you're feeling more specifically than saying, "I wish you'd be more considerate." Describing what you feel in specific terms increases the persuasive power of your message and reduces the risk that the other person will misunderstand or discount it.

b) Communicate what you want the other person to do in the form of a firm *request* rather than a demand or ultimatum. Saying, "I would like you to . . ." is less likely to put the person on the defensive than saying, "I insist . . ." or "I demand . . ."

c) Be *specific* about what you want the person to *do* to resolve the conflict. Saying, "I would like for you to call me at least once a day" is more specific than saying, "I want you to keep in touch with me."

 Reflection 9.10

You're working on a group project and your teammates aren't carrying their weight. You're getting frustrated and angry because you're doing almost all of the work yourself.

Construct an "I" message that communicates your concern to your teammates in an assertive, nonthreatening way.

2. **Approach the conflict with the attitude you're going to solve a problem, not win an argument.** Don't approach conflict with the attitude that you're going to get even or prove you're right. Winning the argument but not persuading the person to change the behavior that's causing the conflict is like winning a battle and losing the war. Instead, approach conflict resolution in a way that allows both parties to win—both of you can end up with a better relationship in the long run.

3. **Pick a private place and time to resolve the conflict.** Don't discuss the issue while others are present. As the old expression goes, "Don't air your dirty laundry in public." Criticizing someone in the presence of others is akin to a public stoning; it's likely to cause resentment and intensify the conflict.

<u>Note</u>

Things are better left unsaid until you find the right time and place to say them.

4. **Decompress emotionally before you express yourself verbally.** Sensitive issues shouldn't be discussed during a fit of anger (Daniels & Horowitz, 1997). Your objective should be to solve the problem and resolve the conflict, not release your emotions. Impulsively dumping on the other person and saying the first thing that comes to your mind may give you a short-lived sense of relief, but it's unlikely to improve the other person's attitude or behavior. Instead of unloading on the person, take the load off yourself—cool down by taking some downtime to gather your thoughts and respond rationally, not emotionally (e.g., count to 10 and give your emotions time to settle down). Taking the time to reflect, weigh your words, and respond in a mellow manner also communicates to the other person that you've given serious consideration to the matter and are not just storming in and firing away like a "loose cannon."

5. **Give the person a chance to respond.** Just because you're angry doesn't mean the person you're angry with must forfeit all rights to free speech and self-defense. By giving the other person a fair chance to be heard, you increase the likelihood that you'll receive a cooperative response. Don't jump the gun and pull the trigger before hearing the other side of the story and getting all the facts straight.

    After listening to the other person's response, check your understanding by summarizing it in your own words (e.g., "What I hear you saying is . . ."). This is an important step in the conflict-resolution process because conflicts often stem from a simple misunderstanding or failure to communicate. Sometimes just taking time to hear each other's side of the story can go a long way toward resolving the conflict.

6. **Acknowledge the person's perspectives and feelings.** After hearing the person's response, if you disagree with it, don't dismiss or discount the person's feelings. Avoid saying things like, "That's ridiculous!" or "That's no excuse!" Instead, acknowledge the persons' response by saying, "I can understand what you were thinking" or "I see how you might feel that way." Then follow by expressing how you believe your complaint is still justified.

7. **If things begin to get nasty, call for a time-out or cease-fire and postpone the discussion to allow both of you time to cool off.** When emotions and adrenaline run high, logic and reason run low. This can result in one person saying something during a fit of anger that triggers an angry response from the other person; then the anger of both combatants continues to escalate until it turns into a blow-by-blow volley of verbal punches and counterpunches. An emotionally heated conversation may end up going something like this:

Person A: "You're way out of control."

Person B: "I'm not out of control; you're the one that's overreacting."

Person A: "*I'm* overreacting? You're the one who's acting like a jerk!"

Person B: "I may be *acting* like a jerk, but you're a real jerk!"

Blow-by-blow exchanges such as these are likely to turn up the emotional heat to a level so high that resolving the conflict takes a back seat to winning the fight. Both boxers need to back off, retreat to their respective corners, and try again later when neither is about to throw a knockout punch.

> "Seek first to understand, then to be understood."
>
> *—Stephen Covey, international best-selling author of* Seven Habits of Highly Effective People

8. **Avoid absolute judgments or blanket statements.** Compare the following three pairs of statements:
   a) "You're no help at all." versus "You don't help me enough."
   b) "You never try to understand how I feel." versus "You don't try hard enough to understand how I feel."
   c) "I always have to clean up." versus "I'm doing more than my fair share of the cleaning."

   The first statement in each of the preceding pairs represents an absolute statement that covers all times, situations, and circumstances. Such extreme, blanket criticisms send the message that the person is doing nothing right with respect to the issue in question. The second statement in each of the above pairs phrases the criticism in terms of degree or amount—the person is doing something right, but needs to do more of it—which is likely to be less threatening or humiliating (and probably closer to the truth).

9. **Conclude your discussion of the conflict on a warm, constructive note.** End it by ensuring that there are no hard feelings, and by letting the person know you're optimistic that the conflict can be resolved and your relationship strengthened.

10. **If the person makes a change in response to your request, express your appreciation.** Even if your complaint was legitimate and your request justified, the person's effort to accommodate your request shouldn't be taken for granted. (The last thing you want to say is something like: "That's more like it" or "It's about time!")

    Expressing appreciation to the other person for making a change is not only a socially sensitive thing to do, it's also a self-serving thing to do. By recognizing and reinforcing the other person's changed behavior, you increase the likelihood that the positive change in behavior will continue and you'll continue to benefit from the change.

> "To keep your marriage brimming with love ... when you're wrong, admit it; when you're right, shut up."
> —*Ogden Nash, American poet*

(Review the personality report of the "Do What You Are" survey that deals with your preferences for dealing with interpersonal conflict. What do the results suggest about how you deal with interpersonal conflict? Which strategies suggested in this chapter might work well with or improve your style of handling conflict?)

Emotional Intelligence

Excelling in college is a challenging task that will test your emotional strength and your ability to persist to task completion (graduation). Research indicates that college students who score higher on tests of emotional intelligence, such as the ability to identify their emotions and moods, are better able to focus their attention and stay absorbed ("in the zone") when completing challenging tasks and less likely to become frustrated or bored (Harris, 2006; Wiederman, 2007).

Research also indicates that experiencing positive emotions, such as optimism and excitement, promotes academic success. In one study involving nearly 4,000 first-year college students, it was found that students' level of optimism or hope for success during their first term on campus was a more accurate predictor of their first-year grades than was their SAT score or high school grade point average (Snyder, et al., 1991). In contrast, negative emotions—such as anxiety and fear—can interfere with the brain's ability to (a) store and retrieve memories, and (b) engage in higher-level thinking (Caine & Caine, 1994; Hertel & Brozovich, 2010).

Discussed below are research-based strategies for minimizing negative emotions that sabotage success and maximizing positive emotions that promote success.

Stress and Anxiety

One of the most common emotions we must monitor and manage is stress. Students report experiencing higher levels of stress in college than they did in high school (Bartlett, 2002; Sax, 2003).

But what exactly is stress? Stress has its roots in the "fight-or-flight" response—an automatic physical reaction wired into the body that enabled our human ancestors to engage in fight (attack) or flight (run away) when confronted by life-threatening predators. The word "stress" derives from a Latin root that means "to draw tight." This suggests that stress isn't necessarily bad; in the right amount, it can actually be productive. For instance, a tightened guitar string generates better sound than a string that's too lax or loose, a tightened bow delivers a more powerful arrow shot, and a tightened muscle provides more strength or speed. Such productive stress is sometimes referred to as eustress—deriving from the root *eu* meaning "good"—as in the words "euphoria" (good mood) and "eulogy" (good words).

Keep in mind that stress can work for you as well as against you; it can either energize or sabotage your performance, depending on its level of intensity and the length of time it continues. Don't expect to stop or eliminate stress completely, nor should you want to; your goal should be to contain it and maintain it at a level where it's more productive than obstructive or destructive. Many years of research indicate that peak performance (mental and physical) is attained under conditions of *moderate* stress. (See **Figure 9.1**.) At an intermediate level, stress can enhance energy, attention, and motivation (Halvorson, 2010; Sapolsky, 2004).

FIGURE 9.1: **Relationship between Arousal and Performance**

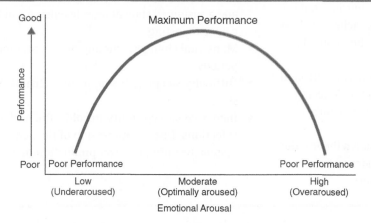

Moderate challenge that produces moderate stress typically promotes maximum (peak) performance.

Source: Williams, Landers, & Boutcher (1993)

 **Reflection 9.11**

Can you think of a situation in which you performed at a higher level because you were slightly nervous or were experiencing a moderate amount of stress?

However, if stress becomes intense, excessive, and persistent, it now may be defined as *anxiety* (Mayo Clinic, 2015a). Studies also show that students who experience high levels of academic stress and performance anxiety are more likely to use ineffective, "surface" approaches to learning that rely on memorization rather than effective, deep-learning strategies—such as reflection and seeking meaning (Biggs & Tang, 2011; Ramsden, 2003). Anxiety can interfere with mental performance on exams because anxious feelings and thoughts begin to preoccupy our mind, taking up valuable space in our limited attention span, leaving less room to process test information and engage in memory retrieval (Fernández-Castillo & Caurcel, 2014).

Anxiety experienced over an extended period of time can also suppress the immune system, leaving us more vulnerable to flu, colds, and other infectious diseases. Studies show that the immune system of college students is suppressed (produces fewer antibodies) at very stressful times during the academic term—such as midterms and finals (Bosch, et al., 2004; Deinzer, et al., 2000).

Box 9.3 provides a summary of the signs or symptoms of anxiety. If these symptoms are experienced for more than a week, help should be sought to reduce them.

Box 9.3

Recognizing the Symptoms of Anxiety

- Jitteriness or shaking—especially the hands
- Accelerated heart rate or heart palpitations (irregular heartbeat)
- Muscle tension. Tightness in the chest or upper shoulders or a tight feeling (lump) in the throat (the expressions "uptight" and "choking under pressure" derive from these symptoms of upper body tension)
- Body aches. Due to heightened muscle tension that can also lead to tension headaches, backaches, or chest pain (in extreme cases, it can feel like a heart attack)
- Sweating—especially sweaty (clammy) palms
- Cold, pale hands or feet. These symptoms are reflected in the expressions "white knuckles" and "cold feet," which have been used to describe someone who's highly anxious
- Dry mouth. Decreased production of saliva (hence, the expression "cotton mouth" and the tendency for nervous speakers to repeatedly sip water)

- Stomach discomfort or indigestion. Caused by increased secretion of stomach acid (as noted in the expression, "I feel like I have butterflies in my stomach")
- Gastrointestinal discomfort (e.g., stomach cramps, constipation, or diarrhea)
- Feeling faint or dizzy. Due to blood vessels constricting, which reduces oxygen flow to the brain
- Weakness and fatigue. A prolonged state of arousal and a sustained state of muscle tension can be physically exhausting
- Menstrual changes—missing or irregular menstrual periods
- Difficulty sleeping. Insomnia or interrupted (fitful) sleep
- Increased susceptibility to colds, flu, and other infections. Due to suppression of the body's immune system, resulting in lower production of antibodies

"My stress has caused me to lose a lot of weight; my appetite is cut in half. My sleep pattern is off; I have trouble falling/staying asleep. No matter how stressed I was in high school, this never happened [before]. What can I do to de-stress?"

—First-term college student

Effective Methods for Managing Stress

If you perceive your level of stress reaching a point where it's beginning to interfere with the quality of your academic performance or your personal life, here are three key stress-management methods that are well-supported by research in psychology and biology (Benson & Proctor, 2011; Lehrer, et al., 2007).

1. Deep (Diaphragmatic) Breathing

When people are experiencing excessive stress, their breathing pattern becomes fast, shallow, and irregular; they breathe through the mouth rather than the chest. Breathing associated with relaxation is just the opposite—slow, deep, and regular breathing that originates from the stomach.

Breathing is something we do involuntarily—without conscious awareness. However, with some concentration and effort, we can gain voluntary control of our breathing by controlling our diaphragm—the body's muscle that enables us to expand and contract our lungs. By intentionally controlling our diaphragm muscle, we slow our breathing rate, which, in turn, brings down our stress level. In fact, studies show that when we slow down our breathing rate, other systems of our body slow down—e.g., our heart rate and blood pressure drop (Benson & Proctor, 2011).

2. Progressive Muscle Relaxation

Similar to stretching exercises to relax and loosen muscles before and after physical exercise, total body (head-to-toe) muscle relaxation can be achieved by progressively tensing and releasing the five sets of muscles listed below. Hold tension in each muscle area for about five seconds and then release slowly.

1. Wrinkle your forehead muscles and then release them.
2. Shrug your shoulders up as if to touch your ears and then drop them.
3. Make a tight fist with both hands and then open them.
4. Tighten your stomach muscles and then release them.
5. Tighten your toes by curling them under your feet and then raise them as high as you can.

> "To relax, I like to stretch a lot."
> —First-year college student

When relaxing your muscles, take a deep breath and think or say: "Relax." By breathing deeply and thinking or hearing the word "relax" each time you release your muscles, the sound of the word "relax" becomes associated with your muscles being relaxed. When you find yourself in a stressful situation, take a deep breath and think or say the word "relax"; your stress level will drop because your muscles have been conditioned to relax in response to that word.

3. Mental Imagery

You can also reduce stress by *imagining* yourself in a calm, comfortable, and relaxing setting. Visualize images such as ocean waves, floating clouds, sitting in a warm sauna, or any sensory experience that tends to relax you. Try to use all of your senses—see it, hear it, smell it, touch it, and feel it. You can also create imaginary calming music in your head to accompany the visual image. The more senses you use, the more real the scene will seem and the more powerful its relaxing effects will be (Fezler, 1989).

AUTHOR'S EXPERIENCE

My wife, Mary, is a kindergarten teacher. Whenever her young students start misbehaving and the situation becomes especially stressful (e.g., during lunchtime when kids are running around wildly, arguing vociferously, and screaming at maximum volume), she "plays" relaxing songs in her head. Mary reports that her musical imagination always works to soothe her nerves, enabling her to remain calm and even-tempered when she must deal with children who are out of control or need to be disciplined.

—*Joe Cuseo*

Reflection 9.12

What are your most common sources or causes of stress?

What is your top strategy for coping with stress?

Would you say that you cope with stress well?

Simple Stress-Reduction Strategies and Habits

In addition the formal stress-management techniques of diaphragmatic breathing, progressive muscle relaxation, and mental imagery, stress may be managed by simpler strategies and habits, such as those discussed below.

> "There are thousands of causes for stress, and one antidote to stress is self-expression. That's what happens to me every day. My thoughts get off my chest, down my sleeves, and onto my pad."
>
> —Garson Kanin, American writer, actor, and film director

1. **Exercise.** Exercise reduces stress by increasing release of serotonin—a mellowing brain chemical that reduces feelings of tension (anxiety) and depression. It is for these reasons that counselors and psychotherapists recommend exercise for patients experiencing milder forms of anxiety or depression (Johnsgard, 2004). Exercise also elevates mood because it enhances self-esteem—by giving us a sense of accomplishment and an improved physical self-image. Studies show that people who exercise regularly tend to report feeling happier (Myers, 1993).

2. **Journaling.** Writing about our feelings in a personal journal helps us identify and express the emotions we're experiencing (a form of emotional intelligence), and provides us with a safe outlet for releasing stress (Seaward, 2011). Writing about our emotions also reduces the risk that we'll deny or repress them (push them out of conscious awareness).

AUTHOR'S EXPERIENCE

I'm the kind of person who carries the worries of the day with me and it really affects my sleep. I'm also the type of person who juggles many balls during the day, which also adds to my stress level. By chance, I discovered a great strategy for managing my stress. I was doing a conflict-resolution workshop about 15 years ago and I asked the participants to write down in a journal all the stressors they encountered during the day for 30 consecutive days. We would then come together as a group at the end of the 30 days to identify those stressors.

I decided to try this experiment on my own stressors. Every night before I went to bed I wrote down the categories or sources of stress I experienced during the day. After 30 days, I was able to recognize patterns in the causes of my stress and what strategies I could use to combat them. I also noticed that over the 30 days my stress level decreased and the quality of my sleep improved. I still use this strategy whenever I'm under stress or not sleeping well.

—Aaron Thompson

3. **Substitute positive thoughts for negative thoughts.** Research indicates that the part of the human brain involved in thinking (the cortex) has many connections to the part of the brain responsible for emotions (the limbic system) (Goleman, 1995; Zull, 2002). Thus, our brain is wired in such a way that our thinking can directly influence our feelings. If thoughts influence emotions, then changing the way we think can change the emotions we experience, including our feelings of stress and anxiety.

We can attack negative, anxiety-producing thoughts and replace them with positive, relaxing thoughts. For instance, you see some students turning in their tests before you're finished and you start having negative thoughts like: "They must all be smarter than I am." You can stop that anxiety-producing thought and substitute the following thought: "They're getting up and getting out because they're giving up." Or, "They're rushing out without taking the time to carefully review their answers before turning their test in."

One of the keys to substituting positive for negative thoughts is to think about what you want to happen, not what you're afraid is going to happen (Halvorson, 2010). If you're a pitcher in a baseball game and you start thinking you're going to walk a batter, stop thinking about whether you're going to throw balls and start thinking about throwing strikes. Similarly, if you're taking a test, stop thinking (and worrying) about losing points and start thinking (and focusing) on earning points. This will reduce your level of test anxiety.

4. **Take time for humor and laughter.** Research on the benefits of humor for reducing tension is clear and convincing. In one study, college students were suddenly told they had to give an impromptu (off the top of their head) speech. This unexpected assignment typically caused students' heart rate to elevate to an average of 110 beats per minute during delivery of the speech. However, students who watched humorous episodes of sitcoms before delivering their impromptu speech had an average heart rate during the speech that was significantly lower (80–85 beats per minute)—indicating that experiencing humor reduces their level of anxiety (O'Brien, cited in Howard, 2014).

Research also shows that humor strengthens our immune system after it's been suppressed or weakened. It does so by blocking the body's production of the stress hormone cortisol—a biochemical that suppresses our immune system when we're under stress (Berk, cited in Liebertz, 2005b).

> The arrival of a good clown exercises a more beneficial influence upon the health of a town than the arrival of twenty asses laden with drugs."
>
> —Thomas Sydenham, 17th-century physician

Depression

Along with anxiety, depression is the other major emotional problem that can afflict us. Research indicates that depression is associated with poorer academic performance in college and higher risk of withdrawing from college, even among highly motivated and academically well-prepared students (Eisenberg, Golberstein, & Hunt, 2009). Depression may be succinctly described as an emotional state characterized by a feeling of sadness accompanied by loss of interest, hope, and energy (Mayo Clinic, 2015b). As the term implies, when we're depressed, our mood is lowered or pushed down. In contrast to anxiety, which typically involves worrying about something that's currently happening or is about to happen, depression more often relates to something that has already happened, particularly a *loss*, such as a lost relationship (e.g., broken romance or death of a family member), or a lost opportunity (e.g., losing a job or being rejected by a school) (Bowlby, 1980; Price, Choi, & Vinokur, 2002).

It's natural and normal to feel dejected after losses such as these. However, if the dejection reaches a point where we can't concentrate and complete our day-to-day tasks, and if this continues for an extended period of time, we may be experiencing what psychologists call *clinical depression* or *depressive disorder*—that is, depression so serious that we should receive immediate professional help. **Box 9.4** provides a summary of symptoms or signs of depression. If these symptoms continue to occur for two or more weeks, you should take action to relieve them.

Box 9.4

Recognizing the Symptoms of Depression

- Feeling low, down, dejected, sad, or blue
- Pessimistic feelings about the future (e.g., expecting failure or feeling helpless or hopeless)
- Decreased sense of humor
- Difficulty finding pleasure, joy, or fun in anything
- Lack of concentration
- Loss of motivation and interest in things previously found to be exciting or stimulating (e.g., loss of interest in school, sudden drop in rate of class attendance or completion of course assignments)
- Stooped posture (e.g., hung head or drawn face)
- Slower and softer speech rate
- Decreased animation and slower bodily movements
- Loss of energy
- Changes in sleeping patterns (e.g., sleeping more or less than usual)
- Changes in eating patterns (e.g., eating more or less than usual)

- Social withdrawal
- Neglect of physical appearance
- Consistently low self-esteem (e.g., thinking "I'm a loser")
- Strong feelings of worthlessness or guilt (e.g., thinking "I'm a failure")
- Suicidal thoughts (e.g., experiencing thoughts such as: "I can't take it anymore," "People would be better off without me," or "I don't deserve to live")

Note: Depression and suicidal thoughts occur at alarmingly high rates among college students. In one national study of more than 26,000 students at 70 campuses, it was found that 15% of the students surveyed reported they "seriously considered" suicide and more than 5% reported they actually attempted suicide. Unfortunately, however, only half the students who had suicidal thoughts sought counseling or treatment (Drum, et al., 2009).

Note

There's a difference between feeling despondent or down and being depressed. When psychologists use the word "depression," they're usually referring to clinical depression—a mood state so low that it's interfering with a person's ability to cope with day-to-day tasks, such as getting to school or going to work.

 Reflection 9.13

Have you, or any member of your family, experienced clinical depression?

What do you think was the primary cause of it?

Strategies for Coping with Depression

Depression can vary widely in intensity. Moderate and severe forms of depression often require professional counseling or psychotherapy, and are often rooted in genetic or hereditary factors that cause imbalances in brain chemistry. The coping strategies described below can also be used for milder forms of depression that may be overcome through self-help and self-management. These strategies may be used in conjunction with professional help or medication to reduce the intensity and frequency of clinical depression.

1. **Focus on the present and the future, not the past.** Consciously combat the tendency to dwell on past losses or failures that can no longer be changed or controlled. Instead, focus on things you can control now.

2. **Make extra effort to engage in positive, emotionally uplifting behavior.** If our behavior is upbeat, our mind (mood) often follows suit. The expression, "Put on a happy face" can actually be an effective depression-reduction strategy because smiling produces changes in our facial muscles that trigger changes in brain chemistry—which, in turn, elevate our mood (Liebertz, 2005a). In contrast, frowning activates a different set of facial muscles that tend to interfere with production of mood-elevating brain chemicals (Myers, 1993).

3. **Continue to engage in activities that are fun and enjoyable.** When we're down, we can fall into the downward spiral of not doing the things that bring us joy (because we're too down to do them); this brings us down further because we fail to do the very things that bring us up. When we're emotionally low, we should try even harder to continue doing the things that bring us joy, such as socializing with friends and engaging in our usual recreational activities. Interestingly, the root of the word "recreation" means to re-create (create again), suggesting that recreational activity can revive, restore, and renew us—both physically and emotionally.

4. **Intentionally seek humor and opportunities to laugh.** In addition to reducing anxiety, laughter can lighten and brighten a dark mood. Furthermore, humor improves memory (Nielson, cited in Liebertz, 2005a), which can combat the memory loss that typically accompanies depression.

5. **Continue getting things done.** When we're feeling down, staying busy and accomplishing things helps boost our mood because it provides us with a sense of achievement. Helping others less fortunate than ourselves can also be a particularly effective way to boost our mood because it gets us outside ourselves, increases our sense of self-esteem, and helps us realize that our issues may be minor compared to the problems faced by others.

6. **Make a conscious effort to focus on personal strengths and accomplishments.** Another way to drive away the blues is by keeping track of the positive developments in our life. We can do this by keeping a "positive events journal" in which we note the good things that happen to us and for us, such as the fortunate experiences in our life, the things we're grateful for, and our personal accomplishments or achievements. Positive journal entries leave us with a visible uplifting record that we can review anytime we're feeling down.

7. **If you're unable to overcome depression on your own, seek help from others.** In some cases, we may be able to help ourselves overcome emotional problems through personal effort and use of effective coping strategies—particularly if we experience depression or anxiety in milder forms and for shorter periods of time. However, overcoming more serious and long-lasting episodes of depression or anxiety isn't as simple as people make it out to be when they insensitively use expressions like: "Just deal with it," "Get over it," or "Snap out of it." More serious cases of depression and anxiety can be strongly associated with genetic factors, which are not completely within the person's control. In these cases, we shouldn't be reluctant to or embarrassed about seeking professional help.

Reflection 9.14

If you thought you were experiencing a serious episode of anxiety or depression, would you feel comfortable seeking help from a professional? If yes, why? If no, why not?

How do you think other students would respond to the above question?

> The best way to cheer yourself up is to try to cheer somebody else up."
>
> —*Samuel Clemens, a.k.a. Mark Twain, writer, lecturer, and humorist*

Chapter Summary and Highlights

Intellectual ability is only one form of human intelligence. Social and emotional intelligence are equally, if not more, important for living a successful, healthy, and happy life. The strategies discussed in this chapter should not be viewed merely as "soft skills," but as "hard core" skills essential for success in college and beyond.

Good communication skills (verbal and nonverbal) and good human relations skills ("people skills") are critical for the development of successful social relationships. We can improve our interpersonal interactions and relationships by working hard at remembering the names and interests of people we meet, being a good listener, and being open to different topics of conversation.

Interpersonal conflicts are an inevitable aspect of social life; we can't completely eliminate them, but we can minimize and manage them by using effective strategies to resolve conflicts assertively rather than aggressively, passively, or passive–aggressively.

Students report experiencing higher levels of stress in college than they did in high school. Strategies for reducing excess stress include formal stress-management techniques (e.g., deep, diaphragmatic breathing and progressive muscle relaxation), as well as simple stress-management strategies (e.g., exercising and journaling).

Along with anxiety, depression is the other major emotional problem that can afflict us. Research on college students indicate that depression is associated with poorer academic performance in college and higher risk of withdrawing from college, even among highly motivated and academically well-prepared students. Mild depression may be overcome with a variety of self-help strategies. However, if symptoms of depression are severe and continue for two or more weeks, this suggests "clinical depression" or a "depressive disorder" is being experienced and professional help should be immediately sought.

Learning More through the World Wide Web: Internet-Based Resources

For additional information on social and emotional intelligence, see the following websites:

Social Intelligence and Interpersonal Relationships:
https://nationalvetcontent.edu.au/alfresco/d/d/workspace/SpacesStore/5c14c044-6d26-4ab8-aef1-530948605d36/ims/shared/resources/mag/web_conflict.htm

http://www.livestrong.com/article/132246-effective-interpersonal-communication-strategies/

http://www.yesintlcampus.com/index.asp?Cid=20&Tid=140&Sid=51680

Emotional Intelligence and Mental Health:
www.eqi.org/eitoc.htm

http://www.nimh.nih.gov/health/publications/depression-easy-to-read/index.shtml

http://www.activeminds.org/issues-a-resources/mental-health-resources/student-resources

References

AhYun, K. (2002). Similarity and attraction. In M. Allen, R. W. Preiss, B. M. Gayle, & N. A. Burrell (Eds.), *Interpersonal communication research* (pp. 145–167). Mahwah, NJ: Erlbaum.

Alberti, R. E., & Emmons, M. L. (2008). *Your perfect right: Assertiveness and equality in your life and relationships.* Atascadero, CA: Impact Publishers.

Avolio, B., & Luthans, F. (2006). *The high impact leader*. New York: McGraw Hill.

Avolio, B. J., Walumbwa, F. O., &. Weber, T. J. (2009). Leadership: Current theories, research, and future directions. *Annual Review of Psychology, 60*, 421–449.

Barker, L., & Watson, K. W. (2000). *Listen up: How to improve relationships, reduce stress, and be more productive by using the power of listening*. New York: St. Martin's Press.

Bartels, A., & Zeki, S. (2000). The neural basis of romantic love. *European Journal of Neuroscience, 12*, 172–193.

Bartlett, T. (2002). Freshman pay, mentally and physically, as they adjust to college life. *Chronicle of Higher Education, 48*, 35–37.

Bassham, G., Irwin, W., Nardone, H., & Wallace, J. M. (2013*). Critical thinking: A student's introduction* (5th ed.) New York: McGraw-Hill.

Benson, H., & Proctor, W. (2011). *The relaxation revolution: The science and genetics of mind body healing*. New York: Scribner.

Berndt, T. J. (1992). Friendship and friends' influence in adolescence. *Current Directions in Psychological Science, 1*(5), 156–159.

Biggs, J., & Tang, C. (2011). *Teaching for quality learning at university*. New York: Open Education Press.

Bippus, A. M., & Young, S. L. (2005). Owning your emotions: Reactions to expressions of self- versus other-attributed positive and negative emotions. *Journal of Applied Communication Research 33*(1), 26–45.

Bosch, J. A., de Geus, E. J., Ring, C., Nieuw-Amerongen, A. V. (2004). Academic examinations and immunity: Academic stress or examination stress? *Psychosomatic Medicine, 66*(4), 625–627.

Bowlby, J. (1980). *Attachment and loss: Vol. 3. Loss, sadness, and depression*. New York: Basic Books.

Caine, R., & Caine, G. (1994). *Making connections: Teaching and the human brain*. Menlo Park, CA: Addison-Wesley.

Carneiro, P., Crawford, C., & Goodman, A. (2006). *Which skills matter?* Centre for the Economics of Education, London School of Economics, Discussion Paper 59. Retrieved from http://cee.lse.ac.uk/ceedps/ceedp59.pdf.

Daniels, D., & Horowitz, L. J. (1997). *Being and caring: A psychology for living*. Prospect Heights, IL: Waveland Press.

Deinzer, R., Kleineidam, C., Stiller–Winkler, R., Idel, H., & Bachg, D. (2000). Prolonged reduction of salivary immunoglobulin A (S-IgA) after a major academic exam. *International Journal of Psychophysiology, 37*, 219–232.

Driver, J. (2010). *You say more than you think: A 7-day plan for using the new body language to get what you want*. New York: Crown Publishers.

Drum, D., Brownson, C., Denmark, A. B., Smith, S. E. (2009). New data on the nature of suicidal crises in college students: Shifting the paradigm. *Professional Psychology: Research and Practice, 40*(3), 213–222.

Eisenberg, D., Golberstein, E., Hunt, J. (2009). Mental health and academic success in college. *B.E. Journal of Economic Analysis & Policy, 9*(1), 1–40.

Ekman, P. (2009). *Telling lies: Clues to deceit in the marketplace, politics, and marriage* (revised ed.). New York: W. W. Norton.

Fernández-Castillo, A., & Caurcel, M. J. (2014). State test-anxiety, selective attention and concentration in university students. *International Journal of Psychology, 50*(4), 265–271.

Festinger, L. (1954). A theory of social comparison processes. *Human Relations, 7*, 117–140.

Fezler, W. (1989). *Creative imagery: How to visualize in all senses*. New York: Simon & Schuster.

Fisher, E. E. (2004). *Why we love: The nature and chemistry of romantic love*. New York: Henry Holt & Co.

Foreman, J. (2009, June 22). "Dear, I love you with all my brain." *Los Angeles Times*. Retrieved from http://www.latimes.com/features/health/la-he-love22-2009jun22,0,6897401.column.

Fromm, E. (1970). *The art of loving*. New York: Bantam.

Fromme, A. (1980). *The ability to love*. Chatsworth, CA: Wilshire Book Company.

Gabric, D., & McFadden, K. L. (2001). Student and employer perceptions of desirable entry-level operations management skills. *American Business Law Journal, 16*(1), 50–59.

Gardner, H. (1993). *Frames of mind: The theory of multiple intelligences* (2nd ed.). New York: Basic Books.

Gardner, H. (1999). *Intelligence reframed: Multiple intelligences for the 21st century*. New York: Basic Books.

Giles, L. C., Glonek, F. V., Luszcz, M. A., & Andrews, G. R. (2005). Effect of social networks on 10-year survival in very old Australians: The Australia longitudinal study of aging. *Journal of Epidemiology and Community Health, 59*, 574–579.

Goleman, D. (1995). *Emotional intelligence: Why it can matter more than IQ*. New York: Random House.

Goleman, D. (2000). *Working with emotional intelligence*. New York: Bantam Dell.

Goleman, D. (2006). *Social intelligence: The new science of human relationships*. New York: Dell.

Goleman, D., Boyatzis, R., & McKee, A. (2013). *Primal leadership: Realizing the potential of emotional intelligence*. Boston, MA: Harvard Business School Press.

Gottman, J. (1994). *Why marriages succeed and fail*. New York: Fireside.

Gottman, J. (1999). *The seven principles for making marriage work*. New York: Three Rivers Press.

Grasz, J. (2014). *More employers finding reasons not to hire candidates on social media, finds Career Builder Survey*. Retrieved from http://www.careerbuilder.com/share/aboutus/pressreleasesdetail.aspx?sd=6/26/2013&id=pr766&ed=12/31/2013.

Halvorson, H. G. (2010). *Succeed: How we can reach our goals*. New York: Plume.

Harris, M. B. (2006). Correlates and characteristics of boredom and proneness to boredom. *Journal of Applied Social Psychology, 30*(3), 576–598.

Hatfield, E., & Rapson, R. L. (1993). *Love, sex, and intimacy: Their psychology, biology, and history*. New York: HarperCollins.

Hatfield, E., & Rapson, R. L. (2000). Love. In W. E. Craighead & C. B. Nemeroff (Eds.), *The concise Corsini encyclopedia of psychology and behavioral science* (pp. 898–901). New York: John Wiley & Sons.

Hertel, P. T., & Brozovich, F. (2010). Cognitive habits and memory distortions in anxiety and depression. *Current Directions in Psychological Science, 19*, 155–160.

Howard, P. J. (2014). *The owner's manual for the brain: Everyday applications of mind-brain research* (4th ed.). New York: HarperCollins.

Johnsgard, K. W. (2004). *Conquering depression and anxiety through exercise*. New York: Prometheus.

Johnson, S. D., & Bechler, C. (1998). Examining the relationships between listening effectiveness and leadership emergence: Perceptions, behaviors, and recall. *Small Group Research, 29*(4), 452–471.

Latané, B., Liu, J. H., Nowak, A., Bonevento, N., & Zheng, L. (1995). Distance matters: Physical space and social impact. *Personality and Social Psychology Bulletin, 21*, 795–805.

Lehrer, P., Barlow, D. H., Woolfolk, R. L., & Sime, W. E. (Eds.). (2007). *Principles and practice of stress management* (3rd ed.). New York: The Guilford Press.

Liebertz, C. (2005a). A healthy laugh. *Scientific American Mind, 16*(3), 90–91.

Liebertz, C. (2005b). Want clear thinking? Relax. *Scientific American Mind, 16*(3), 88–89.

Matthews, G., Zeidner, M., & Roberts, R. D. (2007). *The science of emotional intelligence: Knowns and unknowns*. New York: Oxford University Press.

Mayo Clinic. (2015a). *Anxiety: Definition*. Retrieved from http://www.mayoclinic.org/diseases-conditions/anxiety/basics/definition/con-20026282.

Mayo Clinic. (2015b). *Depression: Definition*. Retrieved from http://www.mayoclinic.org/diseases-conditions/depression/basics/definition/con-20032977.

McKay, M., Davis, M., & Fanning, P. (2009). *Messages: The communication skills book* (2nd ed.). Oakland, CA: New Harbinbger.

Myers, D. G. (1993). *The pursuit of happiness: Who is happy—and why?* New York: Morrow.

Myers, D. G. (2000). *The American paradox: Spiritual hunger in an age of plenty*. New Haven, CT: Yale University Press.

Navarro, J. (2008). *What every BODY is saying*. New York: Harper Collins.

Nichols, M. P. (2009). *The lost art of listening*. New York: Guilford Press.

Oloritun, R. O., Madan, A., Pentland, A., & Khayal, I. (2013). Identifying close friendships in a sensed social network. *Procedia-Social and Behavioral Sciences, 79*(6), 18–26.

Pascarella, E., & Terenzini, P. (2005). *How college affects students: A third decade of research* (Vol. 2). San Francisco: Jossey-Bass.

Peele, S., & Brodsky, A. (1991). *Love and addiction*. New York: Signet Books.

Price, R. H., Choi, J. N., & Vinokur, A. D. (2002). Links in the chain of adversity following job loss: How financial strain and loss of personal control lead to depression, impaired functioning, and poor health. *Journal of Occupational Health Psychology, 7*(4), 302–312.

Purdy, M., & Borisoff, D. (Eds.). (1996). *Listening in everyday life: A personal and professional approach*. Lanham, MD: University Press of America.

Putman, R. D. (2000). *Bowling alone: The collapse and revival of American community*. New York: Simon & Schuster.

Ramsden, P. (2003). *Learning to teach in higher education* (2nd ed.). London: RoutledgeFalmer.

Ruggiero, V. R. (2011). *Beyond feelings: A guide to critical thinking*. New York: McGraw-Hill Education.

Salovey, P., & Mayer, J. D. (1990). Emotional intelligence. *Imagination, Cognition, and Personality, 9*, 185–211.

Sapolsky, R. (2004). *Why zebras don't get ulcers*. New York: W. H. Freeman.

Sax, L. J. (2003). Our incoming students: What are they like? *About Campus* (July–August), 15–20.

Seaward, B. L. (2011). *Managing stress: Principles and strategies for health and well-being*. Burlington, MA: Jones & Bartlett Learning.

Seirup, G. E. (2004). *College dating*. Retrieved from writing.colostate.edu/gallery/talkingback/v3.1/seirup.htm.

Snyder, C. R., Harris, C., Anderson, J. R., Holleran, S. A., Irving, L. M., Sigmon, S. T., et al. (1991). The will and the ways: Development and validation of an individual-differences measure of hope. *Journal of Personality and Social Psychology, 60*, 570–585.

Suls, J., Martin, R., & Wheeler, L. (2002). Social comparison: Why, with whom and with what effect? *Current Directions in Psychological Science, 11*(5), 159–163.

Tinto, V. (2012). *Completing college: Rethinking institutional action*. Chicago: The University of Chicago Press.

Viorst, J. (1998). *Imperfect control: Our lifelong struggles with power and surrender*. New York: Simon Schuster.

Wiederman, M. W. (2007). Gender differences in sexuality. *Family Journal—Counseling and Therapy, 9*(4), 468–471.

Wolvin, A. D. (2010). *Listening and communication in the 21st century*. Malden, MA: Blackwell.

Zull, J. E. (2002). *The art of changing the brain: Enriching teaching by exploring the biology of learning*. Sterling, VA: Stylus.

Chapter 9 Exercises

9.1 Quote Reflections

Review the sidebar quotes contained in this chapter and select two that were especially meaningful or inspirational to you.

For each quote, provide a three- to five-sentence explanation why you chose it.

9.2 Reality Bite

Caught Between a Rock and a Hard Place: Romantic Involvement versus Academic Commitment

Lauren has been dating her boyfriend (Nick) for about two months. She's convinced this is the real thing and that she's definitely in love. Lately, Nick has been asking her to skip class to spend more time with him. He tells Lauren: "If you really love me, you would do it for our relationship." Lauren feels that Nick truly loves her and wouldn't do anything to intentionally hurt her or interfere with her goals. So she accommodates Nick's request and begins skipping some classes to spend time with him. However, Lauren's grades soon start to slip; at the same time, Nick continues to demand more of her time.

Reflection and Discussion Questions

1. What concerns you most about Lauren's behavior?
2. What concerns you most about Nick's behavior?
3. Would you agree with Lauren's decision to start skipping classes?
4. If you were Lauren's friend, what advice would you give her?
5. If you were Nick's friend, what advice would you give him?
6. What might Lauren do to keep her grades up and still keep her relationship with Nick strong?

9.3 Assessment of Interpersonal Skills

1. Complete the "Do What You Are" survey and review the description of your personality type. This description included your strengths and blind spots when it comes to forming and maintaining interpersonal relationships.
2. Do you think the results accurately reflect your interpersonal characteristics?
3. What strategies described in this chapter might help you address your blind spots?

9.4 Identifying Major Ways of Handling Interpersonal Conflict

Think of a social situation or relationship that's currently causing the most conflict in your life. Describe how this conflict could be approached in each of the following ways:

1. Passively:
2. Aggressively:
3. Passive–aggressively:
4. Assertively:

(See p. 215 for descriptions of each of these four approaches.)

Practice the *assertive* approach by role-playing it with a friend or classmate and consider applying it to the actual situation or relationship that's currently causing you the most conflict.

9.5 College Stress: Identifying Sources and Solutions

Read through the following 29 college stressors and rate them in terms of how much stress each one is currently causing you—on a scale of 1 to 5 (1 = lowest, 5 = highest).

Potential Stressors		Stress Rating			
Tests and exams	1	2	3	4	5
Assignments	1	2	3	4	5
Class workload	1	2	3	4	5
Pace of courses	1	2	3	4	5
Performing up to expectations	1	2	3	4	5
Handling personal freedom	1	2	3	4	5
Time pressure (e.g., not enough time)	1	2	3	4	5
Organizational pressure (e.g., losing things)	1	2	3	4	5
Living independently	1	2	3	4	5
The future	1	2	3	4	5
Decisions about a major or career	1	2	3	4	5
Moral and ethical decisions	1	2	3	4	5
Finding meaning in life	1	2	3	4	5
Emotional issues	1	2	3	4	5
Physical health	1	2	3	4	5
Social life	1	2	3	4	5
Intimate relationships	1	2	3	4	5
Sexuality	1	2	3	4	5
Family responsibilities	1	2	3	4	5
Family conflicts	1	2	3	4	5
Family pressure	1	2	3	4	5
Peer pressure	1	2	3	4	5
Loneliness or isolation	1	2	3	4	5
Roommate conflicts	1	2	3	4	5
Conflict with professors	1	2	3	4	5
Campus policies or procedures	1	2	3	4	5
Transportation	1	2	3	4	5
Technology	1	2	3	4	5
Safety	1	2	3	4	5

Review your ratings and record your three, highest-rated stressors in the space below—along with: (a) a coping strategy you may use on your own to deal with that source of stress and (b) a campus resource you could use to obtain help with that source of stress.

Stressor #1: _____

Personal coping strategy:

Campus resource:

Stressor #2: _____

Personal coping strategy:

Campus resource:

Stressor #3: _____

Personal coping strategy:

Campus resource:

Diversity

LEARNING ABOUT AND FROM HUMAN DIFFERENCES

This chapter clarifies what "diversity" really means and demonstrates how experiencing diversity can deepen learning, promote critical and creative thinking, and contribute to your personal and professional development. Strategies are provided for overcoming cultural barriers and biases that block the development of rewarding relationships with diverse people and learning from others whose cultural backgrounds differ from our own. Simply stated, we learn more from people that are different from us than we do from people similar to us. There's more diversity among college students today than at any other time in history. This chapter will help you capitalize on this learning opportunity.

Gain greater appreciation of human differences and develop skills for making the most of diversity in college and beyond.

 Reflection 10.1

Complete the following sentence:

When I hear the word *diversity*, the first thing that comes to my mind is . . .

What Is Diversity?

Literally translated, the word "diversity" derives from the Latin root *diversus*, meaning "various" or "variety." Thus, human diversity refers to the variety that exists in humanity (the human species). The relationship between humanity and diversity may be compared to the relationship between sunlight and the variety of colors that make up the visual spectrum. Similar to how sunlight passing through a prism disperses into the variety of colors that comprise the visual spectrum, the human species on planet earth is dispersed into a variety of different groups that comprise the human spectrum (humanity). **Figure 10.1** illustrates this metaphorical relationship between diversity and humanity.

FIGURE 10.1: **Humanity and Diversity**

> "We are all brothers and sisters. Each face in the rainbow of color that populates our world is precious and special. Each adds to the rich treasure of humanity."
>
> —*Morris Dees, civil rights leader and cofounder of the Southern Poverty Law Center*

SPECTRUM
of
DIVERSITY

HUMANITY →

Gender (male-female)
Age (stage of life)
Race (e.g., White, Black, Asian)
Ethnicity (e.g., Native American, Hispanic, Irish, German)
Socioeconomic status (job status/income)
National *citizenship* (citizen of U.S. or another country)
Native (first-learned) *language*
National *origin* (nation of birth)
National *region* (e.g., raised in north/south)
Generation (historical period when people are born and live)
Political ideology (e.g., liberal/conservative)
Religious/spiritual beliefs (e.g., Christian/Buddhist/Muslim)
Family status (e.g., single-parent/two-parent family)
Marital status (single/married)
Parental status (with/without children)
Sexual orientation (heterosexual/homosexual/bisexual)
Physical ability/disability (e.g., able to hear/deaf)
Mental ability/disability (e.g., mentally able/challenged)
Learning ability/disability (e.g., absence/presence of dyslexia)
Mental health/illness (e.g., absence/presence of depression)

_ _ _ _ _ _ = dimension of diversity

*This list represents some of the major dimensions of human diversity; it does not constitute a complete list of all possible forms of human diversity. Also, disagreement exists about certain dimensions of diversity (e.g., whether certain groups should be considered races or ethnic groups).

As depicted in the above figure, human diversity is manifested in a multiplicity of ways, including differences in physical features, national origins, cultural backgrounds, and sexual orientations. Some dimensions of diversity are easily detectable, others are very subtle, and some are invisible.

 Reflection 10.2

Look at the diversity spectrum in **Figure 10.1** and look over the list of groups that make up the spectrum. Do you notice any groups missing from the list that should be added, either because they have distinctive backgrounds or because they've been targets of prejudice and discrimination?

Diversity includes discussion of equal rights and social justice for minority groups, but it's a broader concept that involves much more than political issues. In a national survey of American voters, the vast majority of respondents agreed that diversity is more than just "political correctness" (National Survey of Women Voters, 1998). Diversity is also an *educational* issue—an integral element of a college education that contributes to the learning, personal development, and career preparation of *all* students. It enhances the quality of the college experience by bringing multiple perspectives and alternative approaches to *what* is being learned (the content) and *how* it's being learned (the process).

Note

Diversity is a human issue that embraces and benefits all people; it's not a code word for "some" people. Although one major goal of diversity is to promote appreciation and equitable treatment of particular groups of people who've experienced discrimination, it's also a learning experience that strengthens the quality of a college education, career preparation, and leadership potential.

What Is Racial Diversity?

A *racial group (race)* is a group of people who share distinctive physical traits, such as skin color or facial characteristics. The variation in skin color we now see among humans is largely due to biological adaptations that have evolved over thousands of years among groups of humans who migrated to different climatic regions of the world. Currently, the most widely accepted explanation of the geographic origin of modern humans is the "Out of Africa" theory. Genetic studies and fossil evidence indicate that all Homo sapiens inhabited Africa 150,000–250,000 years ago; over time, some migrated from Africa to other parts of the world (Mendez, et al., 2013; Meredith, 2011; Reid & Hetherington, 2010). Darker skin tones developed among humans who inhabited and reproduced in hotter geographical regions nearer the equator (e.g., Africans). Their darker skin color helped them adapt and survive by providing them with better protection from the potentially damaging effects of intense sunlight (Bridgeman, 2003). In contrast, lighter skin tones developed over time among humans inhabiting colder climates that were farther from the equator (e.g., Scandinavia). Their lighter skin color enabled them to absorb greater amounts of vitamin D supplied by sunlight, which was in shorter supply in those regions of the world (Jablonksi & Chaplin, 2002).

Currently, the U.S. Census Bureau has identified five races (U.S. Census Bureau, 2013b):

White: a person whose lineage may be traced to the original people inhabiting Europe, the Middle East, or North Africa.

Black or African American: a person whose lineage may be traced to the original people inhabiting Africa.

American Indian or Alaska Native: a person whose lineage may be traced to the original people inhabiting North and South America (including Central America), and who continue to maintain their tribal affiliation or attachment.

Asian: a person whose lineage may be traced to the original people inhabiting the Far East, Southeast Asia, or the Indian subcontinent, including: Cambodia, China, India, Japan, Korea, Malaysia, Pakistan, the Philippine Islands, Thailand, and Vietnam.

Native Hawaiian or Other Pacific Islander: a person whose lineage may be traced to the original people inhabiting Hawaii, Guam, Samoa, or other Pacific islands.

It's important to keep in mind that racial categories are not based on scientific evidence; they merely represent group classifications constructed by society (Anderson & Fienberg, 2000). No identifiable set of genes distinguishes one race from another; in fact, there continues to be disagreement among scholars about what groups of people constitute a human race or whether distinctive races actually exist

> "Ethnic and cultural diversity is an integral, natural, and normal component of educational experiences for all students."
>
> —National Council for Social Studies

(Wheelright, 2005). In other words, you can't do a blood test or some type of internal genetic test to determine a person's race. Humans have simply decided to categorize themselves into races on the basis of certain external differences in their physical appearance, particularly the color of their outer layer of skin. The U.S. Census Bureau could have decided to divide people into "racial" categories based on other physical characteristics, such as eye color (blue, brown, and green), hair color (brown, black, blonde, or red), or body length (tall, short, or mid-sized).

AUTHOR'S EXPERIENCE

My father stood approximately six feet tall and had straight, light brown hair. His skin color was that of a Western European with a very slight suntan. My mother was from Alabama; she was dark in skin color with high cheekbones and had long curly black hair. In fact, if you didn't know that my father was of African American descent, you would not have thought he was black.

All of my life I've thought of myself as African American and all people who know me have thought of me as African American. I've lived half of a century with that as my racial identity. Several years ago, I carefully reviewed records of births and deaths in my family history and discovered that I had less than 50% African lineage. Biologically, I am no longer black; socially and emotionally, I still am. Clearly, my "race" has been socially constructed, not biologically determined.

—*Aaron Thompson*

While humans may display diversity in the color or tone of their external layer of skin, the reality is that all members of the human species are remarkably similar at an internal biological level. More than 98% of the genes of all humans are exactly the same, regardless of what their particular race may be (Bronfenbrenner, 2005). This large amount of genetic overlap accounts for our distinctively "human" appearance, which clearly distinguishes us from all other living species. All humans have internal organs that are similar in structure and function, and despite variations in the color of our outer layer of skin, when it's cut, all humans bleed in the same color.

AUTHOR'S EXPERIENCE

I was sitting in a coffee shop in the Chicago O'Hare airport while proofreading my first draft of this chapter. I looked up from my work for a second and saw what appeared to be a white girl about 18 years of age. As I lowered my head to return to work, I did a double-take and looked at her again because something about her seemed different or unusual. When I looked more closely at her the second time, I noticed that although she had white skin, the features of her face and hair appeared to be those of an African American. After a couple of seconds of puzzlement, I figured it out: she was an *albino* African American. That satisfied my curiosity for the moment, but then I began to wonder: Would it still be accurate to say she was "black" even though her skin was not black? Would her hair and facial features be sufficient for her to be considered or classified as black? If yes, then what would be the "race" of someone who had black skin tone, but did not have the typical hair and facial features characteristic of black people? Is skin color the defining feature of being African American or are other features equally important?

I was unable to answer these questions, but found it amusing that all of these thoughts were crossing my mind while I was working on a chapter dealing with diversity. On the plane ride home, I thought again about that albino African American girl and realized that she was a perfect example of how classifying people into "races" isn't based on objective, scientific evidence, but on subjective, socially constructed categories.

—*Joe Cuseo*

Categorizing people into distinct racial or ethnic groups is becoming even more difficult because members of different ethnic and racial groups are increasingly forming cross-ethnic and interracial families. By 2050, the number of Americans who identify themselves as being of two or more races is projected to more than triple, growing from 7.5 million to 26.7 million (U.S. Census Bureau, 2013a).

 Reflection 10.3

What race(s) do you consider yourself to be?

Would you say you identify strongly with your racial identity, or are you rarely conscious of it? Why?

What Is Cultural Diversity?

"Culture" may be defined as a distinctive pattern of beliefs and values learned by a group of people who share the same social heritage and traditions. In short, culture is the whole way in which a group of people has learned to live (Peoples & Bailey, 2011); it includes their style of speaking (language), fashion, food, art and music, as well as their beliefs and values. **Box 10.1** contains a summary of key components of culture that a group may share.

Box 10.1

Key Components of Culture

Language: How members of the culture communicate through written or spoken words; their particular dialect; and their distinctive style of nonverbal communication (body language).

Space: How cultural members arrange themselves with respect to social–spatial distance (e.g., how closely they stand next to each other when having a conversation).

Time: How the culture conceives of, divides, and uses time (e.g., the speed or pace at which they conduct business).

Aesthetics: How cultural members appreciate and express artistic beauty and creativity (e.g., their style of visual art, culinary art, music, theater, literature, and dance).

Family: The culture's attitudes and habits with respect to interacting with family members (e.g., customary styles of parenting their children and caring for their elderly).

Economics: How the culture meets its members' material needs, and its customary ways of acquiring and distribut-ing wealth (e.g., general level of wealth and gap between the very rich and very poor).

Gender Roles: The culture's expectations for "appropriate" male and female behavior (e.g., whether or not women are able to hold the same leadership positions as men).

Politics: How decision-making power is exercised in the culture (e.g., democratically or autocratically).

Science and Technology: The culture's attitude toward and use of science or technology (e.g., the degree to which the culture is technologically "advanced").

Philosophy: The culture's ideas or views on wisdom, goodness, truth, and social values (e.g., whether they place greater value on individual competition or collective collaboration).

Spirituality and Religion: Cultural beliefs about a supreme being and an afterlife (e.g., its predominant faith-based views and belief systems about the supernatural).

Reflection 10.4

Look at the components of culture cited in the previous list. Add another aspect of culture to the list that you think is important or influential. Explain why you think this is an important element of culture.

I was watching a basketball game between the Los Angeles Lakers and Los Angeles Clippers when a short scuffle broke out between the Lakers' Paul Gasol—who is Spanish—and the Clippers' Chris Paul—who is African American. After the scuffle ended, Gasol tried to show Paul there were no hard feelings by patting him on the head. Instead of interpreting Gasol's head pat as a peace-making gesture, Paul took it as a putdown and returned the favor by slapping (rather than patting) Paul in the head.

This whole misunderstanding stemmed from a basic difference in nonverbal communication between the two cultures. Patting someone on the head in European cultures is a friendly gesture; European soccer players often do it to an opposing player to express no ill will after a foul or collision. However, this same nonverbal message meant something very different to Chris Paul—an African American raised in urban America.

—*Joe Cuseo*

What Is an Ethnic Group?

A group of people who share the same culture is referred to as an *ethnic group*. Thus, "culture" refers to *what* an ethnic group shares in common (e.g., language and traditions) and "ethnic group" refers to the *people* who share the same culture that's been *learned* through common social experiences. Members of the same racial group—whose shared physical characteristics have been *inherited*—may be members of different ethnic groups. For instance, white Americans belong to the same racial group, but differ in terms of their ethnic group (e.g., French, German, Irish) and Asian Americans belong to the same racial group, but are members of different ethnic groups (e.g., Japanese, Chinese, Korean).

Currently, the major cultural (ethnic) groups in the United States include:

- Native Americans (American Indians)
  - Cherokee, Navaho, Hopi, Alaskan natives, Blackfoot, etc.
- European Americans (Whites)
  - Descendents from Western Europe (e.g., United Kingdom, Ireland, Netherlands), Eastern Europe (e.g., Hungary, Romania, Bulgaria), Southern Europe (e.g., Italy, Greece, Portugal), and Northern Europe or Scandinavia (e.g., Denmark, Sweden, Norway)
- African Americans (Blacks)
  - Americans whose cultural roots lie in the continent of Africa (e.g., Ethiopia, Kenya, Nigeria) and the Caribbean Islands (e.g., Bahamas, Cuba, Jamaica)
- Hispanic Americans (Latinos)
  - Americans with cultural roots in Mexico, Puerto Rico, Central America (e.g., El Salvador, Guatemala, Nicaragua), and South America (e.g., Brazil, Columbia, Venezuela)
- Asian Americans
  - Americans whose cultural roots lie in East Asia (e.g., Japan, China, Korea), Southeast Asia (e.g., Vietnam, Thailand, Cambodia), and South Asia (e.g., India, Pakistan, Bangladesh)

- Middle Eastern Americans
  - Americans with cultural roots in Iraq, Iran, Israel, etc.

©neelsky/Shutterstock.com

Culture is a distinctive pattern of beliefs and values that develops among a group of people who share the same social heritage and traditions.

 Reflection 10.5

What ethnic group(s) are you a member of, or do you identify with? What would you say are the key cultural values shared by your ethnic group(s)?

European Americans are still the majority ethnic group in the United States; they account for more than 50% of the American population. Native Americans, African Americans, Hispanic Americans, and Asian Americans are considered to be *minority* ethnic groups because each of these groups represents less than 50% of the American population (U.S. Census Bureau, 2015).

As with racial grouping, classifying humans into different ethnic groups can be very arbitrary and subject to debate. Currently, the U.S. Census Bureau classifies Hispanics as an ethnic group rather than a race. However, among Americans who checked "some other race" in the 2000 Census, 97% were Hispanic. This finding suggests that Hispanic Americans consider themselves to be a racial group, probably because that's how they're perceived and treated by non-Hispanics (Cianciatto, 2005). It's noteworthy that the American media used the term "racial profiling" (rather than ethnic profiling) to describe Arizona's controversial 2010 law that allowed police to target Hispanics who "look" like illegal aliens from Mexico, Central America, and South America. Once again, this illustrates how race and ethnicity are subjective, socially constructed concepts that reflect how people perceive and treat different social groups, which, in turn, affects how members of these groups perceive themselves.

> "I'm the only person from my race in class."
>
> —*Hispanic student commenting on why he felt uncomfortable in his class on race, ethnicity, and gender*

The Relationship between Diversity and Humanity

As previously noted, diversity represents variations on the same theme: being human. Thus, humanity and diversity are interdependent, complementary concepts. To understand human diversity is to understand both our differences and *similari-*

ties. Diversity appreciation includes appreciating both the unique perspectives of different cultural groups as well as universal aspects of the human experience that are common to all groups—whatever their particular cultural background happens to be. Members of all racial and ethnic groups live in communities, develop personal relationships, have emotional needs, and undergo life experiences that affect their self-esteem and personal identity. Humans of all races and ethnicities experience similar emotions and reveal those emotions with similar facial expressions (see **Figure 10.2**).

FIGURE 10.2

Humans all over the world display the same facial expressions when experiencing and expressing different emotions. See if you can detect the emotions being expressed in the following faces.
(To find the answers, turn your book upside down.)

Answers: The emotions shown. Top, left to right: anger, fear, and sadness.
Bottom, left to right: disgust, happiness, and surprise.

All images ©JupiterImages Corporation.

Other characteristics that anthropologists have found to be shared by all humans in every corner of the world include: storytelling, poetry, adornment of the body, dance, music, decoration with artifacts, families, socialization of children by elders, a sense of right and wrong, supernatural beliefs, and mourning of the dead (Pinker, 2000). Although different cultural groups may express these shared experiences in different ways, they are universal experiences common to all human cultures.

Reflection 10.6

In addition to those already mentioned, can you think of another important human experience that is universal—that is experienced by all humans?

You may have heard the question: "We're all human, aren't we?" The answer to this important question is "yes and no." Yes, we are all the same, but not in the same way. A good metaphor for understanding this apparent contradiction is to visualize humanity as a quilt in which we're all united by the common thread of humanity—the universal bond of being human (much like the quilt below). The different patches comprising the quilt represent diversity—the distinctive or unique cultures that comprise our shared humanity. The quilt metaphor acknowledges the identity and beauty of all cultures. It differs from the old American "melting pot" metaphor, which viewed cultural differences as something to be melted down and eliminated. It also differs from the old "salad bowl" metaphor that depicted America as a hodgepodge or mishmash of cultures thrown together without any common connection. In contrast, the quilt metaphor suggests that the unique cultures of different human groups should be preserved, recognized, and valued; at the same time, these cultural differences join together to form a seamless, unified whole. This blending of diversity and unity is captured in the Latin expression *E pluribus unum* ("Out of many, one")—the motto of the United States—which you'll find printed on all its currency.

©steven r. hendricks/Shutterstock.com

> "We are all the same, and we are all unique."
>
> *—Georgia Dunston, African American biologist and research specialist in human genetics*

> "We have become not a melting pot but a beautiful mosaic."
>
> *—Jimmy Carter, 39th president of the United States and winner of the Nobel Peace Prize*

Note

When we appreciate diversity in the context of humanity, we capitalize on the variety and versatility of human differences while preserving the collective strength and synergy of human unity.

AUTHOR'S EXPERIENCE

When I was 12 years old and living in New York City, I returned from school one Friday and my mother asked me if anything interesting happened at school that day. I told her that the teacher went around the room asking students what they had for dinner the night before. At that moment, my mother became a bit concerned and nervously asked me: "What did you tell the teacher?" I said: "I told her and the rest of the class that I had pasta last night because my family always eats pasta on Thursdays and Sundays." My mother exploded and fired back the following question at me in a very agitated tone, "Why didn't you tell her we had steak or roast beef?" For a moment, I was stunned and couldn't figure out what I'd done wrong or why I should have lied about eating pasta. Then it dawned on me: My mom was embarrassed about being Italian American. She wanted me to hide our family's ethnic background and make it sound like we were very "American."

As I grew older, I understood why my mother felt the way she did. She grew up in America's "melting pot" generation—a time when different American ethnic groups were expected to melt down and melt away their ethnicity. They were not to celebrate their diversity; they were to eliminate it.

—Joe Cuseo

What Is Individuality?

It's important to keep in mind that there are individual differences among members of any racial or ethnic group that are greater than the average difference between groups. Said in another way, there's more variability (individuality) within groups than between groups. For example, among members of the same racial group, individual differences in their physical attributes (e.g., height and weight) and psychological characteristics (e.g., temperament and personality) are greater than any average difference that may exist between their racial group and other racial groups (Caplan & Caplan, 2008).

Note

While it's valuable to learn about differences between different human groups, there are substantial individual differences among people within the same racial or ethnic group that should neither be ignored nor overlooked. Don't assume that individuals with the same racial or ethnic characteristics share the same personal characteristics.

As you proceed through your college experience, keep the following key distinctions in mind:

- **Humanity.** All humans are members of the *same group*—the human species.
- **Diversity.** All humans are members of *different groups*—such as, different racial and ethnic groups.
- **Individuality.** Each human is a *unique individual* who differs from all other members of any group to which he or she may belong.

Major Forms or Types of Diversity in Today's World

Ethnic and Racial Diversity

America is rapidly becoming a more racially and ethnically diverse nation. Minorities now account for almost 37% of the total population—an all-time high; in 2011, for the first time in U.S. history, racial and ethnic minorities made up more than half (50.4%) of all children born in America (Nhan, 2012). By the middle of the 21st century, minority groups are expected to comprise 57% of the American population and more than 60% of the nation's children will be members of minority groups (U.S. Census Bureau, 2015).

More specifically, by 2050 the American population is projected to be more than 29% Hispanic (up from 15% in 2008), 15% Black (up from 13% in 2008), 9.6% Asian (up from 5.3% in 2008), and 2% Native Americans (up from 1.6% in 2008). The Native Hawaiian and Pacific Islander population is expected to more than double between 2008 and 2050. During this same timeframe, the percentage of white Americans will decline from 66% (2008) to 46% (2050). As a result of these demographic trends, today's ethnic and racial minorities will become the "new majority" of Americans by the middle of the 21st century (U.S. Census Bureau, 2015) (see **Figure 10.3**).

The growing racial and ethnic diversity of America's population is reflected in the growing diversity of students enrolled in its colleges and universities. In 1960, whites made up almost 95% of the total college population; in 2010, that percentage had decreased to 61.5%. Between 1976 and 2010, the percentage of ethnic minority students in higher education increased from 17% to 40% (National Center for Education Statistics, 2011). This rise in ethnic and racial diversity on American campuses is particularly noteworthy when viewed in light of the historical treatment of minority groups in the United States. In the early 19th century, education

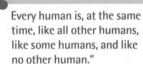

" I realize that I'm black, but I like to be viewed as a person, and this is everybody's wish."

—*Michael Jordan, Hall of Fame basketball player*

" Every human is, at the same time, like all other humans, like some humans, and like no other human."

—*Clyde Kluckhohn, American anthropologist*

FIGURE 10.3: The "New Majority"

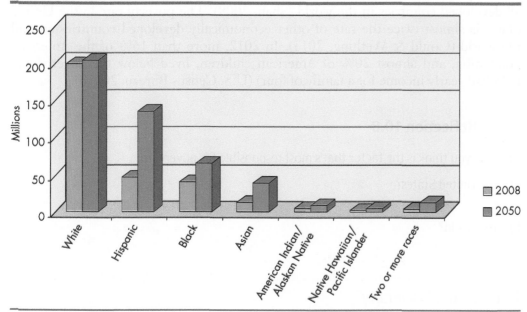

©Kendall Hunt Publishing Company

was not a right, but a privilege available only to those who could afford to attend private schools, which was experienced largely by Protestants of European descent (Luhman, 2007).

Reflection 10.7

1. What diverse groups do you see represented on your campus?

2. Are there groups on campus you didn't expect to see or to see in such large numbers?

3. Are there groups on campus you expected to see but don't see or, see in smaller numbers than you expected?

Socioeconomic Diversity

Human diversity also exists among groups of people in terms of their socioeconomic status (SES), which is determined by their level of education, level of income, and the occupational prestige of the jobs they hold. Groups are stratified (divided) into lower, middle, or upper classes, and groups occupying lower social strata have less economic resources and social privileges (Feagin & Feagin, 2007).

Young adults from high-income families are more than seven times likely to have earned a college degree and hold a prestigious job than those from low-income families (Olson, 2007). Sharp discrepancies also exist in income level among different racial, ethnic, and gender groups. In 2012, the median income for non-Hispanic white households was $57,009, compared to $39,005 for Hispanics and $33,321 for African Americans (DeNavas-Walt, Proctor, & Smith, 2013). From 2005 to 2009, household wealth fell by 66% for Hispanics, 53% for blacks, and 16% for whites, largely due to the housing and mortgage collapse—which had a more damaging effect on lower-income families (Kochlar, Fry, & Taylor, 2011).

Despite its overall wealth, the United States is one of the most impoverished of all developed countries in the world (Shah, 2008). The poverty rate in the United States is almost twice the rate of other economically developed countries around the world (Gould & Wething, 2013). In 2012, more than 16% of the American population, and almost 20% of American children, lived below the poverty line ($23,050 yearly income for a family of four) (U.S. Census Bureau, 2013b).

 Reflection 10.8

What do you think is the factor that's most responsible for poverty in:

a)   the United States?

b)   the world?

International Diversity

If it were possible to reduce the world's population to a village of precisely 100 people, with all existing human ratios remaining about the same, the demographics of this world village would look something like this:

61 would be Asians; 13 would be Africans; 12 would be Europeans; 9 would be Latin Americans; and 5 would be North Americans (citizens of the United States and Canada)
50 would be male, 50 would be female
75 would be non-white; 25 white
67 would be non-Christian; 33 would be Christian
80 would live in substandard housing
16 would be unable to read or write
50 would be malnourished and 1 would be dying of starvation
33 would be without access to a safe water supply
39 would lack access to modern sanitation
24 would have no electricity (and of the 76 who have electricity, most would only use it for light at night)
8 people would have access to the Internet
1 would have a college education
1 would have HIV
2 would be near birth; 1 near death
5 would control 32% of the entire world's wealth; all 5 would be U.S. citizens
48 would live on less than $2 a day
20 would live on less than $1 a day (Family Care Foundation, 2015).

In this world village, English would not be the most common language spoken; it would be third, following Chinese and Spanish (Lewis, Paul, & Fennig, 2014).

The need for American college students to develop an appreciation of international diversity is highlighted by a study conducted by an anthropologist who went "undercover" to pose as a student in a university residence hall. She found that the biggest complaint international students had about American students was their lack of knowledge of other countries and the misconceptions they held about people from different nations (Nathan, 2005). When you take the time to learn about other countries and the cultures of people who inhabit them, you move beyond being just a citizen of your own nation, you become *cosmopolitan*—a citizen of the world.

Generational Diversity

Humans are also diverse with respect to the historical time period in which they grew up. The term "generation" refers to a cohort (group) of individuals born during the same period in history whose attitudes, values, and habits have been shaped by events that took place in the world during their formative years of development. People growing up in different generations are likely to develop different attitudes and beliefs because of the different historical events they experienced during their upbringing.

Box 10.2 contains a brief summary of different generations, the key historical events they experienced, and the personal characteristics commonly associated with each generational group (Lancaster, Stillman, & Williams, 2002).

Box 10.2

Generational Diversity: A Snapshot Summary

- The Traditional Generation (a.k.a. "Silent Generation") (born 1922–1945). This generation was influenced by events such as the Great Depression and World Wars I and II. Characteristics associated with people growing up at this time include loyalty, patriotism, respect for authority, and conservatism.
- The Baby Boomer Generation (born 1946–1964). This generation was influenced by events such as the Vietnam War, Watergate, and the civil rights movement. Characteristics associated with people growing up at this time include idealism, emphasis on self-fulfillment, and concern for social justice and equal rights.
- Generation X (born 1965–1980). This generation was influenced by Sesame Street, the creation of MTV, AIDS, and soaring divorce rates. They were the first "latchkey children"—youngsters who used their own key to let themselves into their home after school—because their mother (or single mother) was working outside the home. Characteristics associated with people growing up at this time include self-reliance, resourcefulness, and ability to adapt to change.
- Generation Y (a.k.a. "Millennials") (born 1981–2002). This generation was influenced by the September 11, 2001, terrorist attack on the United States, the shooting of students at Columbine High School, and the collapse of the Enron Corporation. Characteristics associated with people growing up at this time include a preference for working and playing in groups, familiarity

with technology, and willingness to engage in volunteer service in their community (the "civic generation"). This is also the most ethnically diverse generation, which may explain why they're more open to diversity than previous generations and are more likely to view diversity positively.

> You guys [in the media] have to get used to it. This is a new day and age, and for my generation that's a very common word. It's like saying 'bro.' That's how we address our friends. That's how we talk."
>
> —Matt Barnes, 33-year-old, biracial professional basketball player, explaining to reporters after being fined for using the word "niggas" in a tweet to some of his African American teammates

- Generation Z (a.k.a. "The iGeneration") (born 1994–present). This generation includes the latter half of Generation Y. They grew up during the wars in Afghanistan and Iraq, terrorism, the global recession and climate change. Consequently, they have less trust in political systems and industrial corporations than previous generations. During their formative years, the world wide web was in place, so they're quite comfortable with technology and rely heavily on the Internet, Wikipedia, Google, Twitter, MySpace, Facebook, Instant Messaging, image boards, and YouTube. They expect immediate gratification through technology and accept the lack of privacy associated with social networking. For these reasons, they're also referred to as the "digital generation."

 **Reflection 10.9**

Look back at the characteristics associated with your generation. Which of these characteristics accurately reflect your personal characteristics and those of your closest friends? Which do not?

Sexual Diversity: Gay, Lesbian, Bisexual, and Transgender (GLBT)

Humans experience and express sexuality in diverse ways. "Sexual diversity" refers to differences in human *sexual orientation*—the gender (male or female) an individual is physically attracted to, and *sexual identity*—the gender an individual identifies with or considers himself or herself or to be. The spectrum of sexual diversity includes:

Heterosexuals—males who are sexually attracted to females, and females who are sexually attracted to males

Gays—males who are sexually attracted to males

Lesbians—females who are sexually attracted to females

Bisexuals—individuals who are sexually attracted to males and females

Transgender—individuals who do not identify with the gender they were assigned at birth, or don't feel they belong to a single gender (e.g., transsexuals, transvestites, and bigender)

College campuses across the country are increasing their support for GLBT (gay, lesbian, bisexual, transgendered) students, creating centers and services to facilitate their acceptance and adjustment. These centers and services play an important role in combating homophobia and related forms of sexual prejudice on campus, while promoting awareness and tolerance of all forms of sexual diversity. By accepting individuals who span the spectrum of sexual diversity, we acknowledge and appreciate the reality that heterosexuality isn't the one-and-only form of human sexual expression (Dessel, Woodford, Warren, 2012). This growing acknowledgment is reflected in the Supreme Court's historic decision to legalize same-sex marriage nationwide (Dolan & Romney, 2015).

The Benefits of Experiencing Diversity

Thus far, this chapter has focused on *what* diversity is; we now turn to *why* diversity is worth experiencing. National surveys show that by the end of their first year in college, almost two-thirds of students report "stronger" or "much stronger" knowledge of people from different races and cultures than they had when they first began college, and the majority of them became more open to diverse cultures, viewpoints and values (HERI, 2013; HERI, 2014). Students who develop more openness to and knowledge of diversity are likely to experience the following benefits.

Diversity Increases Self-Awareness and Self-Knowledge

Interacting with people from diverse backgrounds increases self-knowledge and self-awareness by enabling you to compare your life experiences with others whose

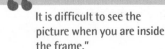
"It is difficult to see the picture when you are inside the frame."

—*An old saying (author unknown)*

experiences may differ sharply from your own. When you step outside yourself to contrast your experiences with others from different backgrounds, you move beyond ethnocentrism and gain a *comparative perspective*—a reference point that positions you to see how your particular cultural background has shaped the person you are today.

A comparative perspective also enables us to learn how our cultural background has advantaged or disadvantaged us. For instance, learning about cross-cultural differences in education makes us aware of the limited opportunities people in other countries have to attend college and how advantaged we are in America—where a college education is available to everyone, regardless of their race, gender, age, or prior academic history.

Note

The more you learn from people who are different than yourself, the more you learn about yourself.

Diversity Deepens Learning

Research consistently shows that we learn more from people who differ from us than we do from people similar to us (Pascarella, 2001; Pascarella & Terenzini, 2005). Learning about different cultures and interacting with people from diverse cultural groups provides our brain with more varied routes or pathways through which to connect (learn) new ideas. Experiencing diversity "stretches" the brain beyond its normal "comfort zone," requiring it to work harder to assimilate something unfamiliar. When we encounter the unfamiliar, the brain has to engage in extra effort to understand it by comparing and contrasting it to something we already know (Acredolo & O'Connor, 1991; Nagda, Gurin, & Johnson, 2005). This added expenditure of mental energy results in the brain forming neurological connections that are deeper and more durable (Willis, 2006). Simply stated, humans learn more from diversity than they do from similarity or familiarity. In contrast, when we restrict the diversity of people with whom we interact (out of habit or prejudice), we limit the breadth and depth of our learning.

Diversity Promotes Critical Thinking

Studies show that students who experience high levels of exposure to various forms of diversity while in college—such as participating in multicultural courses and campus events and interacting with peers from different ethnic backgrounds—report the greatest gains in:

- thinking *complexly*—ability to think about all parts and sides of an issue (Association of American Colleges & Universities, 2004; Gurin, 1999),
- *reflective* thinking—ability to think deeply about personal and global issues (Kitchener, Wood, & Jensen, 2000), and
- *critical* thinking—ability to evaluate the validity of their own reasoning and the reasoning of others (Gorski, 2009; Pascarella, et al., 2001).

These findings are likely explained by the fact that when we're exposed to perspectives that differ from our own, we experience "cognitive dissonance"—a state of cognitive (mental) disequilibrium or imbalance that "forces" our mind to consider multiple perspectives simultaneously; this makes our thinking less simplistic, more complex, and more comprehensive (Brookfield, 1987; Gorski, 2009).

When the only tool you have is a hammer, you tend to see every problem as a nail."

—*Abraham Maslow, humanistic psychologist, best known for his self-actualization theory of human motivation*

Diversity Stimulates Creative Thinking

Cross-cultural knowledge and experiences enhance personal creativity (Leung, et al., 2008; Maddux & Galinsky, 2009). When we have diverse perspectives at our disposal, we have more opportunities to shift perspectives and discover "multiple partial solutions" to problems (Kelly, 1994). Furthermore, ideas acquired from diverse people and cultures can "cross-fertilize," giving birth to new ideas for tackling old problems (Harris, 2010). Research shows that when ideas are generated freely and exchanged openly in groups comprised of people from diverse backgrounds, powerful "cross-stimulation" effects can occur, whereby ideas from one group member trigger new ideas among other group members (Brown, Dane, & Durham, 1998). Research also indicates that seeking out diverse alternatives, perspectives, and viewpoints enhances our ability to reach personal goals (Stoltz, 2014).

Note

By drawing on ideas generated by people from diverse backgrounds and bouncing your ideas off them, divergent or expansive thinking is stimulated; this leads to synergy *(multiplication of ideas) and* serendipity *(unexpected discoveries).*

In contrast, when different cultural perspectives are neither sought nor valued, the variety of lenses available to us for viewing problems is reduced, which, in turn, reduces our capacity to think creatively. Ideas are less likely to diverge (go in different directions); instead, they're more likely to converge and merge into the same cultural channel—the one shared by the homogeneous group of people doing the thinking.

Diversity Enhances Career Preparation and Career Success

Whatever line of work you decide to pursue, you're likely to find yourself working with employers, coworkers, customers, and clients from diverse cultural backgrounds. America's workforce is now more diverse than at any other time in history and will grow ever more diverse throughout the 21st century; by 2050, the proportion of American workers from minority ethnic and racial groups will jump to 55% (U.S. Census Bureau, 2008).

National surveys reveal that policymakers, business leaders, and employers seek college graduates who are more than just "aware" of or "tolerant" of diversity. They want graduates who have actual *experience* with diversity (Education Commission of the States, 1995) and are able to collaborate with diverse coworkers, clients, and customers (Association of American Colleges & Universities, 2002; Hart Research Associates, 2013). Over 90% of employers agree that all students should have experiences in college that teach them how to solve problems with people whose views differ from their own (Hart Research Associates, 2013).

The current "global economy" also requires skills relating to international diversity. Today's work world is characterized by economic interdependence among nations, international trading (imports/exports), multinational corporations, international travel, and almost instantaneous worldwide communication—due to rapid advances in the world wide web (Dryden & Vos, 1999; Friedman, 2005). Even smaller companies and corporations have become increasingly international in nature (Brooks, 2009). As a result, employers in all sectors of the economy now seek job candidates who possess the following skills and attributes: sensitivity to human differences, ability to understand and relate to people from different cultural backgrounds, international knowledge, and ability to communicate in a second language

"What I look for in musicians is generosity. There is so much to learn from each other and about each other's culture. Great creativity begins with tolerance."

—Yo-Yo Ma, French-born, Chinese-American virtuoso cellist, composer, and winner of multiple Grammy Awards

"When all men think alike, no one thinks very much."

—Walter Lippmann, distinguished journalist and originator of the term "stereotype"

"The benefits that accrue to college students who are exposed to racial and ethnic diversity during their education carry over in the work environment. The improved ability to think critically, to understand issues from different points of view, and to collaborate harmoniously with co-workers from a range of cultural backgrounds all enhance a graduate's ability to contribute to his or her company's growth and productivity."

—Business/Higher Education Forum

(Fixman, 1990; National Association of Colleges & Employers, 2014; Office of Research, 1994; Hart Research Associates, 2013).

As a result of these domestic and international trends, *intercultural competence* has become an essential skill for success in the 21st century (Thompson & Cuseo, 2014). Intercultural competence may be defined as the ability to appreciate and learn from human differences and to interact effectively with people from diverse cultural backgrounds. It includes "knowledge of cultures and cultural practices (one's own and others), complex cognitive skills for decision making in intercultural contexts, social skills to function effectively in diverse groups, and personal attributes that include flexibility and openness to new ideas" (Wabash National Study of Liberal Arts Education, 2007).

 Reflection 10.10

What intercultural skills do you think you already possess?

What intercultural skills do you think you need to develop?

Note

The wealth of diversity on college campuses today represents an unprecedented educational opportunity. You may never again be a member of a community with so many people from such a wide variety of backgrounds. Seize this opportunity to strengthen your education and career preparation.

Overcoming Barriers to Diversity

Before we can capitalize on the benefits of diversity, we need to overcome obstacles that have long impeded our ability to appreciate and seek out diversity. These major impediments are discussed below.

Ethnocentrism

A major advantage of culture is that it builds group solidarity, binding its members into a supportive, tight-knit community. Unfortunately, culture not only binds us, it can also blind us from taking different cultural perspectives. Since culture shapes thought and perception, people from the same ethnic (cultural) group run the risk of becoming *ethnocentric*—centered on their own culture to such a degree they view the world solely through their own cultural lens (frame of reference) and fail to consider or appreciate other cultural perspectives (Colombo, Cullen, & Lisle, 2013).

Optical illusions are a good example of how our particular cultural perspective can influence (and distort) our perceptions. Compare the lengths of the two lines in **Figure 10.4**. If you perceive the line on the right to be longer than the one on the left, your perception has been shaped by Western culture. People from Western cultures, such as Americans, perceive the line on the right to be longer. However, both lines are actually equal in length. (If you don't believe it, take out a ruler and measure them.) Interestingly, this perceptual error isn't made by people from non-Western cultures—whose living spaces and architectural structures are predominantly circular (e.g., huts or igloos)—in contrast to rectangular-shaped build-

FIGURE 10.4:
Optical Illusion

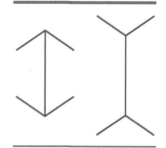

©Kendall Hunt Publishing Company

©James Michael Doresey/Shutterstock.com

People whose cultural experiences involve living and working in circular structures would not be fooled by the optical illusion in Figure 10.4.

ings with angled corners that typify Western cultures (Segall, Campbell, & Herskovits, 1966).

The optical illusion depicted in Figure 10.4 is just one of a number of illusions experienced by people in certain cultures, but not others (Shiraev & Levy, 2013). Cross-cultural differences in susceptibility to optical illusions illustrate how strongly our cultural experiences can influence and sometimes misinform our perception of reality. People think they are seeing things objectively (as they actually are) but they're really seeing things subjectively—as viewed from their particular cultural perspective.

If our cultural experience can influence our perception of the physical world, it can certainly shape our perception of social events and political issues. Research in psychology indicates that the more exposure humans have to somebody or something, the more familiar it becomes and the more likely it will be perceived positively and judged favorably. The effect of familiarity is so prevalent and powerful that social psychologists have come to call it the "familiarity principle"—that is, what is familiar is perceived as better or more acceptable (Zajonc, 1968, 1970, 2001). Thus, we need to be mindful that the familiarity of our cultural experiences can bias us toward seeing our culture as normal or better. By remaining open to the viewpoints of people who perceive the world from different cultural vantage points, we minimize our cultural blind spots, expand our range of perception, and position ourselves to perceive the world with greater clarity and cultural sensitivity.

Stereotyping

"Stereotype" derives from two different roots: *stereo*—to look at in a fixed way—and *type*—to categorize or group together, as in the word "typical." Thus, to stereotype is to view individuals of the same type (group) in the same (fixed) way.

Stereotyping overlooks or disregards individuality; all people sharing the same group characteristic (e.g., race or gender) are viewed as having the same personal characteristics—as in the expression: "You know how they are; they're all alike." Stereotypes can also involve *bias*—literally meaning "slant"—a slant that can tilt toward the positive or the negative. Positive bias results in favorable stereotypes (e.g., "Asians are great in science and math"); negative bias leads to unfavorable stereotypes (e.g., "Asians are nerds who do nothing but study"). Here are some other examples of negative stereotypes:

- Muslims are religious terrorists.
- Whites can't jump (or dance).
- Blacks are lazy.
- Irish are alcoholics.
- Gay men are feminine; lesbian women are masculine.
- Jews are cheap.
- Women are weak.

While few people would agree with these crass stereotypes, overgeneralizations are often made about members of certain groups. Such negative overgeneralizations malign the group's reputation, rob group members of their individuality, and can weaken their self-esteem and self-confidence (as illustrated by the following experience).

When I was six years old, I was told by a six-year-old girl from a different racial group that all people of my race could not swim. Since I couldn't swim at that time and she could, I assumed she was correct. I asked a boy, who was a member of the same racial group as the girl, whether her statement was true. He responded emphatically: "Yes, it's true!" Since I was from an area where few other African Americans were around to counteract this belief about my racial group, I continued to buy into this stereotype until I finally took swimming lessons as an adult. After many lessons, I am now a lousy swimmer because I didn't even attempt to swim until I was an adult. Moral of this story: Group stereotypes can limit the confidence and potential of individual members of the stereotyped group.

—Aaron Thompson

©Kendall Hunt Publishing Company

Whether you are male or female, don't let gender stereotypes limit your career options.

Reflection 10.11

1. Have you ever been stereotyped based on your appearance or group membership? If so, what was the stereotype and how did it make you feel?

2. Have you ever unintentionally perceived or treated a person in terms of a group stereotype rather than as an individual? What assumptions did you make about that person? Was that person aware of, or affected by, your stereotyping?

Prejudice

If all members of a stereotyped group are judged and evaluated in a negative way, the result is *prejudice*. The word "prejudice" literally means to "pre-judge." Typically, the prejudgment is negative and involves *stigmatizing*—ascribing inferior or unfavorable traits to people who belong to the same group. Thus, prejudice may be defined as a negative stereotype held about a group of people that's formed before the facts are known.

People who hold a group prejudice typically avoid contact with members of that group. This enables the prejudice to continue unchallenged because there's little opportunity for the prejudiced person to have a positive experience with members of the stigmatized group that could contradict or disprove the prejudice. Thus, a vicious cycle is established in which the prejudiced person continues to avoid contact with individuals from the stigmatized group; this, in turn, continues to maintain and reinforce the prejudice.

Once prejudice has been formed, it often remains intact and resistant to change through the psychological process of *selective perception*—the tendency for biased (prejudiced) people to see what they *expect* to see and fail to see what contradicts their bias (Hugenberg & Bodenhausen, 2003). Have you ever noticed how fans rooting for their favorite sports team tend to focus on and "see" the calls of referees that go against their own team, but don't seem to react (or even notice) the calls that go against the opposing team? This is a classic example of selective perception. In effect, selective perception transforms the old adage, "seeing is believing," into "believing is seeing." This can lead prejudiced people to focus their attention on information that's consistent with their prejudgment, causing them to "see" what supports or reinforces it and fail to see information that contradicts it.

Making matters worse, selective perception is often accompanied by *selective memory*—the tendency to remember information that's consistent with one's prejudicial belief and to forget information that's inconsistent with it or contradicts it (Judd, Ryan, & Parke, 1991). The mental processes of selective perception and selective memory often work together and often work *unconsciously*. As a result, prejudiced people may not even be aware they're using these biased mental processes or realize how these processes are keeping their prejudice permanently intact (Baron, Byrne, & Brauscombe, 2008).

> "See that man over there? Yes.
> Well, I hate him.
> But you don't know him.
> That's why I hate him."
> —*Gordon Allport, influential social psychologist and author of* The Nature of Prejudice

> "We see what is behind our eyes."
> —*Chinese proverb*

 ### Reflection 10.12

Have you witnessed selective perception or selective memory—people seeing or recalling what they believe is true (due to bias), rather than what's actually true? What happened and why do you think it happened?

Discrimination

Literally translated, the term *discrimination* means "division" or "separation." Whereas prejudice involves a belief, attitude or opinion, discrimination involves an *act* or *behavior*. Technically, discrimination can be either positive or negative. A discriminating eater may only eat healthy foods, which is a positive quality. However, discrimination is most often associated with a harmful act that results in a prejudiced person treating another individual, or group of individuals, in an unfair manner. Thus, it could be said that discrimination is prejudice put into action. For instance, to fire or not hire people on the basis of their race, gender, or sexual orientation is an act of discrimination.

Box 10.3 below contains a summary of the major forms of discrimination, prejudice, and stereotypes that have plagued humanity. As you read through the following list, place a check mark next to any item that you, a friend, or family member has experienced.

Box 10.3

Stereotypes, Prejudices, and Forms of Discrimination: A Snapshot Summary

- **Ethnocentrism:** viewing one's own culture or ethnic group as "central" or "normal," while viewing different cultures as "deficient" or "inferior."

  Example: Viewing another culture as "abnormal" or "uncivilized" because its members eat animals our culture views as unacceptable to eat, although we eat animals their culture views as unacceptable to eat.

- **Stereotyping:** viewing all (or virtually all) members of the same group in the same way—as having the same personal qualities or characteristics.

  Example: "If you're Italian, you must be in the Mafia, or have a family member who is."

- **Prejudice:** negative prejudgment about another group of people.

  Example: Women can't be effective leaders because they're too emotional.

- **Discrimination:** unequal and unfair treatment of a person or group of people—prejudice put into action.

  Example: Paying women less than men for performing the same job, even though they have the same level of education and job qualifications.

- **Segregation:** intentional decision made by a group to separate itself (socially or physically) from another group.

  Example: "White flight"—white people moving out of neighborhoods when people of color move in.

- **Racism:** belief that one's racial group is superior to another group and expressing that belief in attitude (prejudice) or action (discrimination).

  Example: Confiscating land from American Indians based on the unfounded belief that they are "uncivilized" or "savages."

- **Institutional Racism:** racial discrimination rooted in organizational policies and practices that disadvantage certain racial groups.

  Example: Race-based discrimination in mortgage lending, housing, and bank loans.

- **Racial Profiling:** investigating or arresting someone solely on the basis of the person's race, ethnicity, or national origin—without witnessing actual criminal behavior or possessing incriminating evidence.

  Example: Police making a traffic stop or conducting a personal search based solely on an individual's racial features.

- **Slavery:** forced labor in which people are considered to be property, held against their will, and deprived of the right to receive wages.

  Example: Enslavement of Blacks, which was legal in the United States until 1865.

- **"Jim Crow" Laws:** formal and informal laws created by whites to segregate Blacks after the abolition of slavery.

  Example: Laws in certain parts of the United States that once required Blacks to use separate bathrooms and be educated in separate schools.

- **Apartheid:** an institutionalized system of "legal racism" supported by a nation's government. (Apartheid derives from a word in the Afrikaan language, meaning "apartness.")

  Example: South Africa's national system of racial segregation and discrimination that was in place from 1948 to 1994.

" Let us all hope that the dark clouds of racial prejudice will soon pass away and . . . in some not too distant tomorrow the radiant stars of love and brotherhood will shine over our great nation."

—Martin Luther King, Jr., Civil rights leader, humanitarian, and youngest recipient of the Nobel Peace Prize

" Never, never, and never again shall it be that this beautiful land will again experience the oppression of one by another."

—Nelson Mandela, anti-apartheid revolutionary, first Black president of South Africa after apartheid, and winner of the Nobel Peace Prize

(continued)

Box 10.3 *(continued)*

- **Hate Crimes**: criminal action motivated solely by prejudice toward the crime victim.

  Example: Acts of vandalism or assault aimed at members of a particular ethnic group or persons of a particular sexual orientation.

- **Hate Groups**: organizations whose primary purpose is to stimulate prejudice, discrimination, or aggression toward certain groups of people based on their ethnicity, race, religion, etc.

  Example: The Ku Klux Klan—an American terrorist group that perpetrates hatred toward all non-white races.

- **Genocide**: mass murdering of a particular ethnic or racial group.

  Example: The Holocaust, in which millions of Jews were systematically murdered during World War II. Other examples include the murdering of Cambodians under the Khmer Rouge regime, the murdering of Bosnian Muslims in the former country of Yugoslavia, and the slaughter of the Tutsi minority by the Hutu majority in Rwanda.

- **Classism**: prejudice or discrimination based on social class, particularly toward people of lower socioeconomic status.

  Example: Acknowledging the contributions made by politicians and wealthy industrialists to America, while ignoring the contributions of poor immigrants, farmers, slaves, and pioneer women.

- **Religious Intolerance**: denying the fundamental human right of people to hold religious beliefs, or to hold religious beliefs that differ from one's own.

  Example: An atheist who forces nonreligious (secular) beliefs on others, or a member of a religious group who believes that people who hold different religious beliefs are infidels or "sinners" whose souls will not be saved.

"Rivers, ponds, lakes and streams—they all have different names, but they all contain water. Just as religions do—they all contain truths."

—Muhammad Ali, three-time world heavyweight boxing champion, member of the International Boxing Hall of Fame, and recipient of the Spirit of America Award as the most recognized American in the world

- **Anti-Semitism**: prejudice or discrimination toward Jews or people who practice the religion of Judaism.

  Example: Disliking Jews because they're the ones who "killed Christ."

- **Xenophobia**: fear or hatred of foreigners, outsiders, or strangers.

  Example: Believing that immigrants should be banned from entering the country because they'll undermine our economy and increase our crime rate.

- **Regional Bias**: prejudice or discrimination based on the geographical region in which an individual is born and raised.

  Example: A northerner thinking that all southerners are racists.

- **Jingoism**: excessive interest and belief in the superiority of one's own nation—without acknowledging its mistakes or weaknesses—often accompanied by an aggressive foreign policy that neglects the needs of other nations or the common needs of all nations.

  Example: "Blind patriotism"—failure to see the shortcomings of one's own nation and viewing any questioning or criticism of one's own nation as being disloyal or "unpatriotic." (As in the slogan, "America: right or wrong" or "America: love it or leave it!")

Above all nations is humanity."
—Motto of the University of Hawaii

- **Terrorism**: intentional acts of violence committed against civilians that are motivated by political or religious prejudice.

  Example: The September 11, 2001, attacks on the United States.

- **Sexism**: prejudice or discrimination based on sex or gender.

  Example: Believing that women should not pursue careers in fields traditionally filled only by men (e.g., engineering or politics) because they lack the innate qualities or natural skills to do so.

- **Heterosexism**: belief that heterosexuality is the only acceptable sexual orientation.

  Example: Believing that gays should not have the same legal rights and opportunities as heterosexuals.

Box 10.3 *(continued)*

- Homophobia: extreme fear or hatred of homosexuals.

  Example: Creating or contributing to anti-gay websites, or "gay bashing" (acts of violence toward gays).

- Ageism: prejudice or discrimination toward certain age groups, particularly toward the elderly.

  Example: Believing that all "old" people have dementia and shouldn't be allowed to drive or make important decisions.

- Ableism: prejudice or discrimination toward people who are disabled or handicapped (physically, mentally, or emotionally).

  Example: Intentionally avoiding social contact with people in wheelchairs.

 Reflection 10.13

As you read through the above list, did you, a friend, or family member experience any of the form(s) of prejudice listed?

If yes, what happened and why do you think it happened?

Strategies for Overcoming Stereotypes and Prejudices

We may hold prejudices, stereotypes, or subtle biases that bubble beneath the surface of our conscious awareness. The following practices and strategies can help us become more aware of our unconscious biases and relate more effectively to individuals from diverse groups.

Consciously avoid preoccupation with physical appearances. Remember the old proverb: "It's what inside that counts." Judge others by the quality of their inner qualities, not by the familiarity of their outer features. Get beneath the superficial surface of appearances and relate to people not in terms of how they look but who they are and how they act.

Form impressions of others on a person-to-person basis, not on the basis of their group membership. This may seem like an obvious and easy thing to do, but research shows that humans have a natural tendency to perceive individuals from unfamiliar groups as being more alike (or all alike) than members of their own group (Taylor, Peplau, & Sears, 2006). Thus, we need to remain mindful of this tendency and make a conscious effort to perceive and treat individuals of diverse groups as unique human beings, not according to some general (stereotypical) rule of thumb.

Note

It's valuable to learn about different cultures and the common characteristics shared by members of the same culture; however, this shouldn't be done while ignoring individual differences. Don't assume that all individuals who share the same cultural background share the same personal characteristics.

> "I grew up in a very racist family. Even just a year ago, I could honestly say 'I hate Asians' with a straight face and mean it. My senior AP language teacher tried hard to teach me not to be judgmental. He got me to be open to others, so much so that my current boyfriend is half Chinese."
>
> —*First-year college student*

> "Stop judging by mere appearances, and make a right judgment."
>
> —*Bible, John 7:24*

> "You can't judge a book by the cover."
>
> —*1962 hit song by Elias Bates, a.k.a. Bo Diddley (Note: a "bo diddley" is a one-stringed African guitar)*

Reflection 10.14

Your comfort level while interacting with people from diverse groups is likely to depend on how much prior experience you've had with members of those groups. Rate the amount or variety of diversity you have experienced in the following settings:

	high	moderate	low
1. The high school you attended	high	moderate	low
2. The college or university you now attend	high	moderate	low
3. The neighborhood in which you grew up	high	moderate	low
4. Places where you have been employed	high	moderate	low

Which setting had the most and the least diversity?

What do you think accounted for this difference?

> "I am very happy with the diversity here, but it also frightens me. I have never been in a situation where I have met people who are Jewish, Muslim, atheist, born-again, and many more."
>
> —First-year student (quoted in Erickson, Peters, & Strommer, 2006)

(Review your results from the My MI Advantage Inventory. How might the recommendations you received about your interpersonal skills enable you to become more adept at connecting with people from cultural backgrounds that are different from your own?)

Strategies for Increasing Interpersonal Contact and Interaction with Members of Diverse Groups

Place yourself in situations and locations on campus where you will come in regular contact with individuals from diverse groups. Distancing ourselves from diversity ensures we'll never experience diversity and benefit from it. Research in social psychology shows that relationships are more likely to form among people who come in regular contact with one another (Latané, et al., 1995), and research on diversity reveals that when there's regular contact between members of different racial or ethnic groups, stereotyping is sharply reduced and intercultural friendships are more likely to develop (Pettigrew, 1997, 1998). You can create these conditions by making an intentional attempt to sit near diverse students in the classroom, library, or student café, and by joining them for class discussion groups or group projects.

Take advantage of social media to "chat" virtually with students from diverse groups on your own campus, or students on other campuses. Electronic communication can be a convenient and comfortable way to initially interact with members of diverse groups with whom you have had little prior experience. After interacting *online*, you're more likely to feel more comfortable about interacting *in person*.

Engage in co-curricular experiences involving diversity. Review your student handbook to find co-curricular programs, student activities, student clubs, or campus organizations that emphasize diversity awareness and appreciation. Studies indicate that participation in co-curricular experiences relating to diversity promotes critical thinking (Pascarella & Terenzini, 2005) and reduces unconscious prejudice (Blair, 2002).

Consider spending time at the multicultural center on your campus, or joining a campus club or organization that's devoted to diversity awareness (e.g., multicultural or international student club). Putting yourself in these situations will enable you to make regular contact with members of cultural groups other than your own; it also sends a clear message to members of these groups that you value their culture because you've taken the initiative to connect with them on "their turf."

If your campus sponsors multicultural or cross-cultural retreats, strongly consider participating in them. A retreat setting can provide a comfortable environment in which you can interact personally with diverse students without being distracted by your customary social circle and daily routine.

If possible, participate in a study abroad or travel study program that gives you the opportunity to live in another country and interact directly with its native citizens. In addition to coursework, you can gain international knowledge and a global perspective by participating in programs that enable you to actually *experience* a different country. You can do this for a full term or for a shorter time period (e.g., January, May, or summer term). To prepare for international experiences, take a course in the language, culture, or history of the nation to which you will be traveling.

Research on students who participate in study abroad programs indicates that these experiences promote greater appreciation of cross-cultural differences, greater interest in world affairs, and greater commitment to peace and international cooperation (Bok, 2006; Kaufmann, et al., 1992). Additional research shows that study abroad benefits students' personal development, including improved self-confidence, sense of independence, and ability to function in complex environments (Carlson, et al., 1990; IES Abroad News, 2002).

Incorporate diversity courses into your planned schedule of classes. Review your college catalog (bulletin) and identify courses that are designed to promote understanding or appreciation of diversity. These courses may focus on diverse cultures found within the United States (sometimes referred to as multicultural courses) or diverse cultures associated with different countries (sometimes referred to as international or cross-cultural courses).

In a national study of college students who experienced multicultural courses, it was discovered that students of all racial and ethnic groups made significant gains in learning and intellectual development (Smith, 1997; Smith, et al., 1997).

Taking courses focusing on international diversity can help you develop the global perspective needed for success in today's international economy and enhance the quality of your college transcript (Brooks, 2009; Cuseo, et al., 2013; National Association of Colleges & Employers, 2003).

Be on the lookout for diversity implications associated with topics you're reading about or discussing in class. Consider the multicultural and cross-cultural ramifications of material you're studying and use examples of diversity to support or illustrate your points. If you're allowed to choose a topic for a research project, select one that relates to diversity or has implications for diversity.

Seek out the views and opinions of classmates from diverse backgrounds. Discussions among students of different races and cultures can reduce prejudice and promote intercultural appreciation, but only if each member's cultural identity and perspective is sought out and valued by members of the discussion group (Baron, Byrne, & Brauscombe, 2008). During class discussions, you can demonstrate leadership by seeking out views and opinions of classmates from diverse backgrounds and ensuring that the ideas of people from minority groups are included

> "Empirical evidence shows that the actual effects on student development of emphasizing diversity and of student participation in diversity activities are overwhelmingly positive."
>
> —*Alexander Astin*, What Matters in College

> "The classroom can provide a 'public place' where community can be practiced."
>
> —*Susanne Morse*, Renewing Civic Capacity: Preparing College Students for Service and Citizenship

and respected. Also, after class discussions, you can ask students from different backgrounds if there was any point made or position taken in class that they would have strongly questioned or challenged.

If there is little or no diversity among students in class, encourage your classmates to look at topics from diverse perspectives. For instance, you might ask: "If there were international students here, what might they be adding to our discussion?" or, "If members of certain minority groups were here, would they be offering a different viewpoint?"

If you are given the opportunity to form your own discussion groups and group project teams, join or create groups composed of students from diverse backgrounds. You can gain greater exposure to diverse perspectives by intentionally joining or forming learning groups with students who differ in terms of gender, age, race, or ethnicity. Including diversity in your discussion groups not only creates social variety, it also enhances the quality of your group's work by allowing members to gain access to and learn from multiple perspectives. For instance, in learning groups comprised of students that are diverse with respect to age, older students will bring a broad range of life experiences that younger students can draw upon and learn from, while younger students can provide a more contemporary and idealistic perspective to the group's discussions. Gender diversity is also likely to infuse group discussions with different learning styles and approaches to understanding issues. Studies show that males are more likely to be "separate knowers"—they tend to "detach" themselves from the concept or issue being discussed so they can analyze it. In contrast, females are more likely to be "connected knowers"—they tend to relate personally to concepts and connect them with their own experiences and the experiences of others. For example, when interpreting a poem, males are more likely to ask: "What techniques can I use to analyze it?" In contrast, females would be more likely to ask: "What is the poet trying to say to me?" (Belenky, et al., 1986). It's also been found that females are more likely to work collaboratively during group discussions and collect the ideas of other members; in contrast, males are more likely to adopt a competitive approach and debate the ideas of others (Magolda, 1992). Both of these styles of learning are valuable and you can capitalize on these different styles by forming gender-diverse discussion groups.

Form collaborative learning teams with students from diverse backgrounds. A learning *team* is more than a discussion group that tosses around ideas; it moves beyond discussion to *collaboration*—its members "co-labor" (work together) to reach the same goal. Research from kindergarten through college indicates that when students collaborate in teams, their academic performance and interpersonal skills are strengthened (Cuseo, 1996). Also, when individuals from different racial groups work collaboratively toward the same goal, racial prejudice is reduced and interracial friendships are more likely to be formed (Allport, 1954; Amir, 1976; Brown, et al., 2003; Dovidio, Eller, & Hewstone, 2011). These positive developments may be explained, in part, by the fact that when members of diverse groups come together on the same team, nobody is a member of an "out" group ("them"); instead, everybody belongs to the same "in" group ("us") (Pratto, et al., 2000; Sidanius, et al., 2000).

In an analysis of multiple studies involving more than 90,000 people from 25 different countries, it was found that when interaction between members of diverse groups took place under the conditions described in **Box 10.4**, prejudice was significantly reduced (Pettigrew & Tropp, 2000) and the greatest gains in learning took place (Johnson, Johnson, & Smith, 1998; Slavin, 1995).

Box 10.4

Tips for Teamwork: Creating Diverse and Effective Learning Teams

1. Intentionally form learning teams with students who have different cultural backgrounds and life experiences. Teaming up only with friends or classmates whose backgrounds and experiences are similar to yours can actually impair your team's performance because teammates can get off track and onto topics that have nothing to do with the learning task (e.g., what they did last weekend or what they're planning to do next weekend).

2. Before jumping into group work, take some time to interact informally with your teammates. When team members have some social "warm up" time (e.g., time to learn each other's names and learn something about each other), they feel more comfortable expressing their ideas and are more likely to develop a stronger sense of team identity. This feeling of group solidarity can create a foundation of trust among group members, enabling them to work together as a team, particularly if they come from diverse (and unfamiliar) cultural backgrounds.

   The context in which a group interacts can influence the openness and harmony of their interaction. Group members are more likely to interact openly and collaboratively when they work in a friendly, informal environment that's conducive to relationship building. A living room or a lounge area provides a warmer and friendlier team-learning atmosphere than a sterile classroom.

3. Have teammates work together to complete a single work product. One jointly created product serves to highlight the team's collaborative effort and collective achievement (e.g., a completed sheet of answers to questions, or a comprehensive list of ideas). Creating a common final product helps keep individuals thinking in terms of "we" (not "me") and keeps the team moving in the same direction toward the same goal.

4. Group members should work interdependently—they should depend on each other to reach their common goal and each member should have equal opportunity to contribute to the team's final product. Each teammate should take responsibility for making an indispensable contribution to the team's end product, such as contributing: (a) a different piece of *information* (e.g., a specific chapter from the textbook or a particular section of class notes), (b) a particular form of *thinking* to the learning task (e.g., analysis, synthesis, or application), or (c) a different *perspective* (e.g., national, international, or global). Said in another way, each group member should

   assume personal responsibility for a piece that's needed to complete the whole puzzle.

   Similar to a sports team, each member of a learning team should have a specific role to play. For instance, each teammate could perform one of the following roles:
   - manager—whose role is to assure that the team stays on track and keeps moving toward its goal;
   - moderator—whose role is to ensure that all teammates have equal opportunity to contribute;
   - summarizer—whose role is to monitor the team's progress, identifying what has been accomplished and what still needs to be done;
   - recorder—whose role is to keep a written record of the team's ideas.

5. After concluding work in diverse learning teams, take time to reflect on the experience. The final step in any learning process, whether it be learning from a lecture or learning from a group discussion, is to step back from the process and thoughtfully review it. Deep learning requires not only effortful action but also thoughtful reflection (Bligh, 2000; Roediger, Dudai, & Fitzpatrick, 2007). You can reflect on your experiences with diverse learning groups by asking yourself questions that prompt you to process the ideas shared by members of your group and the impact those ideas had on you. For instance, ask yourself (and your teammates) the following questions:
   - What major similarities in viewpoints did all group members share? (What were the common themes?)
   - What major differences of opinion were expressed by diverse members of our group? (What were the variations on the themes?)
   - Were there particular topics or issues raised during the discussion that provoked intense reactions or emotional responses from certain members of our group?
   - Did the group discussion lead any individuals to change their mind about an idea or position they originally held?

When contact among people from diverse groups takes place under the five conditions described in this box, group work is transformed into *teamwork* and promotes higher levels of thinking and deeper appreciation of diversity. A win–win scenario is created: Learning and thinking are strengthened while bias and prejudice are weakened (Allport, 1979; Amir, 1969; Aronson, Wilson, & Akert, 2013; Cook, 1984; Sherif, et al., 1961).

Reflection 10.15

Have you had an experience with a member of an unfamiliar racial or cultural group that caused you to change your attitude or viewpoint toward that group?

Take a stand against prejudice or discrimination by constructively disagreeing with students who make stereotypical statements and prejudicial remarks. By saying nothing, you may avoid conflict, but your silence may be perceived by others to mean that you agree with the person who made the prejudicial remark. Studies show that when members of the same group observe another member of their own group making prejudicial comments, prejudice tends to increase among all group members—probably due to peer pressure of group conformity (Stangor, Sechrist, & Jost, 2001). In contrast, if a person's prejudicial remark is challenged by a member of one's own group, particularly a fellow member who is liked and respected, that person's prejudice decreases along with similar prejudices held by other members of the group (Baron, Byrne, & Brauscombe, 2008). Thus, by taking a leadership role and challenging peers who make prejudicial remarks, you're likely to reduce that person's prejudice as well as the prejudice of others who hear the remark. In addition, you help create a campus climate in which students experience greater satisfaction with their college experience and are more likely to complete their college degree. Studies show that a campus climate which is hostile toward students from minority groups lowers students' level of college satisfaction and college completion rates of both minority and majority students (Cabrera, et al., 1999; Eimers & Pike, 1997; Nora & Cabrera, 1996).

Note

By actively opposing prejudice on campus, you demonstrate diversity leadership and moral character. You become a role model whose actions send a clear message that valuing diversity is not only the smart thing to do, it's the right *thing to do.*

 Reflection 10.16

If you heard another student telling an insulting racial or gender joke, do you think you would do anything about it? Why?

Chapter Summary and Highlights

Diversity refers to the variety of groups that comprise humanity (the human species). Humans differ from one another in multiple ways, including physical features, religious beliefs, mental and physical abilities, national origins, social backgrounds, gender, and sexual orientation. Diversity involves the important political issue of securing equal rights and social justice for all people; however, it's also an important *educational* issue—an integral element of the college experience that enriches learning, personal development, and career preparation.

When a group of people share the same traditions and customs, it creates a culture that serves to bind people into a supportive, tight-knit community. However, culture can also lead its members to view the world solely through their own cultural lens (known as ethnocentrism), which can blind them to other cultural perspectives. Ethnocentrism can contribute to stereotyping—viewing individual members of another cultural group in the same (fixed) way, in which they're seen as having similar personal characteristics.

Stereotyping can result in prejudice—a biased prejudgment about another person or group of people that's formed before the facts are known. Stereotyping and prejudice often go hand in hand because if the stereotype is negative, members of the stereotyped group are then judged negatively. Discrimination takes prejudice one step further by converting the negative prejudgment into behavior that results in unfair treatment of others. Thus, discrimination is prejudice put into action.

Once stereotyping and prejudice are overcome, we are positioned to experience diversity and reap its multiple benefits—which include sharper self-awareness, deeper learning, higher-level thinking, and better career preparation.

The increasing diversity of students on campus, combined with the wealth of diversity-related educational experiences found in the college curriculum and co-curriculum, presents you with an unprecedented opportunity to infuse diversity into your college experience. Seize this opportunity and capitalize on the power of diversity to increase the quality of your college education and your prospects for success in the 21st century.

Learning More through the World Wide Web: Internet-Based Resources

For additional information on diversity, see the following websites:

Stereotyping:
ReducingStereotypeThreat.org at www.reducingstereotypethreat.org

Prejudice and Discrimination:
Southern Poverty Law Center at www.splcenter.org/

Human Rights:
Amnesty International at www.amnesty.org/en/discrimination
Center for Economic & Social Justice at www.cesj.org

Sexism in the Media:
"Killing Us Softly" at www.youtube.com/watch?v=PTlmho_RovY

LGBT Acceptance and Support:
"It Gets Better Project," at www.itgetsbetter.org

References

Acredolo, C., & O'Connor, J. (1991). On the difficulty of detecting cognitive uncertainty. *Human Development, 34,* 204–223.

Allport, G. W. (1954). *The nature of prejudice.* Cambridge, MA: Addison-Wesley.

Allport, G. W. (1979). *The nature of prejudice* (3rd ed.). Reading, MA: Addison-Wesley.

Amir, Y. (1969). Contact hypothesis in ethnic relations. *Psychological Bulletin, 71,* 319–342.

Amir, Y. (1976). The role of intergroup contact in change of prejudice and ethnic relations. In P. A. Katz (Ed.), *Towards the elimination of racism* (pp. 245–308). New York: Pergamon Press.

Anderson, M., & Fienberg, S. (2000). Race and ethnicity and the controversy over the US Census. *Current Sociology, 48*(3), 87–110.

Aronson, E., Wilson, T. D., & Akert, R. M. (2013). *Social psychology* (8th ed.). Upper Saddle River, NJ: Pearson/Prentice Hall.

Association of American Colleges & Universities (AAC&U). (2002). *Greater expectations: A new vision for learning as a nation goes to college.* Washington, DC: Author.

Association of American Colleges & Universities (AAC&U). (2004). *Our students' best work.* Washington, DC: Author.

Baron, et. al. (2008). *Social psychology* (12th ed). Boston, MA: Allyn & Bacon.

Belenky, M. F., Clinchy, B., Goldberger, N. R., & Tarule, J. M. (1986). *Women's ways of knowing: The development of self, voice, and mind.* New York: Basic Books.

Blair, I. V. (2002). The malleability of automatic stereotypes and prejudice. *Personality and Social Psychology Review, 6*(3), 242–261.

Bligh, D. A. (2000). *What's the use of lectures?* San Francisco: Jossey Bass.

Bok, D. (2006). *Our underachieving colleges: A candid look at how much students learn and why they should be learning more.* Princeton, NJ: Princeton University Press.

Bridgeman, B. (2003). *Psychology and evolution: The origins of mind.* Thousand Oaks, CA: Sage Publications.

Bronfenbrenner, U. (Ed.). (2005). *Making human beings human: Bioecological perspectives on human development.* Thousand Oaks, CA: Sage.

Brookfield, S. D. (1987). *Developing critical thinkers.* San Francisco, CA: Jossey-Bass.

Brooks, I. (2009). *Organisational behaviour* (4th ed.). Englewood Cliffs, NJ: Prentice Hall.

Brown, T. D., Dane, F. C., & Durham, M. D. (1998). Perception of race and ethnicity. *Journal of Social Behavior and Personality, 13*(2), 295–306.

Brown, K. T., Brown, T. N., Jackson, J. S., Sellers, R. M., & Manuel, W. J. (2003). Teammates on and off the field? Contact with Black teammates and the racial attitudes of White student athletes. *Journal of Applied Social Psychology, 33*, 1379–1403.

Cabrera, A., Nora, A., Terenzini, P., Pascarella, E., & Hagedorn, L. S. (1999). Campus racial climate and the adjustment of students to college: A comparison between White students and African American students. *The Journal of Higher Education, 70*(2), 134–160.

Caplan, P. J., & Caplan, J. B. (2008). *Thinking critically about research on sex and gender* (3rd ed.). New York: HarperCollins College Publishers.

Carlson, et al. (1990). Individual differences in the behavioral effects of stressors attributable to lateralized differences in mesocortical dopamine systems. *Society for Neuroscience Abstracts, 16*, 233.

Ciancotto, J. (2005). *Hispanic and Latino same-sex couple households in the United States: A report from the 2000 Census.* New York: The National Gay and Lesbian Task Force Policy Institute and the National Latino/a Coalition for Justice.

Colombo, G., Cullen, R., & Lisle, B. (2013). *Rereading America: Cultural contexts for critical thinking and writing* (9th ed.). Boston, MA: Bedford Books of St. Martin's Press.

Cook, S. W. (1984). Cooperative interaction in multiethnic contexts. In N. Miller & M. B. Brewer (Eds.), *Groups in contact: The psychology of desegregation* (pp. 291–302). New York: Academic Press.

Cuseo, J. B. (1996). *Cooperative learning: A pedagogy for addressing contemporary challenges and critical issues in higher education.* Stillwater, OK: New Forums Press.

Cuseo, J. B., et al. (2013). *Thriving in community college & beyond: Strategies for academic success and personal development.* Dubuque, IA: Kendall Hunt Publishing Company.

DeNavas-Walt, C., Proctor, B. D., & Smith, J. C. (2013). *Income, poverty, and health insurance coverage in the United States, 2012.* U.S. Census Bureau, Current Population Reports, P60-245, Washington, DC: U.S. Government Printing Office.

Dessel, A. (2012). Effects of intergroup dialogue: Public school teachers and sexual orientation prejudice. *Small Group Research, 41*(5), 556–592.

Dolan, M., & Romney, L. (2015, June 27). "Law in California is now a right for all." *Los Angeles Times,* pp. A1, A8.

Donald, J. G. (2002). *Learning to think: Disciplinary perspectives.* San Francisco: Jossey-Bass.

Dovidio, J. F., Eller, A., & Hewstone, M. (2011). Improving intergroup relations through direct, extended and other forms of indirect contact. *Group Processes & Intergroup Relations, 14*, 147–160.

Dryden, G., & Vos, J. (1999). *The learning revolution: To change the way the world learns.* Torrance, CA and Auckland, New Zealand: The Learning Web.

Education Commission of the States. (1995). *Making quality count in undergraduate education.* Denver, CO: ECS Distribution Center.

Education Commission of the States. (1996). *Bridging the gap between neuroscience and education.* Denver, CO: Author.

Eimers, M. T., & Pike, G. R. (1997). Minority and nonminority adjustment to college: Differences or similarities. *Research in Higher Education, 38*(1), 77–97.

Erickson, B. L., Peters, C. B., & Strommer, D. W. (2006). *Teaching first-year college students.* San Francisco: Jossey-Bass.

Family Care Foundation. (2015). *If the world were a village of 100 people.* Retrieved from http://www.familycare.org/special-interest/if-the-world-were-a-village-of-100-people/.

Feagin, J. R., & Feagin, C. B. (2007). *Racial and ethnic relations* (8th ed.). Englewood Cliffs, NJ: Prentice Hall.

Fixman, C. S. (1990). The foreign language needs of U.S. based corporations. *Annals of the American Academy of Political and Social Science, 511*, 25–46.

Friedman, T. L. (2005). *The world is flat: A brief history of the twenty-first century: Revitalizing the civic mission of schools.* Alexandria, VA: Farrar, Strauss & Giroux.

Gorski, P. C. (1995–2009). *Key characteristics of a multicultural curriculum.* Critical Multicultural Pavilion: Multicultural Curriculum Reform (An EdChange Project). Retrieved from www.edchange.org/multicultural/curriculum/characteristics.html.

Gould, E. & Wething, H. (2013). Health care, the market and consumer choice. *Inquiry, 50*(1), 85–86.

Gurin, P. (1999). New research on the benefits of diversity in college and beyond: An empirical analysis. *Diversity Digest* (spring). Retrieved from http://www.diversityweb.org/Digest/Sp99/benefits.html.

Harris, A. (2010). Leading system transformation. *School Leadership and Management, 30* (July).

Hart Research Associates. (2013). *It takes more than a major: Employer priorities for college learning and student success.* Washington, DC: Author.

HERI (Higher Education Research Institute). (2013). *Your first college year survey 2012.* Los Angeles, CA: Cooperative Institutional Research Program, University of California-Los Angeles.

HERI (Higher Education Research Institute). (2014). *Your first college year survey 2014.* Los Angeles, CA: Cooperative Institutional Research Program, University of California-Los Angeles.

Hugenberg, K., & Bodenhausen, G. V. (2003). Facing prejudice: Implicit prejudice and the perception of facial threat. *Psychological Science, 14,* 640–643.

IES Abroad News. (2002). *Study abroad: A lifetime of benefits.* Retrieved from www.iesabroad.org/study-abroad/news/study-abroad-lifetime-benefits.

Jablonski, N. G., & Chaplin, G. (2002). Skin deep. *Scientific American, (October),* 75–81.

Johnson, D., Johnson, R., & Smith, K. (1998). Cooperative learning returns to college: What evidence is there that it works? *Change, 30,* 26–35.

Judd, C. M., Ryan, C. S., & Parke, B. (1991). Accuracy in the judgment of in-group and out-group variability. *Journal of Personality and Social Psychology, 61,* 366–379.

Kaufmann, N. L., Martin, J. M., & Weaver, H. D. (1992). *Students abroad: Strangers at home: Education for a global society.* Yarmouth, ME: Intercultural Press.

Kelly, K. (1994). *Out of control: The new biology of machines, social systems, and the economic world.* Reading, MA: Addison-Wesley.

Kitchener, K., Wood, P., & Jensen, L. (2000, August). *Curricular, co-curricular, and institutional influence on real-world problem-solving.* Paper presented at the annual meeting of the American Psychological Association, Boston.

Kochlar, R., Fry, R., & Taylor, P. (2011). Wealth gaps rise to record highs between Whites, Blacks, Hispanics, twenty-to-one. *Pew Research Social and Demographics Trends* (July). Retrieved from http://www.pewsocialtrends.org/2011/07/26/wealth-gaps-rise-to-record-highs-between-whites-blacks-hispanics/

Lancaster, L., et al. (2002). *When generations collide: Who they are. Why they clash.* New York: HarperCollins.

Latané, B., Liu, J. H., Nowak, A., Bonevento, N., & Zheng, L. (1995). Distance matters: Physical space and social impact. *Personality and Social Psychology Bulletin, 21,* 795–805.

Leung, A. K., Maddux, W. W., Galinsky, A. D., & Chie-yue, C. (2008). Multicultural experience enhances creativity: The when and how. *American Psychologist, 63*(3), 169–181.

Lewis, M., Paul, G. W., & Fennig, C. D. (Eds). (2014). *Ethnologue: Languages of the world* (17th ed.). Dallas, TX: SIL International. Online version: http://www.ethnologue.com.

Luhman, R. (2007). *The sociological outlook.* Lanham, MD: Rowman & Littlefield.

Maddux, W. W. & Galinsky, A. D. (2009). Cultural borders and mental barriers: the relationship between living abroad and creativity. *Journal of Personality and Social Psychology, 96*(5), 1047–1061.

Magolda, M. B. B. (1992). *Knowing and reasoning in college.* San Francisco, CA: Jossey-Bass.

Mendez, F., Krahn, T., Schrack, B., Krahn, A. M., Veeramah, K., Woerner, A., Fomine, F. L. M., Bradman, N., Thomas, M., Karafet, T., & Hammer, M. (2013). An African American paternal lineage adds an extremely ancient root to the human Y chromosome phylogenetic tree. *The American Journal of Human Genetics, 92,* 454–459.

Meredith, M. (2011). *Born in Africa: The quest for the origins of human life.* New York: Public Affairs.

Nagda, B. R., Gurin, P., & Johnson, S. M. (2005). Living, doing and thinking diversity: How does pre-college diversity experience affect first-year students' engagement with college diversity? In R. S. Feldman (Ed.), *Improving the first year of college: Research and practice* (pp. 73–110). Mahwah, NJ: Lawrence Erlbaum.

Nathan, R. (2005). *My freshman year: What a professor learned by becoming a student.* London: Penguin.

National Association of Colleges and Employers (NACE). (2003). *Job outlook 2003 survey.* Bethlehem, PA: Author.

National Association of Colleges & Employers. (2014). *Job Outlook 2014 survey.* Bethlehem, PA: Author.

National Center for Education Statistics. (2011). *Digest of education statistics, table 237. Total fall enrollment in degree-granting institutions, by level of student, sex, attendance status, and race/ethnicity: Selected years, 1976 through 2010.* Alexandria, VA: U.S. Department of Education. Retrieved from http://neces.ed/gov/programs/digest/d11/tables/dt11_237.asp.

National Survey of Women Voters. (1998). *Autumn overview report conducted by DYG Inc.* Retrieved from http:www.diversityweb.org/research_and_trends/research_evaluation_impact_/campus_community_connections/national_poll.cfm.

Nhan, D. (2012). "Census: Minorities constitute 37 percent of U.S. population." *National Journal: The Next America—Demographics 2012.* Retrieved from http:www.nationaljournal.com/thenextamerica/demographics/census-minorities-constitute-37-percent-of-u-s-population-20120517.

Nora, A., & Cabrera, A. (1996). The role of perceptions of prejudice and discrimination on the adjustment of minority college students. *The Journal of Higher Education, 67*(2), 119–148.

Office of Research. (1994). *What employers expect of college graduates: International knowledge and second language skills.* Washington, DC: Office of Educational Research and Improvement, U.S. Department of Education.

Olson, L. (2007). What does "ready" mean? *Education Week, 40,* 7–12.

Pascarella, E. T. (2001, November/December). Cognitive growth in college: Surprising and reassuring findings from the National Study of Student Learning. *Change,* 21–27.

Pascarella, E. T., & Terenzini, P. T. (2005). *How college affects students: A third decade of research* (Vol. 2). San Francisco, CA: Jossey-Bass.

Pascarella, E., Palmer, B., Moye, M., & Pierson, C. (2001). Do diversity experiences influence the development of critical thinking? *Journal of College Student Development, 42*(3), 257–291.

Peoples, J., & Bailey, G. (2011). *Humanity: An introduction to cultural anthropology.* Belmont, CA: Wadsworth, Cengage Learning. Retrieved from http://www.aacu.org/leap/documents/2009-employersurvey.pdf.

Pettigrew, T. F. (1997). Generalized intergroup contact effects on prejudice. *Personality and Social Psychology Bulletin, 23,* 173–185.

Pettigrew, T. F. (1998). Intergroup contact theory. *Annual Review of Psychology, 49,* 65–85.

Pettigrew, T. F., & Tropp, L. R. (2000). Does intergroup contact reduce prejudice? Recent meta-analytic findings. In S. Oskamp (Ed.), *Reducing prejudice and discrimination* (pp. 93–114). Mahwah, NJ: Lawrence Erlbaum Associates.

Pinker, S. (2000). *The language instinct: The new science of language and mind.* New York: Perennial.

Pratto, F., Liu, J. H., Levin, S., Sidanius, J., Shih, M., Bachrach, H., & Hegarty, P. (2000). Social dominance orientation and the legitimization of inequality across cultures. *Journal of Cross-Cultural Psychology, 31,* 369–409.

Reid, G. B. R., & Hetherington, R. (2010). *The climate connection: Climate change and modern evolution.* Cambridge, UK: Cambridge University Press.

Roediger, H. L., Dudai, Y., & Fitzpatrick, S. M. (2007). *Science of memory: concepts.* New York, NY: Oxford University Press.

Shah, A. (2009). *Global issues: Poverty facts and stats.* Retrieved from http://www.globalissues.org/artoc;e/26/poverty-facts-and-stats.

Sherif, M., Harvey, D. J., White, B. J., Hood, W. R., & Sherif, C. W. (1961). *The Robbers' cave experiment.* Norman, OK: Institute of Group Relations.

Shiraev, E. D., & Levy, D. (2013). *Cross-cultural psychology: Critical thinking and contemporary applications* (5th ed.).Upper Saddle River, NJ: Pearson Education.

Sidanius, J., Levin, S., Liu, H., & Pratto, F. (2000). Social dominance orientation, anti-egalitarianism, and the political psychology of gender: An extension and cross-cultural replication. *European Journal of Social Psychology, 30,* 41–67.

Slavin, R. E. (1995). *Cooperative learning* (2nd ed.). Boston: Allyn & Bacon.

Smith, D. (1997). How diversity influences learning. *Liberal Education, 83*(2), 42–48.

Smith, D. G., Guy, L., Gerbrick, G. L., Figueroa, M. A., Watkins, G. H., Levitan, T., Moore, L. C., Merchant, P. A., Beliak, H. D., & Figueroa, B. (1997). *Diversity works: The emerging picture of how students benefit.* Washington, DC: Association of American Colleges and Universities.

Stangor, C., Sechrist, G. B., & Jost, J. T. (2001). Changing racial beliefs by providing consensus information. *Personality and Social Psychology Bulletin, 27,* 484–494.

Stoltz, P. G. (2014). *Grit: The new science of what it takes to persevere, flourish, succeed.* San Luis Obispo: Climb Strong Press.

Taylor, S. E., Peplau, L. A., & Sears, D. O. (2006). *Social psychology* (12th ed.). Upper Saddle River, NJ: Pearson/Prentice-Hall.

Thompson, A., & Cuseo, J. (2014). *Diversity and the college experience.* Dubuque, IA: Kendall Hunt.

U.S. Census Bureau. (2008). *Bureau of Labor Statistics.* Washington, DC: Author.

United States Census Bureau. (2013a, July 8). *About race.* Retrieved from http://www.census.gov/topics/population/race/about.html.

U.S. Census Bureau. (2013b). *Poverty.* Retrieved from https://www.census.gov/hhes/www/poverty/data/threshld/.

United States Census Bureau. (2015, March). *Projections of the size and composition of the U.S. population: 2014 to 2060.* Retrieved from http://www.census.gov/content/dam/Census/library/publications/2015/demo/p25-1143.pdf.

Wabash National Study of Liberal Arts Education. (2007). *Liberal arts outcomes.* Retrieved from http:www.liberalarts.wabash.edu/ study-overview/.

Wheelright, J. (2005, March). Human, study thyself. *Discover,* 39–45.

Willis, J. (2006). *Research-based strategies to ignite student learning: Insights from a neurologist and classroom teacher.* Alexandria, VA: ASCD.

Zajonc, R. B. (1968). Attitudinal effects of mere exposure. *Journal of Personality and Social Psychology, 9,* Monograph Supplement, No. 2, Part 2.

Zajonc, R. B. (1970). Brainwash: Familiarity breeds comfort. *Psychology Today,* (February), 32–35, 60–62.

Zajonc, R. B. (2001). Mere exposure: A gateway to the subliminal. *Current Directions in Psychological Science, 10,* 224–228.

Chapter 10 Exercises

10.1 Quote Reflections

Review the sidebar quotes contained in this chapter and select two that were especially meaningful or inspirational to you.

For each quote, provide a three- to five-sentence explanation why you chose it.

10.2 Reality Bite

Hate Crime: A Racially Motivated Murder

Jasper County, Texas, has a population of approximately 31,000 people. In this county, 80% of the people are White, 18% are Black, and 2% are of other races. The county's poverty rate is considerably higher than the national average, and its average household income is significantly lower. In 1998, the mayor, the president of the Chamber of Commerce, and two councilmen were Black. From the outside, Jasper appeared to be a town with racial harmony, and its Black and White leaders were quick to state that there was no racial tension in Jasper.

However, one day, James Byrd Jr.—a 49-year-old African American man—was walking home along a road one evening and was offered a ride by three White males. Rather than taking Byrd home, Lawrence Brewer (age 31), John King (age 23), and Shawn Berry (age 23), three men linked to White-supremacist groups, took Byrd to an isolated area and began beating him. They then dropped his pants to his ankles, painted his face black, chained Byrd to their truck, and dragged him for approximately three miles. The truck was driven in a zigzag fashion to inflict maximum pain on the victim. Byrd was decapitated after his body collided with a culvert in a ditch alongside the road. His skin, arms, genitalia, and other body parts were strewn along the road, while his torso was found dumped in front of a Black cemetery. Medical examiners testified that Byrd was alive for much of the dragging incident.

When they were brought to trial, the bodies of Brewer and King were covered with racist tattoos; they were eventually sentenced to death. As a result of the murder, Byrd's family created the James Byrd Foundation for Racial Healing. A wrought iron fence that separated Black and White graves for more than 150 years in Jasper Cemetery was removed in a special unity service. Members of the racist Ku Klux Klan have since visited the gravesite of Byrd several times, leaving racist stickers and other marks that angered the Jasper community and Byrd's family.

Source: *Louisiana Weekly* (February 3, 2003).

Reflection Questions

1. What factors do you think were responsible for this incident?

2. Could this incident have been prevented? If yes, how? If no, why not?

3. How likely do you think an incident like this could take place in your hometown or near your college campus?

4. If this event happened to take place in your hometown, how do you think members of your community would react?

10.3 Gaining Awareness of Your Group Identities

We are members of multiple groups at the same time and our membership in these overlapping groups can influence our personal development and identity. In the following figure, consider the shaded center circle to be yourself and the six unshaded circles to be six different groups you belong to and have influenced your development.

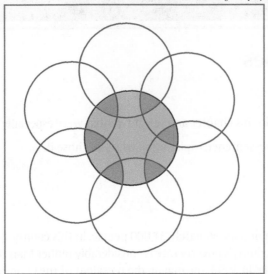

Fill in the unshaded circles with the names of groups to which you think you belong that have had the most influence on your personal development and identity. You can use the diversity spectrum (p. 234) to help you identify different groups to which you may be a member. Don't feel you have to fill in all six circles. What's more important is to identify those groups that you think have had a significant influence on your personal development or identity.

Reflection Questions

1. Which one of your groups has had the greatest influence on your personal development or identity? Why?

2. Have you ever felt limited or disadvantaged by being a member of any group(s) to which you belong? Why?

3. Have you ever felt advantaged or privileged by your membership in any group(s)? Why?

10.4 Intercultural Interview

1. Identify a person on your campus who is a member of an ethnic or racial group that you've had little previous contact. Ask that person for an interview, and during the interview, include the following questions:

    - What does "diversity" mean to you?

    - What prior experiences have affected your current viewpoints or attitudes about diversity?

    - What would you say have been the major influences and turning points in your life?

    - Who would you cite as your positive role models, heroes, or sources of inspiration?

    - What societal contributions made by your ethnic or racial group would you like others to be aware of and acknowledge?

    - What do you hope will never again be said about your ethnic or racial group?

2. If you were the interviewee instead of the interviewer, how would you have answered the above questions?

3. What do you think accounts for the differences (and similarities) between your answers to the above questions and those provided by the person you interviewed?

10.5 Hidden Bias Test

Go to www.tolerance.org/activity/test-yourself-hidden-bias and take one or more of the hidden bias tests on this website. These tests assess subtle bias with respect to gender, age, ethnic minority groups, religious denominations, sexual orientations, disabilities, and body weight.

After completing the test, answer the following questions:

1. Did the results reveal any bias(es) you weren't unaware of?

2. Did you think the assessment results were accurate or valid?

3. What do you think best accounts for or explains your results?

4. If your closest family member and best friend took the test, how do you think their results would compare with yours?

Educational Planning and Academic Decision-Making

MAKING WISE CHOICES ABOUT COLLEGE COURSES AND A COLLEGE MAJOR

Making strategic choices about your courses and your major is essential to reaching your educational goals. You want to be sure your choice of major is compatible with your personal interests, talents, and values. You should also have a strategic plan in mind (and in hand) that enables you to strike a healthy balance between exploring your major options and making a final commitment. This chapter will help you strike this balance and make educational decisions that put you in the best position to reach your long-term goals.

Equip you with effective strategies for choosing courses wisely and pursuing an educational path that's compatible with your personal interests, talents, and goals.

 Reflection 11.1

At this point in your college experience, are you decided or undecided about a major?

1. If you're undecided, what subjects are you considering as possible majors?

2. If you're decided:

   a) What's your choice?

   b) What led you to this choice?

   c) How sure are you about this choice? (Circle one.)

   absolutely sure   fairly sure   not too sure   likely to change

To Be or Not to Be Decided: What Research Shows about Students' Choice of a College Major

"What's your major?" is a question that students are asked over and over again—even before they've stepped foot on a college campus. You probably also saw this question on every one of your college applications and you're likely to hear it again during your very first term in college. Family members are also likely to ask you the same question, particularly if they're paying or helping to pay the high cost of a college education. They want to be sure that their investment will pay off and they're more likely to feel assured if they know you're committed to a major and are on your way to a self-supporting career.

Studies of student decisions about a college major show that:

- Fewer than 10% of new college students feel they know a great deal about the field they intend to major in;
- As students proceed through the first year of college, they grow more uncertain about the major they chose when they entered college;
- More than one-third of new students change their mind about their major during their first year of college; and
- Only one in three college seniors eventually major in the same field they had in mind when they began college (Cuseo, 2005; HERI, 2014).

These findings demonstrate that the vast majority of first-year students are uncertain about their academic specialization. Typically, they don't make a final decision about their major *before* starting college; instead, they reach that decision *during* their college experience.

Thus, being initially undecided about a major isn't something you should be worried or embarrassed about; it doesn't mean you're clueless. It may just mean you're open-minded. In fact, studies show that new students are often undecided for very good reasons. Some are undecided because they have multiple interests; this is a healthy form of indecision indicating they have a wide range of interests and a high level of intellectual curiosity. Students may also be undecided because they are reflective and deliberate decision-makers who prefer to explore their options carefully before making a firm and final commitment. In a national study of students who were undecided about a major at the start of college, 43% of them had some majors in mind but weren't quite ready to make a final commitment to one of them (Gordon & Steele, 2003).

For new students to be at least somewhat uncertain about their educational goals at the start of their college experience is only natural because they haven't yet experienced the variety of subjects included in the college curriculum. One goal of general education courses is to help new students develop the critical thinking skills needed to make wise choices and well-informed decisions, including their decision about a college major.

The college curriculum will introduce you to new fields of study, some of which you never experienced before and all of which represent possible choices for a college major. A key benefit of experiencing the variety of courses in the general education curriculum is that they help you become more aware of the range of academic disciplines and subject areas available to you as potential majors, while at the same time, helping you become more aware of yourself. As you gain experience with the college curriculum, you will gain greater self-insight into your academic interests, strengths, and weaknesses. Take this self-knowledge into consideration when choosing a major because you want to pursue a field that capitalizes on your intellectual curiosity, abilities, and talents.

It's true that some students can take too long to choose a major or procrastinate about making important decisions. However, it's also true that some students make decisions too quickly, resulting in premature choices made without sufficient reflection and careful consideration of their options. Judging from the large number of students who end up changing their major, it's probably safe to say that more students make the mistake of reaching a decision about a major too quickly rather than waiting too long.

If you're currently feeling pressure to make an early decision, we encourage you to respectfully resist it until you've gained more self-knowledge and more experi-

> "All who wander are not lost."
> —*J. R. R. Tolkien, author of* Lord of the Rings

> You have brains in your head. You have feet in your shoes. You can steer yourself any direction you choose.
> —*Theodore Seuss Giesel (a.k.a. Dr. Seuss),* Oh the Places You'll Go

ence with the college curriculum and co-curriculum. As a first-year student, you can still make steady progress toward your destination (a college degree) by taking general education courses that will count toward a college degree in any major you eventually declare.

If you think you're certain about a major right now, be sure to take a course or two in the major to test it out and confirm whether it's a "good fit" for your personal interests, talents, and values. If you discover that your first choice wasn't a good choice, don't think you're "locked" into that major and your only option is to stick with it or drop out of college. You still have time to change your mind without falling far behind. Changing your original educational plans is not necessarily a bad thing. It may mean that your first choice wasn't the best choice for you and that you've discovered another field that's more compatible with your personal interests and talents.

The only drawback to delaying your choice of a major, or changing your original major, is *waiting too long* to make your first choice or to change your mind about your first choice. Prolonged delay in initially choosing a major or late changing of a major can lengthen your time to college graduation. It can also increase the cost of your college education because you may need to complete additional courses for your newly chosen major—particularly if it's in a very different field than your original choice. The key to preventing this late-change scenario from happening to you is by engaging in long-range educational planning *early* in your college experience—beginning now.

> "I see so many people switch [their] major like 4 or 5 times; they end up having to take loads of summer school just to catch up because they invest time and money in classes for a major that they end up not majoring in anyway."
>
> —*College sophomore*

Changing your major this close to graduation will add to the time it takes for you to earn your college degree; it will also add to the cost of your college education.

Note

When students are required to declare a major varies across different campuses and different fields of study. As a general rule, you should reach a firm and final decision about your major during your second (sophomore) year in college. However, no matter how much time you're allowed to make this decision, the process of planning for your major should start now—during your first term in college.

Reflection 11.2

Have you decided on a major?

If yes, how sure are you about your decision? What led you to this decision?

If no, what major(s) are you considering? Why?

The Importance of Long-Range Educational Planning

If you haven't declared a major, it doesn't mean you're indecisive or a hopeless procrastinator. However, it also doesn't mean you can put all thoughts about your major on the back burner and simply drift along until you're forced to make a choice. Being undecided doesn't mean you have no plan; your plan is to find out what your major will be. Now is the time to start the major selection process by testing your interests and narrowing down your choices.

Similarly, if you've already chosen a major, this doesn't mean you'll never have to give any more thought to that decision. Instead, you should continue the exploration process by carefully testing your first choice, making sure it's a choice that is compatible with your abilities and interests. Take the approach that this is your *current* choice; whether it becomes your firm and *final* choice will depend on how well you perform (and how interested you are) in the first courses you take in the field.

Developing a long-range educational plan enables you to take a *proactive* approach to your education—you take charge of it by taking early and preemptive action that anticipates your future. Rather than waiting and passively letting your educational future happen *to* you, advanced planning makes it happen *for* you.

> "Some people make things happen, while others watch things happen or wonder what has happened."
>
> —*Author unknown*

©Kendall Hunt Publishing Company

Don't take the avoidance and denial approach to planning your educational future.

By looking beyond your first year of college and engaging in long-range educational planning, you're able to get a sneak preview and "big picture" overview of your entire college experience. In contrast, looking at and scheduling your classes one term at a time—just before each registration period—carves up your college experience into a choppy series of small, separate snapshots that leaves you with little sense of continuity, connection, and direction. On pp. 293–299, you will find directions and guidelines on how to develop a long-range educational plan. We strongly encourage you to complete this exercise. It's an opportunity for you to begin steering your educational future in a direction that has meaning and purpose for you.

Note

Keep in mind that a long-range educational plan isn't something set in stone. As you gain more educational experience, your specific academic and career interests may change and so may the specifics of your long-range plan. The purpose of a plan is not to tie you up or pin you down, but provide you with a roadmap that keeps you on course and moving in the right direction.

Factors to Consider When Choosing a Major

Self-awareness is the critical first step in the process of making any effective personal decision or choice. You need to know yourself well before knowing what major is best for you. When choosing a major, self-awareness should include awareness of your:

- Mental abilities and talents
- Learning styles and tendencies
- Personal interests and curiosities

As illustrated in **Figure 11.1**, these three pillars provide a solid foundation on which to base your decision about a college major.

FIGURE 11.1: **Three Key Personal Characteristics to Consider when Choosing a College Major**

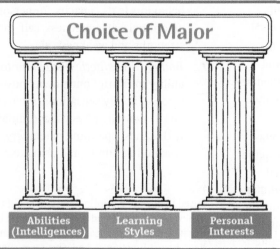

©Kendall Hunt Publishing Company

Research indicates that students who choose majors that are compatible with their personal characteristics are more likely to be academically successful in college and complete their degree (Leuwerke, et al., 2004; Pascarella & Terenzini, 2005).

Multiple Intelligences: Becoming Aware of Your Mental Abilities and Talents

One personal characteristic you should be aware of when choosing a major is your mental strengths, abilities, and talents. Intelligence was once considered to be a single, general trait that could be identified by one intelligence test score. Scholars have since discovered that intelligence doesn't come conveniently wrapped in a one-size-fits-all package. The singular word "intelligence" has been replaced by the plural word "intelligences" to reflect the fact that humans display intelligence (mental ability) in a variety of forms other than that measured by their score on an IQ or SAT test.

Based on studies of gifted and talented individuals, experts in different lines of work, and research on the human brain, psychologist Howard Gardner (1993, 1999, 2006) has identified the multiple forms of intelligence listed in **Box 11.1**. Keep these forms of intelligence in mind when you're choosing a college major because different majors emphasize different intellectual skills (Brooks, 2009). Ideally, you want to pursue an academic field that allows you to utilize your strongest mental attributes and talents. If you do, you're likely to master the concepts and skills required by your major more efficiently and more deeply, excel in courses required by your major, and experience a higher level of academic self-confidence and motivation to continue your education.

> "Exceptional individuals have a special talent for identifying their own strengths and weaknesses."
>
> —*Howard Gardner*, Extraordinary Minds

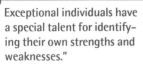

Box 11.1

Multiple Forms of Intelligence

As you read through the following forms of intelligence, place a checkmark next to the type that you think represents your strongest ability or talent. (You can possess more than one type.)

1. *Linguistic* Intelligence: ability to comprehend the meaning of words and communicate through language (e.g., verbal skills relating to speaking, writing, listening, and learning foreign languages).

2. *Logical–Mathematical* Intelligence: aptitude for understanding logical patterns (e.g., making and following logical arguments) and solving mathematical problems (e.g., working well with numbers and quantitative calculations).

3. *Spatial* Intelligence: aptitude for visualizing relationships among objects arranged in different spatial positions and ability to perceive or create visual images (e.g., forming mental images of three-dimensional objects; detecting detail in objects or drawings; drawing, painting, sculpting, and graphic design; strong sense of direction and capacity to navigate unfamiliar places).

4. *Musical* Intelligence: ability to appreciate or create rhythmical and melodic sounds (e.g., playing, writing, or arranging music).

5. *Interpersonal (Social)* Intelligence: ability to relate to others and accurately identify their needs, motivations, or emotional states; effective at expressing emotions and feelings to others (e.g., interpersonal communication skills, ability to accurately "read" the feelings of others and meet their emotional needs).

6. *Intrapersonal (Self)* Intelligence: ability to introspect and understand your own thoughts, feelings, and behaviors (e.g., capacity for personal reflection; emotional self-awareness; self-insight into personal strengths and weaknesses).

7. *Bodily–Kinesthetic (Psychomotor)* Intelligence: ability to control one's own body skillfully and learn through bodily sensations or movements; skilled at tasks involving physical coordination, working well with hands, operating machinery, building models, assembling things, and using technology.

> "I used to operate a printing press. In about two weeks I knew how to run it and soon after I could take the machine apart in my head and analyze what each part does, how it functioned, and why it was shaped that way."
>
> —*Response of college sophomore to the questions: "What are you really good at? What comes easily or naturally to you?"*

Box 11.1 *(continued)*

8. *Naturalist* Intelligence: ability to carefully observe and appreciate features of the natural environment; keen awareness of nature or natural surroundings; ability to understand causes and consequences of events occurring in the natural world.

9. *Existential* Intelligence: ability to conceptualize phenomena and ponder experiences that go beyond sensory or physical evidence, such as questions involving the origin of human life and the meaning of human existence.

Source: Gardner (1993, 1999, 2006).

 Reflection 11.3

Look back at the nine forms of intelligence listed in **Box 11.1**.

Which of these types of intelligence do you think represents your strongest talent(s)?

Which college major(s) do you think may best match your natural talents?

Learning Styles: Becoming Aware of Your Learning Preferences and Tendencies

Another personal characteristic you should be aware of when choosing a major is your learning style. It refers to the way in which you prefer to *perceive* information (receive or take it in) and *process* information (deal with it after taking it in). For instance, students may differ in terms of whether they prefer to take in information by reading about it, listening to it, seeing an image or diagram of it, or physically touching and manipulating it. Individuals may also vary in terms of whether they like to receive information in a structured, orderly format or in an unstructured formats that allows them the freedom to explore, play with, and restructure it in their own way. Individuals may also differ in terms of how they prefer to process (deal with) information after it's been received. Some may like to think about it on their own, while others prefer to discuss it with someone else; some may like to outline it, while others prefer to map it out or draw it.

AUTHOR'S EXPERIENCE

In my family, whenever something needed to be assembled or set up (e.g., a ping-pong table or new electronic equipment), I noticed that my wife, my son, and myself had very different learning styles. I like to read the manual's instructions carefully and completely before I even attempt to touch anything. My son prefers to look at the pictures or diagrams in the manual and use them as models to find parts; then he begins to assemble those parts. My wife seems to prefer not to look at the manual at all. Instead, she likes to figure things out as she goes along, grabbing different parts from the box, assembling those parts that look like they should fit into each other, and piecing them together as if she were completing a jigsaw puzzle.

—*Joe Cuseo*

> Minds differ still more than faces."
>
> *—Voltaire, 18th-century French author and philosopher*

There are tests specially designed to assess your learning style. (If you're interested in taking one, the Learning Center and Career Center are two places on campus where you may be able to do so.) Probably the most frequently used learning styles test is the *Myers-Briggs Type Indicator (MBTI)*—a test based on the personality theory of psychologist Carl Jung. It assesses how people vary along a scale (low to high) on each of four sets of opposing traits, which are illustrated in **Figure 11.2**.

As you read through these pairs of opposite traits, place a mark along the line where you think you fall with respect to each set. Place a mark toward the far left or far right if you think you lean strongly toward that end of the scale; place a mark in the middle of the line if you think you don't lean strongly toward either end of the scale.

FIGURE 11.2: **Traits and Learning Styles Measured by the Myers-Briggs Type Indicator (MBTI)**

Extraversion	*Introversion*
Prefer to focus on the "outer" world of persons, actions, or objects	Prefer to focus on the "inner" world of thoughts and ideas

Sensing	*Intuition*
Prefer interacting with the world directly through concrete, sensory experiences	Prefer dealing with symbolic meanings and imagining possibilities

Thinking	*Feeling*
Prefer to rely on logic and rational thinking when making decisions	Prefer to rely on human needs and feelings when making decisions

Judging	*Perceiving*
Prefer to plan for and control events	Prefer flexibility and spontaneity

Reflection 11.4

For each of the following four sets of opposing traits, make a note about where you fall—low, middle, or high.

MBTI Personality Traits	*Low*	*Middle*	*High*
Extraversion–Introversion			
Sensing–Intuition			
Thinking–Feeling			
Judging–Perceiving			

What majors or fields of study do you think are most compatible with your personality traits?

Research indicates that college students who score high on the introversion scale of the MBTI are more likely to stay engaged and attentive when performing mental tasks that require repetition and involve little external stimulation (Bodanovich, Wallace, & Kass, 2005). This suggests that students may differ in terms of the academic tasks they prefer to perform. For instance, it's been found that students who score differently on the MBTI prefer different writing styles and writing assignments (Jensen & Tiberio, cited in Bean, 2001). These differences are summarized below.

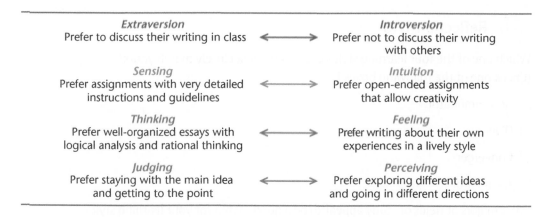

Extraversion
Prefer to discuss their writing in class ⟷ *Introversion*
Prefer not to discuss their writing with others

Sensing
Prefer assignments with very detailed instructions and guidelines ⟷ *Intuition*
Prefer open-ended assignments that allow creativity

Thinking
Prefer well-organized essays with logical analysis and rational thinking ⟷ *Feeling*
Prefer writing about their own experiences in a lively style

Judging
Prefer staying with the main idea and getting to the point ⟷ *Perceiving*
Prefer exploring different ideas and going in different directions

Keep your learning style in mind when choosing your major because different academic fields emphasize different styles of learning. Some fields place heavy emphasis on structured, tightly focused writing (e.g., science and business), while other fields encourage writing with personal style, flair, and creativity (e.g., English). How your writing style meshes with the style emphasized by different academic fields is one factor to consider when choosing a college major.

Another popular learning styles test is the *Learning Styles Inventory* (Dunn, Dunn, & Price, 1990), originally developed by David Kolb, a professor of philosophy (Kolb, 1976, 1985). It's based on how individuals differ with respect to the following two dimensions of the learning process:

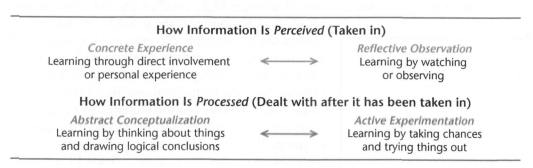

How Information Is *Perceived* (Taken in)

Concrete Experience
Learning through direct involvement or personal experience ⟷ *Reflective Observation*
Learning by watching or observing

How Information Is *Processed* (Dealt with after it has been taken in)

Abstract Conceptualization
Learning by thinking about things and drawing logical conclusions ⟷ *Active Experimentation*
Learning by taking chances and trying things out

When these two dimensions are crisscrossed, four sectors (areas) are created, each of which represents a different learning style—as illustrated in **Figure 11.3**. As you read the characteristics associated with each of the four areas (styles), circle the style that you think reflects your most preferred way of learning.

FIGURE 11.3: **Learning Styles Measured by the Learning Styles Inventory (LSI)**

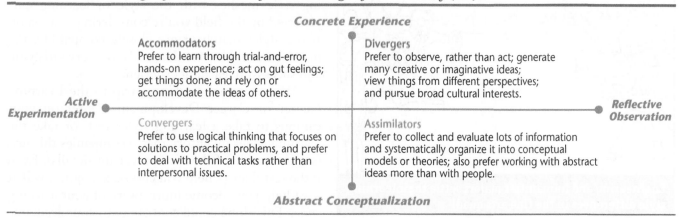

Concrete Experience

Accommodators
Prefer to learn through trial-and-error, hands-on experience; act on gut feelings; get things done; and rely on or accommodate the ideas of others.

Divergers
Prefer to observe, rather than act; generate many creative or imaginative ideas; view things from different perspectives; and pursue broad cultural interests.

Active Experimentation — *Reflective Observation*

Convergers
Prefer to use logical thinking that focuses on solutions to practical problems, and prefer to deal with technical tasks rather than interpersonal issues.

Assimilators
Prefer to collect and evaluate lots of information and systematically organize it into conceptual models or theories; also prefer working with abstract ideas more than with people.

Abstract Conceptualization

Reflection 11.5

Which one of the four learning styles appears to most closely match yours?
(Check one of the following boxes.)

☐ Accommodator

☐ Diverger

☐ Converger

☐ Assimilator

What majors or fields of study appear to be a good match for your learning style?

Research indicates that students who display differences in these four learning styles tend to major in different fields (Svinicki, 2004; Svinicki & Dixon, 1987). "Assimilators" are more often found majoring in mathematics and natural sciences (e.g., chemistry and physics), probably because these subjects emphasize reflection and abstract thinking. In contrast, "accommodators" tend to be more commonly found majoring in business, accounting and law, perhaps because these fields involve taking practical action and making concrete decisions. "Divergers" are more often attracted to majors in the fine arts (e.g., music, art, and drama), humanities (e.g., history and literature), or social sciences (e.g., psychology and political science), possibly because these fields emphasize accommodating multiple (divergent) viewpoints and perspectives. In contrast, "convergers" are more often found majoring in fields such as accounting, engineering, medicine, and nursing, probably because these subjects require students to focus in on (converge on) finding a specific answer to a specific problem (Kolb, 1976). When college instructors were asked to classify academic fields in terms of the type of learning style emphasized by the field, this same pattern of preferences was discovered (Biglan, 1973; Schommer-Aikins, Duell, & Barker, 2003).

Since students have different learning styles and academic fields emphasize different styles of learning, it's important to consider how your learning style meshes with the style of learning emphasized by the field you're considering as a major. If the styles match or are closely compatible, the marriage could be one that leads to a very satisfying and successful learning experience.

We recommend taking a trip to the Learning Center or Career Development Center on your campus to take a learning styles test, or take the learning styles inventory that accompanies this text (see the inside of the front cover for details). Even if the test doesn't help you choose a major, it will at least help you become more aware of your learning style. This alone could contribute to your academic

Engineering and humanities majors settle their learning style differences in the fine arts quad!

success because studies show that when college students gain greater self-awareness of their learning style, their academic performance tends to improve (Claxton & Murrell, 1987; Hendry, et al., 2005).

 Reflection 11.6

In addition to taking formal tests to assess your learning style, you can gain awareness of your learning styles through some simple self-reflection. Take a moment to reflect on your learning style by completing the following statements:

I learn best if...

I learn most from...

I enjoy learning when...

Do you see any pattern in your answers that may suggest that certain majors would be compatible with your learning style?

(Complete Exercise 11.3 at the end of the chapter to see if your learning style and personality traits are a good match for the major you've chosen or are considering.)

AUTHOR'S EXPERIENCE

I first noticed that students in different academic fields may have different learning styles when I was teaching a psychology course to students majoring in nursing and social work. Some students seemed to lose interest (and patience) in class whenever we got involved in extended discussions of controversial issues and theories, while others seemed to love it. On the other hand, during lectures that required students to take notes on factual and practical information, some students seemed to lose interest (and attention) while others perked up, listened attentively, and really got into the process of taking notes.

After one class session that involved quite a bit of student discussion, I reflected on the students who were most involved and those who seemed to drift off or lose interest. I discovered that the students who did most of the talking and seemed most enthused during the class discussion were students majoring in social work. Most of the students who appeared disinterested or a bit frustrated were the nursing majors. The more I thought about this, it dawned on me that nursing students were accustomed to gathering factual information and learning practical skills in their major courses; they were expecting to use that learning style in my psychology course. They felt more comfortable with structured class sessions in which they received lots of factual, practical information from the professor. On the other hand, the social work majors were more comfortable with unstructured class discussions because courses in their major often emphasized debating social issues and processing multiple viewpoints.

When I left class that day, I wondered if the differences in learning styles between the nursing and social work students resulted from their adapting to the primary teaching method used in their major, or if they chose their major because its primary teaching method was a good match for their learning style.

—Joe Cuseo

Discovering a Major that's Compatible with Your Personal Interests and Talents

In addition to knowing your intellectual strengths and learning styles, another key factor to factor into your decisions about a college major are your *interests*. Here are some specific strategies for exploring and confirming whether a major is compatible with your educational interests.

Reflect on past learning experiences you found stimulating and were productive. Think about previous classes that piqued your curiosity and in which you produced your best work. The subjects of these courses may be major fields of study that match up well with your interests, talents, and learning style.

At the website *www.mymajors.com*, you can enter information about your academic performance in high school courses. Your inputted information will be analyzed and you'll receive a report on what college majors appear to be a good match for you. You can do the same analysis for the first courses you complete in college.

Take a look at introductory textbooks in the field you're considering as a major. Review the table of contents and read a few pages of the text to get some sense of the writing style used in the field and whether the topics are compatible with your educational interests. You should be able to conveniently find introductory textbooks for different fields of study in your college bookstore.

Seek out students majoring in the subject you're considering and ask them about their experiences. Talk to several students to get a different and balanced perspective on what the field is like. You can find these students by visiting student clubs on campus related to the major (e.g., psychology club or history club). You could also check the class schedule to see when and where classes in that major are meeting. Go there and speak with students about the major, either before or after class. The following questions may be good ones to ask students in a major you're considering:

- What attracted you to this major?
- What would you say are the advantages and disadvantages of majoring in this field?
- Knowing what you know now, would you choose the same major again?

Also, ask students about the quality of teaching and advising in the department offering the major. Studies show that different departments within the same college or university can vary greatly in terms of the quality of teaching as well as their educational philosophy and attitude toward students (Pascarella & Terenzini, 1991, 2005).

Sit in on some classes in the field you're considering as a major. If the class you'd like to visit is large, you may be able to just slip into the back row and listen. If the class is small, ask the instructor for permission. When visiting a class, focus on the content or ideas being covered rather than the instructor's personality or teaching style. Remember: you're trying to decide whether to major in the subject, not the teacher.

Discuss the major you're considering with an academic advisor. To get unbiased feedback about the pros and cons of majoring in a particular field, it's probably best to speak with an academic advisor who works with students from a variety of majors. If you're still interested, you can follow up by getting more detailed information by consulting with an advisor who works primarily with students in that particular major.

Speak with faculty members in the department. Consider asking them the following questions:

- What academic skills or qualities are needed for a student to be successful in your field?
- What are the greatest challenges faced by students majoring in your field?

- What can students do with a major in your field after graduation?
- What types of graduate programs or professional schools would a student in your major be well prepared to enter?

(See faculty interview exercise on pp. 292–293.)

Surf the website of the professional organization associated with the field you're considering as a major. These websites often contain useful information for students interested in pursuing a major in the field. To locate the professional website for a field you would like to explore as a major, ask a faculty member in that field or complete a search on the web by simply entering the name of the field followed by the word "association." For example, if you're thinking about becoming an anthropology major, check out the website of the American Anthropological Association. If you're considering history as a major, take a look at the website of the American Historical Association. The website of the American Philosophical Association contains information about nonacademic careers for philosophy majors, and the American Sociological Association's website identifies various careers that sociology majors are qualified to pursue.

Visit your Career Development Center to inquire about what college graduates have gone on to do with the major you're considering. Ask if the Center has information about the type of careers the major has led to and what graduate or professional school programs students have entered after completing the major.

Be sure you're aware of all courses required for the major that you've chosen or are considering. You can find this information in your college catalog, university bulletin, or campus website. If you're in doubt, seek assistance from an academic advisor.

Sometimes college majors require courses you never expect would be required. For example, students interested in majoring in the field of forensics are often surprised by the number of science courses for this major. Keep in mind that college majors can require courses in fields outside of the major that are designed to support the major. For instance, psychology majors are often required to take at least one course in biology, and business majors are often required to take calculus.

If you're interested in majoring in a particular field, be sure you are fully aware of such outside requirements and are comfortable with them. Once you've accurately identified all courses required for the major you're considering, ask yourself the following two questions:

1. Do the course titles and descriptions appeal to my interests and values?
2. Do I have the abilities or skills needed to do well in these courses?

Be sure you know if certain academic standards must be met to be admitted to the major. Some college majors may be "impacted" or "oversubscribed," meaning that more students are interested in majoring in these fields than there are openings for students to major in them. Majors that are often most likely to be oversubscribed are pre-professional fields that lead directly to a particular career (e.g., engineering, premed, nursing, or physical therapy). On some campuses, these majors are called "restricted" majors, meaning that departments control their enrollment by restricting the number of students admitted to the major. Admission may be limited to students who earn a GPA of 3.0 or higher in certain introductory courses required by the major, or the department may rank students who apply for the major according to their overall GPA and go down the list until the maximum number of openings has been filled.

If you intend to major in a restricted field of study, be sure to keep track of whether you're meeting the acceptance standards of the major as you continue to complete courses and earn grades. If you're falling short of the academic standards of the major you hope to enter—despite working at your maximum level of effort and regularly using the learning assistance services available on campus—consult with an academic advisor about the possibility of finding an alternative field of study that may be closely related to the restricted major you were hoping to enter.

Use your elective courses to test your interest in subjects that you might major in. As its name implies, "elective" courses are those you elect or choose to take. They come in two forms: free electives and restricted electives. *Free electives* are any courses you take that count toward your college degree but aren't required for general education or a major. *Restricted electives* are courses you must take, but you get to choose them from a restricted list (menu) of possible courses that have been specified by your college to fulfill a requirement in general education or a major. For example, your campus may have a general education requirement in the social or behavioral sciences that stipulates you must take two courses in this field, but you choose what those two courses are from a list of options (e.g., anthropology, economics, political science, psychology, or sociology). If you're considering one of these fields as a possible major, you can take an introductory course in that subject to test your interest in the subject while simultaneously fulfilling a general education requirement needed for graduation. This strategy allows you to use general education as the main highway for travel toward your final destination (a college degree) while using your restricted electives to explore side roads (potential majors) along the way. You can use the same strategy with your free electives.

Naturally, you don't have to use all your electives to explore majors. Up to one-third of your courses in college may be electives. This leaves you with a significant amount of freedom to shape your college experience in a way that best meets your educational and personal goals. **Box 11.2** contains suggestions for making the best use of your free electives.

> "I took it (Biology) to satisfy the distribution requirement and I ended up majoring in it."
>
> —*Pediatrician (quoted in Brooks, 2009)*

Box 11.2

Top Ten Suggestions for Making the Most of Your College Electives

Elective courses give you the academic freedom to take personal control over your coursework. Exercise this freedom responsibly by making strategic selections of electives that allow you to make the most of your college experience and college degree.

Listed below are ten recommendations for making effective use of your college electives. As you read them, note three strategies that appeal most to you and you're most likely to put into practice.

You can make strategic use of your elective to:

1. **Complete a minor or build an area of concentration.** Electives can be used to pursue a field of personal interest that complements and strengthens your major. (See p. 284 for further details.)

2. **Help you choose a career path.** Just as you can use electives to test your interest in a college major, you can use them to test your interest in a career. For instance, you could enroll in:
   - career planning or career development courses; and
   - courses that include internships or service learning experiences in a field you're considering as a possible career (e.g., health, education, or business).

3. **Strengthen your skills in areas that may appeal to future employers.** For instance, courses in foreign language, leadership development, and persuasive communication can develop skills attractive to current employers. (See Chapter 2 for skills sought by today's employers.)

4. **Develop practical life skills.** Courses in managing personal finances, marriage and family, or child

Box 11.2 *(continued)*

development can help you manage your money and your family relationships.

5. Seek balance in your life and develop yourself as a whole person. You can use your electives intentionally to cover all key dimensions of self-development. Electives may be used to promote your emotional development (e.g., stress management), social development (e.g., social psychology), intellectual development (e.g., critical thinking), physical development (e.g., nutrition or self-defense), and spiritual development (e.g., world religions or death and dying).

I discovered an unknown talent and lifelong stress-reducing hobby."

—An attorney talking about an elective ceramics course taken in college (quoted in Brooks, 2009)

6. Make connections between different academic disciplines (subject areas). *Interdisciplinary* courses are courses designed specifically to integrate two or more academic disciplines. For instance, psychobiology is an interdisciplinary course that integrates the fields of psychology (focusing on the mind) and biology (focusing on the body), enabling you to see how the mind influences the body and vice versa.

Making connections across subjects and seeing how they can be combined to create a more complete understanding of personal or societal issues can be a stimulating intellectual experience. Furthermore, the presence of interdisciplinary courses on your college transcript may be attractive to future employers because "real world" work responsibilities and challenges cannot be handled through the lens of a single major; they require the ability to integrate skills acquired from different fields of study (Colby, et al., 2011).

7. Help you develop broader perspectives on the human condition and the surrounding world.

You can intentionally take electives that progressively widen your world perspectives, such as courses that provide a societal perspective (sociology), a national perspective (political science), an international perspective (world geography), a global perspective (ecology), and a cosmological perspective (astronomy). (See pp. 33–37 for more detailed information on these broadening perspectives.)

8. Appreciate different cultural viewpoints and enhance your ability to communicate with people from diverse cultural backgrounds. You could take electives that focus on cultural differences across nations (e.g., international relations) or courses related to cultural differences within America (e.g., race and ethnicity).

9. Stretch yourself beyond your customary learning style to experience different ways of learning and acquire new skills. You'll find courses in the college curriculum you never took before (or even knew existed) that supply you with knowledge and skills you've never had a previous opportunity to acquire or develop. These courses will stretch your mind, allowing you to explore new ideas and expand your skill set in a way that's consistent with a key characteristic of successful people—"growth mindset." (See Chapter 3, pp. 67–69, for information about this personal characteristic.)

10. Learn something you were always curious about. If you've always wondered how members of the other sex think and feel, you could take a course on the psychology of men and women. Or, if you've heard about a particular professor who teaches a course that students find especially interesting, take that course and find out why it's so interesting.

Your college catalog (bulletin) contains descriptions of all courses offered on your campus. Take time to review these course descriptions carefully and explore all the elective options available to you.

 Reflection 11.7

What three strategies for selecting electives listed in **Box 11.2** are you most likely to implement?

Briefly explain why you chose each of these strategies.

> "Try not to take classes because they fit neatly into your schedule. Start by identifying classes that are most important to you and fit your schedule to accommodate them."
>
> —*Katharine Brooks*, You Majored in What?

Note

Your elective courses give you the opportunity to shape and create an academic experience that's uniquely your own. Seize this opportunity to exercise your academic freedom responsibly. Don't make elective choices randomly or merely on the basis of scheduling convenience (e.g., choosing electives to create a schedule with no early morning or late afternoon classes and no classes on Friday). Instead, make course selections strategically so that they contribute most to your educational, personal, and professional development.

©Kendall Hunt Publishing Company

Choosing courses that best enable you to achieve your long-term educational and personal goals should take precedence over creating a schedule that leaves your Fridays free for three-day weekends.

Consider the possibility of completing a college minor in a field that complements your major. A college minor usually requires about half the number of credits (units) required for a major. Most campuses allow you the option of completing a minor along with your major. Check your course catalog or consult with an academic advisor for college minors that may interest you.

If you have a strong interest in two different fields, a minor will allow you to major in one of these fields while minoring in the other. Thus, you're able to pursue two fields of interest without having to sacrifice one for the other. Another advantage of a minor is that it can usually be completed with a major without delaying your time to graduation. In contrast, a double major is likely to lengthen your time to graduation because it requires completing all requirements for both majors.

Another way to complete a second field of study without increasing your time to graduation is by completing a "concentration" or "cognate area"—an academic specialization that requires fewer courses to complete than a minor (e.g., four to five courses vs. seven to eight courses). A concentration area may have even fewer requirements (only three to four courses).

Taking a cluster of courses in a field outside your major can be an effective way to strengthen your resume and your employment prospects; it demonstrates your versatility and ability to acquire knowledge and skills in areas that may be missing or underemphasized in your major. For example, by taking a cluster of courses in fields such as mathematics (e.g., statistics), technology (e.g., computer science), and business (e.g., economics), students majoring in the fine arts (e.g., music or theater) or humanities (e.g., English or history) can acquire knowledge and skills in areas not strongly emphasized by their major, thereby increasing their prospects for employment after graduation.

Myths about the Relationship between Majors and Careers

 Reflection 11.8

Consider the following statement: "Choosing a major is a life-changing decision because it will determine what you will do for the rest of your life."

Would you agree or disagree?

Why?

Numerous misconceptions exist about the relationship between college majors and careers, some of which can lead students to make uninformed or unrealistic decisions about a major. Here are four common myths about the major–career relationship you should be aware of and factor into your decision about a college major.

Myth 1. When you choose your major, you're choosing your career.

While some majors lead directly to a specific career, most do not. Majors leading directly to specialized careers are often called preprofessional or pre-vocational majors; they include such fields as accounting, engineering, and nursing. However, the relationship between most college majors and future careers is often not direct or linear; you don't travel on a monorail straight from your major to a single career that's directly connected to your major. For instance, all physics majors don't become physicists, all philosophy majors don't become philosophers, all history majors don't become historians, and all English majors don't become Englishmen (or Englishwomen). Instead, the same major typically leads you to a variety of career options.

The truth is that for most college students the journey from college major to future career(s) is less like scaling a vertical pole and more like climbing a tree. As illustrated in **Figure 11.4**, you begin with the tree's trunk (the foundation provided by general education (the liberal arts); this leads to separate limbs (choices for college majors), which, in turn, lead to different branches (different career paths or occupational options). Note that different sets of branches (careers) grow from the same limb (major).

> Linear thinking can keep you from thinking broadly about your options and being open-minded to new opportunities."
> —*Katharine Brooks, author,* You Majored in What?

FIGURE 11.4: **The Relationship between General Education (Liberal Arts), College Majors, and Careers**

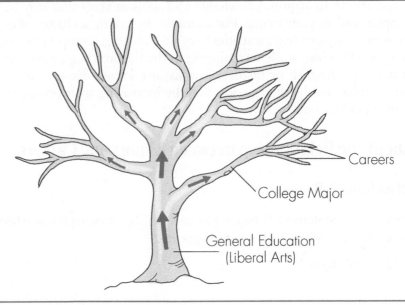

Careers

College Major

General Education
(Liberal Arts)

©Kendall Hunt Publishing Company

I intend on becoming a corporate lawyer. I am an English major. The reason I chose this major is because while I was researching the educational backgrounds of some corporate attorneys, I found that a lot were English majors. It helps with writing and delivering cases."

—*College sophomore*

Things like picking majors and careers really scare me a lot! I don't know exactly what I want to do with my life."

—*First-year student*

Similarly, different career clusters or "career families" grow from the same major. An English major can lead to a variety of careers that involve writing (e.g., editing, journalism, or publishing), and a major in Art can lead to different careers that involve visual media (e.g., illustration, graphic design, or art therapy).

Furthermore, different majors can lead to the same career. For instance, a variety of majors can lead a student to law school and a career as a lawyer; in fact, there's really no such thing as a "law major" or "pre-law major." Students with a variety of majors (or minors) can also enter medical school as long as they have a solid set of foundational courses in biology and chemistry and score well on the medical college admissions test.

Studies show that today's workers change jobs 10 times in the two decades following college and the job-changing rate is highest for younger workers (AAC&U, 2007). Research also indicates that only half of new college graduates expect to be working in the same field in which they're currently employed (Hart Research Associates, 2006); they frequently change positions during their first two decades of employment following college completion, and the further along they proceed in their career path, the more likely they are to be working in a field that's unrelated to their college major (Millard, 2004).

So, don't assume that your major *is* your career, or that your major automatically turns into your lifelong career. It's this belief that can result in some students procrastinating about choosing a major; they think they're making a lifelong decision and fear that if they make the "wrong" choice, they'll be stuck doing something they hate for the rest of their life. Although it's important to think about how your choice of a college major will affect your career path, for most college students—particularly those not majoring in preprofessional fields—choice of a major and choice of a career are not identical decisions made at the same time. Choosing a specific major is a decision that should be made by your sophomore year; choosing a career is a decision that can be made later.

Note

Don't assume that choosing your college major means you're choosing what you'll be doing for the remainder of your working life. Deciding on a major and deciding on a career are not identical decisions that must be made simultaneously.

Myth 2. If you want to continue your education after college graduation, you must continue in the same field as your college major.

After graduating with a four-year (baccalaureate) degree, you have two primary paths available to you: (a) enter the workforce immediately, and/or (b) continue your education in graduate school or professional school. (See **Figure 11.5** for a visual map of the stages and milestones in the college experience and the paths available to you after college.)

FIGURE 11.5: A Snapshot of the College Experience and Beyond

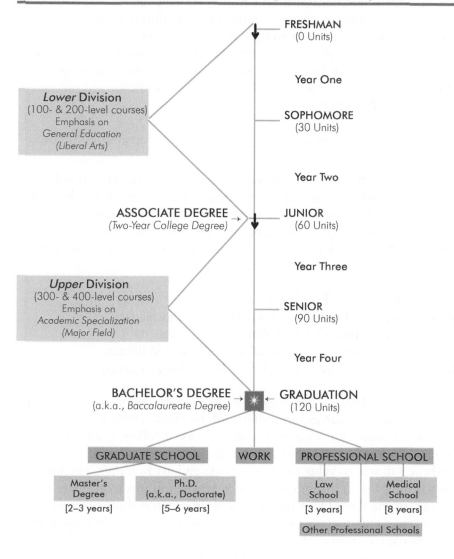

Notes

1. On average, about one-third of the courses required for a college degree are general education courses selected from the liberal arts curriculum. However, the number of required general education courses varies from campus to campus and can vary at the same campus depending on the student's major.

2. The word "freshman" originated in England in 1596, when every college student was a "fresh" (new) "man." Today, the term "freshman" is frequently being replaced by "first-year student" because this is a more gender-neutral term.

3. The term "baccalaureate" derives from "Bacchus"—the Greek god of wine and festive celebration, and "laurel"—a wreath made from the laurel plant that ancient Greeks draped around the neck of Olympic champions.

4. It often takes college students longer than four years to graduate due to a variety of reasons, such as working part-time and taking fewer courses per term, needing to repeat courses that were failed or dropped, or making a late change to a different major and needing to fulfill additional requirements for the new major.

5. Graduate and professional schools are options for continuing to higher levels of education after completion of an undergraduate (college) education.

6. Students going to graduate school on a full-time basis can sometimes support themselves financially by working part-time as a teaching assistant (TA) or research assistant (RA). It's also possible to enroll in some graduate or professional school programs on a part-time basis while holding a full-time job.

7. The term "Ph.D." refers to "Doctor of Philosophy," respecting the fact that the first scholars were the ancient Greek philosophers (e.g., Socrates, Plato, and Aristotle). However, a Ph.D. can be earned in many different academic fields (Mathematics, Music, Economic, etc.).

8. Compared to graduate school, professional school involves advanced education in more "applied" professions (e.g., pharmacy or public administration).

Once you earn a college diploma, you can continue your education in a field that's not directly related to your college major. This is particularly true for students majoring in liberal arts fields that don't lead directly to a specific career after graduation (Pascarella & Terenzini, 1991, 2005). For example, an English major can go to graduate school in a subject other than English, or go to law school, or get a master's degree in business administration. In fact, most students who attend graduate school in the field of business (e.g., MBA programs) were not business majors when they were in college (Zlomek, 2012).

Myth 3. Since most college graduates are employed in business organizations or corporations, you should major in business.

Most college graduates are employed in business settings, so students (and their parents) often conclude that if students are going to work for a business, they better major in business. This belief likely explains why business is the most popular major among college students (National Center for Education Statistics, 2011). However, college graduates now working in business settings have majored in variety of fields besides business, and many CEOs of today's most profitable companies did not major in business. Certainly, if you have an interest in and passion for majoring in business, by all means major in business; however, don't choose a business major because you think it's the only major that will qualify you to work for and succeed in a business organization after graduation.

Myth 4. If you major in a liberal arts field, the only career available to you is teaching.

A commonly held myth is that all you can do with a major in a liberal arts subject is to teach the subject you majored in (e.g., math majors become math teachers; history majors become history teachers). The truth is that students majoring in different liberal arts fields go on to enter, advance, and prosper in a wide variety of careers. College graduates with degrees in the liberal arts who went on to achieve professional success in careers other than teaching include:

- Jill Barad (English major), CEO, Mattel Toys
- Willie Brown (liberal studies major), Mayor of San Francisco
- Ken Chenault (History major), CEO, American Express
- Christopher Connor (Sociology major), CEO, Sherwin Williams
- Robert Iger (Communications major), CEO, Walt Disney Company

Significant numbers of liberal arts majors are also employed in positions relating to marketing, human resources, and public affairs (Bok, 2006; Useem, 1989). An experienced career counselor once tracked the majors of college graduates working in the insurance industry. She found an art history major working at a major insurance firm whose job was to value oriental carpets and art holdings. She found a geology major working for an insurance company whose job was to evaluate beach properties and determine the odds of hurricanes or other natural phenomena causing property damage. This former geology major spent much of her work time traveling to beachfront communities to review new developments and assessing damages after hurricanes or other tragic events (Brooks, 2009).

Research also reveals that the career mobility and career advancement of liberal arts majors working in the corporate world are comparable to business majors. For example, liberal arts majors are just as likely to advance to the highest levels of corporate leadership as majors in such preprofessional fields as business and engineering (Pascarella & Terenzini, 2005). The point we're making here is that if you have a passion for and talent in a liberal arts field, don't dismiss it as being "impractical," and don't be dismayed or discouraged by those who challenge your choice by asking: "What are you going to do with a degree in that major?" (Brooks, 2009).

AUTHOR'S EXPERIENCE

My brother, Vinny, was a philosophy major in college. He came home one Christmas wearing a tee-shirt on which was printed the message: "Philosophy major. Will think for food." With his major in philosophy, my brother went to graduate school, completed a Master's degree in higher education, and is now making a six-figure salary working as a college administrator. Looking back, his old tee-shirt should have read: "Philosophy major. Will think for money."

—*Joe Cuseo*

 Reflection 11.9

Look back at the four myths about the relationships between majors and careers. Which of these four myths did you know were false? Which myths did you previously think were true?

Chapter Summary and Highlights

Studies show that the vast majority of students entering college are uncertain about their academic specialization. Most students do not reach a final decision about their major before starting college; typically, they make that decision during their college experience.

As a new student, it's only natural to be at least somewhat uncertain about educational goals at the early stages of your college experience because you haven't experienced the variety of subjects and academic programs that comprise the college curriculum. The general education curriculum will introduce you to new fields of study, some of which you've never experienced before and all of which represent possible choices for a college major. A key benefit of experiencing the variety of courses that make up the general education curriculum is that they enable you to become more aware of yourself, and at the same time, enable you to become more aware of the academic fields available to you as potential majors. As you gain experience with the college curriculum, you will gain greater self-insight into your academic interests, strengths, and weaknesses. Take this self-knowledge into consideration when choosing a major to help you select a field that capitalizes on your personal interests, abilities, and talents.

You can use your elective courses strategically to help you explore or confirm your choice of a college major as well as to:

- Acquire a minor that complements and augments your major
- Broaden your perspectives on the world around you
- Become a more balanced, well-rounded person
- Handle the practical life tasks that face you now and in the future
- Strengthen your career development and employment prospects after graduation

Compared to high school, higher education allows you more freedom of academic choice and a greater opportunity to determine your own educational path.

Enjoy this freedom and employ it responsibly to make the most of your college experience and college degree.

To make a well-informed choice of a college major, there are several myths you should be aware of:

- **Myth 1. When you choose your major, you're choosing your career.** While some majors lead directly to a specific career, most do not. The relationship between most college majors and careers is not direct or linear. Different career clusters or "career families" can grow from the same major. Furthermore, different majors can lead to the same career.
- **Myth 2. After you graduate with a college degree, any further education you pursue must be in the same field as your college major.** College graduates can continue their education in a field that's not directly related to their college major. This is particularly true for students majoring in liberal arts fields that do not funnel them directly into a specific career after graduation.
- **Myth 3. Since most college graduates work in business settings, you should major business.** Students (and their parents) see most college graduates employed in business settings and conclude that if students are going to work for a business, they better major in business. However, the majority of college graduates now working in business settings didn't major in business when they were in college.
- **Myth 4. If you major in a liberal arts subject, the only career available to you is teaching.** The truth is that students majoring in different fields of the liberal arts go on to enter, advance, and prosper in a wide variety of careers. If you have a passion for and talent in a liberal arts field, consider majoring in it; don't dismiss it as being impractical, and don't be dismayed or discouraged by those who may challenge your choice by asking: "What are you going to do with a degree in that major?"

Learning More through the World Wide Web: Internet-Based Resources

For additional information related to educational planning and choosing a major, see the following websites.

Identifying and Choosing College Majors:
www.mymajors.com
www.princetonreview.com/majors.aspx

Relationships between Majors and Careers:
http://uncw.edu/career/WhatCanIDoWithaMajorIn.html

Careers for Liberal Arts Majors:
Liberal Arts Career Network (www.liberalartscareers.org/)
"What can I do with my liberal arts degree?" (www.bls.gov/ooq/2007/winter/art.01pdf)

References

AAC&U (Association of American Colleges and Universities). (2007). *College learning for the new global century*. A report from the National Leadership Council for Liberal Education & America's Promise. Washington, DC: Association of American Colleges and Universities.

Bean, J. C. (2001). *Engaging ideas: The professor's guide to integrating writing, critical thinking and active learning in the classroom*. San Francisco: Jossey-Bass.

Biglan, A. (1973). The characteristics of subject matter in different academic areas. *Journal of Applied Psychology, 57,* 195–203.

Bodanovich, S. J., Wallace, J. C., & Kass, S. J. (2005). A confirmatory approach to the factor structure of the Boredom Proneness Scale: evidence for a two-factor short form. *Journal of Personality Assessment, 85*(3), 295–303.

Bok, D. (2006). *Our underachieving colleges.* Princeton, NJ: Princeton University Press.

Brooks, K. (2009). *You majored in what? Mapping your path from chaos to career.* New York: Penguin.

Claxton, C. S., & Murrell, P. H. (1987). *Learning styles: Implications for improving practice.* ASHE-ERIC Educational Report No. 4. Washington, DC: Association for the Study of Higher Education.

Colby, A., Ehrlich, T., Sullivan, W. M., & Dolle, J. R. (2011). *Rethinking undergraduate business education: Liberal learning for the profession.* The Carnegie Foundation for the Advancement of Teaching. San Francisco: Jossey-Bass.

Cuseo, J. B. (2005). "Decided," "undecided," and "in transition": Implications for academic advisement, career counseling, and student retention. In R.S. Feldman (Ed.), *Improving the first year of college: Research and patience* (pp. 27–50). Mahwah, NJ: Lawrence Erlbaum.

Dunn, R., Dunn, K., & Price, G. (1990). *Learning style inventory.* Lawrence, KS: Price Systems.

Gardner, H. (1993). *Frames of mind: The theory of multiple intelligences* (2nd ed.). New York: Basic Books.

Gardner, H. (1999). *Intelligence reframed: Multiple intelligences for the 21st century.* New York: Basic Books.

Gardner, H. (2006). *Changing minds. The art and science of changing our own and other people's minds.* Boston, MA: Harvard Business School Press.

Gordon, V. N., & Steele, G. E. (2003). Undecided first-year students: A 25-year longitudinal study. *Journal of the First-Year Experience and Students in Transition, 15*(1), 19–38.

Hart Research Associates. (2006). *How should colleges prepare students to succeed in today's global economy?* Based on surveys among employers and recent college graduates. Conducted on behalf of the Association of American Colleges and Universities. Washington, DC: Author.

Hendry, G., Heinrich, L. P., Barratt, A. L., Simpson, J. M., Hyde, S. J., Gonsalkorale, S., Hyde, M., & Mgaieth, S. (2005). Helping students understand their learning styles: Effects on study self-efficacy, preference for group work, and group climate. *Journal of Educational Psychology, 25*(4), 395–407.

HERI (Higher Education Research Institute). (2014). *Your first college year survey 2014.* Los Angeles, CA: Cooperative Institutional Research Program, University of California-Los Angeles.

Kolb, D. A. (1976). Management and learning process. *California Management Review, 18*(3), 21–31.

Kolb, D. A. (1985). *Learning styles inventory.* Boston: McBer.

Leuwerke, W. C., Robbins, S. B., Sawyer, R., & Hovland, M. (2004). Predicting engineering major status from mathematics achievement and interest congruence. *Journal of Career Assessment, 12*, 135–149.

Millard, B. (2004, November 7). *A purpose-based approach to navigating college transitions.* Preconference workshop presented at the Eleventh National Conference on Students in Transition, Nashville, Tennessee.

National Center for Education Statistics. (2011). U.S. Department of Education Institute of Education Sciences. https://nces.ed.gov/fastfacts/#.

Pascarella, E., & Terenzini, P. (1991). *How college affects students: Findings and insights from twenty years of research.* San Francisco: Jossey-Bass.

Pascarella, E., & Terenzini, P. (2005). *How college affects students: A third decade of research* (Vol. 2). San Francisco: Jossey-Bass.

Schommer-Aikins, M., Duell, O. K., & Barker, S. (2003). Epistemological beliefs across domains using Biglan's classification of academic disciplines. *Research in Higher Education, 44*(3), 347–366.

Svinicki, M. D. (2004). *Learning and motivation in the postsecondary classroom.* Bolton, MA: Anker.

Svinicki, M. D., & Dixon, N. M. (1987). The Kolb model modified for classroom activities. *College Teaching, 35*(4), 141–146.

Useem, M. (1989). *Liberal education and the corporation: The hiring and advancement of college graduates.* Piscataway, NJ: Aldine Transaction.

Zlomek, E. (2012, March 26). As MBA applicants, business majors face an uphill battle. *Bloomburg Business.* Retrieved from http://www.bloomberg.com/bw/articles/2012-03-26/as-mba-applicants-business-majors-face-an-uphill-battle.

Chapter 11 Exercises

11.1 Quote Reflections

Review the sidebar quotes contained in this chapter and select two that were especially meaningful or inspirational to you.

For each quote, provide a three- to five-sentence explanation for why you chose it.

11.2 Reality Bite

Whose Choice Is It Anyway?

Ursula, a first-year student, was in tears when she showed up at the Career Center. She had just returned from a weekend visit home, during which she informed her parents of her plans to major in art or theater. After Ursula's father heard about her plans, he exploded and insisted that she major in something "practical," like nursing or accounting, so that she could get a job after graduation. Ursula replied that she had no interest in these majors, nor did she feel she had the skills in science and math required by these majors. Her father shot back that he had no intention of "paying four years of college tuition for her to end up as a starving artist or unemployed actress!" He went on to say that if she wanted to major in art or theater she'd "have to figure out a way to pay for college herself."

Reflection and Discussion Questions

1. If Ursula were your friend, what would you suggest she do?

2. Do you see any way(s) in which Ursula might pursue a major that's compatible with her interests and talents, while at the same time, ease her father's concern that she'll end up jobless after college graduation?

3. Can you relate to this student's predicament, or know any other students in a similar situation?

11.3 Learning Styles Self-Assessment and Choice of Major

1. Complete the *My PEPS Learning Styles Inventory* that accompanies this book.
    a) Review the results from the report on your preferred modes for learning and working.
    b) Do you think that your learning style preferences are a good match for the major or major(s) you're considering? If yes, why? If no, why not?

2. Complete the *Do What You Are* inventory that provides you with a personality report as well as a list of suggested majors and careers.
    a) How do the suggested majors align with your strengths?
    b) Is your current major or the major you are considering on the list? If it is, explain how the major is a good fit for you. If it's not on the list, explain why you still think it's a good fit or why you think it's not.

11.4 Faculty Interview

Identify a faculty member on campus in a field you've chosen or are considering as a college major. Make an appointment to speak with the faculty member during office hours to learn about that field of study. Let the faculty member know the purpose of your visit. Use the following interview questions, to get to know the faculty member and give you a better understanding of the field.

1. What initially *attracted* you to your academic field?

2. *When* did you decide to pursue a career in your academic field? Was it your *first* choice, or did you *change* to it from another academic area? (If you changed your original major, *why* did you change?)

3. What would you say is the most *enjoyable, exciting,* or *stimulating* aspect of your field of study?

4. Are there any *unexpected* requirements in your academic field that prove to be particularly *challenging* for students?

5. What *careers* are related to your academic field? (Or, what types of careers does a major in your field prepare students to pursue?)

6. What particular *skills, abilities,* or *talents* do you think are needed for *success* in your field of study?

7. What personality *traits* or personal *interests* do you think would *"match up"* well with the type of work required in your academic field?

8. What particular *courses* or *out-of-class experiences* would you recommend to help students decide if your field is a good fit for them?

11.5 Developing a Long-Range Academic Plan for Your Course Work

This exercise is designed to help you design a detailed yet flexible, four-year academic plan. While it may seem a bit overwhelming to develop a long-range plan at this stage of your college experience, you will receive guidance from your course instructor and academic advisor. This is an opportunity to begin customizing your college experience and mapping your educational future. Remember: an educational plan isn't something set in stone; it can change depending on changes in your academic and career interests. As you create, shape, and follow your plan, consult frequently with your academic advisor.

Overview of Courses Comprising Your Plan

Your trip through the college curriculum will involve taking courses in the following three key categories:

1. *General education* courses required of all college graduates regardless of their major;

2. *Required* courses in your chosen *major*; and

3. *Elective* courses you choose to take from any listed in your college catalog.

What follows are planning directions for each of these types of courses. By building these three sets of courses into your educational plan, you can create a roadmap that guides your future coursework. Once you've reserved slots for these three key categories of courses you will have a blueprint to guide (not dictate) your educational future. If you later change your mind about a particular course you originally planned to take, you can do so without interfering with your educational progress by substituting another course from the same category. For instance, if your original plan was to take psychology to fulfill a general education requirement in the Social and Behavioral Sciences, but you decide later to take anthropology instead, you have a space reserved in your plan to make the switch.

As you gain more educational experience, your specific academic and career interests are likely to change and so may the specifics of your long-range plan. The purpose of this plan is not to tie you up or pin you down, but to supply you with a map that keeps you on course and moving in the right direction. Since this is a flexible plan, it's probably best to complete it in pencil or electronically so you can make future changes as needed.

Once you've developed your plan, hold onto it, and keep an up-to-date copy of it throughout your time in college. Bring it with you when you meet with advisors and career development specialists, and come prepared to discuss your progress on the plan as well as any changes you would like to make to it.

Part A. Planning for General Education

Step 1. Use your course catalog (bulletin) to identify the general education requirements for graduation. You're likely to find these requirements organized into general divisions of knowledge (Humanities, Natural Sciences, etc.). Within each of these divisions, courses will be listed that you can take to fulfill the general education requirement(s) for that particular division. (Course catalogs can sometimes be tricky to navigate or interpret; if you run into any difficulty, seek help from your course instructor or an academic advisor.) You'll probably be able to choose courses from a list of different options. Use your freedom of choice to choose general education courses whose descriptions capture your curiosity and contribute to your personal development and career plans. You can use general education courses not only to fulfill general education requirements, but also to test your interest and talent in different fields—one of which may end up becoming your major (or minor).

Step 2. Identify courses in the catalog you plan to take to fulfill your general education requirements and list them on the following form. Some courses you're taking this term may be fulfilling general education requirements, so be sure to list them as well.

Planning Grid for *General Education* Courses

Course Title	Units	Course Title	Units

Total Number of Units Required for *General Education* = _____

Part B. Planning for a College Major

The point of this portion of your educational plan is not to force you to commit to a major right now, but to develop a flexible plan that will allow you to reach a well-informed decision about your major. If you have already chosen a major, this exercise will help you lay out exactly what's ahead of you and confirm whether the coursework required by your major is what you expected and "fits" well with your interests and talents.

Step 1. Go to your college catalog and locate the major you've chosen or are considering. If you're completely undecided, select a field that you might consider as a possibility. To help you identify possible majors, peruse your catalog or go online and answer the questions at *www.mymajors.com.*

Another way to identify a major for this exercise is to first identify a career you might be interested in and work backward to find a major that leads to this career. If you would like to use this strategy, the following website will guide you through the process: *http://uncw.edu/career/WhatCanIDoWithaMajorIn.html.*

Step 2. After you've selected a major, consult your college catalog to identify the courses required for that major. Your campus may also have "major planning sheets" that list the specific course requirements for each major. (To see if these major planning sheets are available, check with the Advising Center or the academic department that offers the major you've selected.)

A college major will require all students majoring in that field to complete specific courses. For instance, all business majors are required to take microeconomics. Other courses required for a major may be chosen from a menu or list of options (e.g., "choose any three courses from the following list of six courses"). Such courses are often called "major electives." For these major electives, read their course descriptions carefully and use your freedom of choice wisely to select courses that interest you and are most relevant to your future plans.

Note: You can "double dip" by taking courses that fulfill a major requirement and a general education requirement at the same time. For instance, if your major is psychology, you may be able to take a course in General or Introductory Psychology that counts simultaneously as a required major course and a required general education course in the area of Social and Behavioral Sciences.

Step 3. Identify courses you plan to take to fulfill your major requirements and major electives and list them on the following form. Courses you're taking this term may be fulfilling requirements in the major you've selected, so be sure to list them as well.

Planning Grid for Courses in Your *Major*

Course Title	Units	Course Title	Units

Total Number of Units Required for Your *Major* = _____

Plan C. Planning Your Free Electives

Now that you've built general education courses and major courses into your educational map, you're well positioned to plan your *free electives*—courses not required for general education or your major but that are needed to reach the minimum number of units required for a college degree. These are courses you are free to choose from any listed in the college catalog.

To determine how many free elective units you have, add up the number of course units you're taking to fulfill general education and major requirements, then subtract this number from the total number of units you need to graduate. The number of course units remaining represents your total number of free electives. (See pp. 282–283 for strategies on choosing electives.)

Planning Grid for Your *Free Electives*

Course Title	Units	Course Title	Units

Total Number of *Free Elective* Units = _____

Part D. Putting It Altogether: Developing a Comprehensive Graduation Plan

In the previous three sections, you built three key sets of college courses into your plan: general education courses, major courses, and free elective courses. Now you're positioned to tie these three sets of courses together and create a comprehensive graduation plan.

Using the "Long-Range Graduation Planning Form" on pp. 297–299, enter the courses you selected to fulfill general education requirements, major requirements, and free electives. In the space provided next to each course, use the following shorthand notations to designate its category:

GE = *general education* course

M = *major* course

E = *elective* course

Notes:

1. If there are courses in your plan that fulfill two or more categories at the same time (e.g., a general education requirement and a major requirement), note both categories.

2. To complete a college degree in four years (approximately 120 units), you should plan to complete about 30 course credits each academic year. Keep in mind that you can take college courses in the summer as well as the fall and spring.

Note

Unlike high school, taking summer courses in college doesn't mean you've fallen behind or need to retake a course you failed during the "normal" school year (fall and spring terms). Instead, summer term can be used to get ahead and reduce your time to graduation. Adopt the mindset that summer term is a regular part of the college academic year; use it strategically to stay on track to complete your degree in a timely fashion.

3. Keep in mind that the number associated with a course indicates the year in the college experience when the course is usually taken. Courses numbered in the 100s (or below) are typically taken in the first year of college, 200-numbered courses in the sophomore year, 300-numbered courses in the junior year, and 400-numbered courses in the senior year.

4. If you haven't decided on a major, a good strategy is to focus on completing general education requirements during your first year of college. This first-year strategy will open more slots in your course schedule during your sophomore year—by that time, you may have a better idea of what you'll major in, so you can fill these open slots with courses required for the major you've chosen. (This first-year strategy will also allow you to use general education courses in different subjects to test your interest in majoring in one of these subjects.)

5. Be sure to check whether the course you're planning to take has any *prerequisites*—courses that need to be completed *before* you can enroll in the course you're planning to take. For example, before you can enroll in a literature course, you may need to complete at least one prerequisite course in writing or English composition.

6. Your campus may have a *degree audit program* that allows you to electronically track the courses you've completed and the courses you still need to complete a degree in your chosen major. If such a program is available, take advantage of it.

7. You're not locked into taking all your courses in the exact terms you originally placed them in your plan. You can trade terms if it turns out that the course isn't offered during the term you were planning to take it, or if it's offered at a time that conflicts with another course in your schedule.

8. Keep in mind that not all college courses are offered every term, every year. Typically, college catalogs do not contain information about when courses will be scheduled. If you're unsure when a course will be offered, check with an academic advisor. Some colleges develop *a projected plan of scheduled courses* that shows what academic term(s) courses will be offered for the next few years. If such a projected schedule of courses is available, take advantage of it. It will enable you to develop an educational plan that not only includes *what* courses you will take, but also *when* you will take them.

Long-Range Graduation Planning Form

FRESHMAN YEAR
Fall Term

Course Title	Course Type General Ed. (GE), Major (M), Elective (E)	Course Units

Total Units = _____

Spring Term

Course Title	Course Type General Ed. (GE), Major (M), Elective (E)	Course Units

Total Units = _____

Summer Term

Course Title	Course Type General Ed. (GE), Major (M), Elective (E)	Course Units

Total Units = _____

SOPHOMORE YEAR
Fall Term

Course Title	Course Type General Ed. (GE), Major (M), Elective (E)	Course Units

Total Units = _____

Spring Term

Course Title	Course Type General Ed. (GE), Major (M), Elective (E)	Course Units

Total Units = _____

Summer Term

Course Title	Course Type General Ed. (GE), Major (M), Elective (E)	Course Units

Total Units = _____

JUNIOR YEAR
Fall Term

Course Title	Course Type General Ed. (GE), Major (M), Elective (E)	Course Units

Total Units = _____

Spring Term

Course Title	Course Type General Ed. (GE), Major (M), Elective (E)	Course Units

Total Units = _____

Course Title	Course Type General Ed. (GE), Major (M), Elective (E)	Course Units

Total Units = _____

SENIOR YEAR
Fall Term

Course Title	Course Type General Ed. (GE), Major (M), Elective (E)	Course Units

Total Units = _____

Spring Term

Course Title	Course Type General Ed. (GE), Major (M), Elective (E)	Course Units

Total Units = _____

Reflection Questions

1. What is the total number of credits in your graduation plan? Does it equal or exceed the total number of credits needed to graduate from your college or university?

2. How many credits will you be taking in the following areas?
   a) General Education =
   b) Major =
   c) Free Electives =

3. Look over the course required for the major you selected:
   a) Are there required courses you were surprised to see or didn't expect would be required?
   b) Are you still interested in majoring in this field?
   c) How likely is it that you will change the major you selected?
   d) If you were to change your major, what would "Plan B" likely be?

4. Did completing this long-range graduation plan help you clarify your educational goals? Why or why not?

11.6 Developing a Co-Curricular Plan for Learning Experiences Outside the Classroom

Now that you've completed a curricular plan for your coursework, let's turn to devising a plan for the second key component of a college education: *experiential* learning—learning from "hands-on" experiences outside the classroom—either on campus (e.g., leadership positions) or off campus (e.g., service experiences, internships, or employment). Learning opportunities available to you beyond the curriculum are known collectively as the *co-curriculum*. Co-curricular experiences complement your coursework, enhance the quality of your education, and increase your employability. Keep in mind that co-curricular experiences are also resume-building experiences.

Ideally, by the time you graduate, you should have co-curricular experiences in each of the following areas:

- *Volunteer work* or *community service* that demonstrates social responsibility and allows you to gain "real world" experience
- *Leadership and mentoring* skills—for example, participating in leadership retreats, student government, peer mentoring, or serving as a student representative on college committees
- *Internships* or work experiences in a field related to your major or career goals
- Interacting and collaborating with members of *diverse racial and cultural groups*—for example, participating in multicultural clubs, organizations, or retreats
- *Study abroad* or *study travel* experiences that allow you to acquire international knowledge and a global perspective

Step 1. Consult your *Student Handbook* or check with professionals working in the offices of Student Life (Student Development) and Career Development to locate co-curricular experiences in each of the above areas.

Step 2. Identify one campus program or opportunity in each of these areas that interests you and note it on the planning form below.

Planning Grid for Co-Curricular Experiences

Volunteer Work/Community Service: _____

Leadership/Mentoring: _____

Diversity (Multicultural) Experience: _____

Study Abroad (International) Experience: _____

Internship or Work Experience Relating to Your Major or Career Goals: _____

Notes:

- Summer term is an excellent time of the year to build experiential learning into your educational plan without having to worry about conflicts with your scheduled classes or doing it while simultaneously handling all the academic work associated with a full load of courses.
- Keep track of the specific skills you develop while engaging in co-curricular experiences, and be sure to showcase them to future employers. Don't just accumulate extracurricular activities to list on your resume, reflect on your experiences and articulate what you learned from them. Identify the thinking processes you used (see Chapter 8, p. 181) as well as the transferable skills and personal qualities you developed while engaging in these experiences (see Chapter 12, p. 317).
- Keep in mind that the professionals with whom you interact while participating in co-curricular experiences can serve as valuable references and sources of letters of recommendation to future employers, graduate schools, and professional schools. (For strategies on requesting letters of recommendation, see Chapter 12, pp. 322–323.)

1. What *challenges* or *obstacles* do you think might interfere with your ability to complete this co-curricular plan? What campus *resources* might help you deal with these challenges or obstacles?

2. What people on or off campus could you *network* with to help you successfully navigate your co-curricular plan?

3. As you pursue your plans for experiential learning outside the classroom, who might be a *mentor* for you, or serve as a personal source of *inspiration and motivation*?

Final Reminder:

Hold onto your curricular and co-curricular plans. Keep an up-to-date copy of them throughout your years in college. Bring these plans with you when you meet with your academic advisor and career development specialists, and come prepared to discuss your progress on these plans as well as any changes you would like to make.

Career Exploration, Preparation, and Development

FINDING A PATH TO YOUR FUTURE PROFESSION

It may seem unusual to find a chapter on career success in a book for beginning college students. Even though career entry may be years away, career exploration and preparation should begin in the first term of college. Career planning gives you a practical, long-range goal to strive for and gets you thinking about how the skills you're using and developing in college align with the skills that promote your professional success beyond college. Career planning is really a form of life planning; the sooner you begin this process, the sooner you start gaining control of your future and steering it in the direction you want it to go.

Acquire strategies you can use immediately and throughout your college experience to explore, prepare for, and gain entry to a future career that's compatible with your talents, interests, needs, and values.

 Reflection 12.1

Before you dig into this chapter, take a moment to answer the following questions:

1. Have you decided on a career or strongly considering one?

2. If yes, why have you chosen this career? (Was your decision strongly influenced by anybody or anything?)

3. If no, what careers are you considering as possibilities?

The Importance of Career Planning

Most of the remaining hours of your life will be spent working; the only other single activity you'll spend more time doing is sleeping. Since such a sizable portion of your life is spent on your vocation, it's easy to see why your career can have such a strong influence on your identity and personal happiness. Choosing a career path is one of the most important decisions you'll make in your life, so the process of career exploration and choice should begin right now—during your first year in college. The need to do so is highlighted by a national survey of first-year college student: almost 60% of them strongly agreed that it's important to be thinking about

> "Love and work . . . work and love . . . what else is there really? Love and work are the cornerstones to our humanness."
>
> —*Sigmund Freud, famous psychologist, responding to the question: "What do you humans need to be happy?"*

their career path; however, only 25% reported they had a clear idea on how to achieve their career goals (HERI, 2014).

Even if you have decided on a career that you've been dreaming about since you were a preschooler, you still need to confirm this choice and will likely need to decide on a specialization within your chosen field. For instance, if you're interested in pursuing a career in law, you'll need to decide what branch of law you will practice (criminal law, corporate law, family law, etc.). You will also need to decide what employment sector or type of industry you'd like to work in (e.g., nonprofit, for-profit, education, or government). Thus, no matter how certain or uncertain you are about your career path, you still need to explore specific career options and begin to devise a career development plan.

Strategies for Career Exploration and Preparation

Reaching an effective decision about a career path involves four key steps:

1.

Awareness of *yourself*—insight into your personal, interests, talents, needs, and values

2.

Awareness of your *career options*—knowing the different career choices available to you

3.

Awareness of what career options provide the *best "fit"* for you— knowing what career(s) best match your personal interests, talents, needs, and values

4.

Awareness of the key *steps and strategies* needed to reach your career goal— knowing how to prepare for and gain entry to the career of your choice

In short, effective career decision-making begins with a clear understanding of who you are, where you can go, where you will go, and how you will get there.

Step 1. Awareness of Self

The career you decide to pursue says a lot about who you are, what you want from life, and how you want to impact the lives of others. Thus, self-awareness is the critical first step in the process of career planning. A wise career choice begins with a clear understanding of who you are; from there you can determine where you want to go and how to get there. You must know yourself before you know what career is best for you. While this may seem obvious, self-awareness and self-discovery are often overlooked aspects of the career decision-making process. By deepening your self-awareness, you put yourself in a better position to choose a career path that's true to the person you are and the person you want to be.

Note

Self-awareness is the first and most important step in the career planning process. Meaningful career goals and effective career choices are built on a deep understanding of self.

You can increase your self-awareness by asking yourself questions that stimulate introspection—reflection on your inner qualities and personal priorities. Introspective questions launch you on an inner quest for self-insight and self-discovery which leads you to a career that's consistent with who you are and who you want to be. You can begin this introspective process by asking yourself questions relating to your personal:

- **Interests:** what you *like* doing;
- **Talents:** what you're *good* at doing;
- **Needs:** what you find personally *satisfying* or *fulfilling*; and
- **Values:** what you believe is *important* to do or is *worth* doing.

 Reflection 12.2

Complete the following sentences:

- My primary interests are . . .

- My strongest abilities or talents are . . .

- What brings me the greatest sense of personal satisfaction and fulfillment is . . .

- What I value the most is . . .

(How do your above answers compare with results from the "Your Career Satisfiers" section of your *Do What You Are* report?)

One way to gain greater self-awareness is by taking psychological tests or assessments. These assessments allow you to see how your interests and values compare with other students and with working professionals who are satisfied and successful with their careers. This comparative perspective provides you with an important reference point for assessing whether your level of interest in a career is high, average, or low relative to other students and to professionals working in that field. To take a career interest test, as well as other career exploration assessments, consult the Career Development Office on your campus.

In addition to your personal interests, another factor you should consider when choosing a career is your personal needs. A *need* may be described as something stronger than an interest. When you do something that satisfies a personal need, you're doing something that you find highly motivating and personally fulfilling (Melton, 1995). Psychologists have identified several important human needs that vary in strength or intensity from person to person (Ryan, 1995; Ryan & Deci, 2000). Listed in **Box 12.1** are personal needs that are especially important to consider when making a career choice.

> The unexamined life is not worth living."
>
> *—Socrates, ancient Greek philosopher and a founding father of Western philosophy*

> In order to succeed, you must know what you are doing, like what you are doing, and believe in what you are doing."
>
> *—Will Rogers, Native American humorist and actor*

> I believe following my passion is more crucial than earning money. I think that would come itself eventually."
>
> *—College sophomore responding to the question, "What are you looking for in a career?*

Box 12.1

Personal Needs to Consider When Making Career Choices

After reading about each need in this box, make a note indicating how strong that need is for you (high, moderate, or low).

1. **Autonomy.** Need for working independently without close supervision or control. Individuals with a high need for autonomy experience greater fulfillment working in careers that allow them to be their own boss, make their own choices or decisions, and control their own work schedule. Individuals low in this need may experience greater satisfaction working in careers that are more structured and allow them to work with a supervisor who provides direction, assistance, and frequent feedback.

Our research [on happiness] indicates prosperity is not the most important factor. Personal freedom is more important, and it's freedom in all kinds of ways . . . political freedom and freedom of choice."

—Ronald Inglehart, happiness researcher, University of Michigan

2. **Affiliation (Belongingness).** Need for social interaction, a sense of belonging, and the opportunity to collaborate with others. Individuals with a high need for affiliation experience greater fulfillment working in careers that involve teamwork and frequent interpersonal interaction with coworkers. Individuals low in this need are more likely to be satisfied working alone or in competition with others.

To me, an important characteristic of a career is being able to meet new, smart, interesting people."

—First-year student

3. **Achievement (Competence).** Need to experience challenge and a sense of personal accomplishment. Individuals with high achievement needs feel more fulfilled working in careers that push them to solve problems, generate creative ideas, and continually learn new information or master new skills. Individuals with a low need for achievement are likely to be more satisfied with careers that don't continually test their abilities and don't repeatedly challenge them to stretch their skills with new tasks and different responsibilities.

I want to be able to enjoy my job and be challenged by it at the same time. I hope that my job will not be monotonous and that I will have the opportunity to learn new things often."

—First-year student

4. **Recognition.** Need for prestige, status, and respect from others. Individuals with high recognition needs are likely to feel satisfied working in high-status careers that society perceives as prestigious. Individuals with a low need for recognition would feel comfortable working in a career that they find self-satisfying, regardless of how impressive or enviable their career appears to others.

5. **Sensory Stimulation.** Need for experiencing variety, change, and risk. Individuals with high sensory stimulation needs are more likely to be satisfied working in careers that involve frequent changes of pace and place (e.g., travel), unpredictable events (e.g., work tasks that require them to think on their feet), and some stress (e.g., working under pressure of competition or deadlines). Individuals with a low need for sensory stimulation may feel more comfortable working in careers that involve regular routines, predictable situations, and minimal risk or stress.

For me, a good career is very unpredictable and interest-fulfilling. I would love to do something that allows me to be spontaneous."

—First-year student

Sources: Baumeister & Leary (1995); Chua & Koestner (2008); Deci & Ryan (2002); Ryan (1995)

Don't expect a recluse to be motivated to sell, a creative thinker to be motivated to be a good proofreader day in and day out, or a sow's ear to be happy in the role of a silk purse."

—Pierce Howard, The Owner's Manual for the Brain (2000)

Reflection 12.3

Looking back at the five needs listed in **Box 12.1**, which one(s) did you identify as being strong needs for you?

What career or careers do you think would best match your strongest needs?

As a college junior with half of my degree completed, I had an eye-opening experience. I wish this experience had happened in my first year, but better late than never. When I chose a career during my first year of college, my decision-making process was not systematic and didn't involve critical thinking. I chose a major based on what sounded prestigious and would pay me the most money. Although these are not necessarily bad factors, I failed to use a systematic and reflective process to evaluate my career choice. In my junior year I asked one of my professors why he decided to get his Ph.D. and become a professor. He simply answered, "I wanted autonomy." This was an epiphany for me. He explained that when he reflected on what mattered most to him, he realized that he needed a career that offered independence. So, he began looking at career options that would allow him to work independently. After hearing his explanation, "autonomy" became my favorite word, and this story became a guiding force in my life. After going through a critical introspective process, I determined that autonomy was exactly what I desired and a professor is what I became.

—Aaron Thompson

In sum, four key personal characteristics should be considered when exploring and choosing a career: abilities, interests, values, and needs. As illustrated in **Figure 12.1**, these core characteristics are the pillars that provide the foundational support for making effective career choices and decisions. Ideally, you want to be in a career that you're good at, interested in, passionate about, and brings you a sense of personal satisfaction and fulfillment.

FIGURE 12.1: Personal Characteristics Providing the Foundation for Effective Career Choice

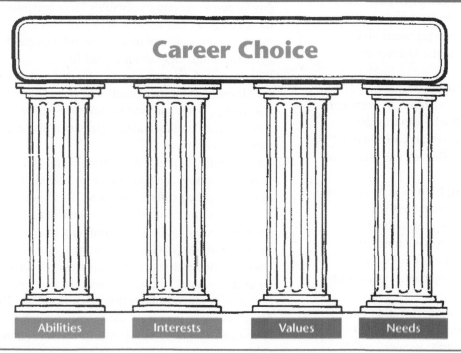

©Kendall Hunt Publishing Company

The opportunity to make a reasonable amount of money is certainly one factor to consider when choosing a career, but a good career choice involves more factors than just starting salary. It's a decision that should also involve deep awareness and strong consideration of your special abilities, what you're passionate about, and what is meaningful to you. It's noteworthy that the word *vocation* derives from the Latin "vocatio" meaning "a calling." This suggests that a career is more than a

> "Know thyself and to thine own self be true."
> —Polonius in Hamlet, *a play by* William Shakespeare

money-making venture; it should call out to you and call forth your true talents and interests.

Step 2. Awareness of Career Options

In addition to self-awareness and knowledge about yourself, effective career decision-making requires knowledge about your range of career options and the realities of the work world. If you were to ask people to name as many careers as they could, they would not come close to naming the 900 career titles listed by the federal government in its Occupational Information Network. There are many more career choices in today's work world than there were for our early ancestors. When you look at the list of occupations in **Box 12.2**—none of which existed ten years ago—you can see how the nature of today's work world is changing more rapidly than at any other time in history.

Box 12.2

Occupations that Didn't Exist Ten Years Ago

1. **App developer:** When you hear "there's an app for that" it's because a career track emerged for program developers who have professional knowledge and skills into the world of mobile devices.

2. **Market research data miner:** Ever wonder how retailers know how to create customized advertisements especially for you? Market researcher data miners collect data on consumer behaviors and predict trends for advertisers to use to develop marketing strategies.

3. **Educational or admissions consultant:** Some parents take extra steps to ensure their children are accepted at the "right" school (from preschool to college). Educational or admissions consultants are hired to guide families through the application and interview process.

4. **Millennial generation expert:** It's now very common to find people from different generations working together in the same organization. Millennial generation experts help employers maximize the potential of their staff by providing advice on working with their youngest employees and mentoring them for future success.

5. **Social media manager:** The business world now makes greater use of social media to market and advertise their products and services. Social media managers target their marketing to users of different social media sites.

6. **Chief listening officer:** Similar to a social media manager, a chief listening officer uses social media to monitor consumer discussions and shares this information with marketing agents so they can design strategies that appeal to various segments of the population.

7. **Cloud computing services:** Most websites used every day by consumers store incredibly large amounts of data. Computer engineers with expertise in data management, store and index tremendous volumes of bytes for companies—about a quadrillion!

8. **Elder care:** Life expectancy is increasing and along with it the need for individuals who possess the knowledge, skills, and compassion to serve the elderly, their families, and the agencies and companies that assist them.

9. **Sustainability expert:** For environmental and economic reasons, companies are now seeking ways to minimize their carbon emissions. This has created a demand for professionals with expertise in the science of sustainability and the ability to develop "green" business practices that are also cost-effective.

10. **User experience design:** User experience designers do exactly what their titles suggest: they create experiences for consumers through technology. These designers use current technology to create color, sound and images by using tools like HTML, Photoshop, and CSS.

Source: Casserly (2012)

(Complete Exercise 12.5 to get an idea about what careers may best match your personal characteristics and life goals.)

Career Information Resources

Listed below are some of the best sources of information about careers. The primary place on campus for locating these sources is likely to be your Career Center. In addition to helping you assess your career interests and abilities, this is also the place where you can learn about the nature of different careers and locate career-related work experiences. Your College Library is another campus resource where you can find a wealth of reading material on careers, either in print or online.

Dictionary of Occupational Titles (DOT) (www.occupationalinfo.org). This is the largest printed resource on careers; it contains concise definitions of more than 17,000 jobs. It also includes information on:

* Work tasks typically performed in different careers
* Background experiences of people working in different careers that qualified them for their positions
* Types of knowledge, skills, and abilities required for different careers
* Personal interests, values, and needs of individuals in different occupations who are satisfied and successful in their line of work

Occupational Outlook Handbook (OOH) (www.bls.gov/oco). This is one of the most widely available and used resources on careers. It contains descriptions of approximately 250 positions, including information on: the nature of the work; work conditions; places of employment; training or education required for career entry and advancement; salaries and benefits; and additional sources of information about particular careers (e.g., professional organizations and governmental agencies associated with a career). A distinctive feature of this resource is that it also contains information about the *future employment outlook* for different careers.

Encyclopedia of Careers and Vocational Guidance (Chicago: Ferguson Press). As the name suggests, this is an encyclopedia of information on entry qualifications, salaries, and advancement opportunities for a wide variety of careers.

Occupational Information Network (O*NET) Online (www.online.onetcenter. org). This is America's most comprehensive online source of online information about careers. It contains up-to-date descriptions of almost 1,000 careers, plus lots of other career-related information similar to what you would find in the *Dictionary of Occupational Titles.*

In addition to these general sources of information, your Career Development Center and College Library should have resources relating to specific careers or occupations (e.g., careers for English majors). You can also learn a great deal about specific careers by simply reading advertisements for position openings in your local newspaper or online (e.g., www.careerbuilder.com and college.monster.com). When reading position descriptions, make special note of the tasks, duties, or responsibilities they involve and ask yourself whether these positions are compatible with your personal talents, interests, needs, and values.

Career Planning and Development Workshops

Periodically during the academic year, your campus is likely to offer programs devoted to career exploration and career preparation. For example, the Career Center may sponsor career exploration or career planning workshops that you can attend for free. Research indicates that career development workshops are effective in helping students plan for and choose careers (Brown & Krane, 2000; Hildenbrand & Gore, 2005). Your Career Center may also organize career fairs on campus, at which professionals working in different career fields have booths where you can visit with them and ask questions about their careers. (See pp. 329–330 for interview questions you can ask working professions about their career.)

Career Development Courses

Your college may offer career development courses for elective credit. These courses typically include self-assessments of your career interests, information about different careers, and strategies for career preparation. Since you need to do career planning while you're enrolled in college, why not do it by enrolling in a career planning course that gives you college credit for doing it? Studies show that students benefit from participating in these courses (Pascarella & Terenzini, 2005).

You may also be able to explore career interests in a writing or speech course that allows you to choose the topic that you write or speak about. If you're given the freedom to choose any topic to research, consider researching a career you're exploring and make that the topic of your paper or presentation.

Another possibility is doing an independent study of a career field you're considering. Typically, an independent study involves an in-depth project you select, write a paper or detailed report, while receiving guidance from an instructor. An independent study allows you to receive academic credit for in-depth study of a topic of your choice without enrolling in a classroom-based course that you attend on a fixed schedule. You could use this independent study option to work on a project related to a career you're exploring. To see if this independent study option is available on your campus, check the college catalog or consult with an academic advisor.

Information Interviews

One of the best and most overlooked ways to get accurate information about a career is to interview professionals working in that career. Career development specialists refer to this strategy as information interviewing. Don't assume that working professionals aren't interested in taking time to speak with a student; most are open to being interviewed and many report they like doing it (Crosby, 2002).

Information interviews provide you with "inside information" about what the career is really like because you're getting it directly from the horse's mouth—the person actually working in the career on a day-to-day basis. Information interviewing also helps you gain experience and confidence in interview situations, which may help you prepare for future job interviews. Furthermore, if you make a good impression during information interviews, the people you interview may suggest that you contact them again after graduation to see if there's a position opening. If there is an opening, you might find yourself being the interviewee instead of the interviewer, and find yourself being hired.

Because interviews can supply you with valuable information about careers and provide possible contacts for future employment, we strongly encourage you to complete the information interview assignment at the end of this chapter.

Career Observation (Shadowing)

In addition to reading about careers and interviewing professionals, you can also learn about careers by observing professionals performing their daily duties in their place of work. Two college-sponsored programs may be available on your campus that will allow you to observe working professionals:

- **Job Shadowing Program.** Following (shadowing) and observing a professional during a typical workday.
- **Externship Program.** An extended version of job shadowing that lasts for a longer time period (e.g., two to three days).

Visit your Career Development Center to learn about what job shadowing or externship programs may be available on your campus. If you're unable to find a campus program for the career field you're exploring, consider finding one on your own by using strategies similar to the recommendations for information interviews at the end of this chapter. It's basically the same process; the only difference is that instead of asking the person for an interview, you're asking if you could observe that person at work. In fact, you could ask the person who granted you an information interview if you could observe (shadow) that person at work. Just a day or two of job shadowing can give you valuable information about a career.

Reflection 12.4

If you were to interview or observe a working professional in a career that interests you, what type of work would that person be doing?

Information interviewing, job shadowing, and externships supply you with great information about a career. However, information is not experience. To get career-related work *experience*, you've got four major options:

* Internships
* Cooperative education programs
* Volunteer work or service learning
* Part-time work

Internships

In contrast to job shadowing and externships—which involve observing someone at work—an internship actively involves you in the work itself and gives you an opportunity to perform career-related work duties. A distinguishing feature of internships is that you can receive academic credit and sometimes financial compensation for the work you do. Usually, an internship involves a total of 120 to 150 work hours, which may be completed at the same time you're enrolled in classes, or at a time when you're not taking classes (e.g., summer internship).

A key advantage of internships is that they enable you to escape the classic catch-22 situation that college graduates often run into when interviewing for their first career position. The interview scenario usually goes something like this: The potential employer asks the college graduate, "What work experience have you had in this field?" The recent graduate replies, "I haven't had any work experience because I've been a full-time student." You can avoid this scenario by completing an internship during your college experience. Participating in at least one internship while you're enrolled in college will enable you to beat the "no experience" rap after graduation and distinguish yourself from other college graduates. Surveys show that more than 75% of employers prefer candidates with internships (National Association of Colleges & Employers, 2010); students with internships are more likely to acquire career-relevant work skills while in college and find immediate employment after college (Hart Research Associates, 2006, 2014; Pascarella & Terenzini, 2005).

Internships are typically available to college students during their junior or senior year; however, some campuses offer internships for first- and second-year students as well. Check with your Career Center if this option may be available to you.

> "Give me a history major who has done internships and a business major who hasn't, and I'll hire the history major every time."
>
> —*William Ardery, senior vice president, Investor Communications Company*

You can also pursue internships on your own by consulting published guides that list various career-related internships and provide information on how to apply for them (e.g., *Peterson's Internships* and the *Vault Guide to Top Internships*). You can also find internships on websites such as www.internships.com or www.vaultreports. com. Lastly, information on internships may be available from the local chamber of commerce in your hometown, or in the city where your college is located.

Cooperative Education (Co-op) Programs

Co-op programs are similar to internships but involve work experiences that last longer than one academic term and often require students to stop their coursework temporarily to participate in the program. Some co-op programs, however, allow you to continue to take classes while working part time at a co-op position; these are sometimes referred to as "parallel co-ops." Students are paid for participating in co-op programs and their co-op experience is officially noted on their college transcript, but no academic credit is awarded (Smith, 2005).

Typically, co-ops are only available to juniors or seniors, but you can begin now to explore co-op programs by reviewing your college catalog and visiting your Career Development Center to see if co-op programs are available in a career field you're pursuing. If you find one, build it into your educational plan because it can provide you with authentic and extensive career-related work experience.

The value of co-ops and internships is strongly supported by research, which indicates that students who have these experiences during college:

- Are more likely to report that their college education was relevant to their career;
- Receive higher evaluations from employers who recruit them on campus;
- Have less difficulty finding an initial position after graduation;
- Are more satisfied with their first career position following graduation; and
- Earn higher starting salaries (Gardner, 1991; Knouse, Tanner, & Harris, 1999; Pascarella & Terenzini, 1991, 2005).

When employers are asked to rank various factors they consider important when hiring new college graduates, internships or cooperative education programs receive the highest ranking (National Association of Colleges & Employers, 2012a, 2014a). Employers also report that when full-time positions open up in their organization or company, they usually turn first to their own interns and co-op students (National Association of Colleges & Employers, 2013).

Volunteer Work or Service Learning

Volunteer service not only gives you the opportunity to serve your community, it also gives you the opportunity to explore different work environments and gain work experience in career fields relating to your area of service. For example, volunteer work performed for different age groups (children, adolescents, or the elderly) and in different work environments (hospital, school, or laboratory) provides you with firsthand, resume-building experience and the opportunity to test your interest in careers related to these age groups and work environments. Volunteer experience also enables you to network with professionals who can serve as personal references for you and provide you with letters of recommendation. Furthermore, if these professionals are impressed with your service, they may hire you on a part-time basis while you're still in college, or full-time after you graduate.

To get an idea of the wide range of career-related service opportunities that may be available to you, go to: www.usa.service.org. You may also get volunteer experience through *service learning* courses at your college that integrate these experiences into coursework. Volunteer service may be incorporated into the course as a required or optional assignment whereby you participate in the volunteer experience and then reflect on your experience in a paper or class presentation.

Another course-integrated option for gaining work experience is by enrolling in courses that include a *practicum* or *field work*. For instance, if you're interested in working with children, courses in child psychology or early childhood education may offer experiential learning opportunities in a preschool or daycare center on campus.

Lastly, it may be possible to do volunteer work on campus in different college offices, or by assisting a faculty member. Volunteering as a research or teaching assistant can be a very valuable experience if you intend to go to graduate school. If you have a good relationship with faculty members in an academic field that interests you, consider asking them whether they would like some assistance with their teaching or research responsibilities. You might also check out your professors' web pages to find out what type of research projects they're working on; if any of these projects interest you or relate to a career path you're considering, contact the professor and offer your help. Volunteer work done for a college professor could lead to your making a presentation with your professor at a professional conference or may even result in your name being included as a coauthor on an article published by the professor.

AUTHOR'S EXPERIENCE

I was once advising two first-year students, Kim and Christopher. Kim was thinking about becoming a physical therapist and Chris was thinking about becoming an elementary school teacher. To help Kim get a better idea if physical therapy was the career for her, I suggested that she visit a hospital near our college to inquire about whether she could do volunteer work in the physical therapy unit. As it turned out, the hospital did need volunteers, so she volunteered in the physical therapy unit and loved it. That volunteer experience confirmed for Kim that a physical therapist is what she wanted to be. She completed a degree in physical therapy and is now a professional physical therapist.

Similarly, I suggested to Chris that he test his interest in possibly becoming an elementary school teacher by visiting some local schools to ask about whether they could use a volunteer teacher's aide. One of the schools did need his services, so Chris volunteered as a teacher's aide for about 10 weeks. About two weeks into his volunteer experience, he came into my office to tell me that the kids were just about driving him crazy and he no longer had any interest in becoming a teacher! He ended up majoring in communications.

Kim and Chris were the first two students I advised to get involved in volunteer work to test their career interests. Their volunteer experiences proved to be so useful in helping them identify their career path that I continued to encourage all students I advised to get volunteer experience in the career field they were considering.

—*Joe Cuseo*

 Reflection 12.5

If you have participated in volunteer experiences, did you learn anything about yourself from these experiences that might influence your career plans, or acquire skills that could be applied to a future career?

Part-Time Work

Jobs you hold during the academic year or summer break shouldn't be overlooked as career development experiences. Part-time work can supply you with opportunities to develop skills and personal qualities that may be relevant to any future career you decide to pursue, such as organizational skills, communication skills, and ability to work effectively with coworkers from diverse backgrounds and cultures. It's also possible that work in a part-time position may eventually turn into a full-time career—as illustrated in the following story.

AUTHOR'S EXPERIENCE

While he was enrolled in college a former student of mine (Matt), an English major, worked part-time for an organization that provides special assistance to mentally handicapped children. After he completed his English degree, the organization offered him a full-time position that he accepted. While working full-time at this position with handicapped children, Matt decided to go to graduate school part-time and eventually completed a master's degree in special education. This degree qualified him for a promotion to a more advanced position in the organization, which he also accepted. Moral of the story: Part-time work in college can play an important role in opening up a future career path.

—*Joe Cuseo*

It might also be possible for you to obtain part-time work experience on campus through your school's work-study program. Work-study jobs can be done in a variety of campus settings (e.g., Financial Aid Office, Library, Public Relations Office, or Computer Services Center), and they can be built around your course schedule. Just like off-campus work, on-campus work can provide you with valuable career exploration and resume-building experiences, and the professionals for whom you work can also serve as excellent references for letters of recommendation to future employers. To see whether you are eligible for your school's work-study program, visit the Financial Aid Office on your campus. If you don't qualify for work-study jobs, ask about other forms of campus employment that are not funded through the work-study program.

There's simply no substitute for gaining knowledge about careers than direct, hands-on learning experience in actual work settings—such as shadowing, internships, volunteer services, and part-time work. These firsthand experiences represent the ultimate career "reality test." They allow you direct access to what careers are really like—as opposed to the glamorized and unrealistic picture of them portrayed in the media.

> "As entertainment, TV shows are great. As reality, they fall a little short. So enjoy your TV and movies, but don't make career decisions based on them."
>
> —*Katharine Brooks, author,* You Majored in What? Mapping Your Path from Chaos to Career

Note

A key characteristic of effective goal setting is to set goals that are realistic. In the case of career goals, getting firsthand experience in actual work settings allows you to get a realistic view of what work in a field is really like—before committing to that field as your career goal.

Tying it altogether, experiencing work in real-life work settings has five powerful career advantages:

- You get a realistic picture of what work is like in a particular field
- You get to test your interests and skills for certain types of work
- You strengthen your resume by adding experiential learning to academic (classroom) learning
- You acquire contacts who can serve as personal references and sources for letters of recommendation

- You network with employers who may hire you or refer you for a position after graduation.

In addition, getting work experience *early* in college makes you a more competitive candidate for internships and part-time positions you may apply for later in your college experience.

To locate and participate in work experiences that relate to your career interests, use all resources available to you, including campus resources (e.g., the Career Development Center and Financial Aid Office), local resources (e.g., Chamber of Commerce), and personal contacts (e.g., family and friends). Take these experiences seriously, learn as much as you can from them, and build relationships with the people you work with—these are the people who can provide you with future contacts, references, and referrals. Don't forget that almost three of every four jobs are obtained through personal relationships, a.k.a. "networking" (Brooks, 2009).

 Reflection 12.6

1. Have you had work experiences that may influence your future career plans, or provided you with skills you can include on your resume?

2. If you could get work experience in any career field right now, what would it be?

Step 3. Awareness of Career Options that Provide the Best "Fit" for You

As we've emphasized throughout this chapter, the factor that should carry the greatest weight in career decision-making is the match between your career choice and your personal talents, interests, needs, and values. Since a career choice is a long-range decision that affects your life well beyond college, the process of self-awareness should not only involve reflection on who you are now, but also on how your career choice relates to where you see yourself in the future. Ideally, your choice of a career should be one that leads to the best-case future scenario in which your typical day goes something like this: You wake up in the morning and hop out of bed enthusiastically—eagerly looking forward to what you'll be doing at work that day. When you're at work, time flies by; before you know it, the day's over. When the workday is done, you feel good about what you did and how well you did it. For this ideal scenario to become a reality, you should make every attempt to select a career path that is true to yourself—a path that leads you to a career that's "in sync" with your abilities (what you do well), your interests (what you like to do), your values (what you feel good about doing), and your needs (what provides you with a sense of satisfaction and personal fulfillment).

Effective career decision-making requires identifying all relevant factors that should be factored into your decision and determining how much weight (influence) each of these factors should carry. A good career decision should involve more than determining whether a career is currently "hot" (in demand) and lucrative (high starting salary). It should involve thoughtful consideration of how the career affects different dimensions of yourself (social, emotional, physical, etc.) at different stages of your life (young adulthood, middle age, and late adulthood). Your career will influence your life in ways beyond earning a living; it will affect the balance between the demands of work and family, your level of stress, and how much

> More people today have the means to live, but no meaning to live for."
>
> *—Viktor Frankl, Austrian neurologist, psychiatrist, and Holocaust survivor*

> "I think that a good career has to be meaningful for a person. It should give a person a sense of fulfillment."
>
> —First-year student

difference you make in the lives of others. In short, an effective career choice is one that not only enables you to earn a living, but also brings meaning and purpose to your life.

 Reflection 12.7

Answer the following questions about a career you're considering or have chosen:

1. Why are you attracted to this career? (What led or caused you to become interested in it?)

2. Would you say that your interest in this career is characterized primarily by *intrinsic* motivation—something "inside" of you, such as your personal abilities, interests, needs, and values? Or, would you say that your interest in the career is driven by *extrinsic* motivation—something "outside" of you, such as starting salary, pleasing your family, or meeting expectations of your gender (i.e., an expected career role for a male or female)?

3. If money weren't an issue and you could earn a comfortable living working in another career, would you still continue to pursue the same career you're currently considering?

> "It's easy to make a buck. It's a lot tougher to make a difference."
>
> —Tom Brokaw, award-winning television journalist and author

Step 4. Awareness of the Major Steps Needed to Reach Your Career Goal

Whether you're keeping your career options open or you think you've already decided on a particular career, you can start now by taking early steps for successful entry into any career by using the following strategies.

Self-Monitoring: Watching and Tracking Your Skills and Attributes

Keep in mind that the *academic* skills you're developing in college are also *professional* skills you'll use beyond college. Said in another way, learning skills become earning skills. When you're engaged in the process of completing academic tasks—such as note-taking, reading, writing papers and taking tests—you're also developing career-relevant skills—such as listening, interpreting, analyzing, and problem solving.

What matters more to employers of college graduates than their degree credentials or the courses on their transcript are the skills and personal qualities they've developed and can bring to the position (Education Commission of the States, 1995; Figler & Boles, 2007). You can start building these skills and qualities through effective *self-monitoring*—that is, monitoring (watching) yourself and tracking the skills you're using and developing during your college experience. Skills are habits, and like other habits which are repeatedly practiced, their development can be so gradual and subtle that you may not even notice how much growth has taken place (like watching grass grow). Thus, career development specialists recommend that you consciously and carefully reflect on the skills you're using so you remain aware of their development and are able to articulate them to potential employers (Lock, 2004).

One way to track your developing skills is by keeping a *learning journal* in which you reflect on the academic tasks and assignments you've completed, along with the skills you developed while completing them. Your journal should also include skills developed outside the classroom—such as those acquired through co-curricular experiences, leadership development programs, volunteer experiences, and part-time jobs.

Since skills are actions, it's best to track and record them in your journal as *verbs*. You're likely to find that many of these action verbs reflect the type of work-related skills that employers seek in today's job candidates. **Box 12.3** contains a sample of action-oriented career skills you're likely to develop in college that are relevant to successful performance in a variety of careers.

Box 12.3

Transferable Skills Relevant to Successful Career Performance

The following behaviors represent a sample of flexible skills that are relevant to success in virtually all careers (Bolles, 1998; Figler & Bolles, 2007). As you track your learning experiences in college, remain mindful of whether you're developing these (and other) skills, both inside and outside the classroom.

advise	create	initiate	present	sequence
assemble	delegate	measure	produce	summarize
calculate	design	motivate	research	supervise
coach	evaluate	negotiate	resolve	synthesize
coordinate	explain			

In addition to tracking your skills, also keep track of the positive traits and attributes you're developing. While skills are best recorded as *verbs* because they represent actions you can perform for anyone who hires you, personal attributes are best recorded as *adjectives* because they describe who you are and what positive qualities you can bring to any position. **Box 12.4** below identifies examples of personal traits and attributes that are relevant to successful performance in any career.

Box 12.4

Personal Traits and Attributes Relevant to Successful Career Performance

As you proceed through college, keep track of these and other personal attributes or character traits you are developing.

collaborative	conscientious	considerate	curious	dependable
determined	energetic	enthusiastic	ethical	flexible
imaginative	industrious	loyal	observant	open-minded
outgoing	patient	persuasive	positive	precise
prepared	productive	prudent	punctual	reflective
sincere	tactful	team player	thorough	thoughtful

 Reflection 12.8

Look back at the personal skills and traits listed in **Boxes 12.3** and **12.4**. Underline or highlight those that you think are relevant to the career(s) you're considering.

After class one day, I had a conversation with a student of mine (Max) about his personal interests. He said he was considering a career in the music industry and was working part-time as a disc jockey at a night club. I asked him what it took to be a good disc jockey, and in less than five minutes of talking about his part-time work, we discovered that there were many transferable career skills embedded in his job than he realized. Each night he worked, he was responsible for organizing three to four hours of music; he had to read the reactions of his audience (customers) and adapt or adjust his selections to their musical tastes; he had to arrange his selections in a sequence that varied the tempo of music he played throughout the night; and he had to continually research and update his music collection to track the latest trends in hits and popular artists. His job also required him to deliver public announcements, which enabled him to overcome his fear of public speaking.

Although we were just having a short, friendly conversation after class about his part-time work, Max ended up reflecting on and identifying multiple skills he was developing on the job. We both agreed that it would be a good idea for him to get these skills down in writing so he could use them as selling points for future jobs in the music field, or any other line of work he might eventually pursue.

—Joe Cuseo

Note

Embedded in your work and class experiences are transferable skills and personal qualities that are applicable to a variety of careers. Tracking these skills and qualities and articulating them to potential employers is as important to successful entry into a future career as the courses listed on your transcript and the major listed on your resume.

Self-Marketing: Packaging and Presenting Your Personal Strengths and Achievements

> "Man who stand on hill with mouth open will wait long time for roast duck to drop in."
>
> *—Confucius, Chinese philosopher*

Studies show that students who convert their college degree into a successful career have two common characteristics: personal initiative and a positive attitude (Pope, 1990). They don't take a passive approach and assume a good position will just fall into their lap; nor do they believe they are owed a position simply because they have a college degree or credential. Instead, they take an active role involved in defining their strengths and showcasing them in the job-search process (Brown & Krane, 2000).

One way you can convert your college degree into gainful employment is to view yourself (a college graduate) as a product and view employers as customers who may be interested in purchasing your product (your skills and attributes). As a first-year student, it could be said that you're in the early stages in the process of developing your product. Begin the process now by identifying and packaging your skills and attributes so by the time you graduate you'll have a well-developed product that potential employers will be interested in purchasing.

> "The bottom line for most employers is 'Will this person fit in our environment?' One of the keys to marketing yourself is to make a connection, to get out of your mindset and into your audience's."
>
> *—Katharine Brooks, author, You Majored in What? Mapping Your Path from Chaos to Career*

By developing an effective self-marketing plan, you give employers a clear idea of what you can bring to the table and do *for them*. You can market your personal skills, qualities, and achievements to future employers through the following formats.

Course Transcript

Your course transcript is a listing of all courses you enrolled in and the grades you received in those courses. Two pieces of information included on your college transcript can strongly influence employers' hiring decisions or admissions committee decisions about your acceptance to a graduate or professional school: (a) the grades you earned in your courses and (b) the types of courses you completed.

Simply stated, the better grades you earn in college, the better are your employment prospects after college. Research on college graduates indicates that the higher their grades, the higher is:

* The prestige of their first job
* Their total earnings (salary and fringe benefits)
* Their job mobility (ability to change jobs or positions).

This relationship between higher college grades and career advantages holds true for students at all types of colleges and universities, regardless of the perceived reputation or prestige of the school they attended (Pascarella & Terenzini, 1991, 2005).

Co-curricular Experiences

Participation in student clubs, campus organizations, and other types of cocurricular activities represent a valuable source of experiential learning that complements classroom-based learning and contributes to career preparation and development. A sizable body of research supports the power of these experiences for career success (Astin, 1993; Hart Research Associates, 2006, 2014; Kuh, 1993; Pascarella & Terenzini, 1991, 2005). Co-curricular experiences that are especially relevant to career development and career success are those that:

* Allow you to develop leadership and mentoring skills—such as, participating in leadership retreats, student government, college committees, peer counseling, or peer tutoring.
* Enable you to interact with others from diverse ethnic and racial groups—such as, multicultural or international clubs and organizations.
* Relate to your academic major or career interests—such as, involvement in student clubs in your college major or intended career field.

Don't forget that co-curricular experiences are also resume-building experiences; they serve as evidence of social responsibility to your communities on and off campus. Be sure to showcase these experiences to prospective employers. Also, don't forget that campus professionals with whom you may interact while participating in co-curricular activities (e.g., the director of student activities or dean of students) can serve as valuable references and provide you with letters of recommendation to future employers, graduate schools, or professional schools.

Personal Resume

A resume may be described as a listed or bulleted summary of your most important accomplishments, skills, and credentials. If you haven't yet accumulated enough experiences to construct a fully developed resume, you can start building a "skeletal resume" that contains major categories or headings (the skeleton) which you'll eventually flesh out with your specific experiences and accomplishments. (See **Box 12.5** for a sample skeleton resume.)

Box 12.5

Constructing a Skeletal Resume

Use this skeletal resume as an outline or template or blueprint to begin constructing your personal resume and setting future goals. (If you have already created a resume, use this template to identify and add categories that may be missing from your current one.)

NAME
(First, Middle, Last)

Current Addresses: *Permanent* Addresses:
Postal address   Postal address
E-mail address   E-mail address
Phone no.   Phone no.

EDUCATION: Name of College or University, City, State
                  Degree Name (e.g., Bachelor of Science)
                  College Major (e.g., Accounting)
                  Graduation Date
                  GPA

RELATED WORK   Position Title, City, State   Start and stop dates
EXPERIENCES: (Begin the list with the most recent experiences.)

(List skills you used or developed.)

VOLUNTEER (COMMUNITY SERVICE) EXPERIENCES
(List skills you used or developed.)

NOTABLE COURSEWORK
(e.g., leadership, interdisciplinary, or intercultural courses; study abroad experiences)

CO-CURRICULAR EXPERIENCES
(e.g., student government or peer leadership)
(List skills you used or developed.)

PERSONAL SKILLS AND POSITIVE QUALITIES
(List as bullets; be sure to include those that are especially relevant to the position for which you're applying.)

HONORS AND AWARDS
(Include those received prior to college and outside of college)

PERSONAL INTERESTS:
(Include special hobbies or talents that may not be directly tied to your school or work experiences)

Portfolio

Unlike a resume, which simply lists your experiences, a portfolio contains actual products or samples of your work. You may have heard the word "portfolio" referred to as a collection of artwork that professional artists put together to showcase or advertise their artistic ability. However, the term *portfolio* has a broader meaning;

it can be a collection of any material that depicts a person's skills and talents, or demonstrates educational and personal development. For example, a portfolio could include items such as:

- Outstanding papers, exam performances, research projects, and lab reports
- Work samples and photos from study abroad experiences, service learning, and internships
- Video footage of oral presentations and public performances
- Performance evaluations received from professors, student development professionals, and employers
- Letters of recognition or commendation from professors, student development professionals, and employers.

©Kendall Hunt Publishing Company

The ritual of burning completed coursework in high school is not recommended in college. Instead, save your best work, and include it in a personal portfolio.

As a first-year student, you can begin the process of portfolio development right now by saving your best work and performances, including those done in classes, co-curricular experiences on campus, or service and work experiences off campus. Store them in a traditional portfolio folder, or save them on your computer to create an electronic portfolio. You could also create a website and upload your materials there. Eventually, you should be able to build a well-stocked portfolio that showcases your skills and demonstrates your achievements to future employers or future schools.

Reflection 12.9

What do you predict will be your best work products in college—those that you would most likely showcase in a portfolio?

Why?

Letters of Recommendation (Letters of Reference)

The quality of your letters of recommendation will be strengthened if you give careful thought to (a) who will serve as your references, (b) how to approach them, and (c) what to provide them. Specific strategies for doing so are summarized in **Box 12.6**.

Box 12.6

The Art and Science of Requesting Letters of Recommendation: Effective Strategies and Common Courtesies

1. Select recommendations from people who know you well. Think about individuals with whom you've had an ongoing relationship, who know you by name, and who have observed your strongest performances and skills. Good candidates are instructors who you've had for more than one course, an academic advisor whom you see often, or an employer who has witnessed your work habits for an extended period of time.

2. Seek a balanced blend of letters from people who have observed your performance in different settings or situations. The following are performance-based settings where people may have observed how well you performed:
    *   The classroom—a professor who can speak to your academic performance
    *   On campus—a student life professional who can comment on your contributions to a club or organization
    *   Off campus—a professional for whom you've performed volunteer service, part-time work, or an internship

3. Pick the right time and place to make your request. Be sure to request letters of recommendation well in advance of the letter's deadline date (at least two weeks). First, ask the person if he or she is willing to write you a letter of recommendation. Don't approach the person with the form in your hand because it may send the message that you have assumed the person will say yes or are pressuring the person to say yes. This isn't the most socially sensitive message to send someone whom you're about to ask a favor.

    Also, pick a place and time where the person can give full attention to your request. Make a personal visit to the person's office, rather than making the request in a busy hallway or in front of a classroom full of students.

4. Provide your references with a fact sheet about yourself. Include your experiences and achievements—both inside and outside the classroom. This will help make your references' job a little easier by providing points for them to focus on. It's also likely to make your letter stronger because it will contain specific examples that draw directly from your personal experiences and accomplishments. On your fact sheet, be sure to include high grades you may have earned in certain courses, as well as volunteer services, leadership experiences, awards or forms of recognition, and special interests or talents relevant to your academic major and career choice. Your fact sheet is the place to "toot your own horn," so don't fear coming across as a braggart. You're not being boastful or showboating; you're just highlighting your strengths.

5. If the letter is to be mailed, provide your references with a stamped, addressed envelope. This is a simple courtesy that makes their job easier and demonstrates your social sensitivity.

6. Waive your right to see the letter. If you have the option to waive (give up) your right to see the letter of recommendation, waive your right—as long as you feel reasonably certain that you will receive a good

Box 12.6 *(continued)*

letter of recommendation. By waiving your right to see the letter, you show confidence that the letter will be positive and assures the person reading the letter that you didn't inspect or screen it to ensure it was good before sending it.

7.   Follow up with a thank you note. Send this note at about the time your letter of recommendation should be sent. This is the right thing to do because it shows your appreciation; it's also the smart thing to do because if the letter hasn't been sent, the thank you note serves as a gentle reminder to your reference that the letter should be sent soon.

8.   Let your references know the outcome of your application. If you've been offered the position or been admitted to the school to which you applied, let your references know. This is the socially sensitive thing to do, plus your references are likely to notice and remember your social sensitivity—which should strengthen the quality of any future letters of recommendation you may request from them.

 Reflection 12.10

Have you met anyone on campus who you think could write a letter of recommendation for you?

If you have, who is this person, and what position does he or she hold on campus?

If you haven't, who might be a good future candidate?

Chapter Summary and Highlights

Reaching an effective decision about a career path involves four forms of awareness:

1.   Awareness of *self*—insight into your personal interests, talents, needs, and values
2.   Awareness of your *career options*—knowledge of different career fields available to you
3.   Awareness of what options provide the *best "fit" for you*—knowing what careers most closely match your personal interests, talents, needs, and values
4.   Awareness of the major *steps needed to reach your career goal*—knowing how to prepare for and gain entry into the career of your choice

You can gain valuable information about careers by:

•   Accessing printed and online career resources (e.g., *Dictionary of Occupational Titles; Occupational Outlook Handbook*)
•   Taking career development courses
•   Attending career fairs on campus
•   Conducting information interviews with professionals in careers that interest you
•   Shadowing (observing) professionals at work
•   Engaging in service learning, internships, or cooperative education programs

Here's what you can do while you're in college to increase your prospects for career success after college:

- **Take time for self-reflection and introspection**—deepen your self-awareness so that you choose a career path that's compatible with your personal interests, talents, values, and needs. Also reflect on and keep track of the skills and personal qualities you're developing so you can successfully "sell yourself" to future employers.
- **Use your Career Center**—capitalize on all the career exploration, preparation, and placement opportunities this campus resource has to offer.
- **Get involved in work-related experiences outside the classroom**—such as job shadowing, service learning, internships, and co-op programs.
- **Interact and collaborate**—network with students in your major, college alumni, and career professionals.
- **Create a skeletal resume**—one that contains major categories or headings (the skeleton), which you'll eventually flesh out with your experiences and accomplishments.
- **Start building a portfolio**—save your best work and performances, including those that take place in courses, co-curricular experiences on campus, and service or work experiences off campus. Store them in a traditional portfolio folder, or save them on your computer to create an electronic portfolio.

> "Life just doesn't hand you things. You have to get out there and make things happen."
>
> *—Emeril Lagasse, award-winning American chef, cookbook author, and TV celebrity*

In national surveys, employers rank attitude of the job applicant as the number one factor in making hiring decisions. They rate this factor higher in importance than reputation of the applicant's school, previous work experience, and recommendations of former employers (Education Commission of the States, 1995; Institute for Research on Higher Education, 1995; National Association of Colleges & Employers, 2012b, 2014b). However, many college students think that it's the degree itself—the credential or piece of paper—that will get them the career they desire (Association of American Colleges & Universities, 2007).

Graduating from college with a diploma in hand may make you a more competitive job candidate, but you still have to compete by documenting and selling your strengths and skills. Your diploma doesn't work like a merit badge or passport that's flashed to gain automatic access to your dream job. Your college experience opens career doors for you, but it's your attitude, initiative, and effort that enable you to step through those doors and into a successful career.

Learning More through the World Wide Web: Internet-Based Resources

For additional information on career exploration, preparation, and development, see the following websites:

Assessing Your Strengths, Talents and Values:
www.authentichappiness.sas.upenn.edu

www.viacharacter.org

Developing a Personalized Career Plan:
www.mappingyourfuture.org

Navigating the Job Market:
http://meldi.snre.umich.edu/navigating_the_job_market/Salary+Negotiations

Career Descriptions and Future Employment Outlook:
www.bls.gov/

Internships:
www.internships.com

http://www.vault.com/

Position Openings and Opportunities:
www.rileyguide.com

www.monster.com

Resume Writing and Job Interviewing:
www.quintcareers.com

References

AAC&U (Association of American Colleges and Universities). (2007). *College learning for the new global century*. A report from the National Leadership Council for Liberal Education & America's Promise. Washington, DC: Association of American Colleges and Universities.

Astin, A. W. (1993). *What matters in college?* San Francisco: Jossey-Bass.

Baumeister, R., & Leary, M. R. (1995). The need to belong: Desire for interpersonal attachments as a fundamental human motivation. *Psychological Bulletin, 117*, 497–529.

Bolles, R. N. (1998). *The new quick job-hunting map*. Toronto, Ontario, Canada: Ten Speed Press.

Brooks, K. (2009). *You majored in what? Mapping your path from chaos to career*. NY: Penguin.

Brown, S. D., & Krane, N. E. R. (2000). Four (or five) sessions and a cloud of dust: Old assumptions and new observations about career counseling. In S. D. Brown & R. W. Lent (Eds.), *Handbook of counseling psychology* (3rd ed., pp. 740–766). New York: Wiley.

Casserly, M. (2012). "10 jobs that didn't exist 10 years ago." *Forbes*. Retrieved from http://www.forbes.com/sites/meghancasserly/2012/05/11/10-jobs-that-didnt-exist-10-years-ago/.

Chua, S. N., & Koestner, R. (2008). A self-determination theory perspective on the role of autonomy in solitary behavior. *The Journal of Social Psychology, 148*(5), 645–647.

Crosby, O. (2002). Informational interviewing: Get the scoop on careers. *Occupational Outlook Quarterly* (Summer), 32–37.

Deci, E., & Ryan, R. (Eds.). (2002). *Handbook of self-determination research*. Rochester, NY: University of Rochester Press.

Education Commission of the States. (1995). *Making quality count in undergraduate education*. Denver, CO: ECS Distribution Center.

Figler, H., & Bolles, R. N. (2007). *The career counselor's handbook*. Berkeley, CA: Ten Speed Press.

Gardner, P. D. (1991, March). *Learning the ropes: Socialization and assimilation into the workplace*. Paper presented at the Second National Conference on the Senior Year Experience, San Antonio, TX.

Hart Research Associates. (2006). *How should colleges prepare students to succeed in today's global economy?* Based on surveys among employers and recent college graduates. Conducted on behalf of the Association of American Colleges and Universities. Washington, DC: Author.

Hart Research Associates. (2014. July). *How should colleges prepare students to succeed in today's global economy?* Retrieved from http://dpdproject.info/details/how-should-colleges-prepare-students-to-succeed-in-todays-global-economy-peter-d-hart-research-associates/.

HERI (Higher Education Research Institute). (2014). *Your first college year survey 2014*. Los Angeles, CA: Cooperative Institutional Research Program, University of California-Los Angeles.

Hildenbrand, M., & Gore, P. A., Jr. (2005). Career development in the first-year seminar: Best practice versus actual practice. In P. A. Gore (Ed.), *Facilitating the career development of students in transition* (Monograph No. 43, pp. 45–60). Columbia: National Resource Center for the First-Year Experience and Students in Transition, University of South Carolina.

Institute for Research on Higher Education. (1995). Connecting schools and employers: Work-related education and training. *Change, 27*(3), 39–46.

Knouse, S., Tanner, J., & Harris, E. (1999). The relation of college internships, college performance, and subsequent job opportunity. *Journal of Employment Counseling, 36*, 35–43.

Kuh, G. D. (1993). In their own words: What students learn outside the classroom. *American Educational Research Journal, 30*, 277–304.

Lock, R. D. (2004). *Taking charge of your career direction* (5th ed.). Belmont, CA: Brooks Cole.

Melton, G. B. (1995). *The individual, the family, and social good: Personal fulfillment in times of change*. Nebraska Symposium on Motivation, Volume 42. Lincoln, NE: University of Nebraska Press.

National Association of Colleges & Employers. (2010). *2009 experiential education survey*. Bethlehem, PA: Author.

National Association of Colleges & Employers. (2012a). *Internship and co-op survey*. Bethlehem, PA: Author.

National Association of Colleges & Employers. (2012b). *Job outlook: The candidate skills/qualities employers want*. Bethlehem, PA: Author.

National Association of Colleges & Employers. (2013). *Job outlook: The candidate skills/qualities employers want.* Retrieved from http://www.naceweb.org/s10022013/job-outlook-skills-quality.aspx.

National Association of Colleges & Employers. (2014a). *2014 Internship and co-op survey, executive summary.* Retrieved from https://www.naceweb.org/uploadedFiles/Content/static-assets/downloads/executive-summary/2014-internship-co-op-survey-executive-summary.pdf.

National Association of Colleges & Employers. (2014b). *Job outlook 2015: The candidate skills/qualities employers want, the influence of attributes.* Retrieved from http://www.naceweb.org/s11122014/job-outlook-skills-qualities-employers-want.aspx.

Pascarella, E., & Terenzini, P. (1991). *How college affects students: Findings and insights from twenty years of research.* San Francisco: Jossey-Bass.

Pascarella, E., & Terenzini, P. (2005). *How college affects students: A third decade of research* (Vol. 2). San Francisco: Jossey-Bass.

Pope, L. (1990). *Looking beyond the Ivy League.* New York: Penguin Press.

Ryan, R. (1995). Psychological needs and the facilitation of integrative processes. *Journal of Personality, 63,* 397–427.

Ryan, R. M., & Deci, E. L. (2000). Self-determination theory and the facilitation of intrinsic motivation, social development, and well-being. *American Psychologist, 55,* 68–78.

Smith, D. D. (2005). Experiential learning, service learning, and career development. In P. A. Gore (Ed.), *Facilitating the career development of students in transition* (Monograph NO. 43 pp. 205–222). Columbia, SC: National Resource Center for the First-Year Experience and Students in Transition, University of South Carolina.

Chapter 12 Exercises

12.1 Quote Reflections

Review the sidebar quotes contained in this chapter and select two that were especially meaningful or inspirational to you. For each quote, provide a three- to five-sentence explanation why you chose it.

12.2 Reality Bite

Career Choice: Conflict and Confusion

Josh is a first-year student whose family has made a great financial sacrifice to support his college education. He deeply appreciates the sacrifice his family members have made and wants to pay them back as soon as possible. Consequently, he's been looking into careers that offer the highest starting salaries immediately after graduation. Unfortunately, none of these careers seem to match Josh's natural abilities and personal interests. He's now conflicted, confused, and worried. He knows he'll have to make a decision soon because the careers with high starting salaries involve majors that have many course requirements. If he expects to graduate in four years, he'll have to start taking some of these courses next semester.

Reflection and Discussion Questions

1. If you were Josh, what would you do?

2. Do you see any way that Josh might balance his desire to pay back his family as soon as possible with his desire to pursue a career that's compatible with his interests and talents?

3. What questions or factors do you think Josh should consider before making his decision about a career?

4. Can you relate to Josh's story, or do you know of students in a similar predicament?

12.3 Gaining Self-Awareness of Personal Interests, Talents, and Values

No one is in a better position to discover who you are, and who you want to be, than *you*. One effective way to gain deeper self-insight is through self-questioning. You can become more self-aware by asking yourself questions that cause you to think carefully about your inner qualities and characteristics. Responding honestly to the following questions can sharpen awareness of your true interests, abilities, and values. As you read each question, briefly note what thought(s) come to mind about yourself.

Personal Interests

1. What tends to grab your attention and hold it for long periods of time?

2. What sorts of things are you naturally curious about or frequently intrigue you?

3. What do you really enjoy doing and do as often as you possibly can?

4. What do you look forward to, or get excited about?

5. What are your favorite hobbies or pastimes?

6. When you're with your friends, what do you like to talk about or spend time doing?

7. What has been your most stimulating or enjoyable learning experience?

8. If you've had previous work or volunteer experience, what jobs or tasks did you find most interesting or stimulating?

9. When time seems to "fly by" for you, what are you usually doing?

10. What do you like to read about?

11. When you open a newspaper or log onto the Internet, where do you tend to go first?

12. When you find yourself daydreaming or fantasizing about your future, what is it usually about?

From your responses to the above questions, identify a career that appears to be most compatible with your personal *interests*? Note the career and your interests that are compatible with it.

Personal Talents and Abilities

1. What seems to come naturally to you?

2. What would you say is your greatest talent or personal gift?

3. What are your most advanced or well-developed skills?

4. What seems to come easily to you that others have to work harder to do?

5. What would you say has been your greatest personal accomplishment or achievement in life thus far?

6. What about yourself are you most proud of, or that you take most pride in doing?

7. When others come to you for advice or assistance, what is it usually for?

8. What would your best friend(s) say is your best quality, trait, or characteristic?

9. When you've done something that left you feeling like you really were successful, what was it that you did?

10. If you have received awards or other forms of recognition, what have they been for?

11. On what types of learning tasks or activities have you experienced the most success?

12. In what types of courses do you tend to earn the highest grades?

From your responses to the above questions, identify a career that appears to be most compatible with your personal *talents* and *abilities*. Note the career and your talents and abilities that are compatible with it.

> Never desert your line of talent. Be what nature intended you for and you will succeed."
>
> —Sydney Smith, 18th-century English writer and defender of the oppressed

Personal Values

1. What matters most to you?

2. If you were to single out one thing you really stand for or believe in, what would it be?

3. What would you say are your highest priorities in life?

4. Whenever you get the feeling you've done what was good or right, what was it that you did?

5. If there were one thing in the world you could change, improve, or make a difference in, what would it be?

6. When you have extra spending money, what do you usually spend it on?

7. When you have free time, what do you usually find yourself doing?

8. What does living a "good life" mean to you?

9. How would you define success? (What would it take for you to feel that you achieved success?)

10. How do you define happiness? (What would it take for you to be happy?)

11. Do you have a hero or anyone you admire, look up to, or feel has set an example worth following? (If yes, who and why?)

12. Would you rather be thought of as:

    a) smart,

    b) wealthy,

> To love what you do and feel that it matters— how could anything be more fun?"
>
> —Katharine Graham, former CEO of the Washington Post and Pulitzer Prize–winning author

> Success is getting what you want. Happiness is wanting what you get."
>
> —Dale Carnegie, author of the best-selling book, How to Win Friends and Influence People and founder of The Dale Carnegie Course—a worldwide program for business based on his teachings

c) creative, or

d) caring?

(Rank from 1 to 4, with 1 being the highest)

From your responses to the above questions, identify a career that appears to be most compatible with your personal *values*. Note the career and your values that are compatible with it.

12.4 Visualizing Your Ideal Career

Project yourself ten years into the future and visualize your ideal career and your ideal life.

1. What are you spending most of your time doing during your typical workday?

2. Where and with whom are you working?

3. How many hours are you working per week?

4. Where are you living?

5. Are you married? Do you have children? How does your work influence your home life?

12.5 Career Self-Assessment Survey

1. Complete the *Do What You Are* survey, and review the results about the careers recommended to you.
   a) How well do you think these suggestions match your personal identity and life goals?
   b) Which suggestions match more closely? Which don't seem to match. Why?

2. Click on the "Career Titles" for the suggested careers that interest you and then click on the "Tasks and Activities" tab for the careers you think are a good fit. Read the descriptions provided.
   a) How closely do they match what you thought these careers to be? Are the knowledge and skills required what you expected they'd be?
   b) Do these descriptions excite or disappoint you? Explain.

12.6 Conducting an Information Interview

One of the best ways to acquire accurate information about a career is to interview a working professional in that career. This career exploration strategy is known as an *information interview*. An information interview enables you to (a) get an insider's view of what the career is really like, (b) network with a professional in the field, and (c) gain confidence in interview situations that prepares you for future job interviews.

Steps in the Information Interview Process

1. Select a career you may be interested in pursuing. Even if you're currently keeping your career options open, pick a career that might be a possibility. You can use the resources cited on p. 309 in this chapter to help you identify a career that may be most appealing to you.

2. Find someone in the career you've selected and set up an information interview with that person. To locate possible interview candidates, consider members of your family, friends of family members, and family members of your friends. Any of these people may be working in the career you are considering and may be good interview candidates, or they may know others who could be good candidates. The Career Development Center on your campus, as well as the Alumni Association or the Rotaract Club may also be able to provide you with contacts who are willing to talk about their careers with students—such as alumni or professionals working in the local community near your campus. The Yellow Pages or the Internet may be other sources for locating interview candidates.

3. Once you've identified someone you would like to interview, send that person a short letter or e-mail asking about the possibility of scheduling a short interview and mention that you would be willing to conduct the interview in person or by phone—whichever would be more convenient. If you don't hear back within a reasonable period (7–10 days), send a follow-up message. If you don't receive a response to the follow-up message, try contacting someone else.

4. After you have found someone to interview, here are some strategies for conducting the interview:

- **Thank the person for taking the time to speak with you.** This should be the first thing you do after meeting the person—before you officially begin the interview.

- **Prepare your interview questions in advance.** Here are some questions that you might consider asking:

    1) During a typical day's work, what tasks occupy most of your time?

    2) What do you like most about your career?

    3) What are the most difficult or frustrating aspects of your career?

    4) What personal skills or qualities do you see as being critical for success in your career?

    5) How did you decide on your career?

    6) What personal qualifications or prior experiences enabled you to enter your career?

    7) How does someone find out about openings in your field?

    8) What steps did you take to locate your current position?

    9) What advice would you give first-year students about what they might do at this stage of their college experience to begin preparing for a career in your field?

    10) How does someone advance in your career?

    11) Are there any moral issues or ethical challenges that tend to arise in your career?

    12) Are members of diverse groups likely to be found in your career? (This is an especially important question to ask if you're a member of an ethnic, racial, or gender group that is underrepresented in the career field.)

    13) What impact does your career have on your home life or personal life outside of work?

    14) If you had to do it all over again, would you choose the same career?

    15) Would you recommend that I speak with anyone else to obtain additional information or a different perspective on your career field? (If the answer is "yes," you may follow up by asking: "May I mention that you referred me?") It's always a good idea to obtain more than one person's perspective before making any important choice, such as your career choice.

- **Take notes during the interview.** This not only helps you remember what was said, it also sends a positive message to the persons you interview because it shows them that their ideas are important and noteworthy (worth taking notes on).

- **If the interview goes well, consider asking if it might be possible to observe or shadow that person at work.**

Self-Assessment Questions

After completing your interview, take a moment to reflect on it and answer the following questions:

1. What information did you receive that impressed you about the career?

2. What information did you receive that distressed (or depressed) you about the career?

3. What was the most useful piece of information you took away from the interview?

4. Based on the information you acquired during the interview, would you still be interested in pursuing a career in this field? Why?

12.7 Creating a Skeletal Resume

Review the headings of a skeletal resume described on p. 320.

1. Under each heading, list any experiences or skills that you've already acquired.

2. Add to each heading (in a different color) any experiences or skills you plan to acquire during your college years.

3. Review your entries under each heading and identify those skills that might result in work products you could include in a personal portfolio. (See p. 321 for samples of work products that could be included in a portfolio.)

Financial Literacy

MANAGING MONEY AND MINIMIZING DEBT

Research shows that accumulating high levels of debt in college is associated with higher stress, lower academic performance, and greater risk of withdrawing from college. The good news is that research also shows that students who learn to use effective money-management strategies are able to minimize unnecessary spending, reduce accumulation of debt and stress, and improve the quality of their academic performance. This chapter identifies effective strategies for tracking income and expenses, minimizing and avoiding debt, balancing time spent on schoolwork and employment, and making wise financial choices in college.

Chapter Preview

Become more aware, knowledgeable, and strategic about managing money, financing your college education and handling your future finances.

Learning Goal

 Reflection 13.1

Ignite Your Thinking

Complete the following sentence with the first thought that comes to mind:

To me, money is . . .

For many students, starting college marks the start of greater personal independence and greater responsibilities for financial self-management and decision-making. The issue of money management for college students is growing in importance for a number of reasons. The rising cost of a college education has resulted in more students working more hours while attending college (Perna & DuBois, 2010). The higher cost of a college education also requires more difficult fiscal decisions about what options (or combination of options) to use to meet college expenses. Unfortunately, research indicates that many students today are making decisions about financing their college education in ways that do not effectively promote their academic success and progress to graduation (King, 2005).

Another reason why money management is growing in importance for college students is the availability and convenience of credit cards. It's never been easier for college students to access, use, and abuse credit cards. Credit agencies and bureaus now closely monitor college students' credit card payments and routinely report their "credit score" to credit card companies and banks. Since research shows that there is a statistical relationship between using credit cards responsibly and being a responsible employee (Rivlin, 2013), employers check these credit scores and use them as indicators or predictors of how responsible a student will be as an employee. Thus, being irresponsible with credit while in college can affect a student's ability to land a job after (or during) college. Students' credit scores also affect their likelihood of qualifying for car loans and home loans as well as their ability to rent an apartment (Pratt, 2011). College graduates today can do everything right while they were in college, such as get good grades, get involved on campus, and get work experience before graduating, but a poor credit history as college students can harm them after college—reducing their chance of obtaining credit and their job prospects (Rivlin, 2013). Furthermore, accumulating high levels of debt while in college is associated with higher levels of student stress (Nelson, et al., 2008), lower academic performance (Susswein, 1995), and greater risk of withdrawing from college (Ring, 1997). On the positive side of the ledger, studies show that when college students learn to use effective money-management strategies (such as those discussed below), they can reduce unnecessary spending, minimize accumulation of debt, and lower their overall level of stress (Kidwell & Turrisi, 2004; Palan, et al., 2011).

Sources of Income for Financing a College Education

College students' income typically comes from three sources:

- Loans that must be repaid,
- Scholarships or grants that are not repaid, and
- Salary earned from part-time or full-time work.

The *Free Application for Federal Student Aid (FAFSA)* is the application used by the U.S. Department of Education to determine financial aid eligibility for students. It asks for personal and family financial information to determine a student's eligibility for federal, state, and college-sponsored financial aid, including grants, loans, and work-study employment. A formula is used to determine the student's *estimated family contribution (EFC)*—the amount of money estimated by the government that a family can contribute to the educational costs incurred by a family member attending college.

No fee is charged to complete the application, so you should complete an application every year to determine your eligibility for financial aid. (See the Financial Aid Office on your campus for a copy of the FAFSA form and for help completing it.)

Student Loans

Loans need to be repaid after a student graduates from college. Listed below are some of the more well-known, federally funded student loan programs.

- *The Federal Perkins Loan:* a low-interest loan awarded to exceptionally needy students. Repayment of the loan begins nine months after a student is no longer enrolled at least half-time.
- *The Federal Subsidized Stafford Loan:* available to students enrolled at least half-time has a fixed interest rate established each year on July 1. The federal government pays the interest on the loan while the student is enrolled. Repayment for this loan begins six months after a student is no longer enrolled at least half-time.

- *The Federal Unsubsidized Stafford Loan:* a loan not based on need that has the same interest rate as the Federal Subsidized Stafford Loan. Students are responsible for paying the interest on this loan while they're enrolled in college.

Keep in mind that federal loans and private loans differ in the following ways:

- *Federal* loans have fixed interest rates that are comparatively low (currently less than 7%) and cannot go higher.
- *Private* loans have variable interest rates that are very high (currently more than 15%) and can go higher at any time.

Despite the much higher interest rate of private loans, they're the fastest growing type of loans taken out by college students—largely because of aggressive, and sometimes misleading, irresponsible, or unethical advertising on loan-shopping websites. Students sometimes think they're getting a federal loan only to find out later they've taken on a more expensive private loan (Hamilton, 2012; Kristof, 2008).

Keep in mind that not all loans are created equal. Compared to private loans, federally guaranteed student loans are relatively low-cost and may be paid off slowly after graduation. On the other hand, private lenders of student loans are like credit card companies; they charge extremely high interest rates (that can go even higher at any time) and the loans must be paid off quickly. Private loans should not be used as a primary loan to help pay for college and they should only be used as a last resort—when no other options are available for covering college expenses.

Also, keep in mind that federal and state regulations require that if you're receiving financial aid, you must maintain "satisfactory academic progress." In most cases this means you must do the following:

1. Maintain a satisfactory GPA—such as, 2.0 or above. Your entire academic record will be reviewed, even if you have paid for some of the classes with your own resources.
2. Make satisfactory academic progress—such as, 12 to 15 units per semester. Your academic progress will be evaluated at least once per year, usually at the end of each spring semester to determine if you have earned at least 67% of your attempted credits.
3. Complete a degree or certificate program within an established period of time. (Check with your institution's Financial Aid Office for details.)

If you happen to find yourself temporarily short of funds and need just a small loan to recover, many colleges have an *emergency student loan program*, whereby they provide students with an immediate, interest-free loan to help them cover short-term expenses (e.g., cost of textbooks) or deal with financial emergencies (e.g., accidents and illnesses). Emergency student loans are typically granted within 24–48 hours, sometimes even the same day, and usually need to be repaid within two months.

Scholarships

Typically, scholarships are awarded at the time of admission to college, but some scholarships may be awarded to students at a later point in their college experience. Scholarships tend to fall into two general categories:

> Apply for as much grant aid as possible before borrowing, and then seek lower-interest federal student loans before tapping private ones. There is a lot of student aid that can help make the expense [of college] more manageable."
>
> *—Sandy Baum, senior policy analyst, College Board (quoted in Gordon, 2009)*

- *Merit-based scholarships*—awarded on the basis of performance or achievement, and
- *Need-based scholarships*—awarded on the basis of financial need.

To find out about scholarships you may still be eligible to receive, either a merit-based or need-based scholarship, visit your Financial Aid Office.

Scholarships are also available from sources other than the institution you've chosen to attend. You can conduct an Internet search to find sites that offer scholarship information. Keep in mind that scholarships are very competitive and deadlines are strictly enforced.

Grants

Grants are considered to be "gift" aid because they don't have to be repaid. Grants vary in amount, depending on such factors as: (a) the anticipated contribution of the family to the student's education (EFC), (b) the cost of the postsecondary institution that the student is attending, and (c) the enrollment status of the student (part-time or full-time).

The Federal Pell Grant is the largest grant program; it provides need-based aid to low-income undergraduate students. The percentage of undergraduate students receiving Pell Grants increased from 23% in 2002–03 to 36% in 2012–13 (College Board, 2013).

Veterans Benefits

If you are currently a veteran, you may be eligible for the GI Bill benefits. The Montgomery GI Bill (MGIB) provides educational benefits for eligible veterans that include, but are not limited to, tuition and fees, housing allowance, and stipends for books or supplies. Veterans need to maintain certain academic standards to receive the benefits. For details, see if your campus has an office for veteran affairs, or consult the following website: http://www.benefits.va.gov/gibill/.

Salary Earnings

If you're relying on salary from off-campus work to pay for college tuition, check with your employer to see if the company you're working for offers tuition reimbursement. Also, check with the Student Accounts Office on your campus to determine whether payment plans are available that allow you to pay tuition costs on an installment schedule that aligns with the timing of your paychecks. These tuition-payment plans may provide you with some flexibility in terms of amount due per payment, deadlines for payments, and how remaining debt owed to the institution is dealt with at the end of the term. (Keep in mind that your college may not allow you to register for the following term until tuition for the previous term has been completely paid.)

If possible, try to find work *on campus* rather than off campus. Research shows that when students work on campus they're more likely to succeed in college (Astin, 1993; Pascarella & Terenzini, 1991, 2005). This is probably due to the fact that they become more connected to the college (Cermak & Filkins, 2004; Tinto, 1993) and because on-campus employers are more flexible than off-campus employers in allowing students to meet their academic commitments (Leonard, 2008). For instance, on-campus employers are more willing to schedule students' work hours around their class schedule and allow students to modify their work schedule when their academic workload increases (e.g., at midterm and finals). Thus, if at all possible, rather than seeking work off campus, try to find work on campus and capitalize on its proven capacity to promote college success.

 Reflection 13.2

If you're using any of the following financial resources to help pay for your college education, circle it: loans, grants, scholarships, salary earnings, savings, monetary support from parents or other family members, other resources.

Which of the above resources is the primary or main source of funding for your college education?

Developing a Money Management Plan

Gain Financial Self-Awareness

Development of any good habit begins with the critical first step of self-aware-ness. Developing effective money-management habits begins with awareness of your *cash flow*—the amount of money you have coming in and going out. As illustrated in **Figure 13.1**, cash flow is tracked by monitoring:

- Income—the amount of money you have coming in versus the amount going out (expenses or expenditures), and
- Savings—the amount of money you've earned and not spent versus the amount of you've borrowed and haven't paid back (debt).

Once you're aware of the amount of money you have coming in (and from what sources) plus the amount of money you're spending (and for what reasons), your next step is to develop a plan for managing your cash flow. The bottom line is to ensure that the sum of money you have coming in (income) is equal to or greater than the sum of money you have going out (expenses). If the amount of money going out exceeds the amount coming in, you're "in the red" or have "negative cash flow."

FIGURE 13.1: **The Two-Way Street of Cash Flow**

Income ⟷ Expenses

Savings ⟷ Debt

©Kendall Hunt Publishing Company

> Never spend your money before you have it."
>
> —Thomas Jefferson, third president of the United States and founder of the University of Virginia

Track Your Cash Flow

You can track cash flow by using any of the following tools:

- Checking accounts
- Credit cards
- Charge cards
- Debit cards

Checking Accounts

Long before credit cards were created, a checking account was the method most people used to keep track of their money. Many people still use checking accounts in addition to (or instead of) credit cards. A checking account may be obtained from a bank or credit union; its typical costs include a deposit ($20–$25) to open the account, a monthly service fee (e.g., $10), and small fees for checks. Some banks charge customers a service fee based on the number of checks written; this is a good option if you don't plan to write many checks each month. Look for a checking account that doesn't charge you if your balance drops below a certain minimum figure. If you maintain a high enough *balance* (deposited money in your account) the bank may not charge any extra fees, and if you're able to maintain an even higher balance, some banks may also pay you interest—known as an interest-bearing checking account.

Along with your checking account, banks usually provide you with an automatic teller machine (ATM) card that you can use to get cash. Look for a checking account that offers a free service along with your checking account, rather than one that charges a separate fee for ATM transactions.

A checking account has several advantages:

- You can carry checks instead of cash.
- You have access to cash at almost any time through an ATM.
- You can keep a visible track record of your income and expenses in your checking account.
- If you manage a checking account responsibly, it can serve as a good credit reference for future loans and purchases.

To make the best use of your checking account, apply the following strategies:

- Whenever you write a check or make an ATM withdrawal, immediately subtract its amount from your *balance* (the amount of money remaining in your account) and determine your new balance.
- Keep a running balance in your checking account; this will ensure you know exactly how much money you have in your account at all times. It also reduces your risk of *bouncing* a check—writing a check for an amount that exceeds the total amount you have in your account. If you do bounce a check, you'll probably have to pay a charge to the bank and possibly to the business that attempted to cash your bounced check.

Double-check your checking account balance with each monthly statement you receive from the bank. Be sure to include the service charges your bank makes to your account; these charges will appear on your monthly statement. Checking your checking account on a regular basis will enable you to catch errors that you've made or the bank has made. (Banks can and do occasionally make mistakes.) Also, track your monthly statements to ensure that the charges that appear were not the result of identity theft.

Credit Cards

A credit card is basically money loaned to you by the credit card company issuing the card, which you pay back to the company on a monthly basis. You can pay the whole bill or a portion of the bill each month—as long as some minimum payment is made. However, for any remaining (unpaid) portion of your bill, you're charged a high interest rate—which can be as much as 30%. Consequently, if you decide to use a credit card, be sure you're able to pay off your whole bill (loan) each month.

If a credit card is used responsibly, it has some key advantages as a money management tool:

- It helps you track your spending habits because the credit card company sends you a monthly statement with an itemized list of all your card-related purchases. This list supplies you with a "paper trail" of what you purchase each month and when you purchased it.

- It provides a convenient way for you to purchase things you need online, which can save time and money that would otherwise be spent traveling to and from stores.

- It allows access to cash whenever and wherever you need it because any bank or ATM that displays your credit card's symbol will give you cash up to a certain limit (usually for a small transaction fee). Keep in mind that some credit card companies charge a higher interest rate for cash *advances* than credit card *purchases*.

- It enables you to establish a personal credit history. If you use a credit card responsibly, you can establish a good credit history that can be used later in life for big ticket purchases—such as a car or home. In effect, responsible use of a credit card shows others from whom you wish to seek credit (or borrow money) that you will pay it back. However, don't buy into the belief that the only way you can establish a good credit history is by using a credit card. It's not your only option; you can also establish a good credit history by responsible use of a checking account and by paying your bills on time.

If you decide to use a credit card, pay attention to its *annual percentage rate (APR)*—the interest rate you pay for previously unpaid monthly balances. This rate can vary from one credit card company to another. Credit card companies also vary in terms of their annual service fee. You'll find that companies charging higher interest rates also charge lower annual fees, and vice versa. As a general rule, if you expect to pay the full balance every month, you're probably better off choosing a credit card that doesn't charge you an annual service fee. On the other hand, if you think you'll need more time to make the full monthly payments, you're probably better off with a credit card company that offers a low interest rate.

Credit card companies also differ from one another in terms of whether they allow a *grace period*—the amount of time you have after receiving your monthly statement to pay back the company without paying additional interest fees. Some companies may allow you a grace period of a full month, while others may provide no forgiveness period and begin charging interest immediately after a payment isn't received by the bill's due date.

Credit cards also differ in terms of their *credit limit* (also known as a "credit line" or "line of credit"), which is the maximum amount of money the credit card company will make available to you. If you're a new customer, most companies will set a credit limit beyond which no additional credit will be granted.

There are advantages of using a credit card, but those advantages are only reaped by using credit cards strategically. If not, its advantages are quickly and greatly outweighed by its disadvantages. Listed here are some strategies for using a credit card that maximize its advantages and minimize its disadvantages.

- **Use a credit card for making purchases conveniently and for tracking the purchases you make; don't use it as a tool for obtaining a long-term loan.** A credit card's main money-management advantage is that it enables you to make purchases with plastic instead of cash. It saves you the inconvenience of having to carry cash or checks and conveniently supplies you with a monthly statement of your purchases, making it easier for you to track and analyze your spending habits.

     The credit provided by a credit card should be seen simply as a short-term loan that must be paid back at the end of every month. Don't use credit cards for long-term credit or long-term loans because their interest rates are outrageously high. Paying such a high rate of interest for a loan is an ineffective (and irresponsible) money-management strategy.

- **Limit yourself to one credit card.** Having more than one credit card means having more accounts to keep track of and more opportunities to accumulate debt. You don't need additional credit cards from department stores, gas stations, or any other profit-making business because they duplicate what your personal credit card already does (plus they typically charge extremely high interest rates for late payments).

- **Make sure you know the specific terms of the agreement.** Credit card companies vary in terms of what they will charge you for not paying your full bill on time and what restrictions they will impose on further use of your card if you accumulate debt. Be sure to read the fine print on your contract; if you have any doubts or questions, contact a representative of the credit card company.

- **Pay off your balance each month** *in full* and *on time*. If you pay the full amount of your bill each month, this means you're using your credit card effectively to obtain an interest-free, short-term (1-month) loan. You're just paying *principal*—the total amount of money borrowed and nothing more. However, if your payment is late and you end up paying interest, you're paying more for the items you purchased than their actual ticket price. For instance, if you have an unpaid balance of $500 on your monthly credit bill for merchandise purchased the previous month and you're charged the typical 18% credit card interest rate for late payment, you end up paying $590: $500 (merchandise) + $90 (18% interest to the credit card company).

Credit card companies make their profit by the interest they collect from cardholders who don't pay back their credit on time. Just as procrastinating about completing schoolwork is a poor time-management habit that hurts your grades, procrastinating about paying your credit card bills is a poor money-management habit that hurts your pocketbook by forcing you to pay high interest rates.

Don't allow credit card companies to make profit at your expense. Pay your total balance on time and avoid paying exorbitantly high interest rates. If you can't pay the total amount owed at the end of the month, instead of making the minimum monthly payment, pay as much as you possibly can. If you keep making only the minimum payment each month, you'll begin piling up huge amounts of debt.

Note

If you keep making charges on your credit card while you have an unpaid balance (debt), you no longer have a grace period to pay back your charges; instead, interest is charged immediately on all your purchases.

> "What I don't do that I know I should do is pay my bills on time, like my cell phone and credit cards."
> —*First-year student*

> "I need to pay attention to my balance more closely and actually allot certain amounts for certain things."
> —*First-year student*

> "You'll never get your credit card debt paid off if you keep charging on your card and make only the minimum monthly payment. Paying only the minimum is like using a Dixie cup to bail water from a sinking boat."
> —*Eric Tyson, financial counselor and national best-selling author of Personal Finance for Dummies*

Reflection 13.3

Do you have a credit card? Do you have more than one?

If you have at least one credit card, do you pay off your entire balance each month?

If you don't pay off your entire balance each month:

a) What's your average unpaid balance per month?

b) What changes would you have to make in your money-management habits to be able to pay off your entire balance each month?

Charge Cards (a.k.a. Smart Cards)

A charge card works similar to a credit card in that you're given a short-term loan for one month; the only difference is that you must pay your bill in full at the end of each month and you cannot carry over any debt from one month to the next. Its major disadvantage relative to a credit card is that it has less flexibility—no matter what your expenses may be for a particular month, you must still pay up or lose your ability to obtain credit for the following month. However, if you're someone who consistently has trouble paying your monthly credit card bill on time, this is an advantage of a charge card because it will prevent you from accumulating debt.

Debit Cards

A debit card looks almost identical to a credit card (e.g., it has a *MasterCard* or *Visa* logo), but it works differently. When you use a debit card, money is immediately taken out or subtracted from your checking account. Like a check or ATM withdrawal, any purchase you make with a debit card is immediately subtracted from your balance. Thus, you can only use money that's already in your account (rather than borrowing money). At the end of the month, you don't receive a bill; instead, you get a statement with information about checks you deposited and cashed, as well as your debit card transactions. If you attempt to purchase something with a debit card that costs more than the amount of money you have in your account, your card will not allow you to do so. Similar to a bounced check, a debit card will not permit you to pay out any money that's not in your account.

Like a credit card, a major advantage of the debit card is that it provides you with the convenience of plastic; however, unlike a credit card, it prevents you from spending beyond your means and accumulating debt. For this reason, many financial advisors recommend using a debit card rather than a credit card (Knox, 2004; Tyson, 2012).

Box 13.1

Minimize Your Risk of Identity Theft

Identity thieves steal your personal information to make transactions or purchases in your name. This can damage your credit status and cost you time and money to restore your financial credibility. Listed below are key strategies for reducing your risk of identity theft.

- Don't share personal identity information over the phone with anyone you don't know and trust, especially your social security or credit card number.
- Don't share identity information over the phone with anyone who claims to be an Internal Revenue Service (IRS) agent and threatens you with arrest or deportation, or who requests personal information for the purpose of sending you a refund. The IRS will contact you in writing if it needs anything.
- Don't respond to e-mails from anyone claiming to be from the IRS. This is always a scam because the IRS doesn't initiate contact with taxpayers by e-mail or social media to request personal or financial information. (The only legitimate communication you will receive from the IRS is through postal mail.)
- Don't click on links or open e-mail attachments from anyone unfamiliar to you. Scam artists create fake websites and send "phishing" e-mails—which are attempts to acquire personal information such as usernames, passwords, and credit card details, often using the names of trustworthy electronic sources (e.g., an Internet service provider).
- Don't enter your credit card or bank account information on any websites.
- Install firewalls and virus detection software on your computer to protect yourself against "cyber crime."
- When using your laptop in public, shield your screen from "shoulder surfers."
- Don't carry your Social Security (SSN) card in your wallet or write it on your checks. Only give out your SSN to people you know and trust.

(continued)

Box 13.1 *(continued)*

- Conceal your personal identification number (PIN). Don't supply it to anyone and don't keep it in your wallet.
- Shred documents containing personal information you no longer need. (Some identity thieves are "dumpster divers" who go through the garbage to get your personal information.)
- Compare your receipts with your account statements and credit card statements to be sure there are no transactions you didn't authorize. If you have an online account, you can check your account at any time. It's a good idea to get in the habit of checking it at least once a week (e.g., every Sunday evening).
- If you believe you've been victimized by identity theft, contact your local police department and any of the following credit reporting companies to place a fraud alert:

Experian: https://www.experian.com/freeze/center.html

TransUnion: https://freeze.transunion.com/sf/security-Freeze/landingPage.jsp

Equifax: https://www.freeze.equifax.com/Freeze/jsp/SFF_PersonalIDInfo.jsp

Sources:
Prevent and Report Identity Theft: https://www.irs.gov/Individuals/Identity-Protection

Identity Protection Tips—Internal Revenue Service: https://www.irs.gov/Individuals/Identity-Protection-Tips

Tips to Avoid Identity Theft: http://www.bbb.org/sacramento/news-events/consumer-tips/2015/03/how-to-avoid-identity-theft/

Developing a Plan for Managing Money and Minimizing Debt

The ultimate goal of money management is to save money and dodge debt. Here are some strategies for accomplishing both of these goals.

Prepare a personal budget. A budget is simply a plan for coordinating income and expenses in a way that ensures you're left with sufficient money to cover your expenses. It enables you to be your own accountant who keeps an accurate account of your own income and expenses.

Sources of expense for college students typically fall into three categories:

1. *Basic needs or essential necessities*—these are "fixed" expenses because you can't live without them—such as, expenses for food, housing, tuition, textbooks, phone, transportation to and from school, and health-related costs
2. *Incidentals or extras*—these are "flexible" expenses because they're optional or discretionary—you choose to spend at your own discretion or judgment. These expenses usually include:
   - money spent on entertainment, enjoyment, or pleasure (e.g., music, movies, and Spring break vacations), and
   - money spent on promoting personal status or self-image (e.g., buying expensive brand name products, fashionable clothes, jewelry, and other personal accessories)
3. *Emergency expenses*—unpredicted, unforeseen, or unexpected expenditures (e.g., costs incurred by unanticipated car repairs or medical services)

 Reflection 13.4

What are your most expensive incidentals (optional purchases)?

What could you do to reduce or eliminate these expenses?

Similar to managing your time, the first step in planning and managing money is to prioritize. Identify your most important expenses—the indispensable necessities you can't live without—and separate them from incidentals—dispensable luxuries you can live without and can be reduced or eliminated if necessary. People easily confuse *essentials* (things they really *need*) with *desirables* (stuff they just *want*). For instance, if a piece of merchandise happens to be on sale, it may be a desirable purchase at that time because of its reduced price; however, it's not an essential purchase if you don't need that piece of merchandise at that particular time.

Note

Remaining aware of the distinction between essentials *that must be purchased and* incidentals *that may or may not be purchased is an important first step toward budgeting effectively and minimizing debt.*

> I shouldn't buy random stuff (like hair dye) and other stuff when I don't need it."
> —*First-year student*

Postponing short-term satisfaction of material desires contributes to long-term financial success. Unfortunately, humans are often more motivated by short-range thinking because it produces quicker results and more immediate gratification (Goldstein & Hogarth, 1997; Lowenstein, Read, & Baumeister, 2003). This is why so many people pile up credit card debt; they choose to experience the short-term pleasure of the immediate purchase instead of postponing gratification to save money in the long run.

We need to remain mindful of whether we're spending money *impulsively* on what we want rather than *reflectively* on what we need. The truth is that humans spend money for a host of psychological reasons (conscious or subconscious), many of which are unrelated to actual need. Some people spend money to build their self-esteem or self-image, to combat personal boredom, or because of the emotional "high" they experience when they buy things for themselves (Dittmar, 2004; Furnham & Argyle, 1998). Other people can become obsessed with spending money, shop compulsively, and develop an addiction to purchasing products. Just as Alcoholics Anonymous (AA) functions as a support group for alcoholics, Debtors Anonymous serves as a support group for shopaholics that has a similar 12-step recovery program.

> I need to save money and not shop so much and impulse buy."
> —*First-year student*

> My money management skills are poor. If I have money, I will spend it unless somebody takes it away from me. I am the kind of person who lives from paycheck to paycheck."
> —*First-year student*

AUTHOR'S EXPERIENCE

I was a student who had to manage my own college expenses, so I soon became an expert in managing small budgets. The first thing I always took care of was my tuition. I was going to go to school even if I starved. The next thing I budgeted for was food, housing, clothing, and transportation needs. If I ran out of money, I would then work additional hours if it didn't interfere with my school work.

Rather than making and spending money while I was in college, I was working to make a better future life for myself. To be successful, I had to be a great money manager because there was so little of it to manage. This took a lot of focus and strong will, but did it pay off? Absolutely.

—*Aaron Thompson*

Note

What you're willing to sacrifice and save for, and what you're willing to spend on and go into debt for, says a lot about who you are and what you value.

Make all your bills visible and, if possible, pay them as soon as you see them. When bills are in your sight, they're on your mind and you're less likely to forget to pay them, or forget to pay them on time. Try to get in the habit of paying a bill as soon as you open it and have it in your hands, rather than setting it aside and running the risk of forgetting to pay it (or losing it altogether).

You can increase the visibility of your bill payments by creating and posting a financial calendar on which you record key fiscal deadlines for the academic year (e.g., due dates for tuition payments, residential bills, and financial aid applications). Also, consider setting up an online banking program that will enable you to visually track your transactions and make credit card payments automatically. The advantage of an online account is that it's paperless and you don't have to deal with bills sent to you through postal mail. However, its disadvantage is that it doesn't appear in tangible form in your mailbox—which provides you with clear, visual reminder to pay it. So, if you set up an online account, get into an ongoing habit of checking it. Otherwise, what's out of sight stays out of mind and your bills may not get paid on time.

Live within your means. Simply stated: Don't purchase what you can't afford. If you're spending more money than you're taking in, it means you're living *beyond* your means. To begin living *within* your means, you have two options:

1. Decrease your expenses (reduce your spending), or
2. Increase your income (earn more money).

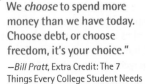

> We *choose* to spend more money than we have today. Choose debt, or choose freedom, it's your choice."
>
> —*Bill Pratt,* Extra Credit: The 7 Things Every College Student Needs to Know About Credit, Debt & Cash

Most college students work while attending college (Kingkade, 2014) and they work so many hours that it interferes with their academic performance and educational progress (King, 2005). Thus, for most college students who find themselves in debt, their best option is not to work more hours for more money, but to reduce their spending on nonessentials and live within their means.

 Reflection 13.5

Are you working while attending college?

If you're working:

a) How many hours per week do you currently work?

b) Are you working for things you need or want?

c) Do you think that working is interfering with your academic performance or progress?

Economize. Intelligent consumers use critical thinking skills when purchasing products. We can be frugal or thrifty without compromising the quality of our purchases. We could pay less to see the same movie in the late afternoon than to see it at night. Why pay more for brand name products that are exactly the same as less expensive products? For instance, why pay 33% more for Advil or Tylenol when we can get the same pain-relieving ingredient (ibuprofen or acetaminophen) from a generic brand? When we buy brand name products, what we're often paying for is all the advertising these brand name companies pay the media and celebrities to promote their products.

Note

Advertising creates product familiarity, not product quality. The more money manufacturers pay for advertising and creating well-known brands, the more money we pay for their product.

Downsize. Cut down or cut out spending for products you don't need. Avoid conspicuous consumption or exhibitionistic (look-at-me) spending just to keep up with or show off to your friends. Don't allow peer pressure to determine your spending habits; your consumer decisions should reflect your ability to think critically, not your desire to conform socially.

Save money by living with others rather than living alone. You lose some privacy when you share living quarters, but you save a substantial amount of money. Living with others may also bring with it the fringe social benefit of spending time with people (roommates or housemates) with whom you're compatible and whose company you enjoy.

Give gifts of time instead of money. Spending money on gifts for family, friends, and romantic partners isn't the only way to show you care. The point of gift giving isn't to show others you aren't cheap, it's to show you care. You can demonstrate caring by making something special or doing something meaningful for those you care about. Gifts of time and kindness are often more personal and special than store-bought gifts.

> "It is preoccupation with possessions, more than anything else, that prevents us from living freely and nobly."
>
> —Bertrand Russell, British philosopher and mathematician

AUTHOR'S EXPERIENCE

When my wife (Mary) and I were first dating, I was trying to gain weight because I was on the thin side. One day when I came home from school, I found this hand-delivered package in front of my apartment door. I opened it up and there was a homemade loaf of whole wheat bread made from scratch by Mary. That gift didn't cost her much money, but she took the time to do it and she remembered to do something that was important to me (gaining weight). That gift really touched me; it's a gift I've never forgotten. Since I eventually married Mary and we're still happily married, I guess you could say that inexpensive loaf of bread was a "gift that kept on giving."

—*Joe Cuseo*

Develop your own money-saving strategies and habits. You can save money by doing little things that eventually add up to big savings over time. The following tips for saving money were suggested by students in a first-year seminar class. Some of these strategies may work for you as well.

> "If you would be wealthy, think of saving as well as getting."
>
> —Benjamin Franklin, 18th-century inventor, newspaper writer, and cosigner of the Declaration of Independence

- Don't carry a lot of extra money in your wallet. (It's just like food; if it's easy to get to, you'll be more likely to eat it up.)
- Shop with a list—get in, get what you need, and get out.
- Put all your extra change in a jar.
- Put extra cash in a piggy bank that requires you to smash the piggy to get at it.
- Seal your savings in an envelope.
- When you get extra money get it immediately into the bank (and out of your hands).
- Bring (don't buy) your lunch.
- Take full advantage of your meal plan—you've already paid for it, so don't pay twice for your meals by buying food elsewhere.
- Use e-mail instead of the phone.
- Hide your credit card or put it in the freezer so that you don't use it on impulse.

> "The safest way to double your money is to fold it over and put it in your pocket."
>
> —Kin Hubbard, American humorist, cartoonist, and journalist

- Use cash (instead of credit cards) because you can set aside a certain amount of it for yourself and you can clearly see how much of it you have at the start of a week (as well as how much is left at any point during the week).

 **Reflection 13.6**

Do you use any of the money-saving strategies on the above list?

What money-saving strategies do you use that could be added to the above list?

AUTHOR'S EXPERIENCE

When I was a four-year-old boy living in the mountains of Kentucky, it was safe for a young lad to walk the roads and railroad tracks alone. Knowing this, my mother would send me to the general store to buy a variety of small items we needed for our household. Since we had very little money, she was very aware of the fact that we needed to be cautious and spend money only on the basic necessities for survival. I could only purchase items from the general store that my mother strictly ordered me to buy. In the early 1960s, most of these items cost less than a dollar and many times you could buy multiple items for a dollar. At the store's checkout counter there were jars with different kinds of candy or gum. You could buy two pieces for one cent. I didn't think there would be any harm in rewarding myself for completing my shopping errand with two pieces of candy. I could even devour the evidence of my disobedience during my slow walk home. When I returned home from the store, my mother— being the protector of the vault and the sergeant-of-arms in our household— would count each item I bought to make sure I had been charged correctly. My mother never failed to notice if I was even one cent short! She always found that I had either been overcharged by one cent or that I had spent one cent. After she gave me a scolding, she would say: "Boy, you better learn how to count your money if you're ever going to be successful in life." I learned the value of saving money and the danger of overspending at a very young age!

—*Aaron Thompson*

"Ask yourself how much of your income is being eaten up by car payments. It may be time to admit you made a mistake . . . sell it [and] replace it with an older or less sporty model."

—*Bill Pratt*, Extra Credit: The 7 Things Every College Student Needs to Know About Credit, Debt & Cash

When making purchases, always factor in their total, long-term cost. Short-term thinking leads to poor long-term money management and financial planning. Those small (monthly) installment plans that businesses offer to entice you to buy expensive products may make the cost of those products appear attractive and affordable in the short run. However, when you factor in the interest rates you pay on monthly installment plans, plus the length of time (number of months) you're making installment payments, you get a more accurate picture of the product's total cost in the long run. Taking this long-range perspective can quickly alert you to the reality that a product's sticker price represents its partial and seemingly affordable short-term cost—not its total long-term cost—which is much less affordable and more likely to exceed your budget.

Furthermore, the total long-term cost for purchases sometimes involves additional "hidden costs" that don't relate directly to the product's initial price but must be paid to enable you to continue using the product. For example, the sticker price paid for clothes doesn't include the hidden, long-term costs of having those clothes dry-cleaned. By just taking a moment to check the inside label, you can save yourself this hidden, long-term cost by purchasing clothes that are machine washable. Similarly, deciding to buy a new car instead of a used car brings with it not only the cost of a higher sticker price, but also the higher hidden costs of licensing and insuring the new car (plus any interest fees that must be paid if the new car was purchased on an installment plan). When you add in these hidden, long-term payments to a new car's total cost, buying a good used car is clearly a much more effective money-management strategy.

Long–Range Fiscal Planning: Financing Your College Education

Thus far, our discussion has focused primarily on short-range and mid-range financial planning strategies that will keep you out of debt on a monthly or yearly basis. We turn now to issues involving long-term financial planning for your entire college experience. While there's no one "correct" strategy for financing a college education, certain strategies are more effective than others. Studies show that financing a college education by obtaining a student loan and working no more than 15 hours per week is an effective long-range strategy for students at all income levels. Students who use this strategy are more likely to graduate from college, graduate in less time, and graduate with higher grades than full-time college students who work part-time for more than 15 hours per week, or students who work full-time and attend college part-time (King, 2002; Perna & DuBois, 2010).

Unfortunately, less than 6% of all first-year students use the college financing strategy of borrowing money in the form of a student loan, attending college full-time and working part time for 15 or fewer hours per week. Instead, almost 50% of first-year students choose a strategy that research indicates is the least likely to be associated with college success: borrowing nothing and trying to work more than 15 hours per week. Students who use this strategy increase their risk of lowering their grades significantly and withdrawing from college altogether (King, 2005), probably because they can't handle the academic work load required of a full-time student on top of all the hours they're working each week. Working longer hours also increases the likelihood that students switch from full-time to part-time enrollment, which delays their time to graduation and increases their risk of not graduating at all (Tinto, 2012). Thus, a good strategy for balancing learning and earning is to try to limit work for pay to 15 or fewer hours per week.

> People don't realize how much work it is to stay in college. It's its own job in itself, plus if you've got another job you go to, too. I mean, it's just a lot."
> —*College student (quoted in Engle, Bermeo, & O'Brien, 2006)*

Some students decide to finance their college education by working full-time and attending college part-time. They believe it will be less expensive in the long run to attend college part-time because it will allow them to avoid any debt from student loans. However, studies show that when students use this strategy, it lengthens their time to degree completion and increases the risk that they will never complete a degree (Perna & DuBois, 2010).

Students who work more than 15 hours per week not only take longer to graduate from college, they end up losing money in the long run. The hourly pay most part-time jobs students earn while they're in college is less than half than what they'll earn from working in full-time positions as college graduates (King, 2005). Thus, the longer they take to graduate, the longer they must wait to enter higher-paying, full-time positions that a college diploma qualifies them for; this delays their opportunity to "cash in" on the monetary benefits of a college degree.

Reflection 13.7

Do you need to work part-time to meet your college expenses?

If you answered "yes" to the above question, are you working more than 15 hours per week?

If you answered "yes" to the above question, can you reduce your work time to 15 or fewer hours per week and still make ends meet?

Furthermore, studies show that two out of three college students have at least one credit card and nearly one-half of students with credit cards carries an average balance of more than $2,000 per month (Sallie Mae, 2009). A debt level this high is likely to force many students into working more than 15 hours a week to pay it off. ("I owe, I owe, so off to work I go.") These students often end up taking fewer courses per term so they can work more hours to pay off their credit card debt, which results in their taking longer to graduate and to start earning a college graduate's salary.

Instead of paying almost 20% interest to credit card companies for their monthly debt, these students would be better off obtaining a student loan at a much lower interest rate, which they will start paying back six months after graduation—when they'll be making more money in full-time positions as college graduates. Despite this clear advantage of student loans compared to credit card loans, only about 25% of college students with credit cards take out student loans (King, 2002).

Note

Student loans are provided by the American government with the intent of helping its citizens become better educated. In contrast, for-profit businesses (such as credit card companies) lend students money with no intent of helping them become better educated, but with the clear intent of helping themselves make money—from the high rates of interest they collect from students who fail to pay off their debt in full at the end of each month.

"Unlike a car that depreciates in value each year that you drive it, an investment in education yields monetary, social, and intellectual profit. A car is more tangible in the short term, but an investment in education (even if it means borrowing money) gives you more bang for the buck in the long run."

—*Eric Tyson, financial counselor and national best-selling author of* Personal Finance for Dummies

"If a man empties his purse into his head, no one can take it away from him. An investment in knowledge always pays the best interest."

—*Benjamin Franklin, 18th-century scientist, inventor, and a founding father of the United States*

Keep in mind that not all debt is bad. Debt can be good if it represents an investment in something that will appreciate with time—that is, something that will gain in value and eventually turn into profit for the investor. Purchasing a college education on credit is a good investment because you're investing in yourself and your future, which, over time, will *appreciate*—that is, increase its monetary return in the form of higher salaries and benefits accumulated over the remainder of your life. In contrast, purchasing a new car is a bad long-term investment because it begins to *depreciate* or lose monetary value immediately after it's purchased. The instant you drive that new car off the dealer's lot, you become the proud owner of a used car that's worth much less than what you just paid for it.

You may have heard the expression: "Time is money." One way to interpret this expression is that the more money you spend, the more time you must spend making money. College students who spend more time earning money to cover the costs of material things they want, but don't need, typically spend less time studying, complete fewer classes, and earn lower grades. You can avoid this negative cycle by viewing academic work as work that "pays" you back in terms of completed courses and higher grades. If you put in more academic time to earn more course credits in less time, you're paid back sooner by graduating sooner and beginning to earn the full-time salary of a college graduate—which will pay you about twice as much per hour than you'll earn doing part-time work without a college degree (plus additional "fringe benefits" like health insurance and paid vacation time). Furthermore, the time you put into earning higher grades in college will earn you more pay in your first full-time position after college because research shows that for students graduating in the same field, those with higher grades earn higher starting salaries (Pascarella & Terenzini, 2005).

Reflection 13.8

In addition to college, what might be other good, long-term investments you could make now or in the near future?

Box 13.2

Financial Literacy: Understanding the Language of Money Management

As you can tell from the number of financial terms used in this chapter, there's an entire language we must master to be *financially literate*. As you read the financial terms listed below, place a checkmark next to any term you didn't know.

Account. A formal business arrangement in which a bank provides financial services to a customer (e.g., checking account or savings account).

Annual Fee. Yearly fee paid to a credit card company to cover the cost of maintaining the cardholder's account.

Annual Percentage Rate (APR). Interest rate that must be paid when monthly credit card balances aren't paid in full.

Balance. Amount of money in a person's account or amount of unpaid debt.

Bounced Check. A check written for a greater amount of money than the amount contained in a personal checking account; it typically requires the person paying a charge to the bank and possibly to the business that attempted to cash the bounced check.

Budget. A plan for balancing income and expenses to ensure that sufficient money is available to cover personal expenses.

Cash Flow. Amount of money flowing in (income) and flowing out (expenses); "negative cash flow" occurs when the amount of money going out exceeds the amount coming in.

Credit. Money obtained with the understanding that it will be paid back.

Credit History. Past record of how timely and completely a credit card holder has paid off credit.

Credit Line (a.k.a. Credit Limit). The maximum amount of money (credit) made available to a borrower.

Credit Score. Measure used by credit card companies to determine if someone applying for a credit card is "credit worthy," that is, likely to repay. (An applicant with a low credit score may be denied credit.)

Debt. Amount of money owed.

Default. Failure to meet a financial obligation (e.g., a student who fails to repay a college loan "defaults" on that loan).

Emergency Student Loan. Immediate, interest-free loan provided by a college or university to help financially strapped students cover short-term expenses (e.g., cost of textbooks) or deal with financial emergencies (e.g., accidents and illnesses). Emergency student loans are typically granted within 24–48 hours, sometimes even the same day, and usually need to be repaid within two months.

Deferred Student Payment Plan. A plan allowing student borrowers to temporarily defer or postpone loan payments for some acceptable reason (e.g., to pursue an internship or do volunteer work after college).

Estimated Family Contribution (EFC). Amount of money the government has determined a family can contribute to the educational costs of a family member attending college.

Fixed Interest Rate. A loan with an interest rate that stays the same for the entire term of the loan.

Free Application for Federal Student Aid (FAFSA). Free application that asks for personal and family financial information to determine a student's eligibility for federal, state, and college-sponsored financial aid, including grants, loans, and work-study employment.

Grace Period. Amount of time a credit card holder has—after a monthly credit card statement has been issued—to pay back the company without paying added interest fees.

Grant. Money received that doesn't have to be repaid.

Gross Income. Income generated before taxes and other expenses are deducted.

(continued)

Box 13.2 *(continued)*

Identity Theft. A crime committed by obtaining someone's personal identity information and assumes that person's identity to make financial transactions or purchases.

Insurance Premium. Amount of money paid in regular installments to an insurance company to remain insured.

Interest. Amount of money paid to a customer for deposited money (as in a bank account) or paid by a customer for borrowed money (e.g., interest on a loan). Interest is usually calculated as a percentage of the total amount of money deposited or borrowed.

Interest-Bearing Account. A bank account that earns interest if the customer keeps a minimum amount of money in the bank.

Loan Consolidation. Consolidating (combining) separate student loans into one larger loan to make the process of tracking, budgeting, and repayment easier. Loan consolidation typically requires the borrower to pay slightly more interest.

Loan Premium. The amount of money loaned without interest.

Merit-Based Scholarship. Money awarded to a student on the basis of performance or achievement that doesn't have to be repaid.

Need-Based Scholarship. Money awarded to a student on the basis of financial need that doesn't have to be repaid.

Net Income. Money earned after all expenses and taxes have been paid.

Principal. Total amount of money borrowed or deposited, not counting interest.

Variable Interest Rate. An interest rate on a loan that can vary (up or down) over the term of the loan.

Work Study. Financial assistance that college students earn by working on campus (funded by the federal government).

Yield. Revenue gained beyond amount invested or paid. (For example, revenue gained by college graduates through higher lifetime salaries beyond the amount they paid for a college education.)

 Reflection 13.9

Which of the terms in **Box 13.2** were unfamiliar to you?

Which of these unfamiliar terms apply to your current financial decisions or money management plans?

Chapter Summary and Highlights

Similar to time management, if you manage your money effectively and gain control of how you spend it, you gain greater control over the quality of your life. Research shows that accumulating high levels of debt while in college is associated with higher levels of stress, lower academic performance, and greater risk of withdrawing from college. The good news is that research demonstrates that students who learn to use effective money-management strategies are able to reduce unnecessary spending, decrease their risk of debt and stress, and increase the quality of their academic performance.

In this chapter, effective strategies for money management were identified and discussed, such as the following:

- **Financing your college education wisely.** Explore all sources of income for financing your college education, including FAFSA, scholarships, grants, loans, salary earnings, and personal savings.

- **Utilizing your Financial Aid Office.** Check periodically to see if you qualify for additional sources of income, such as part-time employment on campus, low-interest loans, grants, or scholarships.
- **Gaining financial self-awareness.** Become aware of your cash flow—amount of money coming in versus going out.
- **Managing money effectively.** Use available financial tools and instruments to track and maximize cash flow, such as checking accounts, credit cards, or debit cards.
- **Preparing a personal budget.** Keep an accurate account of your money to ensure you have a sufficient amount to cover your expenses.
- **Paying your bills when they arrive.** Take care of bills when you first get them to reduce the risk of forgetting to pay them or paying them late.
- **Living within your means.** Don't purchase what you can't afford.
- **Economizing.** Be an intelligent consumer who uses critical thinking skills to evaluate and prioritize purchases.
- **Downsizing.** Don't buy products you don't need and don't allow peer pressure to dictate your spending habits.
- **Working for better grades now and better pay later.** Taking out a student loan and working part-time for 15 or fewer hours per week is the most effective long-range financial and educational strategy for students at all income levels. It improves grades, enables students to earn their degree sooner, and allows them to gain earlier entry to higher-paying jobs that require a college degree.

Learning More through the World Wide Web: Internet-Based Resources

For additional information on fiscal literacy, money management, and financial planning, see the following websites.

Fiscal Literacy and Money Management:
www.360financialliteracy.org

www.cashcourse.org

Financial Aid and Federal Funding Sources for a College Education:
https://studentloans.gov/myDirectLoan/index.action

Student Loan Management Strategies:
https://firsttechfed.studentchoice.org/.../managing.../student-loan-repayment strategies

Spending Habits and Consumer Self-Awareness:
beyondthepurchase.org

References

Astin, A. W. (1993). *What matters in college?* San Francisco: Jossey-Bass.

Cermak, K., & Filkins, J. (2004). *On-campus employment as a factor of student retention and graduation.* DePaul University. Retrieved from www.http://oipr.depaul.edu/open/gradereten/oce.asp.

College Board. (2013). *Trends in student aid, 2013.* Retrieved from http://trends.collegeboard.org/sites/default/files/student-aid-2013-full-report.pdf.

Cude, B. J., Lawrence, F. C., Lyons, A. C., Metzger, K., LeJeune, E., Marks, L., & Machtmes, K. (2006). College students and financial literacy: What they know and what we need to learn. *Proceedings of the Eastern Family Economics and Resource Management Association Conference* (pp. 102–109).

Dittmar, H. (2004). Understanding and diagnosing compulsive buying. In R. Coombs (Ed.), *Handbook of addictive disorders: A practical guide to diagnosis and treatment* (pp. 411–450). New York: Wiley.

Engle, J. Bermeo, A., & O'Brien, C. (2006). *Straight from the source: What works for first-generation college students.* Washington, DC: The Pell Institute for the Study of Opportunity in Higher Education.

Furnham, A., & Argyle, M. (1998). *The psychology of money.* New York: Routledge.

Goldstein, W. M., & Hogarth, R. M. (Eds.). (1997). *Research on judgment and decision making*, Cambridge, UK: Cambridge University Press.

Gordon, L. (2009, Oct. 21). College costs up in hard times. *Los Angeles Times*, p. A13.

Hamilton, H. (2012). Student loan blues. *Los Angeles Times*, pp. B1, B8.

Kidwell, B., & Turrisi, R. (2004). An examination of college student money management tendencies. *Journal of Economic Psychology, 25*(5), 601–616.

King, J. E. (2002). *Crucial choices: How students' financial decisions affect their academic success.* Washington, DC: American Council on Education.

King, J. E. (2005). Academic success and financial decisions: Helping students make crucial choices. In R. S. Feldman (Ed.), *Improving the first year of college: Research and practice* (pp. 3–26). Mahwah, NJ: Lawrence Erlbaum.

Kingkade, T. (2014, August 27). "Sleepy college students are worried about their stress levels." *The Huffington Post.* Retrieved from http://www.huffingtonpost.com/2014/08/27/college-students-sleep-stress_n_5723438.html.

Knox, S. (2004). *Financial basics: A money management guide for students.* Columbus: Ohio State University Press.

Kristof, K. M. (2008). Hooked on debt: Students learn too late the costs of private loans. *Los Angeles Times*, pp. A1, A18–19.

Leonard, G. (2008). *A study on the effects of student employment on retention.* Retrieved from https://uc.iupui.edu/Portals/155/uploadedFiles/Deans/StudEmpRetentionRprt.pdf.

Lowenstein, G., Read, D., & Baumeister, R. G. (Eds.). (2003). *Time and decision: Economic and psychological perspectives on intertemporal choice.* New York: Russell Sage Foundation.

Nelson, M. C., Lust, K., Story, M., & Ehlinger, E. (2008). Credit card debt, stress and key health risk behaviors among college students. *American Journal of Health Promotion, 22*(6), 400–407.

Niederjohn, M. S. (2008). First-year experience course improves students' financial literacy. *ESource for College Transitions* [Electronic newsletter published by the National Resource Center for the First-Year Experience and Students in Transition], *6*(1), 9–11.

Palan, K. M., Morrow, P. C., Trapp, A., & Blackburn, V. (2011). Compulsive buying behavior in college students: The mediating role of credit card misuse. *Journal of Marketing Theory and Practice, 19*(1), 81–96.

Pascarella, E., & Terenzini, P. (1991). *How college affects students: Findings and insights from twenty years of research.* San Francisco: Jossey-Bass.

Pascarella, E., & Terenzini, P. (2005). *How college affects students: A third decade of research* (Vol. 2). San Francisco: Jossey-Bass.

Perna, L. W., & DuBois, G. (Eds.). (2010). *Understanding the working college student: New research and its implications for policy and practice.* Sterling, VA: Stylus.

Pratt, B. (2011). *Extra credit: The 7 things every college student needs to know about credit, debt & cash* (2nd ed.). Winterville, NC: Financial Relevancy.

Rivlin, G. (2013, May 11). "The long shadow of bad credit in a job search." *The New York Times.* Retrieved from http://www.nytimes.com/2013/05/12/business/employers-pull-applicants-credit-reports.html.

SallieMae. (2009). "How undergraduate students use credit cards." Sallie Mae's National Study of Usage Rates and Trends 2009. Available at http://static.mgnetwork.com/rtd/pdfs/20090830_iris.pdf.

Susswein, R. (1995). College students and credit cards: A privilege earned? *Credit World, 83*, 21–23.

Tinto, V. (1993). *Leaving college: Rethinking the causes and cures of student attrition* (2nd ed.). Chicago: University of Chicago Press.

Tyson, E. (2012). *Personal finance for dummies* (7th ed.). Hoboken, NJ: John Wiley & Sons.

Chapter 13 Exercises

13.1 Quote Reflections

Review the sidebar quotes contained in this chapter and select two that were especially meaningful or inspirational to you.

For each quote, provide a three- to five-sentence explanation why you chose it.

13.2 Reality Bite

Problems Paying for College

A college student posted the following message on the Internet:

"I went to college for one semester, failed some of my classes, and ended with $900 in student loans. Now I can't even get financial aid or a loan because of some stupid thing that says if you fail a certain amount of classes you can't get aid or a loan. And now since I couldn't go to college this semester they want me to pay for my loans already, and I don't even have a job."

Any suggestions?

Reflection and Discussion Questions

1. What suggestions do you have for this student? What should the student do immediately? Eventually?
2. What should the student have done to prevent this from happening in the first place?
3. Do you know of any students who are in a similar predicament or soon could be?

13. 3 Connecting Financial and Career Goals

1. Using the Career and Majors tab on the "Do What You Are" survey, review the potential earnings associated with your career interest.
2. For the career(s) that interest you:
    a) Are the earnings what you expected?
    b) Would you be satisfied with these salaries? If not, would this information cause you to reconsider your career interests? What other related careers might allow you to earn the salary you desire?

13.4 Self-Assessment of Financial Attitudes and Habits

Answer the following questions about yourself as accurately and honestly as possible.

	Agree	Disagree
1. I pay my rent or mortgage on time each month.	_____	_____
2. I avoid maxing out or going over the limit on my credit cards.	_____	_____
3. I balance my checking account each month.	_____	_____
4. I set aside money each month for savings.	_____	_____
5. I pay my phone and utility bills on time each month.	_____	_____
6. I pay my credit card bills in full each month to avoid interest charges.	_____	_____
7. I believe it's important to buy the things I want when I want them.	_____	_____
8. Borrowing money to pay for college is a smart thing to do.	_____	_____
9. I have a monthly or weekly budget that I follow faithfully.	_____	_____

10. The thing I enjoy most about making money is spending money. ____ ____

11. I limit myself to one credit card. ____ ____

12. Getting a degree will get me a good job and a good income. ____ ____

Sources: Cude, et al. (2006), Niederjohn (2008).

Give yourself one point for each item that you marked "agree"—except for items 7, 9, and 10. For these items, give yourself a point if you marked "disagree."

A perfect score on this short survey would be 12.

Reflection Questions

1. What was your total score?

2. Which items lowered your score?

3. Do you detect any pattern across the items that lowered your score?

4. Do you see any realistic way(s) to improve your score on this test?

13.5 Financial Self-Awareness: Monitoring Money and Tracking Cash Flow

Step 1. Use the "Financial Self-Awareness" worksheet on the next page to *estimate* your income and expenses per month, and enter them in column 2.

Step 2. *Track* your actual income and expenses for a month and enter them in column 3. (To help you do this accurately, keep a file of your cash receipts, bills paid, and credit card or checking account records for the month.)

Step 3. After one month of tracking your cash flow, answer the following questions.

a) Were your estimates generally accurate?

b) On what items were there the largest discrepancies between your estimated cost and their actual cost?

c) Comparing your bottom-line total for income and expenses, are you satisfied with how your monthly cash flow is going?

d) What changes could you make to create more positive cash flow—that is, to increase your income or savings and reduce your expenses or debt?

e) How likely is it that you'll make the changes you mentioned in the previous question?

Financial Self-Awareness Worksheet

	Estimate	Actual
Income Sources		
Parents/Family		
Work/Job		
Grants/Scholarships		
Loans		
Savings		
Other:		
TOTAL INCOME		
Essentials (*Fixed* Expenses)		
Living Expenses: Food/Groceries		
Rent/Room and Board		
Utilities (gas/electric)		

	Estimate	Actual
Essentials (*Fixed* Expenses) *(continued)*		
Living Expenses (continued):		
Clothing		
Laundry/Dry Cleaning		
Phone		
Computer		
Household Items (dishes, etc.)		
Medical Insurance Expenses		
Debt Payments (loans/credit cards)		
Other:		
School Expenses:		
Tuition		
Books		
Supplies (print cartridges, etc.)		
Special Fees (lab fees, etc.)		
Other:		
Transportation:		
Public Transportation (bus fees, etc.)		
Car Insurance		
Car Maintenance		
Fuel (gas)		
Car Payments		
Other:		
Incidentals (*Variable* Expenses)		
Entertainment:		
Movies/Concerts		
DVDs/CDs		
Restaurants (eating out)		
Other:		
Personal Appearance/Accessories:		
Hairstyling/Coloring		
Cosmetics/Manicures		
Fashionable Clothes		
Jewelry		
Other:		
Hobbies:		
Travel (trips home, vacations)		
Gifts		
Other:		
TOTAL EXPENSES		

CHAPTER 14

Health and Wellness

BODY, MIND, AND SPIRIT

Humans cannot reach their full potential without attending to their physical well-being. Sustaining health and attaining peak levels of performance depend on how well we treat our *body*—what we put into it (healthy food), what we keep out of it (unhealthy substances), what we do with it (exercise), and how well we rejuvenate it (sleep). This chapter examines strategies for maximizing wellness by maintaining a balanced diet, attaining quality sleep, promoting total fitness, and avoiding risky behaviors that jeopardize our health and impair our performance.

Chapter Preview

Acquire wellness strategies that can be immediately practiced in the first year of college and beyond.

Learning Goal

 Reflection 14.1

Ignite Your Thinking

What would you say are the three most important things that college students could do to preserve their health and promote peak performance?

1.

2.

3.

What Is Wellness?

Wellness may be defined as a high-quality state of health in which our risk of illness is minimized and the quality of our physical and mental performance is maximized. Research indicates that people who attend to multiple dimensions of self-development and live a well-rounded, well-balanced life are more likely to be healthy (physically and mentally) and successful (personally and professionally) (Covey, 2004; Goleman, 1995; Heath, 1977).

There's still some debate about the exact number and nature of the components that define the "whole self" (Miller & Foster, 2010; President's Council on Physical Fitness and Sports, 2001). However, the following seven dimensions of personal de-

> "Wellness is a multidimensional state of being describing the existence of positive health in an individual as exemplified by quality of life and a sense of well-being."
>
> —*Charles Corbin and Robert Pangrazi, President's Council on Physical Fitness and Sports*

355

velopment are commonly cited as the key elements of the "wellness wheel"; they provide the foundation for a well-rounded life.

1. *Physical* Wellness: adopting a healthy lifestyle (e.g., balanced diet and regular exercise) and avoiding health-threatening habits (e.g., smoking and drug abuse).
2. *Intellectual* Wellness: openness to new ideas, learning from new experiences, and willingness to continue learning throughout life.
3. *Emotional* Wellness: being aware of personal feelings, effectively expressing feelings, and handling stress in a productive manner.
4. *Social* Wellness: interacting effectively with others and maintaining healthy relationships with family, friends, and romantic partners.
5. *Occupational (Vocational)* Wellness: finding personal fulfillment in a job or career and having positive, productive experiences with employers and coworkers.
6. *Environmental* Wellness: preserving the quality of key elements of the surrounding world that humans depend on for their health (i.e., air, land, and water).
7. *Spiritual* Wellness: finding meaning, purpose, and peace in life.

These elements of wellness correspond closely to the components of holistic ("whole person") development, which is a primary goal of a college education. One of the multiple advantages of the college experience is that college graduates are more likely to live longer, healthier lives and experience higher levels of psychological well-being. Apparently, students learn something important about wellness in college that improves the overall quality of their lives.

AUTHOR'S EXPERIENCE

On my office door, I posted a list of the key components of wellness to remind me to keep my life balanced. Every Sunday night I reflect on the previous week and ask myself if I've ignored any component of the holistic wheel. If I have, I try to make an earnest attempt to pay more attention to that aspect of my life during the upcoming week. For instance, if my previous week's activities reveal that I've neglected to spend enough time on my social self, I plan to spend more time the following week with family and friends. If I've neglected to attend to my physical self, I plan to exercise more consistently and eat more healthily the next week. Having the holistic wheel posted on my door provides me with a constant visual reminder to strive for "wholeness" and "balance" in my life.

—*Joe Cuseo*

Physical Wellness

The physical component of wellness is the primary focus of this chapter. It could be said that physical health is a precondition or prerequisite that enables all other elements of wellness to be experienced. It's hard to grow intellectually and professionally if you're not well physically, and it's hard to become wealthy and wise without first being healthy.

Promoting physical wellness involves more than treating illness or disease after it occurs. Instead, it's engaging in health-promoting behaviors that proactively prevent illness from happening in the first place (Corbin, Pangrazi, & Franks, 2000). Wellness puts into practice two classic proverbs: "Prevention is the best medicine" and "An ounce of prevention is worth a pound of cure."

As depicted in **Figure 14.1**, there are three potential interception points for preventing illness, preserving health, and promoting peak performance; they range from reactive (after illness) to proactive (before illness). Wellness goes beyond maintaining physical health to attaining a higher quality of life that includes vitality (energy and vigor), longevity (longer life span), and life satisfaction (happiness).

FIGURE 14.1: Potential Points for Preventing Illness, Preserving Health, and Promoting Peak Performance

Proactive   Reactive

1.	2.	3.
Feeling great and attaining peak levels of performance	Not sick, but could be feeling better and performing at a higher level	Sick, unable to perform, and trying to regain health

©Kendall Hunt Publishing Company

During any major life transition, such as the transition to college, unhealthy habits add to the level of transitional stress (Khoshaba & Maddi, 2005). In contrast, engaging in healthy habits is one way to manage and reduce stress at all stages of life—especially during stages of transition.

 Reflection 14.2

If you could single out one thing about your physical health right now that you'd like to improve or learn more about, what would it be?

Essential Elements of Physical Wellness

A healthy physical lifestyle includes three key components:

1. Supplying our body with effective fuel (nutrition) and transforming that fuel into bodily energy (exercise)
2. Giving our body adequate rest (sleep) so that it can recover and replenish the energy it has expended
3. Avoiding risky substances (alcohol and drugs) and risky behaviors that can threaten personal health and safety.

Nutrition

Similar to the way in which high-performance fuel improves the performance of an automobile, a high-quality (nutritious) diet improves the performance of the human body and mind, enabling each to operate at peak capacity. Unfortunately, we frequently pay more attention to the quality of fuel we put in our cars than to the quality of food we put into our bodies. We often eat without any intentional plan about what they should eat. We eat at places where we can get food fast and conveniently without having to step out of our car (or off of our butts). America has become a "fast food nation"; we have grown accustomed to consuming food that can be accessed quickly, conveniently, cheaply, and in large (super-sized) portions (Schlosser, 2005). National surveys reveal that less than 40% of American college students report that they maintain a healthy diet (Sax, et al., 2004).

> "Tell me what you eat and I'll tell you what you are."
>
> —Anthelme Brillat-Savarin, French lawyer, gastronomist, and founder of the low-carbohydrate diet

> "If we are what we eat, then I'm cheap, fast, and easy."
>
> —Steven Wright, award-winning comedian

Reflection 14.3

Have your eating habits changed since you've begun college? If yes, in what ways?

We should eat in a thoughtful, nutritionally conscious way, rather than solely out of convenience, habit, or pursuit of what's most pleasing to our taste buds. We should also "eat to win" by consuming the types of food that will best equip us to defeat disease and enable us to reach peak levels of physical and mental performance. The following nutrition management strategies may be used to enhance your body's ability to stay well and perform well.

Nutrition Management Strategies

1. **Develop a nutrition management plan that ensures your diet has variety and balance.** Planning what we eat is an essential step toward ensuring we eat what best preserves health and promotes wellness. If we don't plan in advance to obtain food we should eat, we're more likely to eat food that can be accessed conveniently and doesn't require advanced preparation. Unfortunately, the types of foods that are readily available, easily accessible, and immediately consumable are usually fast foods and prepackaged or processed foods, which are often the least healthy options. If we are serious about eating in a way that's best for our health and performance, we need to do more advanced planning.

   Figure 14.2 depicts the *The MyPlate* chart; this is the new version of the former Food Guide Pyramid created by the Academy of Nutrition and Dietetics. Since foods vary in terms of the nature of nutrients they contain, no single food group can supply all the nutrients our body needs. Therefore, our diet should contain a balanced blend of all food groups, albeit in different proportions or percentages.

FIGURE 14.2: MyPlate

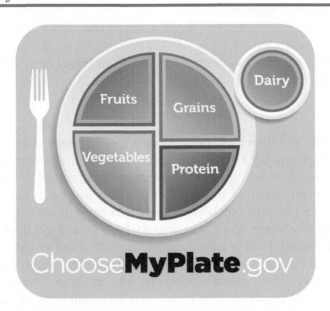

Source: USDA

To find the daily amount of food that should be consumed from each of the major food groups for your age and gender, go to *www.ChooseMyPlate.gov* or *www.cnpp.usda.gov/dietaryguideilines*. You can use these guidelines to create a personal dietary plan that ensures you consume each of these food groups every day, which will result in a balanced diet that minimizes your risk of nutritional deficiencies and disorders, and maximizes your health and performance.

"Eating the rainbow" is a phrase used by nutritionists to help people remember that including a variety of colorful fruits and vegetables in our diet is a simple way to get an ample amount of vitamins, minerals, and disease-fighting nutrients. The colors of certain fruits and vegetables can serve as indicators of the specific nutrients contained within them. For instance, fruits and vegetables that are:

- Orange and yellow (e.g., carrots, squash, melons): contain high amounts of vitamins A and C as well as nutrients that prevent cataracts and other types of eye disease
- Green (e.g., spinach, broccoli, avocado): contain high levels of vitamins B, E, and K as well as anticancer agents
- Red (e.g., tomatoes, strawberries, cherries): contain an antioxidant that reduces the risk of cancer and heart disease.
- Purple and blue (e.g., grapes, eggplant, red cabbage): contain abundant amounts of vitamins C and K as well as antioxidants that reduce the risk of cancer and cardiovascular disease
- Brown and white (e.g., cauliflower, mushrooms, bananas): contain chemicals that reduce the risk of infectious diseases by attacking viruses and bacteria (Nutrition Australia, 2015).

Reflection 14.4

Do you eat fruits and vegetables regularly that fall into each of the above five color categories?

What are your weakest categories? What could you eat, and would be willing to eat, to strengthen your weakest color category?

2. **Monitor your eating habits.** In addition to planning our diet, effective nutrition management requires that we remain aware of our daily eating habits. We can monitor our eating habits by simply taking a little time to read the labels on food products before we put them into our shopping cart and into our body. Keeping a nutritional log or journal of what we eat in a typical week is an effective way to track the nutrients and caloric content of what we're consuming.

When choosing our diet, you should also be mindful of your family history. Are there members of your immediate and extended family who have shown tendencies toward heart disease, diabetes, or cancer? If so, intentionally adopt a diet that reduces your risk for developing the types of illnesses that you may have genetic tendencies to develop. (For regularly updated information on dietary strategies for reducing the risk of common diseases, see the following website: https://fnic.nal.usda.gov/diet-and-disease).

Reflection 14.5

Are you aware of any disease or illness that tends to run in your family?

If yes, are you aware of how you may reduce your risk of experiencing this disease or illness through your diet?

Eating Disorders

While some students experience the "freshman 15"—a 15-pound weight gain during the first year of college (Levitsky, et al., 2006)—others experience eating disorders related to weight loss and losing control of their eating habits. These disorders are more common among females (National Institute of Mental Health, 2014), largely because Western cultures place more emphasis and pressure on females to maintain lighter body weight and body size. Studies show that approximately one of every three college females reports worrying about her weight, body image, or eating habits (Leavy, Gnong, & Ross, 2009).

Box 14.1 provides a short summary of the major eating disorders experienced by college students. These disorders are often accompanied by emotional issues (e.g., depression and anxiety) that are serious enough to require professional treatment (National Institute of Mental Health, 2014). The earlier these disorders are identified and treated, the better the prognosis or probability of complete and permanent recovery.

Box 14.1

Major Eating Disorders

Anorexia Nervosa

Individuals experiencing anorexia nervosa are dangerously thin, yet they see themselves as overweight and have an intense fear of gaining weight. Anorexics typically deny that they're severely underweight; even if their weight drops to the point where they may look like walking skeletons, they may continue to be obsessed with losing weight, eating infrequently, and eating extremely small portions. Anorexics may also use other methods to lose weight, such as compulsive exercise, diet pills, laxatives, diuretics, or enemas.

Bulimia Nervosa

This eating disorder is characterized by repeated episodes of "binge eating"—consuming excessive amounts of food within a limited period of time. Bulimics tend to lose self-control during their binges and then try to compensate for overeating by engaging in behavior to purge their guilt and prevent weight gain. They may purge themselves by self-induced vomiting, consuming excessive amounts of laxatives or diuretics, using enemas, or fasting. The binge–purge pattern typically takes place at least twice a week and continues for three or more months.

> I had a friend who took pride in her ability to lose 30 lbs. in one summer by not eating and working out excessively. I know girls that find pleasure in getting ill so that they throw up, can't eat, and lose weight."
>
> —*Comments written in a first-year student's journal*

Unlike anorexics, bulimics are harder to detect because their binges and purges typically take place secretly and their body weight looks about normal for their age and height. However, similar to anorexics, bulimics fear gaining weight, aren't happy with their body, and have an intense desire to lose weight.

Binge-Eating Disorder

Like bulimia, binge-eating disorder involves repeated, out-of-control episodes of consuming large amounts of food. However, unlike bulimics, binge eaters don't purge after binging episodes.

Box 14.1 *(continued)*

Those suffering from binge-eating disorder demonstrate at least three of the following symptoms, two or more times per week, for several months:

1. Eating at an extremely rapid rate
2. Eating until becoming uncomfortably full
3. Eating large amounts of food when not physically hungry

4. Eating alone because of embarrassment about others seeing how much they eat
5. Feeling guilty, disgusted, or depressed after overeating.

Sources: American Psychiatric Association (2015); National Institute of Mental Health (2014).

Exercise and Fitness

Wellness depends not only on fueling the body but using that fuel to move the body. We know that eating natural (unprocessed) foods is better for our health because those were the foods eaten by our ancient human ancestors, which has contributed to the survival of our species. Similarly, exercise is another "natural" health-promoting activity that contributed to the health and survival of the human species (World Health Organization, 2012). Our ancient ancestors didn't have the luxury of motorized vehicles to transport them from point A to point B, nor could they stroll up leisurely to grocery stores and buy food or have food served to them while seated in restaurants. Instead, they had to roam and rummage for fruit, nuts, and vegetables, or chase down animals for meat to eat. Thus, exercise was part of their daily routine.

The benefits of physical exercise for improving the longevity and quality of human life are simply extraordinary. If done regularly, exercise may well be the most effective "medicine" available to humans for preventing disease and preserving lifelong health. The major health-promoting benefits of exercise are described below.

> "
> If exercise could be packaged into a pill, it would be the single most widely prescribed and beneficial medicine in the nation."
> —*Robert N. Butler, former director of the National Institute of Aging*

Benefits of Exercise for the Body

1. **Exercise promotes cardiovascular health.** Simply stated, exercise makes the heart stronger. Since the heart is a muscle, like any other muscle in the body, its size and strength are increased by exercise. A bigger and stronger heart pumps more blood per beat, reducing the risk for heart disease and stroke (loss of oxygen to the brain) by increasing circulation of oxygen-carrying blood and increasing the body's ability to dissolve blood clots (Khoshaba & Maddi, 2005).

    Exercise further reduces the risk of cardiovascular disease by: (a) decrease the levels of triglycerides (clot-forming fats) in the blood, (b) increasing the levels of "good" cholesterol (high-density lipoproteins), and (c) preventing "bad" cholesterol (low-density lipoproteins) from sticking to and clogging up blood vessels.

2. **Exercise stimulates the immune system.** Exercise enables us to better fight off infectious diseases (e.g., colds and the flu) for the following reasons:

    * It reduces stress—which normally weakens the immune system.
    * It increases blood flow throughout the body, which increases circulation of antibodies that flush germs out of our system.
    * It increases body temperature, which helps kill germs in a way similar to how a low-grade fever kills germs when we're sick (Walsh, et al., 2011).

3. **Exercise strengthens muscles and bones.** Exercise reduces muscle tension, which helps prevent muscle strain and pain; for example, strengthening abdominal muscles reduces the risk of developing lower back pain. Exercise also maintains bone density and reduces the risk of osteoporosis (brittle bones that bend and break easily). It's noteworthy that our bone density before age 20 affects the bone density we will have for the remainder of life. Thus, by engaging in regular exercise early in life, we minimize risk of bone deterioration throughout life.

AUTHOR'S EXPERIENCE

I kept in shape when I was young by playing sports such as basketball and baseball. Whenever time in my schedule would allow, I'd play these sports for hours at a time. I enjoyed it so much that I didn't even realize I was exercising. My body fat was practically nonexistent, energy was ever flowing, and my athletic skills were ever-growing. Age has caught up with me and I can no longer play these sports. At this point in my life, I attempt to remain active through regularly scheduled workouts to keep my body fat in a reasonable double-digit category. This requires effective planning, time management, and willpower.

—*Aaron Thompson*

> "
> I'm less active now than before college because I'm having trouble learning how to manage my time."
> —*First-year student*

 Reflection 14.6

Have your exercise habits changed (for better or worse) since you've begun college?

If yes, why has this change taken place?

4. **Exercise promotes weight loss and weight management.** In a study of 188 countries, the highest proportion of overweight and obese people live in the United States, and the rate is increasing (Ng & Associates, 2014). The national increase in overweight Americans is due not only to our consuming more calories but also to our lower levels of physical activity (NIDDK, 2010). We're now playing double jeopardy with our health by eating more and moving less. Much of our reduced level of physical activity has resulted from the emergence of modern technological conveniences that make it easier for us to go about our daily business without exerting ourselves in the slightest. TVs now come with remote controls; we don't have to move to change channels, change volume, or turn the TV on and off. We now have instant access to video games that can be played virtually without actually running, jumping, or even getting on our feet.

Intentional exercise is our best antidote to all the inactivity that characterizes modern life. As a weight-control strategy, it's superior to dieting in one key respect: It raises the body's rate of metabolism—the rate at which consumed calories are burned as energy rather than stored as fat. In contrast, dieting lowers the body's rate of metabolism and the rate at which calories are burned (Agus, et al., 2000; Leibel, Rosenbaum, & Hirsch, 1995). After two to three weeks of low-calorie dieting without exercising, the body "thinks" it's starving, so it compensates by conserving more calories as fat so that the fat can be used for future energy (Mayo Clinic, 2014). In contrast, exercise speeds up basal metabolism—the body's rate of metabolism when it's resting. Thus, in addition to burning fat directly while exercising, exercise burns fat by continuing to keep the body's metabolic rate higher after we stop exercising.

Benefits of Exercise for the Mind

In addition to its multiple benefits for the body, exercise benefits the mind. Here's a summary of the powerful effects that physical exercise has on our mental health and mental performance.

1. **Exercise increases mental energy and improves mental performance.** Have you noticed how red our face gets when we engage in strenuous physical activity? This rosy complexion occurs because physical activity pumps enormous amounts of blood into our head region and more oxygen into our brain. Exercise increases blood flow to all parts of the body, but since the brain uses more oxygen than any other organ of the body, it's the organ that benefits most from exercise. Moreover, aerobic exercise (exercise that increases respiratory rate and circulates oxygen throughout the body) has been found to: (a) enlarge the frontal lobe—the part of the brain responsible for higher-level thinking (Colcombe, et al., 2006; Kramer & Erickson, 2007) and (b) increase production of brain chemicals that enable neurological connections to form between brain cells (Howard, 2014; Ratey, 2013). As noted in Chapter 5, these are the connections that provide the biological basis of learning and memory. One well-designed study of more than 250 college students discovered that students who regularly engaged in vigorous physical activity had higher GPAs (Parker-Pope, 2010).

   Furthermore, exercise is a stimulant whose stimulating effects are similar to those provided by popular energy drinks (e.g., Red Bull, Full Throttle, and Monster). However, exercise delivers these stimulating effects without the sugar, caffeine, and negative side effects of energy drinks—such as nervousness, irritability, increased blood pressure, and a sharp drop in energy ("crash") after the drink's stimulating effects wear off (Malinauskas, et al., 2007).

2. **Exercise elevates mood.** Exercise stimulates release of: (a) endorphins—morphine-like chemicals found in the brain that produce a natural high; and (b) serotonin—a mellowing brain chemical that reduces feelings of tension, anxiety, and depression. It is for these reasons that psychotherapists often prescribe exercise for patients experiencing mild cases of anxiety and depression (Johnsgard, 2004). Studies show that people who exercise regularly report feeling happier (Myers, 1993; National Institutes of Health, 2012).

3. **Exercise improves self-esteem.** Exercise can enhance our sense of self-worth by providing us with a feeling of accomplishment and improving our physical self-image (e.g., better weight control, muscle tone, and skin tone).

4. **Exercise deepens and enriches the quality of sleep.** Sleep research indicates that if we engage in exercise at least three hours before bedtime, it helps us fall asleep, stay asleep, and sleep more deeply (Youngstedt, 2005). This is why exercise is a common component of treatment programs for people suffering from insomnia (Dement & Vaughan, 2000).

Guidelines and Strategies for Maximizing the Effectiveness of Exercise

Although specific types of exercises benefit the body and mind in different ways, there are general guidelines that can be followed to maximize the positive impact of any exercise routine or personal fitness program. These guidelines are discussed below.

1. **Warm up before exercising and cool down after exercising.** Start with a 10-minute warm up of low-intensity movements similar to the ones you'll be using during the actual exercise. This will increase circulation of blood to the

> "
> To keep the body in good health is a duty, otherwise we shall not be able to keep our mind strong and clear."
>
> *—Buddha, founder of Buddhism*

> "
> It is exercise alone that supports the spirits, and keeps the mind in vigor."
>
> *—Marcus Cicero, ancient Roman orator and philosopher*

muscles you'll be exercising, which will reduce muscle soreness and risk of muscle pulls.

Finish your exercise routine with a 10-minute cool down that involves stretching the muscles you used while exercising. Stretch the muscle until it burns a little bit, and then release it. By cooling down after exercise, you improve circulation to the muscles you exercised, enabling them to return more gradually to a tension-free state; this minimizes the risk of muscle tightness, cramps, pulls, and tears.

2. **Engage in cross-training to attain total body fitness.** A balanced, comprehensive fitness program includes cross-training—a combination of different exercises to achieve total-body fitness. We should strive to combine exercises that enable us to achieve all of the following physical benefits:

- Endurance and weight control (e.g., running, cycling, or swimming);
- Muscle strength and tone (e.g., weight training, push-ups, or sit-ups); and
- Flexibility (e.g., yoga, Pilates, or tai chi).

Cross-training also entails exercising different muscle groups on a rotational basis (e.g., upper body muscles one day, lower body muscles the next). This gives different sets of muscle tissue extra time to rest, repair, and recover before they're exercised again.

3. **Include *interval training* as part of your exercise plan.** Interval training involves interspersing high-intensity exercise workouts with low-intensity exercise or short rest periods (Roxburgh, et al., 2014), such as interspersing walking with short bursts of running. Research indicates that alternating between higher- and lower-intensity exercises effectively strengthens the heart muscle and increases its oxygen-carrying capacity; it also burns calories faster and enables you to exercise longer and at more intense levels (Mayo Clinic, 2015; Mazurek, et al., 2014).

4. **Exercise regularly, allowing strength and stamina to increase gradually.** The key to attaining fitness and avoiding injury is body training, not body straining. One strategy for ensuring you're not straining your body is to see if you can talk while you're exercising. If you can't continue speaking without stopping to catch your breath, this may indicate you're overdoing it. Drop the intensity level and allow your body to adapt or adjust to a less strenuous level. After continuing at this lower level for a while, try again at the higher level and try to talk simultaneously. If you can do both, you're ready to continue at that level for some time. Continue to use this strategy and gradually increase the intensity, frequency, or duration of your exercise routine to a level that produces maximum benefits with minimal post-exercise discomfort.

AUTHOR'S EXPERIENCE

I had a habit of exercising too intensely—to the point where my body felt sore for days after I worked out. I eventually discovered a way to avoid overdoing it. When listening to music through headphones while exercising, I'd see if I could sing along with the music without having to stop and catch my breath. If I could, I knew I wasn't overextending myself. This strategy has helped me manage my exercise intensity level and reduce my day-after exercise soreness. (Plus, I've gained more confidence as a vocalist because my singing sounds a lot better when my ears are covered with headphones.)

—*Joe Cuseo*

5. **Take advantage of exercise and fitness resources on your campus.** Your college tuition pays for use of the campus gym or recreation center so take advantage of it. Also, consider taking physical education courses offered by your

college. They count toward your college degree, and typically they carry one unit of credit so that they can be easily added to your course schedule. If exercise groups or clubs meet on campus, join them; they can provide you with a motivational support group that converts exercise from a solitary routine into a social experience. (It's also a good way to meet people.)

6. **Take advantage of natural opportunities for physical activity that present themselves during the day.** Exercise can take place in places beyond a gym or fitness center and outside scheduled workout times. Opportunities for exercise are available to us as we go about our daily activities. If you can walk or ride your bike to class, do that instead of driving a car or riding a bus. If you can climb some stairs instead of taking an elevator, take the route that requires more bodily activity.

 Reflection 14.7

Do you have a regular exercise routine?

If yes, what do you do and how often do you do it? If no, why not?

What more could you do to improve your:

a) Endurance?

b) Strength?

c) Flexibility?

Rest and Sleep

Sleep experts agree that humans in today's information-loaded, multitasking world aren't getting the quantity and quality of sleep needed to perform at peak levels (Centers for Disease Control and Prevention, 2015a). We often underestimate the power of sleep and think we can cut down on the time we spend sleeping without compromising the quality of our lives. However, as discussed below, the amount of sleep we get plays a pivotal role for preserving our health and enhancing our performance.

> "Sleep deprivation is a major epidemic in our society. Americans spend so much time and energy chasing the American dream that they don't have much time left for actual dreaming."
>
> —*William Dement, pioneering sleep researcher and founder of the American Sleep Disorders Association*

The Value and Purpose of Sleep

Resting and reenergizing the body are the most obvious purposes of sleep. Listed below are other benefits of sleep that are less well known but equally important (Dement & Vaughan, 2000; National Institutes of Health, 2012).

1. **Sleep restores and preserves the power of the immune system.** Studies show that when humans and other animals lose sleep, it lowers their production of disease-fighting antibodies, making them more susceptible to illness, such as common colds and the flu (Bryant, Trinder, & Curtis, 2004).

2. **Sleep helps us cope with daily stress.** Sleep research shows that when we're experiencing stress, we spend more time in the REM (rapid eye movement) stage of sleep, which is the stage when most dreaming takes place (Suchecki, Tiba, & Machado, 2012). This suggests that dreaming is our brain's natural way

of coping with stress. When we lose dream sleep, emotional problems—such as anxiety and depression—worsen (Voelker, 2004). It's thought that the biochemical changes that take place in our brain during dream sleep help restore imbalances in brain chemistry that occur when we experience anxiety or depression. Thus, getting high-quality sleep (especially high-quality dream sleep) helps us maintain our emotional stability and keeps us in a positive frame of mind. Indeed, surveys reveal that people who report sleeping well also report feeling happier (Myers, 1993).

3. **Sleep helps the brain form and retain memories.** When we're sleeping, our brain isn't bombarded with sensory input from the outside world. This allows the brain—particularly during dream sleep—to devote more of its energy (metabolism) to processing and storing information taken in during the day (Willis, 2006). Studies show that loss of dream sleep at night results in poorer memory for information learned during the day (Greer, 2004). For instance, teenagers who get less than adequate amounts of sleep have more difficulty retaining information they learn in school (Wolfson & Carskadon, 2003). Studies also show that increasing sleep time from six or fewer hours per night to eight hours can increase memory by as much as 25% (Frank, Issa, & Stryker, 2001). Additional research indicates that when students study before going to bed and stop studying when they begin to feel drowsy (rather than trying to continue studying after drowsiness sets in), their memory for the studied material is superior (Willis, 2006).

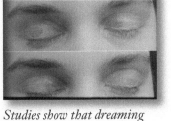

Allan Hobson/Getty Images

Studies show that dreaming during the REM stage of sleep helps us cope with stress and retain memories.

The Importance of Sleep for College Students

College students tend to have poorer sleep habits and experience more sleep problems than the general population. Heavier academic workloads, more opportunities for late-night socializing, and more frequent late-night (or all-night) study sessions often lead to more irregular sleep schedules and more sleep deprivation among college students. It's estimated that 60% of college students get an insufficient amount of sleep—a rate twice that of the general population (Kingkade, 2014).

How much sleep do we need and should we get? The answer lies in our genes and varies from person to person. On average, adults need seven to eight hours of sleep each day and teenagers need slightly more—about nine hours (Ohayon, et al., 2004). Research shows that college students get an average of less than seven hours of sleep per night (Gaultney, 2010), which means they're not getting the amount of sleep needed for optimal academic performance.

Attempting to train our body to sleep less is likely to be an exercise in futility because it's attempting to make our body do something it's not naturally (genetically) "hard-wired" to do. When our body is deprived of the amount of sleep it's genetically designed to receive, it accumulates "sleep debt," which, like financial debt, must be paid back (Dement & Vaughan, 2000; National Institutes of Health, 2015). If our sleep debt isn't repaid, it catches up to us and we pay for it by experiencing lower energy, lower mood, poorer health, and poorer performance (Van Dongen, et al., 2003). For example, studies show that the negative effects of sleep loss on driving an automobile are similar to the effects of drinking alcohol (Arnedt, et al., 2001; Fletcher, et al., 2003). Studies of sleep-deprived college students indicate that their academic performance is poorer than students who get sufficient sleep (Spinweber, cited in Zimbardo, Johnson, & McCann, 2012).

The best way to open up more time for sleep is by using our time more effectively and efficiently to get things done during the day that are cutting into our sleep time at night. (For time management strategies, see Chapter 4.)

> "I'm not getting enough sleep. I've been getting roughly 6–7 hours of sleep on weekdays. In high school, I would get 8–9 hours of sleep."
>
> —*First-year student*

> "First of all, you should probably know that your body will not function without sleep. I learned that the hard way."
>
> —*Words written by a first-year student in a letter of advice to incoming college students*

**Reflection 14.8**

How much sleep do you think you need to perform at a peak level?

How many nights per week do you typically get this amount of sleep?

If you're not getting this optimal amount of sleep each night, what's preventing you from doing so?

Adjusting Academic Work Tasks to Your Biological Rhythms

Attaining peak performance in college requires attention to both time management and energy management. Listed below are strategies for connecting these two forms of self-management to maximize your academic performance.

When planning your daily work schedule, be aware of your "biological rhythms"—that is, your natural *peak periods* and *down times*. Studies show that humans vary in terms of when they naturally prefer to fall asleep and wake up; some are "early birds" who prefer to go to sleep early and wake up early; others are "night owls" who prefer to stay up late at night and get up late in the morning (Smolensky & Lamberg, 2001). As a result of these differences in sleep patterns, individuals vary with respect to the time of day when they experience their highest and lowest levels of energy. Naturally, early birds are more likely to be "morning people" whose peak energy period takes place before noon; night owls are likely to be more productive in the late afternoon and evening. Most people, whether they're night owls or early birds, tend to experience a "post-lunch dip" in energy in the early afternoon (Monk, 2005).

Become aware of your most productive hours of the day and schedule your highest priority work and most challenging tasks at times when you tend to work at peak effectiveness. For instance, schedule out-of-class academic work so that you tackle tasks requiring intense thinking (e.g., technical writing or complex problem-solving) at times of the day when you tend to be most productive; schedule lighter work (e.g., light reading or routine tasks) at times when your energy level tends to be lower.

Also, when scheduling your courses, be mindful of your natural peak and down times. Try to arrange your schedule in such a way that you're sitting in your most challenging courses at times of the day when your body and mind are most ready to tackle those challenges.

(Take Self-Assessment Exercise 14.5 at the end of this chapter to identify your peak performance times.)

Strategies for Improving Sleep Quality

Since sleep has such powerful benefits for both the body and mind, if you can improve the quality of your sleep, you can improve your physical and mental well-being. Listed below are specific strategies for improving sleep quality, which, in turn, should improve your health and performance.

1. **Become more aware of your sleep habits by keeping a sleep log or sleep journal.** Make note of what you did before going to bed on nights when you slept well or poorly. Tracking your sleep experiences in a journal may enable

you to detect a pattern or relationship between certain things you do (or don't do) during the day on those nights when you sleep well. If you discover a pattern, you may have found yourself a routine to follow that gets you a good night's sleep on a consistent basis.

2. **Try to get into a regular sleep schedule by going to sleep and getting up at about the same time each day.** The human body functions best when it's on a biological rhythm of set cycles. If you can get your body on a regular sleep cycle, you can get into a biological rhythm that makes it easier for you to fall asleep, stay asleep, and wake up naturally from sleep—according to your body's own "internal alarm clock."

   Establishing a stable sleep schedule is particularly important around midterms and finals. Unfortunately, however, these are the times during the term when just the opposite happens. Normal sleep cycles are disrupted by cramming in last-minute studying, staying up later, getting up earlier, or pulling all-nighters and not sleeping at all. Sleep research shows that if students want to be at their physical and mental best for upcoming exams, they should get themselves on a regular sleep schedule of going to bed about the same time and getting up about the same time for at least one week before exams are to be taken (Dement & Vaughan, 1999). To help you get into this pattern, use the "distributed" practice strategies and the "part-to-whole" study method. (See Chapter 5 for a discussion of these techniques.)

3. **Attempt to get into a relaxing pre-bedtime ritual each night.** Taking a hot bath or shower, consuming a hot (noncaffeinated) beverage, or listening to relaxing music are bedtime rituals that can get you into a worry-free state before sleep and help you fall asleep sooner. Also, making a list of things you intend to do the next day before going to bed may help you relax and fall asleep because you know you're organized and ready to handle the following day's tasks.

   A light review of class notes or reading highlights just before bedtime can be a good nighttime ritual because sleep helps you retain what you experienced just before falling asleep. Many years of research indicate that the best thing you can do after attempting to learn information is to "sleep on it," probably because your brain can focus on processing and storing that information without interference from external stimulation or outside distractions (Kuriyama, et al., 2008; National Institutes of Health, 2013).

 Reflection 14.9

What do you do on most nights immediately before going to bed? Do you think this helps or hinders the quality of your sleep?

4. **Avoid intense mental activity just before going to bed.** Light mental work may serve as a relaxing pre-sleep ritual, but cramming frantically for a difficult exam or doing intensive writing before bedtime will put you in a state of mental arousal, which can interfere with your ability to wind down and fall asleep (National Institutes of Health, 2012).

5. **Avoid intense physical exercise before bedtime.** Physical exercise elevates muscle tension and increases oxygen flow to the brain, both of which will hinder your ability to fall asleep. If you like to exercise in the evening, it should be done at least three hours before bedtime (Epstein & Mardon, 2007).

6. **Avoid consuming sleep-interfering foods, beverages, or drugs in the late afternoon or evening.** In particular, avoid the following substances near bedtime:

   • **Caffeine.** It's a stimulant drug; for most people, it will stimulate their nervous system and keep them awake.
   • **Nicotine.** Another stimulant drug that's also likely to reduce the depth and quality of your sleep. (Note: Smoking hookah through a water pipe delivers the same amount of nicotine as a cigarette.)
   • **Alcohol.** It's a depressant (sedative) that makes you feel sleepy in larger doses; however, in smaller doses, it can have a stimulating effect. Furthermore, alcohol in any amount disrupts the quality of sleep by reducing the amount of time we spend in dream-stage sleep. (Marijuana does the same.)
   • **High-fat foods.** Eating just before bedtime (or during the night) increases digestive activity in the stomach. This "internal noise" is likely to interfere with the soundness of our sleep. Peanuts, beans, fruits, raw vegetables, and high-fat snacks should especially be avoided because these are harder-to-digest foods.

Note

Substances that make us feel sleepy or cause us to fall asleep (e.g., alcohol and marijuana) typically reduce the quality of our sleep by interfering with dream sleep.

7. **Make sure the temperature in the room where you're sleeping is not warmer than 70 degrees (Fahrenheit).** Warm temperatures often make us feel sleepy, but they usually don't help us stay asleep or sleep deeply. This is why people have trouble sleeping on hot summer evenings. High-quality, uninterrupted sleep is more likely to take place at room temperatures around 65 degrees (Lack, et al., 2008).

©Kendall Hunt Publishing Company

Wellness is built on a balanced foundation of nutrition, exercise, and rest.

Substance Abuse and Risky Behavior

In addition to putting healthy nutrients into our body, as well as exercising and resting it, there are two other important elements of physical wellness: (a) keeping risky substances out of our body and (b) avoiding risky behaviors that threaten our body's well-being.

Alcohol Use among College Students

In the United States, alcohol is a legal beverage (drug) for people 21 years of age and older. However, whether you're of legal age or not, it's likely that alcohol has already been available to you and will continue to be available to you as a college student. Since it's a substance commonly accessible at college parties and social gatherings, you'll be confronted with two choices:

1. To drink or not to drink
2. To drink responsibly or irresponsibly

If you decide to drink, here are some quick tips for drinking safely and responsibly:

- **Eat well before drinking and snack while drinking.** This will help lower the peak level of alcohol in your bloodstream.
- **Drink slowly.** Sip, don't gulp, and avoid "shot-gunning" or "chug-a-lugging" drinks.
- **Space out drinking over time.** (This gives the body time to metabolize the alcohol you've consumed and keeps your blood-alcohol level manageable.)
- **Maintain awareness of how much you're drinking while you're drinking by monitoring your physical and mental state.** Slow down or stop drinking after you've reached a state of moderate relaxation or a mild loss of inhibition. When folks drink to the point of slurring their speech, nodding out, or vomiting in the restroom, they're not exactly the life of the party.

Also, remember that alcohol is costly—both in terms of money and calories. Thus, reducing the amount we drink is not only a better way to manage our health; it's also a better way to manage our money and weight.

Research indicates that first-year college students drink more than they did in high school (Johnston, et al., 2005) and that alcohol abuse is higher among first-year college students than students at more advanced stages of their college experience (Bergen-Cico, 2000; White, Jamieson-Drake, & Swartzwelder, 2002). The most common reason why first-year students drink is to "fit in" or to feel socially accepted (Meilman & Presley, 2005). However, college students overestimate the number of their peers who drink and the total amount they drink; this overestimation can lead them to believe that if they don't conform to this "norm," they're not "normal" (LaBrie, et al., 2010). If you choose to drink, make sure that it's *your* choice, not a choice imposed on you through social pressure or conformity.

Alcohol Abuse among College Students

College students' expectations that they should drink (or drink to excess) accounts, at least in part, for the fact that the number one drug problem on college campuses is *binge drinking*—periodic drinking episodes during which a large amount of alcohol (four to five drinks) is consumed in a short period of time, resulting in an acute state of intoxication, a.k.a., a "drunken state" (Marczinski, Estee, & Grant, 2009). Although alcohol is a legal substance (if you're 21 or older) and a substance that's consumed as a beverage rather than injected, smoked, or snorted, it still acts as a drug when consumed in large quantities (doses), and it does contain a mind-altering ingredient: ethyl alcohol (see **Figure 14.3**). Consumed in moderate amounts, alcohol is a relaxing beverage; in larger doses, it's a mind-altering drug. Like any other mind-altering substance, it has the potential to be addictive; approximately 7% to

8% of people who drink develop alcohol dependency (alcoholism) (Julien, Advokat, & Comaty, 2011). If there's a history of alcohol dependency in your family, be particularly cautious about your drinking habits.

Although binge drinking isn't necessarily a form of alcohol dependency, it's still a form of alcohol abuse because it has direct, negative effects on the health and well-being of the drinker (as well as others who have contact with the drinker). Research indicates that repeatedly getting drunk reduces the size and effectiveness of the part of the brain involved with memory formation (Brown, et al., 2000). These findings have led researchers to a simple conclusion: Each time we get drunk, the dumber we get (Weschsler & Wuethrich, 2002).

Binge drinking also reduces our inhibitions about engaging in risk-taking behavior, which, in turn, increases our risk of personal accidents, injuries, and illnesses. It's noteworthy that the legal age for consuming alcohol was once lowered to 18 years; it was raised back to 21 because the number of drunk-driving accidents and deaths among teenage drinkers increased dramatically after the legal age was lowered (Mothers Against Drunk Driving, 2015; NHTSA/FARS & U.S. Census Bureau, 2012). Traffic accidents still account for more deaths of Americans between the ages of 15 and 24 than any other single cause (Centers for Disease Control & Prevention, 2015b).

Arguably, no other drug reduces a person's inhibitions as dramatically as alcohol. When people consume a substantial amount of alcohol, they often become substantially less cautious about doing things they normally wouldn't do. This chemically induced sense of confidence—sometimes referred to as "liquid courage"—can override the process of logical thinking and decision making, increasing the drinker's willingness to engage in irrational, risk-taking behavior (e.g., engaging in dangerous stunts). Binge drinkers are also more willing to engage in reckless driving—increasing their risk of injury or death—and reckless (unprotected) sex—increasing their risk of accidental pregnancy or contracting sexual transmitted infections (STIs). It could be said that binge drinking leads drinkers to think they're invincible, immortal, and infertile.

This lack of inhibition is because alcohol is a depressant drug, which depresses (slows down) signals normally sent from the upper, front part of the brain (the "human brain") that's responsible for rational thinking. This is the part of the brain that normally controls or inhibits the lower, middle part of the brain (the "animal brain")—which is responsible for basic animal drives, such as sex and aggression (see **Figure 14.4**). When the upper (rational) brain's messages are slowed by alcohol, the animal brain is freed from the signals that normally restrain or inhibit it, allowing its basic drives to be released or expressed. This is the underlying biological reason why excessive alcohol use increases the risk of aggressive behavior, such as: reckless driving, damaging property, fighting, sexual harassment, sexual abuse, and relationship violence (Abbey, 2002; Bushman & Cooper, 1990).

The point we're making here is not to scare you away from even thinking about drinking, nor is it to "guilt" you if you already drink. The point being made is: If you don't drink and don't care to drink, don't be pressured into drinking; and if you do drink, don't do it in excess or in binges.

(Read your Interpersonal Intelligence and Intrapersonal Intelligence descriptions on the *My MI Advantage* survey. (a) What are your strengths when dealing with challenging situations with peers that enable you to stand your ground against pressure? (b) How do you use your strengths to resist peer pressure? (c) What areas do you need to work on when dealing with pressure from peers?)

FIGURE 14.3: **Ethyl Alcohol: The Mind-Altering Ingredient Contained in Alcohol**

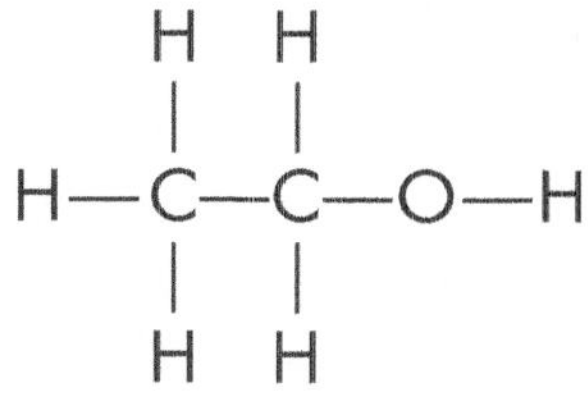

©Kendall Hunt Publishing Company

If you drink, don't park. Accidents cause people."

—*Steven Wright, American comedian*

FIGURE 14.4: How Alcohol Works in the Brain to Reduce Personal Inhibitions

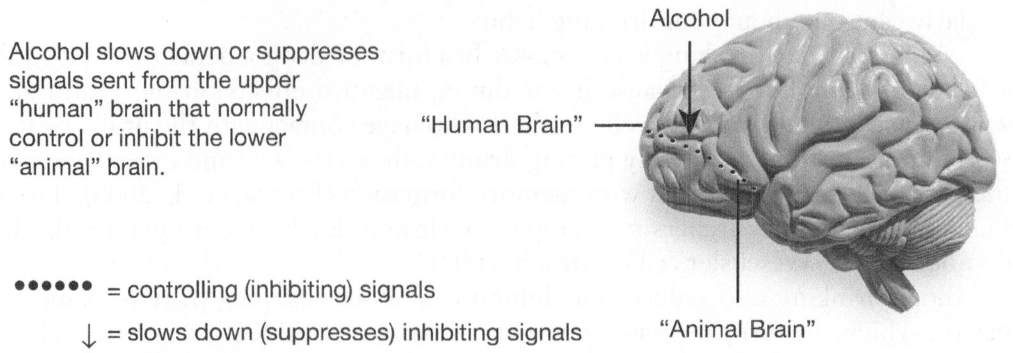

Alcohol slows down or suppresses signals sent from the upper "human" brain that normally control or inhibit the lower "animal" brain.

Alcohol

"Human Brain" —

"Animal Brain"

●●●●●● = controlling (inhibiting) signals

↓ = slows down (suppresses) inhibiting signals

©Kendall Hunt Publishing Company

Use and Abuse of Illegal Drugs

Alcohol can be legally used by anyone 21 years of age and older; other substances cannot be legally used by anyone at any age. While the college years are often a time for exploring and experimenting with different ideas, feelings, and experiences, experimenting with illegal drugs can be risky. Even if we know how an illegal drug affects people in general, we don't know how it will affect us individually because each person has a unique genetic makeup. Furthermore, unlike legal drugs, which have to pass through rigorous testing by the U.S. Federal Drug Administration before being approved for public consumption, we don't have similar safeguards for the production and packaging of illegal drugs. For instance, we don't know if or what the drug may have been "cut" (mixed) with during the production process. Thus, we're not just taking a criminal risk by using an illegal substance, we're also taking a health risk by consuming an *unregulated* substance. Our bottom-line recommendation is: When in doubt, keep it out. Don't put anything into your body that's unregulated and whose impact may be unpredictable.

Listed below are the major types of illegal drugs, accompanied by a short description of their effects. Following the list, **Box 14.2** contains a summary of the major motives or reasons why people use drugs.

- **Cocaine (coke, crack).** A stimulant that's typically snorted or smoked and produces a strong "rush" (an intense feeling of euphoria)
- **Amphetamines (speed, meth).** A strong stimulant that increases energy and general arousal; it's usually taken in pill form but may also be smoked or injected
- **Ecstasy (X).** A stimulant typically taken in pill form that speeds up the nervous system and reduces social inhibitions
- **Hallucinogens (psychedelics).** Drugs that alter or distort perception—such as, LSD ("acid") and hallucinogenic mushrooms ("shrooms")
- **Narcotics (e.g., heroin and prescription pain pills).** Sedative drugs that slow down the nervous system and produce feelings of relaxation. (Heroin is a particularly powerful narcotic that's typically injected or smoked and produces an intense "rush" of euphoria.)
- **Marijuana (weed, pot).** Still an illegal drug in most states, it's primarily a depressant or sedative drug that slows down the nervous system and induces feelings of relaxation
- **Date rape drugs.** Depressant (sedative) drugs that induce sleepiness, memory loss, and possible loss of consciousness; they're typically colorless, tasteless, and

odorless, so they can be easily mixed into a drink without the person noticing it, rendering that person vulnerable to rape or other forms of sexual assault. The most common date rape drugs are Rohypnol ("roofies") and GHB ("liquid E").

 Reflection 14.10

What drugs (if any) have you seen being used on your campus?

How would the type and frequency of drug use on your campus compare to what you saw in high school?

Box 14.2

Motives (Reasons) for Drug Use

People use drugs for a variety of reasons, the most common of which are listed below. If we remain aware of these motives, we reduce the risk that we'll do drugs for unconscious or subconscious reasons.

1. Social Pressure. To "fit in" or be socially accepted (e.g., drinking alcohol because everyone seems to be doing it)
2. Recreational (Party) Use. For fun, stimulation, or pleasure (e.g., smoking marijuana at parties to relax, loosen inhibitions, and have a "good time")

 For fun." "To party." "To fit in." "To become more talkative, outgoing, and flirtatious."

To try anything once." "To become numb." "To forget problems." "Being bored."

—*Responses of freshmen and sophomores to the question, "Why do college students take drugs?"*

3. Experimental Use. Doing drugs out of curiosity—to test out its effects (e.g., experimenting with LSD to see what it's like to have a psychedelic or hallucinogenic experience)
4. Therapeutic Use. Using prescription or over-the-counter drugs for medical purposes (e.g., taking Prozac for depression or Adderall to treat attention deficit disorder)
5. Performance Enhancement. To improve physical, mental, or social performance (e.g., taking steroids to improve athletic performance, stimulants to stay awake all night and cram for an exam, or alcohol to reduce social inhibitions and become more outgoing)
6. Escapism. To escape a personal problem or an unpleasant emotional state (e.g., taking ecstasy to escape depression or boredom)
7. Addiction. Physical or psychological dependence resulting from habitual use of a drug (e.g., continuing to use nicotine or cocaine because stopping triggers withdrawal symptoms such as anxiety and depression)

 Reflection 14.11

What motives for drug use listed in **Box 14.2** would you say are the most common reasons for drug use on your campus?

Any drug has the potential to be addictive (habit forming), especially if it's injected intravenously (directly into a vein) or smoked (inhaled through the lungs). These routes of delivery are particularly dangerous because they allow the drug to reach the brain faster and heighten its peak effect (the intensity of its highest point of impact). This rapid and high-peak effect is immediately followed by a rapid and sharp drop ("crash") (see **Figure 14.5**). This peak-to-valley, roller coaster experi-

FIGURE 14.5: **Drugs Smoked Produce a Higher and More Rapid Peak Effect**

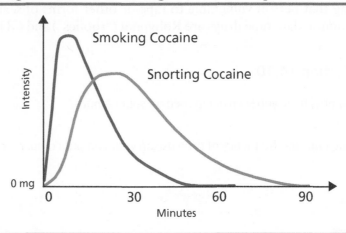

©Kendall Hunt Publishing Company

ence creates a greater risk for craving the drug again, thereby increasing the user's risk of dependency (addiction).

Here's a list of the most common signs that a person's drug use (including alcohol) is moving in the direction of *dependency* (*addiction*):

- Steadily increasing the amount (dose) of the drug and/or using it more often
- Difficulty cutting back (e.g., unable to use the drug less frequently or in smaller amounts)
- Difficulty controlling or limiting the amount taken after starting
- Keeping a steady supply of the drug on hand
- Spending more money on the drug than the person can afford
- Using the drug alone
- Hiding or hoarding the drug
- Lying about drug use to family and friends
- Reacting angrily or defensively when questioned about use of the drug
- Being "in denial" about abusing the drug (e.g., "I don't have a problem")
- Rationalizing drug abuse (e.g., "I'm just partying. It's a normal part of the college experience.")
- When continuing to use the drug matters more to the user than the personal and interpersonal problems caused by its use.

Unhealthy Relationships

Relationships can become unhealthy and pose threats to our physical or psychological well-being. If you're in a relationship where you feel you're being repeatedly disrespected, excessively controlled, or are concerned for your safety, it's essential that you acknowledge and act upon these signals. Relationship abuse—whether emotional, psychological, physical, or sexual—is another threat to wellness and should *never* be tolerated. If you're in such a situation, or you have a friend who is, it's essential to address the issue immediately. See **Box 14.3** for a summary of the major types of relationship abuse and violence.

Sometimes the victims and offenders of relationship abuse don't recognize that they are, in fact, involved in an abusive relationship. Behaviors that characterize relationship violence include, but are not limited to, degrading language, dominating or dictating a partner's actions, as well as physical and/or sexual assault (Murray & Kardatzke, 2007). Unfortunately, the prevalence of relationship abuse is high among college-aged women and men. In a study conducted on relationship violence among college students by the National Institute of Health, 44.7% of the respondents experienced partner or nonpartner violence. Of this group, 72.8% of the women and 27.2% of the men reported being either victims or perpetrators (Forke, et al., 2008).

It's important to note that relationship violence occurs among college students of all races, ethnicities, and socioeconomic groups (Malik, Sorenson, & Aneshensel, 1997). Comparable levels of relationship violence have also been found among victims and perpetrators who are gay, bisexual, or straight (Freedner, et al., 2002). Taken together, these data highlight the unfortunate fact that relationship abuse is all too common among college students and needs to be detected and addressed early in relationships—before it escalates to more violent levels.

Victims of relationship abuse are often reluctant to seek help because they fear embarrassment or retribution. If you find yourself in a violent relationship, it is important that you tell someone what's going on and get support. Don't let fear immobilize you. Talking to a trusted friend who has your health and safety in mind is a good place to start. Connecting with your college's counseling center is especially helpful because you can get professional assistance. Campus counseling centers are often staffed with professionals who have experience working with victims and perpetrators of relationship abuse, or they can refer you to professionals who do.

Box 14.3

Sexual Abuse and Violence

Listed below are various forms of relationship abuse and violence. Note that these examples are not just physical or sexual in nature—emotional and psychological violence can be just as harmful to victims.

Sexual Harassment

Sexual harassment in college settings includes any unwanted or unwelcome sexual behavior initiated by another student or an employee of the college that interferes with one's education. Sexual harassment can take the following forms:

1. Verbal—such as, making sexual comments about someone's body or clothes; sexual jokes; or teasing—including spreading sexual rumors about a person's sexual activity or orientation; requesting sexual favors in exchange for a better grade, job, or promotion.
2. Nonverbal—such as, staring or glaring at someone's body; making erotic or obscene gestures toward the person; sending obscene messages or unsolicited pornographic material.
3. Physical—such as, contact by touching, grabbing, pinching, or brushing up against someone's body.

Recommendations for dealing with sexual harassment:

- Make your objections clear and firm. Tell the harasser directly that you're offended by the unwanted behavior and that you know it constitutes sexual harassment.
- Keep a written record of any harassment. Record the date, place, and specific details about the harassing behavior.
- Become aware of the sexual harassment policy at your school. (Your school's policy is likely to be found in the *Student Handbook* or may be available from the Office of Human Resources.)
- If you're unsure about whether you're experiencing sexual harassment, or what to do about it, seek help from the Counseling Center or Office of Human Resources.

Note: Sexual harassment is one form of *peer harassment*, which is a broader category of harassment that includes taunting, bullying (in person or online), as well as harassment based on race or sexual orientation. All these behaviors violate the law, which guarantees all students the right to a learning environment that's conducive to learning. If you experience any of these forms of harassment, don't tolerate them silently, report them to school authorities.

(continued)

Box 14.3 *(continued)*

Title IX of the Education Amendment of 1972 is a federal civil rights law that prohibits discrimination on the basis of sex, which includes sexual harassment, rape, and sexual assault. A college or university may be held legally responsible when it knows about and ignores sexual harassment or assault in its programs or activities, whether the harassment is committed by a faculty member, staff member, or student. If you have been sexually harassed and believe that your campus has not responded effectively to your concern, you can contact or file a complaint with the Department of Education's Office of Civil Rights (http://www2.ed.gov/about/offices/list/ocr/docs/howto.html).

Abusive Relationships

An abusive relationship may be defined as a relationship in which one partner abuses the other—physically, verbally, or emotionally. Abusers are often dependent on their partners for their sense of self-worth; they commonly have low self-esteem and fear their partner will abandon them, so they attempt to prevent this abandonment by over-controlling their partner. Frequently, abusers feel powerless or weak in other areas of their life and overcompensate by attempting to gain power and personal strength by exerting power over their partner.

Potential Signs of Abuse

- The abuser is possessive and tries to dominate or control all aspects of the partner's life (e.g., discourages the partner from having contact with friends or family members)
- The abuser frequently yells, shouts, intimidates, or makes physical threats toward the partner
- The abuser constantly puts down the partner and attempts to damage the partner's self-esteem
- The abuser displays intense and irrational jealousy (e.g., accusing the partner of infidelity without evidence)
- The abuser demands affection or sex when the partner is not interested or willing
- The abuser often appears charming to others in public settings, but is abusive toward the partner in private
- The abused partner behaves differently and is more inhibited when the abuser is around
- The abused partner fears the abuser

Strategies for Avoiding or Escaping Abusive Relationships

- Avoid relationship isolation; continue to maintain social ties with friends outside of the relationship.

- Don't make excuses for or rationalize the abuser's behavior (e.g., he was under stress or she was drinking)
- Get an objective, "third party" perspective by asking close friends for their views on your relationship. (Love can be "blind," so it's possible to be in denial about an abusive relationship and not "see" what's really going on.)
- Speak with a professional counselor on campus to help you see your relationships more objectively and for help with any relationship that you sense is becoming abusive.

Sexual Assault, a.k.a. Sexual Violence

Sexual assault refers to nonconsensual (unwanted or unwilling) sexual contact, which includes rape, attempted rape, and any other type of sexual contact that a person forces on another without consent. *Rape* is a form of sexual assault or sexual violence that involves forced sexual penetration (intercourse), which takes place through physical force, by threat of bodily harm, or when the victim is incapable of giving consent due to alcohol or drug intoxication. Rape can be classified into two major categories:

1. Stranger Rape—when a total stranger forces sexual intercourse on the victim.
2. Acquaintance Rape or Date Rape—when the victim knows, or is dating, the person who forces unwanted sexual intercourse.

It's estimated that about 85% of reported rapes are committed by an acquaintance. Alcohol is frequently associated with acquaintance rapes because it lowers the rapist's inhibitions and reduces the victim's ability to judge whether it's a potentially dangerous situation. Since the partners are familiar with each other, the victim may feel that what happened was not sexual assault. However, here's the bottom line: Acquaintance rape *is* rape and it's still a crime because it involves nonconsensual sex.

Recommendations for women to reduce the risk of experiencing sexual assault:

- Don't drink to excess or associate with others who do.
- If you drink, or go to places where others drink, remain aware of the possibility of date rape drugs being dropped into your drink. To guard against this risk, don't let others give you drinks, and hold onto your drink at all times (e.g., don't leave it, go to the restroom, and come back to drink it again).
- When you attend parties, go with friends so you can keep an eye out for one another.

Box 14.3 *(continued)*

- Clearly and assertively communicate what your sexual limits are. Use "I messages" to firmly resist unwanted sexual advances by rejecting the behavior rather than the person (e.g., "I'm not comfortable with your touching me like that").
- Carry mace or pepper spray and be prepared to use it if necessary.
- Take a self-defense class. Studies show that courses in resisting sexual assault reduce the risk of rape by almost 50% (Senn, et al., 2015).

Recommendations for men for reducing the risk of committing sexual assault:

- Don't assume a woman wants to have sex just because she's:

a) very friendly or flirtatious,
b) dressed in a provocative way, or
c) drinking alcohol.

- If a woman says "no," don't interpret that to mean she's really saying "yes."
- Don't think that just because you're "the man," you have to be the sexual initiator or aggressor.
- Interpret rejection of sexual advances by a woman to mean that the woman just doesn't want to have sex; don't take it as a personal insult or blow to your masculinity.

Sources: Karjane, Fisher, & Cullen (2002, 2005); National Center for Victims of Crime (2012); Ottens & Hotelling (2001); Penfold (2006)

Reflection 14.12

Have you ever known anyone who was involved in an abusive relationship?

In what way(s) was it abusive?

How did the abused partner handle it?

Sexually Transmitted Infections (STIs)

STIs represent a group of contagious infections spread through sexual contact that can threaten our health and well-being. Latex condoms provide the best protection against STIs (Holmes, Levine, & Weaver, 2004). Also, having sex with fewer partners reduces the risk of contracting an STI. Obviously, not engaging in sexual intercourse is the most foolproof way to eliminate the risk of an STI (and unwanted pregnancy). When it comes to sexual intercourse, we have three basic options: Do it recklessly, do is safely, or don't do it. If you choose the last option (abstinence), it doesn't mean you're a cold or unaffectionate prude. All it means is that you're choosing not to have sexual intercourse at this particular time in your life.

More than 25 types of STIs have been identified and virtually all of them are effectively treated if detected early. However, if ignored, some STIs can progress to the point where they result in serious infection and possible infertility (Cates, et al., 2004). Experiencing pain during or after urination, or unusual discharge from the penis or vaginal areas, are common early symptoms of STI. But the symptoms can sometimes be subtle and undetectable. If you have any doubt, play it safe and check it out immediately by visiting the Health Center on your campus. Any advice or treatment you receive there will remain confidential. If you discover that you have a STI, immediately inform anyone you've had sex with, so he or she can receive early treatment before the disease progresses. This isn't just a polite thing to do; it's the right (ethical) thing to do.

> Last night I discovered a new form of oral contraceptive. I asked a girl to go to bed with me and she said no."
>
> —Woody Allen, actor, writer, director, and comedian

Campus Safety

College campuses are generally safe and no more prone to crime than other locations or organizations. However, crimes do occur on campuses and one element of wellness is reducing your risk of being victimized by crimes, particularly crimes that threaten your physical well-being. Listed below are some top tips on doing so.

- After dark, don't walk alone; use a buddy system.
- At night or when walking alone, don't get so absorbed in texting or listening to iTunes that you tune out or block out what's going on around you.
- If you're carrying valuable electronics, keep them concealed.
- Check if your campus has an escort service at night; if it does, take advantage of it.
- Call ahead for campus shuttles and escort services to reduce the amount of time you're waiting for a ride.
- Have your keys out and ready before entering your building or your car, and double-check to be sure the door locks behind you.
- Know the phone number and location of the office for campus safety.
- Be aware of the location of emergency phones in academic buildings.
- Put emergency numbers in your cell phone.

Sources: Lucler, 2015; "Staying Safe on Campus," 2012.

Mobile apps are also available to promote your safety. For instance, "Circle of 6" (www.circleof6app.com/) is a free mobile map that allows you to choose a network of six friends whom you can contact with emergency text messages, such as: "Call me immediately," "Come and get me," or "I need help getting home safely." When you text a message, your GPS location is included. This app was a co-winner of the national "Apps Against Abuse Challenge" sponsored by the White House (Rivera, 2015).

"ArcAngel" (www.patrocinium.com/arcangel) is another mobile safety app that notifies you within seconds of an emergency or if you're near danger (e.g., a crime scene, fire, or flood); it also provides ongoing status reports throughout the emergency and recommends evacuation routes as needed. If you need help, you can click a button that informs local authorities, campus security teams, and family members of your exact location.

Take advantage of these new safety technologies to lower your risk of being victimized by crime and avoiding dangerous situations.

Chapter Summary and Highlights

Wellness is a state of high-quality health and personal well-being that promotes peak physical and mental performance. It requires a healthy lifestyle that includes the following key elements: (a) supplying our body with effective fuel (nutrition) for optimal energy, (b) using energy to engage in heath-preserving exercise, and (c) giving our body adequate rest (sleep) so that it can recover and replenish the energy it has expended.

Research findings and recommendations from health care professionals indicate that physical wellness is most effectively promoted by adopting the following strategies:

- **Watch what we eat.** In particular, we should increase consumption of natural fruits, vegetables, legumes, whole grains, fish, and water and decrease consumption of processed foods, fatty foods, fried foods, fast foods, and foods purchased from vending machines. Although the expression, "you are what you eat" may be a bit of an exaggeration, it contains a kernel of truth because the food we consume does affect our health, our emotions, and our performance.

- **Become more physically active.** To counteract the sedentary lifestyle created by life in modern society and attain total fitness, we should engage in a balanced blend of exercises that build stamina, strength, and flexibility.
- **Don't cheat on sleep.** Humans typically do not get the amount of sleep they need to perform at peak levels. College students, in particular, need to get more sleep than they usually do and develop more regular (consistent) sleep habits.
- **Drink alcohol responsibly or not at all.** Avoid excessive consumption of alcohol or other mind-altering substances that can threaten our physical health, impair our mental judgment, and reduce our inhibitions about engaging in dangerous, risk-taking behavior.
- **Avoid use of illegal substances that are unregulated**—particularly substances whose effects may be unpredictable and that pose a high risk for dependency (addiction).
- **Avoid unhealthy relationships that are abusive or violent.** If involved in such a relationship, don't tolerate it and allow it to escalate. Instead, escape it, or seek immediate help to address it.
- **Minimize the risk of contracting sexually transmitted infections.** There are three basic strategies for doing so: using latex condoms during sex, limiting the number of sexual partners, or choosing not to be sexually active.
- **Minimize the risk of being victimized by crime.** Be mindful of surroundings, particularly when alone and at night, use social support strategies and emerging technological tools (e.g., apps) to enhance personal safety.

The wellness-promoting strategies discussed in this chapter are effective ways to preserve health and promote peak performance, both in college and beyond.

Learning More through the World Wide Web: Internet-Based Resources

For additional information on health and wellness, see the following websites.

Nutrition:
www.eatright.org

Physical Activities and Fitness:
http://archive.ncppa.org/resources/coalitions/

Sleep:
www.sleepfoundation.org

Drugs and Abuse (including alcohol):
http://www.drugabuse.gov/drugs-abuse

http://www.wise-drinking.com/ (an app on responsible drinking)

Mental Health:
http://www.activeminds.org/issues-a-resources/mental-health-resources/student-resources

Sexual Harassment, Assault, and Abuse:
http://uhs.princeton.edu/medical-services/sexual-health-and-wellness

References

Abbey, A. (2002). Alcohol-related sexual assault: A common problem among college students. *Journal of Studies on Alcohol, 14*, 118–128.

Agus M. S., Swain, J. F., Larson, C. L., Eckert, E. A., & Ludwig, D. S. (2000). Dietary composition and physiologic adaptations to energy restriction. *American Journal of Clinical Nutrition, 74*(4), 901–907.

American Psychiatric Association. (2015). *Diagnostic and statistical manual of mental disorders, DSM-IV-TR* (5th ed.). Washington, DC: Author.

Arnedt, J. T., Wilde, G. J. S., Munt, P. W., & MacLean, A. W. (2001). How do prolonged wakefulness and alcohol compare in the decrements they produce on a simulated driving task? *Accident Analysis and Prevention, 33*, 337–344.

Bergen-Cico, D. (2000). Patterns of substance abuse and attrition among first-year students. *Journal of the First-Year Experience and Students in Transition, 12*(1), 61–75.

Brown, S. A., Tapert, S. F., Granholm, E., & Delis, D. C. (2000). Neurocognitive functioning of adolescents: Effects of protracted alcohol use. *Alcoholism: Clinical & Experimental Research, 24*(2), 164–171.

Bryant, P. A., Trinder, J., & Curtis, N. (2004). Sick and tired: does sleep have a vital role in the immune system? *Nature Reviews Immunology, 4*, 457–467.

Bushman, B. J., & Cooper, H. M. (1990). Effects of alcohol on human aggression: An integrative research review. *Psychological Bulletin, 107*(3), 341–354.

Cates, J. R., Herndon, N. L., Schulz, S. L., & Darroch, J. E. (2004). *Our voices, our lives, our futures: Youth and sexually transmitted diseases.* Chapel Hill, NC: University of North Carolina at Chapel Hill School of Journalism and Mass Communication.

Centers for Disease Control & Prevention. (2015a). *Insufficient sleep is a public health problem.* Retrieved from http://www.cdc.gov/features/dssleep/.

Centers for Disease Control & Prevention. (2015b). *Teen drivers: Fact sheet.* Retrieved from http://www.cdc.gov/motorvehiclesafety/teen_drivers/.

Colcombe, S. J., Erickson, K., Scalf, P. E., Kim, J. S., Prakash, R., & McAuley, E. (2006). Aerobic exercise training increases brain volume in aging humans. *Journal of Gerontology: Medical Sciences, 61A*(11), 1166–1170.

Corbin, C. B., Pangrazi, R. P., & Franks, B. D. (2000). Definitions: Health, fitness, and physical activity. *President's Council on Physical Fitness and Sports Research Digest, 3*(9), 1–8.

Covey, S. R. (2004). *Seven habits of highly effective people* (3rd ed.). New York: Fireside.

Dement, W. C., & Vaughan, C. (2000). *The promise of sleep: A pioneer in sleep medicine explores the vital connection between health, happiness, and a good night's sleep.* New York: Dell.

Epstein, L., & Mardon. S. (2007). *The Harvard medical school guide to a good night's sleep.* New York: McGraw Hill.

Fletcher, A., Lamond, N., van den Heuvel, C. J., & Dawson, D. (2003). Prediction of performance during sleep deprivation and alcohol intoxication using a quantitative model of work-related fatigue. *Sleep Research Online, 5*, 67–75.

Forke, C. M., Myers, R. K., Catallozzi, M., & Schwarz, D. F. (2008). Relationship violence among female and male college undergraduate students. *National Institutes of Health.* Retrieved from http://archpedi.jamanetwork.com/article.aspx?articleid=379815.

Frank, M., Issa, N., & Stryker, M. (2001). Sleep enhances plasticity in the developing visual cortex. *Neuron, 30*(1), 275–297.

Freedner, N., Freed, L. H., Yang, Y. W., & Austin, S. B. (2002). Dating violence among gay, lesbian, and bisexual adolescents: Results from a community survey. *Journal of Adolescent Health, 21*, 469–474.

Gaultney, J. F. (2010). The prevalence of sleep disorders in college students: Impact on academic performance. *Journal of American College Health, 59*(2), 91–97.

Goleman, D. (1995). *Emotional intelligence: Why it can matter more than IQ.* New York: Random House.

Greer, M. (2004). Strengthen your brain by resting it. *American Psychological Association, 35*(7), 60.

Heath, H. (1977). *Maturity and competence: A transcultural view.* New York: Halsted Press.

Holmes, K. K., Levine, R., & Weaver, M. (2004). Effectiveness of condoms in preventing sexually transmitted infections. *Bulletin of the World Health Organization, 82*, 254–464.

Howard, P. J. (2014). *The owner's manual for the brain: Everyday applications of mind-brain research* (4th ed.). New York: HarperCollins.

Johnsgard, K. W. (2004). *Conquering depression and anxiety through exercise.* New York: Prometheus.

Johnston, L. D., O'Malley, P. M., Bachman, J. G., & Schulenberg, J. E. (2005). *Monitoring the future national survey results on drug use, 1975–2004: Vol 2. College students and adults ages 19–45.* National Institute on Drug Abuse: Bethesda, MD: 2005. NIH Publication No. 05-5728.

Julien, R. M., Advokat, C. D., & Comaty, J. E. (2011). *A primer of drug action.* New York: Worth.

Karjane, H. K., Fisher, B. S., & Cullen F. T. (2002). *Campus sexual assault: How America's institutions of higher education respond.* Final Report, NIJ Grant #1999-WA-VX-0008. Newton, MA: Education Development Center, Inc.

Karjane, H. K., Fisher, B. S., & Cullen F. T. (2005). *Sexual assault on campus: What colleges and universities are doing about it.* Retrieved from https://www.ncjrs.gov/pdffiles1/nij/205521.pdf.

Khoshaba, D., & Maddi, S. R. (2005). *HardiTraining: Managing stressful change* (4th ed.). Newport Beach, CA: Hardiness Institute.

Kingkade, T. (2014, August 27). "Sleepy college students are worried about their stress levels." *The Huffington Post.* Retrieved from http://www.huffingtonpost.com/2014/08/27/college-students-sleep-stress_n_5723438.html.

Kramer, A. F., & Erickson, K. I. (2007). Capitalizing on cortical plasticity: Influence of physical activity on cognition and brain function. *Trends in Cognitive Sciences, 11*(8), 342–348.

Kuriyama, K., Mishima, K., Suzuki, H., Aritake, S., & Uchiyama, M. (2008). Sleep accelerates improvement in working memory performance. *The Journal of Neuroscience, 28*(4), 10145–10150.

LaBrie, et al. (2010). Bacteriophage resistance mechanisms. *Nat. Rev. Microbiology, 8,* 317–327. 10.1038/nrmicro2315.

Lack, L. C., Gradisar, M., Van Someren, E. J. W., Wright, H. R., & Lushington, K. (2008). The relationship between insomnia and body temperatures. *Sleep Medicine Reviews 12*(4), 307–317.

Leavy, P., Gnong, A., & Ross, L. S. (2009). Femininity, masculinity, and body image issues among college-age women: An in-depth and written interview study of the mind-body dichotomy. *The Qualitative Report, 14*(2), 261–292.

Leibel, R. L., Rosenbaum, M., & Hirsch, J. (1995). Changes in energy expenditure resulting from altered body weight. *New England Journal of Medicine, 332,* 621–628.

Levitsky, D. A., Garay, J., Nausbaum, M., Neighbors, L., & Dellavalle, D. M. (2006). Monitoring weight daily blocks the freshman weight gain: A model for combating the epidemic of obesity. *International Journal of Obesity, 30*(6), 1003–1010.

Lucler, K. L. (2015). "15 ways to stay safe while in college." Retrieved from http://collegelife.about.com/od/healthwellness/qt/SafetyTips.htm.

Malik, S., Sorenson, S. B., & Aneshensel, C. S. (1997). Community and dating violence among adolescents: Perpetration and victimization. *Journal of Adolescent Health, 21*(5), 291–302.

Malinauskas, B. M., Aeby, V. G., Overton, R. F., Carpenter-Aeby, T., & Barber-Heidal, K. (2007). A survey of energy drink consumption patterns among college students. *Nutrition Journal, 6*(1), 35.

Marczinski, C., Estee, G., & Grant, V. (2009). *Binge drinking in adolescent and college students.* New York: Nova Science Publishers.

Mayo Clinic. (2014, September 19). "Metabolism and weight loss: How you burn calories." Retrieved from http://www.mayoclinic.org/healthy-lifestyle/weight-loss/in-depth/metabolism/art-20046508?pg=1.

Mayo Clinic. (2015). "Rev up your workout with interval training: Interval training can help you get the most out of your workout." Retrieved from http://www.mayoclinic.org/healthy-living/fitness/in-depth/interval-training/art-20044588?pg=1.

Mazurek, K., Karwczyk, K., Zemijeeski, P., Norkoski, H., & Czajkowska, M. (2014). Effects of aerobic interval training versus continuous moderate exercise programme on aerobic and anaerobic capacity, somatic features and blood lipid profile in collegiate females. *Annals of Agricultural and Environmental Medicine, 21*(4), 844–849.

Meilman, P. W., & Presley, C. A. (2005). The first-year experience and alcohol use. In M. L. Upcraft, J. N. Gardner, & B. O. Barefoot & Associates (Eds.), *Challenging and supporting the first-year student: A handbook for improving the first year of college* (pp. 445–468). San Francisco: Jossey-Bass.

Miller, G. D., & Foster, L. T. (2010). *Critical synthesis of wellness literature.* Victoria: University of Victoria. Retrieved from http://www.geog.uvic.ca/wellness.

Monk, T. H. (2005). The post-lunch dip in performance. *Clinical Sports Medicine, 24*(2), 15–23.

Mothers Against Drunk Driving. (2015). *Why 21?: Addressing underage drinking.* Retrieved from http://www.madd.org/underage-drinking/why21/.

Murray, C. E., & Kardatzke, K. N. (2007). Dating violence among college students: Key issues for college counselors. *Journal of College Counseling, 10*(1), 79–89.

Myers, D. G. (1993). *The pursuit of happiness: Who is happy—and why?* New York: Morrow.

National Center for Victims of Crime. (2012). *About sexual assault.* Retrieved from https://www.victimsofcrime.org/our-programs/dna-resource-center/untested-sexual-assault-kits/about-sexual-assault.

National Institute of Mental Health. (2014). *What are eating disorders?* Washington, DC: U.S. Department of Health and Human Services. Retrieved from http://www.nimh.nih.gov/health/publications/eating-disorders-new-trifold/index.shtml.

National Institutes of Health. (2012). *Why is sleep important?* Retrieved from http://www.nhlbi.nih.gov/health/health-topics/topics/sdd/why.

National Institutes of Health. (2013). *Sleep on it: How snoozing strengthens memories.* Retrieved from https://newsinhealth.nih.gov/issue/apr2013/feature2.

National Institutes of Health. (2015). *What are some myths about sleep?* Retrieved from https://www.nichd.nih.gov/health/topics/sleep/conditioninfo/Pages/sleep-myths.aspx.

Ng, M., & Associates. (2014). Global, regional, and national prevalence of overweight and obesity in children and adults during 1980–2013: A systematic analysis for the Global Burden of Disease Study 2013. *The Lancet, 384* (No. 9945), 766–781.

NHTSA/FARS, & U.S. Census Bureau. (2012). *Underage drunk driving fatalities.* Retrieved from www.centurycouncil.org/drunk-driving/underage-drunk-driving-fatalities.

NIDDK (National Institute of Diabetes & Digestive Kidney Diseases). (2010). *Overweight and obesity statistics.* Washington, DC: U.S. Department of Health and Human Services.

Nutrition Australia. (2015). *Eat a rainbow*. Retrieved from http://www.nutritionaustralia.org/national/resource/eat-rainbow.

Ohayon, M. M., Carskadon, M. A., Guilleminault, C., & Vitiello, M. V. (2004). Meta-analysis of quantitative sleep parameters from childhood to old age in healthy individuals: developing normative sleep values across the human lifespan. *Sleep, 27*, 1255–1273.

Ottens, A. J., & Hotelling, K. (2001). *Sexual violence on campus: Policies, programs, and perspectives*. New York: Springer Publishing Company, Inc.

Parker-Pope, T. (2010). "Vigorous exercise linked with better grades." Retrieved from http://query.nytimes.com/gst/fullpage.html?res=9A03EEDE103EF93BA35755C0A9669D8B63.

Penfold, R. B. (2006). *Dragonslippers: This is what an abusive relationship looks like*. New York: Grove/Atlantic.

President's Council on Physical Fitness and Sports. (2001). Toward a uniform definition of wellness: A commentary. *Research Digest, 3*(15), 1–8.

Ratey, J. J. (2013). *Spark: The revolutionary new science of exercise and the brain*. New York: Little, Brown & Company.

Rivera, C. (2015, July 1). "College safety gets a tech boost." *Los Angeles Times*, p. B2.

Roxburgh, et al. (2014). Is moderate intensity exercise training combined with high intensity interval training more effective at improving cardiorespiratory fitness than moderate intensity exercise training alone? *Journal of Sports Science and Medicine, 13*(3), 702–707.

Sax, L. J., Bryant, A. N., & Gilmartin, S. K. (2004). A longitudinal investigation of emotional health among male and female first-year college students. *Journal of the First-Year Experience and Students in Transition, 16*(2), 29–65.

Schlosser, E. (2005). *Fast food nation: The dark side of the all-American meal*. New York: Harper Perennial.

Senn, C. Y., Eliaslw, M., Barata, P. C., Thurston, W. E., Newby-Clark, I. R., Radtke, H. L., & Hobden, K. L. (2015). Efficacy of a sexual assault resistance program for university women. *New England Journal of Medicine, 372*, 2326–2335.

Smolensky, M., & Lamberg, L. (2001*). The body clock guide to better health: How to use your body's natural clock to fight illness and achieve maximum health*. New York: Henry Holt.

"Staying Safe on Campus". (2012 July 20). Retrieved from http://www.nytimes.com/2012/07/20/education/edlife/students-fear-venturing-out-alone-at-night-on-campus.html?pagewanted=all.

Suchecki, D., Tiba, P. A., & Machado, R. B. (2012). REM sleep rebound as an adaptive response to stressful situations. *Frontiers in Neurology, 3*, 41.

Van Dongen, H. P. A., Maislin, G., Mullington, J. M., & Dinges, D. F. (2003). The cumulative cost of additional wakefulness: Dose–response effects on neurobehavioral functions and sleep physiology from chronic sleep restriction and total sleep deprivation. *Sleep, 26*, 117–126.

Voelker, R. (2004). Stress, sleep loss, and substance abuse create potent recipe for college depression. *Journal of the American Medical Association, 291*, 2177–2179.

Walsh, N. P., Gleeson, M., Shephard, R. J., Woods, J. A., Bishop, N. C., Fleshner, M., Green, C., Pedersen, B. K., Hoffman-Goetz, L., Rogers, C. J., Northoff, H., Abbasi, A., & Simon. P. (2011). Position statement. Part one: Immune function and exercise. *Exercise Immunology Review, 17*, 6–63.

Weschsler, H., & Wuethrich, B. (2002). *Dying to drink: Confronting binge drinking on college campuses*. Emmaus, PA: Rodale.

White, A. M., Jamieson-Drake, D. W., & Swartzwelder, H. S. (2002). Prevalence and correlates of alcohol-induced blackouts among college students: results of an e-mail survey. *Journal of American College Health, 51*(3), 117–9, 122–31.

Willis, J. (2006). *Research-based strategies to ignite student learning: Insights from a neurologist and classroom teacher*. Alexandria, VA: ASCD.

Wolfson, A. R., & Carskadon, M. A. (2003). Understanding adolescents' sleep patterns and school performance: A critical appraisal. *Sleep Medicine Reviews, 7*(6), 491–506.

World Health Organization. (2012). *Obesity and overweight*. Retrieved from http://www.who.int/entity/mediacentre/factsheets/fs311/en/index.html.

Youngstedt, S. D. (2005). Effects of exercise on sleep. *Clinical Sports Medicine, 24*(2), 355–365.

Zimbardo, P. G., Johnson, R. L., & McCann, V. (2012). *Psychology: Core concepts* (7th ed.). Boston: Pearson.

Chapter 14 Exercises

14.1 Quote Reflections

Review the sidebar quotes contained in this chapter and select two that were especially meaningful or inspirational to you.

For each quote, provide a three- to five-sentence explanation why you chose it.

14.2 Reality Bite

Drinking to Death: College Partying Gone Wild

At least 50 college students nationwide die each year as a result of drinking incidents on or near campus. During a single month one fall, three college students died as a result of binge drinking at college parties. One involved an 18-year-old, first-year student at a private university who collapsed after drinking a mixture of beer and rum, fell into a coma at his fraternity house, and died three days later. He had a blood-alcohol level of more than .40, which is about equal to gulping down 20 shots in one hour.

The second incident involved a student from a public university in the south who died of alcohol poisoning (overdose). The third student died at another public university in the northeast where, after an evening of partying and heavy drinking, he accidentally fell off a building in the middle of the night and fell through the roof of a greenhouse. Some colleges in the northeast now have student volunteers roaming the campus on cold, winter nights to make sure that no students freeze to death after passing out from an intense episode of binge drinking.

Listed below are some strategies that have been suggested by politicians to stop or reduce the problem of dangerous binge drinking:

1. A state governor announced that he was going to launch a series of radio ads designed to discourage underage drinking.
2. A senator filed bills to toughen penalties for those who violate underage drinking laws, such as producing and using fake identification cards.
3. A group of city council members was looking into stiffening penalties for liquor stores that deliver directly to fraternity houses.

Source: *Los Angeles Times*

Reflection and Discussion Questions

1. Rank the above three strategies in terms of how effective you think they'd be for reducing the problem of binge drinking (1 = the most effective strategy, 3 = the least effective).
2. Comparing your highest ranked and lowest ranked choices, why did you rank:
   a) the first one as most effective?
   b) the last one as least effective?
3. What other strategies do you think would be effective for stopping or reducing dangerous binge drinking among college students?

14.3 Wellness Self-Assessment for Self-Improvement

For each aspect of wellness listed below, rate yourself in terms of how close you are to doing what you should be doing (1 = furthest from the ideal, 5 = closest to the ideal).

	Nowhere Close to What I Should Be Doing		Not Bad but Should Be Better		Right Where I Should Be
	1	2	3	4	5
Nutrition	1	2	3	4	5
Exercise	1	2	3	4	5
Sleep	1	2	3	4	5
Alcohol and Drugs	1	2	3	4	5

For each area in which there's a gap between where you are now and where you should be, identify the best action you could take to reduce or eliminate the gap.

14.4 Nutritional Self-Assessment and Self-Improvement

1. Go to: *www.ChooseMyPlate.gov.*

2. For each of the five food groups listed below, record in the first column the amount you *should* be consuming daily; in the second column, estimate the amount you *do* consume daily.

Basic Food Type	Amount Recommended	Amount Consumed
Fruits		
Vegetables		
Grains		
Protein Foods		
Dairy		

3. For any food group that you're consuming less than the recommended amounts, use the website to find foods that would enable you to meet the recommended daily amount. Write down those food items, and answer the following questions about each of them:

   (a) How likely is it that you'll actually add these food items to your regular diet?

   Very Likely   Possibly   Very Unlikely

   (b) For those food items you identified as "very unlikely," why would you be very unlikely to add these items to your regular diet?

14.5 Identifying Your Peak Performance Times

Refer to your results from the *My PEPS Learning Style Inventory*, under the section Time of Day Preference.

What do the results suggest about times during the day when you're at your best and when it would be best to schedule your most challenging academic work?

How could you set up a study schedule that allows you to make the best use of the time when you're most productive while still balancing your other responsibilities?

Glossary and Dictionary of College Vocabulary

Academic Advisors: faculty or professional staff who advise college students on course selection, help them understand college procedures, and guide their academic progress toward completion of a college degree.

Academic Affairs: unit or division of the college that deals primarily with the college curriculum, course instruction, and campus services supporting academic success (e.g., library and learning center).

Academic Calendar: the scheduling system used by a college or university to divide the academic year into shorter terms (e.g., semesters, trimesters, or quarters).

Academic Credits (Units): how students receive credit for courses counting toward completing college degree. Academic credit is typically counted in terms of how many hours the class meets each week (e.g., a course that meets for three hours per week counts for three credits).

Academic Discipline: a field of study (biology, psychology, philosophy, etc.).

Academic Dismissal: a student is denied enrollment at a college because of a cumulative GPA that is below a minimum standard (e.g., below 2.0).

Academic Probation: a period of time (usually one term) during which students with a grade point average that does not meet the college's minimum requirement for graduation (e.g., less than 2.0) are given a chance to improve their grades. If grades improve to the point that they meet or exceed the college's minimum requirement, probation is lifted; if not, the student may be academically dismissed from the college.

Academic Standing: where a student stands academically (cumulative GPA) at a given point in the college experience (e.g., after one term or one year of coursework).

Academic Support Center: place on campus where students can obtain individual assistance from professionals and trained peers to support and strengthen their academic performance.

Academic Transcript: an official list of all courses a student has enrolled in, the grades received in those courses, and the student's grade point average for all courses.

Active Involvement (a.k.a. Engagement): the amount of *time* a student devotes to learning in college and the degree of personal *effort* or *energy* (mental and physical) the student puts into the learning process.

Advanced Placement (AP) Tests: tests designed to measure knowledge and skills mastered in high school. If a student scores high enough, college credit is awarded in the subject area tested, or the student is granted advanced placement in a college course.

Analysis (Analytical Thinking): a form of higher-level thinking skill, which involves breaking down information, identifying its key parts or underlying elements, and detecting what's most important or relevant.

APA Style: a particular style of citing references in a research report or term paper that is endorsed by the American Psychological Association (APA) and is most commonly used in fields that comprise the Behavioral Sciences (e.g., Psychology and Sociology) and Natural Sciences (e.g., Biology and Chemistry).

Aptitude: ability to do something well or the potential to do it well.

Associate Degree (A.A./A.S. Degree): two-year college degree that represents completion of general education and pre-major requirements needed for transfer to a four-year college or university.

Bachelor's (Baccalaureate) Degree: degree awarded by four-year colleges and universities that represents completion of general education requirements and requirements for a major.

Breadth Requirements: required general education courses that span a wide range of subject areas.

Career: the sum total of vocational experiences throughout an individual's work life.

Career Advancement: working up the career ladder to higher levels of authority and socioeconomic status.

Career Development Center: key campus resource where students learn about the nature of different careers and acquire strategies for locating career-related work experiences.

Career Development Courses: college courses that typically include self-assessment of career interests, information about different careers, and strategies for career preparation.

Certificate: credential received by students at a community college or technical college to signify completion of a vocational or occupational training program, which qualifies them for a specific job or occupation.

Citation: an acknowledgment of the source of any piece of information included in a written paper or oral report that is not the writer's original work.

Co-curricular Experiences: student learning and development that results from experiences taking place outside the classroom.

Collaborative Learning: two or more students working interdependently toward a common goal that involves true teamwork, whereby teammates support each other's success and take equal responsibility for helping the team move toward its shared goal.

College Catalog (a.k.a. College Bulletin): an official publication of a college or university that identifies its mission, curriculum, academic policies and procedures, as well as the names and educational background of its faculty.

Combined Bachelor/Graduate Degree Program: a program offered by some universities that allows students to apply for simultaneous admission to both undergraduate and graduate school in a particular field. The student receives both a bachelor's degree and a graduate degree in that field after completing the combined program (e.g., a Bachelor's and Master's degree in physical therapy).

Communication Skills: skills necessary for accurate reception and articulate expression of ideas (e.g., reading, writing, speaking, listening, and multimedia skills).

Commuter Students: college students who do not live on campus.

Concentration: a cluster of approximately three courses in the same subject area.

Concept: a system or network of related ideas.

Concept (Idea) Map: a diagram that represents or maps out main categories of ideas and depicts their relationships in a visual–spatial format.

Cooperative Education (Co-op) Program: program in which students gain work experience relating to their college major, either by stopping their course work temporarily to work full-time at the co-op position, or by continuing to take classes while working part-time at the co-op position.

Core Courses: courses required of all students, regardless of their particular major.

Counseling Services: personal counseling provided by professionals with expertise in promoting self-awareness and self-development, particularly with respect to social and emotional aspects of life.

Cover (Application) Letter: letter written by an applicant applying for an employment position or admission to a school.

Cramming: packing study time into one study session immediately before an exam.

Creative Thinking: a form of higher-level thinking that generates unique ideas, strategies, or products.

Critical Thinking: a form of higher-level thinking that involves making well-informed evaluations or judgments.

Cross-registration: a collaborative program offered by two colleges or universities that allow students enrolled at one institution to register for and take courses at another institution.

Culture: a distinctive pattern of beliefs and values learned by a group of people who share the same social heritage and traditions.

Cum Laude: graduating "with honors" (e.g., achieving a cumulative GPA of 3.3).

Cumulative GPA: a student's grade point average for all academic terms combined.

Curriculum: the total set of courses offered by a college or university.

Dean: a college or university administrator who is responsible for running a particular unit of the college (e.g., Dean of Fine Arts).

Dean's List: achieving an outstanding GPA for a particular term (e.g., 3.5 or higher).

Distance Learning: courses taken online rather than in person.

Diversity: the variety of different groups that comprise the human species (humanity).

Diversity Appreciation: valuing the experiences of different groups of people and interest in learning from their experiences.

Diversity (Multicultural) Courses: courses designed to promote diversity awareness and appreciation of multiple cultures.

Doctoral Degree: an advanced degree obtained after completion of the bachelor's (baccalaureate) degree, which typically requires five to six years of full-time study in graduate school, including completion of a thesis or doctoral dissertation.

Documentation: sources of information that serve as references to support or reinforce conclusions in a written paper or oral presentation.

Double Major: a bachelor's degree in two majors that is attained by meeting course requirements in both fields of study.

Drop/Add: the process of changing an academic schedule by dropping courses or adding courses to a preexisting schedule.

Electives: courses that students are not required to take, but which they elect (choose) to take.

Ethnic Group (Ethnicity): a group of people who share the same culture.

Experiential Learning: out-of-class experiences that promote learning and development.

Faculty: the collection of instructors on campus whose primary role is to teach courses offered in the college curriculum.

FAFSA (Free Application for Federal Student Aid): a form prepared annually by current and prospective college students (undergraduate and graduate) in the United States to determine their eligibility for student financial aid.

Fine Arts: a division of the liberal arts curriculum that focuses largely on artistic performance and appreciation of artistic expression by pursuing such questions as: What is beautiful? How do humans express and appreciate aesthetic (sensory) experiences, imagination, creativity, style, grace, and elegance?

Free Electives: courses that students may elect to enroll in, which count toward a college degree, but are not required for general education or an academic major.

Freshman Fifteen: a phrase commonly used to describe the 15-pound weight gain that some students experience during their first year of college.

Full-time Student: a student enrolled in at least 12 units of coursework during the academic term.

General Education Curriculum: collection of courses designed to provide breadth of knowledge and transferable skills needed for success in any major or career.

Grade Points: number of points earned for a course, which is calculated by multiplying the course grade by the number of credits carried by the course.

Grade Point Average (GPA): translation of students' letter grades into a numeric system, whereby the total number of grade points earned in all courses is divided by the total number of course units.

Graduate Assistant (GA): a graduate student who receives financial assistance to pursue graduate studies by working in a university office or for a college professor.

Graduate Record Examination (GRE): a standardized test for admission to graduate schools, similar to how SAT and ACT tests are used for admission to undergraduate colleges and universities.

Graduate School: education pursued after completing a bachelor's degree.

Graduate Student: student who has completed a four-year (bachelor's) degree and is enrolled in graduate school to obtain an advanced degree (e.g., Master's or Ph.D.).

Grant: money received that does not have to be repaid.

Greek Life: a term that refers to both fraternities (usually all male) and sororities (usually all female).

Hazing: a rite of induction to a social or other organization, most commonly associated with fraternities.

Health Services: on-campus services to treat students experiencing physical illnesses or injuries, and to educate students on matters relating to health and wellness.

Higher Education: formal education beyond high school.

Higher-Level Thinking: thinking at a higher or more complex level than merely acquiring factual knowledge or memorizing information.

Holistic (Whole Person) Development: development of the total self, which includes intellectual, social, emotional, physical, spiritual, ethical, and vocational aspects of personal development.

Honors Program: a special program of courses and related learning experiences designed for students who have demonstrated exceptionally high levels of academic achievement.

Humanities: division of the liberal arts curriculum that focuses on the human experience, human culture, and questions relating to the human condition, such as: Why are we here? What is the meaning or purpose of our existence? How should we live? What is the good life? Is there life after death?

Humanity: common elements of the human experience shared by all human beings.

Hypothesis: an informed guess that might be true, but still needs to be tested to confirm or verify its truth.

Impacted Major: a college major in which there are more students wishing to enter the program than there are spaces available in the program; thus, students must formally apply and qualify for admission to the major by going through a competitive screening process.

Independent Study: a project in which students receive academic credit for in-depth study of a topic of their choice by working independently with a faculty member, rather than enrolling in a classroom-based course.

Information Interview: an interview with a professional currently working in a career to obtain inside information about what the career is really like.

Information Literacy: the ability to access, retrieve, and evaluate information.

Intellectual (Cognitive) Development: acquiring knowledge, learning how to learn, and learning how to think deeply.

Intercultural Competence: ability to appreciate and capitalize on human differences, and to interact effectively with people from diverse cultural backgrounds.

Interdisciplinary: courses or programs that are designed to help students integrate knowledge from two or more academic disciplines (fields of study).

International Student: a student attending college in one nation, but who is a citizen of another nation.

International Study (Study Abroad) Program: taking courses at a college or university in a foreign country.

Internship: work experience related to a college major for which students receive academic credit and, in some cases, financial compensation.

Interpret: to draw a conclusion about something and support that conclusion with evidence.

Interdisciplinary: courses or programs that are designed to help students integrate knowledge from two or more academic disciplines (fields of study).

Inter-term (a.k.a. January Interim or Maymester): a short academic term, typically running three to four weeks, during which students enroll in only one course that is studied intensively.

Job Shadowing: a program that allows a student to follow (shadow) and observe a professional during a typical workday.

Leadership: ability to influence people in a positive way (e.g., motivating peers to do their best), or the ability to produce positive change in an organization or institution (e.g., improving the quality of a school, business, or political organization).

Learning Community: a program in which the same group of students takes the same block of courses together during the same academic term.

Learning Habits: the usual approaches, methods, or techniques a student uses while learning.

Learning Style: the way in which an individual prefers to perceive information (receive or take it in) and process information (deal with it once it has been taken in).

Liberal Arts: the component of a college education that represents the essential foundation or backbone for the college curriculum, which is designed to equip students with a versatile set of skills that promotes their success in any academic major or career.

Lifelong Learning: learning how to learn and how to continue learning throughout life.

Living-Learning Environment: on-campus student residence designed and organized in such a way that student learning experiences are integrated into the living environment (e.g., in-residence study groups, tutoring, and student development workshops).

Lower-Division Courses: courses taken by college students during their freshman and sophomore years.

Magna Cum Laude: graduating with "high honors" (e.g., achieving a cumulative GPA of 3.5).

Major: the academic field students choose to specialize in while in college.

Master's Degree: degree obtained after completion of the bachelor's (baccalaureate) degree that typically requires two to three years of full-time study in graduate school.

Matriculation: the process of initially enrolling in or registering for college (the term derives from the term *matricula*—a list or register of persons belonging to a society or community).

Mentor: someone who serves as a role model and personal guide to help students reach their educational or occupational goals.

Merit-Based Scholarship: money awarded on the basis of performance or achievement that does not have to be repaid.

Metacognition: thinking about how you are thinking while you are thinking.

Midterm: the midpoint of an academic term.

Minor: a field of study designed to complement and strengthen a major, which usually consists of about half the number of courses required for a college major (e.g., six to seven courses for a minor).

MLA Style: a style of citing references adopted by the Modern Language Association (MLA) and commonly used by academic fields in the Humanities and Fine Arts (e.g., English and Philosophy).

Mnemonic Device (Mnemonic): a memory improvement method for retaining and recalling information (e.g., an acronym or rhyming pattern).

Multicultural Center: place on campus designed for interaction among and between members of diverse cultural groups.

Multidimensional Thinking: a form of higher-level thinking that involves taking multiple perspectives and vantage points.

Multiple Intelligences: the theory that humans display intelligence and mental ability in a variety of ways (e.g., social intelligence and emotional intelligence).

Natural Sciences: a division of the liberal arts curriculum that focuses on the systematic observation of the physical world and underlying explanations of natural phenomena, asking such questions as: "What causes the physical events that take place in the natural world?" "How can we predict and control natural events?"

Need-Based Scholarship: money awarded to students on the basis of financial need that does not have to be repaid.

Netiquette: applying principles of social etiquette and interpersonal sensitivity when communicating online.

Nonresident Status: out-of-state students who typically pay higher tuition than in-state students because they are not residents of the state in which their college is located.

Nontraditional Students (a.k.a. Re-entry Students): students who do not begin college immediately after high school.

Online Resources: resources that can be used to search for and locate information including online card catalogues, Internet search engines, and electronic databases.

Oral Communication Skills: ability to speak in a concise, confident, and eloquent manner.

Orientation: an educational program experienced before the first academic term in college that's designed to help new students make a smooth transition to higher education.

Oversubscribed (a.k.a. Impacted) Major: a major that has more students interested in it than there are openings for it.

Paraphrase: restating or rephrasing information in your own words.

Part-Time Student: a college student who enrolls in fewer than 12 units during an academic term.

Part-to-Whole Study Method: a study strategy in which material to be learned is divided into smaller parts and studied in a series of short sessions in advance of an exam; on the day before the exam, the previously studied parts are reviewed as a whole.

Pass/Fail (Credit/No Credit) Grading: a grading option offered in some courses whereby students can choose to receive a grade of "pass" (credit) or "fail" (no credit), rather than a letter grade (A–F).

Persuasive Speech: an oral presentation intended to persuade the audience to agree with a certain position by providing supporting evidence.

Phi Beta Kappa: a national honor society that recognizes outstanding academic achievement of students at four-year colleges and universities.

Phi Theta Kappa: a national honor society that recognizes outstanding academic achievement of students at two-year colleges.

Placement Tests: tests administered to new students upon entry to a college or university that are designed to assess their basic academic skills (e.g., reading, writing, mathematics) and place them in courses that are neither too advanced nor too elementary for their particular level of skill development.

Plagiarism: intentional or unintentional use of someone else's work without acknowledging it, giving the impression that it is one's own work.

Portfolio: a collection of work materials or products that illustrates an individual's skills and talents, or demonstrates educational and personal development.

Postsecondary Education: formal education beyond secondary (high school) education.

Pre-professional Coursework: undergraduate courses that are required or strongly recommended for gaining entry into professional school (e.g., medical school or law school).

Prerequisite Course: a course that must be completed before a more advanced course can be taken.

Prewriting: an early stage in the writing process where the focus is on generating and organizing one's own ideas, rather than expressing or communicating ideas to someone else.

Primary Sources: information obtained from firsthand sources or original documents.

Process-of-Elimination Method: test-taking strategy for multiple-choice exams whereby choices that are clearly wrong are "weeded out" or eliminated until the best possible answer is identified.

Professional School: formal education pursued after a bachelor's degree in a school that prepares students for an "applied" profession (e.g., Pharmacy, Medicine, or Law).

Proficiency Tests: tests given to college students before graduation that are designed to assess whether they can perform certain academic skills (e.g., writing) at a level high enough to qualify them for college graduation.

Proofreading: final stage of editing that focuses on detecting mechanical errors relating to referencing, grammar, punctuation, and spelling.

Quarter System: a system for scheduling courses in which the academic year is divided into four quarters (fall, winter, spring, and summer terms), each of which lasts approximately 10–11 weeks.

Recall Test Question: a type of test question that requires students to generate or produce the correct answer on their own (e.g., essay question).

Recitation (Reciting): a study strategy that involves recalling and speaking aloud information to be remembered without looking at it.

Recognition Test Question: a type of test question that requires students to select or choose a correct answer from answers that are provided to them (e.g., multiple-choice, true–false, and matching questions).

Reference (Referral) Letter: a letter of reference typically written for students who are applying for entry into positions or schools after college, and for students applying for special academic programs, student leadership positions on campus, or part-time employment.

Reflection: a thoughtful review of what one has already done, is in the process of doing, or is planning to do.

Registrar's Office: campus office that maintains college transcripts and other official records associated with student coursework and academic performance.

Research Skills: ability to locate, access, retrieve, organize, and evaluate information from a variety of sources, including library and technology-based (computer) systems.

Resident Assistant: undergraduate student (sophomore, junior, or senior) whose role is to enforce rules in student residences and help new students adjust successfully to residence hall life.

Resident Director: student development professional in charge of residential (dormitory) life to whom resident assistants report.

Resident Status: in-state students who typically pay lower tuition than out-of-state students because they are residents of the state in which their college is located.

Residential Students: students who live on campus or in a housing unit owned and operated by the college.

Restricted Electives: courses that students choose to take from a restricted set or list of possible courses that have been specified by the college.

Resume: a list of an individual's credentials, accomplishments, skills, and awards.

Rough Draft: an early stage in the writing process whereby the writer's major ideas are expressed without close attention to the mechanics of writing (e.g., punctuation, grammar, or spelling).

Scholarly: a criterion or standard for evaluating the quality of an information source; typically, a source is considered "scholarly" if it has been reviewed by a panel or board of impartial experts in the field before being published.

Secondary Source: a publication that relies or builds on a previously published source (e.g., a textbook that draws its information from published research studies or journal articles).

Self-Assessment: the process of reflecting on and evaluating personal characteristics, such as personality traits, personal interests, or learning habits.

Self-Monitoring: maintaining self-awareness of what you're doing and how well you're doing it.

Self-Regulation: adjusting one's learning strategies in a way that best meet the specific demands of the subject being learned.

Semester System: a system for scheduling courses in which the academic year is divided into two terms (fall and spring) that are approximately 15–16 weeks long.

Semester (Term) GPA: GPA calculated for one semester or academic term.

Senior Seminar (Capstone) Course: course designed to put a "cap" or final touch on the college experience, helping seniors to tie ideas together in their major and to make a smooth transition from college to post-college life.

Service Learning: a form of experiential learning in which students serve or help others while also acquiring skills through hands-on experience that can be used to strengthen their resumes and explore potential careers.

Sexually Transmitted Infections (STIs): a group of contagious infections spread through sexual contact.

Shadow Majors: students who have been admitted to their college or university, but have not yet been admitted to their intended major.

Shallow (Surface) Learning: an approach to learning in which the student's study time is spent repeating and memorizing information in the exact form in which it's presented, rather than transforming it into words that are meaningful to the student.

Social and Behavioral Sciences: a division of the liberal arts curriculum that focuses on the observation of human behavior, individually and in groups, asking such questions as: What causes humans to behave the way they do? How can we predict, control, or improve human behavior?

Socially Constructed Knowledge: knowledge that is built up through interaction and dialogue with others.

Student Activities: co-curricular experiences offered outside the classroom that are designed to promote student learning and student involvement in campus life.

Student-Designed Major: an academic program offered at some colleges and universities in which a student works with a college representative or committee to develop a major that is not officially offered by the institution.

Student Development Services (Student Affairs): division of a college or university that provides student support on issues relating to social and emotional adjustment, involvement in campus life outside the classroom, and leadership development.

Student Handbook: an official college publication that identifies student roles and responsibilities, violations of campus rules and policies, and opportunities for student involvement in co-curricular programs, such as student clubs, campus organizations, and student leadership positions.

Summa Cum Laude: graduating with "highest honors" (e.g., achieving a cumulative GPA of 3.8 or higher).

Summer Session: courses offered during the summer between spring and fall terms, which typically run for four to six weeks.

Syllabus: an academic document that outlines course requirements, attendance policies, grading scale, course topics by date, test dates and dates for completing reading and other assignments, as well as information about the instructor (e.g., office location and office hours).

Synthesis: a form of higher-level thinking that involves integrating (connecting) smaller, separate pieces of information into a more comprehensive and coherent product.

Teaching Assistant (TA): a graduate student who receives financial assistance to pursue graduate studies by teaching undergraduate courses, leading course discussions, and/or helping professors grade papers or conduct labs.

Test Anxiety: a state of emotional tension that can weaken test performance by interfering with concentration, memory, and ability to think at a higher level.

Test-Wise: using characteristics of the test question itself (such as its wording or format) to increase the probability of choosing the correct answer.

Theory: a body of conceptually related concepts and general principles that help organize, understand, and apply knowledge that has been acquired in a particular field of study.

Thesis Statement: a one- to three-sentence statement contained in the introduction to a paper, which serves as a summary of the key point or main argument the writer intends to make and support with evidence.

Transfer Program: two-year college program that provides general education and pre-major coursework to prepare students for successful transfer to a four-year college or university.

Transferable Skills: skills that can be transferred or applied across different subjects, careers, and life situations.

Trimester System: a system for scheduling courses in which the academic year is divided into three terms (fall, winter, and spring) that are approximately 12–13 weeks long.

Undeclared: students who have not declared (committed to) a college major.

Undergraduate: student enrolled in a two-year or four-year college.

Upper-division Courses: courses taken by college students during their junior and senior years.

Visual Aids: charts, graphs, diagrams, or concept maps that improve learning and memory by enabling the learner to organize information into a picture or image.

Visual Memory: memory that relies on the sense of vision.

Visualization: a memory improvement strategy that involves creating a mental image or picture of what is to be remembered, or by imagining it in a familiar site or location.

Vocational (Occupational) Development: exploring career options, making career choices wisely, and developing skills needed for career success.

Vocational/Technical Programs: community college programs of study that train students for a particular occupation or trade and immediate employment after completing a two-year associate degree (e.g., Associate of Applied Science) or a one-year certificate program.

Volunteerism: volunteering personal time to help others without being rewarded with pay or academic credit.

Waive: to give up one's right to access information (e.g., waiving the right to see a letter of recommendation).

Wellness: a state of optimal health, peak performance, and positive well-being that results from balancing and integrating different dimensions of the "self" (body, mind, and spirit).

Withdrawal: dropping a class after the drop/add deadline, which results in a student receiving a "W" for the course and no academic credit.

Work-Study Program: a federal program that supplies colleges and universities with funds to provide on-campus employment for students who are in financial need.

Writing Center: a campus support service where students receive assistance at any stage of the writing process, whether it be collecting and organizing ideas, composing a first draft, or proofreading a final draft.

Index